OTHER BOOKS BY THE AUTHOR

Desert Island Wine

(2007, Ambeli Press)

a collection of humorous pieces about many aspects of wine appreciation

Greek Salad: A Dionysian Travelogue

(2004, The Wine Appreciation Guild)

an enophile's rollicking travels through the Greek islands and mainland

The Wines of Greece

(1990, Faber and Faber)

the definitive account of contemporary Greek wine, with all due attention to antiquity

TOKAJI WINE

FAME, FATE, TRADITION

A-Z through the history of Tokaji wine

by Miles Lambert-Gócs

Ambeli Press
Williamsburg, Virginia

Tokaji Wine: Fame, Fate, Tradition

Published in the U.S. by:

Ambeli Press
1008 Settlement Drive
Williamsburg, VA 23188

Distributed by:
The Wine Appreciation Guild
360 Swift Avenue
South San Francisco, CA 94080
(650) 866-3020
www.wineappreciation.com

Text copyright 2010, Miles Lambert-Gócs

Library of Congress CIP Data:

Lambert-Gócs, Miles Tokaji wine : fame, fate, tradition : A-Z
through the history of Tokaji wine / by Miles Lambert-Gocs.
p. cm. Includes bibliographical references and index.
ISBN 978-1-934259-49-8

1. Wine and wine making--Hungary--Tokaj--History. 2. Wine
and wine making--Hungary--Hegyalja--History. I. Wine Appreciation Guild (San Francisco, Calif.) II. Title. TP559.H9L35 2010
641.2'209439--dc22
2010017501

Printed in the United States of America
Signature Book Printing, www.sbpbooks.com

Front Cover Illustrations:

Upper left-hand corner: detail from the first map of Hungary (1528), showing Hegyalja hills, from 'Tokay'-'Tarzal'-'Talija'-'Zanto' north to 'Zemlin,' plus commercial center of 'Cassovia' (Košice)

Upper right-hand corner: entry about 'Tockay' from Encylopaedia Britannica of 1771

Lower left-hand corner: portrait of Prince Francis Rákóczi II; and the opening notes of Franz Liszt's Rákóczi March

Lower middle: a bottle carrying the old Latin name for Tokaji Aszú – Vinum Tokajense Passum

Lower right-hand corner: early-20th century English-language poster for the cooperative 'Tokaj Winegrowers Association' (with emblem of the Hungarian kingdom in the upper left-hand corner); and Thomas Jefferson's portrait and signature

Two things were in front of me as I worked on this book: an empty bottle of Tokaji wine (post-communist), and this photo from 1960. Grandpa Gócs was a headstone carver by trade, and by avocation, a maker of wine (white). When I lived with him, in Brooklyn, he would often tell me, "Make a good job," if I was busy creating something. Those words have never left me, and I hope that it will be apparent on the pages that follow.

"Ritka eset, hogy egy meghatározott táj, meghatározott bora egy nemzet Himnuszában is helyet kaphasson és ez ilyen teljes formában csak a tokaj-hegyaljai nektárral történhetett meg. Ez többet jelent minden világ-hírnévnél."

"It's a rare case that a particular locale, its particular wine might gain a place even in a nation's anthem, and this could have happened in such an integral way only with the nectar of Tokaj-Hegyalja. This means more than any world renown."

Iván Balassa

TABLE OF CONTENTS

A PERSONAL NOTE FROM THE AUTHOR

Everything about the history of Tokaji wine fascinates me. It has been that way for over three decades now. My curiosity was by turns slaked and intensified by having ready access during most of that time to the National Agricultural Library and Library of Congress holdings, because of employment at the U.S. Department of Agriculture. Virtually all of the needed Hungarian-language source materials were at my disposal.

But dry scholarship was not motivation in itself. There was a liquid stimulus, to be sure. In fact, this entire project was set off by a specific bottle, a 5-*puttonyos* Tokaji Aszú from 1969, drunk at Christmas 1977. That vintage is rated only three out of four possible stars, but it seems that we opened it in the optimum time-range. I was no stranger to Tokaji at the time, but the quality of that one was, as they say, an eye-opener. After that, I simply had to look into the bottom of the bottle.

Even so, some readers may be surprised by the breadth of the subject matter herein. It is a considerable leap from a narrow focus on the Tokaj-Hegyalja region to its broader geographical context, that of the Upper Tisza region of Old Hungary, the former kingdom. The explanation is family history, and this, too, was a strong motivation. As the years of research went on, I found myself shifting back and forth between Tokaji wine itself and family connections. It was as if the one interest fed off the other.

Some of the place-names and family names listed in the pages that follow were ones that I had heard my grandparents mention as a child. The names sounded so mysterious then, but my research on Tokaji brought them to life and they were always a spur to further investigation. The familial connections grew, too. I discovered that my grandfather, Stephan Gócs, to whom this book is dedicated, was the last in a row of persons with that name, going back to one from Transylvania, who, along with other Székler soldiers, was raised to the minor nobility (tax-exempt status) by Prince George Rákóczi II in 1655, and given some land and a vineyard just north of Hegyalja, so as to be available for action against either the Ottomans or the Habsburgs. The family kept the vineyard going for 300 years, but, alas, it was located two or three hills north of the later appellation zone. But that irony made me feel no less duty-bound to research and write.

Still, this book would not have been written were there not significant new information, perspectives, and interpretations to present on the subject of Tokaji. Some topics, notably the Hegyalja-Balkan connection (which owes to my long involvement with Greece and Bulgaria), will be novel even for Hungarians. However, I have tried to keep my enthusiasm in check and to cull the material carefully. But, on the other hand, readers might appreciate some of the esoteric observations, speculations, and humor.

I hope you will find yourself pulling this volume from your bookshelf nearly as often as you pull corks from bottles of Tokaji.

Miles Lambert-Gócs
April 2010

i

PREFACE

The comeback of Hungary's Tokaj-Hegyalja wine region since 1989 after four cloistered decades under a communist regime has been marked by new interest among wine professionals, journalists, merchants, and enthusiasts worldwide about the pre-communist past of Tokaji. Indeed, a more fundamental curiosity is being displayed by non-Hungarian enophiles than ever before in the wine's long history.

But the widespread audience has had to make do with narrowly focused accounts, often insouciantly researched, and typically with no foundation in Hungarian-language source materials. Not infrequently, too, the writing has been polemical in nature, in connection with the differing viewpoints that have surfaced about how to make Tokaji wine, not to mention lingering finger-pointing with regard to the recently passed communist era. All this has led to sketchy accounts, and unreliability of information. No Tokaji enthusiast has been well-served by this situation.

It is time for a new approach. To begin with, for anyone who wants to have a context in which to understand Tokaji, it is not enough just to pore over appellation-zone maps and topographical features. No gleanings from those will make it comprehensible to non-Hungarians why Tokaji is lauded in Hungary's national anthem, let alone why the Rákóczi March of Liszt and Berlioz is forever linked with Tokaji in the Hungarian psyche. It is the names of clans, places, and vineyard-tracts that explain 'why.'

It is hoped that this volume will make clear that the history of Tokaji is far-ranging indeed. Emphatically, too, it is about the wine's *history*, not about today's producers and labels. But it will be an exploration of how the past has shaped the contemporary scene, and a consideration of why people who really care about Tokaji's future should look at that past. While I would gladly have left this to Hegyalja wine professionals, they are, after all, practical people, and have not had time to spend rummaging in old books and archival documents for obscure notations from bygone eras.

An encyclopedic-style A-Z format was chosen as the most digestible way to present the depth of background to the non-Hungarian audience. This is new in the literature on Tokaji. The explanation for it is that a presentation of many of the most fascinating and instructive details in a narrative format would be daunting for most readers, and therefore, counterproductive. Nevertheless, the A-Z entries in the four sections have been tied together in the five appendix essays. To my knowledge, nothing like these essays, either, has appeared in the literature on Tokaji.

Even having said all this, readers may still be surprised at the variety of topics covered. I have tried to bring together information from an array of authors and specialists who were focused on varied aspects of Tokaji. At the same time, I have pointed out some of the gaps in what is known, and, whenever necessary, have couched the subject matter so as to reflect the historical uncertainties.

Miles Lambert-Gócs

PART I

POPULACE and ACTORS:

peoples, clans, persons, entities

"the interpretation of interethnic occurrences in Hegyalja...needs to be given greater significance than it has received to date..."

Iván Balassa, 1991

1

INTRODUCTION

Tokaji may be the quintessential national expression of Hungary in wine, but it has broader ethnic 'roots.' The Hegyalja region where the wine is grown is located at the southern end of the Upper Tisza (northeastern) section of the old Kingdom of Hungary, mostly in the county of Zemplén. Several ethnic groups settled in the Upper Tisza, between the Carpathian border with the Polish lands to the north and the Hungarian Great Plain (Alföld) in the south, and all of those groups contributed to making Tokaji wine what it became. Also, extraneous groups came into the region and had an impact. It can truly be said that Tokaji stands as an inter-ethnic achievement in wine.

*

Tokaji wine emerged from a fascinating history of peoples, clans, families, individuals, and religious or secular entities during the past 1,200 years. The landmark date is 896, when the Magyars, known to us now as Hungarians, migrated westward from southern Russia and arrived at the Carpathian mountains. They crossed over into the Carpathian basin and followed the tributaries of the Tisza river down to the Zemplén area near the Bodrog and Latorca rivers. Thus began the so called 'Homeland Occupation' (*Honfoglalás*), or Conquest of Hungary. Zemplén was the first encampment area, and became the Magyars' first base in their new land.

The Magyars did not enter an entirely vacant space. The Upper Tisza had a scattered population that was mainly Slavic in speech, and whose main pursuit was agriculture, including some viticulture. Indeed, it is likely that the Magyars decided to remain in Zemplén in part because it was already an inhabited and sustaining region. At the same time, the population was not very considerable in number and lacked political cohesiveness. Zemplén, and the greater Upper Tisza region surrounding it, was frontier territory, positioned between early Slavic kingdoms but rather too peripheral and dangerously open to the south for those budding political entities to be able to make a vigorous defense of territorial claims, much less enable any but minor settlements.

At the time of the Magyar arrival, a number of small, rudimentary fortification points were the chief manmade feature of the landscape. The main ones seem to have been located at the later village of Zemplén and the later town of Tokaj. These were located respectively at the northern and southern ends of what would eventually comprise the Tokaj-Hegyalja region. According to the account of the Magyars' arrival, recorded from oral history by the scribe Anonymous three centuries later, the Magyar leader, Árpád, allocated territory to his chief lieutenants, and much of the area which today is Hegyalja was included among those distributions. It is a safe presumption that vineyards were already a feature of the hills stretching along the Bodrog river, albeit sporadic and very limited in extent. Certainly nothing like Tokaj-Hegyalja existed.

*

There is a lack of documentary evidence about wine-growing in Zemplén and Hegyalja around the year 900. However, various proofs can be cited to demonstrate that vines were cultivated. This evidence is best viewed chronologically *backwards* through the earliest period of Hungarian history, which was the era of the Árpád Dynasty (or, the Árpád kings), the original Magyar royal family, who ruled the country from its founding until they died out in 1301.

The names of two Hegyalja vineyard-tracts strongly suggest an origin in the Árpád era: Baksó (or Baksa) in Tarcal, and Káté (Káta) in Slovenské Nové Mesto (now in East Slovakia). Both were names of leading clans from that period and could date to at least the early-13th century. Káté could be even older since the clan of that name may have been one of the Magyar clans at the time of the Conquest. It is worth noting, too, that the Baksó and Káté tracts are located at opposite ends of Hegyalja, respectively the southern and northern, which indicates that wine-growing was pursued throughout the region in the Árpád era. Already in the early-12th century, King Kálmán apparently had large wine cellars in Tarcal, in southern Hegyalja. Lending credence to this is the fact that his predecessors had brought Walloons to Hegyalja in the mid-11th century. The cellars beneath the Zemplén fortress dated to that time. Also, a major area of Walloon settlement was Sárospatak, probably because vines were already cultivated there.

Documents from the 11th century mention three other villages, now in East Slovakia, that would later become associated with Hegyalja wine: Kistoronya (now Malá Tŕňa), Szőlőske (Viničky), and Csörgő (Čerhov), all immediately northeast of Sátoraljaújhely. Although nothing substantial is known about the three, Szőlőske's very name refers to vineyards (szőlő = vineyard); and it is a name found in a document of 1029, in the form Zeuleus. It also appears that settlements existed by Szerencs, Mád, and Tokaj, in the south of Hegyalja, at the time of the Conquest of Hungary. There is every reason to think that vines were cultivated in the region at that time, since a pruning knife from the 7th century was unearthed at Abaújvár, just northwest of Hegyalja. Abaújvár (Aba-new-fortress) belonged to the Aba clan, one of the earliest clans to own extensive lands in the Upper Tisza region; and the pruning knife indicates an earlier habitation at that locale.

*

As concerns wine-growing, the key factor about the Magyars' new territory in the Upper Tisza was that it had fallen beyond the dominion of Rome. As is evident from its scant population and lack of towns, Zemplén was distant from the Romans west of the Danube. The Romans in effect had largely left the region to the Huns and Avars during the 5th to 7th centuries. Subsequently, the expanding Bulgarian Empire took an interest in the region, and by the early-9th century had pushed its hold around 112 km (70 miles) further north than Hegyalja. [See the entries for Anonymous, Bulgaro-Slavs, and Presian, below; and the entry for Strachyna, in Part II.]

The role of the Bulgaro-Slavs in Hegyalja, and in the Upper Tisza region generally, is a chapter that has been insufficiently studied. Writing of Hegyalja in 1903, J. Kossuth went so far as to deny a Bulgar presence prior to the Kingdom of Hungary [see the entry Bulgars: Bulgaro-Phobia]. Yet, in the history section of the same volume in which Kossuth wrote, it was stated that Slavs (who would have been Bulgaro-Slavs) from north of the Greek port city of Thessaloniki were brought to Zemplén in the 9th century. The chronicler Anonymous, writing around 1200, indicated that the Bulgaro-Slavs had dominion over the Upper Tisza when the Magyars arrived, and Bulgarian historians have no doubt that the medieval Bulgarian Empire extended that far to the northwest of present-day Bulgaria. A number of geographical names in the Upper Tisza indicate that this view is correct. [See Map #3 and the entry for Bulgarian Empire, in Part II.]

All sorts of evidence suggest that it was the wine-growing habits of the Bulgaro-Slavs that the Magyars encountered in Hegyalja, and which became the foundation of Tokaji wine. The researcher Iván Balassa, in 1991, was surprised at the extent to which Balkan and Aegean grape varieties predominated in the early period of Hegyalja. Some of these might well have dated to the time of the Slavs from Macedonia. Besides grape varieties, virtually every peculiarity of Hegyalja wine-growing and wine-making that distinguishes it from Roman and Frankish habits has been recorded at various locales in the southeastern Balkans [see the entry for Balkan Influences, in Part IV]. Clearly, this is a subject that deserves much more research than it has received to date.

*　*　*

PART I

THE A-Z LISTING

Aba
Andrássy
Angevin Kings
Anna Ivanovna, Czarina
Anonymous
Aristocracy
Armenians
Árpád Dynasty
Aspremont
Ásvány
Avars
Baksa
Barkóczi
Báthory
Bél
Béla IV, King
Bimbólázár
Bogát-Radvány
Bollman
Boner
Brankovich
Bretzenheim
Bright
Bulgaro-Slavs
Bulgars: Bulgaro-Phobia
Chelebi
Columella
Cooperatives
Csáky
Csirke
Dercsényi
Dobó
Dombi
Douglass
Draheim
Draskovics
Drugeth
Dujardin
Eger Bishopric
Eugénie, Empress
Ferenczi
Frosch
Fugger
Germans
Görög
Grassalkovich
Greek Merchant Society
Greeks
Gyöngyösi

Habsburgs
Halápi
Herodotus
Hungarian Chamber
Hungarian Wine Commission
Italians
Jefferson
Jews
Joseph II, Emperor
Jullien
Kabars
Kádár
Kálmán, King
Kalmár
Katha
Keczer
Klobusiczky
Kölcsey
Kosinszky
Kossuth
Kossuth, J.
Lórántffy
Louis I, King
Lubomirski
Madocsányi
Mágochy
Magyars
Magyars: Observation
Maria Theresa
Mathiász
National Wine-Qualifying Institute
Oláh
Ond
Ossoliński
Ottlik
Ottoman Turks
Paget
Pálóczi
Paracelsus
Paraskevich
Pauline Order
Perényi
Peter I, Czar
Pethő
Poles
Presian II, Czar
Preysz
Rákóczi

Ratold
Redding
Rosa
Rozgonyi
Rumpolt
Russians
Rusyns
Sapjeha
Schams
Schwendi
Scots
Selbstherr
Serbs
Sforza
Slovaks
Smallholders
Soós
Sperfogel
Stegner
Szabó, J.
Szabó, L.
Szápolyai
Széchenyi
Szepes Chamber
Szepsi
Szepsi: Mystique
Szerviczky
Szirmay
Szirmay, A.
Szuhay
Tarcal Institute
Tatars
Teitelbaum
Thököly
Thurzó
Timon
T-H Committee
T-H Facility
Trautsohn
Upori
Usz
Valenczvella..?
Vishnyevski
Waldbott
Walloons
Windischgrätz
Zada
Zudar

Note: All persons or families mentioned in any entry below have their own entry, or else are found in Part III. All place-names and wine terms will be found respectively in Part II and Part IV. Hungarian names of religious or secular entities are listed by their English equivalent. Obviously, a great many more names of families could be mentioned, but the list has been restricted to those that add something to an understanding of the history of Hegyalja. Numerous aristocratic families [see the entry for Aristocracy] that had vineyards in Hegyalja in recent centuries have been left out, although mention is made of some of them in Part II, under the entries for specific communities, or in Part III, in the listing of vineyard-tract names.

*

Aba. One of the oldest clans in the Upper Tisza, the Abas were based primarily in what became Abaúj County, Zemplén County's neighbor on the southwest. At the same time, though, the Abas were in all probability the earliest clan to hold extensive lands in Zemplén, where they had estates ranging throughout the southern half of later Hegyalja, from Tállya and Rátka in the south, to Erdőbénye further north. This is presumed to have happened well before the Tatar invasion of 1241-1242, even though there is no documentation about the Aba clan until the early 1200s. The Abas are thought to have descended from a related people, probably the Kabars, who joined with the Magyars around the time of the Conquest of Hungary [see the entry for Kabars.]. Subsequently, the clan branched off into many family lines, such that their later influence on Hegyalja cannot be determined. The names of vineyard-tracts do not indicate a specific link to the Abas, although any that belonged to the Regéc Domain might have been theirs originally [see Regéc, in Part II].

Andrássy. One of the major aristocratic families in the more recent history of Hungary, the Andrássys began coming into their high rank at the beginning of the 16th century, just when Hegyalja was making a name for itself. The family remained Roman Catholic, and deftly straddled the conflict between the Habsburgs and the anti-Habsburg aristocrats of the Upper Tisza. Consequently, they did not suffer from the property confiscations by the Habsburgs during the late-17th and early-18th centuries. Their vineyard properties were largely concentrated in southern Hegyalja, at Tállya, Mád, Monok, Bekecs, Mezőzombor, and Tarcal, but also at Tolcsva in middle Hegyalja. Further, in the late-19th century, Count Julian Andrássy, whose manor was just north of Hegyalja, created a model vineyard estate in Szőlőske, at the northeastern end of the region as it would be demarcated in 1893 and 1908. The Szőlőske estate became one of the focal points of the region's efforts to recover from phylloxera [see the entry for Mathiász]. Also notable is that, in 1857, George Andrássy founded the Tokaj-Hegyalja Wine-Grower Association (*Tokaj-Hegyaljai Bormívelő Egyesület*), which was an effort at bringing major growers together for the common good. It was the Association that published the classic *Tokaj-Hegyaljai Album* of 1867.

Angevin Kings. When the original dynasty of the Magyars, the Árpád kings, died out in 1301, they were replaced by the Anjous from western Europe. The Angevin kings ruled Hungary until 1387. The period of their rule was notable for contact with Croatia, especially the Italian-speaking towns along the Dalmatian coast. It can be presumed that this resulted in the migration of people and grape varieties to Hegyalja, although the specifics of what this might have meant can only be surmised as yet. [See the entries for Louis I; and for Bardejov and Dalmatia, in Part II.]

Anna Ivanovna, Czarina. (1693-1740) A singular chapter in Hegyalja history opened when Anna Ivanovna, who ruled from 1730 to 1740, ordered the establishment of the Hungarian Wine Commission in 1733. Her aim was to ensure supplies of Tokaji wine while continuing to take advantage of a tariff reduction that Habsburg Emperor Joseph I granted to Russia in 1729. Polish authorities had been interfering with the shipments and confiscating substantial amounts as a tariff. [See the entry for Hungarian Wine Commission.]

Anonymous. (12th c.) Also referred to in Hungarian as *Névtelen* (Nameless), this person is variously thought to have been a royal scribe or a high royal court personage, most likely towards the end of the 12th century, but possibly somewhat earlier. He wrote the *Gesta Hungarorum* (Deeds of the Hungarians), an account of the Conquest of Hungary by the Magyars 300 years previously, with reference to the earliest years. During the past century, it has been supposed that much of what he recorded tells more about circumstances and geography in his own time. However, it may be countered that even if some of his details were inaccurate, or the result of mixing legends, he was coming out of an oral tradition that probably had the outline right, especially since only 300 years had elapsed. Of particular note, Anonymous related that the Bulgaro-Slavs dominated as far north as the Beskids, which not only comports with the research of historians of the medieval Bulgarian Empire, but also appears to be borne out by the Bulgaro-Slav toponym Ostrachina near the Beskids [see the entry for Strachyna, in Part II], and Bulgarian Czar Presian's selection of the region as his place of exile in the 11th century [see Presian, below].

As regards Hegyalja, his account places some focus on the Zemplén region. He tells of scouting the region by a route that virtually encompasses the later Hegyalja [see the entry for Szerencs, in Part II]. He also mentioned a bestowal of territory that roughly coincides with Hegyalja; and in this case, it does *not* seem as if he was transposing the situation in his day to the earlier era. Sometimes, too, what Anonymous does *not* say is also significant. Notably, while he indicates that contact was made with Bulgaro-Slavs in the Upper Tisza region [see the entry for *Szlankamenka*, in Part IV], he does not mention encountering Great Moravia there. This jibes with the absence in Hegyalja of the viti-vinicultural features of the Frank-oriented Great Moravia in the era of the Hungarian Conquest. Also, Anonymous did not mention a geographical area with a name suggestive of Hegyalja [see the entry for Hegyalja, in Part II].

Aristocracy. For many Hungarians of earlier generations, the 'history' of Tokaji wine, as indeed of Hungary itself, was entirely intertwined with the doings of the aristocracy, the great magnates of the country. It amounted to viewing Hegyalja from the perspective of 'who owned what' and venerating vineyard-tracts on that basis. This perhaps was to be expected in a society that was retarded in outgrowing its feudal period (because of the Ottomans and Habsburgs). In any case, its aura and luster carried over into how non-Hungarians looked at the region since the time when Westerners started visiting Hungary. Thus, too, it became decidedly detrimental to Tokaji's reputation once the grand old names of the upper nobility disappeared during the 20th century. Of course, it is obvious that the aristocracy had made crucial contributions to Hegyalja, such as expanding cellar capacity, advancing changes in grape varieties, and not least of all, spreading the wine's fame amongst the upper echelon in other countries. But the role of municipalities, religious orders, and smallholders, as well as foreign traders, particularly the Greeks, was grossly neglected by the fixation on the aristocracy. It can even be argued that many details of Hegyalja history were not preserved and are not known precisely because of that fixation.

In the long era of their primacy, roughly from the mid-13th century to the mid-19th century, the aristocracy did have distinct advantages. As the ultimate lords of the land, though not all of the vineyards upon it, they enjoyed the right of 'advance-purchase' of a portion of the output of smallholders who owned and worked vineyards within the respective domains of the lords. It was, in effect, a system of 'monopoly' pricing. Thus, the regulation of 1655 that required the separate collection of botrytized berries was a boon for the aristocracy above all; they could claim 'the pick of the crop,' as it were. The aristocracy also enjoyed tariff dispensations on exports [see the entries for Kalmár and Mágochy], which is why they were the class most vehemently opposed to the Greek traders, who found ways to circumvent regulatory requirements during the 18th century. Also, the upper nobility had advantages with regard to selling their table wines on tap at taverns. On the other hand, the aristocracy did not necessarily enjoy more advantages than smallholders when it came to tithes and taxes on vineyard properties, since those depended on the fiscal classification of the tract of land in question.

Coming out of the Ottoman period, at the end of the 17th century, the aristocracy could certainly be characterized as a 'regressive' class [see the entry for Szabó, L.]. They remained so, practically in their entirety, for another century. Although there is little if any historical evidence that they sought directly to inhibit the activity of smallholders, they were decidedly against free trade until Antal Szirmay and Stephan Széchenyi [see those entries]; and free trade was a beacon that held promise for smallholders [see the entry for Mád, in Part II]. In fact, the opposition of the aristocracy first to Greek and then to Jewish participation in the Hegyalja wine trade was motivated in no small part by fear of competition in the purchase of *aszú* berries or wine from smallholders, who were being offered higher prices (even if marginally so) by the merchant class.

The aristocracy was, of course, vilified during the communist era of Hungary, and not least of all in Hegyalja. Only the memory of certain 'national' figures, notably Francis Rákóczi II, was to be promoted, because they could be interpreted as representative of a transitional phase in the gradual social evolution towards communism. But this was hardly a faithful representation of the aristocracy, and certainly not in Hegyalja. For one thing, from phylloxera until the Second World War, the aristocracy was in the forefront of bolstering the image of Tokaji wine by organizing the smallholders into cooperatives [see the entries for Cooperatives and Smallholders].

Armenians. Mostly coming from the European area of the Ottoman Empire, Armenians engaged in Central European wine trade originally dealt mainly in Balkan wines and Greek Malvasia wines. But they began gaining some significance in exporting Tokaji to Poland in the late-18th century, as Greek participation in the Hegyalja wine trade started to fall off. Regional historians have mentioned that Armenians were present in the trading towns of the Upper Tisza, including East Slovakia; and the English visitor John Paget noted that Armenians, along with Greeks and Jews, were present in the town of Tokaj itself in the early-19th century. But, unlike the Greeks, little if any information is available about specific families. Komoróczi's (1944) research led him to conclude that the Armenians "did not shrink from [Tokaji] wine fraud on even the grandest scale." [See the entry for Széchenyi; and for Falsification, in Part IV.]

Árpád Dynasty. Prince Árpád led the Magyars during their final westward trek, and brought them into the Carpathian basin, the later Kingdom of Hungary, at the end of the 9th century. This so called 'Conquest,' or in Hungarian, *Honfoglalás* ('occupation of the homeland') is traditionally dated to the year 896. Árpád's direct descendants continued to rule Hungary for 400 years, until dying out in 1301. Two of the most notable kings of the dynasty were Stephan I, who converted to Christianity and set Hungary on a course of Westernization, and Béla IV, who took measures to rebuild the country following the Tatar invasion of 1241-1242. Both of them, and other members of the dynasty, were notable for enhancing Hegyalja. [See the entry for Kálmán; and for Cellars, in Part IV.]

Aspremont. In Hegyalja history, the Counts Aspremont are the preeminent instance of accumulating a large vineyard estate beginning from a marriage. In 1693, the Aspremonts acquired a toehold when Austrian General Ferdinand Aspremont married the daughter, Juliana, of none other than Francis Rákóczi I. At that time, the outcome of the Rákóczi conflict with the Habsburgs could not be foreseen. But after the failure of the last Rákóczi rebellion, Juliana was allowed to keep a small part of the family's vineyard holdings. The Habsburgs certainly had no quarrel with the Aspremonts (though it might be supposed that the Aspremonts were sorely disappointed that the Rákóczis lost their realm). Thereafter, members of the family went on to acquire properties on their own, and to become one of the most widespread wine-growing families in Hegyalja, with holdings (from north to south) in Kistoronya, Bodrogkisfalud, Mád, Mezőzombor, Ond, Szerencs, and Legyesbénye. Additionally, they were in the northerly villages of Nagytoronya and Nagy Bári, whose status as Hegyalja locales was as yet uncertain.

Ásvány, Ákos. (1923-1994) Arguably the foremost enological expert on Tokaji wine in the 20th century, Ásvány was definitely a leading expert during the communist era. Sadly, his writings have been ignored even by Hungarian commentators of the post-communist era. Ásvány's professionalism, authoritativeness, and integrity were such that he was chosen as the first president of the Hungarian Wine Academy. He is simply indispensable to knowledge of Tokaji enological developments during the second-half of his century.

Augustine Order. [See the entry for Bodroghalász, in Part II.]

Avars. The origin of the Avars was in Central Asia, and their graves in northeastern Hungary and eastern Slovakia show that they were short, black-haired, and yellowish, though not of mongoloid race. Beginning around the second-half of the 6th century, they had stepped into the power vacuum left in the Upper Tisza area by the Huns under Attila, who had held sway in the 5th century. But the Avars were defeated by combined Frank and Bulgar attacks in 796, just one-hundred years before the Magyar arrival. Although the Avars mixed with the Slavs under their control and may have been on the verge of total linguistic absorption, their cultural continuity in the Upper Tisza in the 9th century is suggested by the apparent ability of some inhabitants to communicate with the newly arrived Magyars and allied tribes. Such a late survival of the Avars likely was facilitated by the extension of the Bulgarian Empire into the Upper Tisza [see the entry for Bulgarian Empire, in Part II]. Of great significance is that without the onetime Avar dominion over the Upper Tisza area of future Hungary, the Magyars would probably have found no people at all, let alone viticulture, when they arrived in Zemplén. The basis for agriculture was stability that derived from authority, and the Avars had provided it for over two centuries. Although no place-names have been definitively linked to them by Hungarian etymologists, it is possible that the ending –*bénye* in the Hegyalja village names Erdőbénye and Legyesbénye might have originated in the Avar term *bény*, which signified a fortified site.

Baksa. (also as Baksó, Boksa, Bokcsa) One of the earliest Magyar clans in Zemplén, the Baksas seem to have been of extraordinary importance during the period of the Árpád kings (*i.e.*, before 1300), and also well into the subsequent era of the Angevin kings. The Baksas account for the name of the Baksó vineyard-tract in southern Hegyalja, and also for the locale of Baksó on the northwestern rim of Zemplén County (now Bokša, in East Slovakia). They were also in the Hegyalja locale of Bodroghalász (then Petrahó) in the second-half of the 13th century. This indicates a considerable territorial presence and influence during the 13th-14th centuries, when viticulture was spreading throughout the region. [See the entry for Baksó, in Part III.] Later, the Baksa (or Baxa) family owned a variety of excellent properties in central and northern Hegyalja, such as in the Diókút tract (of Erdőbénye), Ciróka and Kútpatka (Tolcsva), and Kis-Oremus (Sátoraljaújhely) at the beginning of the 17th century (UC 108:55).

Barkóczi. Another of the ancient Magyar families, the Barkóczis came from southwestern to northeastern Hungary in the 16th century, and became prominent throughout the counties of the Upper Tisza, particularly the ones central to Hegyalja history: Zemplén, Abaúj, and Sáros. It can perhaps be said that wine-growing was not a priority with them early on, even though they did have vineyard property in Mezőzombor by 1567, and later in nearby Mád. Their connection to the Pethő family, by marriage, certainly raised their awareness of the value of the Tokaji trade with Poland. When Francis Barkóczi became the Bishop of Eger (1745-1761), some tension arose between his concerns as bishop and the family's interests as wine-growers, namely, to stimulate production for the benefit of the bishopric (through wine tithes), even though it could result in price reductions unfavorable to the family. In 1749, the bishop involved himself in Zemplén County's ongoing feud with the Russian commission for Hegyalja wine purchases by charging that it was really a 'front' for fomenting religious conflict (inasmuch as the Orthodox church was already well-established because of the Greek merchants). The incident provoked Imperial Russian indignation, but did not hold back the work of the commission. In the long run, the devout Roman Catholicism of the Barkóczis served them well in Hegyalja, and generally, too, because they kept in step with the Catholic Habsburgs. [See the entry for Hungarian Wine Commission.]

Báthory, Stephan (István). (1533-1586) Neither the first nor the last of the Transylvanian princes to take an interest in Hegyalja wine, Báthory nevertheless is of special importance because he became the king of Poland in 1576, through his marriage to a daughter of Polish King Sigismund I and Queen Bona Sforza [see the latter entry]. He eased the entry of Hungarian wine into Poland by granting tariff exemptions, thereby spreading the good name of Hegyalja wine, which was particularly helpful following Queen Bona's indignant attitude towards Hungarian wines (vis-à-vis Italian wines). Also, Báthory brought with him a large contingent of military and other persons from Hungary, whose families steadfastly continued to demand Hegyalja wines even after having settled permanently in Poland. [See the entry for Báthori, in Part III.]

Bél, Matthias. (1684-1749) Hungary's first geographer, Bél wrote a manuscript that provided details about the country's population and resources, county by county, settlement by settlement, at the beginning of the 18th century: the *Notitia Hungariae novae historico-geographica* (1735-1742). His careful description of the geographical confines of Hegyalja [see the Part II Essay] is particularly valuable as the earliest extant exposition on the subject, and indisputably demonstrates that by the late-1600s most observers had agreed that the region included most, but not all, of the same territory specified as Hegyalja by Hungarian legislation of 1893 and 1908. However, it is incorrect to think that Bél was the person who first classified the Hegyalja vineyards, as this had occurred in the mid-17th century. Further, Hegyalja vineyard rankings mentioned by Bél early in the 18th century no doubt followed the earlier judgment, particularly since he had no particular connection to either Hegyalja or the Upper Tisza.

Béla IV, King. (1206-1270) One of the last of the original Árpád Dynasty kings, Béla's reign began in 1235, and he played a crucial role in Hegyalja history by seeing to the rebuilding of the region following the Tatar invasion of 1241-1242. More than just rebuilding it, he actually extended wine-growing compared to the pre-invasion period, in effect setting the stage for a new era in the region's development. Indeed, the very notion 'Hegyalja' may have arisen in the second-half of the 13th century as a result of the region's new conformation. Where wine-growing was concerned, Béla's efforts were concentrated on bringing in knowledgeable foreign settlers, perhaps mostly Italians and Croatians (Dalmatians), but also Greeks from the Peloponnesus ('Morea'). However, he was equally active in strengthening the Upper Tisza region generally, through fortification and settlement, which eventually resulted in building a substantial regional market for Hegyalja wine even before the period of its great fame. He is also considered the king who firmly established Zemplén as a county.

Bimbólázár. (or Bimbolassar) John Bimbólázár was a Greek merchant in Tokaj in the early 18th century, but the family is noted here mainly because his son, George, who was born in Tokaj, went on to become an officer in the Imperial Russian army, and was called upon to arrange for vine-cuttings from Hegyalja to be procured for shipment to the czar's vineyard estate in the Crimea in 1784. [See the entry for *Gohér*, in Part IV.]

Bogát-Radvány. Among the early clans of Zemplén and the Upper Tisza, the Bogát-Radvány clan was among the most prolific. They apparently originated in the Czech lands, but were given a large estate in Hegyalja and further north along the Ondava river by at least the first-half of the 12th century [see the entry for Ondava River, in Part II]. A number of noble families descended from them and had an impact on the development of Hegyalja, but none more so than the Rákóczis. [See the entries for Rákóczi and Upori.] Another offshoot was the Kolcs clan, and it is possible that the Kócsag vineyard-tract in Tokaj was one of their holdings, since an early variation of the spelling was Kotts-ág, or 'Kolcs-branch' ('branch' in the sense of a hill spur).

Bollman, Justus Erich. (mid-18th c. – early-19th c.) A German merchant resident in the United States, Bollman procured Tokaji wines for Thomas Jefferson at the beginning of the 19th century. He is more generally notable for hoping to introduce Tokaji and other Hungarian wines to the well-to-do American public. In fact, his efforts are the earliest known aimed at supplying Tokaji to the New World on a regular basis. However, he was unsuccessful because the wines were not to the American taste of the day (which was accustomed to fortified, more spirituous wines), and on top of that were quite expensive, two factors that perhaps overlapped.

Bona, Queen. [See the entry for Sforza.]

Boner. Amongst the many 16th-century Polish traders in Tokaji and other Hungarian wines, the German-origin Boner family stands out because of the extent of their commitment and vision. Far from being occasional or opportunistic traders, they were looking at the long-term market for Tokaji, and organized themselves for it. Although a major supplier to the Polish royal court, Hans Boner had grander plans. He maintained representatives in Bohemia, Germany, and Russia, as well as in Hungary. Endeavors expanded under his son Sigmund, who had the assistance of three brothers. Remarkably, the Boners persisted despite the opposition of Queen Bona Sforza to the consumption of Hungarian wines in Poland. But the enterprise did not survive Sigmund's death. (The Boner family, incidentally, were involved with far more than just wine, and have a significant place in Polish economic history of the late Middle Ages.)

Bornemissza. [See the entries for Bornemissza and Hétszőlő, in Part III.]

Brankovich. The Serbian Brankovich family became involved in Hegyalja in the 1420s, when the despot George Brankovich acquired Abaújszántó and Szerencs. In 1433, the Hungarian king presented him with the Tállya and Tokaj estates that earlier had belonged to the Debrei branch of the Aba clan. But ownership of the latter two was rescinded by the king in 1459. Nevertheless, the family continued to own vineyards in highly-regarded tracts of Szántó (Gelencsér), Tállya (Remete), Tarcal (Tárczy), and even Bodrogkeresztúr (Henye) into the 1730s. A Count Brankovich was still a landowner in Zemplén County and Hegyalja as late as 1764. The interest of Serbian merchants in Tokaji presumably was sparked by the Brankoviches in the 16th century.

Bretzenheim, Ferdinand. (late-18th c. – 1855) Prince Bretzenheim took over the Regéc Domain in 1783, including Abaújszántó. In 1806, he purchased the extensive Hegyalja estate of the Trautsohns from the (Habsburg) Royal Treasury, and moved there from his estate in Germany. He took a great interest in developing varietal selection for the region. In 1845, he organized a varietal plantation at Sárospatak, with the aim of collecting all the varieties found in Hegyalja and seeing to the propagation of the best-suited ones and the exclusion of the rest. However, little is known about the project, and it seems to have been abandoned after the Hungarian revolution of 1848-1849. Afterward, in 1853, Bretzenheim turned his attention to the Hegyalja Shareholding Society, which was concerned primarily with wine trade.

Bright, Richard. (late-18th c. – early-19th c.) An integral part of the history of Tokaji wine is the dissemination of incorrect information abroad. Sometimes it was spread in printed form. Apparently oblivious to the 1773 report of Sylvester Douglass, Dr. Bright, in his 1818 book, *Travels from Vienna through Lower Hungary*, gave a sketchy report on Tokaji and perpetuated the misperception (of which Douglass had tried to disabuse the British) that "the greater part of these vineyards are the property of the Emperor; several, however, are in the hands of nobles." This erroneous belief prevailed until at least 1839, when it was assailed again by John Paget.

Bulgaro-Slavs. Like the Magyars, the Bulgars came from the east, and in the 7th century they occupied what would become Bulgaria. They amalgamated with the more numerous Slav inhabitants and adopted their language even while preserving an ethno-cultural identity as Bulgars. Their empire expanded westward and northward, and in the 9th century reached the Upper Tisza region, which is hardly to be wondered at, considering that Greek traders, coming from the same part of the Balkans, had been passing through the Upper Tisza for far more than a millennium. Thus did the Bulgars take over from the Avars in Hegyalja and most river valleys to its north. Further, Bulgaro-Slavs from central Macedonia (now north-central Greece and the Struma valley of Bulgaria) were brought to the southern Zemplén area, which includes Hegyalja, in the 9th century [see the entries for Mánta Creek and Sárazsadány, in Part II; and Rány, in Part III]. Their interest in the region may have lasted even longer [see the entry for Presian].

The Bulgaro-Slavs are of seminal importance to the development of Tokaji wine. Before the arrival of the Bulgars, the Slavs who migrated south from the Carpathian mountains to later Bulgaria mixed with the earlier Thracians, who were closely associated with wine in antiquity. These Slavs thus acquired Thracian wine-making habits (closely entwined with those of the Greeks), which the Bulgaro-Slavs took to Hegyalja. Evidence for this is in the old grape varieties of Zemplén, which were of Balkan origin; the treading of grapes by foot in the manner of the Thracians, rather than the use of presses in the Roman fashion; performing the treading outdoors, either in or beside the vineyards; the passing of the trampled grape mass through fibrous containers; and the storage of wine in goatskins. Much circumstantial evidence for a Bulgaro-Slav presence is to be found in geographical names [see the entry for Bulgarian Empire, in Part II]. Certain vocabulary terms are of interest [see the entry for Balkans, in Part II]. The greatest curiosity is the identical use in Hegyalja of the word 'kasha' that the Bulgaro-Slavs used for the thoroughly mashed skins and pulp of grapes [see #6, in the entry for Balkan Influences, in Part IV].

Bulgars: Bulgaro-Phobia

"There is no sign that our hill-country would have had any kind of contact with the Bulgars." So wrote the Hungarian J. Kossuth in 1903 in his paragraph on "Tokajhegyalja's first vineyard-planters." Such a robust denial is surprising, in view of the paucity of work that had been done on the subject. But, 70 years later, the Slovak historian B. Varsik, in his 3-volume work on the early history of the area just north of Hegyalja, felt compelled to address 'the Bulgar question,' and similarly concluded that the Bulgaro-Slavs had not been there. Varsik stated this view without consulting a single Bulgarian source. For Kossuth and other Hungarians of his era, the thought of being lumped in with the Balkan peoples was repugnant. For Varsik and other Slovak historians of his time, it was imperative to emphasize (even without demonstrating) that the Bulgarian Empire had never held 'historical Slovak territory' (lest Hungary seek to reclaim the Upper Tisza at some future date). But the cosmopolitan enophile can dismiss such stances in considering the roots of Hegyalja wine-growing. There is an abundance of 'prima facie' evidence refuting Kossuth and Varsik. Certainly it is supremely ironic that, in 'substantiating' his view, Varsik referenced the Hungarian historian E. Moór, who found little Bulgar influence in Hungarian agricultural terminology. Too bad neither Moór nor Varsik delved into Hegyalja [see the entries for Balkan Influences and Grape Varieties, in Part IV].

Caraffa. [See the entry for Klobusiczky.]

Charles Robert, King. [See the entry for Angevin Kings; and for Bardejov, in Part II.]

Chelebi, Evlia. (1611-1679) As noted wryly by almost every Christian traveler in Ottoman Europe, not all Muslims there foreswore wine. But the Turk who stood apart was Chelebi. A voracious traveler in Ottoman Europe, he displayed the instincts of a wine *amateur* while on the road. He wrote detailed journals in which he seems never to have failed to make note of wine-growing locales that impressed or pleased him. Chelebi even reached the Upper Tisza region, though it was not under Ottoman control, and mentioned a "marvelous vine" of Tokaj. This was around 1665, or after the inception of botrytis wines. Thus, he likely was praising the wine rather than a grape variety, under the misapprehension that a single varietal was responsible for it.

College of Sárospatak. [See the entry for Lórántffy; and for Sárospatak, in Part II.]

Columella. (1st c. AD) The stratum of educated Hungarians, able to read Latin and Greek, grew immensely during the 15th century, hence the spread of the name Deák (from the Greek for 'scholar'). The ancient books read by this literate class must have been broad, but Columella's *De Re Rustica* stands out as the one that might have had some influence in Hegyalja. First of all, it seems that his mention of overripe berries being 'soaked' in ordinary must was noticed and considered, probably because ordinary ripe grapes were already being treated that way in the case of *főbor* [see that entry, in Part IV]. Yet Hegyalja did not switch from sacks to baskets ("*in fiscellam*") or begin using a wine-press ("*prelo*") as prescribed by Columella for that sort of wine. (He said that he learned of the technique by reading the work of Mago, a Carthaginian. Mago, though, based much of his viti-vinicultural commentary on Greek authors.) [See the entry for *Aszú*: Aegean Echo, in Part IV.] Second, Columella's statement that berries were fully ripe when the seeds had achieved full color was repeated by F. Pethe, in 1797: "When the seed is not green, but brown: such is the real *aszú* grape [of Hegyalja]." But, as Columella admitted up front, he was strongly influenced by the earlier Greek agricultural and scientific writers. Surely, Aristotle's discussion of "concoction" in *Meteorologica* explains Columella's comment on seeds.

Compagnia Graecorum. [See the entry for Greek Merchant Society.]

Cooperatives. Understandably, the word 'cooperative' conjures the 'joint-labor associations' imposed during the communist era in Hungary. But the historic fact is that cooperatives were spreading in the preceding decades. Several factors were responsible for this trend. First, recovery from phylloxera could only be achieved amongst smallholders by joining together to replant Hegyalja's vineyards in an appropriate manner (notably, American root-stocks). Second, it would be difficult for smallholders to adhere to the Hungarian wine laws of 1893 and 1908 without mutual support; and most of all, the advantage of marketing wine in bottle would be out of reach. Further, the wine glut of the Interwar Period generally could not be weathered by individual smallholders acting alone. Yet another factor was the threat to the worldwide availability and reputation of Tokaji wine, which is why the nobility – the class with the greatest organizational skills – was a leading force behind the creation of cooperatives.

In 1903, Baron Maillot undertook the formation of the Tokaji Wine-Growers' Shareholding Society, in Mád, which was subsequently continued by Prince Windischgrätz under the name Tokaji Wine-Growers' Society. This led to a farsighted proposal in 1909 to organize 12 coops in the region, under state supervision. But little action was taken on it, except for the creation of the Sátoraljaújhely Hungarian Royal State Joint-Cellar in 1914. This was followed in 1931 by the Tokaj-hegyalja Wine Growers' Cellar-Cooperative, and in 1938 by the Hungarian Hill-Country Wine-Growers' Marketing Cooperative. These were focused mostly on sales, though with attention to enhancing quality. However, the world market and financial conditions of the period were such that these cooperative efforts could not resolve the region's problems, particularly not for smallholders.

The cooperatives of the communist era were, of course, of a different nature and had a different purpose. Most especially, because they were motivated by ideology and were seen as interim structures on the road to collectivization (which would spell the end of privately owned vineyards except for backyard plots), they did not have the long-term good of smallholders in mind. In that framework, the smallholder was just a convenient caretaker of a parcel. During the first-half of the era, smallholders had no prospect of marketing wine on their own, which meant a lack of incentive. Even in the second-half, under liberalized conditions, prices for grapes and must were manipulated in favor of the purchasing agencies. Rather late, there was some scope for joint effort by small groups of smallholders ('mini-coops'), but it was out of the question financially for all but a very few. Additionally, at this point in Hegyalja history, most smallholders had become dependent on industrial jobs for their livelihood, with wine-growing only a sideline.

Csáky – The Csákys were among the first major aristocratic families from outside the Upper Tisza region to become involved in Hegyalja. This could have started in the early-15th century. The family was from Bihar County, to the southeast, and probably was aware of Hegyalja wine because of the Csojka fort in Bihar [see the entry for Csojka, in Part III]. From the mid-16th century to the beginning of the 18th century, they skillfully switched allegiances between the Habsburgs and the anti-Habsburg Hungarian nobility, but always came out in favor of the crown just in time to be recipients of Habsburg largesse. Thus did Stephan Csáky gain the Nagy Sáros and Medgyes forts in Sáros County, and their vineyards in Hegyalja, at the beginning of the 17th century [see the entries for Sáros and Medgyes, in Part III]. His son, also named Stephan, acted in a like way and received from the Habsburgs the extensive domain belonging to the Szepes fortress, west of the Upper Tisza region, and also ownership of the important Hegyalja town of Tarcal. It is estimated that in the mid-17th century Stephan exported up to one-quarter of the family's wine production, mostly to Poland, and gave another one-fifth as gifts, mostly to important wielders of Habsburg power. This was of considerable promotional benefit to Hegyalja just when its fame was spreading because of modern botrytis *aszú* wine. Later, in 1749, the widow of Francis Csáky gave vineyard land adjoining the Szarvas tract to the Habsburgs for their expansion of Szarvas, in exchange for other Habsburg vineyard property [see the entry for Grassalkovich].

Csirke. Resident mainly in neighboring Abaúj County, the Csirke family became a significant owner of vineyards in Zemplén County, apparently in the aftermath of the Tatar invasion of 1241-1242. By the late 1300s, Margaret (Margit) owned vineyards throughout Hegyalja, which is an early indication that the region was developing an identity of its own well before later-harvested wines started to be produced. The vineyard-tract Csirke in Szegi and Bodrogkisfalud almost certainly refers to this family, as might Margitasor in Erdőbénye, as well [see the entries for those tracts, in Part III].

Czudar. [See the entry for Zudar.]

Dercsényi, John (János). (1755-1837) A Hungarian-German born in the Szepesség region, John Dercsényi (Derczeni in older literature) became a physician, worked briefly for Zemplén County (1780-1782), and married into local nobility, the Kazinczy family. Thus did he become a significant writer on the subject of Tokaji, and leave behind a variety of interesting notations. Most of all, in 1825, he mentioned *aszú* wines of greater than 6-*puttonyos* sweetness: 8-, 10- and 12-*puttonyos aszú*, with 12-*puttonyos aszú* being known as "the queen of *eszencias*." This information contradicts 20th-century explanations of the term *aszú-eszencia* as originating from the addition of *eszencia* to a 3-, 4-, 5- or 6-*puttonyos aszú* wine. Also, in his book of 1796 about Tokaji production, Dercsényi listed the *gohér* as the chief Hegyalja grape variety, followed by *furmint*, *fejérszőlő*, *hárslevelű* (all of which were white), the red *rózsásszőlő* and black *feketeszőlő*, as well as the white *muskotály* and *szekfű* [see the entry for Grape Varieties, in Part IV]. Further, he emphatically stated that different sorts of Tokaji wine were preferred in various countries. He specified the Poles and Hungarians as preferring spicy, extractive *aszú* and *máslás* wines, while Germans prefer "sweet and unctuous" wine, and value "*eszencia* above all."

Dobó. Any student of Hungarian wine is familiar with this name from the story of Egri Bikavér and the improbable defeat of the Ottomans at Eger by the vastly outnumbered Hungarians under Stephan Dobó in 1552. The Dobós were actually from Ung County, on the northeastern side of Zemplén, and did not have any substantive connection to the wine of Eger (west of Hegyalja, in Heves County). But, by at least the first decade of the 16th century, they had become involved in Hegyalja wine-growing. At that time, Sofia Dobó was recorded as a vineyard owner in Bodrogkeresztúr, Bodrogkisfalud, Vámosújfalu, and Kistoronya (now Malá Tŕňa), as well as Csarnahó (Černochov) and Csörgő (Čergov), which later were disputed Hegyalja locales. Also, in the late 1500s, Francis Dobó planted a vineyard in Sárospatak, in the Somlyód tract. The Dobós died out in 1602 [see the opening to the Part I Essay; and the entry for Somlyód, in Part III].

Dombi, Samuel. (18th century) In his thesis of 1758 for the University of Utrecht, *Dissertatio inauguralis Physico-Chemico Medica de vino Tokaiense*, the Hungarian doctoral candidate Dombi gave the names of the principal Hegyalja varieties in Latin: Augusta, Albula, Tumidula, and Gemma, which correspond in Hungarian to *gohér*, *fehérszőlő*, *kövérszőlő*, and *gyöngyszőlő* [see those entries, in Part IV]. In view of other varietal accounts in the course of Hegyalja history, it is far less surprising that Dombi seems not to have mentioned *furmint*, than that he included *gyöngyszőlő*. But some persons of that era, notably Matthias Bél, seemed to think that the *furmint* was indicated by the name *tumidula* [see the latter entry, in Part IV]. Dombi is also notable for his comment that the highest Hegyalja vineyards in his day mostly produced "thin" (*híg*) and "biting" (*csípős*) wine [the subject of altitude is discussed in the Part III Essay].

Dominican Order. [See the entries for Szemince and Szent Vince, in Part III.]

Douglass, Sylvester. (18th century) Having found that "the popular [British] notions concerning [Tokaji] are in general erroneous," Douglass, in 1768, became the first western European to visit Hungary for the express purpose of learning and writing about the subject. His report of 1773, "An Account of the Tokay and other Wines of Hungary," contains a number of notations of interest, the more so because he was informed by "the chief proprietors." He specified several characteristics of Tokaji [see the entry for Color: Historical Enigma, in Part IV], and generalized that "all Tokay wine has an aromatic taste; so peculiar, that nobody, who has ever drank it genuine, can confound it with any other species of wine." As to wine types, Douglass made no mention of the terms *ordinárium* or *szamorodni* [see those entries, in Part IV]. His most notable comments are about *máslás* [Part IV]. For one thing, he mentioned the use of hands instead of feet in obtaining it, whereas Paget connected hand-squeezing with *aszú* [see #9 in the entry for Balkan Influences, in Part IV]. Regarding exports to England, Douglass mentioned that "the late Mr. Wortley Montague" had been involved with it and had even stayed in Tokaj for several months so as to be sure of procuring only "the best and most genuine wine." [See the Part I Essay; and also the entry for Uzhhorod, in Part II.]

Draheim, Wilhelm Leopold. (1640-1693) A Hungarian-German from the Szepesség region, Draheim was appointed in 1678 as the director of the vineyards administered for the Habsburgs by the Szepes Chamber [see that entry]. He immediately set about making an intensive inquiry into how the vineyards were being worked. This was at a time when the Habsburg vineyards were widely scattered around Hegyalja. He found the vineyards so poorly managed that income hardly covered expenses, a situation he attributed in part to insufficient attention by experts, and in part to the unstable political and civil situation in Hegyalja owing to anti-Habsburg activities. Draheim gave a lot of attention to Tarcal, where the crown's most valuable properties were located. This became a legacy to the overall Habsburg view of Hegyalja, and thus a reason that the Imperial properties were eventually concentrated at Tarcal. Draheim's work was so well-regarded that he was allowed to continue even when Tarcal fell into the hands of the anti-Habsburg nobility during the Thököly rebellion of 1683-1685. [See the entry for Halápi.]

Draskovics, George (György). (1515-1587) The bishop of Pécs, in southwestern Hungary, then under Ottoman occupation, Draskovics became the unlikely first publicist for Tokaji wine abroad. As the representative of King Ferdinand of Austria at the Council of Trent in 1562, his worldly interests led him to have some Hegyalja wine brought from Tállya for Pope Pius IV, because he thought it better than any of the other wines being served. (Alternatively, the incident is dated to the early 1550s and Pope Julian III.) The pope praised it as "worthy of the Supreme Pontiff," and thus did the West first take note of Hegyalja. Draskovics had no connection to the Upper Tisza region where Hegyalja is located, but Tokaji apparently had begun to gain repute west of the Danube by the middle of the 16th century, despite the Ottoman occupation.

Drugeth. This family is usually referred to in Hungarian history by the name Homonnai Drugeth, in reference to the northeastern Zemplén County town of Homonna (now Humenné, in East Slovakia). The Drugeths were a noble clan from Naples that came to Hungary with the Angevin kings after 1300 and quickly rose to regional and national prominence. By mid-century, they were routinely occupying the position of Lord-Lieutenant of Zemplén County. The Drugeths played an important role in extending and solidifying the county's control further north (up to today's Slovakian-Polish border), into what was still newly developing territory. Their main seat was the Homonna Domain centered in the Ciróka (Ciroché) river valley. The family's interests extended to wine, including efforts to cultivate the vine on sunny southern slopes along the Ciróka [see the entry for Upper Tisza, in Part II]. They also paid particular attention to Hegyalja during its early development, hence the old vineyard-tract in Tolcsva still known as Ciróka. By at least the mid-15th century, the Drugeths were exporting Hegyalja wine to Poland by normal commercial means, and when customs regulations became onerous in the 16th century, they became heavily involved in smuggling Tokaji, which was facilitated by the Homonna Domain being a borderland fringed by forested uplands. The family used the Rusyns, who inhabited the northeasternmost area, to transport the wine along little known paths, and to carve out new ones. The Drugeths' political downfall came at the hands of the Rákóczis in the 17th century, when they supported the Habsburgs. They died out in 1684.

Dujardin, Karl. (18th century) Dujardin was perhaps the most impressive administrator in Hegyalja history. He was brought from Germany in 1740 by Leopold Trautsohn to manage the family's domain, which in that era comprised by far the largest collection of vineyard properties in the region, with holdings in 28 communities. One of his notable efforts was the reconstruction of the old Somlyód vineyard-tract [see that entry, in Part III]. He resided in Sáros County, in Eperjes, a key locale for sales to Poland. Where wine sales were concerned, Dujardin certainly cooperated with the Russian wine-buying commission, and thus, presumably, dealt with the Greek merchants as well. Yet, perhaps his greatest coup was in finding ways to circumvent the export restrictions imposed by the Habsburgs, to the advantage of his benefactors, the Trautsohns. Unfortunately, no specific information is available about that.

Eger Bishopric. Founded at the beginning of the 11th century by King St. Stephan, this bishopric had virtually the whole Upper Tisza region, including Hegyalja and Zemplén County, under its ecclesiastical authority from the late Middle Ages onward. The bishopric played a major role in developing the vineyards of Zemplén by bringing various religious orders into the region. It also helped repopulate Hegyalja following calamities such as the Tatar invasion. The bishopric had a vested interest in keeping wine production high since the secular domains of the area were subject to an annual wine tithe. At the same time, it was a major factor in spreading markets for Tokaji wine before the era of later-harvested wines, particularly in the Upper Tisza region. [See the entry for Barkóczi.]

Eugènie, Empress. (1825-1920) Tokaji had many admirers and devotees, but Napoleon III's wife, Eugènie is, in retrospect, remarkable for having noticed something about Tokaji that only modern science has proven to be true. Namely, she attributed not only her health, but also her well-preserved complexion to drinking two small glasses of *aszú* every morning. Recent research has shown Tokaji *aszú* to have a significant content of superoxide-dismustase, which enhances skin tone [see the entry for SOD, in Part IV].

Ferenczi, Alexander (Sándor). (20th c.) An enologist active in Hegyalja since pre-communist times, Ferenczi was preoccupied with the question of how to stabilize the Tokaji sweet wines without harming their quality or affecting their character. He developed a stabilization technique that bore his name, the 'Ferenczi heat-treatment,' which employed pasteurization in a highly innovative and complex way, specifically designed for the maturation process used for the Tokaji specialty wines. It became standard procedure during the 1970s and remained in use during most of the remainder of the communist period. It is not an exaggeration to say that it was because of Ferenczi that more Tokaji arrived at its destination in a healthy state than ever before in the wine's history. Western connoisseurs of the era had no idea about Ferenczi's procedure and Tokaji's continued ability to develop beneficially in bottle afterward. [See the entry for Ferenczi heat-treatment, in Part IV.]

Frosch. (also as Froos and Frus in old Hungarian documents) This German-origin commercial family resided in the towns of the Upper Tisza area north of Hegyalja during the late Middle Ages. The fact that one of them (Froos) was in the earliest list of Eperjes (Prešov) citizens, from 1428, suggests that they were already a trade-oriented family of the region at that time, and probably became involved in the trade of Tokaji wine from its early period as a major commercial article outside Hegyalja. Another family member (Frus) was also a prominent townsman of Sztropkó (Stropkov), in northern Zemplén, in the first-half of the 16th century, during the era of contraband exports of Tokaji wine from that town to Poland. Some family members resided in Poland to take care of business at that end, for instance, Andreas Frosch at Troppau (Opava), in Silesia, in the second-half of the 16th century.

Fugger. (also as Fukker, Fuker, Fukier) Mentioned mostly for the old stocks of Tokaji in their former Warsaw cellar, the Fugger family had far more than anecdotal significance in Tokaji history. The Fugger merchant house of Augsburg, under Jacob Fugger, partnered with Hungarian-born John Thurzó of Cracow in 1496 in exploiting mining in northern Hungary (now north-central Slovakia). This happened precisely in the period when wine-growing in Hegyalja was shifting to later-harvested white wine, and since the Thurzós were well aware of Hegyalja, they drew the Fuggers' attention to it. Thus, the Fuggers may be credited for some of the early marketing of later-harvested Tokaji in the markets of southern Poland. Moving further north, the family also became active in Warsaw towards the end of the 18th century; and in 1805, Florian Fukier established the cellar that would hold the stocks of 17th century Tokaji which later became entrenched in wine lore. One source of those ancient wines likely were the remaining stocks of Martin Fukker, who had been involved with the smuggling of Tokaji during the mid-17th century from his base in Ó-Lubló (now Stará Ľubovňa, East Slovakia), one of the towns under Polish rule in the Szepesség region [see that entry, in Part II]. Also, one of the early books about Tokaj-Hegyalja was written by Andreas Fuker of Eperjes in 1749 [see the entry for Prešov, in Part II]. His son settled in Tállya, whence he continued to conduct his father's wine trade business, and also acquired a vineyard. Additionally, the family owned a vineyard in Olaszliszka. Regarding the Thurzó-Fugger connection, it is also to be noted that in the late-16th century, George Thurzó married Anna Fugger. [See the entry for Thurzó.]

Garai. [See the entry for Garai, in Part III.]

Germans. It is impossible to overstate the role of German-speaking people in the development of Tokaji wine. The Germans in the Hungarian towns north of Hegyalja were enormously influential as buyers of wine during the 14th-16th centuries, and their initial 'approval' of later-harvested white wine was instrumental in ushering in the region's broader fame. [See the entry for Selbstherr, below; and for Szepesség, in Part II.]

The permanent and significant presence of Germans in the Upper Tisza dates to the earliest centuries of the Kingdom of Hungary, to the era of the Árpád kings. For instance, the later Tokaji trading town of Eperjes (Prešov) received its first large influx of Germans around 1150, and a document of 1249 referred to that area as *terra Saxonum*, or 'Saxon land.' Germans founded most of the Hungarian towns north of Hegyalja [see Pentapolitana, in Part II], or else imbued largish villages with an urban character; and they created new hamlets as well. They were also significant in Hegyalja itself, in the towns of Sárospatak and Sátoraljaújhely. Further, German settlement in the Upper Tisza recurred several times during Hungarian history, even as late as the 18th century. In many locales, a German identity was preserved to some extent, and not until well into the 19th century did the German language lose its influence in commerce and culture. Several of the earliest books about Tokaji were written in German in the towns to the north.

Direct German influence on wine-growing in Hegyalja (as opposed to their indirect influence as consumers) seems to have been negligible. There is nothing to suggest that either grape varieties or wine-growing and wine-making techniques were brought from the German lands. It is noteworthy that the wine-press was not being used in Hegyalja around 1500, even though Germans had already brought it to some nearby areas just to the west [see the entry for Vizsoly, in Part II]. However, a particular German addition to the wine culture of Hegyalja was the term *eszencia*, which first made its appearance in the German form, *essentz*.

Two German settlements are of special note. First, and the earliest, is Gönc, to the west of the Zemplén hills, in Abaúj County. It developed in the 13th century and became specialized in cooperage. Gönc is where Hegyalja and other regional growers went for casks and other wine-making equipment. Here, too, is where the so called *gönci* barrel, which became identified with Tokaji wine, was developed. The other notable settlement, further north in Abaúj, was Mecenzéf, which provided Hegyalja with a variety of skilled laborers and excellent tools. [See the entries for Gönc and Medzev, as well as Hercegkút, Józseffalva, Károlyfalva, and Rátka, in Part II.]

Ghyllányi. [See the entry for Gilányi, in Part III.]

Görög, Demeter. (1760-1833) Although Hungarian, Görög established a vine collection near Vienna. But he made a point of collecting varieties from throughout the lands that traditionally belonged to the Kingdom of Hungary, thus including parts of Croatia and Dalmatia. He noted that numerous very good varieties, some for wine, some for the table, were to be found in Hegyalja, and that some had therefore been brought to Western lands for cultivation, particularly to the Rheinland. Görög's collection was maintained after his death and was a source of cuttings purchased for Ágoston Haraszthy in California by General Lázár Mészáros. The Hungarian aristocrats of Hegyalja were keenly aware of Görög's collection in the period, mostly the mid-19th century, when they were looking into the best varieties and clones to plant in the region. But the particulars of his influence in that regard are not known.

Grassalkovich, Antal. (1694-1771) A supporter of Habsburg rule, the Hungarian nobleman Grassalkovich was made president of the Hungarian Chamber under Queen Maria Theresa. He took a direct interest in her Hegyalja vineyard properties, and in 1748 reported that the crown's holdings needed to be consolidated in the interest of better management and producing wine befitting the royal court. Having gained the queen's approval, Grassalkovich concentrated on increasing the area of prime holdings in Tarcal, on Tokaj-hill, through purchases and exchanges, while disposing of lesser or distant vineyards through sales and exchanges. The result was an expansion of the crown's Szarvas tract onto adjacent tracts, and creation of the Terézhegy (Theresa-hill) vineyard-tract through acquisition and expansion on Henye-hill. It was this 'unification' of the crown's Hegyalja properties that later lent the term 'Imperial Tokay' a geographical significance amongst people thoroughly versed in Hegyalja wine-growing. Grassalkovich also made careful observations about aspects of cultivation, and it is quite likely that he was responsible for *furmint* becoming the major variety in the Habsburgs' Tarcal vineyards, since it is known that *furmint* was grown to only a very minor extent in the Szarvas tract in the first-half of the 18th century, whereas in the second-half of the century the *furmint* was being planted and harvested separately there.

Greek Merchant Society. (*Compagnia Graecorum*, or *Görög Kereskedő Társaság*). This association of Greek traders in Tokaji wine was unique in Hegyalja history, as no other ethnically based trading association was ever formed. To some extent, this reflects the considerable size of the Greek community when the society was founded early in the 18th century. But the motivations behind its formation are not clear. It seems less likely that it was intended as a joint effort in exporting Tokaji, than as a joint effort to protect the Greeks' interests against actions being taken against them by Zemplén County. In that regard, the society may have resorted to some sort of 'self-policing' regarding the falsification of Tokaji wine, which was what the County was most concerned about [see the entry for Falsification, in Part IV]. In any case, it certainly seems as though it was successful in keeping the Greeks in the Tokaji trade, and the society was still in existence as late as 1772 (UC 58:32). It was headquartered at Tokaj. The major Greek families of Hegyalja included the following (the names in italics have separate entries herein): Altentzis, *Bimbólázár*, Constantin, Despu, Draskovszky, Kallona, Karácsony, Kefala, Kiró, Koszta, Lefter, Mane, Morally, Pap, *Paraskevich*, Parda, Polity, *Rosa*, *Stegner*, *Szerviczky*, and Zákó. Their presence in the town of Tokaj itself was so large in the second-half of the 18th century, that Douglass mentioned only Magyars and Greeks as inhabitants of the town.

Greeks. Since mention of the Greeks in Hegyalja history is invariably limited to their utter domination of the region's wine trade from the late-17th century to the late-18th century, it needs to be emphasized that this has led to a gross underestimation of Greek influence. The historical Balkan orientation of what became Hegyalja is most effectively demonstrated by the presence and activity of Greeks in the part of the Upper Tisza region directly north of Hegyalja since very early times. The Greeks since antiquity had plied the trade routes from the Aegean to the Baltic (about 1,610 km/1,000 miles), which is primarily why the Bulgaro-Slavs learned of the Upper

Tisza in the first place [see the entry for Molyvás, in Part II]. They were so well-acquainted, that in the late-13th century Greeks were the first owners of Raslavice and Koprivnica at the northern end of the Eperjes-Tokaj Hill-Chain [see that entry, in Part II]. Also, the first registry of citizens at Eperjes, in 1428, records a man named Samarrumnyoo, in which the otherwise bizarre ending –*rumnyoo* is only explicable as a distorted rendering of *romyós* (ρωμιός), the name by which the Greeks called themselves in that era (Samar- = Saddler). The Greeks thus appear to have been traders in the Upper Tisza from the time when Tokaji wine became a significant commodity.

In Hegyalja itself, the Greeks made two important appearances. The first occurred after the Tatar invasion of 1241-1242, when King Béla IV brought foreign vine-dressers to help repopulate the region. Hungarian historians seem to understand that all of these newcomers were Italians, or other neo-Latin speakers, even while mentioning that some came from 'Morea.' But Morea has nothing to do with Italy, and instead is synonymous, in colloquial Greek, with the Peloponnesus. While Béla IV might have dealt with aristocratic Italian families in arranging the migrations, settlers could easily have been sourced in the northern Peloponnesus, since it had fallen under the rule of the so called Frankish (Roman Catholic) princes early in the 13th century, several decades before Béla brought 'Italians.' Migration from the Peloponnesus and the island of Zakynthos could explain some of the old Greek grape sorts of Hegyalja [see the entry for *Malozsa*, in Part IV].

The second major influx of Greeks was more gradual and began in the 17th century. This influx was of a commercial nature rather than agricultural. These were the Greek traders usually spoken of in Hegyalja history. The Macedonian Greeks, in particular, had been active in Poland, trading in Macedonian as well as Aegean wines (for one, the anciently famous Chian was still known in Poland because of these merchants) [see the entry for Chios, in Part II]. Thus, they had become aware of Tokaji when it first started acquiring a name in Poland during the 15th century. It is known that one of the earliest traders in Tokaji was the Rosa family, in the early-17th century. Many of these merchants originated in the major Macedonian wine-producing and trading towns, such as Siatista, Naoussa, and Melenikon (now Melnik, in Bulgaria), places averaging around 700 km (450 miles) in distance from Tokaj. Some others came into Hungary and Hegyalja with the Serbian exodus into southern Hungary near the end of the 17th century.

In addition to taking up residence in the trading towns north of Hegyalja, the merchants eventually settled in Hegyalja itself. How early this might have begun is uncertain, but the cellar of the Honétzy house in Tokaj has Greek writing on the walls, and several dates, including 1460 (the same era as the aforementioned Samarrumnyoo in Eperjes). The Greeks must have been significant in number by the late-17th century, since a *taxa graecorum* ('Greek tax') was imposed in 1689 (UC 5:15). Some acquired vineyards as well as cellars. Although the Greeks initially tended to migrate back and forth between Hungary and Macedonia, they increasingly stayed and became Hungarian subjects, especially after a law of 1741 required them to do so if they were to retain vineyard ownership [see the entry Gangalus: Scholar's or Merchant's?, in Part III]. A census of Greeks in Tokaj and Tarcal was taken in 1760, and included their vineyards. Unfortunately, some tampered with Tokaji [see Falsification, in Part IV], which led to anti-Greek sentiment amongst the nobility, Upper Tisza towns, and scrupulous Polish traders. A county regulation of 1723 excluded foreigners (mostly Greeks) from the wine trade, though it was not much enforced.

It is a mistake to imagine these Greeks as mere wine-traders. Those from the well-known wine regions of Macedonia oftentimes were from families that operated the most considerable wine-making facilities in their hometowns, and were far removed conceptually from the peasant wine-grower. Thus, those Greeks in Hegyalja possessed, collectively, a large fund of knowledge about viti-vinicultural techniques. The Hegyalja Greeks were a veritable repository of wine techniques that had come down from antiquity; and they probably shared their knowledge with one another.

While this comes to mind mostly when thinking of the fraudulent practices of some Greek traders, it is quite possible that positive contributions were made both in the vineyard (because of familiarity with some of the grape varieties) and in the cellar (because of analogous cellaring conditions in Macedonia). As well, the northern Greeks, because of the natural environment of their homeland, were ahead of most Europeans in familiarity with the properties of woods other than oak in the aging of wines.

Finally, in connection with their ancient heritage, the Greeks knew various possibilities for the use of shriveled grapes, including those that shriveled on the vine rather than being dried in the sun after harvesting [see the entry *Aszú*: Aegean Echo, in Part IV]. Also, e*szencia* could have been an addition of theirs to Tokaji tradition. The first recorded mention of *eszencia* is from 1707, or at least three decades after the arrival of Greek merchants in Hegyalja, and several decades longer in the case of the Rosas. The *eszencia* technique is identical to that for the ancient Greek *protropon* [see the entries for Nectar and *Protropon*, in Part IV]. Also, the use of such a wine to improve other wines was another practice that the Greeks had inherited from antiquity.

Gyöngyösi, Gabriel (Gábor). (late-17th c. – mid-18th c.) Gabriel Gyöngyösi was both a Hegyalja wine-grower and an advisor to the Hungarian Chamber in the early-18th century. In 1736, he cautioned against over-production of *eszencia* and *aszú*, lest it be at the quantitative and qualitative expense of the table wines that were the region's perennial mainstay in commerce. His remark serves to indicate the period when *eszencia* and *aszú* were at their historic peak as a proportion of production, and thus also suggests when and why the more botrytis-prone *furmint* variety began to receive much greater attention from major growers.

Habsburgs. No wine name was ever so closely connected to an imperial and royal house as Tokaji was to the Habsburgs. Indeed, the end of the Habsburg Empire after the First World War was in some eyes tantamount to the fall of Tokaji. But the story of the Habsburgs and Tokaji is more complicated. The Habsburgs had no part in the early development of Hegyalja, were rather late in exerting significant influence on the region, and did not always have the region's best interests in mind (if we distinguish the overall region from the Habsburgs' own properties). To be sure, the Habsburgs got a foothold in Hungary at a fairly early date in Hegyalja history, when Ferdinand I became king of rump Royal Hungary in 1541 (as part of the tripartite partition with the Ottomans and the Transylvanian princes). As a result, they also gained some vineyard properties in Hegyalja, though not extensive or notable ones. Their attention to the region grew only with the extension of Transylvanian influence in the Upper Tisza that was supposed to be Habsburg territory, and particularly when the Rákóczis during the second-half of the 17th century used revenues from Tokaji wine to finance their anti-Habsburg activities. The first significant Habsburg 'intervention' in the region came in the late-17th century, when the vineyard properties of the pro-Thököly and pro-Rákóczi nobility were confiscated for the Royal Treasury.

This history was reflected as well in the Habsburg involvement with wine-growing in Hegyalja. Initially, the royal house viewed the region quite like any other wine-growing territory in its realm and, without any particular knowledgeableness, acquired a motley collection of properties through bequeathals, donations, and purchases, all administered through the Royal Treasury. The properties were widely scattered over nine communes, both in the north and the south of Hegyalja. Numbering over 50, they varied in size and quality, and none were adjoining, all of which encumbered management. The basis for a new outlook was laid when the Habsburgs took over the most prized property of the Rákóczis after 1711, the Szarvas tract in Tarcal. Even so, the possibilities were not realized until Maria Theresa decided to go along with the recommendation of Hungarian Chamber president Grassalkovich's proposal, in 1748, to consolidate the Royal vineyard holdings on the Tarcal side of Tokaj-hill (which included Szarvas). It was only as a result of that action that the notion of 'Imperial Tokay' began to develop, *i.e.*, in reference to a specific, integral property. Following the First World War, the Habsburg vineyard estate was managed by The Royal Family Vineyard Administration, in the expectation of a Habsburg restoration. After the Second World War, the property was nationalized and put under the direct management of the Tarcal Viti-Vinicultural Institute. [See the entry for Szarvas, in Part IV.]

Halápi, Martin (Márton). (17th century) A member of the Sáros County nobility, Halápi had a position with the Szepes Chamber, including responsibility for inspecting vineyards that it held. This was in the time of Wilhelm Draheim's management of the Chamber's vineyards [see the entries for Draheim and Szepes Chamber]. Doing the legwork for Draheim, Halápi compiled information on 23 communities of Hegyalja (*"Submontanarum"*) in 1674-1675 (UC 158:31(a); UC 158:31(b); UC 158:32). The timing is close enough to the Rákóczis' mid-century Hegyalja vineyard classification, that the 22 present-day communities mentioned in Halápi's report must have reflected the Rákóczis' conception of what constituted Hegyalja, although not including villages where the Chamber did not have fiscal properties. [See the Part II Essay.]

Henderson, Alexander. [See the entries for Color and Tokaji Character, in Part IV.]

Herodotus. (5th c. B.C.) The Greek historian is included in connection with the word *aszú*. In Book IV (22-23) of *History* (*circa* 440 B.C.), he wrote of the Scythian territory north of the Black Sea, and mentioned inhabitants of a foothill region who "speak a tongue of their own" and drink "a thick black liquid" called "aschu" (ἄσχυ). He attributed the drink to a tree called "pontic," which he said was about the size of a fig tree, with a fruit the size of a bean, but with a stone in it. The scholar Ernst Herzfeld identified this as the coffee tree from the Arabian land of Punt; hence, a 'pontic' tree, but having nothing to do with the Pontus (Black Sea) region. Herodotus indicates that the fruit was fully ripe and black before ἄσχυ could be made, which suggests an ultra-ripe, dry state, as is meant by *aszú*. His term ἄσχυ would have sounded like 'ahz-khy,' not 'ahs-chu,' but he might have distorted the sound of a word he picked up secondhand or even third-hand. Still, he put the accent on the first syllable, as in *aszú*. It seems possible that Herodotus could have been referring to a language from which the Magyars picked up a root word while living in Scythia during their gradual westward migration to Hungary at a much later date.

Homonnay. [See the entry for Drugeth.]

Hungarian Chamber. (*Magyar Kamara*) The Habsburgs established the Hungarian Chamber to administer their Hungarian territories, partly to ensure fealty to the Empire, and partly to develop Hungary's economic resources for the benefit of the Crown. The Chamber was headquartered in Bratislava (formerly Pozsony), which was also the Hungarian capital, and located near to Vienna. Acting through its regional subsidiary, the Szepes Chamber, the Hungarian Chamber also had a hand in Hegyalja. This interest was quite direct. For example, in 1738, the Royal Treasury had 31 vineyard properties throughout Hegyalja: Tállya, Mád, Szerencs, Tarcal, Bodrogkisfalud, Bodrogzsadány, Erdőbénye, Tolcsva, and Sárospatak (UC 83:89). In 1783, the Chamber had vineyards in 18 separate tracts in the town of Sátoraljaújhely alone (UC: 191:10). It should be emphasized that such properties were primarily a source of revenue for the Crown, and had little to do with producing wine for consumption at the Imperial Court.

Hungarian Wine Commission. (or 'Tokaji Russian Wine-Purchasing Commission') Established by Czarina Anna Ivanovna in 1733, the Commission continued to operate virtually throughout the rest of the 18th century, in the service of Russian rulers. The only hiatus was during 1740-1744, when purchasing was temporarily entrusted to private merchants, notably Paraskevich. As its title indicates, the Commission was initially meant to obtain quantities of

Tokaji simply by making purchases. But the quantities sought by the Imperial Court soon trebled from 250 to 750 *antal*-s (1 *antal* = 1/2 *gönci* barrel [Part IV]). Thus, in 1745, Czarina Elizabeth I instructed Commission chief Vishnyevski to purchase not only wine, but also large quantities of *aszú* grapes for vinification, and to rent vineyards and facilities. For instance, Vishnyevski rented two vineyards in the Melegoldal tract in Tokaj in 1746 for 15 years, another in Zsoltár in Tokaj the same year, also for 15 years, and two more in Veres and Szappanos in Tokaj in 1747 for 20 years. This practice continued until at least the 1770s.

But these activities of the Commission were illegal, in that only foreigners owning vineyard estates could purchase *aszú* grapes or rent vineyards. The result was ongoing disputes with Zemplén County virtually throughout the life of the Commission, although the Habsburgs sometimes overrode the Hungarians, depending on the political climate between Russia and Austria. [Also, see the entry for Barkóczi.] The last major dispute was in 1784-1785, when the Commission purchased 30,000 vine cuttings for planting in the Crimea, a purchase that was also prohibited by Hungarian law. Habsburg Emperor Joseph II favored the sale, but after 19,000 cuttings had been sent, Zemplén authorities had the remainder destroyed before shipment. [See the entry for *Gohér*, in Part IV.]

The Commission had one last flurry of wine purchases during 1790-1795, after Czarina Catherine II prohibited imports of French wine (particularly Champagne) into Russia because of the French Revolution. But her son, Paul I, quietly disbanded the Commission in 1798. The loss of the Imperial Russian market could not have come at a worse time for Hegyalja, since it was already suffering from losses of sales on the Polish market because of political developments there.

Italians. The Italians occupy a relatively well-known place in Tokaji's history because of their participation in repopulating Hegyalja following the Tatar devastation of 1241-42, when King Béla IV sought people with vineyard skills to rebuild the region. However, the Italian presence in this era was greater than that one occurrence suggests. Italians first came to Zemplén around the beginning of the 12th century, when King Kálmán granted Sátoraljaújhely to the Ratold clan of Caserta. It can also be presumed that Italians came with the Roman Catholic religious orders that reached Zemplén in the late-12th and early-13th centuries.

Later even than the post-Tatar reconstruction, some Italians would have arrived in the early-14th century with the Neapolitan Drugeth clan, which had been presented with the Hommona Domain of northern Zemplén, and then became the lords-lieutenant of the county. Duke Ladislao of Apulia also occupied the latter position briefly in the 1380s, and presumably brought a few Apulians. Further, in about that same era, Italians settled along the Tapoly (Topľa) valley that extended from west-central Zemplén into eastern Sáros County [see the entry for Bardejov, in Part II]. Since all of these places were little more than a day's ride apart, it is likely that, from around 1250 to 1450, there was an Italian cultural presence in the small towns and lowlands of the western Upper Tisza region, facilitated as well by the use of Latin as a *lingua franca* in Hungary.

The Italian influence on agriculture in general must have been extensive. Notably, the Italians were the first skilled gardeners to inhabit the area, and the parts of west-central Zemplén and east-central Sáros where they settled became known for market-gardening, including both vegetables and fruit trees. The Italians likely introduced wine-growing in some areas, such as the Tapoly valley in east-central Sáros, near Girált (Giraltovce), whose name apparently was derived from the Italian original, Giroalto. It can also be presumed that the Drugeths encouraged wine-growing in the Ciróka (Ciroché) river valley running northeast from Homonna. A likely Italian bequest was the cultivation of vines amidst vegetables and fruit trees (including Mediterranean fruits) in warm areas, although this habit did not survive. Also, because of their stone masonry skills, early

Italians might have suggested methods for separating and enclosing vineyard parcels, which in the course of time became the basis for vineyard classification in Hegyalja.

Regarding Hegyalja specifically, Italian settlement in the 13th century apparently occurred all along the north-to-south length of the region. Popular lore attributes several village names to the Italians: Tállya, on the assumption that it derives from the name Italia; as well as Olaszliszka (originally Liszka-Olaszi) and Bodrogolaszi, in which *olasz* is the Hungarian word for Italian. But Hungarian researchers now doubt that these names actually indicated settlement by Italians. The name Tállya likely dates to earlier settlement by Walloons and derives from a word they used for cleared forest land, *taille*. Also, the term *olasz* in the Middle Ages did not refer only to Italians, but instead was applied collectively to persons speaking any of the neo-Latin languages, and thus could just as well have been applied to the earlier Walloons. Nevertheless, Italians settled in these places as a result of King Béla IV's efforts; and the founding of Olaszliszka and Bodrogolaszi seems to coincide with that period. In any case, no one has challenged the old tradition that Bári, north of Sátoraljaújhely, was resettled by people from the Bari area of Apulia.

Despite their presence in Hegyalja, it is exceedingly difficult to specify the Italian contribution to Tokaji wine. They seem to have had but a minimal impact on wine techniques, since they obviously did not replace the earlier Balkan methods of handling the grape harvest. Further, they arrived in an era when reddish dry wine likely was still either dominant or widespread in Hegyalja, and seem not to have left any trace of introducing sweet wine of any color. However, immigrant Italians of an early era presumably introduced the type of wine called 'Italian wine' (*olaszbor*), which was made by immediately pouring water over the grape skins left from making ordinary wine, then letting the skins soak up the water, and finally pressing the mixture. It was a relatively 'richer' wine than *lőre* [see that entry, in Part IV]. The fact that this particular wine was attributed by name to Italians virtually rules out their contribution to other Hegyalja wine types.

The Italian influence on grape varieties, which a century ago was taken for granted, and even in the recent past was thought by some Hungarian researchers to have been significant, seems on closer examination to have been minimal. It possibly amounted to nothing more than the *bakator*, presumably from the Italian name *bocca d'oro*; but even that is open to question since no such grape is known in Italy, while the name *bakator* also occurred in Hungary as an early surname. It is especially surprising that links have not been established between Hegyalja grape varieties and the southern Italian regions whence settlers were brought. Without such links, there is not even a basis for thinking that the Italians influenced a broad change in favor of white grape varieties. [See the entries for *Bakator* and Grape Varieties, in Part IV.]

Jefferson, Thomas. (1743-1826) The first American connoisseur of wines was also the first person in the New World to be a regular customer for Tokaji, and to leave some record of his interest. He first encountered Tokaji wines while serving as the American ambassador to France (1785-1789). He certainly thought them among the best he had tasted in Europe, even though his preference was not for sweet wine. After becoming president, in 1801, Jefferson continued to order a variety of Hungarian wines, including Tokaji, through the merchant Bollman [see that entry], despite their considerable expense. He was sufficiently enamored that he included cuttings of 'Tokay' vines among those he brought to Monticello, although the exact variety is unknown.

Jesuit Order. [See the entry for Uzhhorod, in Part II.]

Jews. Mostly heading south into Hungary from Galicia, Jews became an increasing presence in the Upper Tisza beginning in the second-half of the 17th century [see the entry for Dukla, in Part II].

They grew in number during the 18th century, when Hungary needed to repopulate the region following the considerable loss of life that took place during the Rákóczi rebellion at the beginning of the century. Late in that century, Galicia came under Austrian rule, and its inhabitants (Poles, Rusyns, Jews) were able to migrate freely to Hungary. This resulted in large-scale Jewish migration into the Upper Tisza, including Hegyalja. The Jews thereafter became Hungarian subjects, and quickly assimilated linguistically. They began taking over the wine trade from the Greeks, who by that time either were married into Hungarian families or had returned to Macedonia. From the 19th century, especially the second-half, until the Second World War, Jews were closely tied to the Tokaji wine trade generally, not just trade in kosher wines [see the entry for Teitelbaum-Beiler, below; and for Kosher Wine, in Part IV].

Early on, Jews were allowed to own vineyards in Hegyalja, but this was curtailed by a law of 1741, when the Hungarian authorities grew fearful that too many vineyards would fall into the hands of persons who were not Hungarian subjects, whether Jews, Greeks, or Armenians. Certainly there were cracks and laxity in enforcement of the law, which enabled some Jews and others to retain vineyard property, particularly if they had become Hungarian subjects. [See the entry for Agáros, in Part III.] Further, during the reign of Joseph II (1780-1790), Jews were free to participate in Tokaji wine production and trade [see the entry for Joseph II]. But after Joseph's death, the freedom of commercial activity was rescinded or severely abridged from time to time, although occasionally champions of free commercial activity managed to liberalize the conditions for Jews. Finally, a law of 1839-1840 again allowed Jews to purchase vineyard land freely, and Jews were given full equality after 1867. [See the entry for Zemplén County, in Part II.]

There is little evidence by which to think that Zemplén County officialdom was particularly concerned about the Jews from an ethnic perspective. The county to begin with was an ethnic and religious tapestry (almost on a par with Ottoman Macedonia), and of course there were the traders of exogenous origin who were already ensconced. Further, Jews were welcome in diminished communities throughout the long north-south extent of Zemplén. But it is clear from the detailed record of County regulations in the 18th century, that the Jews were perceived as posing a very particular threat to Hegyalja owing to the production of kosher wine. Because of large-scale Jewish purchases of grapes, kosher wine was viewed as having the potential to detract from the quality of the botrytis wines. This led to measures forbidding Jews to purchase botrytized grapes, let alone make kosher *aszú* wines whose only market would be Jews (of course, this demonstrates that Jews had previously been involved to some extent in making botrytis wines, even if they had to rely on local Christians for overall procedural guidance).

Basically, Jews were constrained to make kosher wine in the seasonal period after Christians had made table wines from fresh grapes. This meant that Jews were mostly vinifying over-ripe grapes in non-botrytis years, which inadvertently kept alive, or revived, the tradition of the late-harvest, semi-sweet wines that antedated botrytis wine. Also, since Jews typically made their communal kosher wines in facilities rented from Christians, they helped in setting Hegyalja wine-making on the road to modernity by starting to bring to an end the antique habit of rubbing the interior of old barrels with fat bacon when preparing them for the new vintage. The fat was meant to preserve the barrels and prevent re-fermentation, but Jewish refusal of such barrels eventually led to replacing the bacon treatment with the burning of sulfur inside the barrels. Oftentimes, however, Jews would use only new wooden barrels (lest old ones had been rubbed with bacon), and ones, moreover, that had no metal fittings.

As regards exports of Tokaji, the Jews did not have a particular importance before the 19th century. This is not to say that they were not involved, but that they had a minor role in sales other than to their co-religionists in Galicia and Poland. This was not an especially lucrative market in terms of the barrel-price of the wines. Further, records from as far back as the 18th century show that this trade was fraught with difficulties for the average Polish-Jewish trader, as some Jewish customs officials on the Polish side of the border with Hungary were disposed to demand bribes on kosher wines. At the same time, however, a few Jewish and Polish traders cooperated on sales of non-kosher Tokaji to Christian Poles [see the entry for Sapjeha]. This can perhaps be thought of as the 'seed' for later Jewish participation in the general trade of Tokaji wine. [A detailed account of the regulations regarding Jews is in Balassa's 1991 book, pages 581-619.]

Joseph II, Emperor. (1741-1790) Maria Theresa's son, Joseph II became emperor upon her death in 1780. A reform-minded ruler, he sought to equalize economic possibilities throughout the Habsburg lands by imposing uniform measures. He was committed to free trade, and among other actions, he permitted free enterprise for Jews, which included the right to trade in the Tokaji botrytis wines. In Hungary, he wanted to dismantle the old multi-county system and replace it with ten large territorial units, the better to centralize direction. It can only be speculated how the disappearance of Zemplén County would have affected Hegyalja. In contrast to his mother, Joseph II was not seen in Zemplén as a friend. When he went to Hegyalja, to Sárospatak, for hearings, none of the county nobility invited him for dinner. He had to eat in a hostelry. No Tokaji wine would have been on that table. While he had no desire to undermine a good source of income left to him by his mother, neither did he put much store by wine. An anecdote survives from his visit to Tokaj during that same trip: "the teetotal ruler was offered a glass of Tokaji wine, in the belief that [he] would derive some good from it. The emperor, however, raised the glass, held it to the light, gazed at its color a while, and said, 'So, this is Tokaji.' With that, he put it down. He did not take a sip." (Nagy, 1963) The Catholic Joseph's furtive, sudden disbanding in 1786 of the Catholic but patriotically Hungarian Pauline Order, so prominent in Hegyalja history, sealed the distaste for him in Zemplén. [See the entry for Józseffalva, in Part II.]

Jullien, André. (1766-1832) The author of the first 'wines-of-the-world' book, *Topographie de Tous Les Vignobles Connus* (1816), Jullien gave more space to Tokaj-Hegyalja than to most other non-French regions. He even went so far as to call Tokaji "the premier *vin de liqueur* of the world," which French connoisseurs of the day would have known to be quite a slap in the face to Grimod de la Reynière, who had heaped nationalistic discredit on Tokaji just a decade earlier [see the Part I Essay]. However, Jullien's opinion of Tokaji's place in the wine hierarchy is of far less interest than his remark that Tokaji "refreshes the mouth, rinses away the taste of all dishes which have preceded it, and does not leave but a delectable savor." This could only have been an allusion to the remarkably lengthy 'tang' characteristic of excellent *aszú* wine, which is a feature that requires more or less significant barrel aging in the Hegyalja cellars. [See the entry for Redding, below; and that for Tokaji Character and the last paragraph under Wine-delicacy, in Part IV.]

Kabars. Having previously allied themselves with the Magyars, several once Turkic-speaking Kabar tribes entered Hungary at the time of the Conquest. They probably would have been the chief linguistic conduit between the Magyars and any Bulgaro-Slavs they found in the region. In any case, they seem to have been significant in the early Magyar occupation of Zemplén [see the entry for Aba, above; and that for Bodrogköz, in Part II]. The Kabars are thought to have had more appreciable wine-growing skills than the Magyars, although nothing specific is known about that. They obviously did not jettison the wine-growing practices of Hegyalja; on the contrary, they probably recognized and perpetuated most of them. The Kabars likely were very comfortable with the storage of wine in goat-skins, too. Another aspect of the Kabars is that they had already had contact with Byzantine Christianity when they entered Hungary. This could account for some indications of Byantine Christian influence in the Upper Tisza region around that time. [See the entry for Ondava: Turkic Remnant? and the two for Turany nad Ondavou, in Part II.]

Kádár, János. (1912-1989) The history of Tokaji wine naturally drifts to thoughts of Hungarian kings and Habsburg emperors, without any mention of heads of government. But the nearness of the communist era, upon which commentary is still focused, makes it difficult to shelve Kádár. A 'proletarian pragmatist,' he managed, after the failed Hungarian Revolution of 1956, to convince the Soviet leadership that it was in their interest to give the Hungarians some economic breathing space. The result was that Kádár was able to carry through with the New Economic Mechanism (NEM), which did not bring back large-scale private entrepreneurship, but did allow for some independent decision-making by large firms, including wineries. Leeway was also given for small-scale private ventures; and in agriculture, compulsory deliveries to the state were ended, and larger private plots were allowed than anywhere else in the Soviet empire. The NEM became known popularly as 'goulash communism,' and without resorting to national stereotypes or trivialization, it enabled the Hungarians to make a significant return towards their once lauded tradition of food and wine. Of course this had some benefit for Hegyalja and Tokaji wine, and we might just note the provision for individual cooperatives to bottle and market their own wines. However, this was countered a bit because cooperatives sometimes cut corners (*e.g.*, not replacing barrels in a timely way) to remain profitable. [See the Appendix Essay.]

Kálmán, King. (1070-1116) Ascending to the throne in 1095, Kálmán was one of the major Árpád kings, and apparently the most educated, hence his moniker, 'the Learned' (*Könyves Kálmán*, literally 'bookish Coloman'). Though involved with numerous affairs of state, he took a particular interest in developing the Zemplén area, especially Hegyalja, and is thought to have had the first large wine cellars built there, in Tarcal, at the beginning of the 12th century. Further, he bestowed Sátoraljaújhely and its environs on Count Ratold of Caserta, which resulted in the first settlers from Italy coming to Hegyalja, probably with wine-growing partly in mind. The extent of Kálmán's interest suggests that the region's wine-growing potential was already being noticed by the mid-11th century. [See the entry for Boszorkány, in Part III; and Cellars, in Part IV.]

Kalmár, Gregory (Gergely). (late-15th c. – mid-16th c.) Gregory Kalmár was a trader in Kassa in the early-16th century [see the entry for Košice, in Part II]. Some historians of Tokaji wine trade have considered him a key figure in gaining the Polish market, by assiduously cultivating several urban markets in Poland. Judging from the presence of the surname Kalmár further north in Bártfa and Sztropkó, near the Polish border, in that same era, it is possible that the family was also involved with transshipping Tokaji through those places. But this is uncertain because the name, which means 'merchant' in Hungarian, was not uncommon in that era. It is known, though, that the Kalmárs had the confidence of the nobility, and a number of families routinely exported their wines to Poland through them.

Katha. (also spelled Káta) One of the earliest Magyar clans in the Upper Tisza region, the Kathas were involved in wine-growing in Hegyalja before the Tatar invasion of 1241-1242. This is proven by the existence of the two Káté vineyard tracts in Slovenské Nové Mesto (the Slovakian portion of Sátoraljaújhely) [see the entry for Káté, in Part III]. Since record of the clan disappears after the Tatar invasion, as if branching out into differently named families as a result of the event, these tracts must have dated to an earlier time. Very possibly, this was as early as the 11th century, because the village of Toronya (later, Kistoronya and Nagytoronya) was already in existence, and the Kathas did have an estate there, although it is not known how early. The clan presumably constructed some of the earliest of the wine cellars at Kistoronya, that is, well before the arrival of the Pauline Order in the 13th century.

Keczer. A major family involved in Hegyalja from its early days, the Keczers descended from one of the leading Magyar clans that had stayed in the Upper Tisza region since the time of the Conquest of Hungary. They became centered in southern Sáros County, and were among its preeminent families (several old southern villages had Keczer- as a forename). From their location in southern Sáros, they had ready access to Hegyalja, especially by way of the Hernád river, and they took advantage of it. A vineyard bearing their name was located in Mezőzombor (easily reached by way of the Hernád valley), in southern Hegyalja. They were also owners in Tállya and Bodrogkisfalud. As supporters of the anti-Habsburg rebellions, the Keczers' properties were confiscated by the Habsburgs in the late-17th century.

Klobusiczky. The bestowal of a vineyard in Hegyalja became a typical Habsburg reward for their prominent supporters in the Upper Tisza region, as exemplified by the Klobusiczky family, who came from northwestern Hungary to Sáros County in the mid-17th century. In 1683, Francis Klobusiczky fought against the anti-Habsburg forces of Thököly at Tarcal, in southern Hegyalja, and by 1684 he had a vineyard in Tolcsva (UC 70:15). But despite his alignment with the Habsburgs, he took gold and 24 barrels of *aszú* wine to Eperjes in 1686 to assuage, if not actually to mellow, the Habsburg general, Caraffa, at a time when the latter was bent on executing or otherwise exacting revenge upon the Sáros County nobility and notables suspected of anti-Habsburg activity. Klobusiczky's wily act at least had the effect of keeping Caraffa out of Zemplén County and Hegyalja. During 1688-1694, he was the general administrator of the Rákóczi vineyard properties for the orphans of Francis Rákóczi I [see the entry for Madocsányi]. The Klobusiczkys also acquired vineyards in the famous tracts of Szerelmi in Tokaj and Cserfás in Tarcal. They remained notable growers into the 20th century.

Kolcs. [See the entry for Bogát-Radvány, above; and for Kócsag, in Part III.]

Kölcsey, Francis (Ferenc). (1790-1838) A leading literary figure of his day, Kölcsey in 1828 wrote a vaguely anti-Habsburg poem, *Himnusz*, that was adopted as the Hungarian national anthem in 1844, while the Habsburgs still had full authority over Hungary. In one of its stanzas, Kölcsey praises the "nectar" that God has dripped "through the vine-shoots of Tokaj" (*Tokaj szőlővesszein / nektárt csepegtettél*). His use of the word nectar (*nektár*) is thought to be a poetical allusion to *aszú* wine generally; although he might have had *eszencia* in mind. [See the entries for Nectar and *Protropon*, in Part IV.]

Kosinszky, Viktor. (late-19th c. – early-20th c.) A major figure in Hegyalja's recovery from phylloxera, Kosinszky headed the Vintner Training Institute in Tarcal, which had the key role in propagating the use of American root-stocks. He saw to establishing several model plots in various parts of Hegyalja, which were used to instruct growers in the new methods. The work of the Institute was supported by a loan program whereby growers of all social classes could readily acquire the necessary American root-stocks. In the course of the replanting, Kosinszky saw to it that only the most suitable grape varieties were planted, which culminated in the specification of only three authorized varieties (*furmint, hárslevelű, sárga muskotály*) in the legislation of 1908.

Kossuth. It is hardly possible for Hungarians to think of Hegyalja without remembering the Kossuth family. This is entirely because of the illustrious patriot, Louis Kossuth, who was born in Monok and became the driving force behind the war for independence against the Habsburgs in 1848-1849 [regarding Louis, see the entry for Botrytis: Stellar Conditions, in Part IV]. The Kossuths appeared in northern Zemplén, at Sztropkó, as early as the end of the 16th century, when the town was already involved with Tokaji wine exports to Poland [see the entry for Stropkov, in Part II]. A short time later, in 1631, a John "Kusitt" was mentioned in connection with a wine cellar in Sárospatak. By the early-18th century, they were Hegyalja officials, as well as vineyard owners. The magistrate Andrew Kossuth was entrusted by Zemplén County to look into Czarina Anna Ivanovna's request of 1733 that the Russian Commission be allowed to purchase *aszú* grapes, which ended up being allowed, despite the County's misgivings [see the entry for Zemplén County, in Part II]. As vineyard owners, the Kossuths generally sold their wines to Poland through the Ossolińskis [see that entry]. The family had vineyard property in Sátoraljaújhely at the northern end of Hegyalja, but eventually resided in the south at Monok.

Kossuth, John (János). (late-19th c. – early-20th c.) A special case amongst the Kossuths, John stands out because of his 1903 report on Zemplén County wine-growing. Writing in the immediate aftermath of phylloxera, while reconstruction was underway, he gave one of the earliest assurances to the Hungarian public that the region was going to recover, not least of all in quality: "The reconstructed vineyards, with the uniformity of row and vinestock distance that had been lacking until now…practically carries us away with a new vision of old Hegyalja. After the good [vintage] of 1901 convinced even the skeptics that the product of the American root-stocks does not lag the [pre-phylloxera] wines, confidence in the new culture became general."

Kozma, Paul. [See the entry for Tokaj-Hegyalja Reconstruction Committee.]

Lórántffy. (also as Lorándfi in old documents) The Lórántffys are remembered in Tokaji wine history principally because of Susanna Lórántffy (1600-1660), whose chaplain and vineyard manager, László Szepsi, made the first modern botrytis *aszú* wine, purportedly from the harvest of her Oremus vineyard in Sátoraljaújhely. But the real significance of the family, as such, was their extensive properties in the northern part of Hegyalja. Those properties became part of the Rákóczi lands after Susanna married George Rákóczi I in 1616. When the Rákóczis acquired the Tokaj Domain in 1640, virtually the whole of the later Hegyalja wine district came under their control. In 1659, Catherine Lórántffy donated twelve vineyards to the college of Sárospatak. The Lórántffys descended from the mid-13th century Lóránt of the Ratold clan [see that entry], which suggests a long presence in Hegyalja. [See Somlyód, in Part III.]

Louis I, King. (1326-1382) 'Louis the Great' (Nagy Lajos) was the major Angevin king, reigning from 1342 to 1382. In between extensive wars, he seems to have fostered wine production, since the vine spread to virtually every corner of the country were it could grow. One measure of considerable importance to Hegyalja was a prohibition on imported wine. Hegyalja wine was not widely known in Hungary at that time, and the curb on imports, together with immigration and population build-up in northern Hungary, created new opportunities for marketing it. Louis's reign might also have seen the first large wine exports from Hegyalja to Poland, since he was also the king of Poland from 1370 to 1382. Louis also deepened Hungary's ties to Dalmatia. [See the entries for Dalmatia, in Part II; Lajos, in Part III; and *Malozsa*, in Part IV.]

Lubomirski. An intense interest in Hegyalja wine began in this family of Polish princes in the first-half of the 17th century, when Stanley Lubomirski was the governor-general of the Szepes towns that Hungary had pawned to Poland [see the entry for Szepesség, in Part II]. In 1632, he was given a permit to purchase 200 barrels of Tokaji duty-free annually for his own use. Whether or not he adhered strictly to the permit, and did not ship any wine to Poland for personal profit, the privilege was in line with the general practice of allowing the Hungarian aristocracy to export specified quantities of Hegyalja wine to Poland without paying Hungarian duties. However, the peculiar administrative situation of the Szepes towns, *i.e.*, as a Hungarian region under Polish guardianship, caused the Hungarian Chamber to withdraw the privilege in 1636 and require that Lubomirski pay a duty, on the grounds that the Hungarian state was owed an income from his wine sales. Later in the century, though, the Lubomirski princes began routinely receiving tariff dispensations from the Chamber on limited export amounts to Poland. They definitely abused the privilege. In 1731, an emissary of the Hungarian Chamber dryly noted in his report, "Prince Lubomirski annually has several hundred barrels of wine sent to Poland without paying the least tariff or duty, and I was unable to clarify how he feels entitled to do so."

Madocsányi, Emerich (Imre). (mid-17th c. – early-18th c.) After the death of Francis Rákóczi I, Madocsányi was appointed by the Habsburgs as general-inspector of the family's Hegyalja vineyards on behalf of the Rákóczi orphans. In 1689, he was entrusted specifically with seeing to the upkeep of every sort of activity that would allow reconstruction of the vineyards. His assignment is clear indication of the damage and neglect that had occurred in the preceding years, particularly during the Thököly rebellion of 1683-1685. [See the entries for Draheim and Klobusiczky.]

Mágochy. (or Mágócsi) The old Hungarian aristocracy is usually portrayed as having had no inclination for direct involvement with trade. Be that as it may as a generalization, it was not wholly true during the 15th and 16th centuries, and the Mágochy family seems to have been a most notable exception. Their acquaintance and dealings with Hegyalja began in the late-16th century, when Gaspar Mágochy became an owner of the nearby Regéc Domain [see that entry, in Part II]. Mostly, the Mágochys relied on regular customers amongst the Polish nobility, but the court of the Polish chancellor was also an important customer periodically. Gaspar and his two brothers then became vineyard-owners in Tállya. At times, they also bought wines from around Hegyalja and then sold them to the Kalmárs [see that entry], who worked with traders in Poland. Francis Mágochy kept up the family's trade activity into the early-17th century. It is a question whether Gaspar Mágochy's interest in wine began when he was the captain of the Eger fortress during 1564-1567 and expelled the Bishop of Eger. Apparently, he converted the diocesan cathedral into a storehouse for wine and other goods belonging to the bishopric.

Magyars. The founding ethnic group of the former Kingdom of Hungary, the Magyars were a collection of non-mongoloid Central Asian tribes that originated in the Ural Mountains but gradually moved, or were driven, westward over the centuries [see the entry for Herodotus]. Shortly before 900, they finally landed in the Carpathian basin, where they encountered a mostly scattered population that offered little resistance when they stepped into the overlord role that the Avars had vacated. Further, the Magyars readily intermingled with the still mostly pagan, agrarian Slav populace; and the Slavs, who were just being introduced to Christianity, apparently were agreeable to backsliding towards the pagan customs of the Magyars. But the long-term impact was on the Magyars, who at last abandoned the semi-nomadic way of life they had followed ancestrally, and became Christians.

Based on their vocabulary in connection with grapes, there is no doubt that the Magyars were familiar with wine, and to some extent with wine-growing, prior to reaching the Carpathian basin. It is also likely that Zemplén appealed to them in part because they found vines and wine there. But none of this means that the Magyars, as an ethnic group, had any particular influence on wine-growing itself in Hegyalja in the early centuries of the Hungarian kingdom, or at least not an influence that would move the region out of habits already acquired before the Magyars arrived. However, through their political activity in connection with clans and the fledgling Christian church of the Upper Tisza region, the Magyars of the original Árpád dynasty likely laid the groundwork, so to speak, for later geographical conceptions of the Hegyalja region.

By the time Tokaji started to become known as a somewhat sweet white wine, around 1500, we can begin thinking of this ethnic group as 'neo-Magyars,' since their genetic heredity by this time diverged significantly from that of their ancestors before the Tatar invasion of the mid-13th century, as a result of the ongoing assimilation of native Slavs, as well as incoming Poles, Germans, Walloons, Italians, and others. At the same time, the Upper Tisza region was minimally affected by the arrival and admixture of the Turkic Jazygs and Cumans further south in Hungary during the 12th and 13th centuries. The amalgam that occurred in the Upper Tisza area yielded a distinctly modern, European Hungarian, who now began to accumulate regional cultural taste preferences that exerted a strong influence on the further development of Tokaji wine.

In historical literature, the Magyars, neo- or not, were usually portrayed as being averse to direct involvement in commerce. This includes the trade in Hegyalja wine. However, the historical record does not bear this out. The cellars of the Rozgonyi family indicate that they were involved in the trade from at least the 15th century; and they were followed not long after by their regional rivals, the Perényis. In the 16th century, when Tokaji was just beginning to make its mark, a significant number of Hungarian noble families, such as the Mágochys, became involved in shipping northwards to Poland. Records also demonstrate that in this same era Magyars of the burgher class were involved in the trade as a career throughout the Upper Tisza, including the towns of Kassa, Eperjes, Varannó, and Sztropkó. Subsequent retraction in their interest had to do with disadvantages imposed by the Habsburgs, as well as the influx of Greek Macedonians who, over the centuries, had built up a much wider network of trade contacts in Europe.

Magyars: Ethno-historical Observation

Beginning in the era when Tokaji was becoming a later-harvested wine, around 1500, a native inhabitant of an appreciable settlement in the Upper Tisza would usually have understood himself to be *Hungaros*, no matter language or any other source of identity (usually religion). Indeed, many persons spoke more than one language: a 17th century German visitor noted that children acquired Hungarian, Slav, and German speech in the streets. Further, many people by that time descended from more than one group, and in that sense had a 'complex' identity that would have made them amenable to describing themselves as *Hungaros*. Put simply, there was more than just co-existence between people of various backgrounds; in towns and lowland places, they were continually intermarrying. Before the Reformation, there was no compunction about it, since virtually everyone was Catholic; and it was facilitated by bi- and tri-lingualism. During the Reformation, there was a tendency for separation by religion and language, according to the dominant language in local churches, but once the Counter-Reformation was underway, many Protestants returned to Roman Catholicism or became Greek Catholics, which resulted in a new round of ethnic intermixture. This is not a subject touched on by nationalistic historians who write as if the ethnic groups self-consciously kept their distance from one another, but it is nonetheless the *Hungaros* cultural milieu from which Tokaji wine emerged as the quintessential gustatory expression of the Upper Tisza region.

Maria Theresa. (1717-1780) Reigning from 1740 to 1780, Maria Theresa was the most pro-Hungarian of all Habsburg rulers. She never forgot that the Hungarian aristocracy had wholeheartedly supported her ascendancy to the throne (it may also be said that no Habsburg was ever viewed so favorably by Hungarians as was Maria Theresa). Where Hegyalja was concerned, it is to her everlasting credit that she entrusted development of the crown's vineyard lands to a loyal Hungarian, Count Grassalkovich, who transformed it into the most estimable and progressive property in the region. But, on the negative side, Maria Theresa caved in to the wishes of the Vienna Trade Council to restrain Hungarian wine exports, and Tokaji above all.

Mathiász, John (János). (1838-1921) Without qualification, Mathiász was the most gifted vineyard manager in the history of Hegyalja. In particular, he managed the property of Count Andrássy in Szőlőske (now Viničky, in East Slovakia), beginning in 1881, and led it through the post-phylloxera period. He was not only a viticulturalist, but also one of the most important grape-breeders in Europe. His work, together with Andrássy's backing, may have been instrumental in securing a place for Szőlőske amongst the Hegyalja locales specified in the Hungarian legislation of 1893 and 1908. Mathiász was a native of Sáros County, which illustrates the close ties within the Upper Tisza region where Hegyalja was located.

Matthias Corvinus. (1443-1490) King Mátyás, or Matthias, was a Transylvanian nobleman who reigned as the Hungarian king in the second-half of the 15th century, from 1458 to 1490. Towards the end of his reign, he conducted protracted warfare against Polish armies in northern Zemplén and adjacent areas, and left soldiers behind as settlers, since the region was still developing. He thus heralded the Transylvanian interest in Zemplén and Hegyalja [see the entry for Szápolyai], which grew following the Ottoman Turkish occupation of Lower Hungary, beginning in 1526, and culminated in the Rákóczis' intensive involvement in the 17th century. An action taken by Corvinus that strongly favored Hegyalja for a time was a decree of 1482 prohibiting the shipment of the esteemed Szerémség wines of southern Hungary further north than Tiszalúc (west of Tokaj), in order to stifle its sale to Poland. As for his direct interest in Hegyalja, there is a distinct possibility that he created the famous Szarvas vineyard-tract in Tarcal as his own property. [See the entries for Fulóhegy, Parlag, and Szarvas, in Part III.]

Micsk. [See the entries for Perényi; for Sečovce, in Part II; and for Mecsege and Mestervölgy, in Part III.]

Mongols. [See the entry for Tatars.]

National Wine-Qualifying Institute. (*Országos Borminősítő Intézet*, or OBI) This is the Hungarian government's quality-control organization for the wine industry. All wines destined for marketing either internally or for export must be qualified by the OBI on the basis of chemical testing in its laboratories. Further, all wines to be marketed with the state control band, as is the case with the Tokaji specialty wines, must be submitted to the OBI's National Wine-Expert Committee (*Országos Borszakértő Bizottság*, or OBB) for organoleptic examination and qualification [see the mention of the OBB in the last paragraph of the entry for *Aszú-Eszencia*, in Part IV]. The OBI was the target of much criticism in the early post-communist years: in some Hungarian circles, for allegedly having allowed the commercialization of improperly produced Tokaji botrytis wines during the previous era; and in some non-Hungarian circles, because it was perceived as a communist-era creation intent on preserving alleged *aszú*-aging aberrations of that era in Hegyalja wine-making [see the Appendix Essay]. Actually, as far as its history is concerned, the OBI was the immediate successor to the Wine Inspection Station (*Borvizsgáló Állomás*), established in 1881, even before the first national wine legislation of 1893.

Nobility. [See the entry for Aristocracy.]

Oláh, Nicholas (Miklós). (1493-1568) A figure in the Hungarian royal court who later became the Archbishop of Esztergom, Oláh's name is always encountered in Tokaji history because he mentioned it in his journal of 1553-1559, in which he gave an overview of Hungarian wine trade. Judging by Oláh's account, Tokaji was still not widely traded in Hungary, nor particularly well-known. However, it is considered that his remarks were grounded in what he knew about wine trade before the Ottoman occupation of southern Hungary, or pre-1526. Further, he had resided in western Hungary and was far more familiar with wine trade in Pest. Oláh seems not to have known of the commercial importance that Tokaji had achieved in the Upper Tisza, which would also mean that he was not familiar with the stylistic change in Tokaji wine [see the entry for Sperfogel]. It is also notable that while Oláh did not use the expression Hegyalja, he clearly tried to give a geographic idea of the region. But in doing so, he included the locales of Füzér (Fyzer) and Boldogkőváralja (Buldo-Kő), which are located west of the Zemplén hills. Rather than reflecting a lack of knowledge about Hegyalja, Oláh inadvertently may have left an idea of how the region was perceived geographically before it was associated with later-harvested white wines [see the entry for Timon; and for Hegyalja and Regéc, in Part II].

Ónd. As related in the account written by Anonymous, Ónd was one of the significant Magyar chieftains at the time of the Conquest, in 896. His name (given in Latin as Ound by Anonymous, and Und or Ónd by later Hungarian historians) seems to equate to 'Oldster,' which suggests that it was because of his experience that he was, according to Anonymous, important in scouting the region that would become Hegyalja. The southwestern Hegyalja commune of Ond is believed to bear his name, and indeed, the antique name Ondszőlőhegy (Ond-vineyard-hill) suggests that the chieftain may have laid claim to vineyard land that he found at that site. Some have also thought that Ónd's name accounts for that of the Ondava river further north, although this is problematic [see the two entries for Ondava, in Part II].

Ossoliński. One of the most significant Polish families trading in Tokaji wine during the 18th century, the Ossolińskis were noblemen who catered to the aristocratic market in Poland. Consequently, they dealt largely in *aszú* wines. At a time when Hungarian wine exports were generally burdened by Habsburg impediments, the status of the Ossolińskis was of great advantage to Hegyalja in maintaining a presence in Poland. Also, the Ossolińskis had significant storage facilities in Warsaw, and were second only to the Fuggers in supplying that market. They generally resided in Sáros County.

Ottlik, Paul (Pál). (late-17th c. – early-18th c.) A Hungarian official of the Habsburgs in the early-18th century, Paul Ottlik was an assistant to Prince Trautsohn [see that entry]. In keeping with the latter's efforts to enhance sales (Trautsohn having become a major proprietor in Hegyalja), Ottlik thought to set up a series of storage points along the Hungarian-Polish border. (He once stated, "The Poles can't live without good Hungarian wine, just as fish can't live without water.") The idea was that traders from Galicia and Silesia could thus readily acquire Tokaji without having to travel further south into the Upper Tisza, let alone to Hegyalja itself. But despite Trautsohn's support for the idea, merchants were not won over to it, neither those who might hold the stocks, nor those who would obtain supplies from them. One consequence was that the Greek merchants of Hegyalja remained indispensable to large-scale trade in Tokaji wine during the 18th century.

Ottoman Turks. ['Ottoman' is specified to set these Turks apart from Turkic-speakers mentioned in other entries.] The major reason for attention to the Turks is basically the same as with the Tatars: the devastation they visited upon Hungary. The Ottomans occupied southern Hungary beginning in 1526, and did not leave until 1683. During that time, they rarely ceased marauding and trying to push further north, especially into Hegyalja. But their successes were minor (mostly in the southerly Szerencs hills area) and short-lived, though disruptive of wine-growing. However, their occupation caused major demographic changes, as large numbers of Hungarians sought refuge in Royal Hungary (Upper Hungary generally, and the Upper Tisza area specifically) [see those entries, in Part II]. This had the effect, though, of creating a populous market for Hegyalja wine in the era when it was becoming a later-harvested wine. Also, the Ottoman relationship with the Hungarians outside the area under their control was not always antagonistic, and in some cases was even cordial. This likely resulted mostly from political maneuvering as a result of sharing with the Transylvanian princes a common enemy: the Habsburgs. The Rákóczis for a time in the mid-17th century were on good terms with the Ottoman pasha of nearby Eger, a certain Murát, and may even have given him a vineyard in Hegyalja. [See the entries for Chelebi and Tatars (b); and Agáros and Murát, in Part III. Also note the second paragraph of Balkans, in Part II.]

Paget, John. (19th century) Although his two-volume work of 1839, *Hungary and Transylvania*, was a typical travel journal of the period, the Englishman Paget took care in reporting on Tokaji and Hegyalja. It is notable that despite the 1773 report of Douglass, Paget stated that the British public still associated Tokaji entirely with the Habsburg emperor. His opinion of Tokaji (or at least the best of it) was indeed high: "It is a sweet, rich, but not cloying wine; strong, full-bodied, but mild, bright, and clear [he also described it as "topaz"]; and has a peculiar flavour of most exquisite delicacy." It is difficult to read this and not think that Paget was consciously countering the opinion published in 1833 by the wine-writer Cyrus Redding [see that entry, below]. Indeed, unlike Redding, Paget was strongly in favor of importing Tokaji into England, and recommended a specific merchant in Pest. Paget's account of the production of the Tokaji wines contains two peculiarities. First, "the grapes are of many different kinds, of which the Formint and Champagne are considered the best." The latter grape variety will forever remain unknown. Second, the grapes for *aszú* are "gently pressed with the hand" [see #9 in the entry for Balkan Influences, in Part IV]. Douglass had indicated that technique in connection with *máslás* rather than *aszú*, but in either case it would seem possible only when relatively small quantities were involved.

Pajzos. [See that entry, in Part III.]

Pálóczi. This was one of the early major families involved with Hegyalja. Of special interest, Ladislaus Pálóczi, the lord of the Sárospatak Domain, sent two barrels of Sátoraljaújhely wine to the town of Bártfa in 1467, along with a letter inviting them to see how good the wine was. This seems to be an early expression of faith in the quality of Hegyalja wine, whether or not it is indicative of a particular change in wine-making habits (such as, perhaps, a general switchover to white wine). No matter Pálóczi's immediate effect, trade records show that Bártfa was a regular buyer by 1500. But that was also a result of the Poles' increased awareness of Hegyalja after their military incursions into Zemplén and Sáros counties in the latter part of the 15th century.

Paracelsus. (1493-1541) The renowned Swiss alchemist visited Hegyalja in 1524, spurred by stories of occasional vines that had a gold content. He finessed the issue by concluding that vegetal and mineral matter can fuse to become something like a 'liquid gold.' While Paracelsus may only have been thinking metaphorically, the effect was that he perpetuated the legend for another couple of centuries. [See the entry for Gold Content, in Part IV.]

Paraskevich. During the early period of Russian interest in Tokaji, in the first-half of the 18th century, members of this Greek merchant family were occasionally called upon by the czar to assist in procuring large quantities of wine. Their services were crucial during 1740-1744, when the work of the (Russian) Hungarian Wine Commission was temporarily suspended. This was at a time when other Greeks whom the Paraskeviches could rely upon were still dominant in the Tokaji wine trade. Interestingly, their purchases for the czar in 1744 included 20 barrels of Hegyalja *red* wine, in addition to botrytis and other white wines [see the entry for Siller, in Part III].

Pauline Order. Among the several Roman Catholic religious orders that came to Zemplén County and Hegyalja, the Pauliners were not only the earliest, but also the most active in wine-growing. They were brought in the first-half of the 13th century, to their historical center, Sátoraljaújhely, where they were especially associated with the famous Oremus vineyard-tract. In that era, they also had vineyards in nearby Kistoronya and Bodroghalász (then Petrahó). In 1476, Szápolyai donated Ond and Golop to them, as well as vineyards in Tarcal and Tokaj; and, early in the 16th century, they were given two vineyards in Tolcsva. But during most of the 16th and 17th centuries, the Pauliners suffered vicissitudes because of the Reformation and Counter-Reformation, such that they had to remove to places further north (Trebišov) and further south (Sárospatak). They also lost and gained properties. They were ousted from their original properties in the 16th century, but in 1665 they once again received a property in Oremus. In 1678, they also received properties in Bodrogolaszi and Sárazsadány. The widespread presence of the Pauline Order during these early centuries likely accounts for a number of vineyard-tract names indicating religiosity. [See the entry for Joseph II, above; and those for Bahomalja, Barát, Oremus, and Szentvér, in Part III].

Peasantry. [See the entry for Smallholders.]

Perényi. The Perényis were major aristocrats in 14th-to-16th-century Hungary, and impacted Hegyalja. They had become princes of Transylvania, but were originally from the Upper Tisza region, and endeavored to exert power there as well. As descendants of the Micsk clan, they had extensive influence in Abaúj, Sáros, and Zemplén counties. In the 15th century, the king bestowed on them dominion over most of Zemplén County, including much of Hegyalja. It is known specifically that they received vineyard properties in Tolcsva and Vámosújfalu in 1512; but it is probable that they had properties in the region earlier than that [see the entry for Por-törő, in Part III]. Beginning in 1534, Peter Perényi began the construction of the Sárospatak castle, including the vast subterranean network of wine cellars (all of which would later belong to the Rákóczis). Since the family also had territory in southwestern Hungary, it is likely that the Perényis brought some Croatian (*horvát*) settlers to Hegyalja (hence the village of Erdő-*horváti*), and generally increased the region's population. More intriguing is the possibility that the Perényis were instrumental in bringing Walloons to Hegyalja from the famous Szerémség wine region of southern Hungary. But there was a notably sinister side to the Perényis: they were known to interfere with commercial trade, by confiscating wine enroute from Hegyalja to the Upper Tisza towns or Poland, and using it for their own gain.

Peter I, Czar. (1672-1725) The extraordinary interest of the Russian Imperial Court in Tokaji wine began when Peter the Great (1689-1725) was introduced to it by Prince Francis Rákóczi II while they were negotiating a treaty in Warsaw in 1707. Rákóczi continued to send much appreciated gifts of Tokaji. (The morning after another meeting with Rákóczi, in 1711, the Czar stated, "Until now I haven't been defeated by anyone or anything, but Tokaji wine defeated me last evening.") In 1714, Peter sent a delegation to Hegyalja to buy 300 barrels. He was so enamored that he even had thoughts of experimenting with making a similar wine somewhere in Russia. This could explain how Hegyaljan grape varieties came to be grown in Astrakhan [see the entry for *Góhér*, in Part IV].

Pethő. (or Pető) Originally from the village of Gerse in western Hungary (hence their full name, 'Pethő de Gerse'), the Pethős acquired estates in Zemplén in the 16th century, and the entire Sztropkó Domain in the northernmost part of the county in 1664. Vineyard cultivation had ceased at Sztropkó during that era, but the Pethős acquired vineyards in Hegyalja. One of the best vineyard-tracts in Tolcsva still bears their name: Pethő-*dűlő*. The marriage of Sigmund Pethő to the Polish noblewoman Helen Skavinsky in the mid-18th century of course was a stimulus to Pethő wine sales in Poland. [See the entries for Bel-, Henye, and Pethő, in Part III.]

Piarist Order. [See the entry for Szent Kereszt, in Part III.]

Poles. The Poles are prominent in accounts of Tokaji wine history chiefly because they were the primary customers for Tokaji sweet wine in its early centuries, and always exerted an influence on Hegyalja wine types [see the Part IV Essay]. However, their acquaintance with Hegyalja wine almost certainly predates that. When a Polish army invaded Zemplén in 1490, they went as far south as Hegyalja and sent wagonloads of wine back to Poland. Records show that even before that they were quite familiar on the territory of Sáros County, which was a major market for Hegyalja wine. Nevertheless, the Hungarian wine mostly known in southern Poland was from the Szerémség region of southern Hungary (now in the Vojvodina area of Serbia). But Szerém wine became unavailable in the early-16th century because of the Ottoman occupation. The Poles had a taste for old but sweetish Szerém white wine, and it was fortuitous that Hegyalja had begun producing later-harvested wines. Early on, the main Polish markets were in southern Poland, particularly Cracow, but also Biecz, Dukla, Gorlice, Grybow, Krosno, Nowy Targ, and other places. Later, exports of Tokaji spread further north, to Warsaw and all the way to the Baltic Sea. During the 16th and 17th centuries, many of the actual traders were Poles or German-Poles, but for the most part, they were small-scale and not specialized, and were easily displaced by the geographically widely based and wine-knowledgeable Greeks of Macedonia.

Mention is never made of the Polish role in populating the western part of the Upper Tisza region. According to the *Chronica Hungarorum* of the Warsaw Codex, Poles comprised most of the population from the vicinity of Eperjes (Prešov) northwest to the Szepes region in the early-11th century. In that era, when wine-growing was still known in southern Poland, Poles might have influenced wine-growing in the northern area of the Upper Tisza [see that entry, in Part II]. Roman Catholic Poles continued to trickle in throughout the centuries, and at times of political crisis in Poland were far more than a trickle. Slovak and Hungarian historians have largely overlooked it, but the Poles likely were a substantial element in populating the Upper Tisza during the 13th to 18th centuries (surnames and even some place-names bear this out). They mostly gravitated to the lowlands, especially along the river valleys, which brought them down to Hegyalja as well. However, immigration into this part of Hungary was not confined to the agricultural classes. Upper-class and titled Poles assimilated to their social equals in the counties of Zemplén, Sáros, and Abaúj, and also acquired vineyards in Hegyalja [see the entry for Bialka, in Part III].

Prémontré Order. [See the entry for Darnó, in Part III.]

Presian II, Czar. (c. 996 – c. 1060) Perhaps the most intriguing indication of a strong connection between the Upper Tisza region and the medieval Bulgarian Empire is the grave marked 'Prince Presian' at Michalovce (formerly Nagy Mihály), in central Zemplén, 51 km (32 miles) north-northeast of Hegyalja. Having fallen out of favor and being in fear for his life, Czar Presian II apparently exiled himself. His presumed grave near Michalovce suggests that he found refuge on territory well-known to Bulgarian royalty. He had been born before 1000, which was but a century after the Bulgarian Empire had a serious stake in the Upper Tisza. During his lifetime, Bulgaria may still have had various interests there, perhaps mostly commercial, but maybe even residual territorial pretensions, *i.e*, if the Kingdom of Hungary were to collapse there would be a power vacuum for the Bulgarian Empire to fill. That would have been attractive in an era when Bulgaria was constantly in a power struggle with the Byzantine Empire. Incidentally, the story of Presian tends to corroborate Anonymous's account of the Magyar Conquest as regards the Bulgaro-Slav presence [see the entry for Anonymous].

Preysz, Morris (Mór). (1829-1877) A chemist, Preysz was the first researcher to experiment with using a heat-treatment to prevent the re-fermentation of the Tokaji sweet wines. In 1861, he demonstrated that the wines could be stabilized by being heated to 70-80° C in a closed vessel. This was three years before Pasteur, but Preysz received no recognition because his findings were published only in Hungarian. [See the entry for Ferenczi.]

Rákóczi. The premier family in the early history of modern Hegyalja botrytis wine, the Rákóczis were princes of Transylvania, though with roots in the Upper Tisza region. They returned to Zemplén County during the late-16th century, when Transylvania was at its peak of power and had extended its authority into what is now eastern Slovakia. By the early-17th century, the greater part of Zemplén was in their possession, including most of Hegyalja. Prince George Rákóczi I acquired the Sárospatak Domain by his marriage to Susanna Lórántffy in 1616, and in 1624 he acquired the Tokaj Domain. Additionally, they held the Regéc Domain, which gave them the Hegyalja parts of Abaúj County, and they purchased Mád in 1700. As a result of these acquisitions, the Rákóczis had tremendous interest in the development of wine-growing in the region. They also added vastly to cellar capacity [see the entry for Cellars, in Part IV].

However, being Protestant Transylvanians set on liberating the Kingdom of Hungary from the Catholic Habsburgs, the Rákóczis were equally active in politics and warfare. Indeed, their interest in the development of Hegyalja stemmed in part from their recognition that Tokaji wine could finance their anti-Habsburg activities. One measure was taken in 1667, to charge a wine export fee. The Rákóczis famously used gifts of Tokaji to win support amongst European rulers. However, the anti-Habsburg campaign of Francis Rákóczi I in the 17th century failed, and resulted in confiscation of his vineyard properties and those of his aristocratic allies. Control came back to the Rákóczis for a time under Francis II, but his final defeat came in 1711 (despite having sent 150 barrels of Tokaji to the Prussian king in 1710 to gain his intervention). This final defeat led to a redistribution of vineyards to aristocratic allies of the Habsburgs, many of whom were Austrians or Germans. Altogether, 21 Rákóczi vineyard properties in Hegyalja were confiscated, with only two kept for the Imperial Court [see the entry for Grassalkovich].

Special note must be made of the Rákóczis' efforts, in the mid-17th century, to delimit the Hegyalja region and classify its vineyard hills and tracts. Unfortunately, their own documentation of their determinations has not survived. But a variety of documents from the second-half of the 17th century testify to the fact that the determinations were made. For instance, in the case of vineyard-tract classifications, a document of 1676 listed the tracts of Bodrogkisfalud in three classes (UC 116:15). Of greater pertinence, though, is the delineation of the Hegyalja region. Three Szepes Chamber documents of 1674-1675 [see the entry for Halápi] specifically concerning Hegyalja ("*Submontanarum*") include virtually the geographic entirety of present-day Hegyalja, even though only those locales where the Chamber had properties were included (22 communities). Documents like those, from that time period, must have reflected the the Rákóczi determinations. This strongly undercuts the idea (Balassa, 1991) that a palpable 'dilution' of the geographical concept of Hegyalja occurred over the centuries. Or else, it must be argued that dilution started with the Rákóczis in the mid-17th century, presumably to increase military funding from Tokaji. [The Part II Essay and Part III Essay consider these topics in detail.]

Ratold. (also spelled Rathold) Invited to Zemplén by King Kálmán in 1110, this Italian clan from Caserta was given the area of Sátoraljaújhely in northern Hegyalja. They may have extended wine-growing thereabouts by the establishment of monasteries belonging to Roman Catholic orders. Settlers from Italy were also brought at that time, and are presumed to account for the settlement of Bári just to the northeast of Sátoraljaújhely. Despite this significant presence, it was highly localized, and any erstwhile Italian-inspired influences in wine-growing lost out to the pre-existing indigenous habits of Balkan origin. The stronghold of the Ratolds was the fort of Nagy Kövesd, east of Bári, and it is likely that the onetime Nagy-Kövesd vineyard-tract in Tarcal was originally theirs. The family name became Hungarian-ized as Rátót. [See the entries for Lórántffy; those for Bara and Veľký Kamenec, in Part II; and for Kakas and Kövesd, in Part III.]

Redding, Cyrus. (1785-1870) Redding's book, *A History and Description of Modern Wines* (1833), places him alongside Jullien as a founder of modern wine-writing. On the subject of Tokaji, he was more descriptive than Jullien, and his comment that "it should appear oily in the glass and have an astringent twang, a little earthy" was not only notable at the time, but held its validity for another two centuries. Yet, in contrast to Jullien, Redding was ambivalent in his appraisal of Tokaji. While recognizing its quality, he thought its "value" rested mostly on "empty repute." He did not see the contradiction (from a connoisseur perspective) in adding that "[its] flavour itself has nothing more than *its singularity* to recommend it" (emphasis added). [See the entry for Paget, above.]

Rosa. This was the most important of the early Macedonian Greek families that traded in Tokaji wine. They were already operating in the early-17th century, whereas the commercial interest of Greeks in Tokaji wine developed mostly later in that century. It is significant that the Rosa family resided in and conducted their business from the royal free town of Eperjes, a strategic commercial location from which to transship to destinations either to the north (Galicia) or northwest (Silesia). In 1739, three of the other major Tokaji trading towns (Kassa, Lőcse, Bártfa) lodged a complaint with the Hungarian Chamber about the export dealings of Stephan Rosa, with the intention of barring him from further participation in the wine trade. But because of Rosa's significance in exports to Poland, the Chamber decided that he could continue trading, provided that he abstain from falsifying wines or substituting low-quality for high-quality wine, and also that he scrupulously pay the export tariff at the collection stations of the Szepes Chamber.

Rozgonyi. This was one of the early native families that gained prominence following the Tatar invasion in the mid-13th century, first in Abaúj (the village of Rozgony, now Rozhanovce), and then in neighboring Zemplén. John Rozgonyi became the Royal Chief Justice in 1471. The family built the Csicsva fortress in central Zemplén at the beginning of the 14th century, and quickly gained vineyard property in Hegyalja. Headquartered at Monyorós, the seat of a military district, the Rozgonyis also acquired the alias Monyorósi. They subsequently held the Varannó Domain, which succeeded Monyorós-Csicsva. The Dobra vineyard-tract in Sárazsadány likely was an appurtenance of the commune of Dobra in the Varannó Domain. Also, during 1465-1470, the family gained estates in the Hegyalja villages of Erdőbénye and Szegi, as well as the Makovica Domain, which would have included the Makovica vineyard-tract in Mád. Trade records indicate that around 1500, Stephan Rozgonyi was selling Hegyalja wine from the family cellars at Varannó to merchants in Bártfa for further sale to Poland; and the existence of these cellars suggests that his forebears were similarly involved with Tokaji wine trade. The family might have been using the alias Roszwalt in trade with Poland. [See the entry for Monyorós-Csicsva, in Part II; and those for Alsobénye, Cigány, Dobra, Makovica, Mocsár, and Peres, in Part III.]

Rumpolt, Marx. (16th c.) This Hungarian-German cook published a book in Germany in 1581, which was translated into Hungarian in 1680 [S. Török, *Borgazdaság* [Viniculture] Vol. 33, No. 4 (1985), pp. 145-151]. Rumpolt told of a wine made by fermenting raisins in must, which conforms to pre-botrytis Hegyalja sweet wines, (*i.e.*, in Rumpolt's time); it can only be speculated, though, that he meant grapes left to dry on the vine, rather than ones dried after harvesting. He also looked at the problem of maintaining the health of wine in barrels that were partly empty. Hegyalja growers who read the German edition may have been spurred to experiment further during the 17th century. [See the entries for Barrel Aging and *Darabbantartás*, in Part IV.]

Russians. Although prominent in Hegyalja lore, the Russians feature almost entirely in the context of the lengths to which the czars and czarinas went to ensure the Imperial Court's supply of Tokaji. Little information is available about ordinary commercial trade that might have made Tokaji available to other Russians, especially outside St. Petersburg. Furthermore, most shipments to St. Petersburg traveled by sea via Gdańsk (Danzig), rather than overland. Nevertheless, it may be presumed that some Tokaji reached the bourgeoisie in Moscow and elsewhere as a result of transshipments through Lviv in western Ukraine. [See the entries for Michalovce and Uzhhorod, in Part II.]

Rusyns. (or Ruthenians) In the view of some ethnographers, the Rusyns are Ukrainians by another, earlier name, and distinguishable primarily by the territory they inhabit, which is on both sides of the rim of the east-central Carpathians, and also by their traditional occupations, namely, lumbering and carting. But difference in 'ethnic origin' from the Ukrainians proper resulted from intermixture with Romanian Vlachs from the eastern Carpathians and early Galician German colonists. The Rusyns in any case are the westernmost of the eastern Slavs, and adhere to Greek (Byzantine-rite) Catholicism and the Cyrillic alphabet. They were certainly in the Upper Tisza area very early. The *Chronica Hungarorum* of the Warsaw Codex mentions their presence along with Hungarians and Poles in the 11th century. They also migrated deeply into northern and central Zemplén County in large numbers in the 14th century. But in these early times they were mostly upland and forest dwellers without knowledge of wine-growing.

The major contribution of the Rusyns to Tokaji sweet wine in its early era was in hauling it to the markets of Poland and Russia. But sometimes they were traders as well, most of all in the period of rampant smuggling of Tokaji in the 16th century, when a lot of contraband Tokaji passed through the Rusyn mountain and hill districts of Upper Zemplén and northern Sáros counties. The Rusyns were familiar with many paths not known to authorities or tariff officials. However, after the end of the Rákóczi rebellion in 1711, they increasingly moved south into the river valleys of Lower Zemplén to replace population lost to strife and epidemics. Some acquired wine-growing skills from the Hungarians after this time, at first mostly as seasonal laborers, but later as settlers in wine-growing locales. Several of the smaller Hegyalja settlements (Bekecs, Végardó, Bodrogkeresztúr) were able to survive in no small part because of Rusyn migration.

Sapjeha. (18th century) A major Polish nobleman in Lithuania, Count Sapjeha informed an advisor of the Szepes Chamber [see that entry] that whenever Polish noblemen were associating with Jewish wine traders, it was invariably a sign of abuse in exports to Poland, inasmuch as a nobleman's interest in assisting the trader would only be to get a share of the profit. This was during the period, in the 18th century, when Hungarian decrees or Zemplén County regulations barred or encumbered Jewish participation in the trade of *aszú* wines. Sapjeha's familiarity with the issue also stands as an indication that Tokaji was reaching the Baltic countries at that time.

Schams, Franz. (1780-1839) A German from Bohemia, Schams came to Hungary at the beginning of the 19th century and became the country's first viticultural scientist. In 1834, he addressed a letter to Zemplén County, in which he decried the chaotic situation that prevailed in grape varietal names, *i.e.*, the difficulty of identifying varieties accurately [see the entry for *Tumidula*, in Part IV]. In his book of 1832, he noted one of the key characteristics of an abundant botrytis vintage in commenting on the 1797 vintage: "for every barrel of regular [non-botrytis] wine, a *puttony* of *aszú* grapes was produced, with the result that less of our *ordinárium* wine will remain." The implication was that, from the commercial perspective, there was a fine balance between having too much *aszú* wine and too little of the best table wine on hand.

Schwendi, Lazarus von. (1522-1584) A German-born general in the service of the Habsburgs, Schwendi directed a campaign against the Protestant Hungarian aristocracy in the Hegyalja region beginning in 1565 and ending in 1568. For a time, he held the fortresses of Tokaj and Szerencs in southern Hegyalja. He is reputed to have become something of an aficionado of Tokaji. Legend has it that Schwendi took vine cuttings from Hungary to Alsace, hence the name Tokay d'Alsace for a grape variety grown there. However, if he in fact did so, he did not bring the varieties for which Hegyalja is known today, *furmint* and *hárslevelű*, which is readily understandable, since these varieties were not of any particular importance in Hegyalja in the 16th century. However, Schwendi was in Hegyalja after later-harvested wine had become the region's best wine. Thus, it can be speculated that any vine cuttings he brought from Hungary to

Alsace were for the purpose of making wine of that type. This might explain the origin of the varietal name Tokay d'Alsace, that is, to designate a grape used to make wine of Tokaji type.

Scots. Unlikely as it might seem, Scots played a role in marketing Tokaji wine. This came about as a result of those who left Britain for the continent, beginning in the late-16th century, and eventually settled in Poland. Most became involved in trade, and a few of them realized the opportunity that Tokaji wine afforded. Their activity was mostly during the 17th century. Balassa (1991) noted that one in particular, a certain "Robert, Béla de Lanxet Portius" [*sic*], became quite wealthy from the Tokaji trade while residing in Cracow during 1623-1661, which was the period when the wine was coming into its full glory in Poland.

Selbstherr. German traders, as opposed to Hungarian-German ones, were a rarity in Hegyalja even after Tokaji acquired Europe-wide fame. This may have been largely because of Greek and Jewish dominance of the trade, respectively in the 18th and 19th centuries. But, additionally, the impediments to Hungarian wine exports instituted by Austria and Prussia during the 18th century had a discouraging effect on would-be German merchants in Tokaji wine. However, the Selbstherr brothers of Silesia were an exception, and were active in Hegyalja by the late-18th century. They settled in Mád at the very beginning of the 19th century, and operated a significant trading firm there for nearly the rest of the century, until the phylloxera episode. They were especially interested in sales to the German lands, but to Western Europe generally. One of the brothers, Karl, is notable for having been not merely a merchant, but a genuine devotee of Tokaji, perhaps singularly so amongst the foreign merchants who dealt with Hegyalja over the centuries. His deep concern for the integrity and reputation of Tokaji led him to write a lengthy letter to Zemplén County authorities, in 1839, detailing the deficiencies he found in viti-viniculture and wine trade, and recommending specific improvements. One of his proposals included keeping an official registry as to the owner (producer), type, and vintage-date of each barrel of wine. Despite the fact that the Hegyalja vineyard-tracts had been classified for almost two centuries, Selbstherr's letter appears to be the earliest time when serious thought was given to the potential for using village names, or even vineyard-tract names, in the Tokaji trade.

Serbs. Hungarian historians of Hegyalja consider that Serbs were amongst the foreigners who traded in Hegyalja wine. This would seem to be so, since Serbs resided in not too distant Eger, to the west, and certainly would have taken an interest in Hegyalja if they were involved with trade in Eger's wine. Their presence in Hungary dated mostly to the end of the 17th century (after the Turks had left), when a Serbian Orthodox bishop obtained permission to lead a large migration of Serbs from Ottoman-controlled Serbia into southern Hungary. A few of the incoming 'Serbs' were actually Greek merchants who had been resident in Serbia, which, like Greece, was just another part of European Turkey and therefore open to Greek traders. However, Serb commercial awareness of Hegyalja could date to the 15th century [see the entry for Brankovich].

Serédi. [See that entry in Part III.]

Sforza, Bona. (1494-1558) The Italian wife of Polish King Sigismund I, Queen Bona, much like Catherine de Medici in France, is credited with transforming gardening and gastronomy amongst the upper classes of Poland. She even had garden-plots of vines planted in central Poland, which reportedly were still producing a century later. Her influence included greatly increased demand for wine, such that by the mid-16th century complaints about over-consumption of wine were expressed by some prominent Poles. But the favorable effect for Hegyalja was somewhat muted during Bona's lifetime by her personal efforts to satisfy the royal court's large wine needs with imports from Italy, while intentionally ignoring neighboring Hungary. Ironically, two of her daughters married Hungarian noblemen, John Szápolyai and Stephan Báthory, both of whom fostered sales of Tokaji in Poland. [See the entries for Báthory and Szápolyai.]

Slovaks. Some of the ancestors of today's East Slovaks were already in the Hegyalja region when the Magyars arrived at the end of the 9th century. But we are speaking of the pre-Hungary Slavs of eastern Slovakia, whose ethnic relationship to the ancestors of the Slovaks of central and western Slovakia is not so easy to ascertain because of a lack of documentary and artifact evidence. For one thing, it is not known what sort of political relationship, if any, the inhabitants of the Upper Tisza area had with the short-lived 9th century Great Moravia to the west, which is the cradle of Slovak ethnicity. Some historians have thought that Great Moravia did not extend nearly as far east as Zemplén; moreover, because of the paucity of concrete information about Great Moravia, the question of just where it was situated has been the subject of scholarly dispute. At the same time, it is clear that the Bulgarian Empire in that period exerted real dominance in the river valleys of the Upper Tisza. This is supported by the fact that the early grape varieties and wine-making practices of Hegyalja were of Balkan/Greek origin, and dissimilar from those of western Slovakia, which instead show a cultural overlap with Roman and Frankish Europe. [See the entry for Bulgarian Empire, in Part II; and those for Balkan Influences and Grape Varieties, in Part IV.]

But, no matter the ethnic position they occupied along the spectrum of Slavic languages and dialects, these particular ancestors of today's East Slovaks presented the incoming Magyars with a tradition of wine-growing in southern Zemplén, albeit a tradition of Balkan type. This occurred largely through their gradual absorption by the Magyars who settled there (Magyar speech predominated much further north in eastern Slovakia until 1700 than it did later). The wine-growing habits were so ingrained that they prevailed even over those of later settlers, such as the Walloons, Italians, and Saxons [but, see the entry for Upper Tisza Region, in Part II]. An especially salient bequest to Hegyalja wine culture by the early East Slovaks was the typical wine 'cellar,' a sort of large earthen mound, usually built against a slope of land, which had evolved from the typical domicile in use by the native Slavs before the Magyars' arrival. The basic idea was not forgotten during later Hegyalja history [see the entry for Bodrogköz, in Part II; and for Cellars, in Part IV]. Incidentally, these constructions had no parallel among the Slovaks to the west, and again point to a distinct Slav or Slav-Avar culture in at least the southern half of the Upper Tisza area.

During the 15th century, most of the Roman Catholic Slavs of the northern Upper Tisza region had become more Slovak than Polish linguistically owing to the Hussite occupation, the resultant influence of the Czech bible, as well as some migration from northwestern Slovakia. Some persons in the northernmost towns entered the trade in Hegyalja wine beginning early in the 16th century. The town of Bardejov (formerly Bártfa) is the most notable instance, with Slovak traders moving back and forth between there and the town of Dukla in Poland. Also, as Slovak and Slovak-Rusyn dialects spread southwards after 1700, the proportion of Slovak peasants grew in the seasonal labor force of Hegyalja. Consequently, large-scale emigration by this class around 1900 was a setback for Hegyalja owing to the consequent rise in the cost of day-labor.

Smallholders. This term oftentimes tends to equate to 'peasants' in common parlance, and to their antecedents, the presumed 'serfs,' even though land ownership is implicit. For a long time, this minimized any interest in this class of Hegyalja producers, but the fact remains that this was a class to be reckoned with throughout the region, throughout its history. The sheer number of owners in various vineyard-tracts in past centuries (as shown by old documents) demonstrates that smallholders, and not the nobility, were ever the backbone of regional wine output. It is hardly possibly to imagine the recovery of the region after Tatar, Ottoman, Habsburg, and phylloxera destructions without thinking of them and their modest holdings and facilities. We have only to remember John Paget's (1839) mention of the need of even the Habsburg court to fill their cellars with the product of wine-growers much further down on the social scale.

It cannot be doubted that there were aspects in which the smallholders could not keep pace with the nobility [see the entry for Aristocracy]. Their small production of botrytized berries generally ruled out the production of *eszencia*, and even *aszú* wines higher than 3-*puttonyos* level. They were also slower to adapt to varietal change. But they did produce and market *aszú* wines, oftentimes actually carting the wines to the towns further north in the Upper Tisza region, whether for consumption there or for transshipment to Poland by professional traders. None of this is to be discounted in the building and maintenance of the market for Tokaji. (As to wine quality, note the bronze medal certificate awarded to the smallholder Antal Kicsinkó at the Paris Exhibition of 1900, on page 179 of Miklós Pap's 1985 book, *A Tokaji*. [See the entry for Cooperatives; and that for Szabó, Louis.]

Because of their common interest in promoting Tokaji wine outside Hungary, and especially in retaining the all-important Polish market, the smallholder class generally did not defy or counter the wishes of the aristocracy, their 'social enemy.' But, by the early-18th century, they were showing signs of following their own interests and contradicting the aristocracy on wine 'policy' in Hegyalja. Their initial incentive for doing so was the presence of Greek merchants, who simply offered slightly higher prices than the aristocracy was willing to pay under their centuries-old privilege of 'first-dibs' on buying the best of the harvest. The clearest sign of this was the cooperation of the smallholders with the Greek merchants even in fraudulent practices (Komoróczi, 1944). Eventually, by 1800, this class of growers became outright supporters of free trade and enterprise, which at that time favored the participation of Jewish traders [see the entry for Mád, in Part II]. This alignment spelled the end of aristocratic primacy in Hegyalja history.

Soós. Descended from the ancient Baksa clan, the Soós family shows up in the background of many major landholding families of Hegyalja of the late Middle Ages. The extent of their own holdings is unclear. However, from the mid-13th to the mid-15th centuries, they owned or built various fortresses, and Hegyalja vineyard property certainly came along with doing so. They are often referred to as the Sóvári Soós family, because of their early ownership of Sóvár ('Salt-fort') in Sáros County; the surname Soós actually means 'Salter.' [See the entry for Solivar, in Part II.] The family was important in Sáros for several centuries, which favored the county's acquaintance with Tokaji wine, and also spurred interest in acquiring vineyards there. However, the family later moved into Zemplén as well, where they owned part of the Bodrogköz area abutting Hegyalja on the east, and also, further north, the Céke (or Czéke) fortress (now Cejkov, in East Slovakia). The latter's lands included Mészpest, which became the name of a vineyard-tract in Hegyalja [see the entries for Cseke, Poklos, and Sóhajó, in Part III].

Sperfogel, Conrad. (late-15th c. – early-16th c.) Towards the end of the 15th century, the Swiss Sperfogel came to Lőcse, one of the German-speaking trading towns of the Szepesség region of Upper Hungary, and at times during the early-16th century served as town notary and judge. In a diary entry of 1524, he wrote that Tokaji wine at that time was "so good and generous, as it had never been before." This notation, coming from someone who had known Tokaji for three decades or more, suggests that a significant change in wine-making had occurred in Hegyalja during the preceding years, most likely in connection with the later harvesting that began towards the end of the 15th century. [See the entry for *Főbor*, in Part IV.]

Stegner. This prominent Macedonian-Greek wine trading family was resident in Hegyalja since the late-17th century, and played a financial role in the anti-Habsburg wars of the Rákóczis when Francis Rákóczi II pawned his vineyards and other holdings in Erdőbénye to them around the end of the century. It is testimony to their influence and commercial significance that the Stegners were allowed to retain the property, as a so called 'pawn-estate' (*zálog-birtok*), even after the Habsburgs confiscated the Rákóczi lands. The family's continued involvement in the wine trade was mentioned by Antal Szirmay in his book of 1798. This was several decades after the Greeks had receded considerably in importance, especially relative to the incoming Jews from Galicia.

Szabó, Julian (Gyula). (19th c. – 1934) A native of the historic Tokaji trading town of Bártfa, in northern Sáros County, Szabó became a vineyard owner in Tállya and distinguished himself in the wake of phylloxera. At his own expense, he went to France to study how phylloxera was being combated there, then returned to Hegyalja and became the first grower to undertake the use of American root-stocks. Most growers had not dared to bear that expense, in the belief that phylloxera could not be stopped, but Szabó's example and results entirely changed that way of thinking. [See the entry for Kosinszky.]

Szabó, Louis (Lajos). (mid-19th c. – early-20th c.) Appointed director of the Cellar-master Training Institute established in Tarcal in 1873, Szabó is especially notable for trying to put not only Tarcal but also the wider region on guard against phylloxera by around 1880. Although there is little likelihood that the disastrous outcome could have been prevented, he met resistance amongst smallholders in particular, many of whom, in Szabó's words, believed that "the lords just invented the whole thing" (*i.e.*, the approach of a devastating pest) for a presumed benefit of theirs. The episode of course speaks volumes about social relations in Hegyalja.

Szápolyai. (alternatively as Zápolyai) In the early-16th century, the Szápolyais were the first of the Transylvanian princes to bring Zemplén County into their sphere of protection, in effect challenging Habsburg rule there. After the Ottoman Turks had occupied Lower Hungary, John Szápolyai managed to gain their agreement to Transylvania's continued independence by, in effect, abetting the Ottomans in their opposition to the Habsburgs in Royal Hungary. However, at the same time, this stymied Ottoman aims because Szápolyai embarked on expansion of Transylvanian over-lordship northwestward into the Upper Tisza region, Zemplén County, and Hegyalja, with the goal of eventually restoring the Kingdom of Hungary to native rule (in place of the Habsburgs). This gave Hegyalja some nominal insurance against Ottoman control, though in actuality it required military rebuffs of repeated Ottoman attempts on the Upper Tisza area throughout the following century-and-a-half.

The Szápolyais had already acquired vineyards in Hegyalja, at Tokaj and Tarcal, in the late-15th century, when they were headquartered in the Szepes region to the northwest, at the fortress of Szepesvár (now Spišské Podhradie, in eastern Slovakia). By courting Rome's favor in opposition to Habsburg rule in rump Royal Hungary, the Szápolyais possibly were behind Tokaji wine's first international triumph, when it was supplied to the Council of Trent, in 1562 [see the entry for Draskovics]. However, the main effect of the Szápolyais on the region's wine-growing was indirect, namely, their anti-Ottoman, anti-Habsburg, and pro-Hungary activities paved the way for another family of Transylvanian princes, the Rákóczis, who would take far more direct interest in Hegyalja's potential and bring it into its modern era.

Széchenyi, Stephan (István). (1791-1860) The central figure of the Hungarian 'Age of Reform,' Count Széchenyi was focused on economic advancement, but most of all on agriculture. He initiated the National Hungarian Economic Association (OMGE), in 1830, which worked to update agriculture, including the problem of credit availability for smallholders. The OMGE led to a number of national and regional organizations to assist wine-growing, and their usefulness proved crucial following phylloxera. Széchenyi thought Hungary every bit as suited as France in natural conditions for wine-growing, but that Hungary lagged in every aspect of viti-viniculture.

He also contradicted the general aristocratic viewpoint in not attributing export difficulties in that era primarily to tariffs, but to Hungarian wines being unable to withstand long travel. In his book of 1830 (*Hitel*/Credit), Széchenyi alluded to the falsification of Hegyalja wines: "In Tokaj there were more raisins, ripened in Syria, than [stored] in all three of our seaports [along the Adriatic]."

Szepes Chamber (*Szepesi Kamara* in Hungarian; *Zipser Kammer* in German). Established in 1567, the Chamber was the body through which the Habsburgs exerted financial, economic, and trade control over the eastern part of Royal Hungary (non-Ottoman Hungary). Technically a regional subsidiary of the Hungarian Chamber, in actuality it often operated with considerable autonomy. However, during the late-16th and early-17th centuries, the Chamber was frequently undermined by the expanding power of the anti-Habsburg Transylvanian princes, especially the Rákóczis, in the eastern areas under the Chamber's purview, including the counties of Zemplén, Sáros, and Abaúj, as well as the royal free towns of Kassa, Eperjes, and Bártfa, all of which were key to wine trade. The Szepes Chamber lasted until 1848. [See the entries for Draheim and Halápi.]

Although its name derived from Szepes County [see the entry for Szepesség, in Part II], on the southeastern side of the Tatra mountains, the Chamber had oversight for much territory to the east, notably most of present-day eastern Slovakia and Hegyalja. Indeed, the Chamber had its seat not in the Szepes region, but at Kassa, and sometimes Eperjes, both off to the southeast and much closer to Hegyalja. Because all the major trade routes for Tokaji wine passed through the customs stations operated by the Chamber, its practices had a huge impact on exports of Tokaji, at times inadvertently spurring smuggling and falsification because of efforts by merchants to circumvent restrictive measures that interfered with trade or reduced profits. Additionally, the Chamber supervised the administration of royal vineyards for the Habsburgs, and also saw to the confiscation and redistribution of their opponents' vineyards following the rebellions of the late-17th and early-18th centuries. [Also, see the entry for Gönci Barrel, in Part IV.]

Szepsi, László (Laczkó) Máté. (1576-1633) The 'invention' of *aszú* wine as it is known today is attributed to Szepsi. Born in Szepsi (now Moldava nad Bodvou, in East Slovakia), a wine-growing locale in neighboring Abaúj County, about 54 km (33 miles) west of Sátoraljaújhely, he spent much of his life in Hegyalja, at various times in Sárospatak, Olaszliszka, and Erdőbénye. Szepsi was a Protestant clergyman, but also had a great interest in wine-growing, and became the manager of Susanna Lórántffy's Oremus vineyard in Sátoraljaújhely. Tradition holds that because of warfare with the Ottoman Turks, he postponed a vintage and used the large harvest of botrytized grapes to make a new sort of later-harvested *aszú* wine. By most accounts, this happened around 1620, although others have thought it might have been earlier [see the entry for Barrel Aging, in Part IV]. But Szepsi only presented Lórántffy with the wine at Easter 1631 (sometimes this is dated to around 1640 or 1650, but that would have been after Szepsi's death). However, oral tradition may be wrong as to Szepsi's actual contribution. The fact that a 4-*puttonyos* wine of 1646 was exported to Poland and a law of 1655 required separate harvesting of botrytized fruit strongly suggests that *aszú* wine production was taking place since at least around 1600, and that any innovation by Szepsi had to do with some particular detail. It might be speculated that his knowledge of Latin had given him access to the discussion of sweet wines in Columella's *De Re Rustica*, which perhaps caused him to ponder alternative possibilities for their production [see the entry for Columella].

Szepsi: Mystique and Mystery

Undeniably, there is an aura about Szepsi: he ranks among the very few persons to whom a kind of wine is attributed. He could be called the Dom Perignon of Hungary. From all the fanfare about him in Hungarian wine history, it can hardly be doubted that he made a major contribution of some sort, a contribution that profoundly affected the fabrication of botrytis wines in Hegyalja. But just what was his contribution? Did he actually 'discover' botrytis or 'invent' botrytis *aszú* wine? Not likely, since over one-hundred years had passed since very overripe grapes were being used in Hegyalja. Was he the first person to 'soak' the mass of *aszú*-grape material before fermentation? Again, not likely, since this was a Balkan method known in Hegyalja long before his time; however, he could have been influenced in some way by Columella [see the entry for Soaking, in Part IV]. Did he notice the self-squeezed run-off from botrytis-affected grapes in an exceptional vintage and obtain *eszencia* that could be added to his mixture in making *aszú* wine? It cannot be absolutely ruled out since there is no indication that *eszencia* was known earlier than Szepsi's lifetime. Or, was he simply the first to notice the special qualities of *furmint* [see the entry for Furmint, in part III]. But, in the end, without any documentation, it seems destined always to remain guesswork.

Szerviczky. Greeks, the Szerviczkys originally bore the surname Papademos. Their ancestor, Charis Papademos, arrived in Hungary at the end of the 17th century, possibly with the mass migration into southern Hungary of Serb refugees from Ottoman rule at that time, which would account for the alias Szerviczky. Late in the 18th century, the family took up residence in the town of Tokaj as wine merchants. They became Hungarian subjects, and in 1802 were raised to noble status. The fact that a vineyard hill was depicted on their crest indicates that the family had become growers as well as merchants. Presumably because they were growers, their cellar was one of only three from which the Imperial Court was able to obtain a barrel of the illustrious 1811 'comet year' *aszú* wine for the coronation of Habsburg Emperor Ferdinand V in 1830 [see the entry for Botrytis: Stellar Conditions, in Part IV]. The Szerviczkys were still growers at the time of the *Tokaj-Hegyaljai Album* of 1867.

Szirmay. To the extent that the Szirmay name is known in the West, it is because of Antal Szirmay [see the following entry] and his book of 1798 about Zemplén County wine-growing. But the basis for his knowledgeableness, and authoritativeness, was the Szirmay family's considerable, long involvement with the region. Being especially prominent in Sáros County for several centuries, they would have been keenly aware of Tokaji wine developments from at least the 15th century. In the mid-17th century, their close relationship with the Rákóczis and the Drugeths brought them into neighboring Zemplén County. Thereafter, members of the family acquired vineyard properties at various times in Tállya, Mád, Ond, Mezőzombor, Tarcal, Tokaj, Bodrogkeresztúr, Bodrogkisfalud, Erdőbénye, Erdőhorváti, Tolcsva, Vámosújfalu, and Sátoraljaújhely, with the most valuable of them being located in Tolcsva, in the famed Gyapáros tract [see the latter entry, in Part III]. In Erdőbénye, they also acquired the largest cellaring facility in Hegyalja, with a capacity of 2,000 barrels; the cellar had once been the property of the Rákóczis. Count George Szirmay acquired the community of Szerencs in the late-19th century, which may have been of influence in the ultimate decision, after two centuries of uncertainty, to include Szerencs in the legal roster of Hegyalja communities in 1893. Indicative of the Szirmays' breadth of experience and substantial influence is that, in 1736, when the Crown appointed a deputation to investigate the problem of falsified Tokaji wine (one year before the 1737 royal delimitation of the Hegyalja region), three of the seven members were Szirmays, respectively representing Zemplén, Abaúj, and Sáros counties.

Szirmay, Antal. (1747-1812) Scion of a major Hegyalja family [see the previous entry], Antal Szirmay made a mark in his own right because of his book of 1798, *Notitia historica, politica, oeconomica montium et locorum viniferorum comitatus Zempleniensis* [Historical, political, economic notes on the wine-bearing hills and places of Zemplén County]. Although it covered wine-growing throughout the county, its focus was preponderantly on Hegyalja [see the listing of authors in the entry for Grape Varieties, in Part IV], with no discussion at all of wine-making habits or grape varieties that differed from those of Hegyalja. Written in Latin of a quite technical nature, the book was intended for a Europe-wide audience of wine specialists, and it may be said that, thereafter, no classically educated European could think of Hegyalja in any sense but as a wine-growing entity [see the entry for Hegyalja, in Part II]. A significant historical detail mentioned by Szirmay was that a third hoeing, so crucial to pushing the vintage further into fall and promoting the onset of botrytis, did not occur until around 1560, though he gave no explanation for that timing. Also, he evinced the concern of the Zemplén officialdom of his times about the problem of fraudulent Tokaji. Besides his landmark book, Antal Szirmay is notable for having been at the forefront of the movement for free trade in Hegyalja, which at that time was particularly favorable to Jews, while also being distinctly unfavorable for his own class, the aristocracy. However, it was in line with his concern about fraud, because he saw open competition as the best way to discourage smallholders from cooperating with merchants who dealt in cheap, adulterated Tokaji. [See the entries for Aristocracy, Jews, and Smallholders; and Chios, in Part II.]

Szuhay. The Szuhay family is found (sometimes as 'Zuhai' in early documents) as far back as the early-13th century, and they became major nobility in Sáros County, hence their interest in Hegyalja. The Szuhays are notable for being perhaps the foremost 'losers' amongst anti-Habsburg supporters in the latter part of the 17th century. Little is known about the timing of their acquisition of vineyard properties in Hegyalja, but clearly, they had been amongst the shrewdest 'investors.' Their properties were not only large, but uniformly excellent, including vineyards in the Cserfás and Henye tracts, among others. It was the confiscation of these by the Royal Court that eventually led to the creation of a Habsburg vineyard 'domain' in Hegyalja.

Tarcal Viti-Vinicultural Research Institute. (*Tarcali Szőlészeti-és-Borászati Kutató Intézet*) This name was given to the chief center for research on Tokaji wine during the communist period. However, research activity in Hegyalja had long been centered in Tarcal. Notably, the Vintners Training Institute was established in Tarcal after phylloxera. The choice of location reflected the great esteem in which Tarcal was held amongst Hegyalja communes, and not least of all the fact that the Habsburgs' vineyard property, Szarvas, was located there. During the communist era, the Research Institute was the caretaker of Szarvas.

Tatars. 1) One of the signal events of Hegyalja history, and of Hungarian history generally, was the invasion by the Mongols, or Tatars, in 1241-1242. As devastating as the invasion was, the reconstruction in its aftermath laid the foundation for Hegyalja specifically as a wine-growing region. Indeed, the term Hegyalja, with its wine-growing connotation, likely dates to the decades following the invasion. The Tatars left Eastern Europe and returned to Mongolia only because of the fortuitous death of their Great Khan in 1241. 2) The name Tatar is a bit of a misnomer, as it was applied loosely to the Mongols and allied Turkic tribes. Only one of those tribes was actually the Tatars, and they were the Tatars who later served as mercenaries of the Ottomans, and made brief but destructive incursions into Hegyalja as late as 1566-1567.

Teitelbaum-Beiler. This large Jewish wine-trading firm began operating in Abaújszántó in 1783. They acquired the former Rákóczi cellar there, and began a 'wine museum' in it, where they collected bottles from every vintage. This collection was preserved until the First World War. The Teitelbaums had vineyard property in Abaújszántó by the end of the 18th century, and were listed among prominent vineyard owners in the *Tokaj-Hegyaljai Album* of 1867. Teitelbaum-Beiler played a significant role in helping to maintain Tokaji's presence and reputation on the market in the wake of phylloxera.

Thököly, Emerich (Imre). (1657-1705) The Thököly family was mostly associated with Sáros County, and consequently would have been aware of wine developments in Hegyalja from the region's early days. Their main vineyard property seems to have been the famous Megyer tract of Sárospatak. Emerich Thököly became a high-ranking Protestant nobleman in the Szepesség region, just to the northwest of Sáros, and incited a rebellion against Catholic Habsburg rule in

Upper Hungary during 1683-1685. This led to decades of revolt that were commercially injurious to Hegyalja and also resulted in vineyard confiscations from anti-Habsburg owners, including the Megyer tract. [See the entries for Izdenci and Megyer, in Part III.]

Thurzó. The Thurzós were a family of the Szepesség region of north-central Hungary, adjoining Poland. Having become wealthy through the mining industry there in the late-15th century, the family rose to the ranks of the Hungarian aristocracy. Since a number of the small towns of Szepesség were under Polish administration in this era, John Thurzó became a citizen of Cracow and allied himself financially with the Fugger family. In 1607, George Thurzó paid in gold to gain possession of the Tokaj Domain and castle, and also became palatine, the highest official of the Hungarian royal court under the Habsburgs. During all this time, Hegyalja was coming to prominence in wine, and the Thurzós had quickly acquired vineyard property there, specifically on Tokaj-hill. The Thurzó vineyard-tract in Tarcal still bears their name. [See the entry for Fugger.]

Timon, Samuel. (1675-1736) Otherwise a Jesuit theologian, Timon was a writer of Latin verse. Having spent time in Eperjes, Ungvár, and Kassa in the early-18th century, he wrote a poem about Tokaji in 1728, *De vino Tocaino commune epigramma*, which was peculiar in being as much an orientation to Hegyalja as a poem. Timon could practically be called a proselytizer, since he obviously was writing for (classically educated) persons who did not know much about Tokaji or Hegyalja. This audience would have been largely outside the Upper Tisza region, most of all in parts of Hungary rather recently out of the grip of the Ottomans, including Buda. The most surprising aspect of the poem is the amount of territory that Timon seems to have included in Hegyalja. Instead of today's familiar Hegyalja 'triangle,' he left the impression of a 'rectangle' that included the entire Hernád valley to the west, from Szikszó north to Kassa. But his poetical remarks about the wines of individual locales contradict that impression and suggest that he was putting the actual Tokaj-Hegyalja in a broader geographical context. Thus, for instance, the only Hernád locale whose wine Timon singled out for a comment in verse was Abaújszántó, which was an undisputed part of Tokaj-Hegyalja. Timon leaves the impression that Tarcal, Tokaj, Tállya, Mád, and Mezőzombor were the prime locales of his day; and he said that the fame of Sátoraljaújhely was "not very old." He mentioned Tarcal's Szarvas vineyard-tract by name. The poem had some lasting influence, since Antal Szirmay referred to it in 1798. [See the entries for Hegyalja, Hernád River, and Chios, in Part II; as well as Section III (c) of the Part II Essay.]

Tokaj-Hegyalja Reconstruction Committee. Formed in 1970, the committee was under the leadership of the pre-communist era viticulturalist, Paul Kozma. Under his leadership, detailed plans were formulated to improve the quality of Tokaji wine by examination and supervision of where further planting should take place. But the Committee was disbanded without explanation in 1976. Apparently, the function was to be taken over by the Tokaj-Hegyalja State Farm Wine-Facility [see the Appendix Essay], though probably by order of Hungary's central economic authorities, who presumably balked at a few of the Committee's recommendations. Some ideas would have entailed removing from use the lesser-quality but higher-yielding areas, while incurring extra costs to bring higher-quality but lower-yielding areas into use.

Tokaj-Hegyalja State Farm Wine-Facility. (*Tokaj-Hegyalja Állami Gazdaság Borkombinát*) The creation of the Facility, in 1971, can in a sense be thought of as the 'high-water mark' of collectivization in Hegyalja wine-growing. However, this was far from collectivization as foreseen by communist theorists and apparatchiks two decades earlier. By 1971, the thought of bringing all land under state control had been abandoned. The Facility, at its four branches, processed all of the grapes from the *state-cultivated* lands; but cooperatives and smallholders could also sell their product to it. Tarcal became the focal point because it is centrally located amongst the most densely planted area of Hegyalja. Also, the state viti-vinicultural research facility was there. Unfortunately, no systematic research has been presented on the work and financing of the Facility during its almost 20-year existence. [See the Appendix Essay.]

Tokay, Francis. [See the entry for Tokaj: Spelling Lesson, in Part II.]

Tolcsva. [See that entry in Part II.]

Trautsohn. Prince Leopold Trautsohn, of Germany, was the Lord Steward of the Habsburg Court, and the chief German-Austrian aristocrat to benefit from the Court's confiscations of vineyard properties from the rebellious Hungarian aristocrats after the end of the last Rákóczi war in 1711. In 1720, he purchased from the Royal Treasury virtually the entire Rákóczi Hegyalja estate, spread over 28 communes. The family thus became the largest landholder in Hegyalja during the 18th century (in 1773, Sylvester Douglass mentioned "Prince Trautzon" as "the greatest proprietor"). Leopold did not take much direct interest in Hegyalja, and instead relied on an able representative, Paul Ottlik [see that entry]. In contrast, his son Johann actually moved there. Johann's notable contribution was in trying to repopulate and bolster wine-growing at several locales by bringing German settlers from the Trautsohn estates in the Black Forest region. Three settlements were started in the area between Sárospatak and Sátoraljaújhely: Hercegkút (originally Trautsohnfalva), Józseffalva, and Károlyfalva (or Karlsdorf). Settlers were also brought to Rátka in the south. The Trautsohns' notable properties included the Oremus tract of Sátoralaújhely. [See the entries for Dörzsik, Hercegköves, Oremus, and Somlyód, in Part III.]

Turks. [See the entry for Ottoman Turks.]

Upori. Although just one of a number of early families involved in the region, the Uporis are worthy of note because in 1446 their property in Hegyalja included estates in Tolcsva, Vámosújfalu, Kistoronya, Nagytoronya, and Csörgő. This was several decades before the inception of later-harvested wine in Hegyalja. In an era when the mere ownership and proximity of vineyards, as opposed to wine types, counted for a lot in framing perceptions of a wine-growing region, the widespread holdings of a prominent family like the Uporis probably added to confusion as to which locales were actually part of Hegyalja (Nagytoronya and Csörgő would not be included in later delineations of the region). The Uporis were descended from the Bogát-Radvány clan, and thus, distantly related to the Rákóczis.

Usz. One of the very old noble clans of Sáros County, they were descended from the ancient Magyar conquerors. Uszhegy hill in Mád suggests early involvement in Hegyalja. Their interest must have extended to Tokaj during the late-17th century, when Anna Usz married a Dessewffy. [See the entries for Dessewffy and Uszhegy, in Part III.] The family seat was in Usz-Peklén, in Sáros, and their castle there had substantial wine-cellaring capacity. A document of 1756 noted five cellars, respectively capable of holding 10, 26, 30, 35, and 50 *gönci* barrels; however, although the cellars were in good condition, they were empty (UC 143:6), possibly reflecting a contraction in vineyard land in Hegyalja in that period [see the Introduction to Part III].

Valenczvella: Who the Heck?

How far and how early did the fame of Tokaji spread westward on the Continent? Judging from what is easily the most 'outlandish' name in the annals of Hegyalja history, the answer must be southwestern Spain by the late-17th century. The name is Valenczvella and it is tucked away in several documents from 1737. Mention was made of "Valenczvella's vineyard" in the community of Tállya (UC 83:131). The owner's full name was recorded as "Petrus de Valenczvella." But, in actuality, he seems to have been 'Pedro de Valenzuela.' Why this Andalusian gentleman came to Hegyalja is anyone's guess. Was he a friend of Trautsohn, or even the Royal Court? After all, the likelihood is that he acquired the vineyard only after the

1711 defeat of the Rákóczis. The curiosity of Señor Valenzuela is that his vineyard marks the only instance of ownership interest in Hegyalja from the western Mediterranean. But his ownership probably was brief, and seems to have ended, judging from the documents, by 1737.

Vay. Despite being a prominent family, the Vays were only marginally connected to the Upper Tisza region, and came into Hegyalja relatively late, probably in the late-17th century (UC 83:1). The principal reason for listing them here is that Baron Nicholas Vay, in the mid-19th century, experimented with sparkling wine production at his vineyard estate in Golop. At first, he used typical regional varieties, such as *furmint* and *fehérszőlő*, but later tried cultivating several French varieties. But he eventually abandoned the project, and the French varieties never spread in Hegyalja. Also, Baron Vay became the president of the Hegyalja Wine-Growing Society (*Hegyaljai Bormívelő Társaság*) in 1871. [See the entry for Serédi-Vay, in Part III.]

Vishnyevski, Feodor. (late-17th c. – 1749) Appointed by Czarina Anna Ivanovna in 1733, Lieutenant-Colonel Vishnyevski was charged with establishing the Hungarian Wine Commission in the town of Tokaj. With him came a retinue of about 40 persons that became known locally as the 'Russian colony.' Vishnyevski retained his position for most of the next 16 years, until his death at Tokaj in 1749. As time went on, he frequently found himself in disputes with Zemplén County and the Hungarian Chamber because of the Commission's failure to observe laws and regulations relating to foreign nationals in Hegyalja. The underlying cause of the infractions was the Commission's need to double wine purchases during the period of Vishnyevski's supervision, and he apparently felt certain that the Habsburgs would usually override the Hungarians in some way in order to favor the czarina or czar. In that way, Vishnyevski set a precedent that would be followed by his successors until the discontinuation of the Commission in 1798. [See the entry for Hungarian Wine Commission.]

Vlachs. [See the entry for Rusyns; and for Levoča, in Part II.]

Voltaire. [See the opening to the Part I Essay, and the entries for Color and Tokaji Character, in Part IV.]

Waldbott. The barons Waldbott were among the Austrian-German families that came to prominence in Hegyalja in the 18th century through the auspices of the Habsburgs. They went on to become major owners, with 160 hectares (395 acres) spread in seven locales throughout the region: Mezőzombor, Mád, Erdőbénye, Erdőhorváti, Tolcsva, Bodrogolaszi, and Sátoraljaújhely. Further, all of their properties were situated in prime tracts, most notably Kincsem in Tolcsva and Rákóczi's Várhegy between Tolcsva and Erdőbénye. The Rákóczis' huge cellar at Erdőbénye was also acquired by them. Following phylloxera, towards the end of the 19th century, Friedrich Waldbott was a leading figure in the reconstruction of Hegyalja, and had nearly half of his vineyard area replanted with American root-stocks by the time J. Kossuth wrote in 1903.

Walloons. Amongst the ethnic groups that populated Hegyalja, the Walloons are the most mysterious, both as to who they were and what they did. They seem to have made two appearances, first during the 12th century, when King Kálmán brought them to the vicinity of Sárospatak, and second, in the 16th century, when they were brought from southern Hungary to transfer some of the wine traditions of the famous Szerémség region to Hegyalja. But it is not at all certain whether these two influxes involved, strictly speaking, the same ethnic group. The most that can be said is that they both spoke neo-Latin languages or dialects of Western Europe. Also, because of their neo-Latin speech, the early Walloon settlers were sometimes identified by the term *olasz*, which was also how the Hungarians of that era referred to Italians. Consequently, the Hegyalja town of Tállya is now thought to come from the Walloon word *taille*, in reference to land cleared for vineyards, instead of Talia in reference to Italia, which was an old folkloric explanation. Apparently, the Walloons also settled further north than Hegyalja, since a village recorded as Vallyon/Vallon existed by Tőketerebes (Trebišov) in the 15th century.

Wesselényi. [See the entries for Henye and Murány, in Part III.]

Windischgrätz. The princes Windischgrätz were prominent among the beneficiaries of the distribution of Hegyalja properties following the confiscations from pro-Rákóczi nobles at the beginning of the 18th century. Their vineyard holdings were originally concentrated in Sátoraljaújhely, but the family went on to acquire vineyards in Sárospatak, Bodroghalász (then Petrahó), Végardó, and Makkoshotyka, as well. During the Interwar Period of the 20th century, Louis Windischgrätz directed the Tokaji Wine-Growers Association in Mád [see the front cover].

Zada. Early records show the Zada family (also spelled Szada) to have been significant owners of vineyard properties in Hegyalja by the 14th century. In 1307, they gave use of a new vineyard in Sátoraljaújhely to the Pauline Order. Conceivably, the family might have had a connection to the vineyard hill called Zsadányi-hegy, by Sárazsadány.

Zápolyai. [See the entry for Szápolyai.]

Zudar. (Czudar in old records) The Zudars were an important noble family of the Upper Tisza beginning around the mid-13th century, and lasting until they died out near the end of the 15th century. They were especially active in fortifying the region after the Tatar invasion of 1241-1242. That task of course took precedence over involvement with wine, but it seems that the Zudars assisted wine-growing by providing virtually all of the fortresses with a vineyard-tract in Hegyalja. One of the most important of the Zudar fortresses was Boldogkő (by present-day Boldogkőváralja), just north of Abaújszántó, one of Hegyalja's earliest flourishing wine-growing locales [see the entry for Oláh.]. The fortress was an important contribution to trade because it guarded the route along the Hernád river from southern Hegyalja north towards Sáros County and Poland. At the same time, the Zudars also had the Makovica fortress near Poland [see the entry for Makovica, in Part III]. It is thus likely that they were involved with some of the earliest exports from Hegyalja to Poland. Further, in the latter part of the 15th century, Peter Zudar owned the fortress of Tállya, ever the largest producer of Hegyalja wine.

*   *   *

PART I

ESSAY

A History of the Popularity and Reputation of Tokaji Wine

At the Council of Trent (1545-1563), Hungarian bishop George Draskovics in 1562 had wine brought from Tállya, which prompted Pope Pius IV to pun that *"talia* ('such') wine is worthy of the Supreme Pontiff."

While campaigning for the Habsburgs against Hungary during 1565-1568, General Lazarus von Schwendi did not pass up the opportunity to confiscate 4,000 barrels of Tokaji for his own cellars.

Upon the death of the important Hegyalja grower and merchant Francis Dobó, in 1602, Habsburg Emperor Rudolf sent an express-courier to Sárospatak to seize Dobó's wine stocks.

In 1606, 300 casks of excellent Tokaji wine were sent to Russia for the wedding of false-czar Dmitri and the Polish noblewoman Maria Mniszek.

Voltaire found in Tokaji an aid to his literary muse, and famously became a devotee.

One year towards the mid-18th century, Habsburg Empress Elizabeth used two casks of Tokaji *aszú* as a dip for bread with which to nurse her aging parrot, thus restoring its plumage, mood, and talkativeness.

In the 19th century, Habsburg Emperor Franz Josef I made a tradition of sending Queen Victoria an annual birthday present of 12 bottles of *aszú* for each year of her life.

Flaubert, in his *Sentimental Education*, of 1869, knew it would have a literary effect to have a bourgeois table graced with "a York ham cooked in Tokay."

In the late-19th century, the physician of a gravely ill Baron Rothschild prescribed Imperial Tokay, succeeded in procuring some from the Emperor himself, and the Baron soon recovered.

In her 1927 autobiography, *My Life*, the dancer Isadora Duncan confided that after meeting a dashing Hungarian "over a glass of golden Tokay" she would no longer be "the chaste nymph" she had been.

*   *   *

So they go, more than four centuries of anecdotal history testifying to the onetime status of Tokaji wine. But by probing beneath this layer of trivia we find a remarkable story of how a wine from what was still a remote and little-known nook of Europe gained a widespread clientele and went on to became virtually a symbol of Hungary worldwide.

Lack of documentary evidence makes it difficult to say how early Hegyalja began to gain a good name for wine in its corner of Hungary. But it must have happened by 1400, since a new hamlet towards the north of Zemplén County was given the same name around that time [see the entry for Tokajík, in Part II]. Still, the marketing of Tokaji spread only gradually, and had rather modest beginnings. Considering that it eventually became a source of Hungarian national pride, it is no little irony that, with the exception of Hegyalja itself, Tokaji had practically no market on the territory of present-day Hungary. Its earliest market was almost entirely regional, and mostly on territory now in eastern Slovakia, from just southeast of the Tatra Mountains east to around the current border with Ukraine. Most of this area was part of the Upper Tisza region of the former

Kingdom of Hungary, and for both geographical and historical reasons it constituted a distinct, integral 'regional market.'

The difference between the Upper Tisza market and the broader Hungarian market is readily seen by contrasting the notations of Nicholas Oláh and Conrad Sperfogel in the first-half of the 16th century. For Oláh, in western Hungary, Tokaji was the name of a far-off wine that the merchants of Pest hardly bothered with, whereas for Sperfogel, in the Szepes region northwest of Hegyalja, Tokaji was familiar for so long that he was able to comment on its improved quality. The fact that Bishop Draskovics, of southwestern Hungary, presented Hegyalja wine at the Council of Trent, in 1562, suggests that it was around the mid-16th century that Tokaji started gaining recognition west of the Danube. Nevertheless, the Ottoman occupation of western and southern Hungary, beginning in 1526, and the growth of population in the Upper Tisza, focused Hegyalja's commercial interests northward. Notably, although Hegyalja was just as well situated to market its wine in the lowlands to its south as it was in the Upper Tisza, the lowlands were nearly depopulated because of the Ottoman occupation and consequent out-migration.

Transylvania was a special case. The Ottomans had allowed this eastern part of the Hungarian kingdom to exist as an autonomous principality. Since a major trade route in that era ran from the Upper Tisza town of Kassa to Transylvania, a market for Tokaji developed in the towns of Transylvania. But more importantly for the fame of Tokaji, most of the princes of Transylvania had roots in the Upper Tisza, and for the next 150 years exerted dominant influence over the region, not least of all in Hegyalja. In particular, the Princes Rákóczis (five in a row during the 17th century) laid the foundation for the modern Hegyalja region and set Tokaji on the road to becoming a national emblem. Especially, they used the wine as their calling card in trying to win support in royal courts throughout Europe in their efforts to oust the Habsburgs from Hungary. This proved a marketing tour de force, even though the Rákóczis failed in their political goal.

*

Although Tokaji had a market, even outside Hungary, prior to the 15th century, there is no question that it burgeoned subsequently. This was partially because of the Ottoman occupation of southern Hungary, which cut off wine exports from the famous Szerémség region. Additionally, a change had taken place in the style of Tokaji wine, as alluded to by Sperfogel in 1524. Judging from the timing of his comment, it is probable that the change was the introduction of the earliest kind of sweet wine, a later-harvested wine made in part with grapes that had shriveled somewhat on the vine, but not harvested late enough to have a significant amount of botrytized berries.

Tokaji's earliest appearance as a commercial article outside Hungary naturally was to the north, in southern Poland, since the roads and rivers through the Upper Tisza region led there. However, this trade was also propelled by growing Polish demand for wine, especially amongst the nobility and bourgeoisie. In the early-16th century, the frequent and lavish parties of the Italian-born Queen Bona (Sforza) brought wine into far greater fashion in Poland than it had ever been before. At the time, there was scattered, small-scale wine-growing in southern Poland, but utterly insufficient to meet demand in either quantity or quality. Subsequently, local production disappeared because of climatic cooling and the availability of wine from nearby Hegyalja.

Trade in Tokaji was directed above all at Cracow, which at that time was the capital of Poland. Cracow was quite familiar to the nobility and bourgeoisie of the Upper Tisza in the late Middle Ages. Moreover, because of its renown, Cracow was also a center of Greek mercantile trade. As Polish demand for wine increased, Greek merchants stepped in and brought wines from Greek Macedonia and some Aegean islands, notably, Malvasia wines and the Ariousian, or Nectar, of

Chios [see the latter entry, in Part II]. They were quick to notice the increasing Polish affinity for Tokaji during the 16th century, and began visiting Hegyalja to satisfy that demand. (The early importance of Cracow as a market is reflected in the name of the Krakó vineyard-tract, in Abaújszántó.)

From Cracow, demand for Tokaji spread further north, all the way to the Baltic coast at Danzig (Gdańsk). (Again, there is the old Danczka tract, in Mád.) Exports to the Baltic coast of Poland in turn led to exports to Scandinavia, mostly Sweden, but also Denmark. When George Rákóczi II formed an alliance with Swedish King Charles X, in 1656, Tokaji again served as an ambassador. By the late-17th century, Tokaji wine was quite well known amongst the upper class of Sweden. In his 1711-1712 travel notes about Greece, Michael Olofsson Eneman wrote that the sweet wine of Chios, famous since antiquity, reminded him of Tokaji ("Ptokaiska"). It is also clear from a letter written by Voltaire in 1722 that Tokaji was readily available in the Low Countries (Best.D.125/2 October 1722).

German-speaking markets were hardly behind the Poles. The contacts between Germans in southern Poland and northern Hungary were extensive, and German townspeople from Silesia eastward through Galicia and into Ukraine were early customers for Tokaji. Germans to the west also knew about Tokaji early on, but towards the end of the 17th century the Habsburgs barred Hungarian wine exports to those German lands, and this restriction lasted until 1775. Of course, the German upper classes managed to procure quantities via personal connections or roundabout commercial dealings, but it was not really until the German nobility started acquiring vineyards in Hegyalja in the 19th century that Germany itself became a significant market.

Russian interest in Hegyalja developed largely as a result of exports of Tokaji to eastern Galicia, especially to Lemberg (Lviv) in Ukraine. In this sense, Russia was taking cues from Poland. However, the Russian market differed considerably in that interest was concentrated at the topmost segment of society. Tokaji became an ultimate status symbol during the reign of Anna Ivanovna in the 18th century, when vineyards were rented in Hegyalja and a commission was assigned to Tokaj to ensure the accomplishment of the vintage and safeguard the output's journey to Russia. The Imperial Russian obsession went so far as to transplant Hegyalja grape varieties to Astrakhan and Crimea with the thought of imitating Tokaji.

*

Tokaji faced greater challenges outside central, eastern, and northern Europe. Certainly there is little to suggest that it had much market presence in the wine-producing countries of western and southern Europe [see the entry for Valenczvella]. Nevertheless, Tokaji had reached France by the 17th century, when Jacques Savary indicated that its main foreign competition was sweet wine from the Canary Islands. But even without large quantities of Tokaji going to France, it did gain a certain cachet there amongst the elite. Judging from the remarks of Grimod de la Reynière, in his *Almanach des Gourmands* of 1803-1812, Tokaji even inspired some nationalistic huffiness over a non-French wine that succeeded in impressing sophisticated French palates. Grimod strongly urged French growers to come up with something comparable, and the switch to botrytis wine in Sauternes shortly thereafter suggests that someone had paid attention to him.

British interest in Tokaji lagged, not only because of distance from Hegyalja, but also the long established predilection for other, fortified sweet wines. The fact that Tokaji was not mentioned in Samuel Pepys's 17th century diary is indicative. However, the works of subsequent British writers show that Tokaji had become known to the upper classes of England in the first-half of the 18th century. Beginning with Sylvester Douglass's account in 1773, Britons were traveling to

Hungary and usually made a point of visiting Hegyalja and discussing Tokaji wine at some length in their published travel notes.

However, Tokaji was never made to cater to English tastes, and accordingly, some Englishmen did not take to it. Robert Townson was outspoken about his qualms in 1737: "Tokay is no doubt a fine wine, but I think no ways adequate to its price: there are few of my countrymen, except on account of its scarceness, who would not prefer to it good claret or burgundy, which do not cost above one-fourth of its price. Some of the sweetest Spanish wines, begging its pardon, are in my opinion equally good; and unless [Tokaji] be very old, it is too sweet for an Englishman's palate…" He was echoed by Cyrus Redding in 1836: "The value of Tokay is another example of the caprice of taste or fashion in wine…Few Englishmen would prefer Tokay to wines very much its inferior in fame, did they dare to contradict the decision of fashion in its favour."

The fame of Tokaji reached beyond Europe. This may have resulted in part from actual exports across the seas, since Szirmay, in his 1803 book about Zemplén County history, noted that the wines of Tolcsva and Erdőbénye withstood sea voyages better than other Hegyalja wines. But observations about seaworthiness may have started a century earlier, when Tokaji was being shipped to Russia via Danzig (Gdańsk) and the Baltic Sea, and the wine too frequently arrived in poor condition. In any case, shipments beyond Europe were rare until the early-20th century. Some wine was shipped overseas in bottle even in the early-19th century, but the amounts were utterly insignificant, and generally resulted from special orders placed by well-connected persons (Thomas Jefferson being the most prominent example). Consequently, Tokaji's reputation overseas was largely hearsay, a circumstance that would make it all the easier for New World vintners to produce 'Tokay' wines that were facsimiles, at least as regards color and sweetness.

*

Proximity to Hegyalja and taste preferences in wine determined the direction of exports of the Tokaji sweet wines during the 16th and 17th centuries. But this was still the pre-mercantilism, pre-nationalism era of trade. The rulers of the dynastic regimes of east-central Europe were content to charge merchants a certain amount relative to the value of goods traded across borders, without being concerned as to how this prerogative might be used to serve the statist philosophy that was coming to the fore towards the 18th century. But even though royalty and aristocracy remained ascendant, they came ever more under the influence of minds that were focused on 'domestic economy' and saw unrestrained trade as a drawback, or even a threat. The policies fomented by this thinking became known as mercantilism, or the use of commerce for the benefit, the financial welfare, of the nation-state. This would become an obstacle to exports of Tokaji virtually throughout the 18th century and well into the 19th century.

Worst of all for Tokaji, the mercantilist philosophy took deep hold amongst the administrative intelligentsia in Poland in the early-18th century. Hungary, hardly out of the clutches of the Ottomans, and too preoccupied with the imposition of autocratic rule by the Austrian Habsburgs to be paying much attention to new trends in political philosophy, was caught off guard and did not think about impacts on its wine production. Gradually, Polish statesmen began having serious doubts about the Polish predilection for Tokaji wine, because expenditures on it seemed to be draining money away from the domestic economy [see the entry for Ottlik]. This outlook went so far as to envision that Polish tastes could be switched away from grape wine altogether, to the advantage of producers of domestic wines from other fruits or honey.

The general European export situation began deteriorating during the 18th century. In mid-century, the Vienna Trade Council persuaded the Habsburgs, under Maria Theresa, to prohibit

Hungarian wine exports by way of the Danube, and after 1775, to favor Austrian wine exports by allowing exports of Hungarian wine along the Danube, that is, towards Western Europe, only to the extent that equivalent amounts of Austrian wine were exported. Since Austrian wine was not in demand, this was a severe constraint on westward exports of Tokaji. Also, because Austria took a nationalistic stance vis-à-vis the importation of Prussian goods, Prussia prohibited imports of Tokaji and other Hungarian wines. Further, Russia laid a heavy duty on Hungarian wines in 1766, which affected all buyers except the Russian Imperial Court.

Additionally, after southern Poland, or Galicia, was absorbed by the Habsburg Empire in the late-18th century, exports of Tokaji to Poland were doubly burdened. Hegyalja wine then faced both a tariff on exports to Galicia and as much again on crossing over into Poland. Elsewhere, the scope for exports to Britain, even if not large because of British tastes, had been minimized ever since 1703 by the Methuen Treaty, which gave a tariff advantage to Portuguese wines made specifically for British tastes. However, the prejudicial tariff policy did not prevent the uppermost British classes from gaining some acquaintance with Tokaji [see the entry for Douglass].

*

Tokaji's image as a luxury wine was encouraged from the beginnng by its close association with the Hungarian landed nobility, particularly in the Upper Tisza region. Virtually all of the very best Tokaji was destined for 'conspicuous appreciation' by the aristocracy, as well as their friends and allies. A loosely historical representation is inadvertently portrayed in an ideologically motivated passage from a communist-era book (1978) about the Sztropkó Domain and its 16th century owner, Count Pethő, a significant Hegyalja owner: "Here [in the Sztropkó castle] the gentlemen [of the aristocracy] enjoyed themselves with good Tokaji wine...While they argued [Zemplén County affairs], and the Tokaji was tasting ever better, the peasants had to catch fish, bring hens, slaughter sheep and lambs, so that the honored gentlemen counts and barons could not say that Pethő had hosted them poorly in Sztropkó" (Beňko/Durkaj).

But the consumption of Tokaji had a much broader social appeal. The bourgeoisie of the Upper Tisza was the real mainstay of Hegyalja during the 16th century, and they were joined and surpassed by their counterparts in Poland in the 17th century. Obviously, when Gabriel Gyöngyösi, in 1736, admonished growers not to squeeze too much *eszencia* and *aszú* out of the Hegyalja vintage, he was in effect pointing to the large domestic and export burgher markets, not to the limited market represented by the nobility. Further, the bourgeoisie constituted by far the largest market for other Hegyalja wines that were the year-in-year-out money-earners. This refers not only to by-product wines of the botrytis vintage, such as *máslás*, but also table wines from vintages that did not produce botrytized berries (this included the dry red wines that hung on in Hegyalja until into the 19th century [see the entry for Paraskevich]). It must be remembered, too, that some of the bourgeoisie, as well as their municipalities, were Hegyalja vineyard-owners.

To return for a moment to the Sztropkó castle, let us be clear that the peasants of the Upper Tisza area knew well what was being drunk by the nobility, and not just because they were pouring it. Serfs from throughout the domains of present-day eastern Slovakia were sent seasonally to work in the vineyards belonging to their lords' Hegyalja properties, or volunteered because of the favorable pay for day-labor. Of course, peasants drank the lesser, common wines of Hegyalja that were sold on tap at taverns, often operated for the benefit of the lords. However, it is clear from old documents that Hegyalja vineyard-tracts usually had many owners, most of whom were neither noblemen nor burghers, but local craftsmen and peasant smallholders. Even the Englishman John Paget alluded to this in 1839: "by far the greater part [of the vineyards] is in the hands of private individuals, and the Emperor himself is often obliged to purchase his Tokay from others." While most small-scale growers did not have the facilities to produce the rarer of Tokaji wines, a few did begin making 2- or 3-*puttonyos aszú*, and carted these wines to sell to independent taverns and craftsmen in the large villages and market towns of the Upper Tisza, a habit which continued into the early-20th century.

Ironically, the 'lower-class' market for the cheaper table wines of Hegyalja eventually collapsed and was another blow to the region. The aristocracy realized that more money could be made through the sale of distilled spirits to peasants and the growing urban working class, and this resulted in the spread of distilleries in the Upper Tisza region. Wine had become increasingly expensive while vineyard land was receding during the 18th century because of trade impediments, and thus, the peasantry in non-producing areas north of Hegyalja were attracted to spirits. Further, by the 19th century, significant population changes had taken place in the Upper Tisza, such that country-folk from non-wine-consuming areas (particularly north-central Slovakia and Galicia) had settled in the Upper Tisza and reduced Hegyalja's nearby market for ordinary wine. Thus did cheap spirits replace table wine and the name Tokaji became virtually an abstraction for the great majority of people even in its own section of the Kingdom of Hungary.

*

While Tokaji never lost its allure on some markets, notably Poland, the history of its repute is not continuous or unsullied. It can even be argued that its period of grandeur lasted only from the mid-16th century (the Trident Council) to the early 1800s. When André Jullien wrote, in 1816, that Tokaji was "regarded with reason as the *premier vin de liqueur* of the world," its fame in fact had peaked and would be in a slow decline the rest of the century, and then faster from the First World War until 1990. This may seem counterintuitive if we consider that the period from 1800 to 1930 was when the modern varietal composition was being established, the chemical nature of the botrytis wines was being analyzed, and the laws and regulations pertaining to production were being adopted (not to mention the many glowing anecdotes from the 19th century).

Nevertheless, two factors worked to cause a downturn in Tokaji's fortunes. First, the circulation of imitation and counterfeit Tokaji hurt its image beginning in the 18th century and lasting until the 20th century. Attempts at imitating Tokaji can be dated to as early as 1565, when Lazarus von Schwendi took vine cuttings from Hegyalja to Alsace in the hope that something similar to Tokaji could be produced elsewhere. However, in that era, so long before the idea of protecting appellations of origin, the 'replication' of wines was not necessarily censurable as long as both seller and customer knew what the product actually was and where it came from. Nor were regular buyers likely to be duped so long as there was plenty of real Tokaji on the market.

The insidious problem of bogus Tokaji began when availability of the real product decreased. It is no little irony that the Habsburgs who so coveted their vineyards in Hegyalja were also responsible for the first downturn in the region's fortunes. This began with a production decline towards the end of the 17th century and into the early-18th century because of the Thököly and Rákóczi wars against the Habsburgs, which caused the Imperial Court to confiscate the Hegyalja properties of the anti-Habsburg Hungarian nobility, and also resulted in ruining several communities. Compounding this, there were the aforementioned impediments to exports of Hungarian wine in the 18th century. The result was a decline in the availability of Tokaji for export, and an increase in prices, which dampened demand for authentic Tokaji.

The reduced amount of genuine Tokaji encouraged the preparation and commercialization of bogus Tokaji wines. This seems to have begun in the early-18th century, in Hungary, indeed in Hegyalja itself. Early on, the main culprits were the Greek merchants, and it was primarily because of this behavior that a law of 1727 was aimed mainly at curtailing the participation of Greeks in the Tokaji trade, although enforcement became ever more lax as time went by. Typically, the Greeks brought similar but cheaper wines from nearby places into Hegyalja, did some blending with Tokaji (often of an inferior sort), and otherwise 'doctored' the wines [see the entry for Falsification, in Part IV]. Thus did they continue to make a good profit despite unfavorable laws, trade circumstances, and tariff regimes.

Some of these Hungarian products might have reached Western Europe in the 18th century. In any case, Western merchants began accepting and marketing as Tokaji any wine that purported to be that, no matter if it came from Hungary or not, let alone from Hegyalja. The fact that Grimod put his stamp of approval on imitating Tokaji in France early in the 1800s suggests that imitations were not being made there as yet. But several decades later, in 1845, Alexandre Odart commented on French imitations of Tokaji. Subsequently, Tokaji was plagued by a rash of bogus wines produced outside Hungary.

Most Western consumers, other than the nobility, were not able to distinguish fraudulent Tokaji, because they had never been acquainted with the genuine article. The extent of trade in bogus Tokaji was made embarrassingly evident in a description written by none other than the gourmand Grimod: "The wine of Tokai possesses a taste of rotten apple, extremely disagreeable, and which leaves on the palate a very unpleasant aftertaste, the most sickly; not only is it never clear and never has the diaphanous look, the cast, and the topaz color which our good Muscat wines and those of Malaga present, but it is nearly always murky, thick, and seems to hold in dissolution some foreign substance which renders it disagreeable to drink." In 1875, the *Larousse Grand Dictionnaire Universel* addressed Grimod's comment directly and said that the only possible explanation was that he had never experienced anything but sham Tokaji.

A second wave of counterfeit Tokaji hit after phylloxera struck Hegyalja in 1885. Production declined precipitously, while foreign demand continued. Most of the falsification was now occurring in Hungary again. In an attempt to stem this development, a law of 1893 was passed that included regulation of Hegyalja wine production, with a specific prohibition on bringing any wine into the region in barrels. However, world demand for 'Tokay' was now being met in part by wines produced under that name in the New World, albeit these were frankly meant as replicas rather than being presented as genuine Hungarian Tokaji. Again, many customers were acquainted with the name Tokaji, but were ill-informed about the actual product and region, and so were willing to accept the euphemism.

*

The second factor that undermined Tokaji's reputation had to do with changes in political regime. This occurred first following the First World War and the downfall of the Austro-Hungarian Monarchy. The result was 'bad press' amongst Western wine connoisseurs, who completely misunderstood the situation. It derived mostly from erroneous notions about 'Imperial Tokay,' particularly its misidentification with *eszencia*. As late as 1940, the British wine-writer Maurice Healy went so far as to call *eszencia* "the real Tokay" (*Stay Me With Flagons*).

The history of Hegyalja from the 16th to the 20th century shows that *eszencia* made no contribution to Tokaji's reputation early on, but that its influence grew beginning with the consolidation of the Habsburg properties at Tarcal in the second-half of the 18th century, and reached a peak by the First World War. On the one hand, *eszencia* is not known to have been made much before 1700, which was long after Tokaji's rise to renown. On the other hand, its fame in the West spread thereafter, especially during the 19th century, when many Western connoisseurs were under the mistaken impression that *eszencia* was not merely a type of wine, but also was synonymous with the so called 'Imperial Tokay' produced for the Habsburg court. Thus, the predominant perspective of later-day Western connoisseurs was to attribute Tokaji's fame entirely to *eszencia* produced on Habsburg vineyard properties, which meant that the disappearance of the Habsburgs was tantamount to the disappearance of Tokaji wine. The viewpoint was best expressed in 1921 by George Saintsbury: "Republican Tokay would be a contradiction in terms" (*Notes on a Cellar Book*).

However, the public relations setback did not by itself diminish *sales* of Tokaji. Relatively few consumers had read Saintsbury, and once Hegyalja recovered somewhat from phylloxera, so did sales to a certain extent. It was only the worldwide Depression of the Interwar Period that had a major negative market impact. Nevertheless, because of the dismemberment of Hungary in 1918, many owners of good vineyard properties in Hegyalja were now residing outside Hungary, particularly in eastern Slovakia. These owners lost interest in investing their scarce resources there in an effort to put their vineyards back into production. Generally, there was a loss of native interest in particular vineyard properties. Instead, cooperatives – the bane of the connoisseur class – emerged.

The final blow came when Hungary fell under communist rule after the Second World War. The message from Western connoisseurs was dire. Alec Waugh expressed it succinctly in 1959: "Tokay exists no more" (*In Praise of Wine*). Waugh's clarion call seems to have left other writers little choice but to take heed and, accordingly, to look for aspects by which to fault and downgrade Tokaji. For instance, in 1976, Terry Robards found Tokaji "not quite as soft and velvety" as other botrytis wines, and suggested that it was because of pasteurization (*The New York Times Book of Wines*). Just as Robards did, it became commonplace to place the blame squarely on the shoulders of "the Hungarian Government," as though the commissars in Budapest were dictating wine-making in Hegyalja. The anti-communist viewpoint urged by the connoisseurs was even adopted by foreign enologists, who, without any knowledge of Hungarian laws pertaining to Tokaji, wrote as if the specialty wines were now being made in contravention of those laws. [See the Appendix Essay regarding Hegyalja and the communist period.]

*

In reviewing the history of Tokaji's fortunes on the world market, one might wonder whether all of its admirers, and its doubters, had exactly the same wine in mind. For the fact is that after Hegyalja began producing later-harvested white wines, towards 1500, variations also began to be introduced, mostly as regards the level of sweetness and the amount of aging in barrel. The underlying reason had to do with the variability of ripening in such a northerly land, and this became even more the case when so much wine became botrytis-based after 1600. But as Tokaji's name spread, it also became necessary to take into account the taste preferences encountered on various markets and try to bring the botrytis-wines into line with those demands.

The taste for Tokaji certainly did vary from market to market. Dercsényi addressed it in 1796: "Among nations, some like one, some like another kind of Hegyalja wine. The Poles and Hungarians have a taste and preference for the aged, spicy, spirituous, strong and extractive *aszúszőlő* or *máslás* wines. But the Germans prefer it sweet and oily. Additionally, [the German] prefers young wine and esteems *eszencia* above all." Just as clearly, too, there historically were markets, such as France around 1800, where sweet wines other than of Muscat or Malvasia type were widely regarded as a dubious novelty. Around the same time, England and the United States were standoffish about sweet wines that were not also substantially fortified with spirits.

It was in no small part because of Hegyalja's dependence on trade and the considerable variability in market preferences that caused growers and traders to offer a broad spectrum of wines. A notation about 4-*puttonyos* wine can be found as early as 1646, which indicates a very early start to differentiation by sweetness and aging-time. In 1796, Dercsényi mentioned *aszú* wines of 8-, 10- and 12-*puttonyos* value, which meant both greater sweetness and more aging. During the second-half of the 19th century, curiosities such as 'Old *Aszú*' (*ó-aszú*) and 'Dry-*Aszú*' (*száraz-aszú*) began to be marketed with Western customers in mind. In the early-20th century, muscat-*aszú* (*muskotályos aszú*) became popular, if mainly on the Hungarian market.

In sum, a crucial aspect in the popularity and reputation of Tokaji wine has been that of offering variety and adapting to individual markets. This has continued into the post-communist era of Hegyalja, except that the focus has been on abstracted perceptions of the world market at large. Thus, while conscientious producers and purveyors in the past sought to present the inimitable features of 'Tokaji character' [see that entry, in Part IV], there has been less concern for the integrity and inimitableness of that character during the two decades that have followed communist rule in Hungary. This has been possible because many of the recent foreign customers for Tokaji have been as unconcerned, uninformed, or misinformed about the specifics of 'Tokaji character' as those who gladly purchased bogus Tokaji in past centuries.

*   *   *

PART II

GAZETTEER

place-names, regional geography, Hegyalja wine villages

*"...Tokaji, along with the hard wheat of the Alföld [Great Plain],
will ever be the glory and pride of our beautiful Carpathian-
girded homeland...Hegyalja's typical aspect best meets the eye
when approaching from the Alföld [the south]. The Nagy Kopasz
hill of Tokaj can already be spotted from afar...but for some
time it seems to stand alone. Only gradually do the smaller fore-
hills to its north emerge. Then suddenly appears, almost at once,
the northern line of [the Eperjes-Tokaj] hills. At first intermittent,
the cones of Hegyalja then join together uninterruptedly, as though
an encampment of tents."*

Irén Spotkovszky, 1914

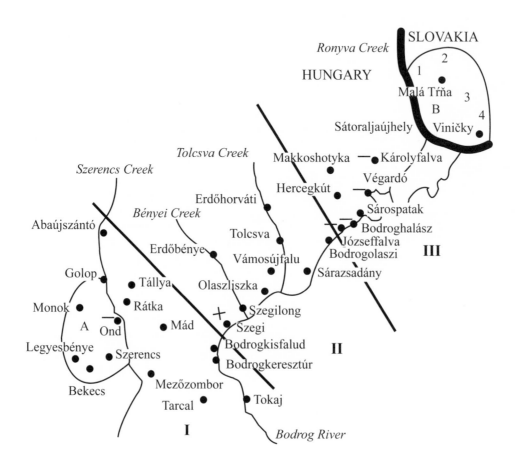

MAP #1. TOKAJ-HEGYALJA APPELLATION REGION, 1893-1994

• Hegyalja communities specified in legislation of 1893, modified by later communal developments

⌐• Hegyalja communities of 1893 that ceased to exist as entities during the 20th century, and thus, were not given separate mention as Hegyalja locales in 1994

+• Szegi became a community separate from Szegilong, and was recognized as a Hegyalja locale

_____ historical sections of Hegyalja: **I** - southern; **II** - central; **III** - northern (as indicated by Balassa; but note the last paragraph of the Introduction)

⌣ geographic units apart from Zemplén Hills: **A** - Szerencs Hills; **B** - Island Hills

• locales added by Slovak legislation of 1959, though excluded in 1893 and 1908:
   1- Čerhov; 2 - Veľká Třňa; 3 - Černochov; 4 - Bara

POLAND / GALICIA

Dukla Pass

Bártfa

SÁROS CTY.

Kisszeben

Sztropkó

Tokaj

ZEMPLÉN CTY.

Lőcse

Eperjes

Sóvár

Homonna

Igló

Csicsva

SZEPES CTY.

Varannó

Vinna

Nagy Mihály

UNG CTY.

ABAÚJ CTY.

Kassa

Mecenzéf

Gálszécs

Ungvár

Jászó

Tőketerebes

Abaújvár

Gönc

Zemplén

Regéc

Vizsoly

Háromhuta

Sátor/újhely

Bold/váralja

Aba/szántó

Tokaj

MAP #2. THE UPPER TISZA REGION of the FORMER KINGDOM OF HUNGARY

The map is centered on the most important administrative units involved in Hegyalja history: the counties of Abaúj, Sáros, and Zemplén. For background, see the entries for Eperjes-Tokaj Hill-Chain, Hegyalja, Pentapolitana, and Upper Tisza, as well as those for the counties. Each indicated place has its own entry. The area shown is about 140 km (87 miles) from north to south, and 120 km (75 miles) from east to west.

POLAND

Strachyna (*Ostrakina*)

Turány (*Trihun*)
Ondalík

Prešov (*Presian I*)

Humenné (*Gumen-*)

Enyicke (*Enyo-*)

Bogdány

Michalovce
(*Presian II*)

K

Migléz (*Mâglizh*)

Mánta Creek (*Mantepa*)

Trebesh (*Trâmbesh*)

Enyicke (*Enyo-*)

Ondava River

Laborc River

Perín (*Pirin*)

Száva (*Sava*)

Zemlin (*Zemlân*)

Makra

Rány

Molyvás (*Molyvos*)
Golop (*Gâlâb*)
Monok (*Monyak*)
Gilip Creek (*Gâlâb*)

Bogdán
Rátka (*Radka*)
Tokaj (*Sâs-toka*)
Szerencs (*Srechen*)

MAP #3. UPPER TISZA AREA and 9TH-10TH C. BALKAN CONTACT

Map #3 shows possibilities of early connections between the Upper Tisza and Macedonia-Thrace. See the entry for Bulgarian Empire; most sites have their own entry, but Trebesh is found as Trebišov, and Zemlin as Zemplín. Also see the entries: Humenné: Hmmm…; Turány: On a Saintly Trail; and Prešov: More than Strawberries?. Makra and Rány are found in Part III. K marks the modern city of Košice. The depicted area conforms to maps of the northwestern extent of the Bulgarian Empire in the 9th century [*e.g.*, see Crampton, p. 13]. The area is about 120 km (75 miles) north to south, and 60 km (37 miles) east to west, not long distances in the 9th century, since the sites are along river valleys quickly traversed by horse.

INTRODUCTION

This gazetteer aims to provide a comprehensive geographical understanding of the Tokaj-Hegyalja wine region and its historical development. Consequently, the Upper Tisza region of the former Kingdom of Hungary is covered, as well as a few outlying areas, all of which had a major influence on the commercialization of Tokaji wine, and thus on geographical conceptions of Hegyalja. Of course, though, special emphasis is given to the towns and villages that comprised the demarcated Tokaj-Hegyalja region after Hungarian national legislation of 1893.

*

Tokaji's home territory was the Upper Tisza region of the Kingdom of Hungary, the area fanning out northwest and northeast from Hegyalja, especially today's East Slovakia up to the border with Poland [see the entry for Upper Tisza]. Within the triangle formed by the town of Tokaj in the south, the Low Beskid mountains to the north, and the Tatras to the northwest, Hegyalja wine began to be known following the Tatar invasion of 1241-1242. This was sparked by the system of fortresses created in the decades of recovery that followed. As the fortresses spread, vine cultivation was encouraged wherever conditions permitted, but it was not sufficient to supply the needs of the garrisons and their serfs. To compensate, each considerable fortress was bestowed with vineyard property in the only potentially extensive wine area of the Upper Tisza: Hegyalja.

A major purpose of the fortresses was to attract settlement that would provide manpower in case of future threats from wandering hordes. This led to the establishment of secular domains around many of the fortresses, with each domain consisting of anywhere from 10 to 50 communities of varying size. Further, the fortresses became the nuclei for greater or lesser urban growth throughout present-day eastern Slovakia, as marked most characteristically by the settlement of German burghers, who sought ample wine supplies as a supplement to their own production of beer. This pattern entirely characterized the adjacent counties of Zemplén, Abaúj, and Sáros, whose combined territory early on was by far the largest market for Hegyalja wine.

Ownership of the domains became highly coveted by the most powerful families of the region during the 14th to 17th centuries, and the historical record demonstrates much jostling for position. This is apparent as early as the late-13th century in the case of the Zudars. By the 15th century, having a guaranteed supply of wine from Hegyalja had become a significant motive in acquiring a domain. The Rozgonyi family, who possessed the Varannó Domain, conducted a lively transshipment trade from there. [See the entries for Zudar and Rozgonyi, in Part I.] However, the spread of Tokaji's fame was augmented when the Transylvanian princes took an interest in the Upper Tisza domains after the Ottomans, who held southern Hungary after 1526, acquiesced in Transylvania's autonomy in 1541. Beginning with the Szápolyais and culminating with the Rákóczis, the Transylvanian princes extended their sway into the Upper Tisza and Hegyalja. From the 1630s through 1700, the Rákóczis laid the foundations of the modern Hegyalja region.

*

The term Hegyalja was used in the Upper Tisza region for possibly as long as five hundred years as a colloquial, general allusion to the region producing Tokaji wine. Since at least the early-17th century, it has been the key geographic notion and name for circumscribing or delimiting the region. However, the term's early history is nebulous and suggests that several centuries elapsed before it denoted a specific area of southern Zemplén County where wine-growing was the major agricultural activity and wines of a similar and distinctive character were produced.

63

The term Hegyalja signifies 'foothills.' But it antedates the wine region as such, and in past centuries had not only a geographic usage, but also an administrative usage in relation to secular and ecclesiastical territories. While it cannot be stated with certainty which of the two usages was more significant at the outset, they were not identical as regards territory covered, although they certainly would have overlapped. The two usages resulted in long-lasting confusion about which areas belong to the Tokaj-Hegyalja wine region, a confusion that was not decisively ended until Hungarian legislation of 1893 and 1908 [see the Part II Essay].

In 1704, "Upper, Middle and Lower Hegyalja" were specified in a solicitation to give military assistance to Francis Rákóczi II against the Habsburgs. Judging from the context, these distinctions apparently were outgrowths of an administrative usage, probably in connection with the domains of geographical Hegyalja: the Tokaj, Sárospatak, and Sátoraljaújhely domains, and possibly Regéc, as well. But documentation about the specific division of the three Hegyaljas is lacking. Balassa (1991) thought it likely that all areas north of Bodrogolaszi, thus including the Sárospatak and Sátoraljaújhely domains, comprised Upper Hegyalja. Assuming that all of the settlements from Abaújszántó southeast to Tokaj and Bodrogkeresztúr comprised Lower Hegyalja, this would leave the area between Tolcsva creek and Bényei creek as Middle Hegyalja.

*

Although Balassa took it for granted that the three Hegyaljas of 1704 had a connection to wine-growing, it is unclear how precisely true that was. Before the Rákóczis gathered up virtually all of modern-day Hegyalja, in the first-half of the 17th century, many people thought of the southernmost towns (Lower Hegyalja) as the wine region proper. But, in 1730, the geographer Bél included territory from the three Hegyaljas, and thus, also, most of today's region. Yet, he noted, "there are those who do not want to list the Sárospatak and Sátoraljaújhely wines" (in other words, Upper Hegyalja). As late as 1838, it was stated, "some people count eight Hegyalja towns, namely Tállya, Mád, Tarcal, Tokaj, Bodrogkeresztúr, Erdőbénye, Olaszliszka and Tolcsva." This excluded Upper Hegyalja, but included some of Middle Hegyalja.

The earliest official indication that parts of all three of the old Hegyaljas would eventually be included was in a royal order of 1737. Specified were (from south to north): Abaújszántó, Golop, Rátka, Ond, Mezőzombor, Tállya, Mád, Tarcal, Tokaj, Bodrogkeresztúr, Bodrogkisfalud, Bodrogszegi (now Szegilong and Szegi), Erdőbénye, Erdőhorváti, Tolcsva, Olaszliszka, Vámosújfalu, Bodrogzsadány (now Sárazsadány), Bodrogolaszi, Sárospatak, Sátoraljaújhely, and Kistoronya. This was repeated in a Zemplén County regulation of 1801 aimed at curtailing the falsification of Tokaji. A new outbreak of bogus Tokaji following phylloxera necessitated a demarcation at the national level, which came in legislation of 1893. At that time, all of the foregoing communities were included, plus (south to north) Legyesbénye, Bekecs, Monok, Szerencs, Józseffalva (later Újpatak), Petrahó (Bodroghalász), Trautsohnfalva (Hercegkút), Károlyfalva, Makkoshotyka, Végardó, and Szőlőske. This listing of 33 towns and villages now definitely included substantial territory from all three of the old sections known as Hegyalja.

Without impacting the territory entitled to the Tokaj-Hegyalja name, slight changes have occurred since the listing of 31 communities in 1908. First, in the northeast, the villages of Kistoronya and Szőlőske were attached to (Czecho-) Slovakia in 1918. Additionally, several small communes either merged or were absorbed by neighboring towns. To reflect the latter changes, Hegyalja was pared down to 27 communities by legislation of 1994, as follows (in alphabetical order): Abaújszántó, Bekecs, Bodrogkeresztúr, Bodrogkisfalud, Bodrogolaszi, Erdőbénye, Erdőhorváti, Golop, Hercegkút, Legyesbénye, Makkoshotyka, Mád, Mezőzombor,

Monok, Olaszliszka, Rátka, Sárazsadány, Sárospatak, Sátoraljaújhely, Szegi, Szegilong, Szerencs, Tarcal, Tállya, Tokaj, Tolcsva, Vámosújfalu. Additionally, Malá Tŕňa (Kistoronya) and Viničky (Szőlőske) in Slovakia were still recognized under the 1908 legislation.

*

Despite the national laws of 1893 and 1908, Hungarian experts have not been entirely unanimous about what constitutes Hegyalja. Some have thought that the greater the territory covered by the official delineation, the greater was the loss in average quality. Balassa (1991) went so far as to refer to it as a 'dilution.' He assumed that as the geographical concept of Hegyalja was extended, more lesser-quality than higher-quality land had been included. He is echoed by some Hegyalja cognoscenti and Hungarian enophiles at this very moment.

Balassa did not get into the specifics of the dilution, or how such dilution might be recognized for what it was. The most likely supposition is that it would concern primarily the small Hegyalja communities. In terms of vineyard area, Hegyalja can easily be broken down historically into communities of three sizes in terms of vineyard acreage: large (Mád, Sárospatak, Sátoraljaújhely, Tállya, Tarcal, Tokaj, Tolcsva); medium (Abaújszántó, Erdőbénye, Mezőzombor, Olaszliszka); and small (all the rest). Since the latter group included the last communities to be officially and conclusively admitted to the ranks of Hegyalja, 'dilution' has to be attributed largely to them. But is that reasonable? [See the last paragraph of the entry for Rákóczi, in Part I.]

The advantage of the large and medium communities was the number and area of 1st and 2nd Class vineyard-tracts. But, one-hundred years ago, the Hungarians were faced with the dilemma that certain hills and vineyard-tracts in the small communities could produce Tokaji botrytis wines almost as good as any in a good botrytis year, and indistinguishable in essential characteristics from equivalent wines of the bigger Hegyalja communities that had the greatest, oldest pedigree. This could be proved time and again in tastings. Was this to be ignored because of debatable notions like 'average quality'? And what about the imperative of an objective display of 'Tokaji character' versus the threat of a subjective pecking order amongst villages?

The fact that only 22 locales were specified in the royal order of 1737 does not necessarily mean that all of the villages added in the 1893 legislation were *really* left out in 1737. The area around Sárospatak merits special attention. Bodroghalász (Petrahó) and Végardó likely were implicitly included as part of Patak [see the entry for Végardó]; and the Patak Domain apparently had within its bounds the vineyard areas of three nearby locales that simply had not yet been established as villages: Trautsohnfalva (later Hercegkút), Józseffalva (Újpatak), and Károlyfalva. Farther south along the Bodrog, Szegi likely included Szegilong. In the Szerencs hills area, Bekecs and Legyesbénye were at their historic nadir, and likely were brushed aside as wholly insignificant.

In 1985, the Hegyalja expert Dezső Szilágyi saw something other than dilution of average quality. He noticed, instead, that the wines of certain parts of Hegyalja had a broad similarity, no matter the relative repute of the communities in each. Indeed, he was recommending that Hegyalja be divided into three parts for practical purposes (such as, presumably, blending), although the appellation itself would remain unitary. He specified the "southernmost" line from Abaújszántó to Tokaj, the "middle section" from Bodrogkeresztúr to Tolcsva, and the "northern area" from Bodrogolaszi to Sátoraljaújhely: "Each of these areas produces a wine of relatively uniform quality" (presumably, he meant 'character'). What a coincidence that he was in effect harking back to the "Upper, Middle and Lower Hegyalja" of 1704.

*   *   *

PART II

THE A-Z LISTING

The names in capital letters are those of present and past towns/villages designated as part of the Tokaj-Hegyalja appellation zone.

Abaúj County
ABAÚJSZÁNTÓ
Abaújvár
Balkans
Bara
Bardejov
BEKECS
Bényei Creek
BODROGHALÁSZ
BODROGKERESZTÚR
BODROGKISFALUD
Bodrogköz
BODROGOLASZI
Bodrog River
Bulgarian Empire
Čerhov
Černochov
Chios
Cotnari
Cracow
Dalmatia
Dukla
Dunajec-Vistula
Eperjes-Tokaj Hill-Chain
ERDŐBÉNYE
ERDŐHORVÁTI
Gdańsk
Gilip Creek
GOLOP
Gönc
Háromhuta
Hegyalja
Hejce
HERCEGKÚT
Hernád River
Humenné
Humenné: Hmmm...
Island-hills
Jasov

JÓZSEFFALVA
KÁROLYFALVA
Košice
Ladmovce
LEGYESBÉNYE
Leles
Levoča
Macedonia
MÁD
MAKKOSHOTYKA
MALÁ TŘŇA
Mánta Creek
Medzev
MEZŐZOMBOR
Michalovce
Molyvás: Greek?
MONOK
Monyorós-Csicsva
Moravia, Great
OLASZLISZKA
OND
Ondava River
Ondava: Turkic Remnant?
Pentapolitana
Perín
Prešov
Prešov: More than Strawberries?
RÁTKA
Regéc
Ronyva Creek
Royal Hungary
Sabinov
SÁRAZSADÁNY
Sáros County
SÁROSPATAK
SÁTORALJAÚJHELY
Sečovce

Slovakia
SLOVENSKÉ
  NOVÉ MESTO
Solivar
Spišská N. Ves
Strachyna
Stropkov
SZEGI
SZEGILONG
Szepesség
Szerémség
SZERENCS
Szerencs Hills
TÁLLYA
TARCAL
TOKAJ
Tokaj: Spelling
Tokajík
TOLCSVA
Tolcsva Creek
Trebišov
Turany
Turány: On a
  Saintly Trail
Upper Hungary
Upper Tisza
Uzhhorod
VÁMOSÚJFALU
VÉGARDÓ
Veľká Tŕňa
Veľký Kamenec
VINIČKY
Vinné
Vizsoly
Vranov
Zakynthos
Zemplén County
Zemplén Hills
Zemplín

Note: The names of the towns and villages belonging to the Tokaji appellation region are bolded in upper-case and also underlined in bold, e.g., **MÁD**. The names of villages that were included in the legislation of 1893 but no longer exist as administrative entities are bolded in lower-case with underlining, and preceded by an asterisk, e.g., * **Monok.** Village names bolded but preceeded by two asterisks and not underlined were included by Slovakian legislation of 1959, despite having been excluded by the 1893 and 1908 laws, e.g., ****Bara**.

Towns now in Slovakia are listed by their Slovak names for ease in finding them on contemporary maps. However, the former Hungarian names are also shown because those are the ones that researchers need to know for the preponderance of sources on the subject of Tokaj-Hegyalja. The names of counties are listed by their old Hungarian names, because even though parts or all of them are now in Slovakia, they have never been used as administrative names in Slovakia. The names of rivers, streams, and hill formations are given in the Hungarian form, although Slovak names are shown as appropriate. For the ease of English-readers, the names of vineyard hills are given in redundant form, such as Feketehegy hill ('hegy' being Hungarian for hill).

In the entries for the wine-growing communities, mention is made of the soil-type known colloquially in Hegyalja as 'nyirok.' It is a valued but somewhat variable clay-based soil, of which more is said in the Part III Essay.

All distances stated as "north of Hegyalja" refer to Sátoraljaújhely, unless otherwise indicated.

*

Abaúj County. (See Map #2) One of the earliest counties of Hungary, Abaúj abutted Zemplén County on the southwest, the western side of Hegyalja. The name refers to the Aba clan and the Abaújvár fort. The interest of the Abas suggests that the area had some habitation at the time of the Hungarian Conquest. Since Abaúj was centered on the Kassa basin, it was probably amongst the most inhabitable areas in terms of arable land. Moreover, the Hernád river is a central feature of the basin, and was no doubt attractive to the Abas as a trade route, as it had been for earlier inhabitants. Abaúj grew in population during the first period of Hungarian history, under the Árpád kings. This development was enhanced by resettlement (mainly German colonization) after the Tatar invasion of 1241-1242; the northward flight of Magyars from Ottoman-occupied southern Hungary during the 16th and 17th centuries; and the settling of Székler (Székely) soldiers from Transylvania by the Hungarian Transylvanian princes in the 17th century to guard against Ottoman military efforts to gain Hegyalja and the Upper Tisza. Notably, Abaúj was a northerly area of the Upper Tisza where very good wine could be grown, and consequently, wine was the habitual drink even after the Germans arrived with beer. But, as population grew, Abaúj was not able to meet its wine consumption needs, which caused innkeepers and merchants to look first to the Szerémség, and then, after the Ottoman occupation, to Hegyalja. Given the Hernád river route, this inevitably led to Abaúj being a major conduit for exports of Tokaji to Poland.

ABAÚJSZÁNTÓ. (colloquially Szántó) Located at the southwestern end of Hegyalja, this small town is the only one of the region's wine locales whose territory always remained entirely outside the historical Zemplén County, and instead belonged to Abaúj County. But as a result of redistricting after the First World War, it became part of the newly constituted Abaúj-Borsod-Zemplén County. Its position close to the Hernád river gave it an early advantage in sending wine northward to the towns of Kassa, Eperjes, and Bártfa, and in turn to Poland.

The general suitability of the Hernád valley for wine-growing suggests that Abaújszántó was one of the locales taking part in it from a very early time. However, it is thought to have received some Italian newcomers in the mid-13th century, following the Tatar invasion, both to renew and extend vine cultivation. Its wine production had to have been estimable by 1275, when the village figured in the Bishop of Eger's list of communal wine-tithes. The Angevin King Charles Robert settled more Italians early in the 14th century, and they are assumed to have brought some dark grape varieties, although nothing specific is known. In any case, Abaújszántó was an early and important source of high-quality later-harvested white wine, and later on, botrytis wine. It is entrenched in town lore that Pope Pius VII, early in the 19th century, was impressed by it, and said: "What the vintage sends from the Szántó lands is the prime glory of Újvár [Abaúj]."

Despite being in Abaúj County, the town was difficult to leave out of notions of Hegyalja. It is situated along the southern line of the most famous Hegyalja locales, and also beside one of the two Sátor hills that gave rise to the centuries-old understanding of Hegyalja as stretching 'from Sátor hill [in Sátoraljaújhely] to Sátor hill [in Abaújszántó].' Consequently, Szántó was almost always included in even the most restrictive notions of what constitutes the Hegyalja wine region. In 1859, the Hegyalja Vinicultural Association (*Hegyaljai Borászati Egylet*), a first, was founded here. Besides quality, the village also had quantity. This drew Galician Jews in significant numbers beginning in the late-18th century. The wine-trading houses of Flegman, Teitelbaum, and Zimmerman were very active in the wine trade there in the second-half of the 19th century, and played a significant role in maintaining the fame of Tokaji on the world market in the wake of the phylloxera crisis [see the entry for Teitelbaum-Beiler, in Part I].

Szántó sustained the largest loss of vineyard land to phylloxera among the major Hegyalja communities, up to 98 percent. In 1950, Hidvéghy noted that numerous old vineyard-tracts had made hardly any recovery from phylloxera, and not a few had gone entirely fallow and disappeared, not least of all in some very good areas. Incidentally, Szabó/Török in 1867 gave only a short list of the village's tracts, and even for those did not mention rankings that might have come down from the mid-17th century Rákóczi classification. As for Szirmay in 1798, he gave no information about Abaújszántó because he did not include Abaúj County locales. But a document of 1783 shows that there were at least 35 tracts at that time (UC 192:6). A tract praised by Szabó/Török in 1867 that did not survive phylloxera was Cserjes.

[Historical vineyard area: 1873 - 363 ha.; 1913 - 56 ha.; 1940 - 125 ha.; 1963 - 127 ha.; 1990 - 142 ha.]

Abaújszántó's wine-growing area consists of two sections, on either side of Szerencs creek. The larger and generally more esteemed part is on the town side of the creek, towards the southeast, and features the Krakóhegy and Sátorhegy hills. The smaller part is to the west, across the creek, and thus actually known as the 'across-the-water' (*vízentúli*) section, where Sulyomhegy hill is found. Both sides have tracts with favorable southwestern expositions, but some more southerly than westerly; the main disadvantage 'across-the-water' is that too many areas face westerly. Soil is frequently a mix of the clayey sort (*nyirok*) with loess and riolite dust (Hidvéghy noted that nowhere except at Tokaj is there such a wide extent of loess covering); but here and there lime is very significant. Otherwise, the best areas are in the upper-middle zone where stone content can reach 50-70 percent. On the basis of these factors, the most highly regarded vineyard-tracts were Felső-Bea, Fövenyes, Krakó, Pendics, and Sátor on the town side of Szerencs creek, and Sulyomtető and Délrefekvő-Sulyom in the 'across-the-water' section.

Abaújvár. The 'Aba-new-fortress' (in reference to the Aba clan) was situated just to the northwest of Hegyalja. It became the focal point of regional development along the Hernád river, and particularly the foundation for Abaúj County. Apparently, a settlement was adjacent to

Abaújvár already at the time of the Magyar Conquest, and vines were being cultivated. A pruning knife from the 7th century was found there. It is identical to the type known to the Bulgaro-Slavs of that era [see the following entry]. Abaújvár would have had an early interest in Hegyalja wine, as it possessed Golop since the 13th century [see the entry for Golop].

Balkans. Although the core Balkan lands are distant by several hundred miles from Hegyalja, old Balkan grape varieties and wine-making habits are of great significance to understanding the viti-vinicultural background of the famous Hungarian region. The territory mainly concerned is the contiguous area of south-central and southwestern Bulgaria, and north-central Greece [see the entry for Macedonia]. The main historical reason for the Balkan influence is that the Romans hardly reached the Upper Tisza region, and never made a cultural impact there. Instead, the Bulgaro-Slavs brought a tradition that had grown out of ancient Thracian and Greek grape varieties and wine-making procedures. [See the entries for Bulgarian Empire; Bulgaro-Slavs, and Greeks, in Part I; and for Balkan Influences and Grape Varieties, in Part IV.]

The Magyar language has several overlaps with the Balkans in grape/wine terminology, although it cannot be demonstrated just when and how these occurred. It might have been because of the Bulgaro-Slavs that the Magyars settled on the word *kád* for 'vat,' though it had come from the Greek *kados*, which had been used since antiquity (κάδος) and might already have been known to the Magyars earlier. There is also a connection between a Hungarian word for marc, *cefre*, and the Bulgarian *dzhibri* and Greek *tsipri* [see Cepre, in Part III]. The Magyar word for the grape-bunch stem, *kocsány*, is shared with the Bulgaro-Slavs (*kochan*) and Greeks (*kotsani*), although it is uncertain whether this borrowing happened after the Magyars arrived in Hegyalja, or was in their older fund of Turkic words, as could also have been the case with the Bulgars. The Magyar term for a 'wine-skin' (for wine storage), *tömlő*, almost certainly shared an origin with the Bulgar *tulum* as a Turkic loan-word from earlier ethnic history. The one word used in Hegyalja that does link the region directly to the Bulgaro-Slavs is *kása* (kasha), as applied to the thoroughly crushed mash of grape skins and pulp [see #6 in the entry for Balkan Influences, in Part IV].

**Bara (Bári). Situated in East Slovakia at the northeastern edge of Hegyalja, Bara lies between the Hegyalja communes of Malá Tŕňa (Kistoronya) and Viničky (Szőlőske), but nevertheless was not considered in recent times to belong to the Hegyalja wine region proper. Notably, Antal Szirmay, in 1798, mentioned it among the Zemplén wine villages that did *not* produce Tokaji. In 1851, Fényes mentioned a vineyard hill in the village, then called Nagy (Big) Bári, but gave no indication that it merited mention among the Hegyalja locales; he said nothing about the twin village of Kis (Little) Bári. The Hungarian legislation on Hegyalja in 1893 and 1908 also did not include Bári. Nevertheless, Slovak legislation of 1959 added Bara to Slovakia's Tokaji wine villages. Hungary has sought, within the European Union, to have the locale excluded again in order for Slovakia to export its Tokaji (Tokajské) wines under that name. The village's best vineyard-tracts are considered to be Kenderes and Hecske.

Bara is of special interest because of its history and location. Archaeological finds indicate settlement there prior to the Kingdom of Hungary; and old documents attest to a settlement in the 9th-10th century. This suggests that wine-growing may have been an activity since that time, and by inference, also in adjacent areas of what later became northern Hegyalja. It also implies rudimentary wine-storage spaces [see the entry for Bodrogköz]. However, the village's present name dates to after the Tatar invasion of 1241-1242, and is attributed, at least in folklore, to Italian settlers brought from Bari, in Apulia, to repopulate the locale and rejuvenate wine-growing [see the entry for Ratold, in Part I]. The folklore has not been challenged.

Bardejov (Bártfa). The second largest town of the former Sáros County, Bártfa was also the northernmost of the Pentapolitana [see that entry], near Poland. In fact, Poland had shown an early ecclesiastical interest in the area during the Árpád era. However, the peculiarity of Bártfa's history is that its development began in earnest when the Angevin king Charles Robert settled Italian soldiers there in 1312, which spurred a string of smaller Italian-initiated settlements, originally bearing Italian names, southeasterly along the Tapoly (Topľa) river. The Italians apparently brought viticulture to the Tapoly, although this was hardly sufficient for Bártfa as it grew [see the entry for Upper Tisza; and for Italians, in Part I]. Further, Charles Robert encouraged commerce by exempting the Italians and any other citizens of Bártfa from paying mercantile taxes. By 1410, it had become a royal free town, and subsequently was part of the Pentapolitana. As such, it was of considerable importance in the early trade of Hegyalja wine [see the entry for Pálóczi, in Part I]. By this time, Bártfa was preponderantly German-speaking.

Although 105 km (65 miles) north of Hegyalja, its immediate proximity to Poland naturally favored Bártfa as a transshipment point. Consequently, numerous merchants operated out of the town. Trade records from the early 1500s demonstrate that these merchants ranged far and wide in the Upper Tisza to acquire wines for sale to Poland, usually Hegyalja wine, no matter the commercial provenance (*i.e.*, Hegyalja wine procured in places north of Hegyalja). Purchases directly from Hegyalja appear to have been made from various communities in the region. The town also purchased vineyards in Hegyalja, as is still apparent from the Bártfai (or Bátfi) vineyard-tract in Tállya. It is interesting, too, that Bártfa owned vineyards both in the south, at Tállya, and in the north, at Sátoraljaújhely, which is an early indication that knowledgeable merchants were developing a clear geographic outline of Hegyalja. [See the entries Bártfai, Esztáva, Németszőlő, Nyergesek, Sátorhegy (3) (4), Seres (1), and Tökösmaj, in Part III.]

Bártfa. [See the previous entry.]

BEKECS. This small village is located at the far southwestern end of Hegyalja, between Szerencs and Legyesbénye. Though perhaps not inhabited when the Magyars arrived around 900, it might be among the second oldest stratum of Hegyalja villages, perhaps dating to the centuries of the Árpád kings beginning in the 10th century. Its name is attributed to the historical figure Beke, of the Bogát-Radvány clan, whose presence in the Zemplén area before the Tatar invasion of 1241-1242 is attested to by documents. An early, integral connection between wine-growing in Bekecs and the nearby Hegyalja villages can be imputed from its transfer along with Monok and Golop, in 1435, to the Dobi family (also descended from the Bogát-Radvány clan).

Bekecs is among the Hegyalja villages which, historically, were not always treated as part of the region, notably in the royal order of 1737. But its omission may have been because of distant location and small size, together with its destruction twice by fire, first during the Turkish attacks on Upper Hungary in the late-16th century, and again in the late-17th century. The village was still deserted in the early 1730s. In short, Bekecs was a minor habitation to begin with, and was at its low-point when modern conceptions of Hegyalja were taking shape. Even in 1774, it was noted that the village produced just enough wine to sell in its own taverns in a year's time. But it seems to have recovered sufficiently to be included by the national legislation of 1893 and 1908.

[Historical vineyard area: 1873 - 47 ha.; 1913 - 17 ha.; 1940 - 17 ha.; 1963 - 5 ha.; 1990 - 18 ha.]

The Bekecs vineyards are situated on the slopes of Nagyhegy hill, northwest of the village. Soil varies between clayey (*nyirok*) and loess, with stone content up to 50-60 percent. Historically, the most esteemed tract was Napos ('Sunny'), named for its southerly exposure. But, in its entirety, the village was rated as 2nd Class by Szirmay in 1798.

Bényei Creek. Arising in the southern Zemplén hills, Bényei creek passes through Erdőbénye and meets the Bodrog at Szegilong. Just to the north of that point is Olaszliszka, some of whose vineyard land is along the northern side of the creek. Together with the Tolcsva creek further north, the Bényei creek seems to have given rise to notions about 'Middle Hegyalja' in past centuries, at least in part because a fairly continuous mass of vineyard hills stretches between the valleys of the two creeks. This land is set off by forested hills that virtually surround the whole.

*Bodroghalász. Situated along the Bodrog just south of Sárospatak, this small village was included in Hegyalja by the Hungarian legislation of 1893 and 1908, but was absorbed by Sárospatak in 1950, and consequently did not appear by name in legislation of 1994. The present name dates only to 1896 and signifies 'Bodrog-fisher' to reflect its riverside site. The older name was Petrahó, which was mentioned in 1248, shortly after the Tatar destruction. However, the village may well have existed before then, since Sárospatak certainly did. Italian settlement in the post-invasion years enlarged the village, and most vineyards might date to that time. The village's wine-growing connection to the rest of Hegyalja was enhanced in 1257, when King Béla IV donated Petrahó to the Augustine Order seated in the northernmost Hegyalja village of Toronya (later divided into Nagy- and Kis-Toronya); and again when it became an estate of the Pauline Order of Sátoraljaújhely in the 15th century. Aristocratic interest was also drawn to the village, and it belonged to the Perényi family in the early-16th century, and to the Rákóczis in the 17th century. Petrahó was confiscated by the Habsburg court and transferred to the Royal Treasury after the failure of the Rákóczi rebellion in 1711, but subsequently was acquired by Prince Bretzenheim. Prince Windischgrätz had an estate in Bodroghalász in the early-20th century. The village was usually considered an integral part of Hegyalja, though not much attention was paid to it because of its small size and minor contribution to wine output.

[Historical vineyard area: 1873 - n/a; 1913 - n/a.; 1940 - 6 ha.; 1963 - 5 ha.; 1990 - n/a]

Bodroghalász for the most part is lowland territory. Its vineyards occupy a small area scattered over the southern, eastern, and western sides of Szemince-hill. Although the soil is clayey (*nyirok*), it is mostly of the less desirable, somewhat loose sort, owing to 'stone-dust' (*kőpor*) content. The riolite-rich higher area with southern exposure was the preferred area historically.

BODROGKERESZTÚR. (colloquially Keresztúr) The southernmost village along the Bodrog before it reaches Tokaj, Keresztúr lies just where the river bends southeastward. Its immediate neighbor to the north is Bodrogkisfalud, and they have much history in common. Both existed before the Tatar invasion, although Keresztúr, first mentioned in 1239, might be slightly younger. It was a fortified place, perhaps belonging to the Knights of St. John, since one explanation for the name is that Keresztúr (signifying 'man of the cross') could indicate 'Crusader.' However, another view holds that the village originally belonged to a monastery, and attributes the name to a church presumed to have been named Holy Cross (Szent Kereszt) [see the entry for Vinné]. Both Keresztúr and Kisfalud were obliterated by the Ottomans in 1566, and again during the last Rákóczi rebellion at the beginning of the 18th century. Both belonged to the Tokaj Domain, and Timon, in 1728, wrote that Keresztúr's fame owed mostly to its being Tokaj's neighbor, and that its wine "is not the best." However, if read the wrong way, that evaluation flies in the face of the village's possession of several excellent old vineyard-tracts.

[Historical vineyard area: 1873 - 172 ha.; 1913 - 84 ha.; 1940 - 109 ha.; 1963 - 148 ha.; 1990 - 379 ha. Includes Bodrogkisfalud, except for 1940.]

As with their general history, wine-growing has overlapped historically between the two neighboring villages [see the following entry]. All of their vineyards lie on the hills northwest of them. Bodrogkeresztúr's vineyard area is twice as large as that of Bodrogkisfalud, and the high-quality parts are almost entirely within the boundaries of Keresztúr, particularly the tracts Csókamáj, Henye, Kakas, Kővágó, Messzelátó, Sajgó, and Újhegy. Soil is mostly clayey (*nyirok*) or loess-clay, but Keresztúr is the last locale heading north along the Bodrog where loess is a major soil type [see the entry for Dereszla, in Part III]. Degraded riolite-tuff is found nearly throughout, while lime is virtually absent.

BODROGKISFALUD. (colloquially Kisfalud) A village along the Bodrog, immediately north of Bodrogkeresztúr and Tokaj, its name means simply 'Small-Village.' It was mentioned as early as 1220, or two decades before the Tatar invasion; but the *–d* ending on the name suggests that it could be much older. As an agricultural locale, it is certainly older than Bodrogkeresztúr. During the 14th and 15th centuries, a surprising number of prominent landed families of the Upper Tisza region had ownership interests in both of these villages: Rozgonyi, Perényi, Keczer, Szápolyai, Rákóczi, and others. Both places became part of the Tokaj Domain. [See the preceding entry.]

[Historical vineyard area: included in Bodrogkeresztúr data, except 1940, at 67 ha.]

In recent centuries, Kisfalud's vineyard area has been only half as large as Keresztúr's. Soil is clayey (*nyirok*), and stoniness is very variable, but up to 20-40 percent on Csirke-hill. The esteemed tracts were Barakonyi on Várhegy-hill and Aranyos on Csirke. Curiously, a document of 1675 (UC 116:15) indicates that at that time all of the vineyards northwest of Bodrogkisfalud and Bodrogkeresztúr belonged to Kisfalud: Kővágó, Sajgó, Somos, Vári. (Inexplicably, the document also mentions Hatalos, Hosszúmáj, Lapis, and Poklos as Kisfalud tracts, although they have usually belonged to Szegi.)

Of special note about the 1675 document is that the vineyards were listed by quality according to three classes, which demonstrates that the Rákóczis had indeed had the Tokaj-Hegyalja vineyards classified in three quality classes earlier in the 17th century.

Bodrogköz. (*Medzibodrozie* in Slovak) Signifying 'land amidst the Bodrog,' this distinct topographic area lies just east of Sátoraljaújhely and northernmost Hegyalja, and is divided between Hungary and Slovakia. As the name suggests, it is an 'island,' surrounded by river waters, the Tisza on the southern side, and the Bodrog and Latorca on the northern side. Mostly a level region, but with hills suitable for wine-growing, the Bodrogköz is thought to have been the only substantially occupied area of the Upper Tisza region at the time of the Hungarian Conquest, perhaps not with a large population, but with numerous hamlets. Historically, its most important settlement was 'Zemlin' [see the entry for Zemplín]. All indications are that this was an Avar-Slav populace, though Slavic 'ethnicity' within the larger tapestry of old Slavdom is not known. The grape varieties and wine-growing habits clearly were not of a Western (Frankish) type that would be expected if they had been brought to the area by Great Moravia. Particularly notable, in terms of regional wine history, is that the early inhabitants dug their homes and storage facilities into earth and rock, which is the origin of the famous underground 'hole-cellar' of Hegyalja [see the entry for Cellars, in Part IV]. Also of interest is that it was specifically the wine-growing Kabars who settled throughout the Bodrogköz, and thus probably in northern Hegyalja as well, after the Hungarian Conquest [see the entry for Kabars, in Part I]. [Also, see the entry for Cseke, in Part III.]

BODROGOLASZI. (colloquially Olaszi) South of Sárospatak and east of Tolcsva, this village lies towards the northern portion of Hegyalja. Balassa (1991) considered that it probably was the southernmost community of what was at one time referred to as Upper Hegyalja, which seems likely in view of its having been part of the Sárospatak Domain. There is uncertainty about the

–olaszi member of the name. King Béla IV apparently settled Italian (*olasz*) vine-dressers there in 1244, after the Tatar invasion, but neo-Latin speakers other than Italians were already there in the 12th century, and they, too, would have been called *olasz* in that era. It might be speculated that colonization was accomplished with assistance from the Pauline Order of Sátoraljaújhely. The Pauliners were instrumental in developing the locale during the 16th and 17th centuries, a period that included recovery following the Ottoman Turkish destruction of the village in 1566.

[Historical vineyard area: 1873 - 227 ha.; 1913 - 59 ha.; 1940 - 62 ha.; 1963 - 213 ha.; 1990 - 164 ha.]

The vineyards of Bodrogolaszi are situated west of the village. Exposition is various, but soil for the most part is clayey (*nyirok*), sometimes mixed with 'stone-dust' (*kőpor*), but with stone content of 20-40 percent in the higher areas. The most highly regarded tracts historically were on the southeastern side of Magoshegy hill, especially the southwestern side of the Kanta tract, and the southeast- and southwest-facing areas of the Somos tract. Hidvéghy (1950) noted that the old Darnó tract had been left largely uncultivated in recent times because of poor easterly exposition.

Bodrog River. The Bodrog is the waterway most closely associated with Hegyalja. It flows past Sárospatak in the northeast all the way south to Tokaj-hill. Consequently, several Hegyalja villages bear, or have borne, the forename Bodrog-. Additionally, the three tributary creeks (north to south) of Ronyva, Tolcsva, and Bényei are the site of still other Hegyalja villages. The name Bodrog apparently reaches back to the Magyar Conquest, or at any rate deep into the era of the Árpád kings who established the Kingdom of Hungary. Indeed, it was the main river of the Zemplén region for about eight centuries, since use of the name spread northward as new territory was developed following the Tatar invasion of 1241-1242. The name ('Bodrug') was still used at Sztropkó, in northernmost Zemplén, in 1355 (DL 4483), and at least as far north as the Tőketerebes Domain in 1601 (per the domain's *urbárium* of that year). Subsequently, it was used only as far north as its confluence with the Latorca river, from which point the Bodrog became the Ondava [see that entry]. Also to be emphasized, the Bodrog makes a significant contribution to botrytization because of its late-fall fogs and mists that penetrate the hills to its west.

Bodrogsára. [See the entry for Sárazsadány.]
Bodrogzsadány. [See the entry for Sárazsadány.]

Bulgarian Empire. The history of Hegyalja, its grape varieties, and its wine-making will never be understood fully without much more research about the medieval Bulgarian Empire and its penetration of the Upper Tisza region. The Empire was in control of what is *now* east-central Hungary since around the 8th century, and during the 9th century pushed north, through what would become Abaúj, Zemplén, and Ung counties. In this Bulgarian 'borderland,' control might have been loose, since population was scanty. Nevertheless, according to Anonymous, the Bulgar Zalán met with the Magyar leader Árpád at the time of the Hungarian Conquest, at the end of the 9th century, and acceded to the Magyars' insistence upon remaining there. As with much of the account given by Anonymous, there are those who question his accuracy on this point. Some Hungarian and Slovak historians have even downplayed the Bulgarian Empire in regional history [see the entry for Bulgars: Bulgaro-Phobia, in Part I]. Certainly some of the strongest evidence bearing Anonymous out is to be found in the mundane subject of viti-viniculture [see the entries for Balkan Influences, Grape Varieties, and *Szlankamenka*, in Part IV].

However, circumstantial evidence is found in unusual place-names in the Upper Tisza, toponyms that can only be called anomalous. These names are few in number relative to names of dialectically muddled northern Slav origin, and of Magyar and German origin, names which mostly date to after the Tatar invasion of 1241-1242. But they may represent the oldest stratum of toponyms, and they point to the south-central Balkans. The name Zemplén itself merits investigation [see the third paragraph of the entry for Zemplín]; the Zemplén (now East Slovakian) place-name Trebišov (pronounced Trebish-ov) is in line with Trâmbesh (Тръмбеш), near the medieval Bulgarian capital of Veliko Târnovo [see the entry for Trebišov]; the old Zemplén village of Migléz (now Milhostov) bore virtually the same name as the Bulgarian locale of Mâglizh (Мъглиж), also near Târnovo, and Migléz is but 8 km (5 miles) southwest of Michalovce, where the grave of Bulgarian Prince Presian was found [see the entry for Michalovce, below; and for Presian, in Part I]; and the name of the Mánta creek, just west of Hegyalja, likely is an ancient Thracian name [see the entry for Mánta Creek]. Further, the old place-name Strachyna [see that entry], just over the border from northernmost Zemplén, in Sáros County, is certainly of Bulgaro-Slav origin.

Other toponyms may reflect the 9th century Christianization of the Bulgaro-Slavs, in being derived from Orthodox saints [see the two entries for Turany nad Ondavou]. These are just the most striking overlaps in toponyms between Bulgaria and the Upper Tisza, and it is worth noting that the places are scattered around the area north of Hegyalja in such a way that one could think they give an accurate idea of the area dominated by the Bulgaro-Slavs at the time of the Magyar Conquest [see the entry for Ondava River]. Indeed, all are solidly accommodated by maps that historians of Bulgaria have drawn to show the extent of the medieval empire [see Map #3].

The potential for scholarly research is considerable, and beyond the scope of this volume. However, the possibility of Bulgaro-Slav toponyms in the Upper Tisza is no more improbable than the Balkan grape varieties brought forward from the pre-Hungary period of regional history.

Čerhov (Csörgő). This small village was declared to be a Tokaji wine producing locale by Slovakian legislation of 1959. But it was not included by the Hungarian legislation of 1893 or 1908, and consequently, Hungary has contested the locale's continued inclusion if Slovakia is to have the right to export its Tokaji (Tokajské) wines under that name. Čerhov is located along the extreme northern periphery of the demarcated Hegyalja area.

Having been mentioned in a document of 1067 as a property of the Sazdice monastery, Čerhov must be one of the oldest villages of Lower Zemplén. Possibly, it pre-dates the Magyar Conquest at the end of the 9th century. However, its name apparently derives from the landholding Csörgő family of the 10th or 11th century. (Incidentally, there is a Csörgő-hill literally at the other end of Hegyalja, between Bekecs, Legyesbénye, and Monok.) Also of note, it is the only village ever associated with Tokaji wine where a Slovak-Rusyn dialect became the communal language before 1800 (*i.e.*, when Szirmay and Vályi wrote). Slovak-Rusyns were brought to repopulate the area towards the middle of the 18th century, after the loss of its Magyar populace during the anti-Habsburg wars. In 1727, only one serf was recorded at Csörgő (UC 153:76).

Čerhov likely was producing good wine by the 14th century, since in 1395 the same Margaret Csirke who owned land there also had vineyards far to the south in the key Hegyalja communities of Tolcsva and Abaújszántó. It must have been a desirable locale much later, too, since the aristocratic Aspremont, Kazinczy, and Wiczmándy families owned land in the early-19th century. Nevertheless, Čerhov's place among the Hegyalja villages must not have been clear. Since at one time the village belonged to the Tokaj Domain under the Rákóczis, there might have been some confusion in favor of its being thought part of Hegyalja. However, Szirmay did not consider it a Hegyalja locale in 1798. The likelihood is that its vineyards generally were of lesser quality and did not regularly yield high-quality botrytis wines. Vályi, in 1796, said it produces "good-tasting table wine." Fényes made no comment about wine at all in 1851; and the village was also passed over in the *Tokaj-Hegyaljai Album* of 1867. Čerhov's best vineyards are on Feketehegy hill and Borsóhegy hill. Szirmay mentioned Feketehegy in 1798.

**Černochov (Csarnahó). Of the several communes added to Slovakia's Tokaji region by Slovakian legislation of 1959 [see the entry for Slovakia], Černochov is the one that can make the relatively strongest historical case for inclusion. Administratively, it was part of the Sárospatak Domain in 1688 (UC 36:25), which no doubt influenced some people to think of it as part of Hegyalja. Additionally, it was mentioned in the listing of Hegyalja vineyard-hill supervisors in 1743. Further, a document of 1790 noted that although the commune was not counted with Hegyalja, its wine was of the same quality (UC 191:112 (a)). Nevertheless, it had been left out of the significant efforts to define Hegyalja during 1730-1750 [see the Part II Essay]. In 1796, Vályi called its wine only "satisfactory." This leaves it unclear whether Černochov was producing any botrytis wine; after all, even Nagy Kövesd, a little further east, was noted in 1903 as producing wines that could be mistaken for Hegyalja wine, at least as far as table wine was concerned. In any case, Szirmay did not include Černochov in 1798, and it was left out of all Zemplén County delimitations of Hegyalja during the 19th century, which is quite in contrast to the sometimes contested locales of southwestern Hegyalja [see the entry for Szerencs Hills and the Part II Essay]. With this easily documented record as a basis, Hungary has sought the exclusion of Černochov as a condition of the European Union's allowing Slovakia to use the Tokaji (Tokajské) name in exporting its wines. The village's vineyard-tracts are Lada, Lada-parlag, Mézes, and Töltés.

Chios. In his poetic paean of 1728, Samuel Timon had Bacchus choose to place his throne in Tokaj, although the god had long cared for the wine of the Aegean island of Chios. Antal Szirmay felt compelled to repeat this in 1798, as if to say that the sweet wine of Chios, famous for over two millennia, had been overshadowed by *aszú*. It was not an esoteric name to invoke. Greek merchants – some of them presumably connected to the same families as those in Hegyalja – had continued bringing Chian sweet wine to Poland well into the 18th century. Some of this wine was 'dropped off' in the Upper Tisza along the way. Thus, for Timon, Szirmay, and their audience, the name Chios was not just a poetic device; they knew the wine whose name was being invoked. It seems to have been virtually a paragon emulated by Hegyalja producers. Chian wine disappeared from the market after the Ottoman destruction on the island in 1822. [See the entries for Timon and Szirmay, A., in Part I; and for Color and Nectar: Macedonian Bequest? in Part IV.]

Cotnari. Wine production at this renowned region of Moldavia (northeastern Romania) was directly influenced by wine-growing in Hegyalja in the 15th century, because of contacts between Hungarian and Moldavian princes that resulted in settlement of Hungarian and Hungarian-German wine-growers at Cotnari. Of special interest is that the chief grape adopted at Cotnari was the *grasă* ('fat'), or *kövérszőlő* ('fat-grape'), thus suggesting that it was a major Hegyalja variety in the 15th century [see *Kövérszőlő*, in Part IV]. Like Hegyalja, the shriveling of grapes was always accomplished on the vine. Also, the early importance of large stone cellars at Cotnari is an indication that some white wine was being given barrel aging in Hegyalja in the 15th century. On the other hand, *eszencia* and *darabbantartás* aging were not known at Cotnari, which suggests that they were not Hegyalja habits in the 15th century [see those entries, in Part IV].

Cracow. The onetime Polish capital, Cracow is located in south-central Poland, about 257 km (160 miles) distant from Hegyalja. Historically, the city had a close relationship with the Upper Tisza region of Hungary. For instance, many Hungarian students from the region matriculated at the University of Cracow. Cracow took an early interest in Hegyalja, both in its wines and its vineyards. Records show that a Cracow citizen owned Hegyalja vineyard land before 1526 (the start of the Ottoman occupation of Lower Hungary), in other words, well before the region became widely renowned, and when Poland still favored the Szerémség wines of southern Hungary. That person's vineyard may have been in the tract later named Krakó, in Abaújszántó. [See the entries for Fugger and Thurzó, in Part I; and for Nyergesek and Krakó, in Part III.]

Dalmatia. The littoral of Croatia, along the Adriatic Sea, had close ties to the Kingdom of Hungary during the Middle Ages, and may have been a source of grape varieties for Hegyalja in that era. Like most of the Balkan Peninsula, Dalmatia is characterized by indigenous grape varieties that differ significantly from those of Western Europe. Some were brought by Greek colonists during antiquity. Even some of the 'Italian' settlers who came to Hegyalja could have been from Dalmatia, since it was a bi-cultural area in those times because of Venetian control and influence. Knowledge of how to make Malvasia wine might also have come to Hegyalja by way of Dalmatia, since the Dalmatian islands had connections with the Ionian islands to the south. Indeed, the sweet wine *prošek*, made from a mixture of certain semi-aromatic varieties, can be considered a Dalmatian replica of the Greek Malvasia wines that were so popular in the late Middle Ages. Dalmatia certainly merits a closer look with respect to Hegyalja history.

Danzig. [See the entry for Gdańsk.]

Dukla. (a) This is the name of the pass in the Low Beskid section of the Carpathian mountains in northern Zemplén County (now on the Slovakian-Polish border), through which exports of Tokaji wine to Poland often were taken, whether from Eperjes, Kassa, Bártfa, or Sztropkó. Dukla led to the Polish towns of Nowy Sacz and Jasło, where Polish traders, and later on Hungarian traders, were positioned to move the wine further north, especially to Cracow. Also, after Galicia's attachment to Austria, in 1772, many Jews entered Hungary through Dukla and settled in Zemplén County, which spurred production of kosher wine in Hegyalja, and encouraged Jewish involvement in the trade of Tokaji wine. (b) The nearby town of Dukla, on the Polish side of the Beskids, was a significant trade center early in the history of Hegyalja wine. It gained importance as a point of sale for kosher Tokaji wines to the Jews of Galicia, which in turn enhanced Sztropkó, on the Hungarian side of the Beskids, as a transshipment point. However, in the 18th century, the trade in kosher and *aszú* wines through Dukla suffered a setback due to a certain tariff official, Wolf Zelmanovich, who caused Jewish merchants in Dukla to abandon the wine trade because of his demand for excessive bribes.

Dunajec-Vistula. The Dunajec river of southern Poland formed a short section of the border between Poland and Old Hungary (and now between Poland and Slovakia) on the eastern side of the Tatra mountains. During the 16th and 17th centuries, it was significant as a water route for shipping Tokaji wine, in barrel, into Poland. Typically, it was first shipped overland from Levoča, and subsequently, after its voyage along the Dunajec, transferred to the Vistula river for inland sales to Poland, and ultimately to the Baltic port of Danzig (Gdańsk). This route declined in importance after the first partition of Poland, in 1772, which made it more practical and less costly to ship entirely overland from the Hungarian trading towns of the Upper Tisza region.

Eperjes. [See the entry for Prešov.]

Eperjes-Tokaj Hill-Chain. (*Eperjes-Tokaj Hegylánc* in Hungarian; *Prešovsko-Tokajski Podhorie* in Slovak). The Eperjes-Tokaj hills run continuously from north to south for a distance of about 105 km (65 miles), from the vicinity of Eperjes [see the entry for Prešov] south to Tokaj. The northern end was marked by the hills on which the Nagy Sáros and Kapi fortresses stood, respectively several kilometers northwest and northeast of Eperjes; while Tokaj-hill by Tokaj marked the southern end. [See the entries for Kapi and Sáros, in Part III.]

The range is bounded on the north by the Sáros Uplands (*Šarišská Vrhovina* in Slovak) that run roughly west to east, and on the south by the Great Plain (Alföld) of Hungary. Hill elevation within the range proper varies from 1,092 meters/3,583 feet above sea level (Simonka near Eperjes) to 198 meters/650 feet (Henye-hill at Bodrogkeresztúr). The Tokaj-Hegyalja wine region is situated in the southern third of the range, along the eastern side, where most of the hill peaks vary from 250 meters/820 feet to 450 meters/1,476 feet above sea level. Tokaj-hill is exceptional at 514 meters/1,686 feet. [It is notable that a document of 1670 about the northerly Zemplén County area of Varannó refers to the Hegyalja wines as "*alföldi*" (lowland) wines, so as to indicate Lower, or southerly, Zemplén (UC 46:64).]

From the portrayal of the Eperjes-Tokaj hills on the first map of Hungary, from 1528, it can easily be imagined that even at that relatively late date, more than halfway into Hungarian history, some natives might have thought of the entire range as a geographic entity, without distinct subunits such as Hegyalja. Indeed, the Slovak term *podhorie* for this entire hill-chain is equivalent to *hegyalja*. Such a notion might have been very widespread before that time, when vines were cultivated even in the northern half of the Eperjes-Tokaj Hill-Chain. At both Eperjes in the north and at the southern end in Mezőzombor there are old sites called Borkút (Wine-font); vines were still cultivated north of Eperjes at Finta (now Fintice) as late as the 1680s (UC 38:41); and south of Eperjes, at Téhány (Ťahanovce), even until the late-18th century. In the 14th century, wine-growing along the Eperjes-Tokaj range could be likened, at least geographically, to Burgundy's Côte d'Or; but climatic cooling led to the abandonment of vines in the northern half of the range. Today's Hegyalja survived rather like a lonely Côte de Beaune.

The demographic history of the range is pertinent to Hegyalja history. Going back to the 11th and 12th centuries, it was one of the relatively most populous parts of the Upper Tisza region, with a continuous line of settlement from Hegyalja to the Sáros Uplands. This of course would favor trade in Hegyalja wine as population grew. Also, there was a notable mélange of ethnic groups. But, most surprising, in light of today's linguistic borders, is that Magyar-speakers were predominant in the river valleys and lowlands from south to north amongst the hills until around 1700. Indeed, wine-growing receded in the early-18th century in part because of war and pestilence that decimated the rural Magyars who grew most of the wine. They were replaced by northern hill-country Slovaks and Rusyns, most of whom were unfamiliar with viticulture.

Of older significance, the Eperjes-Tokaj Hill-Chain made for a break in the landscape from west to east, such that it was of importance in the beginning of Tokaj-Hegyalja wine tradition. The area east of the range was easily dominated from the south by the medieval Bulgarian Empire as it extended its rule northward from the Great Plain in the 8th and 9th centuries, before the arrival of the Magyars, much as was indicated by the chronicler Anonymous [see Map #3, and the entry Turány: On a Saintly Trail]. Conversely, the 9th century Great Moravia to the west appears not to have extended its dominion east of these hills, with the possible exception of a few small pockets along the eastern periphery. The result was that a Balkan ('Byzantine') rather than a Western ('Frankish') tradition of wine-growing took hold, as demonstrated by grape varieties and wine-making procedures [see the entries for Balkans and Bulgarian Empire].

ERDŐBÉNYE. (colloquially Bénye) Located up the Bényei creek from the Bodrog river, and surrounded by the forested Zemplén hills, Erdőbénye is relatively the most isolated of the Hegyalja wine locales. As the location suggests, the village developed relatively late, probably not before the late-14th century. It can be presumed from the name that it was created by removing forest (*erdő*) land; the -*bénye* ending is thought to have been a surname or personal name [but, see the last sentence of the entry for Avars, in Part I]. At first there were two settlements, Felső- (Upper) and Alsó- (Lower) Bénye (hence the vineyard-tract name Alsóbénye). But, by the mid-15th century, they were also known jointly as Erdőbénye.

It is indicative of how far into the hills Erdőbénye is, that the locale originally was part of neighboring Abaúj County, not Zemplén (which is why Szirmay glossed over the village in 1798). But it must have come into the sphere of Zemplén County after becoming part of the Sárospatak Domain in 1604. As a result of that acquisition, the village also became a possession of the Lórántffys [see the entry for Furmint, in Part III]. Consequently, when Susanna Lórántffy married George Rákóczi I, in 1616, the Rákóczis became its owners and built an enormous underground wine cellar as part of their castle there. Of note, too, is Francis Rákóczi II's pawning of his portion of the village to the Stegner family of wine traders [see the entry for Stegner, in Part I]. Later prominent families also were owners, notably the Szirmays, Aspremonts, and Waldbotts, with the latter playing a key role after phylloxera.

[Historical vineyard area: 1873 - 278 ha.; 1913 - 238 ha.; 1940 - 256 ha.; 1963 - 269 ha.; 1990 - 310 ha.]

Erdőbénye was known as a high-quality producer among the middle-size Hegyalja villages, in the best vintages vying with the most renowned locales. However, there is much variability among sites; and vintages are more variable than in most of Hegyalja because of cooler, wetter weather. The prime sites are on the south-facing slopes north and east of the village between Zsuzsonka-hill and Tolcsva-hill, a stretch known colloquially as Felhegy hill. The soil in this area is clayey (*nyirok*), though usually mixed with 'stone-dust' (*kőpor*). Stone content reaches 40-60 percent in the higher sections. The historically esteemed vineyard-tracts were Bajóka, Hosszú, Lőcse, Messzelátó, Nagy Palánkos, Négyszögű, Palásti, Parlag, and Raffai, which Hidvéghy (1950) said produce "the most savory Bénye wines." The lesser areas are to the west and south, such as Alsóbénye, Barnamáj, Becsk, Mulatóhegy, Ösztvérek, Paperdő, and Szárhegy; and generally on lower land, such as Eresztvény, Gömbölyű-Mogyorós, Lapos-Mogyorós, and Lepény.

Regrettably, the tract that historically had the most fame of all, Zsákos, never recovered from phylloxera. Hidvéghy also indicated that quite a few other tracts also sank into obscurity after phylloxera because of height, steep slopes, or water erosion, such as Bodóka, Farkas, Fehérkút, Hidegoldal, Mondoha, Peres, Szenyes, and Verőmáj.

ERDŐHORVÁTI. (colloquially Horváti) Just about at the geographical center of Hegyalja, Erdőhorváti lies upstream from larger Tolcsva along the creek of that name. Going back to its founding, this was a somewhat improbable location since it marks where the Tolcsva valley meets the wooded Zemplén Hills, as indicated by the settlement's name (*erdő* = forest). It was far enough off the main line of Bodrog river vineyard locales that it was originally included in Abaúj County, and not attached to Zemplén County until 1884.

Erdőhorváti did not become a settlement until long after one existed at Tolcsva, probably not until around 1300, after the Tatar invasion and the erection of the Tolcsva fortress on a hill halfway between the two locales. The earliest known habitation was a monastery built in 1353 by the Pauline Order, who may have been the first wine-growers there. However, the second part of the village's name, –horváti, suggests a possible connection with Croatians when the village acquired its name (in earlier times, *horvát* had a somewhat indefinite association with Slavs, but by the 14th century it indicated Croatians). Or, perhaps the Pauliners brought monks from Croatia for their new monastery. Either way, further ampelographic research might reveal that some grape varieties, including *furmint*, were brought from Slavonia or Dalmatia.

[Historical vineyard area: 1873 - 176 ha.; 1913 - 62 ha.; 1940 - 69 ha.; 1963 - 96 ha.; 1990 - 96 ha.]

Though not originally included in Zemplén County, Erdőhorváti was usually treated as part of the Hegyalja wine region. Further, despite its out-of-the-way location, the village historically was one of the largest of the small producers. The soil is clayey (*nyirok*), mostly friable because of degraded stone content. Hidvéghy (1950) stated that the best vineyards were on the south- and southwest-facing parts of the Melegmáj, Haragos, Véghegyek, and Agáros tracts, the latter two having the stoniest composition, ranging from 30 to 50 percent. In 1867, Szabó/Török had mentioned all of those except Haragos, while noting the Szunyogh and Kalap tracts as "very favourably situated." Incidentally, the tract name Véghegyek means 'end-hills' and suggests that this originally was the area of Erdőhorváti furthest up the Tolcsva creek.

Fényes in 1851 made a point of complimenting the wine of Erdőhorváti, if in somewhat opaque fashion: "The crystal-clear and, furthermore, unchanging color makes this wine renowned." He was echoed in 1867 by Szabó/Török, who in English and French translation more specifically indicated that the wine's appearance held up extremely well during long keeping.

Gálszécs. [See the entry for Sečovce.]

Gdańsk. Better known historically by its German name, Danzig, this Baltic port was not at first a major market for Tokaji wine. The city was largely German, and mostly consumed wines from the German lands. Nevertheless, its position as a port city resulted in a healthy interest in Hegyalja wine as a good to be shipped across the Baltic to Sweden and Russia. It also gained a market in Danzig itself because no German wine was like it. The city's interest is apparent from its ownership of the Danczka vineyard-tract in Mád. [See the entry for Dunajec-Vistula.]

Gilip Creek. Running north to south from Monok to Legyesbénye, the Gilip creek in effect marks the southern end of Hegyalja. The south-facing slopes of the hills on the creek's eastern side, from (north to south) Zsebrik through Medgyes, Lete, Pipiske, Fulóhegy, and Nagyhegy, contain the region's last important vineyard-tracts. It was, however, one of the first parts of Hegyalja to be devastated by phylloxera, and amongst the slowest to recover. The name naturally invites thoughts of an ancient connection to Golop, a Hegyalja village less than 6 km (4 miles) to the north, and in that regard favors a Bulgaro-Slav toponymic origin [see the following entry].

GOLOP. Situated on the southwestern rim of Hegyalja, Golop is among the region's smallest settlements in size and wine output, but possibly among the oldest. Certainly its Slavic name suggests an origin prior to the Kingdom of Hungary. Balassa (1991) thought the name derived from Slavic *glup* (stupid); but this seems improbable compared to the alternative possibility of *golub* (pigeon), specifically the Bulgaro-Slav form *gâlâb* (гълъб). It stimulates the historical imagination to find a Bulgarian Gâlâbovo hardly 100 km (62 miles) from the fortress of Monyak that might account for the name of Monok [see the latter entry]. A name of 'Pigeon-hill' (Golopi-hegy) certainly makes more sense than 'Idiot-hill' [see the preceding entry].

Golop was an appurtenance of Abaújvár by the late-13th century. But its subsequent history is not continuous. It was interrupted when the village was destroyed by the Ottoman Turks in 1566. The village's name probably survived mainly because of the continuity of the name Golopi-hegy hill. Golop apparently was left out of some early demarcations of Hegyalja because of its small size and the lingering effects of the Turkish destruction. Even in 1715, only eight taxpayers resided in Golop. Additionally, there had been ambiguity as to whether Golop was part of Zemplén County. Both an Alsó (Lower) and a Felső (Upper) Golop existed until the mid-15th century, with the former in Zemplén County and the latter in Abaúj. The two supposedly were joined and belonged to Zemplén after that time; but Vályi in 1796 and Fényes in 1851 continued to mention two Golops, one each in Zemplén and Abaúj. Finally, in 1875, both Golops were definitively placed in Zemplén.

Being partly in Abaúj did not necessarily exclude Golop from also being part of Hegyalja, but because of its small size it was easy to ignore the village in early delineations, which were not as rigorous as today's appellations of origin. In reference to Golopi-hegy, Fényes (1851) specifically stated that the "vineyard hill" of Alsó Golop in Zemplén is part of Hegyalja; and he also said that the wine of Felső Golop in Abaúj is "famous." The fame may have been relatively recent, and most likely because the noble Vay family had come into possession of both of the Golops in the late-18th century and gave a boost to wine-growing on Golopi-hegy for the first time since the Turkish destruction. Vineyard expansion again took place after phylloxera, and Golop was recognized as part of Hegyalja in the legislation of 1893 and 1908.

[Historical vineyard area: 1873 - 82 ha.; 1913 - 12 ha.; 1940 - 11 ha.; 1963 - 11 ha.; 1990 - 12 ha.]

All of Golop's vineyards are located on Golopi-hegy and face east or west (the hill's superior south-facing slope belongs to Tállya). The soil for the most part is clayey (*nyirok*), with stone content of 20-50 percent on the upper slopes and less than 15 percent on the lower slopes, the former being preferable. The upper part of the Somos-oldal vineyard-tract was considered to produce "the best wine" of Golop (Hidvéghy, 1950).

Gönc. One of very few places associated with a specific kind of barrel, Gönc is the home of Hegyalja's famous *gönci* [see that entry, in Part IV]. The town lies near the Hernád river, in the former Abaúj County, about 29 km (18 miles) west of Sátoraljaújhely, and 40 km (25 miles) northwest of Tokaj. It goes back to the mid-12th century, when it grew as a result of German settlement. The locale was favorable for wine-growing, and the settlers built on the cooperage skills that they brought with them. The coopers developed the small *gönci* barrel that could fit through the narrow entrances to the cellars typical of the Hernád valley and Hegyalja. Because of its location along the way to the regional center of Kassa (Košice), the town served as the seat of Abaúj County from 1570 to 1647. [See the entry for Vizsoly, below; and for Cellars, in Part IV.]

Great Moravia. [See the entry for Moravia, Great.]
Greece. [See the entries for Chios and Macedonia; and for *Aszú*: Aegean Echo, in Part IV.]

Háromhuta. Located in the Zemplén Hills north of Erdőhorváti, the village of 'Three-Hutas' became the local source of bottles for Hegyalja wine, beginning in the time of Francis Rákóczi II, in the late-17th century. At that time, the area was part of the Regéc Domain, which belonged to the Rákóczis. It may be presumed that one of the motives in increasing bottled output was to gain favor for Hungary abroad vis-à-vis the Habsburgs. The word *huta* refers to a foundry, and the village name 'Three-Hutas' refers to the fact that it developed from Old-, New- and Middle-Huta.

Hegyalja. (a) *Geographic Hegyalja.* As a geographical term, *hegyalja* means 'below the mountains' and is usually translated as 'foothills.' Because of this generality of meaning, it was used in several areas of Hungary, not just Tokaj-Hegyalja. Its first documentary occurrences are from the 14th century, and only one of those definitely appears to refer to Tokaj-Hegyalja. That was a document of 1339, in which a man was mentioned as 'Ladislaus of Hegyalja' (DL 56894). Since reference was made to the Ronyva creek in the northernmost part of today's Hegyalja wine region, as well as to several Zemplén locales just to the north, it may be presumed that an area in the Eperjes-Tokaj Hill-Chain was indicated. It is notable, too, that the chronicler Anonymous, circa 1200, did *not* use the name Hegyalja, although he wrote extensively about the territory that is Tokaj-Hegyalja. Thus, it seems that the name did not come into use until the 13th century.

It is uncertain whether the term *hegyalja* necessarily implied wine-growing at the outset of its use as a geographical expression. If it originated in the second-half of the 13th century, after the

Tatar invasion, its use might have coincided with the extension of wine-growing in the region in that period, in which case it might have been introduced in connection with Italian colonization, as a neo-latinism: *submontana* (= *hegyalja*). But at the very least, the term must soon have become associated with wine-growing, since it was typical in the 14th and 15th centuries for vineyards to be created by clearing forested land on the middle or lower slopes of hills and lesser mountains. This practice is clearly demonstrated by the equivalent Slavic term, *podgoria* ('below the mountains'), which actually became the Romanian word for 'vineyard.'

Nevertheless, the term *hegyalja* antedates efforts to delineate a wine region as such; and for a long time the proper name Hegyalja was practically without significance to wine traders. In the context of the Eperjes-Tokaj hills, it might have been a geographically vague name as late as around 1400, since the vine had been cultivated on many hills much further north in the range. But the north was affected by climatic cooling in the 14th and 15th centuries, and was increasingly unable to produce sufficient wine. Also, these wines must increasingly have lagged in quality, a deficiency that would have been exacerbated by the advent of later-harvested white wines in Tokaj-Hegyalja towards 1500, since a longer growing season was needed.

In sum, the use of *hegyalja* as a designation exclusively for vineyard hills, together with the ever decreasing suitability of the northerly Eperjes-Tokaj hills for wine-growing, impelled people to restrict the proper name Hegyalja to the hills of southern Zemplén. [See the entry for Upper Tisza.]

(b) Administrative Hegyalja. Although the term *hegyalja* arose from topography, the original impetus for its use might have been administrative, in order to indicate specific districts or jurisdictional subunits, whether in connection with secular or ecclesiastical domains. It is even uncertain whether 'Ladislaus of Hegyalja' in 1339 was from the general area known as Hegyalja today, or from a particular territorial district known by that name. But it is also unclear what the secular administrative subunits represented. Perhaps they were in some sense forerunners of the feudal domains of the late Middle Ages, and thus had arisen out of clan lands during the period of the early Árpád kings of Hungary. But documentary evidence on these questions is lacking.

The earliest documentary specification occurs late, in 1622, when Mád records refer to "*the* seven Hegyalja towns" (emphasis added). That wording, together with the context of an agreement on payment of vineyard workers, suggests that a bond had existed between the towns for some time, even if limited in scope. Further, it is significant that the places were indicated as municipalities, and thus able to act on their own behalf. The seven towns were not specified, but it can be presumed that all were in Zemplén County and must have included the five towns from Tállya southeast to Tokaj, namely, those two plus Mád, Tarcal, and Bodrogkeresztúr. This was echoed in 1838 by David Szabó: "Some people count eight Hegyalja towns, namely Tállya, Mád, Tarcal, Tokaj, Bodrogkeresztúr, Erdőbénye, Olaszliszka and Tolcsva." The one addition since 1622 certainly would have been Erdőbénye, since earlier it had belonged to Abaúj County, not Zemplén. Abaúj's earlier exclusion from an administrative Hegyalja is clear from the absence of Abaújszántó even in 1838, though it is in a direct line with Tállya, Mád, Tarcal, and Tokaj.

However, the notation about "the seven Hegyalja towns" in 1622 came at the end of an era. Subsequently, the cohesion of the towns diminished, and accordingly, notions about a quasi-political Hegyalja became less administrative, and more expansive and inclusive. Notably, even Abaúj County locales began to be recognized along with those of Zemplén. A meeting of Hegyalja communities in Mád in 1641 included not only 'the seven Hegyalja towns' of two decades earlier, but also the nearby communes of Mezőzombor, Szerencs, Ond, and Rátka, as well as Erdőbénye and the Abaúj town of Abaújszántó. By 1674-1675, the Szepes Chamber regarded 22 communities of modern Hegyalja as part of "*Submontanarum*" [as cited and listed in the Part II Essay]. Yet, despite the increased tendency to define Hegyalja just in terms of geography, a jurisdictional connotation to the term survived, as made clear by Szabó.

In sum, the administrative Hegyalja originally consisted of the towns of Zemplén County where the Eperjes-Tokaj hills approach the Great Plain of Hungary, all of which had wine-growing as a primary economic activity; and this continued to influence the view that some people had of the Tokaji wine region as late as the early-19th century.

Hejce. Located 30 km (19 miles) west of Sátoraljaújhely, on the northwestern side of the Zemplén hills and in the valley of the Hernád river, this wine-growing commune was thought to be part of Hegyalja by some people during the 15th-17th centuries. The reasons are unclear, but it may be supposed that prior to the importance of botrytis wine, the table wine of Hejce was comparable to that of Hegyalja, as was true of the Hernád valley generally [see section III (c) of the Part II Essay]. Certainly its wines were purchased by merchants in the northern towns (now in eastern Slovakia), who also bought Hegyalja wine. However, while Hejce belongs to the contemporary Borsod-Abaúj-Zemplén County, it formerly was in Abaúj, which together with its 'removed' location would have disqualified it from inclusion in Hegyalja in the eyes of most observers by 1700. Somewhat unusually, a document of 1683 stated that Hejce had four classes of vineyards (UC 116:29), which seems to contrast with the three quality classes of Hegyalja. But this probably was in accord with the Szepes Chamber's practice of dividing vineyards into four classes according to productivity, not wine quality (UC 158:31 (a), of 1674).

HERCEGKÚT. One of the small villages of northern Hegyalja, Hercegkút is situated beside the Hotyka creek west of Sárospatak. It lies adjacent to the vineyard area of the vicinity (including Sárospatak), and probably developed exactly because of that proximity, sometime before the Ottoman Turks occupied Lower Hungary in the 16th century. Originally belonging to the Sárospatak Domain, the village became part of the Rákóczis' holdings, and then ceased to exist for a time after the Habsburg defeat of the Rákóczis. Prince Trautsohn acquired the locale subsequently, and in 1754 settled Germans there. The new village was called Trautsohnfalva, under which name it was included in Hegyalja in the legislation of 1893. But it was renamed Hercegkút ('Prince-well') at the turn of the century, and not given mention separate from Patak in the 1908 law. It was again recognized as a self-standing Hegyalja village in 1959 and 1994.

[Historical vineyard area: 1873 - n/a; 1913 - n/a; 1940 - 39 ha.; 1963 - 59 ha.; 1990 - 134 ha.]

Only two vineyard-tracts belong to Hercegkút: Kőporos, and Pogánykút (the latter influenced the choice of the village name Hercegkút). Pogánykút faces south and southeast, and generally produces better wine than the former because of it; Kőporos faces east and is more exposed to wind and cold. The soil is of a relatively easily worked clayey (*nyirok*) sort, with riolite content of 20-30 percent in some of the higher vineyards, particularly to the north and west. However, the name Kőporos means 'stone-powdery,' in reference to its covering of 'stone-dust,' which is an occasional, but lesser, soil type in Hegyalja.

Hernád River. (Hornad in Slovak) Located on the western side of the Zemplén Hills, the Hernád runs through former Abaúj County. The river valley led north to the trade center of Kassa [see the entry for Košice], and became a major route early in the history of the Upper Tisza region. It favored the marketing of Tokaji in the towns of what is now eastern Slovakia, and later on, Poland. This was especially helpful to Abaújszántó, located in Abaúj County. However, since the Hernád also favored wine-growing in other locales northward towards Kassa, there was some confusion early on as to whether the valley was part of Hegyalja, the more so because traders often recorded only the provenance (place of acquisition) of their wines, not the place where the wine was actually grown. But once botrytis wine became the sought-after Hegyalja product, it became clear that the Hernád valley, except for Abaújszántó, did not belong to the region. The Hernád's name is pre-Slav and originated as Hornacht, which dated to Germanic tribes that lived in the area in the 4th and 5th centuries. This continuity in name suggests that it was amongst the longest continuously occupied areas of the Upper Tisza. The Avars and Bulgaro-Slavs likely preserved the name before the Magyars arrived [see the entries for Abaújvár and Mánta Creek].

Homonna. [See the following entry.]

Humenné (Homonna). As the Kingdom of Hungary extended north in the Upper Tisza region, towards Poland, Homonna became the seat of the northeasternmost domain of Zemplén County, situated about 64 km (40 miles) north-northeast of Hegyalja. The territory was given to the Drugeth clan of Naples at the beginning of the 14th century, and they continued to occupy it for the next four centuries [see the entry for Drugeth, in Part I]. There is nothing to suggest that settlers from Italy were brought in great number, but some viticulture was initiated along the Ciróka river valley, the core of the domain, and continued until the 18th century. However, the Drugeths had taken an interest in Hegyalja early on, hence the Ciróka vineyard-tract, and apparently Szentvér as well, both in Tolcsva [see the entries for Ciróka and Szentvér, in Part III]. Although a tariff-collection point since 1330, Homonna never became one of the major trade centers for Tokaji wine, even if much of the Drugeths' wine was transshipped through it. But the heavily forested northern area of the Homonna Domain became an important area for smuggling Tokaji into Poland during the 17th and 18th centuries [see the entry for Rusyns, in Part I]. It is a curiosity that in the early 1800s, the Ciróka valley was the most northerly vineyard area in Zemplén County.

Humenné: Hmmm…

The name Humenné/Homonna is another toponymic anomaly that raises the issue of an early Bulgaro-Slav presence in Hegyalja and vicinity. No name like it is found either north of the Carpathians, in Poland, or to the west, in what was Great Moravia. Further, the local Rusyns pronounce it Gumen-, vice Humen- (*g* vice *h* being a characteristic pronunciation difference between certain Slavic languages). Where we find a similar name is in the ancient Greek province of Paionia in Macedonia, near the present juncture of Greece, Bulgaria, and the Former Yugoslav Republic of Macedonia: the town of Goumenissa, whose first part is also voiced as Gumen- by the Bulgarians (Gumendje) and Slavo-Macedonians (Gumentze). This is the area north of Thessaloniki, the origin of the Bulgaro-Slavs who were brought to Hegyalja in the 9th century. It is also notable that Humenné/Homonna is located at the confluence of the Ciróka and Laborc rivers, the latter bearing the name of Laborc, who, according to the chronicler Anonymous, was the local headman that the Magyars encountered when they arrived in the Upper Tisza. Before the climatic cooling of the 14th century, the south-facing slopes along the Ciróka might have been attractive as vineyard land. In any case, it shall have to be left to Bulgarian and Greek etymologists to argue and tell us about Gumen-.

Hungary. [See the entries for Royal Hungary and Upper Hungary.]
Huta. [See the entry for Háromhuta.]
Igló. [See the entry for Spišská Nová Ves.]

Island-hills. (*Sziget-hegység*) This is the collective name for the hills east of the Ronyva creek valley and northeast of Sátoraljaújhely, which include the northernmost vineyards of Hegyalja. The name signifies that they are outcroppings of the Eperjes-Tokaj Hill-Chain, rather than part of the compact, main mass of the range. Geographically, the Island-hills, which are now entirely in southeastern Slovakia, encompass the wine-growing localities of Čerhov (formerly Csörgő), Černochov (Csarnahó), Bara (Bári), Veľká Tŕňa (Nagytoronya), Malá Tŕňa (Kistoronya), and

Viničky (Szőlőske); but some geographers would stretch them east to Kráľovský Chlemec (Királyhelmec). In the late Middle Ages, before 1500, much of this area might have been commonly thought of as part of Hegyalja, but after the inception of botrytis *aszú* wine in the early-17th century, and especially during the course of the 19th century, it began to be observed systematically that only some parts of the Island-hills had the right geological makeup and soils to yield high-quality *aszú* wine. Hence, the Hungarian legislation of 1908 included only Kistoronya and Szőlőske from among the communites dotting the Island-hills. Slovak legislation of 1959 expanded Slovakia's Tokaji-producing area by, in effect, treating the Island-hills as a geographical entity rather than distinguishing amongst them on the basis of viticultural suitability.

Jasov (Jászó). Located in Abaúj County, about midway between Hegyalja and Košice (Kassa), this village became the site of one of the first Angevin fortresses, at the beginning of the 14th century. A major monastery of the Prémontré Order had already been established there. The village was settled mostly by Germans from the Szepesség region after the Tatar invasion in the mid-13th century, and, typical of Abaúj, it became the seat of a relatively small domain. It probably acquired Hegyalja vineyards when the Rozgonyi family possessed it in the mid-15th century. The most apparent connection is the Rudnok vineyard-tract in Sárazsadány. [See the entries for Rozgonyi, in Part I; and for Perőc and Rudnok, in Part III.]

Jászó. [See the previous entry.]

*Józseffalva. The last of three Hegyalja villages settled by Germans during the 18th century, Józseffalva was established in 1785 (UC 169:10), and named after Habsburg Emperor Joseph II [see that entry, in Part I]. Its proximity to Sárospatak caused it to be renamed Újpatak (New-Patak) at the turn of the 20th century. Thus, while it was included by its earlier name in the listing of Hegyalja communities in the legislation of 1893, it appeared as Újpatak in the legal roster of 1908. Later, it was absorbed by Sárospatak, and was left out of the legislation of 1959. The village was situated just southwest of Bodroghalász, heading towards Bodrogolaszi.

*Károlyfalva. Located between Sárospatak and Sátoraljaújhely, this area belonged to the Sárospatak Domain and thus became property of the Rákóczis. After the Habsburg defeat of the Rákóczis, it was acquired by Prince Trautsohn, who settled Germans there around 1750. Its name is the Magyar version of the name Karlsdorf, or 'Charles-village,' in reference to a son of Trautsohn. Due to the industrial growth of Sátoraljaújhely during the communist era, and consequent urban sprawl, Károlyfalva was administratively attached to that town in 1984, and accordingly, was not given separate mention in the 1994 legislation.

Károlyfalva is encompassed by its vineyard area, namely, the hills called Nagy- and Kis-Kocsárd. The soils are of a very suitable clayey (*nyirok*) sort, with significant riolite content. The south- and southeast-facing vineyards on both Kocsárds were well-regarded for their wines. Hidvéghy, in 1950, put them on a par with the best of Sárospatak (at that time, he treated of Károlyfalva in his discussion of the latter town, not Sátoraljaújhely).

Kassa. [See the entry for Košice.]
Kisszeben. [See the entry for Sabinov.]
KISTORONYA [See the entry for MALÁ TŔŇA.]

Košice (Kassa). The most significant place outside Hegyalja in Tokaji's history, Kassa was the closest to Hegyalja of the five East Slovakian towns that comprised the Pentapolitana of the late Middle Ages [see the entry for Pentapolitana]. At a distance of about 48 km (30 miles) northwest of Hegyalja, Kassa's importance no doubt preceeded the others chronologically simply because of location. Situated along the Hernád river in the Kassa basin, it is supposed that the locale had a population, albeit minor and rural, before the arrival of the Magyars. This is suggested above all by the fact that the Hernád had retained its Germanic name (Hornacht) since the 5th century.

The name Košice has been reason to suppose that it was named for a Slavic clan named Koša; but the identically named Polish village of Koszyce suggests a possible influx of Poles during the Christianization of eastern Slovakia in the 10th and 11th centuries. In either case, the establishment of the Abaúj fortress (Abaújvár) by the Aba clan in the 10th century led to the development of Abaúj County, with Kassa eventually becoming its chief locality. Thereafter, it became the most important town of the Upper Tisza region, such that it was the 'capital' of northeastern Hungary during the Ottoman occupation; the seat of the Szepes Chamber from 1567 to 1848; and the residence of the Bishop of Eger throughout the 17th century [see the entries for Eger Bishopric and Szepes Chamber, in Part I]. Also, it was in Kassa that the Hungarian nobility declared George Rákóczi I the Prince of Hungary, in opposition to the Habsburgs, in 1644.

Kassa grew as a trade and civic center because of its position along the Hernád, together with land routes leading to Poland. Like the other towns of the Pentapolitana, this growth was spurred especially by German settlement that began in the second-half of the 13th century, after the Tatar invasion. However, the Germans never dominated Kassa to the extent they did the rest of the Pentapolitana and other towns of the Upper Tisza region; and indeed, the town was a center of Magyardom from the late Middle Ages until the communist period.

Kassa early on had fairly extensive vineyards within its territory, but already by the 13th and 14th centuries its population growth was outpacing the capacity of its vineyards to supply wine for local consumption. This circumstance favored growers in Hegyalja because of proximity. In the late-15th century, 48 citizens of Kassa owned 72 vineyards in Hegyalja. [See the entries for Hegyes and Kassa, in Part III.] The relationship between Kassa and Hegyalja gave the town an edge when trade in Tokaji with Poland escalated. The town's commercial importance was a reason that the Szepes Chamber was headquartered in Kassa. It was the Chamber that gave Kassa a monopoly on wine trade with Poland for several decades in the 16th century, which may be considered the peak importance of the town's involvement with wine trade. After the Ottoman threat abated at the end of the 17th century, and Greeks became dominant in the Tokaji trade, other routes grew in importance and Kassa lost some of its advantage as the northward conduit for Tokaji wine.

Kővár. [See the entry for Berkec, in Part III.]
Laborc River. [See the entry for Humenné: Hmmm…; and for Michalovce.]
Ladmóc. [See the following entry.]

Ladmovce (Ladmóc/Ladamóc). Ladmóc is a village (now in East Slovakia) along the Bodrog river, just northeast of Szőlőske, the northeasternmost tip of Hegyalja. The mention of Ladmóc alongside Szőlőske in a document of 1743 that specified the so called 'hill-masters' in Hegyalja communities, suggests that it was thought by some to be part of the region in early times. How this notion came about is a matter for conjecture. However, a number of prominent regional families that were owners in Ladmóc also had holdings in Hegyalja proper, notably: the Arancsi, Boda, Keczer, and Paksi families. This circumstance probably caused some confusion between properties and geographical notions about Hegyalja in the late Middle Ages.

LEGYESBÉNYE. This small community is located at the outermost southerly extremity of Hegyalja, where the hills trail off into the Hungarian Great Plain (Alföld). Its history as a settlement was shaped by this location, in that for centuries Legyesbénye's character was mostly that of a 'ranching' environment. Even its name suggests lowlands and livestock, since *legyes-*

alludes to 'flies'; *–bénye* supposedly refers to a family or person with that name [but note the last sentence of the entry for Avars, in Part I]. Apparently, the present-day village is of relatively recent origin, perhaps not earlier than around 1500. However, whatever developed in that era was destroyed by the Ottoman Turks in 1566. The Turks inflicted a second devastation in the late-17th century, such that only two vineyards were being cultivated there in 1678 (UC 39:24). Legyesbénye was reported to be deserted in the 1730s.

[Historical vineyard area: 1873 - 72 ha.; 1913 - 31 ha.; 1940 - 30 ha.; 1963 - 33 ha.; 1990 - 39 ha.]

With this background, it is little wonder that Legyesbénye was often disregarded as an integral part of Hegyalja. However, vineyard land did fall within the village limits, and from the mid-18th century onwards aristocratic owners took an interest in it, no matter that the village overall was assessed by Szirmay as 2nd Class. The prime land is to the north, on Fulóhegy hill, where the averred best wine was produced in the Nagy- and Kis-Cserepes tracts. However, the south-facing side of Monoki-hegy hill also belongs to Legyesbénye, and its Hasznos tract thereon was highly regarded. The Legyesbénye soils are favorably clayey (*nyirok*), with loess-clay on Hasznos. High stone content (35-50 percent) is typical of upper areas.

Leles (Lelesz). This village in southeastern Slovakia is located near the Latorca river in the east-central part of former Zemplén County, 22.5 km (14 miles) northeast of the northeasternmost Hegyalja village of Viničky (Szőlőske). But in a published ditty of 1771, Stephan Losontzi mentioned Lelesz as part of Hegyalja. Balassa (1991) regarded this as an utter error on Losontzi's part; yet, it was repeated in over 70 editions for more than 80 years. The error might have reflected a degree of general confusion about the northern limits of Hegyalja that had been brought forward from earlier times. Before botrytis wines came along, many people might have thought that Hegyalja extended as far north as the juncture of the Bodrog and Latorca rivers, especially since the lands of the Lórántffys, who held the Sátoraljaújhely Domain, extended that far and included Lelesz. But, assuming that Losontzi shared that perception of Hegyalja, he must have mistakenly attributed to Lelesz the wines grown in nearby Kraľovský Chlemec, since it was the latter, not Lelesz, that was known for good table wine. Perhaps adding to the confusion was the fact that four vineyards in Tállya were donated to the Lelesz Monastery in 1628; in other words, Lelesz was a significant owner in Hegyalja. The monastery may also have been the first owner of the Szent-Kereszt vineyard-tract in Tarcal [see the entry for Szent-Kereszt, in Part III].

Levoča (Lőcse). The major town of the Szepesség region in the Middle Ages, situated about 105 km (65 miles) northwest of Hegyalja, Lőcse was a major trade center since German settlement in the Middle Ages (its German name was Leutschau). Involvement with Tokaji wine trade must have been significant during the 16th century, since a vineyard-tract in Erdőbénye bears its name [see the entries for Lőcse, Határi, and Omlás, in Part III]. However, in later centuries, its trade in Tokaji fell off compared to the towns of the Upper Tisza region. Nevertheless, because of its location, Lőcse continued to be a transshipment point to Poland via the Dunajec river; and also to Silesia via the Árva (Orava) area west of the Tatra mountains, where Vlach inhabitants served as knowledgeable carters for both legal and smuggled exports. [See the entries for Pentapolitana and Szepesség, below; and for Rusyns, in Part I.]

Lőcse. [See the previous entry.]

Macedonia. When relating Hegyalja wine history to the Balkans, it is not easy to be very specific geographically about the latter. But, equally, it is hard to skip over Macedonia. The confines of 'Macedonia' have varied somewhat historically. However, from the perspective of Hegyalja's history, we are basically looking at the ancient Strymon river valley of the Greeks, which is the Struma of southwestern Bulgaria. But in the south, near the port of Thessaloniki, the area concerned spreads out widely, from the Gulf of Strymon and the Chalkidiki peninsula on the east, to the Pindos mountains on the west. Virtually everything mentioned in the entries for Balkan Influences and Grape Varieties in Part IV can be 'traced' to this area, as can much of what is pointed out under the entry for the Bulgarian Empire (above). It should not be forgotten either, that this is the area whence Bulgaro-Slavs came to Hegyalja as agricultural people in the 9th century. It was also the origin of Greek merchants since time immemorial, to say nothing of the 17th century Greek traders in Tokaji wine in particular. All of the antique Macedonian territory is due south of Hegyalja, along the ancient routes from the Aegean to the Baltic. Tokaj is separated from Thessaloniki by 950 km (500 miles), but political circumstances in the Middle Ages ensured a perhaps otherwise improbable overlap in grape varieties and wine-making.

MÁD. One of the largest and most esteemed Hegyalja wine-growing locales, Mád is situated about midway along the southern line of communities between Abaújszántó and Tokaj. It is presumed to have a very long history, probably going back to the time of the first Magyar occupants. This presumption is based on its name, thought to derive from the pagan personal name Modu. In early Hungarian history, the locale seems to have been a royal estate (hence, the vineyard-tract Király, or 'King'); but, during the 16th century, it became an appurtenance of the Tállya fortress, which is readily understood from the town's proximity. The Rákóczis were closely associated with the development of wine-growing in Mád from 1596 until their properties there were confiscated in 1715. Hence, the village is well-known for its Rákóczi-*pince* (cellar). It was thanks to the Rákóczis that Mád's status changed from village to market town in 1627, which brought trading privileges with it. However, the town was destroyed by the Ottoman Turks in 1667, a relatively late date for Turkish depredations, and was unable to make much headway in recovering until after the end of the Rákóczi rebellion four decades later.

A noteworthy detail in the town's history is that at an extraordinary session of the Zemplén County assembly in 1808, "the tax-paying public of the town of Mád" (per the record of the assembly) sought free trade in *aszú* wines in the interest of higher prices for smallholders. This was an open challenge to the aristocracy, as well as an implicit demand for the inclusion of Jews and anyone else disaffected by existing County regulations on vineyard ownership or wine trade [see the entries for Aristocracy, Jews, and Smallholders, in Part I].

[Historical vineyard area: 1873 - 508 ha.; 1913 - 365 ha.; 1940 - 390 ha.; 1963 - 416 ha.; 1990 - 958 ha.]

Mád's vineyard hills are found north, east, and west of the town. Like the other top Hegyalja locales, there are an impressive number of 1st- and 2nd-Class vineyard-tracts. But in looking over the list of them, it is notable that, historically, there were differences of opinion about which tracts belonged in which of the top two classes, as if they all fell into a rather narrow band of high quality. This likely reflected the fact that the soil is mostly of a very favorable clayey (*nyirok*) sort, and frequently with iron content sufficient to give a reddish hue to the land. Some of the best tracts are notable for both iron and lime. Pulverized stone, especially riolite tuff, is found in the higher sections. The historically best known tract names of Mád were: Becsek, Birsalmás, Bomboly, Király, Kővágó, Középhegy, Makovica, Nyulászó, Percze, Szent Tamás, Úrágya, and Vilmánok. Hidvéghy (1950) highlighted Király as a "textbook example of good position."

Magita. [See that entry, in Part III.]

MAKKOSHOTYKA. Located along the Hotyka creek west of Sárospatak, this was historically the smallest of the Hegyalja villages. It was also the most unlikely. It was a forest community, literally by nature (*makkos-* refers to acorns). But it was frequented by Sárospatak noblemen for hunting since the early centuries of the Hungarian kingdom; and apparently it did not escape their notice that some of the land would also be suitable for wine-growing if the forested slopes were cleared. This might have happened in the 1200s, because in that era the hamlet was known as Makramál; and the *–mál* suffix was often applied to south-facing slopes used for wine-growing. A name from the time of the Árpád kings is 'Papaj-hill,' or *mons Popol* in old Latin documents, on which vines were cultivated. Papaj likely was the best vineyard area in olden times, but it was abandoned long ago and returned to forest. In any case, 'Hotyka' was mentioned as having vineyards in a document of 1676 (UC 96:25). [See the entry for Makra, in Part III.]

[Historical vineyard area: 1873 - n/a; 1913 - 2 ha.; 1940 - 2 ha.; 1963 - 6 ha.; 1990 - 39 ha.]

Despite its small size, the village has a history of sometimes being treated individually as part of Hegyalja, going back at least to the late-17th century. It was also included by the national legislation of 1893 and 1908. Its vineyard area is to its north on Kishegy hill, which has medium compact clayey (*nyirok*) soil with 20-30 percent stone content. Vályi (1798) mentioned Makkoshotyka's wine as "middling," or 2nd Class. [As with Vámosújfalu (see that entry), the lack of a 1st Class tract perhaps supports Balassa's (1991) consideration that Hegyalja had been somewhat 'diluted' over time. But in this case, too, it is hardly a development of recent times.]

MALÁ TŔŇA (KISTORONYA). The northernmost of the Hegyalja villages, Malá Tŕňa is situated about 6.5 km (4 miles) north of Sátoraljaújhely, in southeastern Slovakia. It is a locale of historical importance to Hegyalja, as the earliest documentary reference to it is from 1067. Even at that time there were two neighboring settlements that shared the name Toronya, but they were referred to then as Alsó (Lower) and Felső (Upper) Toronya, whereas later they became Kis (Little) and Nagy (Big) Toronya. Judging from the early documentary mention, the locale likely was inhabited to some extent at the time of the Magyar occupation at the end of the 9th century.

Malá Tŕňa probably was engaged in wine-growing at a very early date, since the Magyar Katha clan held it from at least the early 1200s. The Pauline Order was also involved with the area in early times; the name Toronya ('tower' or 'spire') is thought by some to refer to a church erected by the Pauliners. The Order most likely encouraged viticulture. A document from 1567 noted that the commune had five vineyard-tracts, mostly belonging to church entities (UC 40:35). The Pauliners may have constructed the ancient wine cellars, which, according to old local lore, were used as a hiding place at the time of the Tatar invasion of 1241-1242. A sure sign that Malá Tŕňa was recognized early for the quality of its vineyard hills is that the Csirke family, once important in Hegyalja wine-growing, had acquired holdings there late in the 14th century.

Malá Tŕňa is the focal point of the Slovakian Tokaji region, and the basis on which Slovakia can claim a capability for quality on a par with Hungarian Hegyalja broadly speaking. Historically, Malá Tŕňa had a reputation in northernmost Hegyalja that can be likened to that of Tarcal in the south. Duly, it has been included in lists of Hegyalja villages since 1737. Szirmay in 1798 mentioned its Mákos and Meleg-oldal tracts, although he included the latter as part of Sátoraljaújhely. He also mentioned Keletka, which seems to have been an alternative name for Királyka. The latter name indicates a onetime royal property, certainly from the Árpád era.

[Historical vineyard area: 1865 - 143 ha.; 1873 - 107 ha.; 1956 - 57 ha.]

Malá Tŕňa has by far the largest amount of vineyard land in Slovakian Hegyalja, and all of it is exposed to the south, though sometimes with an easterly or westerly slant. The vineyard hills are south and southeast of the village, as follows: Királyka (Kráľka is the Slovak translation), Meleg Oldal (Teplá stráň), Sütő (Prahnisko), Farkas (Vlčina), Tájhegy (Tajisko), Domik, Fecske

(Lastovičie), Útalja (Podcestie), Mákos (Makovisko), Határ (Chotár), Kisdomb (Pahorok). Soils are of a very favorable clayey (*nyirok*) nature, with more or less significant stoniness. The steeper inclines and stonier areas are considered to produce the best wine. Fényes (1851) commented about Malá Tŕňa: "its wine is especially appreciated for its spicy [*fűszeres*] taste."

Mánta Creek. To the west of the Zemplén hills, this creek just west of the Hernád river may be relevant to regional wine history because of its name. The origin seems to be Thracian, which suggests that it was a term that had been retained by the Bulgaro-Slavs who came to the Upper Tisza and brought old Thracian viti-viniculture with them. 'Manta' indicates that horses were penned nearby; and the Thracians had used a like name for at least one ancient stream, Mantepa (Manta+apa). (Even today, there is a Mantaritsa nature preserve in the Rhodope mountain region of Bulgarian Thrace.) The Mánta creek runs through Szikszó, several miles west of Hegyalja (Abaújszántó), and heads north towards Košice (Kassa). [See Map #3.]

Mecenzéf. [See the following entry.]

Medzev (Mecenzéf). Of the many localities outside Hegyalja that had a connection to it because of employment, Mecenzéf is in a class by itself. Situated in Abaúj County, about 64 km (40 miles) northwest of Hegyalja, it had become a German settlement by the late-13th century, and its fortunes were closely associated with developments in Hegyalja from that time forward. The major locales of Hegyalja looked to Mecenzéf especially for two things that other locales were not able to supply: expertise in constructing stone walls and stairways between various vineyard-tracts or vineyards; and the guild-level skills with which to craft metal tools for use by vineyard workers. Also, Mecenzéf supplied seasonal vineyard labor. Despite incorporation into East Slovakia, the village remains substantially German-speaking today.

MEZŐZOMBOR. (colloquially Zombor) Among the southernmost Hegyalja communes, Mezőzombor is situated south of Mád, and between Tarcal and Szerencs in heading westward from Tokaj. Its name is a compound of *mező* (Hungarian for meadow) and *zombor*, the latter having been a pagan Slavic personal name that was borne by a onetime castle-fort nearby. While the fort indicates some habitation in the area in the earliest period of Hungarian history, Mezőzombor itself apparently dates only to the late-13th century, in the wake of the Tatar invasion. The village was destroyed by the Ottoman Turks in 1566, and again during the anti-Habsburg rebellions at the end of the 17th century. Otherwise, it was an agriculturally desirable area that attracted numerous prominent landowning families throughout its history; indeed, the first documentary mention of Mezőzombor is from a property suit brought against a high-ranking county official by a member of one of the prominent clans in 1298. Certainly families with an interest in wine-growing were among that number. Even the municipality of Eperjes, at the far northern end of the Eperjes-Tokaj Hill-Chain, became an owner, in 1579, in seeking to secure a supply of good Hegyalja wine [see the entry for Prešov].

[Historical vineyard area: 1873 - 192 ha.; 1913 - 154 ha.; 1940 - 144 ha.; 1963 - 182 ha.; 1990 - 234 ha.]

Situated on the northern perimeter of the Great Plain (Alföld), Mezőzombor hardly seems likely to have been sought after for wine-growing. But its vineyard area lies to its north, abutting that of Mád, Tarcal, and Bodrogkeresztúr. The proximity to more famous locales is not just coincidental, as Mezőzombor has very estimable vineyard land, with clayey (*nyirok*), clay-loess, and loess soils overlaying perlite. Clayey and clay-loess areas with southerly exposure are especially well-regarded. Mezőzombor's most heralded tract was Disznókő, although Csojka, Hangács, and Zombori-Király were always considered 1st Class.

Michalovce (Nagy Mihály). Located about 45 km (28 miles) north-northeast of Hegyalja, in East Slovakia, this locale of central Zemplén is thought to have been inhabited at the time of the Magyar Conquest [see the entry for Vinné]. Having become a town (*oppidum*) by 1400, it was undoubtedly one of the first steady markets for Hegyalja wine. Additionally, it was a tariff collection site by the mid-15th century, which gave it significance in the early days of Tokaji exports to the northeast (Ukraine, Russia). The onetime Nagy-Mihály vineyard-tract in Sárospatak likely belonged to the town at an early date [see the Supplemental List of tract names, in Part III]. The town's name refers to a 'Michael' upon whom the area was conferred at the time of German settlement after the Tatar invasion of 1241-1242. Nothing is known of its earlier name.

Of special note is that Michalovce is the site of a grave marked 'Prince Presian' [see the entry for Presian, in Part I]. In all likelihood, he was the former Czar Presian II of Bulgaria, who died around 1060. It has been presumed that he was forced into exile. As his lifetime was only a century-and-a-half after the Magyar Conquest, Presian's selection of the Michalovce area suggests that the earlier Bulgarian Empire had indeed been quite familiar with the Upper Tisza, and perhaps still had some degree of interest in the region. Also, Michalovce is situated beside the river Laborc, whose name was attributed by Anonymous to a local Bulgaro-Slav potentate at the time of the Magyar arrival [see the entry for Anonymous, in Part I].

Molyvás: More Greek than Magyar?

Pronounced MOLY'-vahsh, this is a peak abut 500 meters/1,640 feet high, east of Abaújszántó and north of Tállya, giving good protection to several excellent vineyard-tracts (notably, Bártfai, Hasznos, and Patócs) arrayed on its lowermost southern hills. The reason for singling it out amongst other such peaks is its name. A Magyar origin cannot be ruled out, but the possibility that it was a magyarization of a Greek name is tantalizing. As 'Molyvos,' it would have originally indicated a slate-gray color (*molyvi*); and in fact, the peak's composition is tufa (*i.e.*, ashen). The historical interest is that it might have carried the name for many centuries. Conceivably, it served as a landmark on the way to the Hernád river valley for Greek traders traveling the Aegean-to-Baltic trade routes. [Note the headland of Molyvos on the northern Aegean island of Lesvos.] It can be presumed that it was largely because of the Greek routes through the Upper Tisza that the Bulgarian Empire became familiar with the region and interested in holding it.

MONOK. Along with Golop and Abaújszántó, Monok marks the far southwestern rim of Hegyalja. Along with Golop, Szerencs, and Rátka, it might mark a Bulgaro-Slav nucleus. The name is believed to be derived from a Slavic word for 'monk,' though without an explanation as to why that would be, since no monastery is known to have existed there. Overlooked is the Monyak (Моняк) fortress that was built in the 12th century along a major route from Bulgarian Thrace to the Aegean, near the present-day Kârdzhali (ancient Achridos). The name of the fort suggests that the reason for Monok's name had nothing to do with monks. Further, there was a fort at Monok long ago. For the sake of completeness, let it be noted that some Hungarian historians have attributed the name to a Cuman tribal leader subsequent to the Conquest of Hungary [see the entry for Bulgars: Bulgaro-Phobia, in Part I.] In any case, Monok must certainly date to the era of the Árpád kings, *i.e.*, before 1300, since the Lete vineyard-tracts apparently date to that time [see the entry for Lete, in Part III]. The village was repopulated several times, notably after being destroyed by the Ottomans in 1566. In 1651, it fell under Ottoman dominion briefly. In 1685, 11 vineyards were confiscated from the anti-Habsburg leader Thököly (UC 152:27).

Monok is far more widely known to Hungarians as the birthplace of the anti-Habsburg leader of 1848-1849, Louis Kossuth, than as a Tokaji village [see the entry for Botrytization: Stellar Conditions, in Part IV]. Actually, it lies amongst the communities on the southern side of the Szerencs creek, whose credentials as Hegyalja villages were long in being affirmed. Timon seems to have included it in 1728, a decade before the Zemplén County delimitation of 1737, although he made the curious comment that "not everybody has a taste for Monok wine" [see the entry for Timon, in Part I]. Neither Vályi nor Szirmay included Monok at the end of the 18th century, but Szabó/Török did include it in 1867; and it was also included in the legislation of 1893 and 1908.

[Historical vineyard area: 1873 - 308 ha.; 1913 - 114 ha.; 1940 - 76 ha.; 1963 - 49 ha.; 1990 - 68 ha.]

The village's vineyards are spread over Monoki-hegy hill, preponderantly with clayey (*nyirok*) soil, and stone content of 50-60 percent in the upper parts. Lime splotches are frequent, most notably on Zsebrik hill. The best growing areas were Nagy-Lete and Kis-Lete, as well as the loess areas on the south-facing slope of Szőlőshegy hill. [See the entry for Lányka, in Part III.]

Monyorós-Csicsva. Hegyalja wine production developed by being able to market wine in quantity in the Upper Tisza territory to its north, as well as in Poland. This was possible because the Hungarian kings undertook to populate the Upper Tisza as far towards Poland as practicable. The basis for doing so was to extend a military presence along the northern fringe of Zemplén and Sáros counties. One of the major early efforts was Monyorós-Csicsva, which initially functioned as a sort of military district about two-thirds of the way between Hegyalja and Poland, in an area not yet fully incorporated into Zemplén County because of sparse settlement. Monyorós was the administrative center; Csicsva was the nearby fortress. The fortress was built in 1310 by the Rozgonyis, and the hamlet of Peres grew alongside it (hence, the Peres vineyard-tract of Erdőbénye). A vineyard-tract might also have been named for Monyorós, but become known by the more familiar name Mogyorós, since several tracts bear the latter name. (There was so much confusion about the name Monyorós, that it was mistakenly recorded as 'Momeros' on the first map of Hungary, in 1528). Well-situated to protect trade routes to Poland, Monyorós-Csicsva was a significant aid to Hegyalja exports in early times, and had a direct interest in it. A document of 1711 stated that the Csicsva fort still had usable wine cellars at that time (UC 4:25). Also, the house in Mád where the wine tithe was collected was called Csicsvár (Csicsva-fortress), which indicates that the Rozgonyis once had vineyard land in Mád, too. In time, Monyorós-Csicsva simply coalesced with the Varannó Domain [see the entry for Vranov nad Topľou].

Moravia, Great. Mention of Great Moravia needs to be made in connection with the sort of viticulture – and culture – the Magyars encountered in the Upper Tisza region and Hegyalja when they entered the area at the end of the 9th century. Great Moravia, or the Great Moravian Empire, had a brief existence in the 9th century, and is generally thought to have been centered mostly in what is now western Slovakia, particularly around Nitra. Some Slovak historians presume that Great Moravia must have extended into the Upper Tisza area, but the documentary record about the empire is extremely scanty and does not address that question. As for physical evidence, Slav artifacts have been found in the Upper Tisza, and although some can be dated roughly to the time of Great Moravia, that does not demonstrate that they were of Great Moravian origin, as opposed to an origin north of the Carpathian mountains. [See the entry for Vinné.]

Certainly there were Slavs, speaking varying dialects, in the the Upper Tisza at the time of the Magyar arrival, and it is likely that the Great Moravians had penetrated the mountain forests to their east and had contact with the region, possibly even creating some rude settlements on the northern and western fringes for trade purposes (alternatively, it has been hypothesized that undesirables were exiled to the area from Moravia). But the utter predominance of Bulgaro-Slav characteristics in all aspects of viti-viniculture in the area between the Hernád and Bodrog rivers casts considerable doubt on a major Great Moravian presence, and points instead to the medieval Bulgarian Empire as the dominant power in eastern Slovakia when the Magyars arrived. [See the entries for Bulgarian Empire, Upper Tisza, and Vinné; and for Bulgaro-Slavs and Slovaks, in Part I.]

Nagy Kövesd. [See the entry for Veľký Kamenec; for Ratold, in Part I; and for Kövesd, in Part III.]
Nagy Mihály. [See the entry for Michalovce.]
Nagy Toronya. [See the entry for Veľká Tŕňa.]

OLASZLISZKA. (colloquially Liszka) This is the largest village along the Bodrog between Tokaj and Sárospatak, and it is situated about equidistant between them, just west of where the Tolcsva creek joins the river. Vályi (1796) called its vineyards "famous," and historically, none of the other medium-size Hegyalja communities had quite as much of a reputation. Olaszliszka dates to at least the 12th century, when its name was simply Liszka, deriving from a Slavic term for either a bare piece of land (*leska*) or a grove of walnut shrubs (*liska*). The name subsequently became Liszka-Olaszi, in allusion to immigrant settlers, though exactly which ones is unclear. The uncertainty arises because *olasz* usually signifies 'Italian,' which would seem to refer to the Italians who were settled in Hegyalja after the Tatar invasion in the mid-13th century. But Balassa (1991) points out that *olasz* originally signified speakers of any neo-Latin language and could more likely have referred to the Walloons who were settled in Hegyalja in the 12th century. But it would seem that both Walloons and Italians might have been among the early inhabitants.

Olaszliszka began as a royal property, and wine-growing was emphasized from the start, as reflected in having Walloon and Italian settlers brought in as the king's vineyard workers. But, in the second-half of the 13th century, the village was donated to the bishopric and chamberlain of the Szepesség district of northern Hungary (now in Slovakia). The 14th and 15th centuries saw much flux in property entitlements (a sure sign of desirable land), and in 1504 the aggrandizing Perényi family bestowed ownership of the village upon the Pauline Order of Tőketerebes, further north in Zemplén. However, the Szepes bishopric still possessed at least ten vineyards in the village in 1681 (UC 10:88(a).

Olaszliszka was given market town status in the early-15th century, and was attached to the Tokaj Domain in 1560. Two calamities were suffered, first the Ottoman obliteration of 1566, and second, a plague in 1739 that wiped out most inhabitants. A very useful tie for Olaszliszka throughout these centuries was its special connection to the Szepesség. Both Olaszliszka growers and Szepes traders benefited once Hegyalja wine became famous; and the Szepes bishop and chamberlain retained properties into the 20th century. Intriguingly, Vályi (1796) commented that "its inhabitants make unusual *aszú*-grape wines," as if they might have had an unusual technique for making some of their botrytis wines, or else had continued to rely on grape varieties that had lost favor. [A document of 1615 inventoried the cellar of the Archbishop of Nagyszombat (now Trnava, in western Slovakia), and listed *red* wine from Olaszliszka (UC 76:19 (h)).]

[Historical vineyard area: 1873 - 251 ha.; 1913 - 228 ha.; 1940 - 258 ha.; 1963 - 239 ha.; 1990 - 468 ha.]

The vineyards belonging to Olaszliszka are found on its northern side, and include a lot of very highly regarded tracts. The best ones have workable clayey (*nyirok*) soil and high stone content, the latter rising to well above 50 percent in the upper vineyards. These areas spread in an arc spanning from the eastern vineyards of Erdőbénye to the western ones of Tolcsva, and are invariably south-facing. The tract names that historically gave Olaszliszka a claim to status as a first-rank Hegyalja village were Csontos, Határi, Magita, Rakottyás, and Rány. However, Hidvéghy (1950) also specified some tracts that included considerably lesser quality land because of rather flat terrain bordering on cropland, and poor stone content: Erdődi, Györgyike, Haraszt, Komoróc, Lókötő, Palandor, and the lower part of the Meszes tracts. Except for Meszes, none of the latter was mentioned in 1798 or 1867.

The tracts called Nagy- (Big) and Kis- (Little) Meszes merit a special notation, not least of all because Szirmay mentioned them (simply as Meszes) in 1798. Hidvéghy (1950) was somewhat puzzled by the name because it means 'Limey' and would seem to belie the fact that there is practically no limestone in the soil, as is true of Olaszliszka generally. But the more likely explanation for the tract name is that it alludes to the hamlet of Meszes that existed as far back as 1255, adjacent to the original Liszka. Apparently, those tracts survive from that era, and had been worked by the inhabitants of Meszes, who conceivably were the Italian settlers presumed to have been brought by King Béla IV immediately after the Tatar invasion.

*Ond. This village in the southwestern corner of Hegyalja had existed as its own entity for over a millennium, and it was recognized as such in the Hungarian legislation of 1893 and 1908 about the confines of Hegyalja. But it has been absorbed administratively by Szerencs, and thus was not included by name in the legislation of 1994. Ond is assumed to be among the oldest Hegyalja settlements because its name refers to one of the Magyar chieftains at the time of the Conquest of Hungary: Ónd or Und (Ound in the original Latin spelling of Anonymous). Supposedly, Ónd and his clan encamped here for a period of time, which suggests that they had found some Slav agriculturalists producing food in the vicinity, and perhaps wine as well.

The earliest mention of a vineyard name is "Ondzeuloshege" (Óndszőlőshegye in modern Magyar spelling), or 'Ond's vineyard hill,' but since it occurred in a document of 1349 (DL 4087), the name probably referred to the village, not to the ancient leader himself. In any case, judging by the town of Kassa's old interest in Ond, the village has been considered a Hegyalja locale ever since people began viewing the region as a wine-growing unit. Timon included it in his poem of 1728 [see the entry for Timon, in Part I]. In 1796, Vályi mentioned its "beautiful vineyard hills" without making any reference to Hegyalja; but two years later, Szirmay rated it a first-class village, which was tantamount to placing Ond in Hegyalja. Fényes, in 1851, wrote: "its vineyard hill [*i.e.*, the total wine-growing area] belongs to Hegyalja, and produces very good wine." More specifically, Timon wrote that in Ond wine "vigor combines with sweetness." Presumably because of its small size, Ond was not described in the *Tokaj-Hegyaljai Album* of 1867.

Ond is the best case in point regarding changes in vineyard-tract names over the centuries. Whereas in the mid-14th century all vineyards were considered to be on Óndszőlőshegye, a document of 1573 (UC 158:29) mentions eight tracts: Fodor Cheel, Zala, Zendy, Boldiser, Kwtss, Barath, Karoly, Zolten (*sic*). But most of these disappeared subsequently, probably because of warfare and destruction at Ond. Only Boldizsár survived (UC 83:126, of 1723). The name Kassai-hegy hill has also come down to modern times (apparently because the important town of Kassa had owned it). Mostly, though, new tract names appeared that bore no apparent relationship to those of 1573, such as: Bábavölgy, Dorgó, Gárdon(y), Hegyfark, and Malomsor.

[Historical vineyard area: 1873 - 130 ha.; 1913 - 35 ha.; 1940 - 35 ha.; 1963 - 30 ha.; 1990 - n/a.]

Ond's good vineyard sites are located west of the village, on the southern and western slopes of Kassai-hegy hill. However, while the soil is mostly of the desirably clayey kind (*nyirok*), exposition often is not very favorable. The most notable exception is the upper part of the Dorgó tract on Gárdontető (Gárdon-peak), where stoniness reaches 30-50 percent. Hidvéghy reported that Dorgó gives "the best Ond wine." He also noted very favorable conditions in Hegyfark and Bábavölgy. Lower areas, such as the Gárdon tract, are sandy and of lesser quality (3rd Class).

Ondava River. The name of this river north of Hegyalja perhaps sheds light on the era when popular perceptions about the northern extent of the region began to contract, since the 'Ondava river' by all documentary indications is a relatively recent distinction, probably no more than 600 years old, at least as an 'official' name. Before that time, it was referred to simply as the Bodrog. For instance, a document from 1355 calls it by that name as far north as Stropkov (DL 4483). Indeed, there is no documentary evidence of the name Ondava before the 15th century, and it was still known as the Bodrog at Trebišov in 1601, per the Terebes Domain *urbárium* of that year. Only around that time did the name Ondava come to refer to the stretch of river north of where Hegyalja's Bodrog river meets the Latorca (Latorica) river, about 14 km (9 miles) northeast of Hegyalja. The new name for that length of the Bodrog suggests new geographical perceptions, which perhaps grew out of political changes with respect to the various domains. Incidentally, this time-line casts doubt on folklore linking the Ondava's name, which signifies Ond's river, to the ancient Magyar chieftain Ónd, since it would have been too long after he lived. But the name might refer to the Sáros County clan recorded as Und/And in the late Middle Ages.

Ondava: Turkic Remnant?

It is notable that the Ondava valley seems to have been a focal point of the Bulgarian Empire's interest in the Upper Tisza (see Map #3). One of the curious names along the valley is the hilltop known as Ondalík, about 77 km (48 miles) north of Hegyalja (and flanked by an Ondava tributary also called Ondalík). The interesting part is the *–lík* ending. It stands rather as a question-mark about the name of the Ondava river, and indeed brings us full circle to the origin of the *Onda-* forename and whether it simply existed colloquially before coming into use amongst Zemplén officialdom. The Slovak historian Varsik speculated that *Onda-* might have an origin earlier than a Magyar or Western Slav presence, but without giving any specific possibility. Varsik was definitely *not* inclined to admit a Bulgaro-Slav origin, and linguistically he might have been correct: a Bulgaro-*Turkic* origin needs to be considered because of the *–lík* ending. It was a characteristic Turkic usage to indicate 'place of…' Thus, there is Hisarlik (of Troy fame) near the Hellespont; and Perelik in Bulgaria. Does Ondalík belong amongst those? It would not necessarily have been the Bulgars who gave that name. It could just as well have been the Turkic Kabars who came into Hungary with the Magyars. They might even have named it for the leader Ónd of that period.

Peloponnesus. [See the entry for Zakynthos; for Greeks, in Part I; and the Part IV Essay (third section).]

Pentapolitana. (also called Pentapolis) Meaning 'the five cities,' this Greco-Latin term was applied collectively to the northern Hungarian towns of Kassa (now Košice), Eperjes (Prešov), Bártfa (Bardejov), Kisszeben (Sabinov), and Lőcse (Levoča), all now in East Slovakia. During the late Middle Ages, the towns were independent municipalities, self-administered and existing apart from their surrounding counties. They were tied largely by their preponderantly German ethnicity (excepting only Kassa); the utter dominance of German as their commercial language (including Kassa); and their mutual interest in trade with Poland, not least of all their trade in Hungarian wine. An early sign of their cohesion is on record from 1454, when all except Kisszeben took part in a congress held in Tőketerebes (Trebišov), Zemplén County. Since none of the towns (excepting only Kassa) was able to grow an appreciable quantity of wine on its own or nearby lands, they purchased wine largely from Hungary's southern Szerémség region both for their own consumption and for sale to Poland. They were compelled to switch their sourcing entirely to Hegyalja after the Szerémség fell to the Ottomans in 1526, although they had started taking serious interest in Hegyalja during the 1400s. Along with changes in Hegyalja wine types, the economic activity of 'the five cities' led to great Polish demand for Tokaji. The trade in wine in turn stimulated the Pentapolitana to ensure their supplies by also becoming, as individual municipalities, Hegyalja vineyard owners; hence, the extant vineyard-tract names Lőcse (in Tolcsva), Bártfai (Tállya), and Kassa-város (Abaújszántó).

Perín (Perény). Although this village provided the historically important Perényi family with their name, the reason for including it here is that its name points to an origin from the Pirin region of southwestern Bulgaria, the same Struma/Strymon river valley area to which the Upper

Tisza region and Hegyalja appear to be linked historically [see the entries for Bulgarian Empire and Macedonia]. Situated on the Slovak-Hungarian border, in what was formerly Abaúj County, Perín's antiquity is suggested by its proximity to the very old site of Abaújvár, and to several toponyms suggestive of Bulgaro-Slav origin, notably Mánta creek [see Map #3].

Petrahó. [See the entry for Bodroghalász.]

Prešov (Eperjes). Lending its name to the Eperjes-Tokaj Hill-Chain, the town of Eperjes is situated at the northern end of the range, now in East Slovakia, about 72 km (45 miles) from Hegyalja. It developed just north of a small pre-Hungarian dwelling place (of unknown name), but acquired a Hungarian name derived from 'strawberry' (*eper*), hence the town's Greco-Latin name, Fragopolis. Like other major towns in the region, German settlement in the 12th and 13th centuries transformed the locale into an urban environment. In the early centuries, the Germans barred non-Germans (or at least persons not German in culture) from residing in Eperjes, and the German language retained its commercial and cultural primacy for several centuries more. Several of the earliest books about Tokaji were written in German by inhabitants of Eperjes.

After the Turks overran Lower Hungary beginning in 1526, Eperjes remained in Royal Hungary, and grew wealthy from trade with Poland. During the 16th century, the town acquired several vineyards in Hegyalja, mostly in the southern part [see Danczka and Kútpatka (1), in Part III]. A document of 1672 mentioned that Eperjes even had its own vintners and cellars in Mád and Erdőbénye (UC 154:2). Its prosperity earned it the moniker 'little Vienna,' and also, because of its schools, 'Athens on the Tarcza' (the latter name refers to the river that runs by Eperjes). Often remarked as one of Hungary's prettiest towns, a number of Hungarian-German, Greek, and Polish traders in Tokaji wine resided there because of its charms and comforts, as well as its favorable geographical position for commerce (most of the old wine cellars still exist). The town's fortunes took a downturn during the Counter-Reformation, after an execution of anti-Habsburg townsmen in 1683 [see the entry for Klobusiczky, in Part I], and continued downward during and after the last Rákóczi rebellion in the early-18th century. Somewhat of a comeback was made when Prince Trautsohn stationed an agency (a 'clearing-house') in Eperjes for sales of his wines to Poland, after plans to hold stocks closer to the Polish-Hungarian border did not come to fruition [see the entry for Ottlik, in Part I]. Eperjes eventually recovered sufficiently that, in 1816, Jullien mentioned it as a major trader in Tokaji; and the Hungarian Potemkin again indicated it as such in his book of 1863 about Sáros County. [Also, see the entry Eszencia: A Literary Aside, in Part IV.]

Prešov: More than Strawberries?

The Bulgaro-Slavs need to be addressed again because of the Slovak historian F. Uličný's anxiety to find a Slovak, or at least a generally Slavic, explanation for the name Prešov. He could not bear the thought that the original name was Eperjes, and that the name Prešov was just a Slovak knock-off. A couple of anecdotes from the 12th century have long been referenced in explaining that strawberries were found here, hence the name Eperjes. Without necessarily putting faith in the tales, the Slovak historian B. Varsik accepted the Magyar origin of the name, and in fact built quite a substantive case for it. But his colleague Uličný (1990) ignored Varsik and, with no documentation whatsoever, insisted that there was a Slavic clan named Preš. Fatuous though he may be, Uličný gives us an idea to work with: Could Preš- be a corrupted, truncated remembrance of Bulgar Czar Presian I (836-852)? There was good farmland by the confluence of the Delne and Tarca rivers just south of Eperjes; the salt deposits of Sóvár were immediately to the east; the village of Enyicke just to the south might allude to the Bulgaro-Slav saint Enyo; and all fell within the outer northwestern rim of the Bulgarian Empire. It is the best historical argument to be made by a vociferous opponent of Magyar strawberries. [See the entry for Turány: On a Saintly Trail.]

RÁTKA. Lying just south of Tállya, Rátka is one of the smaller communes in the southwestern corner of Hegyalja. Its name raises a historical puzzle as to the era when it was founded. The name is usually attributed to the Slavic personal name Radka, which would seem to take it far back into regional history, along with some of the neighboring villages. But, more particularly, Radka is a typically Bulgaro-Slav personal (female) name that conceivably could date to the time of the Magyar occupation. As well, the historically emblematic vineyard hill of Rátka is called Istenhegy (God-hill), a name which suggests an ancient ceremonial site, whether pagan or new-Christian. But the fact that no documentary record of Rátka is found until the 15th century makes it impossible to substantiate a settlement in the earliest centuries of the Hungarian kingdom. It is known, though, that it later became a possession of the Tállya and Tokaj fortresses, and was also within the sphere of the Regéc Domain at one time [see the entry for Regéc].

The village was destroyed by the Ottoman Turks in 1566 and came into the ownership of the Rákóczis by 1598. But it was destroyed by the Turks again towards the end of the 17th century, after which it did not recover. Not one building was standing in 1688 (UC 82:58), and it was still "deserted" in 1709 (UC 22:9). Some build-up occurred subsequently, and Rátka was recognized as belonging to Hegyalja in the royal decree of 1737. This was followed, though, by a loss of inhabitants to plague. After Prince Trautsohn became owner, German settlers were brought in to expand agriculture and wine-growing (this is a relatively recent instance of foreign settlers acquiring the indigenous wine-making habits). One of the chief vineyard hills is known as 'Prince's Stony Hill' (Hercegköves-hegy), in reference to Trautsohn. However, Rátka suffered a dimunition in reputation following phylloxera because much of it was replanted with phylloxera-immune American varieties (*noah*, *othello*) which maintained their place into the communist era.

[Historical vineyard area: 1873 - 173 ha.; 1913 - 58 ha.; 1940 - 60 ha.; 1963 - 115 ha.; 1990 - 267 ha.]

As a wine-growing locale, Rátka is characterized by widely scattered vineyards, all of which lie to the east and southeast of the commune, towards Mád. Much of the vineyard area faces west, with only a lesser part having a more favorable, southerly exposure. Soils are clayey (*nyirok*), though with occasional loess areas. The upper areas have stone content of 40-60 percent, and it is those areas on the south-facing portions of Padihegy and Újhegy hills, as well as on the southwest-facing part of Hercegköves hill, that grow Rátka's best wine. There is a frequency of lime patches virtually throughout, and Újhegy is unusual in its lack of lime content.

Regéc. One of the early feudal domains of the Upper Tisza region, Regéc was situated on the western side of the Zemplén Hills, preponderantly in Abaúj County. Wine-growing was significant in the domain, and furthermore, five of the later Hegyalja communities belonged to it as late as the early-18th century: Abaújszántó and Erdőhorváti (both in Abaúj County); and Tállya, Rátka, and Legyesbénye (all in Zemplén County). Tállya was, moreover, the largest single producer of Tokaji wine. These factors apparently caused many people to think of the entire Regéc Domain territory as part of Hegyalja, even well into the 18th century. In the 17th century, the domain had come under the control of the Rákóczis, who placed the first glass-works there to produce bottles for Tokaji wine locally [see the entry for Háromhuta]. A curious notation was made in the 1644 inventory of the Domain: wines from Szántó, Tállya, and Tokaj were being stored in a cellar otherwise used for the storage of animal-feed (UC 78:34). This suggests short-term holding during transshipment north along the Hernád river valley.

Ronyva Creek. This name belongs to a rivulet, and its valley, in northern Hegyalja, that in former centuries had some influence on perceptions of the region's northern limits. The Ronyva is a tributary of the Bodrog river that extends north from their confluence above Sárospatak, and then passes through Sátoraljaújhely. Since the confluence occurs where the Bodrog turns east, the northerly vista seems to widen and the foothills appear to be set back much farther from the river, beyond the Ronyva, and thus, almost at a remove from the rest of Hegyalja. Although maps show this to be a false impression, the visual circumstance caused some people in the past to presume that all Ronyva valley locales must lie outside Hegyalja; in 1828, David Szabó noted that one viewpoint did not even regard Sátoraljaújhely itself as part of Hegyalja. Actually, the Ronyva follows the line of the last of the contiguous Eperjes-Tokaj Hill-Chain in this part of Hegyalja, and marks their separation from the final eastern outcroppings of the range, the so called Island-hills [see that entry]. However, Hungarian legislation of 1893 and 1908 recognized Sátoraljaújhely as the only Hegyalja locale situated beside the Ronyva. Ronyva valley vineyard locales to the north were excluded, notably Csörgő (now Čerhov, in East Slovakia), where grapes in some vineyards occasionally can reach botrytized condition, as well as Mátyásháza and Alsóregmec (both still in Hungary), which produced only table wine. Today, part of the Ronyva creek forms Hungary's border with southeastern Slovakia (where it becomes the Roňava) [see the entry for Slovakia]. Also to be noted is that, with respect to weather conditions in Hegyalja, the Ronyva lends its name to the so called 'Ronyva-wind' (*Ronyva-szél*), a cold air current from Russia, whose path follows the southwesterly part of the stream.

Royal Hungary. (*Magyar Királyság*) Historians use this term to refer to the northern and western parts of the Kingdom of Hungary that remained outside both the Ottoman Empire and the Principality of Transylvania between 1526 and 1683. It was this part of Hungary that came under Habsburg rule in 1541, and thus became the basis on which the dynasty would claim the entire Kingdom of Hungary, including Transylvania, following the withdrawal of the Ottomans back to the Balkans at the end of the 17th century. Geographically, Royal Hungary included what has been known as Upper Hungary [see that entry], although it extended beyond that.

Ružomberok. [See the entry for Rosenberg, in Part III.]

Sabinov (Kisszeben). As a town of the Pentapolitana [see that entry], Kisszeben participated in exporting Tokaji wine to Poland as early as around 1500. However, it was the smallest of the five towns, and less favorably situated than Prešov (Eperjes) and Bardejov (Bártfa) for acquiring wines from Hegyalja. Being located only about 14 km (9 miles) northwest of Eperjes, legitimate Kisszeben merchants mostly acquired Tokaji wine there and then usually sold it to traders who had come from Poland. On the other hand, Kisszeben's location, just south of the forested Beskids, was conducive to smuggling. The town's lesser role relative to the rest of the Pentapolitana is seen in the disinterest of major traders, such as the Fuggers or the Greek families, in positioning themselves there. [See the entry for Csákány, in Part III.]

Santorini. [See the entry for *Aszú*: Aegean Echo, in Part IV.]

SÁRAZSADÁNY. One of the smaller Hegyalja settlements, this village is situated along the Bodrog river east of Tolcsva, about midway between Sátoraljaújhely and Tokaj. The locale is of very old historical interest because it may have originated as a dwelling place for the Bulgaro-Slavs who came from north of Thessaloniki in the 9th century [see the entry for Bulgaro-Slavs, in Part I; and for Rány, in Part III]. However, the later village apparently was settled in the second-half of the 13th century, after the Tatar invasion, and its history is that of two small communities gradually fusing together. The present name reflects the 20th-century joining of the neighboring villages of Sára and Zsadány (both of which had borne the prefix Bodrog- in the past). Further, Zsadány had developed from two adjoining hamlets, Arbonya and Zsadány (Szirmay referred to "Arbonya-Zsadány" in 1798). The name Zsadány, which is attributed to a pagan Slav personal name, is particularly interesting because old documents show that a family with a surname recorded as Sada and Zada was quite active in northern Hegyalja wine-growing in the 14th and 15th centuries. Notably, in 1307, a married couple named Sada visited the vicar of Sárospatak to bestow a newly planted vineyard of theirs on the Pauline Order of Sátoraljaújhely.

[Historical vineyard area: 1873 - 51 ha.; 1913 - 100 ha.; 1940 - 99 ha.; 1963 - 104 ha.; 1990 - 154 ha.]

Certainly the area that was formerly Zsadány always had by far the most and best vineyard land of the Sárazsadány locale. Some might even call it the best of the small communities along the Bodrog, which can easily be understood when it is seen that its vineyards mostly lie just east of Tolcsva, one of Hegyalja's best areas. The tracts of particular significance are the south- and southwest-facing slopes of the hills called Előhegy and Szárhegy, both of which are located closer to Tolcsva than to Sárazsadány (the two communes share Előhegy). These areas have a highly suitable heavy clayey (*nyirok*) soil, with 30-60 percent riolite content on the steep upper parts of Szárhegy. Hidvéghy (1950) thought highly of the Rudnok and Alsóőrzés tracts, while noting that the Ültetés tract had been left virtually uncultivated in the 20th century because of its unfavorable exposition. All of these were formerly part of Zsadány. The only part of the village's vineyard area that belonged to the former Sára is Dobra hill, whose riolite-covered clayey (*nyirok*) soil area on the south slope was well-regarded historically.

Sáros County. (See Map #2) Situated along the northwestern border of Zemplén County, Sáros was an early major customer for the wines of Hegyalja. The county had developed relatively late, beginning in the 12th century, as a northern extension of Abaúj County, and did not become completely separate until the mid-14th century. The area grew in significance as a result of German settlement and increased economic activity. However, between 1200 and 1700, the Magyar language dominated in rural areas much further north than after 1700; it extended about 24-32 km (15-20 miles) to the north, northwest, and northeast of Eperjes (Prešov), particularly in lowland, river valleys (and also up to Varannó to the east [see the entry for Vranov nad Topľou]). In the time of Francis Rakoczi II, about 130 Magyar settlements covered the southern half of Sáros County (Potemkin, 1863). This facilitated every kind of interaction between Hegyalja and the northern part of the Eperjes-Tokaj Hill-Chain. Only depopulation because of pestilence and the Rákóczi wars with the Habsburgs caused the Hungarian language to recede south of Eperjes.

Wine-growing was fairly widespread in southern Sáros in the early centuries, especially as Magyars from Abaúj and Zemplén moved north along the river valleys. But local wine output was never enough to satisfy demand, and all but disappeared during the 15th and 16th centuries because of climatic cooling. When imports from the Szerémség region were cut off after the Ottoman occupation of Lower Hungary, Sáros merchants looked to Abaúj and Zemplén, but first of all to Hegyalja. At the same time, the county swelled with displaced Magyar nobility (major and minor). Its towns, especially Eperjes, and lowland areas, became synonymous with extravagance and pomp. Sáros was even dubbed 'the Hungarian Gascony' [see the entry Eszencia: a Literary Aside, in Part IV]. Because of its long border with Poland and considerable contacts with that land, Sáros was where Poles first became acquainted with Tokaji (some of the earliest mentions of Sáros County are in Polish documents). Indeed, Poles were a significant part of the rural population of northern Sáros in the Middle Ages (the surname Polyak, Poljak, etc., is very widespread in Sáros).

It is notable about Sáros that its prominent families owned vineyard parcels throughout Hegyalja. This was motivated by the unsuitable climate for vines in Sáros, but also the fondness of the county's upper-class for high-living (Tóth, in 1910, wrote that the oldtime Sáros grandee was "never in want of pals, nor his cellar of wine"). Tracts where Sáros municipalities, fortresses, or families once had vineyards include: Bacskai (in Mád); Bajusz (Tarcal); Bártfai (Tállya);

Bodonyi (Tarcal); Divini-Sulyom (Abaújszántó); Gyapáros (Tolcsva); Hangács (Mezőzombor); Hegymegy (Mezőzombor); Keczer (Mezőzombor); Kún (Tokaj); Kútpatka (Tolcsva); Lete (Monok); Mandulás (Mád); Medgyes (Tállya); Nyergesek (Tállya); Sánczy (Tokaj); Sáros (Erdőbénye); Szent-Margit (Abaújszántó); Tárczi (Tarcal); Tökösmáj (Tállya); Tormás (Tokaj); Uszhegy (Mád); Vitéz (Tarcal). [See the entries for Prešov; and for Rosa and Szirmay, in Part I.]

SÁROSPATAK. (colloquially Patak) This historically important Hegyalja and Zemplén town is situated towards the northern end of the region, along the Bodrog river near its confluence with the Ronyva creek, about 13 km (8 miles) south of Sátoraljaújhely. It has long since swallowed administratively the communities of Végardó to its north and Bodroghalász to its south, as well as Újpatak (the onetime Józseffalva) [see those entries]. The history of the town, whose name means 'Muddy-Creek,' goes far back into the early period of the Kingdom of Hungary. Anonymous told that a fort was erected here by the leader Ketel, immediately after the Magyar occupation. Some Hungarian historians in the past thought it was the center of a 'Patak County' around 1300, but, although it was a royal property, there is no documentary proof that it enjoyed county status.

Sárospatak received Walloon settlers (by some accounts they were Flemish) in the 12th century and Italians in the 13th century. Its early significance is attested by its destruction in 1310 at the hands of Máté Csák, an ambitious lord in northwestern Hungary. Similarly, the Czech Hussite armies repeatedly attacked Sárospatak during their incursion into the Upper Tisza in the 15th century, and actually controlled the fortress for two decades beginning in 1440. It was also the focus of the Ottoman Turkish invasion of Hegyalja in 1566, which resulted in great destruction and population loss in the environs, although the Ottomans did not succeed.

Meanwhile, the Sárospatak Domain had been created in the 13th century and was ever after a prize sought by the most powerful families of northeastern Hungary, notably the Perényis and Pálóczis. Ownership eventually fell to the Rákóczis by their marriage into the Lórántffy family in 1616, and they established the town as the cultural center of Zemplén County. The Calvinist College had been founded in 1531, and it owned significant vineyard acreage, often as a result of donations and bequeathals [see the entry for Lórántffy, in Part I]. In the 18th century, one vineyard-tract actually bore the name Collegiumi [see the Supplemental List, in Part III]. Whether or not the College's vine-dressers and cellar-masters, under the tutelage of the professors, made any contributions to the development of Hegyalja wine is unknown.

It is surprising that Sárospatak was not always or necessarily considered part of Hegyalja. Further viticultural development had occurred under the Rákóczis, as seen in the 17th-century profusion of vineyard names in the Domain. Once the Rákóczis gave some geographical definition to the Hegyalja region, there was really no leaving Sárospatak out, even if it had relatively few of the vaunted vineyard-tracts, especially for a community of its size (the Kútpatka and Mandulás tracts of Sárospatak are not to be confused with the renowned ones of Tolcsva). In 1838, David Szabó wrote that Hegyalja extended as far north as the northern rim of Sárospatak.

[Historical vineyard area: 1873 - 549 ha.; 1913 - 151 ha.; 1940 - 428 ha.; 1963 - 461 ha.; 1990 - 485 ha.]

Sárospatak's vineyard lands are arrayed to its west and northwest, respectively centered on the Szegfű-Hosszúhegy and Királyhegy-Megyer hill complexes. The latter is the most important grouping qualitatively, but specifically the south- or southeast-facing parcels. The soil is clayey (*nyirok*), with significant riolite content. These areas yield what Hidvéghy (1950) characterized as "the typical Patak wine." (In past times, this area also included the Nagy- and Kis-Kocsárd tracts of Károlyfalva.) On the other hand, there are a number of vineyard-tracts with a favorable though thinner layer of stony *nyirok* soils, but with an eastern or western exposition, and thus middling (2nd Class); these include Sárospatak's Kútpatka and Mandulás tracts, as well as Darnó and Gombos. Lesser tracts (3rd Class) have similar soils, but are in the lower belt of vineyards and with exposition towards the east or north, for instance on the eastern side of Hosszúhegy. [See the entries for Bodroghalász, Józseffalva, and Végardó.]

SÁTORALJAÚJHELY. (colloquially Újhely) This most challenging of Hegyalja place-names means 'New-Place-Below-Sátor (hill),' in reference to one of the two identically named hills in the traditional description of Hegyalja as stretching 'from Sátor to Sátor.' It is a name with origins far back in Zemplén history, very possibly to the founding of Hungary, since Anonymous indicated that it was an inhabited place when the Magyars arrived. The earliest known names for the settlement were Sátorhalma (Sátor-mound) and Sátorelő (Sátor-front), and dated at least as far back as the 11th century. But the old settlement was not situated exactly where the modern one is. After the Tatars devastated the vicinity in 1241, the settlement's position was shifted slightly and the name 'new place' (*új hely*) came into use. King Andrew III mentioned it by the name "Saturalia Wyhel" in 1291. But (and mercifully for non-Hungarians) it has long been referred to as Újhely casually. It became the seat of Zemplén County in 1685.

Újhely was one of the earliest Zemplén settlements to acquire an urban character, probably in the mid-12th century. King Andrew III referred to it as a *civitas* in 1291. This development was stimulated in no small part by foreign settlers, above all by Germans in the mid-12th century. However, King Kálmán had earlier presented the town to Count Ratold of Apulia, who probably brought some settlers with him [see the entry for Bara; and those for Kálmán and Ratold, in Part I]. This early Italian connection may be why King Béla IV turned to Italy for settlers a century later when he rebuilt Hegyalja after the Tatar invasion. However, another important outside influence in solidifying Sátoraljaújhely's importance was the founding of a Pauline Order monastery not long after 1200. The Pauliners definitely created vineyards, and inasmuch as they also had land in nearby Kistoronya (now Malá Tŕňa) and Petrahó (later Bodroghalász), it may be presumed that they promoted wine-growing generally in what would become northernmost Hegyalja.

The worst period for the town coincided with the ascent of Tokaji's star. It was targeted by the Hussites in the 15th century, and suffered from minor rebellions in the 16th century, especially destruction at the hands of the ambitious Perényi family [see that entry, in Part I]. The volatile, precarious political situation likely was a major reason why vineyard buyers from the important towns to the north did not take much interest in Sátoraljaújhely early on, despite the appreciable extent of its vineyard hills. Great devastation was also visited on the town by the Ottoman Turks in 1566. In the late-17th and early-18th centuries, wine production was negatively influenced by Habsburg confiscation of vineyards from rebellious noblemen, many of whom had acquired tracts in Sátoraljaújhely because of its growing political prominence after the mid-17th century. All of this explains why Timon, in 1728, wrote that Újhely's fame was "not very old."

Since the Sátor-hill of Újhely is the traditional northeastern marker of Hegyalja, it is odd that there were times when there was some dispute as to whether the town's vineyards should be included. The reason for the indecision can be understood from David Szabó's notation in 1838 that some persons thought Újhely itself should not be included in Hegyalja because of a change in landscape coming north from Sárospatak, especially a 'break' in the chain of hills, and a change in their direction from north-northeast to north [see the entry for Ronyva Creek]. This viewpoint, though, was at odds with long-established county decisions and governances about Hegyalja.

[Historical vineyard area: 1873 - 560 ha.; 1913 - 151 ha.; 1940 - 440 ha.; 1963 - 340 ha.; 1990 - 289 ha.]

Overall, the town has never been deemed one of the very best wine areas of Hegyalja, but it always had among the most extensive vineyard areas, and there was no dearth of 1st Class sites. Those were located west and southwest of the town, along the hillsides lining two valleys protected on the north. Especially respected names were Galambos, Köveshegy, Nagy-Boglyoska, Nagy-Melegoldal, Oremus, Szárhegy, Szemszúró, Tompakő, Vióka, Veresföld, and of course, Sátor. The most favorable sites face mostly south or southeast and have loose or medium compact clayey (*nyirok*) soil, depending on the proportion of 'stone-dust' (*kőpor*). Stone covering reaches 60-70 percent in the higher areas. Historically, the town's vineyards reached the highest elevations in Hegyalja, at around 300 meters/984 feet, and even today reach around 250 meters/820 feet. [See the entries for Károlyfalva and Slovenské Nové Mesto.]

Sečovce (Gálszécs). Located about 34 km (21 miles) north of Hegyalja, Gálszécs had become a town by the mid-15th century, and had a tariff collection station. Innumerable wine barrels passed through the Gálszécs Domain on their way to Poland during the late Middle Ages. It was at this geographical point that shipments, whether ultimately legal or contraband, bifurcated for further transport, either north or northeast through Zemplén County, or northwest through Sáros County. Historically, the locale may have had a very early relationship with Hegyalja because of the old Micsk clan, going back to the early-14th century. Also, the Perényi and Rozgonyi familes were owners here and in Hegyalja. [See the entries for Dorgó and Mestervölgy, in Part III].

Slovakia. Bordering Hungary on the north, Slovakia has had the northeastern tip of Hegyalja since the formation of Czechoslovakia in 1918 (with the exception of 1938-1944, when Hungary once again held those villages). This area is situated in the far southeastern corner of Slovakia, in the area between the Ronyva creek and Bodrog river; for the most part, this coincides with the so called Island-hills [see the entries for Bodrog, Bodrogköz, Island-hills, and Ronyva]. According to the 1908 Hungarian law, only Malá Tŕňa (Kistoronya), Viničky (Szőlőske), and Slovenské Nové Mesto (Slovakia's small portion of Sátoraljaújhely, also east of the Ronyva) qualified for inclusion. But, in 1959, Slovakia passed legislation that expanded its Tokaji territory by adding several neighboring villages, all located between the Ronyva and Bodrog, which had been rejected by the 1908 Hungarian law: Bara (Bári), Čerhov (Csörgő), Černochov (Csarnahó), and Veľká Tŕňa (Nagytoronya) [see those entries]. Hungary has contested this expansion in the European Union as an impermissible reformulation of the region by Slovakia that necessarily disallows Slovakia's marketing of its wines under the name Tokajské within the EU or abroad. [It is instructive to contrast the history of the disputed Slovakian locales with the locales of southwestern Hegyalja, particularly Fényes's comments in 1851. See the entries for Golop, Ond, and Szerencs.]

During the Interwar period, Slovakia's Tokaji production was concentrated in Malá Tŕňa, which has always been the principal wine-growing locale, and the local viti-vinicultural school was also located there (with instruction in Hungarian). During the communist period, bottling took place at the state wine enterprise located in the nearby city of Košice, whence it was also marketed. However, in line with the international Lisbon Agreement of 1958 concerning national rights to appellation names, the Slovakian state wine trading company agreed in 1967 to a compromise whereby its Hungarian counterpart would purchase 1,000 hectoliters of Slovakian sweet *szamorodni* wine annually for hard currency, and the Slovakian firm would market its bottled Tokajské wines only within Czechoslovakia. [See the entry for Slovakian Tokajské, in Part IV.]

Of old historical interest about the rejected area of Slovakia, is that despite its exclusion from Hegyalja, it is apparent that the area had followed in the same viti-viticultural traditions and developments, as regards grape varieties, wine-making, wine-storage, etc., since long ago. This suggests that Bulgaro-Slav (Thracian) habits had once extended from Szerencs and Tokaj in the south to at least as far north as the village of Zemplén [see the entry for Zemplín].

SLOVENSKÉ NOVÉ MESTO. (colloquially called Nové Mesto; also known colloquially in Hungarian as Kisújhely and Tótújhely, respectively Little-újhely and Slavish-újhely) This community is immediately across the Ronyva Creek from Sátoraljaújhely, of which it was an integral part until 1918 [the historical background is found under the latter name]. The Nové Mesto vineyards are concentrated on two hills, Nagy (Big) and Kis (Little) Káté, whose name goes back to the Magyar clan Katha [see that entry, in Part I], from the era of the Árpád kings.

The best tracts have a southerly exposure. Soil is of a typically Hegyalja clayey (*nyirok*) type, occasionally stony. The Káté hills were not mentioned by Szirmay (1798) in giving the names of the chief vineyard hills of Sátoraljaújhely, possibly because they are situated at a remove from the town, at its eastern border near to the vineyard area of Viničky (Szőlőske), which he did not include in Hegyalja.

Solivar (Sóvár). The old settlement of 'Salt-fort' is of considerable importance in the early history of the Upper Tisza region, and consequently, of Hegyalja as well. Located at the northern end of the Eperjes-Tokaj Hill-Chain, abutting Eperjes (Prešov) on the east, these salt deposits were a fundamental reason for settlement along the river valleys that spread north from Hegyalja. Salt likely was being extracted here continuously since the time of the Celts. The site probably explains why Bulgaro-Slav interest in the region took the geographical shape that it did. It no doubt drew the attention of Great Moravia, too, and indeed, is reason to think that Great Moravia settled some people in the vicinity to ensure supplies, though probably with the consent of the Bulgarian Empire, owing to their alliance during the 9th century. An indication of the early importance of Sóvár is the 12th-century Warsaw Codex, which refers to the early-11th century and uses that settlement (rather than whatever existed at Eperjes) as the focal point in stating that Poles lived to the northwest, Rusyns to the northeast, and Hungarians to the south. In the late-13th century, 'Salt-fort' became the property of the regionally important Soós family, who took their surname from the locale. In that era, it was usual for the salt to be transported by river as well as overland routes, which possibly accounts for the name of the Sóhajó ('salt-boat') vineyard-tract in Tarcal. [See the entry for Soós, in Part I; and for Sóhajó, in Part III.]

Sóvár. [See the previous entry.]

Spišská Nová Ves (Igló). Located just south of Levoča (Lőcse), Igló was one of the westernmost transshipment points into Poland, both by overland and water routes, in the early period of Tokaji's fame. Its significance probably peaked in the 16th century, although the Fuggers continued to do some trading from there. In the mid-17th century, Igló was the seat of operations for a significant smuggler of Tokaji, Johannes Mülleter. His activities may have reflected the avid ownership of vineyards in Hegyalja by Igló burghers.

Strachyna. (now Stročin, in East Slovakia) [See Map #3.] This antique name for a locale about 100 km (62 miles) north of Hegyalja is of historical interest in connection with a Balkan Slav (Bulgaro-Slav) presence in the Upper Tisza region, and thus Hegyalja, too, in the period just prior to the arrival of the Magyars. The name was also recorded as Oustrachina, Oostrachina, and Oztrachina in early documents; and it can be no coincidence that the Bulgaro-Slavs also applied the name Ostrakina (still in use today) to a site in the northeastern Peloponnesus, in Arcadia, when they migrated south in the same era. Approximately 1,287 km (800 miles) separate the two Ostrakinas. [Note: the Greeks do not make the *ch* sound, and therefore would have pronounced the name as Ostra*k*ina vice Ostra*ch*ina.] Bulgarian maps portraying the extent of the medieval

Bulgarian Empire indicate that Oustrakina/Strachyna was situated near the outermost rim of its territory in the Upper Tisza along the Ondava river. The locale's name thus is an additional indication as to how Hegyalja came to have Balkan wine-growing roots. [See the entries for Bulgarian Empire, Ondava River, and Turany nad Ondavou.]

Stropkov (Sztropkó). This northernmost Zemplén town along the Ondava river is situated in eastern Slovakia, about 93 km (58 miles) north of Hegyalja. However, its rise and fortunes as an urban entity were closely tied to trade in Hegyalja wine. It seems to have been the last major market town to develop in Zemplén County, and could not much antedate the frontier fortress of Toporó that was erected during the 14th century [see the entry for Por-törő, in Part III]. German settlement beginning in the 14th century led to commercial development and acquisition of town status (German remained the municipal language until around 1600). Sztropkó was conveniently located for trade with Poland, on the far side of the Low Beskid mountains. Duly, a tariff collection point was situated in its vicinity at least as early as the beginning of the 14th century (which perhaps is why the Toporó fort was built). This might mark the first major exports of Hegyalja wine to Poland, since it followed the expansion of the region's wine-growing in the second-half of the 13th century. The town's relative importance early on is indicated by a letter of 1468, in which the assistance of the Sztropkó magistrate was sought in selling several barrels of wine from Mezőzombor. Sztropkó became a convenient entrepôt for Tokaji in the early-16th century, when Hungarian commercial communities were established across the border in Jasło and Nowy Sacz; and this role grew in mid-century, when Sztropkó became a center for contraband trade because of an attempt to give the town of Kassa a virtual monopoly on exports to Poland. The town's stake in Tokaji continued for two centuries more, because in 1569 the Sztropkó Domain came into the possession of the Pethős [see that entry, in Part I], who were important vineyard owners in Hegyalja, and thus had a vested interest in wine exports to Poland.

SZEGI. One of the smaller settlements along the middle stretch of the Bodrog, Szegi is situated just south of Szegilong and north of Bodrogkisfalud. It developed perhaps in the early-14th century, and might have taken its name from the landowning family known as Szegi. Conversely, the family might have taken to calling themselves after the locale, since the place was recorded as 'Zugh' in a document from the late-14th century. The latter name referred to the site's position by the Bodrog, whether the antique spelling indicated *szeg* (angle) or *zug* (nook). At times, the village was also known as Bodrogszegi.

[Historical vineyard area: 1873 - 140 ha.; 1913 - 67 ha.; 1940 - 91 ha.; 1963 - 152 ha.; 1990 - 224 ha.]

Hidvéghy (1950) commented, "As a consequence of its superb position, there are numerous quality vineyards" at Szegi. The best areas are northwest of the village. Exposition is southerly and very favorable, while soil for the most part is of a good, workable clayey (*nyirok*) sort. The upper parts of the Murány, Poklos, and Hosszúmáj vineyard-tracts were the most esteemed in past centuries, with Murány notable for 50-60 percent stony content.

SZEGILONG. One of the smallest Hegyalja communities, Szegilong is located along the Bodrog south of Olaszliszka, near the river's confluence with Bényei creek. The village is immediately north of Szegi, and apparently came into existence in the 14th century as a northward extension of Szegi towards the riverine woods called Long; Balassa (1991) notes *long* as deriving from a Slavic term for a marshy pasture. In the 19th century, the community usually was distinguished from Szegi simply by the name Long. Szegilong became part of the Tokaj Domain by the 15th century, and the Rákóczis became its owners in the late-16th century.

[Historical vineyard area: 1873 - 28 ha.; 1913 - 112 ha.; 1940 - 28 ha.; 1963 - 29 ha.; 1990 - 37 ha.]

Szegilong's vineyard area is similar to that of Szegi, but much smaller and with fewer high-quality sites. Soil is of a favorable clayey (*nyirok*) sort, but has considerably less stone content than at Szegi. The well-regarded vineyards were those on the southeast-facing parts of the Gyertyános and Hosszúmáj tracts (the latter is shared with Szegi).

Szepesség. (formerly known widely in Europe by its German name, Zips; its Slovak name is Spiš) This former region of north-central Hungary is located on the southeastern side of the Tatra mountains of Slovakia, and always had a significant impact on Tokaji wine, despite being 95-155 km (60-80 miles) away from Hegyalja (distance varying depending on the specific communities at either end). Sparsely populated by Slavs at the time of Hungary's founding, Szepesség received an early influx of Magyar settlers as border guards, and later was settled even more thickly by German immigrants who built up a number of important urban centers at pre-existing, though minor, Slav (Slovak/Polish/Rusyn) settlements. These German towns were the basis for the development of a self-governing region, hence an individual identity. The Szepes towns were pawned to the Polish king in 1412, and owed obeisance to Poland during 1412-1772. This close connection with Poland during the era of Tokaji's ascent had a favorable influence on exports; and a number of Polish wine merchants took up residence in the Szepes towns. The prosperity of the Szepesség also led to the Habsburgs' founding of the Szepes Chamber in the 16th century, which had considerable influence over Tokaji wine trade. It was a German resident in the Szepesség who first made note of a change in the nature of Tokaji wine. [See the entries for Lubomirski, Sperfogel, Szepes Chamber, and Thurzó, in Part I.]

Szerémség. Now the Sremska region of southern Vojvodina in Serbia, this former region of southern Hungary is thought to have exerted an influence on Hegyalja after 1500. Prior to the Ottoman occupation in the early-16th century, Szerém wines were one of the most well-known of Hungarian wines and enjoyed a strong market in Poland. It is known that the ones popular in Poland were somewhat sweet, and probably given age in barrel. The method for gaining grapes with extra sugar most likely was drying them in the sun, since Walloons from west Europe had been settled in the region. But that practice was never adopted in Hegyalja, even though it is thought that some Walloons were brought from the Szerémség to Hegyalja during the Ottoman occupation, specifically for the purpose of transferring their know-how. But perhaps a more central question is whether the Walloons brought the *furmint* grape along with them from the Szerémség [see the entry for Furmint (b), in Part IV]. The Szerém wine area extends along the Tarcal mountain, or in Serbo-Croatian, Fruška Gora ('Frankish Mountain,' in reference to the Walloons). About 354 km (220 miles) separate the latter from Hegyalja. [See the entry for Pajzos, in Part III.]

<u>SZERENCS</u>. Situated along the southern rim of Hegyalja, Szerencs faces the creek of the same name on its eastern side, and a hill-group of the same name to its northwest. In recent decades, it became the centerpoint of an agglomeration of four Hegyalja villages, the others being Legyesbénye, Bekecs, and Ond; Szerencs has absorbed the latter for administrative purposes. The locale's relatively muted renown in regional wine history contrasts with its role in early Zemplén history. According to the account of Anonymous, written around 1200, Szerencs was the area where the forward scouting parties of the Magyars encamped during the first days in their new land at the end of the 9th century. Apparently, it remained a seat of major clans during the period of the Árpád kings, since its name was used administratively to cover most of what would become southern Zemplén County, thus encompassing most of Hegyalja.

While Anonymous made no comment about wine-growing at Szerencs at the time of the Magyar occupation, he did mention a topographic feature, namely a hill that he knew by the name

'Szerencse.' He said the Magyar scouts were enchanted by the view from the hill and called the place Szerelmes, signifying 'lovely to behold,' but that the name had changed over time to signify 'good luck' in Hungarian. But Hungarian etymologists have denied a Magyar origin to the name, and instead have put forth ancient Slavic or Turkic possibilities, for instance: Slavic *sreshtan* ('meeting place'), perhaps referring to the confluence of two local streams; or a diminutive form of Serem, an old Turkic personal name. A Bulgaro-Slav possibility that the etymologists have overlooked is *srechen* ('fortunate'), which jibes with the name Anonymous knew, and may even be the origin of the Magyar word *szerencse*. 'Favored Hill' seems a fitting name for a vineyard hill; and, in all likelihood, people at Szerencs were growing wine on it before Anonymous wrote.

There is irony in Szerencs having been often disregarded in delineations of Hegyalja. The account of Anonymous indicates that the Magyar scouting parties had in effect limned the later wine region when they followed the Bodrog river south from Sátor-hill (at Sátoraljaújhely) to Tokaj-hill, and then turned west and alighted at Szerencse-hill. Perhaps the convenience of the expression 'from Sátor-hill to Sátor-hill' made it easy to ignore Szerencs. Vályi, in 1796, was ambiguous about whether it belongs to Hegyalja, in saying that its wine is "middling" relative to Hegyalja (did he mean 'compared to' or 'among'?). Just two years later, Szirmay left Szerencs out of his account of Hegyalja. In 1851, Fényes was equally definite in excluding it, although he seems merely to have deferred to Szirmay's opinion, while having a different personal view: "Although [Szerencs's] vineyard hill does not belong to Hegyalja, nevertheless on some parts of it, namely on Elöhegy [hill] and Berkec, such good wine is grown, that it is not at all inferior to Hegyaljan." The village was not described in the *Tokaj-Hegyaljai Album* of 1867, but opinion thereafter must have swung towards Fényes's way of thinking, because Szerencs was included in the legislation of 1893 and 1908. [See the entry for Szirmay, in Part I.]

[Historical vineyard area: 1873 - 173 ha.; 1913 - 66 ha.; 1940 - 125 ha.; 1963 - 51 ha.; 1990 - 99 ha.]

Perhaps the Elöhegy praised by Fényes is the Szerencse hill mentioned by Anonymous. In any case, Vályi, too, said that Elöhegy produced the village's "best" wine. But 'Favored Hill' notwithstanding, Szerencs has quite variable conditions for growing Hegyalja botrytis wines. According to Hidvéghy's report of 1950, soil for the most part is favorably clayey (*nyirok*), but sometimes loess, or a mix of loess with clay. In all of these cases, the upper areas are the most favorable because of their high content of crushed riolite, up to 40-50 percent; stone content diminishes progressively further down the slopes. But Hidvéghy noted that the exposition of the village's vineyards is "in general unfavorable," because they mostly face east or west. However, there are vineyards that face south, and these are located in the tracts known as Berkec, Kertész, Szemere, and Vida, the first being the same as the one remarked on so favorably by Fényes a century earlier. [See the entry for Aranka, in Part III.]

Szerencs Hills. (*Szerencsi Dombság*) The southwesternmost section of Hegyalja, the Szerencs hills resemble an appendage of the Zemplén hills that is separated from the rest by the Szerencs creek. Six Hegyalja communes encircle the Szerencs hills: Golop, Ond, Szerencs, Bekecs, Legyesbénye, and Monok, with the first three lying along Szerencs creek and the latter three to the rear, westward. The vineyard area behind the six communes is almost continuous throughout, as is the area of habitation between Ond, Szerencs, Bekecs, and Legyesbénye on the southeastern side. The Szerencs hills could well be one of the oldest wine-growing areas of Hegyalja, not least of all because Szerencs was of administrative significance in the centuries right after the Hungarian Conquest. But it might also have been planted to some extent even before that. Despite its age, the Szerencs hills area was not accepted as part of Hegyalja by some observers during the 18th and 19th centuries. One factor influencing that view was the late recovery of the communities from the predations of the Ottomans and the Habsburgs in the last quarter of the

17th century. Eventually, though, it was impossible to overlook that these communes possessed some sites capable of yielding estimable Tokaji wines. It is noteworthy that during the early part of the communist period, there was no drive to bring the Szerencs hills villages into the state (collective) farm framework. Data from 1963 show that 41 percent of the 179 hectares cultivated remained in the private sector, and the remainder in the cooperative sector; however, the total represented less than 4 percent of total Hegyalja vineyard area. [See the entry for Gilip Creek.]

SZŐLŐSKE [See the entry for VINIČKY.]

Sztropkó. [See the entry for Stropkov.]

TÁLLYA. Located towards Abaújszántó at the southwestern end of Hegyalja, Tállya has long been the region's largest community in terms of vineyard acreage, and also one of the most respected as regards wine quality. Its history dates back to the era of the Árpád kings, when a fortress was built on what became known as Várhegy (Fortress-hill). The settlement likely was expanded during that era by bringing in foreign settlers, although there is some doubt about their date and origin. Popular imagination sees 'Italia' in the name Tállya and attributes it to Italian settlers who arrived after the Tatar invasion of 1241-1242. But the name seems to have been in use before that time. There are two theories to explain this: either, 1) Italians came earlier, after having already settled in the Szerémség region of southern Hungary in the mid-12th century; or, 2) the name Tállya actually has nothing to do with Italy, and derives instead from the Old French term *taille* (land cleared of forest), as a result of Walloons who settled in the 12th century.

Both theories about Tállya's name indicate a relatively old origin for wine-growing. Vineyards probably were cultivated at least since the time of the first fortress (*vár*). In fact, Várhegy was the name of one of the oldest vineyard hills. Another famous old name amongst the town's vineyard hills is Patócs, a personal name left over from the pagan era, thus suggesting that it might have been cultivated from the earliest years of the Kingdom of Hungary. [Also, see the entry for Fegyemes, in Part III.] Tállya's fame in the Upper Tisza region of Hungary can be dated to at least 1485. That was when the town of Bártfa, in Sáros County, purchased an existing vineyard-tract that subsequently became known by the name Bártfai (later corrupted as Bátfi). However, it was in 1562 that Tállya became 'a name' in the wider world, when its wine was presented and praised at the Council of Trent (this was still the era before botrytis *aszú* wines, although some botrytized grapes might have been included by chance) [see the entry for Draskovics, in Part I]. At the time, the Tállya fortress was of regional prominence [see the entry for Regéc]. The late-17th and early-18th centuries on the whole were less auspicious because it was the time of the Rákóczis' struggles against the Habsburgs; and Tállya had come into the Rákóczis' sphere in 1647. Nevertheless, botrytis *aszú* wine production had started by that time, and the Rákóczis constructed at Tállya a huge underground network of wine cellars that still bears their name.

[Historical vineyard area: 1873 - 922 ha.; 1913 - 617 ha.; 1940 - 607 ha.; 1963 - 622 ha.; 1990 - 649 ha.]

Most of Tállya's vineyards are northeast of the town, stretching from its border with Abaújszántó east to Mád, with a much smaller area to the west, towards Golop. The soil is mostly clayey (*nyirok*), though very variable in compactness, depending on the proportion of 'stone-dust' (*kőpor*) soil mixed in with the clay. Stone content, reaching 70-75 percent on the upper slopes, is remarkable. Historically, the most highly regarded vineyard-tracts were Dorgó, Kő-Hetény, Kővágó, Patócs, and Várhegy, with Nyergeshegy, Palota, and Sashegy not far behind. However, Szirmay mentioned another dozen as "noble" in 1798. In 1950, Hidvéghy reported that Báthori, Dukát, Galuska, Remete, Őszhegy [see Uszhegy, in Part III], Görbe, Hasznosok, Palota, and Remete still had a "good name" (the last four were amongst the best as noted by Szirmay). But in all of these cases, many of the superior parts were not reconstructed after phylloxera, either because of erosion or compact soil and high stone content that made the land very difficult to work, and also costly at a time of high overseas emigration.

TARCAL. The western neighbor of Tokaj, Tarcal lies below the western side of Tokaj-hill, which was originally known as Tarcal-hill, according to the account of Anonymous. He related that the name was given at the time of the Magyar occupation of Hegyalja, at the end of the 9th century, when a leader named Turzol (or Turcol) won a horse race with fellow chieftains Ónd and Ketel up to the top of the hill. It was still the name of the hill when Anonymous wrote at the beginning of the 13th century. But Tokaj was larger and more important because it showed its face to the world, so to speak, by being located where the Bodrog and Tisza rivers meet. Consequently, Tokaj's name eventually became the one by which the hill was called.

The settlement of Tarcal, taking its name from the hill, developed in the early period of the Hungarian kingdom, perhaps around 1100; the first documentary mention of Tarcal is from 1150. Wine-growing potential might have been a major stimulus for settlement, as suggested by the vineyard-tract named Baksó, from the Baksó (or Baxa) clan that was in the area by at least the mid-12th century. Tarcal's star was forever hitched to Tokaji wine when the community became part of the Tokaj Domain in the mid-15th century. Tarcal certainly benefited from the growing fame of Tokaji wine in the 16th and 17th centuries, as demonstrated by the many vineyard names dating to that period; and it is when the Rákóczis came into possession of vineyard land. But it was also an extremely trying period, arguably worse than for any other Hegyalja town. Tarcal was destroyed by the Ottoman Turks in 1566; burned by Habsburg troops in 1604; repeatedly blackmailed by Habsburg armies in the 1670s; burned by the anti-Habsburg forces of the Transylvanian prince Thököly in 1676; attacked and burned to the ground by the Ottomans in 1678; ravaged by plague in 1679; depleted of able-bodied males sent to defend Tokaj in 1685, while a Habsburg army arrived and destroyed Tarcal's vineyards; given to the Ottoman pasha of Eger in 1689; ransomed by anti-Habsburg forces; and, during 1697-99, largely depopulated for fear of the Habsburg armies during the Rákóczi rebellions.

Were it not for Tokaj's position at the confluence of the Bodrog and Tisza rivers, Tarcal might well have become the name by which Hegyalja wine would be known. The aforementioned Baksó vineyard tract demonstrates that the potential for quality was perceived very early. Further, Tarcal's name apparently became widely known in the Kingdom of Hungary in that era because of wine. Balassa (1991), who wrote as if he did not accept Anonymous's account of the origin of Tarcal's name, noted that the only other place in Hungary where the topographical name Tarcal turned up was in the once famous Szerém wine region in the south (now Srem in Serbia), where Magyar inhabitants in the 16th century applied the name to the vineyard hill later called Fruška Gora ('Frankish Hill') by the Serbs. Balassa thus intimated that the name Tarcal was copied in Szerém exactly because Tarcal in Hegyalja already had a good name as a wine locale.

Tarcal has always been considered one of the very best Hegyalja wine-growing areas, certainly ahead of Tokaj. It is apparent, for instance, that its list of old 1st Class tracts is more extensive than that of any other Hegyalja community. It was one of only three communities (along with Tállya and Tolcsva) whose primacy Vályi (1796) recognized by listing the 1st- and 2nd-Class tracts. But Vályi also made a comment that set Tarcal rather apart from all the other Hegyalja communities in terms of the market value of its wines: "These vineyard hills grow *many expensive wines*" (emphasis added). Tarcal also had what came to be the most prized of all Hegyalja vineyards, Szarvas, which had been the crown of the Rákóczi holdings and then was confiscated for the Habsburgs in 1714. It eventually became synonymous with 'Imperial Tokay,' the single most famous designation in the history of Tokaji wine.

[Historical vineyard area: 1873 - 518 ha.; 1913 - 510 ha.; 1940 - 376 ha.; 1963 - 307 ha.; 1990 - 506 ha.]

The soil at Tarcal is various, being either clayey (*nyirok*) or loess, or a mixture of the two. Lime occurs in conjunction with the loess soils, and comprises 15-32 percent of the loess areas. Andesite is characteristic of all the soil types at Tarcal, though never in a considerable amount. Tarcal's best vineyard-tracts lie to the east of town, ranged along the southwestern side of Tokaj-hill, but particularly the south- and southwest-facing slopes. This is perhaps the single most extensive, sun-drenched locale of Hegyalja, and it is the location of the most famous old vineyard-tracts of Tarcal: Szarvas, Mézesmáj, Cserfás, Királymáj, Agyag, Csuka, Paksi, Görbe, Barát, Forrás, Baksó (per Hidvéghy, 1950). Only somewhat less highly regarded (historically, 2nd Class) are the slopes west of town that also have a somewhat westerly exposition: Cseke, Mandulás, Perőc. Those to the northwest, such as Előhegy hill, once enjoyed a good though lesser reputation (historically, 3rd Class), though 'lesser' mostly in the context of the overall quality of Tarcal wines; this area never recovered significantly from phylloxera. The list of names is much longer in Szirmay's account of 1798, and those tracts are included in Part III.

TOKAJ. The town that lent its name to Hegyalja's wine is situated at the southeastern corner of the region, along the river Bodrog and at the eastern foot of Tokaj-hill. The hill is the southernmost of the Eperjes-Tokaj Hill-Chain, and thus is the first sign when coming north from the Great Plain (Alföld) that a different landscape lays ahead. The chronicler Anonymous, around 1200, related that the Magyars erected an earthen fort at this site when they arrived at the end of the 9th century. He was probably accurate on this point, since Tokaj is at the confluence of the Bodrog and Tisza rivers, and thus must have appeared to have strategic value. But, according to Hungary's first geographer, Matthias Bél, writing at the beginning of the 18th century, there were Slav inhabitants here when the Magyars arrived. Indeed, the most likely explanation of the name Tokaj is that it derives from a Bulgaro-Slavic term for 'confluence' (*sâs-toka*), in allusion to the Bodrog and Tisza rivers. For a time, the place was known as Hímesudvar (the name by which Anonymous knew it), but 'Tokaj' apparently had hung on colloquially. (Etymologists have also theorized a Turkic origin because of early documents in which Tokaj is called Tokota, Tokoyd, Tochol, etc., which are non-Slavic names.)

A number of historical factors led to Tokaj becoming the general name for the wine of Hegyalja. To begin with, it may have been the earliest site of extensive wine-growing in the region because of Tokaj-hill (originally Tarcal-hill), especially along the southern side known as Mézesmáj [see part (c) of that entry in Part III]. This would have happened in tandem with the growing importance of Tokaj after the Magyars erected a more formidable fortress of stone, probably sometime in the early-11th century, when they had ceased marauding and were attending to settling down in their new homeland. The fortress led to Tokaj becoming the seat of a feudal domain. By the mid-15th century, the Tokaj Domain included the entire southeastern corner of Hegyalja: Mezőzombor, Tarcal, Bodrogkeresztúr, Bodrogkisfalud, and even (according to the Tokaj *urbárium* of 1581) Szegi. Together with its key location for land and river transportation, this preeminence in southern Hegyalja made Tokaj an important commercial center regionally, such that it became known to wine traders as the provenance of good Hegyalja wine, even though not all of it was grown there. This accounts for Sylvester Douglass's otherwise surprising notation about the town's populace when he visited in 1768: "The inhabitants are chiefly either Hungarians of the Protestant religion, or Greeks, who came originally from Turkey, but have been *long* settled here *for the purpose of carrying on the wine trade*" (emphasis added).

Tokaj might have been the first Hegyalja locale where, by chance, some botrytized grapes were crushed along with a larger quantity of ordinary shriveled grapes, possibly around 1500, which resulted in *főbor* [see that entry, in Part IV]. While this would not have been botrytis wine as such, it did result in a discernibly different style of wine that was referred to afterward as 'Tokaji.' This would be an implication of Conrad Sperfogel's notation in 1524, that "Tokaji" wine had become "so good and generous as never before." Yet, a document of 1676 demonstrates that both 'black' and 'red' wines were still being produced at Tokaj at that time (UC 117:5).

[Historical vineyard area: 1873 - 447 ha.; 1913 - 474 ha.; 1940 - 367 ha.; 1963 - 329 ha.; 1990 - 231 ha.]

Tokaj has never been the largest producer of 'Tokaji' wine, though it places high. Also, it has never been considered one of the very best communities in terms of overall level of wine quality. The objective reason for this is that too many vineyards face easterly or westerly. Loess is the predominant soil, especially on Tokaj's southern side, and in fact is more significant than at any other Hegyalja vineyard locale. The town has a good number of 1st Class vineyard slopes within its borders, such as Barát, Bornemissza, Gyöpös, Hétszőlő, Kanducs, Kis-Mézesmáj, Kócsag, Melegoldal, Nagyszőlő, Paksi, and Szerelmi, all of which face south. As befits Tokaj's southeasternmost position in Hegyalja, these slopes, especially the loess areas, produce the sweetest wines of Hegyalja. Other vineyard-tracts mentioned by Szirmay in 1798 are listed in Part III. His 2nd Class tracts were east-facing, and the 3rd Class ones west-facing.

Tokaj-Hegyalja. [See the entry for Hegyalja.]

Tokaj: Spelling Lesson

It may be puzzling that since 1990 we have shifted to 'Tokaji' in spelling the wine's name, after centuries of being used to 'Tokay.' The change has been made to reflect the correct modern Hungarian spelling of the town of Tokaj, with the addition of the –*i* ending to signify 'from' (thus, the wine's name corresponds to 'Tokaj-an' or 'Tokaj-er'). However, this does not mean that the old Western spelling was incorrect. On the contrary, Tokay or Tokaÿ was the spelling used by Hungarians in the Middle Ages, when Latin was the administrative language. For instance, it is the spelling used in the 1581 Tokaj Domain *urbárium*, and as recently as the *urbárium* of 1688. That spelling is also seen in the old surname Tokay, which in some families has never been updated. (The most well-known bearer of the name was 'the peasant king' Francis Tokay, who led an uprising against the nobility in 1697 and inflicted considerable harm on wine-growing in Hegyalja.) The name Tokay was easily committed to memory under any of those spellings. One wonders whether the success of the wine would have been achieved nearly so quickly if it had been burdened with the name given to the locale by the Magyars in the 10th century: Hímesudvar.

Tokajík. Originally Tokaj, it is intriguing to find the name of the Hegyaljan Tokaj replicated about 112 km (70 miles) to its north (formerly in Zemplén County, it is now in East Slovakia, hence the name alteration). It long postdates the town in Hegyalja, and does not go back earlier than around 1400. Despite never being more than a hamlet, its existence in Zemplén apparently caused the name 'Tisza-Tokaj' to be used in several 18th-century county documents to distinguish the Hegyalja town. How this distant place acquired its name is unknown. It could not have had anything to do with the confluence of rivers (*sâs-toka*), as in the case of Hegyalja's Tokaj. But its proximity to Turany nad Ondavou [see that entry] is reason to speculate that wine-growing might have been attempted, and that the local lord was thinking of Tokaj-hill. This would mean that Tokaj had acquired a fair reputation throughout Zemplén *before 1400*, even though it was not yet producing later-harvested wines. The place's name association ennabled a Viennese entrepreneur to entice settlers from Lower Austria in 1851; but most returned home upon finding nothing remotely like 'Tisza-Tokaj' in terms of agricultural possibilities.

Tőketerebes. [See the entry for Trebišov.]

TOLCSVA. Situated about midway from Sátoraljaújhely to Tokaj, Tolcsva is the only one of the four most vaunted Hegyalja communes that falls outside the region's southern line between Tokaj and Abaújszántó. The area's singularity is explained by its position along the Tolcsva creek, which offers plenty of slopes with a southerly exposure for wine-growing. Because of its potential for agriculture, the Tolcsva area probably had some habitation at the time of the Magyar arrival, and likely has been growing wine since that time. The name is generally thought to be that of the Magyar Tolcsva clan, partly because Anonymous wrote that Prince Árpád gave the area to one of his lieutentants with that name. However, since the village is beside the Tolcsva creek [see that entry] and the *–va* ending indicates a stream, there is a possibility that the name acturally derives from a Bulgaro-Slav word referring to a 'trickle' (*toch-*), the more so since the nearby locale of Sárazsadány had been settled by Bulgaro-Slavs in the 9th century. Either way, the locale must have acquired regional importance for wine-growing during the time of the Árpád Dynasty. Later, at the beginning of the 18th century, the Compagnia Graecorum was first established at Tolcsva by Greek wine merchants who obviously knew its name and reputation [see the entry for Greek Merchant Society, in Part I]. Timon, in 1728, and Szirmay, in 1803, stated that Tolcsva's wines withstood sea voyages, although the basis for the judgement is unknown.

[Historical vineyard area: 1873 - 550 ha.; 1913 - 410 ha.; 1940 - 427 ha.; 1963 - 464 ha.; 1990 - 539 ha.]

Vályi, in 1796, said that the "famous" Tolcsva wines came from the vineyard tracts "Cziróka, Kútpataka [*sic*], Gyapáros, Előhegy, Várhegy, Nagykő and Bikkoldal, and others." Szirmay, in 1798, specified the first three plus Paczoth as 1st Class, and the last four as 2nd Class. In 1851, Fényes reported Gyapáros and Kútpatka as "famous for the best wines" of Tolcsva. In 1867, Szabó/Török repeated Szirmay. Kossuth, in 1903, lauded Gyapáros as a "jewel" and mentioned Kincsem as one of "the foremost vineyards" of Hegyalja. According to Hidvéghy in 1950: "[Tolcsva's] wines of most outstanding quality are harvested in the vineyard-tracts Kincsem, Boszorkány, Gyapáros, Várhegy, Előhegy, Mandulás, etc." The land around Előhegy is dubbed Borkút (Wine-font) because it produces much of Tolcsva's wine [see Borkút, in Part III].

The town's vineyards are to its west, east, and south. Perhaps more than elsewhere in Hegyalja, it is difficult to link wine quality to soil composition. While all of the once famous names – Bikkoldal, Előhegy, Gyapáros, Kincsem, Kútpatka, Mandulás, Nagykő, Várhegy – are on clayey soil (*nyirok*), there is much variation in friability and stone content, the latter varying from 40-50 percent in the Előhegy-Várhegy area (east of town) to under 3 percent in Kincsem (south). The western area is notable for a wide range in the degree of 'fineness' in its stone-dust (*kőpor*) content. Gyapáros is unusual for volcanic ash in its northern part, as well as scattered splotches of up to 13 percent limestone. Overall, exposition seems to be the factor that accounts most for Tolcsva's high standing in Hegyalja wine quality.

Tolcsva Creek. This stream, arising far up in the Zemplén hills, flows southeastward through the commune of Tolcsva, and meets the Bodrog river nearly in the middle of the river's run along the eastern length of Hegyalja. It is a marked feature of the landscape, and its position likely was a major factor in referring to the surrounding area as 'Middle Hegyalja' during the late Middle Ages [see the entry for Bényei Creek]. The Tolcsva area would have been attractive for agriculture in early times, even before the arrival of the Magyars. Viticulturally, the creek stands out for having along its banks a concentration of famous vineyard names perhaps second only to that around Tokaj-hill. The name Tolcsva supposedly refers to one of the Magyar leaders at the time of the Conquest, but it could just as well be a Hungarianized version of a Bulgaro-Slav toponym and signify 'Trickle-stream.'

Transylvania. This region of today's northwestern Romania may seem far from the Upper Tisza region, but there were very strong historical ties between the two areas. One of the most important trade routes in medieval Hungary ran between Transylvania and the town of Kassa. Further, after Transylvania became an autonomous principality in the 16th century, it persistently sought to extend its control into the Upper Tisza. The leading families of the two regions overlapped considerably, beginning with the Szápolyais and culminating with the Rákóczis. All of the Transylvanian princes had a strong interest in Hegyalja, and the Rákóczis brought the region into its modern era.

Trautsohnfalva. [See the entry for Hercegkút.]

Trebišov (Tőketerebes). Situated in East Slovakia about 29 km (18 miles) north of Hungarian Hegyalja, this town was once the center of the Tőketerebes (or Terebes) Domain. The Domain had its own vineyards, and a document of 1567 stated that the fortress owned the Hegyalja community of Bodrogkeresztúr (UC 40:35). A vineyard sale of 1481 in Sátoraljaújhely shows that individuals in Terebes also owned vineyards in Hegyalja at an early date. Consequently, significant wine cellars were built at Terebes, which made the town a convenient place where merchants from further north, including Poland, could arrange for Hegyalja wine to be delivered for transshipment. But a period of lawlessness and brigandry erupted in the area during the mid-17th century, thus reducing the town's participation in transshipping wine.

Some habitation likely had been at this locale prior to the arrival of the Magyars. The Hungarian name of the place simply combines the Hungarian clan name *Tőke* with the pre-existing Slavic name *Trebesh*, which designated an area that had been cleared of forest. The Slavic name recalls the similarly named locale of Trâmbesh, near Veliko Târnovo, a one-time capital of the medieval Bulgarian Empire. The 11th-century grave of the Bulgarian prince Presian was found about 19 km (12 miles) to the northeast. [See the entry for Bulgarian Empire; and that for Presian, in Part I.]

Turány. [See the following entry.]

Turany nad Ondavou (Turány). Located in the Ondava river valley about 80 km (50 miles) north of Hegyalja, this village's name may be another geographical indication of the Bulgaro-Slav presence in the region at the time of the Magyar Conquest around 900 [see the entries for Bulgarian Empire and Ondava River]. Turány was once the northernmost wine-growing area in Zemplén, and the name suggests that it might also have been the oldest. In the Hungarian Byzantine (Greek) Catholic liturgical calendar, the name Turány equates to that of Saint Trifon, the Eastern Orthodox protector of vines. A conversion from Trifon to Turány in the Upper Tisza region can be explained by the fact that early Bulgaro-Slav Orthodox Christians knew the name as Trihun, rather than Trifon. [See the entry for Kabars, in Part I.] In accordance with Magyar linguistic habits, the name would have evolved as Trihun→Turiun→Turián→Turány. It needs to be added, though, that Slovak and Hungarian historians, unaware of the name Trihun and its connection to wine-growing, have posited other explanations for the name Turány, mainly a supposed pagan Slavic personal name, Tur. They could be right, of course, but the Bulgaro-Slav connection merits consideration in view of Turány's location just 19 km (12 miles) south of the Ondava river locale that originally bore the indisputably Bulgaro-Slav name Oustrachina [see the entry for Strachyna], and generally because of the Bulgarian Empire's interest in the Ondava valley [see Map #3 and the entry for Ondava: Turkic Remnant?].

A Bulgaro-Slav saint's name as a toponym in the northern Upper Tisza may seem unlikely. But maps of the Eperjes-Tokaj Hill-Chain indicate that Trihun would not have been the only Orthodox saint so honored. Between Tokaj in the south and Eperjes (Prešov) in the north, as many as five sites appear to have such an origin. Just south of Erdőbénye, a peak carries the name Bogdán (St. Bogdan); just west of Sátoraljaújhely is a peak named Száva (St. Sava); and in southern Sáros County, between Prešov and Košice, a village was named Bogdány (now Bohdanovce). In addition, south of Kassa (Košice), a village bore the name Enyicke (now Haniska), and abutting Prešov on the south there was a like named village. The Slovak historians Varsik and Uličný attributed the name Enyicke to Slovak *Jan-*. Yet, the earliest spellings all begin with Ene-, Eni-, or Eny-. Enyo is a Bulgaro-Slav 'agrarian' saint; Enyovden, or 'Enyo's Day,' is a rural holiday marking midsummer. How much more likely that two rural locales in an area of interest to the Bulgarian Empire carry Enyo's name instead of two ordinary Johns. As with everything else concerning the Bulgaro-Slavs in the Upper Tisza and Hegyalja, even their saints are ignored, although the Bulgarian Empire had fallen into the sphere of Orthodoxy in the 9th century. Incidentally, the five sites noted are arrayed at intervals along a distance of only about 85 km (50 miles) south to north. [See Map #3.]

Újpatak. [See the entry for Hercegkút.]
Ungvár. [See the entry for Uzhhorod.]

Upper Hungary. (*Felső Magyarország*) Popularly referred to as the Uplands (*Felvidék*), Upper Hungary was the historical quadrant of the Kingdom of Hungary of which Hegyalja was a part. From a strict geographical standpoint, it denoted the mostly hilly areas that ascended towards the Carpathian mountains along the northern rim of the Kingdom; hence, the Eperjes-Tokaj Hill-Chain towards the eastern end was naturally viewed as an integral part of the Uplands, as was Hegyalja because of its location in that chain. But, during the Ottoman occupation (1526-1683), Upper Hungary formed most of Royal Hungary (excepting the western arc of territory), and consequently notions about it expanded to include lowland areas immediately to the south that also remained outside Ottoman control. During that period, the Uplands grew in population because of Hungarian refugees from the Ottoman areas and a further influx of German townspeople and miners. Thus, this section of Hungary became extremely important for the development of Hegyalja, in terms of both consumption and trade of wine. The southern spread of Slavic languages, particularly Slovak in the west and center, and mixed Slovak-Rusyn-Polish dialects in the east, after the Rákóczi debacles that occurred around 1700, led to the 20th century misperception that Upper Hungary had been synonymous with Slovakia, and thus, a historical continuation of Great Moravia [see the entry for Moravia, Great].

Upper Tisza Region. (*Felső Tisza Vidék*) The history of Hegyalja is bound up with that of the greater region of which it is a part: the northern watershed of the Tisza river. This area fans out north of the southern line of Hegyalja (Abaújszántó to Tokaj) along several rivers: (west to east) Hernád (Hornad in Slovak), Tapoly (Topľa), Szekcső (Sekčov), Bodrog, Ondava, Ciróka (Ciroché), Laborc (Laborec), Ung (Uzh in Ukrainian), Tisza (Tisa). As settlement expanded northward towards the old Hungarian border with Poland during the 11th to 13th centuries, trade in wine also grew, and created the first interest in Hegyalja wine outside its own vicinity. Following the Ottoman occupation of Lower Hungary that began in 1526, the population of the Upper Tisza area swelled with refugees from the south, again favoring the purchase of wine from Hegyalja. Virtually throughout the history of the Kingdom of Hungary, a certain cultural 'unity' was fostered by the Bishopric of Eger, which had ecclesiastical dominion over the Roman Catholic Church in all the counties of the Upper Tisza [see the entry Eger Bishopric, in Part I].

Wine-growing in the region was influenced by ethnic developments, and the Upper Tisza is notable for its unique ethnic history within the Kingdom of Hungary. Because of its position relative to the Baltic and the Aegean seas, it had been a major corridor for the the movement of people since ancient times, and a notable trading route for the Greeks in antiquity. Celts and early Germanic tribes spent time there later on [see the entry for Hernád River]. The Romans are thought to have entered the area in the 5th century, but they made no lasting penetration. In the early Middle Ages (roughly around 500-600), Slavs from the north and east began to enter to a minor extent, but were too small in number to resist the Avars [see that entry, in Part I], and the resultant Avar-Slav populace was absorbed into the Bulgarian Empire by the 9th century. [See the entry for Moravia, Great.]. During the 10th to 12th centuries, they were mingling with the Magyars, Germans, Italians, and Vlachs (the Romanians of later history).

With this background in mind, it is understandable that wine-growing in the Upper Tisza was not uniform. Even if the Balkan (Macedonian-Thracian) tradition of the Bulgaro-Slavs was dominant throughout when the Magyars arrived, around 900, it likely receded southward during the 13th-14th centuries, to Abaújvár, in the Hernád valley, eastward to the village of Zemplén, in the Bodrogköz. North of that line, Balkan grape varieties, wine-growing methods, and wine-making practices most likely were supplanted by Italian habits, and to a lesser extent, German. This was a consequence of Italian settlement in the Tapoly and Ciróka valleys, as well as German colonization along the upper Ondava, from the valley of Sztropkó (Stropkov) south to Michalovce. Further, King Louis I, in the 14th century, encouraged wine-growing wherever possible. But climatic cooling beginning in that century rolled back wine-growing in the northern area over the next three centuries, which benefited the marketing of Hegyalja's wines in the region. [See the entries for Bardejov, Tokajík, and Vinné; and also for Drugeth and Italians, in Part I.]

Nothing specific is known about the kind of wine grown in the northern Upper Tisza. Especially, the great retraction in cultivated area left no trace of the grape varieties that had been grown. The only safe presumption is that mostly they were white ones that did not need a long growing season, and that some had been brought from western lands, whether by colonists or religious orders, though possibly also several varieties when Poles came in an earlier times, since wine-growing was still an activity in southern Poland. (Several of the obscure old Hegyalja varieties discussed by Balassa, in 1991, might be relevant.) Still, there are several reasons to suppose that significant differences from Hegyalja emerged in the northern Upper Tisza: performance of the initial wine-making tasks indoors; the absence of 'soaking'; the use of the wine-press; and the use of barrels larger than the Hegyalja *antal* [see the entry for Gönci Barrel, in Part IV]. But, as Hegyalja was coming into its era of commercial significance at this time, it did not feel compelled to alter its ways. Thus did Hegyalja and vicinity become the last outpost of Balkan wine-growing and wine-making in the Upper Tisza.

Uzhhorod (Ungvár). Situated along the Ung (Uzh) river about 53 km (33 miles) east of Hegyalja, the fortress (*vár*) apparently dated to before the arrival of the Magyars at the end of the 9th century. A town grew around it after the Tatar invasion of 1241-1242, and it eventually became the seat of Ung County. It was also the easternmost town in the Upper Tisza region to have an active interest in Tokaji wine. This is hardly surprising since Ungvár was owned by the Drugeths [see that entry, in Part I] from 1318 to 1678. A document of 1683 noted that the town had vineyard property in Erdőbénye and Tállya at that time (UC 88:60 (a)). Further, the Drugeths brought the Pauliners in 1384, and the Jesuits in 1646. In his Tokaji report of 1773, Sylvester Douglass noted that "the Jesuits college at Ungwar has a considerable share of the best wines [*i.e.*, vineyards]" of Hegyalja. Several of the vineyards were in Tállya. Further, Ungvár was a center for Greek traders until well into the 18th century, in other words, during the time of their importance to the Tokaji wine trade. The town's onetime significance to Hegyalja was reflected in the so called 'Ungvár cellar complex' (*Ungvári pince telep*) dug out of stone on the northern side of Sátoraljaújhely. Also indicative of the town's involvement with Hegyalja is the name of the hill called Ingvár [sic], 153 km (95 miles) to the southwest, near Monok. Ungvár was transferred to Czechoslovakia following the First World War, to the Soviet Union after the Second World War, and finally to Ukraine after the breakup of the USSR, hence the spelling Uzhhorod on current maps. [Also, see the second paragraph of *Puttonyos* System, in Part IV.]

VÁMOSÚJFALU. This small village is situated along the Tolcsva creek, between Tolcsva to the north and Olaszliszka to the south. Its name signifies 'tariff-new-village' and reflects its origin in the 14th century as a tariff (*vám*) collection site. Probably because of this function, it was absorbed by the Tokaj Domain at least as early as the mid-15th century. Never large to begin with, Vámosújfalu was much reduced as a result of the Ottoman Turkish incursion into Hegyalja in the late-16th century. For a time, what remained of it was known simply as Kis-Tolcsva (Little Tolcsva). At the beginning of the 17th century, it came into the possession of the Sárospatak Domain and the Lórántffy family; and the the Rákóczis became owners through marriage with the Lórántffys in 1616. However, the confiscation of Rákóczi properties by the Habsburgs towards the end of the 17th century resulted in a virtual depopulation of the village. Only in the first-half of the 18th century did repopulation begin.

[Historical vineyard area: 1873 - 104 ha.; 1913 - 43 ha.; 1940 - 47 ha.; 1963 - 39 ha.; 1990 - 61 ha.]

Even if only a minor activity initially, wine-growing at Vámosújfalu must have been encouraged by proximity to Tolcsva and Olaszliszka, and later been intensified by connection to the Tokaj and Sárospatak domains. The village's vineyards are located along Szőlőhegy (Vineyard-hill), going northwest towards Tolcsva. Soil generally is of a relatively loose clayey sort (*nyirok*), though with high stony content, up to 30-50 percent in the higher parts. But Hidvéghy, in 1950, noted that most of the vineyards have an unfavorable, northeastern exposure "which is also apparent in the quality of the wine." In 1796, Vályi stated that Vámosújfalu had "vineyard hills producing good wine," an appraisal that might have reflected the village's possession of a section of the highly regarded Rány vineyard-tract, even if perhaps a less favorable part than that belonging to Olaszliszka. Although there is a scarcity of historical detail, it is likely that the village's best vineyard sections never recovered after phylloxera. [From the comments noted, the inclusion of Vámosújfalu in demarcations of Hegyalja appears to be a rare instance supporting Balassa's (1991) thought that Hegyalja suffered some qualitative 'dilution' as the appellation region was expanded. But that is hardly 'recent,' since it goes back to the 17th century. (Also, see the entry for Makkoshotyka.)]

Varannó. [See the entry for Vranov nád Topl'ou.]

*Végardó. This onetime village along the Bodrog river was included among the Hegyalja villages specified by Hungarian legislation of 1893 and 1908. But it was absorbed administratively by the town of Sárospatak in 1965. It is known from Anonymous that Végardó originated as a tariff collection site before 1200. Most likely it was founded to serve that purpose for Sárospatak, since *vég-* signifies 'end' or 'limit,' while *ardó* referred to forest land, thus suggesting the outskirts of a settlement. It can be supposed that Végardó continued in that capacity, since during the 14th through 17th centuries it belonged to the Sárospatak Domain. In fact, a document of 1567 stated that Végardó's vineyards "are in Sárospatak" (UC 40:35). Because of the connection to Patak, the village was a property of the Rákóczis. But it ceased to exist for several years after the failure of Francis Rákóczi II's anti-Habsburg rebellion at the beginning of the 18th century. Perhaps this explains why a document of 1712 (UC 6:19 (a)) refers to a *Szőllős Vég-Ardó* ('Vineyard-Vég-Ardó'), as though to distinguish what remained of the place. Prince Trautsohn saw to Végardó's resettlement in 1720.

[Historical vineyard area: 1873 - 5 ha.; 1913 - n/a.; 1940 - 5 ha.; 1963 - 3 ha.; 1990 - n/a]

Végardó was always among the smallest Hegyalja producers, with only one vineyard hill, Somlyód, located to its northwest. It is somewhat peculiar in being a lonely hill outcropping surrounded by level land. Its vineyard area is on the south-facing slope, on medium compact clayey soil (*nyirok*) that sporadically contains a significant amount of crushed stone fragments. Susanna Lórántffy was an owner there, and a letter of hers of 1634 indicates that Somlyód must have been among the earliest Hegyalja vineyard-tracts from which botrytis *aszú* wine ("*Azzu Szeoleo borat*") was produced (Détshy, 1973). [See the entry for Somlyód, in Part III.]

**Veľká Tŕňa (Nagytoronya). Lying just north of Malá Tŕňa in southeastern Slovakia, this village would have been the northernmost Hegyalja village if it had been included by the Hungarian legislation of 1893 or 1908, but it was not. Fényes, in 1851, specifically stated that Nagytoronya did not belong: "Its vineyard hill grows good *table* wine [emphasis added], but this cannot be counted with Hegyalja." Nevertheless, Slovakian legislation of 1959 declared Veľká Tŕňa a Tokaji wine-producing locale. Hungary has disputed this inclusion within the framework of the European Union in order for Slovakia to use the Tokaji name in marketing its wines.

Veľký Kamenec (Nagy Kövesd). Among the easternmost significant wine villages of former Zemplén County, Nagy Kövesd lies to the southeast of the Island-hills, and well east of the Bodrog river. Consequently, it was never given consideration for inclusion in a legally defined Hegyalja. Nevertheless, it is of interest that Kossuth, in 1903, stated that "the wine grown in the better situated vineyards of the Kövesdi hill oftentimes throws into confusion even those most thoroughly acquainted with Hegyalja wine." Presumably, though, he might only have been referring to table wines. Still, the comment illustrates some of the difficulties in earlier centuries in demarcating Hegyalja. [See the entries for Ratold, in Part I; and for Kövesd, in Part III.]

<u>VINIČKY</u> (SZŐLŐSKE). Located about 5.5 km (3.5 miles) east of Sátoraljaújhely, beside the western bank of the Bodrog river, the village of Viničky has an exceptionally long history of settlement and wine production. The earliest documentary mention is from 1029, when it was recorded as *Zeuleus*, in reference to *szőlő*, the Hungarian word for 'vineyard.' But its vineyards might date back earlier than that, since Viničky is close to the village of Zemplén, which was a fortified site at the time of the Magyar Conquest at the end of the 9th century. Incidentally, a number of villages along the Bodrog have carried the river's name as a forename, and around 1700, this one was occasionally recorded as 'Bodrog-Szőlőske' (UC 117:86).

[Historical vineyard area: 1865 - 97 ha.; 1956 - 65 ha.]

Viničky's vineyard hills are arrayed from west to northeast of the village. Most of the area has a southerly exposure, though some vineyards face southwest or west. Soils are clayey (*nyirok*), and more or less stony. The most favorable vineyards are on the steeper, south-facing parts of the Dióska, Gerenda-földek, Hegyköz, Nyúlugró, Pipó, and Pósa tracts; lesser areas are Berek and Hegyfark. [See the entries for Nyúl- and Pósa, in Part III.]

Vinné (Vinna). This village, several miles north of Michalovce, or about 50 km (31 miles) north-northeast of Hegyalja, had ties to that region, but is also of interest with regard to the history of the Upper Tisza. A church architecturally of Roman type was constructed here in the late-9th century, and its name was 'Holy Cross.' But it is not known who caused it to be built. It could have been the Romans themselves, as a challenge to Bulgarian overlordship, or simply to spread Latin Christianity. But Great Moravia is a more likely possibility. At that time, Bulgaria was in alliance with Moravia and also flirting with Rome (to the consternation of the Byzantine Empire), and therefore might have countenanced a Latin church. The locale was very suitable for the vine, and as a presumed 'colony' of Great Moravia, this would intimate Frankish habits in wine-growing. In any case, Holy-Cross (Szent-Kereszt) hill was the major vineyard site during the 15th century, when the noble Eödönffys were at their peak and involved in large-scale wine output. Although wine production declined subsequently, the Szent-Kereszt tract still existed at Vinna in 1761 (UC 146:12). The tract of that name in Tarcal possibly had a connection to Vinna. [See the entries for Gombos and Vinnai, in Part III.] The origin of Vinna's property in Hegyalja owed to its having a fortress, Vinna Vár, which belonged to the Nagy Mihály Domain [see the entry for Michalovce]. A document of 1689 (UC 176:10) shows that Vinna Vár had a vineyard on Tolcsva-hegy hill, presumably in reference to Erdőbénye [see the entry for Peres, in Part III]. Although Vinna was on the border of Zemplén County, it was actually in Ung County.

Vistula. [See the entry for Dunajec-Vistula.]

Vizsoly. Located in the Hernád river valley about midway between the Hegyalja town of Abaújszántó and the trade center of Kassa (Košice) to the north, Vizsoly was the center of a small fiefdom around the 13th century. This was at the height of German settlement in the Upper Tisza, and the Vizsoly fiefdom was unusual in being ethnically based, a German-language island. The craft skills possessed in Vizsoly's little realm were significant, and proved useful in various ways in Hegyalja. The focal point turned out to be Gönc [see that entry], not Vizsoly itself.

Vranov nád Topľou (Varannó). Located 55 km (34 miles) north of Hegyalja, this town of central Zemplén, near the confluence of the Topľa (Tapoly) and Ondava rivers, developed around an early fortress and became the seat of the Varannó Domain. The early owners included the Perényi and Rozgonyi families, both of whom took an active interest in Hegyalja wine. Varannó also became an important tariff collection point as wine exports to Poland grew. But, in the 16th century, predations on commerce by bandits in the area between Varannó and Trebišov (to the south) disrupted wine trade, which resulted in diverting ever more trade through the Sáros County towns to the west. By 1711, the once commercially significant transshipment cellars of the Varannó Domain were hardly even in use. However, the domain possessed vineyards in Hegyalja as late as the end of the 17th century, at Erdőbénye (UC 88:60 (a) – 1683), Bodrogkeresztúr (Szécs-Keresztúr) and Szőlőske (UC 4:24 – 1691). [See the entry for Monyorós-Csicsva.]

Zakynthos. Long known in Europe by its Italian name, Zante, this Greek island in the Ionian Sea holds some interest for researchers of Hegyalja history because of several overlaps that are difficult to explain. Historically, the island's most valued grape variety was the white *goustoulidi*, which very possibly was the same as, or related to, the *gohér* variety that made possible the first *aszú* wines of Hegyalja. The *goustoulidi* was the basis for making a sweet wine, known as *lianorogi* ('small-berry'), using the ancient *protropon* technique that was identical to the method for *eszencia*; and it was noted in 1782 that *gohér* was the variety most suited for making *eszencia*. But Zakynthos also produced red wine, which was being traded under the name Romanía in the 16th century. A variant of that name, *rumonya/romonya*, was a varietal name in Hegyalja. It is uncertain, though, how these varieties might have reached Hegyalja. One possibility is direct transferal, if Zakynthos was included in the migration from the northwestern Peloponnesus arranged in the mid-13th century. Alternatively, Zakynthos may have been a source of grape varieties for Dalmatia, whence some also reached Hegyalja. [See the entry for Greeks, in Part I; and Balkan Influences (#11), *Gohér*, Grape Varieties, and *Protropon*, in Part IV.]

Zemplén. [See the entry for Zemplín.]

Zemplén County. (See Map #2) Certainly for Hungarians, as well as East Slovakians, the geographical concept of Hegyalja, and consequently the name of Tokaji wine, will ever be associated with the former Hungarian county of Zemplén. Historically, all but four of the Hegyalja locales belonged to Zemplén; and by the end of the 19th century, only Abaújszántó did not. By all accounts, the Magyars occupied the area of Hegyalja and its environs right after entering the Carpathian basin. Beginning in the early-13th century, a county began to develop gradually as an administrative unit. Lower, or southern, Zemplén, was the Szerencs district, and it extended from Szerencs to Sátoraljaújhely; Upper, or northern, Zemplén, extended from Sátoraljaújhely to Monyorós-Csicsva [see that entry]. As settlement spread north during the 14th century, the county reached the present Slovakia-Poland border. Zemplén was then spoken of in terms of southern, central, and northern parts. The southern part included Hegyalja, but also the county's territory south of there; this area would become the 'Hegyalja District' (*járás*) in the 1840s. [Regarding the name Zemplén, see the second paragraph of the entry for Zemplín, below.]

During its early history, wine-growing was widespread in the lowland, river valley parts of the county, even if it was not appreciable north of the central area (today's Vranov and Michalovce). Indicative of the importance of viticulture is that, at the beginning of the 18th century, the County established eight price categories according to an average year's output. The categories were geographic, and even at this relatively late date a good deal of territory north of Hegyalja was included. The lowest numbered categories reflected lower quality and were assigned the lowest prices. Consequently, the 'first-class' areas were all in the north of the county, such as Homonna (Humenné) and Varannó (Vranov). Conversely, the highest numbered categories reflected high quality and were assigned the highest prices. Thus, the 'eighth class' included Mád, Mezőzombor, Tállya, Tarcal, and Tokaj. [See the Borovszki volume, which gives no further information about the content of the eight categories. Other sources did not mention the action.]

With the great increase in the economic importance of Tokaji wine in the 17th century, the County administration became ever more active in trying to regulate Hegyalja production and trade, and also in defining the region geographically. Early significant measures include the separate harvesting of botrytized grapes in 1655, a 'tax on Greeks' (*taxa graecorum*) in 1689, and the vineyard classification of 1772. Moreover, the royal order of 1737 delimiting Hegyalja was actually initiated, researched, and pushed by the County. However, the aforementioned 'price classification' of wine-growing areas of the county had the unforeseen effect of causing some merchants to look northward in falsifying Tokaji wine. In the early 18th century, it became common practice for Jewish merchants to buy thin wines from the north, to which illegally obtained *eszencia* was added so as to make either kosher or non-kosher 'Hegyalja' wines.

Virtually a chapter unto itself is occupied by the subject of accommodating Jews in the production and trade of wine (see Balassa, pages 581-619). The period lasted from the mid-18th century to the mid-19th century. From around 1790 until around 1830, it was marked by contradictory actions, though usually aimed at limiting Jewish involvement to kosher wine, and even then with some restrictions. Zemplén being an ethnically diverse county, its officialdom did not show ethnic bias against Jews. For one thing, the Jews at first were small in number and were not seen differently where wine was concerned than other exogenous elements of the population, such as the Greeks, especially not in connection with wine fraud. What made the County view the Jewish situation more critically was the rapid rise in the Jewish population in Zemplén, and throughout the Upper Tisza, in the late-18th century (a result of the partitions of Poland), which caused kosher wine production to threaten the quality of non-kosher wine. The one consistent feature of the various County regulations to restrict Jewish wine activity was the intention to keep botrytis grapes and wine out of their hands. But there was another aspect of the issue that differed greatly from the period when the Greeks were the County's main concern. Namely, the timing of Jewish interest coincided, increasingly in the 19th century, with the political pressure developing behind free trade. Most of the nobility was opposed, and they saw Jewish commercial activity in Hegyalja as a major threat. This proved a correct reading, since the opening of the wine trade to Jews in the mid-19th century in effect spelled the end of aristocratic privilege vis-à-vis smallholders. [See the entries for Mád; for Jews, in Part I; and for Kosher Wine, in Part IV.]

Zemplén Hills. These hills comprise the southernmost area of the Eperjes-Tokaj Hill-Chain. They begin at the Hegyköz ('amidst the mountains') area just north of Sátoraljaújhely, between the Hernád river and Ronyva creek, and extend south to Abaújszántó on the west and Tokaj on the east, roughly a triangle. Although the hills encompass Hegyalja, only their eastern and southern rims actually form it. The area is entirely in Borsod-Abaúj-Zemplén County now, but historically only the westernmost areas belonged to Abaúj County, and the rest to Zemplén.

Of special note about the hills is that ever since Hegyalja switched from skins to wood for wine storage, the hill forests to the rear of the vineyards have been the source of oak for barrels. It turned out to be an exceptionally favorable sort of oak (*quercus petraea*), greatly suited to the long maturation of wine. The reddish highlights of long-aged Tokaji *aszú* are attributed to it.

Zemplín (Zemplén). The village whose name became that of Zemplén County was an existing settlement at the time of the Magyar Conquest. More accurately, it was a fortified site, though no doubt engaged in some agricultural activity. It retained importance later, too, and served as the de facto county seat, with most county meetings taking place there from around 1300 until 1685. According to the chronicler Anonymous, the Magyar leader Árpád received the emissaries of the Bulgarian prince Zalán at Zemplén [see the entry for *Szlankamenka*, in Part IV].

Whether or not it had vines at the time of the Magyar arrival, Zemplén was a wine-growing locale later on and had significant cellaring space beneath the fort by the early-11th century. The cellars might originally have been built because of royal vineyard land in nearby Kistoronya (Malá Třňa). The fort also had early ownership of the locales of Ond and Monok in southern Hegyalja. The village's position along the Bodrog river influenced some people to think of Zemplén as the northeasternmost point of Hegyalja when the region was just a producer of ordinary wine. Even in 1743, Zemplén was listed among the Hegyalja communities having a vineyard 'hill-master,' although that might simply have been an old administrative habit. However, by the 20th century, viticulture had disappeared from the locale. The village is located about 14 km (9 miles) northeast of Sátoraljaújhely, near the confluence of the Bodrog and Latorca (Latorica) rivers.

Except for its derivation from the Slavic word *zem* ('land'), the name's origin is debatable. 'Zem-plén' suggests *zem-plna*, or 'fat (fruitful)-land.' But the name occurred only as 'Zemlin' and 'Zemlyn' (without a *p*) in early times; it appeared as Zemlin on the first map of Hungary, from 1528; and as late as 1684 (UC 18:20). There had been a medieval Bulgaro-Slav fortress with the name Zemlân (Земльн) along the Struma river [see the entry for Macedonia]; and 'Zemlin' (Zemplén), too, was a fortified site. The two locales are separated by about 724 km (450 miles), or less than the two Ostrakinas [see the entry for Strachyna]. No name resembling 'Zemlin' is found in central or western Slovakia (*i.e.*, the onetime Great Moravian part of Slovakia). In short, even in the name Zemplén we likely are looking at 9th-century Bulgaro-Slav territorial expansion. [This explanation of the name contradicts Varsik (see the Bibliography). But Varsik, in failing to look at medieval Bulgarian history, was unaware of Zemlân, or of Bulgaro-Slav interest in the Upper Tisza. Nor did he realize that the Bulgaro-Slavs were merely following in the footsteps – literally – of the Greeks who had been traveling through the Upper Tisza since antiquity. See the entry Bulgars: Bulgaro-Phobia, Part I.]

*   *   *

PART II

ESSAY

The Historical Development and Delineation of the Hegyalja Wine Region

There have been two eras in the delineation of Hegyalja as a wine region: pre-1640 and post-1640. The date 1640 has a double significance: 1) beginning in 1640, the Rákóczi family came into possession of virtually all of Hegyalja, and in 1641 imposed the first regulation of wine-growing for the region; and 2) the rise of botrytis *aszú* wine of the sort known today began its ascent as the premier regional wine type circa 1640.

Before 1640, the name Hegyalja had developed gradually as a colloquial and somewhat vague geographical notion that did not always necessarily relate to wine. It also had an administrative or quasi-political usage, which created confusion, because for a long time it did not coincide with its use as a topographical name [see the entry for Hegyalja]. But, subsequently, the increasing fame and economic importance of *aszú* made it ever more necessary, and practicable, to exclude from the unfolding specification of a Hegyalja wine region those locales that were not suitably situated to produce wine of like kind and quality. Also notable is that the aging of Tokaji wine for several years was already so typical, that it became a means of distinguishing between areas that truly merited the name, and those whose wines resembled Tokaji for only a short time.

I. The Early Era, pre-1640

This period was characterized by indefiniteness about the topographical name Hegyalja. The term had administrative denotations that precluded its exclusive association with a wine-growing area. Further, insofar as wine-growing was intimated by the name, there was ambiguity about the areas that fell within it, because no one type of wine had established itself as a criterion for inclusion. It is instructive that Zemplén County changed the number and composition of its districts (*járás*-es) several times after the 16th century, and not until the 1840s was a 'Hegyalja Járás' created that was centered on the Zemplén hills, though even this included the southernmost stretch of the county that was not part of the topographical, wine-growing Hegyalja.

Hegyalja means 'foothills' and Tokaj-Hegyalja refers to the southernmost section of the foothills known as the Eperjes-Tokaj Hill-Chain, but most of all to the section in southern Zemplén County, or the Zemplén hills. It is unlikely that the name Hegyalja was in use before the 13th century, since the chronicler Anonymous likely would have used it when writing of this very territory, circa 1200. But neither is the term mentioned in later 13th century documents.

The first documentary indication that an area in the Eperjes-Tokaj range had become known as Hegyalja is from 1339, when a man was referred to as "Ladislaus of Hegyalja" (DL 56894). The document concerned what was then northerly Zemplén County, and since the term *hegyalja* might to some extent have become associated with wine-growing, it can be speculated that "Ladislaus of Hegyalja" resided somewhere in the southern part of the Eperjes-Tokaj hills. But it is also possible that Hegyalja in this instance was a district name only tangentially related to wine, since the name retained that aspect much later as well. Nevertheless, in an era long before later-harvested wines, and when the vine was far more widespread along the Eperjes-Tokaj hills, the term Hegyalja may generally have been only a notional one that people understood variously as regards the territory covered by it.

Nevertheless, the first hint of a distinct identity for the area now known as Hegyalja goes back much earlier than the term itself, at least as far back as Anonymous, circa 1200. In recording the story of the Magyar Conquest of Hungary, he related that Árpád presented one of his lieutenants with the territory extending from Sátor-hill, by Sátoraljaújhely, south to the Tolcsva creek (in all likelihood at its confluence with the Bodrog river), which is more than half the distance to Tokaj-hill. Moreover, Anonymous told of the Magyars' arrival at Tokaj-hill (which his contemporaries knew as Tarcal-hill), and then their turn westward to Szerencs. While there can be doubt about his account vis-à-vis realities around 896, Anonymous was conveying the names of the southern Zemplén locales that were familiar to everyone in his time who would be reading his chronicle; and the area covered does largely coincide with what is now the Tokaj-Hegyalja wine district.

Clear indications that the southerly foothills of the Eperjes-Tokaj range would acquire their own identity grew out of political and ecclesiastical circumstances during the late period of the Árpád kings, not long after Anonymous. At that time, in the early-13th century, an ecclesiastical (if not an administrative) distinction was made between Upper (northern) and Lower (southern) Zemplén. Lower Zemplén was referred to as Szerencs, and it extended from the vicinity of the town of that name northeastward along the foothills to just north of Sátoraljaújhely; thus, it was practically identical to today's Hegyalja wine region in north-to-south length, even though it is highly unlikely that wine would have been a motivation in separating Lower from Upper Zemplén in that era, since vines were cultivated throughout.

However, it was of specific importance to wine-growing that in the same century the Roman Catholic Church was focusing its efforts at diocesan organization and development in this Szerencs district, and its religious orders were establishing monasteries and vineyards there; indeed, several piously named vineyard hills and tracts of Hegyalja might date to that time. Yet another early factor favoring eventual recognition of the southern foothills as a wine district was the development of the feudal domains of important landholding families during the late-13th and early-14th centuries, in the wake of the Tatar invasion of 1241-1242. Wine-growing was a significant activity on virtually all the domains in the vicinity of the Eperjes-Tokaj hills.

It was because of the flowering of the feudal domains that an image of Hegyalja as a wine-growing *entity* began to take shape, but most especially in the 16th century, when the domains became the subject of the economic accountings known as *urbária*. In granting the establishment of a domain, the Hungarian kings expected that its economic potential would be exploited fully, not merely as an enrichment of the Royal Treasury, but also to ensure living conditions and sufficient population density to protect against attacks by foreign hordes, as had happened during the Tatar invasion. This threat was again very real after the Ottoman Turks began their conquest of Hungary from the south in 1526; the Ottomans attacked parts of Hegyalja in the 1560s, and as late as the 1670s. During the 16th and 17th centuries, the domains in what remained of the Kingdom of Hungary ('Royal Hungary') occasionally compiled an *urbárium*, or a detailed description of economic resources in each of the towns and villages. The *urbárium* of the Tokaj Domain for 1581 of course gave an account of vineyard resources, and the mention of wine-growing places therein became, in effect, a focus for conceptions about an integral wine region.

Already, though, popular thought had been drifting towards an 'inclusion-exclusion' frame of mind about Hegyalja towns and villages. This was spurred by two key changes that occurred within the space of less than a century, between the late-15th century and the last third of the 16th century. In both instances, the vintage date was pushed back, the first time for uncertain reasons and the second time because of the introduction of a third hoeing. With the vintage moved from September to late-October, shriveled grapes (whether or not affected by botrytis) became the prized product, and it started to be noticed which locales and sites produced the best quality. The southern part of Hegyalja got a headstart in repute because it benefited most, in terms of shriveled grape output, by the first delay in vintage date, towards 1500, and this would color popular notions about the extent of the region for over two centuries more.

By the early 1600s, Zemplén County officialdom was feeling a need to give some shape to the conception of Hegyalja as a wine-growing region. This was, however, incidental to dealing with specific issues rather than an effort at demarcation as such. Hegyaljan wine-growing in this period was a frequent topic of county and municipal meetings, especially in connection with paying vineyard workers, a cost that was increasing dramatically because of competition for day-laborers by owners residing outside Hegyalja. But the scant documentary evidence is sketchy, and indicates a considerable range of viewpoints and motivations. A notation of 1622, from the town records of Mád, refers to "the seven Hegyalja towns," while a Zemplén County document of around 1625 addresses the payment of workers "from Sátoraljaújhely to Tokaj and from Abaújszántó to Tarcal, [and] Monok to Mezőzombor," though without specifying them as 'the locales of Hegyalja' or any similar indication of cohesiveness.

Despite the tendency towards a more restrictive notion of Hegyalja, not even in the late-16th and early-17th centuries was its name always associated with wine. It is notable that when Tokaji wine made its debut on the European stage, at the Council of Trent, in 1562, it was not identified as coming from Hegyalja, but specifically from Tállya. Likewise, commercial records indicate that wine traders did not use the term Hegyalja in their ledgers. The lack of a commonly understood identity for the term reflected its continued use as a quasi-administrative and geographical name outside the context of wine. For instance, in the 17th century, there was a Protestant 'Hegyalja District' (*Districtus Submontaneus*), in the sense of a diocese. As late as 1704, a communiqué urging rebels to join in Francis Rákóczi II's anti-Habsburg war referred to "Upper, Middle and Lower Hegyalja," in the general sense of 'the southern hill country' of Zemplén, not merely the narrow band of hills that supported vines.

II. The Modern Era, post-1640

This period was characterized by conscious effort to narrow the Hegyalja name to wine-growing, and to be specific about its geographical extent. The motivation at first may have been narrowly pecuniary on the part of the Rákóczis, to gain wealth in support of their anti-Habsburg wars, but later more generally commercial, based on the rise of botrytis *aszú* as the characteristic product.

The outset of the modern era is unmistakeably marked by the institution of regulations in 1641 to govern wine-growing virtually throughout the area that would later be Hegyalja. This landmark action had been ushered in by developments in the ownership of domains, whereby the Princes Rákóczi became absolutely predominant in the Upper Tisza region. The Rákóczis had been extending their power from Transylvania in the aftermath of the Ottoman Turkish occupation of Lower Hungary in the early-16th century, and they gradually acquired territories in Zemplén County. They achieved great regional importance in 1616, when George Rákóczi I married Susanna Lórántffy, a member of one of the most prominent landholding families of Zemplén. The marriage made the Rákóczis the lords of the Sárospatak and Sátoraljaújhely domains in northern Hegyalja. But, in 1640, the Rákóczis also acquired the Tokaj Domain in the south, which thus put virtually all of the future Tokaj-Hegyalja within their purview, and led to the regulations of 1641. Furthermore, they acquired the Regéc Domain, which included several later Hegyalja communities, including the most extensive of all, Tállya.

The second-half of the 17th century was extremely difficult for Hegyalja, and for the Rákóczis, first because of renewed military pressure from the Ottomans to bring the Upper Tisza area under their dominion, and subsequently because of the anti-Habsburg activity of the Protestant aristocracy (with the Rákóczis usually at the forefront), as well as peasant unrest in Zemplén County. As a result, further development towards a Hegyalja wine region stalled. Indeed, it suffered a setback because of widespread destruction and out-migration.

However, there is 'negative' documentary proof that the notion of Hegyalja as a wine-growing region was now becoming permanent, namely, in documents pertaining to the Habsburgs' large-scale confiscation of Hegyalja properties from rebellious nobles and patricians in the late-17th and early-18th centuries. These confiscations took place throughout the later demarcated region. One of the most telling documents is from 1674-1677, in which it is recorded that Stephan Baxa's vineyards in Sátoraljaújhely, Erdőbenye, Olaszliszka, Tolcsva, and Tokaj had been confiscated (UC 8:16 (a). This covers the north-south length of present-day Hegyalja, and suggests that the Baxa family had a firm conception of the region [see the entry for Baksa, in Part I]. There is also a document of 1683-1685 (UC 113:36 (a)) that mentions stocks of wine held further north (either at the Vinna fortress or the Makovica Domain); and these wines were from Sátoraljaújhely, Sárospatak, Tokaj, Tállya, and Szerencs, which again covers the length of Hegyalja, and suggests that Polish merchants 'recognized' this expanse of territory as Hegyalja, probably based on the Rákóczis' 'demarcation.'

A particularly valuable set of documents is a threesome from 1674 (two on November 7) and 1675. These were the work of Martin Halápi, of the Szepes Chamber [see those entries, in Part I]. His data pertained specifically to the Chamber's fiscal vineyards of "*Submontanarum*" (Hegyalja). Altogether, the three documents list 22 locales of modern Hegyalja (alphabetically): Bekecs, Bodrogkeresztúr, Bodrogkisfalud, Bodrogolaszi, Erdőbénye, Erdőhorváti, Mád, Makkoshotyka, Mezőzombor, Monok, Olaszliszka, Ond, Rátka, Sárospatak, Sátoraljaújhely, Szegi, Szerencs, Tállya, Tarcal, Tokaj, Tolcsva, Vámosújfalu (UC 158:31 (a); UC 158:31 (b); UC 158:32). Boldogkőváralja, to the west, in the Hernád valley, was also included, but this could have indicated Abaújszántó, only 10 km/6 miles to the south, and apparently an old appurtenance of the Boldogkőváralja fortress (both places belonged to the Regéc Domain). This de facto 'delineation' of Hegyalja must have come from the Chamber itself, on the advice of Draheim. It has to be assumed, therefore, that it followed the Rákóczi view of the region three decades earlier. [One of the three documents (UC 158:31 (a)) mentions four classes of vineyards. But this seems to have had to do with productivity/quantity rather than wine quality, since 1st Class was termed "good-yielding" and 4th Class as "abandoned." That is what most interested the Chamber.]

Although the content of the 1641 Rákóczi regulations did not survive, it can be stated that it must have included a three-tier classification according to wine quality, or else that such a classing followed almost immediately after. This is demonstrated by evidence from other documents in the subsequent decades. For instance, a document of 1675 mentions the Meszes tract in Olaszliszka as "*optima vinea 1 classis*" (UC 116:15); and a document of 1689 lists the vineyards of Bodrogkisfalud according to three quality classes (UC 116:58). The basis for the quality distinctions, and thus for the inclusion of communities within the area called Hegyalja, was the changeover to botrytis *aszú* wine as the characteristic regional product. This development likely was strongly influenced by the Rákóczis. A key landmark is a law of 1655 that required botrytis-affected berries or bunches to be collected separately from the rest of the harvest, and also prohibited taking botrytized berries out of the vineyards. By 1736, Gabriel Gyöngyösi was troubled by over-production of *aszú*; and in 1764, the Cserfás tract in Tarcal was remarked as a producer of "extraordinary *aszú* berries" (UC 122:34), which obviously had long since become the most desirable grapes. Thus, ultimately, the delineation of Hegyalja would come down to proven capacity to produce wines of a certain kind and nature.

Attention to the demarcation of Hegyalja resumed after the Habsburgs had firmly secured their control in the first part of the 18th century and the region began to be repopulated. The crucial period seems to have been from roughly 1730 to 1750. Around 1730, Matthias Bél, in writing the first geography of Hungary, described Hegyalja very specifically and even indicated the disagreements over the inclusion of locales:

> Hegyalja-i or Tokaj-i is the name of all those wines which are grown on Tokaj-hill and on the better vineyard hills that extend on the one hand to the north in a two-league zone to the locales of Tarcal, Mezőzombor, Mád, Tállya, all the way to Abaújszántó, and on the other hand within three leagues in the direction of the summer sunrise to the locales Bodrogkeresztúr, Szegi, Erdőbénye, Olaszliszka, Tolcsva, Bodrogzsadány, Bodrogolaszi, Sárospatak, all the way to Sátoraljaújhely…But there are those who do not want to list the Sárospatak and Sátoraljaújhely wines here, and also those who add those of Szerencs – everyone esteems the wines of this area according to [the location of] their property or the evaluation of their taste.

Whether Bél's description was informed at all by the Rákóczi classification is not known (the document presumably still existed at that time). However, he very likely consulted Zemplén authorities while traversing the county. Hegyalja's proper geographical bounds had been the subject of much scrutiny by the county in the preceding years because of the marketing of fraudulent Tokaji. In 1737, a royal ordinance specified 21 locales, in addition to Tokaj, that "possess the esteem and value of Tokaji wines." This virtually duplicated the Halápi documents of 1674-1675 (although those did not include the several small villages where the Szepes Chamber had no properties), and also covered the same territory specified by Bél. The main divergences were the exclusion of Szerencs, in the far southwest, and the inclusion of Kistoronya (now Malá Tŕňa), just northeast of Sátoraljaújhely. Additionally, this same area, but including Szerencs, was depicted on a map of 1749 titled, "The Vine-bearing Hills of Tokaj" (*Montium vitiferorum Tokaiensis*), published by Andreas Fuker (Fugger) of Eperjes. Clearly, during 1730-1750, wine-growing suitability and commerce had superceded lingering administrative-political notions, such as the domains and their *urbária*, in delineating the Hegyalja region.

Of special significance about the 1730-1750 period, is that for most observers thereafter no major questions remained about the extent of Hegyalja; only minor details around the periphery of the region needed to be settled (as discussed below in Section III). It is clear that the geographer Vályi, in 1796, relied on the determinations of that period. The same is true of Antal Szirmay's decisively influential work of 1798, *Notitia historica, politica, oeconomica montium et locorum viniferorum comitatus Zempleniensis* [Historical, political, economic notes on the wine-bearing hills and places of Zemplén County], which exerted everlasting authority on the subject because it concentrated on Hegyalja, and was written by a member of one of the most important and knowledgeable wine-growing families of the upper nobility.

Meanwhile, Tokaji wine continued to be plagued by falsification, and in 1801, Zemplén County instituted a regulation aimed at curtailing it, in which the following 22 communities were specified: Abaújszántó, Bodrogkeresztúr, Bodrogkisfalud, Bodrogolaszi, Bodrogszegi, Bodrogzsadány, Erdőbénye, Erdőhorváti, Golop, Kistoronya, Mád, Mezőzombor, Olaszliszka, Ond, Rátka, Sárospatak, Sátoraljaújhely, Tállya, Tarcal, Tokaj, Tolcsva, and Vámosújfalu. Zemplén County examined the Hegyalja question again in 1820, and came to the same conclusion. The geographer Fényes, in 1851, echoed Vályi and Bél, and even alluded to Bél's question about Szerencs. The *Tokaj-Hegyaljai Album* of 1867 followed Szirmay scrupulously.

The final stage in the delineation of Hegyalja began with national legislation in 1893, following phylloxera. Preventing the marketing of wines with bogus indication of geographical origin was again a major concern. This time, 33 communities were listed as belonging to Hegyalja. The additions since 1820 were: Bekecs, Józseffalva (later Újpatak), Károlyfalva, Legyesbénye, Makkoshotyka, Monok, Petrahó (later Bodroghalász), Szegilong, Szerencs, Szőlőske, Trautsohnfalva (later Hercegkút), and Végardó. Most of these were on the periphery, and it may be that several of the smaller ones were included implicitly in earlier regulations as being part of the wine-growing area of larger neighboring communities. For instance, it had been noted in a document of 1567 that "[Vég-] Ardó's vineyards are in Sárospatak" (UC 40:35). Further, the Halápi documents of 1674-1675 had included Bekecs, Monok, and Szerencs.

But even 1893 was not the end of it. National legislation on wine in 1908 trimmed the number back to 31 by not mentioning Hercegkút and Makkoshotyka, whose vineyards were treated as part of Sárospatak. Minor legal adjustments to the list of Hegyalja communities were also made thereafter. This was necessitated in part by the transfer of Kistoronya (now Malá Tŕňa) and Szőlőske (Viničky) to (Czecho-) Slovakia in 1918, and partly by slight administrative changes, including new village names for some of the small communities along the Bodrog river. In 1942, though, Kistoronya and Szőlőske were specified again because of Hungary's war-time recovery of that corner of Hegyalja.

The latest official listing of Hegyalja's administratively independent communities in Hungary dates to legislation of 1994: Abaújszántó, Bekecs, Bodrogkeresztúr, Bodrogkisfalud, Bodrogolaszi, Erdőbénye, Erdőhorváti, Golop, Hercegkút, Legyesbénye, Makkoshotyka, Mád, Mezőzombor, Monok, Olaszliszka, Rátka, Sárazsadány, Sárospatak, Sátoraljaújhely, Szegi, Szegilong, Szerencs, Tarcal, Tállya, Tokaj, Tolcsva, and Vámosújfalu. Additionally, Malá Tŕňa (Kistoronya) and Viničky (Szőlőske) are still included under the 1908 legislation, as is the small Slovakian portion of Sátoraljaújhely, or Slovenské Nové Mesto.

III. Circumscribing Hegyalja

General notions about Hegyalja as a wine district had long been guided by the colloquial expression 'beginning at Sátor hill, ending at Sátor hill,' in reference to the 34 km (21 miles) distance between two hills of like name, located respectively at Abaújszántó in the southwest and Sátoraljaújhely in the northeast. But this formulation addressed only the 'core' area, and could not settle uncertainties about the northeastern, southwestern, and western fringes. Thus, while the modern conception of Hegyalja as a wine region was largely worked out by 1740, older notions persisted concerning the periphery. A significant piece of evidence in that regard is a document of 1743, which sets out the apportionment of so called 'hill-masters' (vineyard-hill supervisors) in the Hegyalja area of Zemplén County (Abaúj County was not dealt with). Included in the listing of 25 communities were seven that were in doubt: Nagytoronya, Csarnahó, Ladmóc, Zemplén, and Szőlőske in the northeast; and Szerencs and Monok in the southwest.

Apparently, with the passage of time, a variety of considerations went into defining the periphery of Hegyalja. Some exclusions were made mostly because a locale was literally on the wrong side of the hillocks or waterways generally assumed to limn the region. Also, some of the smaller villages might not have had influential supporters to press the case for their inclusion. Yet, in the end, wine quality considerations appear to have been the determining factor. By the time of the 1893 and 1908 legislation, Hegyalja had become an area of contiguous communities, with a preponderance of 1st and 2nd Class vineyard-tracts.

(a) <u>North.</u> Over the centuries, the knottiest issues concerned the northeastern limits of Hegyalja. The basic difficulty arose from two factors having to do with geographical perceptions in this area: first, a question about the connection between Hegyalja and the Bodrog river this far north; and second, a question about which hills do not really belong to the Eperjes-Tokaj Hill-Chain.

Before 1500, many people must have thought Hegyalja extended northeast to the confluence of the Bodrog and Latorca rivers, near the village of Zemplén. This notion likely had ancient origins, since Zemplén was one of the oldest inhabited locales, going back to the founding of Hungary, and probably was a wine producer since its beginnings. Confusion also occurred because of the old system of domains. Since the Sárospatak Domain in 1686 included Nagytoronya (Felső Toronya) and Csernahó, some persons might have thought that those wine-growing locales must also be part of Hegyalja (UC 154:11). Even the Szepes Chamber [see that entry, in Part I] seems not to have been entirely certain. A Chamber document of 1687 about its fiscal vineyard holdings included Nagy Bári and Nagytoronya along with 15 present-day Hegyalja communities; however, the document did not purport to be about Hegyalja (UC 209:5).

The persistence in connecting Hegyalja with wine-growing along the Bodrog in this northeastern area is demonstrated by the inclusion of Zemplén and the neighboring village of Ladmóc among the 1743 list of Hegyalja locales for which vineyard-hill supervisors were appointed. The habit regarding supervisors probably dated to an earlier time, but in any case contributed to Losontzi's confusion, in 1771, when he indicated that even Lelesz, to the east of these places and of the Bodrog, belonged to Hegyalja. Contradictorily, though, some people in the same era thought that Hegyalja ended even south of Sátoraljaújhely, at the point where the Ronyva creek meets the Bodrog and the river makes a sharp eastward turn away from the Eperjes-Tokaj Hill-Chain.

Also, at this corner of the Hill-Chain, the hills lose continuity and become outcroppings. For this reason, they became known collectively as the 'Island-hills.' Several of the villages located beside the hills in the space between the Bodrog and the Ronyva may have been thought part of Hegyalja centuries ago. Thus, although the 1743 list of Hegyalja communities having vineyard-hill supervisors included Kistoronya, Nagytoronya, Csarnahó, and Szőlőske, the list might simply have followed old custom. In 1798, Szirmay excluded all except Kistoronya, which was the only one widely considered to be on a par qualitatively with Hegyalja communities to the south, as shown earlier by its inclusion in the decree of 1737. Its vineyard hills in effect were viewed as the easternmost outcroppings of the Eperjes-Tokaj Hill-Chain.

Eventually, by the late-19th century, all locales east of the Bodrog had been excluded from conceptions of Hegyalja. Among these, notably, was Nagy Kövesd, whose best wines reportedly were easily confused with those of Hegyalja (according to Kossuth in 1903). But the status of the area to the west, between the Bodrog and the Ronyva, remained somewhat unclear, at least in the popular mind. Only Nagytoronya, though well regarded for its table wines, had been definitively excluded. The crucial decisions were made following the phylloxera episode, at which time the villages of Csörgő, Csarnahó, and Bári, in addition to Nagytoronya, were left out of the 1893 and 1908 Hungarian legislation regarding Hegyalja. In all of those cases, the amount and proportion of suitable Hegyalja-type soils was very small, thus potentially detrimental to the wine district's overall reputation for high-quality botrytis wine. On the other hand, Szőlőske, situated beside the easternmost of the Island-hills, was included because of soil and exposition.

Czechoslovakia adhered to those determinations through the Second World War (Fiala/Sedláček left no doubt about that in their publication of 1936). But, in 1959, the history of confusion about the area between the Bodrog and Ronyva was seized upon by the Slovak wine industry, and legislation added Bári (Bara), Csörgő (Čerhov), Csarnahó (Černochov), and even Nagytoronya

(Veľká Tŕňa) in order to expand Slovakia's output of Tokaji-type wines. However, Hungary has protested this within the European Union, and has sought to exclude those locales once again if Slovakia is to be entitled to use the Tokaji name in marketing its wines outside Slovakia. This would mean that only the vineyard areas between the Ronyva and Bodrog that were included by the Hungarian legislation of 1908 would be recognized [see the entry for Slovakia].

(b) South. At issue in the south were the so called Szerencs hills, about midway from Tokaj to Abaújszántó. Technically, these hills lie somewhat apart from the Eperjes-Tokaj range, and furthermore, they are separated from the rest of Hegyalja by the Szerencs creek. Hidvéghy (1950) said the villages here "could be considered the foreground of the true Hegyalja."

The communes in the Szerencs group are (clockwise from the southeast): Szerencs, Bekecs, Legyesbénye, Ond, Monok, and Golop. The essential problem was that if one of the communes were to be accepted into Hegyalja, it would be difficult to exclude any of the others. Moreover, the three Szepes Chamber documents of 1674 and 1675 about Hegyalja specifically included all but Legyesbénye and Golop, although the latter might have been implicit in the mention of Boldogkőváralja (UC 158:31 (a); UC 158:31 (b); UC 158:32). Otherwise, both Golop and Ond had a long history of inclusion. While none of these villages was ever regarded a paragon – and opinions about their wines differed strongly during recent centuries – each had at least one highly esteemed vineyard-tract, notably: Napos in Bekecs; Somos-oldal in Golop; Cserepes in Legyesbénye; Lete in Monok; Dorgó in Ond; Berkec in Szerencs. Additionally, they had typical Hegyalja soils throughout their vineyard area, in contrast to some villages on the northern fringe.

A factor that held back recognition of the Szerencs group was their exposure to attacks by Ottoman and Habsburg forces in the late-17th century, since this made for a late recovery. It was noted in 1678 that Legyesbénye was largely deserted and had only two vineyards (UC 39:24). A later hurdle for the group may have been that the *furmint* arrived relatively late [see the entry for Aranka, in Part III]. Further, a particular problem of 'status' for these villages was their position immediately southwest of Mád and Tállya, two of the most famous Hegyalja villages; the Szerencs hills villages were bound to fare poorly in terms of 'average quality' in direct comparison with the latter two, although, tellingly, that did not dissuade aristocratic interest in the Szerencs hills during the 19th century.

(c) West. Pap (1985) mentioned that even places on the western side of the Zemplén Hills, in the Hernád river valley, from Abaújszántó north to the environs of Kassa (Košice), were at times in the distant past viewed as falling within conceptions of Hegyalja (at least for some people, but including some wine merchants). [See the entry for Timon, in Part I.] Notably, the village of Hejce was a good yielder of 1-, 2- and sometimes 3-*puttonyos aszú* wines that competed with Tokaji in the towns of Kassa and Eperjes to the north even as late as the early-20th century. Furthermore, Boldogkőváralja and Gönc were two of the earliest known wine-growing locales in the region (broadly considered). Szepes Chamber documents of 1675 (UC 158:32) and 1687 (UC 209:5) listed, respectively, Boldogkőváralja and Fony amongst Hegyalja communities, and in the former case the document was specifically about Hegyalja ("*Submontanarum*"). This was, though, in a period when production of botrytis *aszú* wine may not have been the sole criterion for inclusion.

However, from a geographical perspective, all of these places had 'rounded the bend' of Abaújszántó and its Sátor-hill, and were well north into the valley of the Hernád river, in the heart of Abaúj County. This put them on the far side of both the Zemplén hills and the Bodrog river, and thus, also far to the rear of what had increasingly become perceived as Hegyalja. Further, for administratively minded Hungarian officials, this position also separated them completely from even the broadest sense of Zemplén, whereas Hegyalja had become linked with the name

126

Zemplén, to the point that by the late-19th century only Abaújszántó remained in Abaúj County, all other Tokaji-producing Abaúj locales having been attached to Zemplén County.

*

Incipit in Sator desinit in Sator. 'It begins at Sátor, it ends at Sátor.' So went the Latin phrase used before 1800 as an offhand description of Hegyalja proper. It referred to the two hills called Sátor, one in the northeast at Sátoraljaújhely, and the other in the southwest at Abaújszántó. The two are about 34 km (21 miles) apart, but more territory is involved. Maps of Hegyalja show that Sátor-to-Sátor is just the longest side of a large triangular territory, with vineyards lining both sides of the right angle.

Given the size of the region, it is natural to wonder how much difference there might be amongst the wines of the various locales. Writing in 1888, Stephan Molnár made it clear that the inevitable rivalry was intense: "As to which of these villages produces the best wine, it is still not settled, and the moment [Hegyalja] producers come together and this question is raised, a heated debate concerning primacy ensues amongst them right away…The debate is not easily resolvable even by experts" because of the differing merits of wines from the respective villages (*Az Osztrák-Magyar Monárchia* / The Austro-Hungarian Monarchy). Hungarians were wrestling with this question since at least around 1700, since it touched on the subject of which villages belong to Hegyalja. But Pap (1985) intimated that the controversy was even older than that.

Around 1800, Szirmay recorded some well-established opinions about the character of certain Hegyalja wines. But here we need to be careful in separating 'character' from notions of 'quality,' *i.e.*, we are apposing qualities to quality. Characterizations of the wines (by which are understood *aszú* wines) are found scattered about in Hungarian literature on Tokaj-Hegyalja:

Erdőbénye: among the most "long-lasting" (Szirmay, 1798)
Erdőhorváti: "crystal-clear…unchanging color" (Fényes, 1851)
Mád: "honeyed" (anonymous, 17th century); among the "sweetest" (Szirmay, 1798); "fine flavor and gentle aftertaste" (Molnár, 1888)
Malá Tŕňa (Kistoronya): "especially esteemed for its spicy [*fűszeres*] flavor" (Fényes, 1851)
Mezőzombor: among the "strongest" (Szirmay, 1798)
Ond: "vigor combines with sweetness" (Timon, 1728)
Sárazsadány (Bodrogzsadány): among the "strongest" (Szirmay, 1798)
Szegi (Bodrogszegi): among the "strongest" and "most aromatic" (Szirmay, 1798)
Tállya: "fine flavor and gentle aftertaste" (Molnár, 1888); "generous and savory" (Hidvéghy, 1950)
Tarcal: among the "sweetest" (Szirmay, 1798)
Tokaj: among the "sweetest" (Szirmay, 1798); "relatively greater sweetness" (Molnár, 1888); "the sweetest" [in south-facing, loess areas] (Hidvéghy, 1950)
Tolcsva: among the most "long-lasting" (Szirmay, 1798); "pleasant softness" (Molnár, 1888)

Of course, though, these characterizations were idealized types, perhaps based on the most highly regarded vineyards. Whether the preponderance of wine from those communes is so readily distinguishable seems problematic, except perhaps for the few who have devoted a lifetime going from village to village to sample Hegyalja wines from a multitude of growers and vintages.

In any case, the challenge for Tokaji at this juncture is that wines produced by new precepts, in new styles, might inadvertently bear so much resemblance to wines grown *near* – but not *in* – Hegyalja, as to blur the demarcation that took several centuries to achieve.

*   *   *

PART III

WINE-GROWING HILLS and TRACTS

"Just a few hurriedly extracted examples [of vineyard names], and in it is the entire Hungarian past, the entire history. After the [Soviet] liberation [following the Second World War], the state farms and cooperatives in their industrial plans rechristened the greater part of the beautiful old dűlő *[vineyard-tract] names with industrial designations (I-II-III section, or VI/1, VI/2, VI/3, etc.). Here and there the names of some of the larger members were preserved, for instance: Szarvas, Hétszőlő, Rákóczi, Kincsem, Pajzsos, etc.; but not the smaller members any longer. It can almost be taken for granted that in two or three generations the anxious researcher will find the names of past times only on yellow parchment, on archival papers."*

Miklós Pap, 1985

INTRODUCTION

The hills and tracts where Tokaji is grown are a fundamental aspect of regional history and tradition, and even Hungarian identity. But it should not be imagined that the vineyard names had been widely known outside Hegyalja in the past and then forgotten during the forty years of communism. On the contrary, of all the aspects of Tokaji, the least information was known, outside Hegyalja, about vineyard-tracts. As late as the mid-19th century, many persons outside Hungary assumed that the name 'Tokay' itself was synonymous with a vineyard designation.

A major obstacle to knowledgeability was that Tokaji historically was *not* commercialized on the basis of vineyard names. The growers rarely acted as merchants, especially during the era of great fame, and thus did not indulge any inclination to highlight their properties by name. Further, large growers (landed nobility, municipal councils, church offices, religious orders) were owners of vineyards in tracts in more than one locale, and were not averse to blending if circumstances recommended doing so. As for actual wine-traders, they were not usually Hungarians, and had no stake in names other than Tokaji. Their propensity to blend from various vineyard-tracts would have been even greater. [See the entry for Selbstherr, in Part I.]

This is not to say, though, that the individual tracts were not given individual recognition in wine-making. A document of 1747 inventoried the estate of the late Éva Molnár Keresztessi in the Zemplén village of Parnó (now Parchovany, in East Slovakia), and it recorded wine from her vineyard in the Sajgó tract ("*ex vinea Saygo*") in Olaszliszka (UC 149:43). But outside the Upper Tisza region, and to some extent Poland, the tract names had little market significance, even if the traders were acquainted with the origin. Type of wine was of far greater impact on profits.

*

The annals of Hegyalja suggest that anywhere from 800 to 900 vineyard-tract names were known during the past 700 years. This number may seem extremely, even inconceivably large. But in addition to the extensive size of the region, two factors explain the number. First, not all of the tract names existed throughout those 700 years. Names came and names went, and they did not necessarily cover identical acreage [see the entry for Ond, in Part II]. Second, part of a once single tract could acquire a reputation of its own and a modified name (usually Big/Little or Upper/Lower). Conversely, especially after phylloxera, some once differentiated tracts were combined under one name, with the 'core' name in plural form (*–ak, –ek, –ok*).

It is difficult to specify the time-period during which the greatest number of names were in use. Most likely it occurred roughly between 1655, when it was required that botrytized berries be collected separately, and the Zemplén County vineyard classification of 1772, which was also the period when the demand for botrytis *aszú* wines peaked. However, even in that period, actual cultivation of the existing tracts waxed and waned because of warfare, pestilence, and out-migration. Notations pointing to dropoffs in cultivated vineyard land can be found in documents from various periods, for instance, from 1674 (UC 116:11), 1700 (UC 70:45 & 70:46 (b)), and 1753 (UC 94:36). Even the famous Szerelmi tract in Tokaj was recorded as "deserted" in 1776 (UC 149:2). [Also, see the entry for Somlyód.] Further, as the 18th century moved along, the number of tracts was subject to decline because of trade barriers and the loss of marketing opportunities. Nevertheless, the low point occurred, of course, after the phylloxera episode at the end of the 19th century, when many tracts were left fallow in its wake. In sum, the list of forgotten tract names was long even before Pap wrote his nostalgic and poignant words of 1985.

In view of the large historical number of names, several steps have been taken to prevent this compilation from being unnecessarily daunting for Tokaji aficionados and enthusiasts. The first aim in Part III is to include most of the 1st and 2nd Class tracts recorded in accounts and documents since the classification of 1772, with special attention to Szirmay (1798) and Szabó/Török (1867). Also, whenever possible, only core names are listed, with offshoot names mentioned in the entries. This results in far fewer than 900 entries. However, a supplemental list of old tract names, arranged by village, follows the main list, to give an idea of the many that were known in earlier times. Altogether, close to 700 hill and tract names are mentioned.

*

In consideration of the size of Hegyalja and the vicissitudes of its history, the question of vineyard land and its relationship to wine quality during the past 500 years is a bit unnerving. Can it be answered with much confidence?

The 'objective' factors about the vineyard-tracts can be considered. The three factors that have always played the dominant role are exposition, elevation, and soil type. But they vary in their importance. More or less southern exposure has always been the single indispensable advantage, but with openness to air currents from the east and west so as to facilitate air exchange. At the other extreme, the composition of the soil, especially between clayey (*nyirok*) and loess, and combinations thereof, has always been the most variable, with opinions being prone to subjectivity, except that there should be sufficient compactness so as to retain water. The factor that occupies the middle, in being neither an absolute nor an inconstant, is height above sea level. (These factors are discussed in depth in the Part III Essay.)

More than 200 years passed between the Rákóczi classification and the scientific exploration of the advantages and disadvantages of the various growing sites. In fact, of primary significance about Szabó/Török in 1867 is that it offered the first scientific presentation about the prerequisites for outstanding wine-growing sites in Hegyalja. Thereafter, especially following phylloxera, other research was done by wealthy owners with regard to their own properties. The Hidvéghy report of 1950 elaborated in more detail about specific tracts and areas throughout the region.

The best botrytis wines generally are associated with soil that is predominantly *nyirok*, and preferably of greater than lesser compactness because of longer moisture retention, especially in dry years. But outstanding botrytis wines are grown on a wide range of soils in terms of the proportion between *nyirok* and loess. A covering of stone is desirable because of heat retention. A high proportion of large stones is usually preferable in this regard; conversely, finely ground stone dust (the so called *kőpor*) is not esteemed. But major stoniness occurs mostly in the upper areas of the vineyard-tracts, and as Hidvéghy noted in 1950, the tendency after the phylloxera episode was for cultivation to "slide down" the hillsides. Fortunately, though, the high areas of the middle slopes are extremely well-suited when also south-facing.

All told, the case can be made that, historically, the 'ideal' Hegyalja land has been the south-facing tracts with predominantly *nyirok* soil of observable compactness, especially if also situated in the stony lower portion of the upper zone, or else the higher part of the middle zone. On the other hand, high and stony areas where *nyirok* is extremely compact are not favorable. But this hardly tells the whole story in a region the size of Hegyalja. Historically, exceptions are legion, most famously, the south-facing loess areas on the middle slopes of southern Hegyalja.

*

For the convenience of English-speakers, the term 'vineyard-tract' is used to refer to a section of land designated by name as a single wine-growing 'spread.' The operative Hungarian term is *dűlő*, which in general agricultural usage signifies 'field,' but in wine-growing usually approximates the French term *climat*, not least of all in that, historically, *dűlő*-s usually consisted of vineyards owned by various persons (noblemen, burghers, craftsmen, peasant smallholders) or entities (towns, parochial offices, religious orders). For instance, a 1784 document mentions seven vineyard hills at Erdőhorváti, respectively with 28, 7, 16, 66, 81, 13, and 26 owners, or 237 vineyard properties on the seven hills (UC 143:16). The term *hegy*, or hill, usually refers to a hill with several *dűlő*-s, although the smaller hills were sometimes treated as a *dűlő* in their own right; this seems to have varied from era to era. (Note to researchers: the Latin term *promontorium* is frequent in old documents. Typically, it was used as 'hill,' as in the document of 1784. But, occasionally, it was used as *dűlő*, as in UC 145:123, of 1747, which listed 45 taxable *promontoria* for Tarcal alone.)

The Hungarian term for 'vineyard' is *szőlő* (the same as for 'grape'), and by the late Middle Ages it was generally being used in reference to an individual property, rather than to an entire tract (however, in old Latin documents, the term *vinea* was used). In more recent times, the possessive suffix *–féle* was sometimes applied to an owner's name, *e.g.*, the *Báró Waldbott-féle szőlő* (Kossuth, 1903), was the 'vineyard of Baron Waldbott.' But *–féle* could be applied collectively to a family's total vineyard 'estate,' comprised of properties in several *dűlő*-s and/or villages. For instance, the Waldbotts had vineyards in no less than seven communes, and it was the totality of those that comprised the *Waldbott-féle* 'vineyard.'

Sometimes the names of families became forever attached to certain tracts even though there were both earlier and later owners (earlier names disappeared except in old documents). Such names date mostly to the Habsburg period, or after the mid-16th century. It should also be kept in mind that tract names occasionally became altered over time because some people heard the name in a slightly different way and did not know the significance of the earlier name. Notable examples are Bahomalja vice Pahómalja (in Tállya), Bátfi vice Bártfai (Tállya), Futó- vice Fuló-hill (Legyesbénye), Kendős vice Kanducs (Tokaj), Lajstrom vice Lestár (Tarcal), Narancsi vice Arancsi (Olaszliszka), Ősz vice Usz (Mád), and Szerelmi vice Szerémi (Tokaj).

*

A general purpose in discussing tract names has been to bear out the verity of Pap's statement that "the entire Hungarian past" is to be found in the names of the Hegyalja *dűlő*-s. Thus, some defunct names, or ones not mentioned by Szirmay or Szabó/Török, but found in old documents, are included for historic interest. 'Historic interest' relates in part to the names themselves. While the origin of the names oftentimes is readily apparent, there are cases in which more than one explanation is possible. Sometimes, a name may be an allusion to the domain to which it originally belonged, or else to a family that owned the domain at one time. Thus, for instance, a significant number of Hegyalja tracts bear names relating to places to the north of Hegyalja, and now in East Slovakia, such as Michalovce and Vranov, and to very old families that were important prior to the Habsburg claim to the Upper Tisza in the 1520s, such as the Buttkai, Soós, Pálóczi, Perényi, and Rozgonyi families. The possibilities are set out below.

Finally, while it may be tempting to concentrate on the famous names, readers are encouraged to make a distinction between 'storied' vineyards and ones that 'have a story' to tell. The latter kind adds depth, not to mention a 'romantic' aura, when considering Hegyalja history.

*   *   *

PART III

THE A-Z LISTING

Over 300 tract names have entries in Part III. Because of space limitations on this page, and since most of the names are unfamiliar anyway, the names below have been selected in accord with the historical orientation of this book. They are tracts or hills having particular or unusual historical significance. It is *not* a quality- or fame-based selection [see the following page].

Agáros	Haragos	Paczoth
Alsóbénye	Hatalos	Pajzos
Aranyos	Henye	Palandor
Bahomalja	Hétszőlő	Parlag
Baksó	Kanducs	Peres
Barát	Kapi	Pethő
Becsek/Becsk	Kassa	Poklos
Berkec	Káté	*Por-törő*
Bodonyi	Kincsem	Raffai
Bojták	Király	Rány
Bomboly	Kócsag	Remete
Borkút	Krakó	Rézló
Bornemissza	Kútpatka	Rosenberg
Cepre	Lajos	Serédi(-Vay)
Ciróka	Lete	Sóhajó
Cseke	Lőcse	Somlyód
Cserfás	Makovica	Szarvas
Danczka	Makra	Szegfű
Dereszla	Máriás	Szent-Kereszt
Dessewffy	Medgyes	Szentvér
Disznókő	Megyer	Szerelmi
Dukát	Mestervölgy	Tehéntánc
Esztáva	Meszes	Terézia
Fegyemes	Mézesmáj	Térhegy
Felhegy	Mocsár	Tófelé
Fövenyes	Murát	Uszhegy
Furmint	Napos	Várhegy
Gangalus	Narancsi	Veres
Gyapáros	Nyergesek	Vinnai
Gyöpös	Oremus	Zsadány
		Zsákos

Note for Anglophones on Hungarian pronunciation: It is mostly in connection with tract names that one will be persistently bedeviled by the Hungarian alphabet. The letters to take note of are:

a is pronounced *uh* − *á* is *aah*
e is pronounced *eh* − *é* is as *a* in *hay*
i is pronounced *ih* − *í* is as *ee* in *tee*
o is pronounced *oh* − *ó* is as *o* in *old*
ö is as *ea* in *Earp* (Wyatt) − *ő* is as *ieu* in *adieu*
u is as *ew* in *new* − *ú* is as *oo* in *noose*
ü is as *ou* in *amour* − *ű* is as *u* in *azure*, but longer

c is as *cz* in *czar*
cs is as *ch* in *church*
gy is as *di* in *adieu*
j is as *y* in *yak*
ly is as *le* in *Aleut*
ny is as Spanish ñ
s is as *sh* in *ship* − *sz* is as *s* in *sit*
zs is as *z* in *azure*, or *Zsa Zsa* (Gabor)

Note: 1) The tract names are listed alphabetically, except that only 'core' names are included. Thus, for instance, Kis-Lete and Nagy-Lete will both be found under Lete. Likewise, identically or similarly named tracts are included under only one entry, with the various ones differentiated therein. For instance, all tracts that feature the name Király (King) are found numbered individually under that heading. In this case, the names have been arranged in order of rank or fame. [An accounting of tracts by town/village can be found in Part II.] 2) Regarding quality rank, the date 1798 refers to Szirmay's ranking; the date 1867 to Szabó/Török; and the date 1950 to Hidvéghy. Also noted are qualitative comments from other Hungarian authors, such as Kossuth in 1903, Fényes in 1851, and Hungarian archival documents (as cited). 3) Historical notations about the tracts and their names are drawn primarily from Hungarian studies and documents. In the case of unnumbered documents, the initials MOL are used to refer to the Hungarian National Archives (See the note on Hungarian archival documents at the end of the Bibliography).

* The historically most famous tracts and hills (i.e., greatest name recognition in Hegyalja and the Upper Tisza) are in upper-case letters. The tracts are (alphabetically): Aranyos, Ciróka, Cserfás, Danczka, Disznókő, Dorgó, (Zsadány-)Előhegy, Fövenyes, Görbe, Gyapáros, Hasznos, Hatalos, Henye, Hétszőlő, Kincsem, Király, Királyka, Kócsag, Krakó, Kútpatka, Lőcse, Makovica, Mandulás, Meszes, Mézesmáj, Napos, Oremus, Patócs, Peres, Szarvas, Szentvér, Szerelmi, Várhegy, and Zsákos.

*

Agáros – A *dűlő* of Erdőhorváti, mentioned as "very favourably situated" in 1867, and noted among the village's best in 1950. Historically, and as recently as 1784, there were Nagy- (Big) and Kis- (Little) Agáros hills that were treated as separate vineyard-tracts (UC 143:15). Owners on Kis-Agáros in 1784 included Count Pálffy and David Judaeus ('David the Jew'). The name refers to 'greyhound' (*agár*), and no information suggests that Agáros was a surname. In 1628, Ibrahim Pasha of Eger presented Prince George Rákóczi I with a greyhound, for use in hunting, but it is not known whether the gift had any connection to the name of this vineyard-tract, such as Rákóczi reciprocating by giving a vineyard to Ibrahim Pasha.

Agyag – The name refers to 'clay' land, and sometimes was recorded alternatively as *Agyas*, or 'clayey.' 1) A *dűlő* in Tarcal, on the southern side of Tokaj-hill, mentioned as 1st Class in 1798 and 1867. The Rákóczis had a vineyard here as late as 1686. 2) A *dűlő* in Abaújszántó, mentioned as "distinguished" in 1867, but not mentioned in 1798 because Szirmay did not include Abaúj County. The municipality of Bártfa [see that entry, in Part II] purchased one of its first Hegyalja vineyards here, in the year 1481. At a later date, the Rákóczis were also owners.

Alsó-Bea. See the entry for Bea.

Alsóbénye – This *dűlő* in Erdőbénye was not mentioned in 1798 or 1867, and in 1950 was indicated as not being among the village's best. But the tract perhaps was constituted differently at an earlier time, or else was viewed better before later-harvested wines started to be produced. The name harks back to when there were two villages, Lower Bénye and Upper Bénye. The vineyard-tract named Alsóbénye referred to the former; but it seems there was never a tract named for the other village. The attraction of Lower Bénye and its tract in earlier times is suggested by the attempt of the Rozgonyi family to take them illegally in the late-15th century (DL 16979) [see the entry for Rozgonyi, in Part I].

Alsó-Feketehegy. See the entry for Feketehegy.

Alsó-Gát. See the entry for Gát.

Alsó-Mecsege. See the entry for Mecsege.

Alsó-Mocsár. See the entry for Mocsár.

Alsóőrzés – A *dűlő* in Sárazsadány, noted in 1950 for its excellent vineyard soil. The name signifies 'lower guardpost,' probably with reference to the onetime fortress of Tolcsva.

Alsó-Remete. See the entry for Remete.

Alsó-Thurzó. See the entry for Thurzó.

Aranka – Even though it means 'Goldie,' this *dűlő* name in Szerencs merits consideration apart from the following entry for 'Golden.' It could well be another instance of a tract being named for a grape variety, since Balassa (1991) found it as a varietal name of the early-19th century, and even with one indication that the variety was a variant of the *furmint* ('*Aranka Formint*' – 1829). [See the entries for Furmint, Kecsi, Lányka, Szegfű, and Talyanka]. The *dűlő* name might indicate when the *furmint* reached Szerencs and vicinity (southernmost Hegyalja). This might have been the early-18th century, since an Aranka was recorded in a document of 1737 (UC 145:98). Although the document stated that the tract belonged to nearby Mád, it is quite possible that it was the Szerencs tract, but that it was being used by Mád in a period when Szerencs was still recovering from devastation. No Aranka tract was mentioned for Mád in 1798 or 1867; while it was not mentioned for Szerencs, either, that village was not included.

ARANYOS – The word 'golden' was the basis for several vineyard names, whether as a euphemism for quality; or an allusion to sunny exposure; or even a suggestion of the old Hegyalja myths about vines containing gold [see the entry for Gold Content, in Part IV]. **1)** The famous Aranyos ('Golden') part of the Csirke *dűlő* in Bodrogkisfalud was only mentioned in passing in 1798 (under the listing for the village of Szegi), but was noted as "celebrated" in 1867 (under the listing for Szegi and Long). In 1950, it was specified as one of two tracts producing the "most outstanding" wine of Kisfalud. **2)** The *dűlő* of this name in Tokaj, on the southeastern side of Tokaj-hill, was mentioned as 2nd Class in 1798 and 1867, and was noted in 1764 as inconveniently situated (UC 122:34).

Árokháti – A *dűlő* in Tarcal, on the southern side of Tokaj-hill, mentioned as 1st Class in 1798 and 1867. The name signifies 'on the far side of the ditch.'

Bacskai – A vineyard hill and *dűlő* in Mád, mentioned as 1st Class in 1798; not mentioned in 1867; and mentioned favorably in 1950. It bears the name of the Bacskay family of Sáros County [see the latter entry, in Part II].

Baglyos. See the entry for Boglyos.

Bahomalja – A *dűlő* in Tállya, mentioned as "noble" in 1798 and "eminent" in 1867. The name indicates that it was established by the Pauline Order, since 'Bahom' is an altered form of the name Pahóm (Hungarian for Pachomius), who was the first to bring the Pauliner hermits together in monastic communities. The suffix –*alja* signifies the lower portion of an earlier and larger Bahom/Pahóm tract. [See the entry for Pauline Order, in Part I.]

Bajóka – A *dűlő* in Erdőbénye, mentioned among the village's best in 1950.

Bajusz – A *dűlő* in Tarcal, on the northern side of Tokaj-hill. In past centuries, both a Nagy-(Big) and Kis- (Little) Bajusz were recorded, with both mentioned as 3rd Class in 1798 and 1867. The name means 'moustache,' but most likely indicates the noble Bajusz family of Abaúj and Sáros counties [see the latter entries, in Part II].

Baksó – The name, recorded as Baxo in 1573 (UC 158:29), refers to the Baksa clan, which was significant in the Zemplén region probably as far back as the second-half of the 12th century [see the entry for Baksa, in Part I]. 1) Primarily, it has referred to a *dűlő* in Tarcal, on the southern side of Tokaj-hill, mentioned as 1st Class in 1798, 1867, and 1950. In 1737, it was recorded by the name Nagy- (Big) Baxo, apparently to differentiate it from a neighboring 'Baxo' *dűlő* (UC 145:98). The latter was probably the "Baxy Allya" recorded in 1747 (UC 145:123). More recently, the tract has been known as Görbe-Baksó [see the entry for Görbe (2)]. 2) Boros (1996) included Tokaj's Baksa tract as part of the town's Nagy-Mézesmáj area [see the entry for Mézesmáj (c)]. As at Tarcal in the same era, a Baksa-alja (Baxa Allya), or 'Baksa-bottom,' *dűlő* was recorded in Tokaj in 1736 and 1737 (Balassa; and UC 145:98).

Bánya – Names referring to a 'mine' (*bánya*) mostly suggest the period in Upper Hungary when the mining of ores became a major activity, and thus probably date mostly to the 14th century. 1) Kőbánya, or 'Stone-quarry,' is a *dűlő* in Tarcal, on the southern side of Tokaj-hill, mentioned as 1st Class in 1798 and 1867. 2) Nagy- (Big) and Kis- (Little) Bányihegy are *dűlő*-s in Sátoraljaújhely. A document of 1481 mentioned only a Bányahegy. It was mentioned as Bányai in 1798 and 1867, but only in passing, without qualitative notation. A Felső- (Upper) Bányihegy was also known. 3) Abaújszántó has had several *dűlő*-s that include this name: Nagy- (Big) Bánya, Hátutolsó-(Hindmost) Bánya and Bánya-fark (tail-end). All were mentioned in 1950, but none in 1798 because Szirmay did not include Abaúj County. The first two as well as a Kis-(Little) Bánya were mentioned in a document of 1785-1785 (UC 143:17). 4) A document of 1785 shows that Sárospatak had a Bánya-oldali (-side) tract at that time (Balassa). 5) Tállya has a *dűlő* named Bányász ('Miner'), which was the surname of a prominent family in Zemplén and Sáros counties in the 15th century [but see the entry for Bártfai].

Bányász. See the previous entry (5).
Barakonyi-oldal. See the entry for Várhegy (2).

Barát – Use of the word 'brother' as the name of a vineyard-tract probably goes back to at least the 13th century, in connection with the spread of religious orders and monasteries, especially the Pauliners. At one time, it might have been found throughout Hegyalja as a vineyard name, although the following *dűlő*-s may have been the most significant ones even then. 1) The *dűlő* Barát (or Deák or Deák-Barát) in Tarcal, on the southern side of Tokaj-hill, mentioned as 1st Class in 1798 and 1867. The name dates to a vineyard owned by the Pauline Order in the 15th century. (The term *deák* indicates an educated person.) 2) A *dűlő* in Tokaj, on the southern side of Tokaj-hill, mentioned as 1st Class in 1798, 1867, and 1950. 3) A onetime *dűlő* in Bodrogkeresztúr, mentioned in 1573 (UC 158:29), but not in the 1798 or 1867 listings. [See the entry for Pauline Order, in Part I.]

Barnamáj – A *dűlő* in Erdőbénye, mentioned in passing in 1798, and indicated in 1950 as not being among the village's very best, at least in certain areas. Nevertheless, it was noted as a "principal" *dűlő* of the village in 1867. The name signifies 'brown warm-side,' in reference to soil color, which owes to *nyirok* (clayey) soil, as well as to a sloping southerly exposition (*–máj*).

Bartalos-Térhegy. See the entry for Térhegy.

136

Bártfai – A *dűlő* in Tállya, mentioned as "noble" in 1798 and as "eminent" in 1867. It may originally have been a section of the Bányász *dűlő* [see the entry for Bánya (5)], but increasingly became known as Bártfai after it was purchased in 1485 by the municipality of Bártfa (now Bardejov, in East Slovakia). The name is also corrupted nowadays as Bártfi and Bátfi. [See the entry for Bardejov, in Part II.]

Bátfi. See the previous entry.

Báthori – A *dűlő* in Tállya, not mentioned individually in 1798 or 1867, but noted in 1950 as still having a "good name" for its wines. The Rákóczis had a vineyard here as late as 1686. The name refers to the Báthory family of Protestant Transylvanian princes, most likely dating to Stephan Báthory in the late-16th century [see the entry for Báthory, in Part I].

Bea – The name of two *dűlő*-s in Abaújszántó, Felső- (Upper) and Alsó- (Lower) Bea, on the southern side of Sátor-hill. They were not mentioned by that name in a document of 1783 that listed over 30 tracts in the village (UC 192:6). Nor were they mentioned by Szirmay in 1798, since he did not include Abaúj County. But both were mentioned as "distinguished" in 1867. In 1950, Felső-Bea was mentioned among the *dűlő*-s producing the commune's "best quality wines." In local lore, the name Bea, which was sometimes recorded as Beja, is thought to allude to an unknown Turkish bey who once held claim to its output. That would take the name back to as early as the 16th century.

Becsek – 1) A *dűlő* in Mád mentioned as 1st Class in 1798 and 1867, and included among the village's best in 1950. 2) The similarly named Becsk *dűlő* in Erdőbénye was not mentioned in 1798 or 1867, and was noted in 1950 as not being among the village's best. The name Becsk refers to a family (also recorded as Bechk and Bekcz) of Abaújszántó that gained some regional prominence beginning in the 15th century, *e.g.*, "Georgii Bechk de Zantho" in 1501 (DL 30956). The name Becsek at Mád most likely is a later variant of Becsk.

Becsk. See the previous entry.

Bel- – Two *dűlő*-s with names beginning with Bel- were recorded around the time of the Zemplén County classification of 1772: 1) a Belia-tó (Belia-lake) in Tokaj in 1765 (UC 117:50); and 2) a Bellova in Abaújszántó in 1783 (UC 192:6). 3) A Bellő still exists in Tolcsva. None of these were mentioned in 1798 or 1867. The significance of Bel- is unclear. In at least one case, the Bella *castrum* was probably indicated originally. Certainly, the name Bellova could be left over from Bella-vár (fort). Although the fort was in southwestern Hungary, it was a property of the Pethő family that owned other vineyards in Hegyalja [see the entry for Henye]. A very old possibility would be the Count Belus who was in charge of the Sárospatak fort around 1300.

Berkec – (or Berkecs) A *dűlő* in Szerencs, not mentioned in 1798 or 1867 because Szerencs then was not usually included in Hegyalja. But in 1950 it was mentioned among the village's best tracts. Fényes also praised it in 1851: "…such good wine is grown [on Berkec], that it is not at all inferior to that of Hegyalja." Berkec appears to be among the early Hegyalja vineyard-tract names. The village of Berkec (Berkez, Berkesz, etc.) belonged to the Kővár Domain, located beside Boldogkőváralja in Abaúj County, and Berkec-*dűlő* might first have been planted following the Tatar invasion of 1241-1242, when the Kővár fortress itself was erected.

Bialka – A *dűlő* on Magoshegy hill in Bodrogolaszi, its name is thought to refer to a Bialka family that is supposed to have come to Hegyalja from Poland, presumably in the 16th century, after Hegyalja had become well-known to the Poles. The family perhaps was involved with wine trade, although there is no record of it. It was not given individual mention, *i.e.*, recognition apart from Magoshegy, in 1798 or 1867, but was noted in 1950 for its good conditions. It had been mentioned with the spelling 'Bialaka' in 1748 (Balassa, 1991). [See the entry for Magashegy (*sic*).]

Bigó – Also called Bige, this Tarcal tract, on the southern side of Tokaj-hill, was mentioned as 1st Class in 1798 and 1867. However, as late as 1737, part of it fell within the borders of Tokaj (Balassa). The name apparently refers to Ladislaus Bige, the liege man of Francis Rákóczi II.

Bikkoldal – A onetime *dűlő* in Tolcsva, mentioned as 2nd Class in 1798 (Bikódal), although Vályi called it "famous" in 1796. It was included among the village's favorable vineyards in 1950. The name '*bikk*-side' refers to the '*nemes* (noble) *bikk*,' a tree in the beech (*bükk*) family, and indicates that the vineyard-tract was created by clearing away forest land.

Birsalmás – A *dűlő* in Mád, mentioned as 2nd Class in 1798 and 1867, but listed amongst the village's best in 1950. The name alludes to a onetime quince orchard.

Bodó – A family with this name (also recorded as Boda) apparently once had widespread vineyard holdings in Hegyalja: 1) Bodó *dűlő* in Bodrogolaszi was mentioned very favorably in 1950. 2) Bodóka (diminutive form) in Erdőbénye, also mentioned in 1950. 3) A Boda in Sátoraljaújhely, which was not mentioned in any of the earlier listings.

Bodonyi – A *dűlő* in Tarcal, on the northern side of Tokaj-hill, mentioned as 3rd Class in 1798 and 1867. The name suggests onetime ownership by the Bodon(y) fortress in Sáros County, possibly as early as 1400. But it could be even older, since the fortress itself probably dates to the mid-14th century and the historical Sáros figure Bodun, of the ancient Tekule clan.

Boglyos, Boglyoska – 'Haystack' (*boglyó*) seems to have been a popular name, perhaps because of adjacent land used for other agricultural purposes. 1) Boglyoska in Sátoraljaújhely was mentioned in passing in 1798 and 1867, while in 1950 the section called Nagy- (Big) Boglyoska was remarked as 1st Class. 2) Boglyos is a *dűlő* in Tokaj, on the northern side of Tokaj-hill, mentioned as 3rd Class in 1798 and 1867. It was also recorded in 1736. 3) A document of 1686 mentioned a Boglyoska belonging to Erdőbénye (UC 154:11).

Bojták – A *dűlő* in Mád. The name has been used in plural form (-*ák*), apparently because, at one time, two adjoining *dűlő*-s shared the name. In singular form, Bojta is of interest because of its antiquity as a Magyar personal name left over from pagan times, found in documents as late as the 13th century. However, it must have been converted to use as a surname when last names began to be acquired, and that is likely how and when it came to be attached to a vineyard-tract, perhaps as early as the 14th century.

Bokond – A *dűlő* in Mezőzombor, mentioned as 2nd Class in 1798 and 1867; not mentioned in 1950. The origin of the name is uncertain, although the –*d* ending indicates a very old name, whether or not the tract would be equally old.

Bomboly – A *dűlő* in Mád, not mentioned in 1798 or 1867, but mentioned among the village's best in 1950. The only logical word association for the name is a dialectical Romanian name for shriveled (*aszú*) grapes, recorded by Dr. Richard Bright in 1818 as *bómbele*. He found the term in the Ménes area of southern Hungary (now Miniş, in southwest Romania), 129 km (80 miles) away, where a red botrytis wine was produced. It would seem that the term had somehow migrated to Mád and was applied to a site known for abundant production of botrytized grapes.

Borkút – 1) A *dűlő* of Mezőzombor, mentioned as 2nd Class in 1798, 1867, and 1950. 2) The abundantly producing vineyards around the hill of Előhegy extending northwest from Tolcsva towards Erdőhorváti are collectively known by this name. The name signifies 'wine-font' and was a popular colloquial designation in the late Middle Ages. In that era, a vineyard hill of the same name was situated by Eperjes, at the northern end of the Eperjes-Tokaj Hill-Chain (the name is still in use there, though wine-growing ended centuries ago). [See the entry for Prešov, in Part II.]

Bornemissza – A *dűlő* in Tokaj, on the southern side of Tokaj-hill, mentioned as 1st Class in 1798, 1867, and 1950. The name refers to the early Bornemissza ('Teetotal') family of Sáros County, who became Hegyalja landlords in the 16th century, when presented with an endowment by Habsburg Emperor Rudolf. According to a document of 1695, the tract had earlier been known as Tófelé (UC 116:60) [see the entries for Tófelé and Mézesmáj (c)].

Boszorkány – A *dűlő* in Tolcsva, not mentioned in 1798 or 1867, but mentioned among the village's very best in 1950: "outstandingly situated" and with "first-class quality vineyards." The name means 'witch,' and has some historical interest in that King Kálmán prohibited the persecution of witches in the early-12th century because, he said, there no longer were any. Apparently, some had gone underground, or else witchcraft enjoyed a revival later on.

Cepre – (formerly spelled Czepre) A *dűlő* of Sátoraljaújhely, mentioned in 1798 and 1867; not mentioned in 1950. There was both a Nagy- (Big) and a Kis- (Little) Cepre tract, but only the latter remains. Being pronounced 'TZEH-preh, the name suggests a Balkan origin, from a word for grape-marc ('TZI-pri' in Greek; and TZI-por-i' or 'DZHI-bri' in Bulgarian). This suggests must-making amidst the vineyards. The Hungarians adopted the term in the form *cefre*, not *cepre*. [The use of 'marc' as a toponym is not improbable. Part of the once Greek-inhabited wine town of Assenovgrad, in Bulgarian Thrace, was called Tsiprohori, or 'Marc-ville.']

Cigány – (formerly spelled Czigány) 1) 'Gypsy' *dűlő* in Szegi was mentioned in 1798, and called "celebrated" in 1867 (under the listing for Szegi and Long communes). 2) A document in the late-17th century mentioned Cigányhegy hill in neighboring Bodrogkisfalud (UC 69:81), which suggests that both villages had part of the hill in their boundaries. The name Cigány likely antedates the presence of Roma in Hegyalja, and might refer to the estate of that name owned by the Rozgonyi family in the 14th century (DL 68632) [see the entry for Rozgonyi, in Part I].

CIRÓKA – (formerly spelled Cziróka) A *dűlő* in Tolcsva, mentioned as 1st Class in 1798 and 1867, and mentioned in 1963 (Dömötör/Katona) among the eight "most well-known" *dűlő*-s of Hegyalja At the beginning of the 17th century, there were two tracts, respectively Nagy- (Big) and Kis- (Little) Ciróka (UC 108:55). The name refers to the Ciróka (now Ciroché) river in Upper Zemplén (now in eastern Slovakia), in all likelihood because of onetime ownership by the Drugeths of the Homonna Domain [see the entries for the latter two, respectively in Part I and Part II]. Also, this tract is one of only a few in which it is known that a Greek merchant family, the Constantins, had a vineyard.

Compoly – (formerly spelled Czompoly) A onetime *dűlő* of Bodrogkeresztúr. Mention of it can be found as early as 1573 (UC 158:29), but it was not mentioned in 1798, 1867, or 1950. The name could have originated with an ancestor of the person listed as Compolar in the 1688 *urbárium* of the Tokaj Domain. Or, it might have been a corruption of the name of Kompolt, a descendant of the Aba clan, who lived around 1300 [see the entry for Aba, in Part I].

Csadó. See the entry for Csető.

Csákány – A *dűlő* in Mezőzombor, mentioned as 2nd Class in 1798, 1867, and 1950. The name means 'axe,' but is probably a surname, possibly the Csákánys of Kisszeben in Sáros County, which would be a rare known instance of vineyard ownership in Hegyalja from Kisszeben [see that entry, in Part II]. It is also possible, though, that the reference is to a clan from the earliest period of Hungarian history.

Cseke – (alternatively as Cséke) A *dűlő* in Tarcal, on the western side of Tokaj-hill. It was recorded as Nagy- (Big) and Kis- (Little) Cseke in past centuries, with both mentioned as 2nd Class in 1798 and 1867. In 1950, Cseke was noted as producing wine nearly as good as the town's best *dűlő*-s. The name is an instance of trying to untangle a place-name and a surname. The tract's name might be a direct reference to a village of Bodrogköz [see that entry, in Part II], Cseke/Cséke (now Lácacséke, about 24 km/15 miles east of Sátoraljaújhely), which had been the site of a fort and castle of the prominent Bocskay family in the 15th century. But it could also be an indirect reference to the village, since a significant 15th and 16th century family had adopted Cseke as a surname. Some family members were resident in Bodrogkisfalud in the early-15th century. The Csekes were an offshoot of the very old Soós family, and in turn, of the ancient Baksa clan [see the entries for Soós and Baksa, in Part I]. [Note: A Czékevölgy – 'Czéke-vale' – *dűlő* was recorded in Tarcal in 1565, but this likely referred to the fort of Czéke (now Cejkov), about 8 km/5 miles northeast of Hegyalja. See the Supplemental List of tract names.]

Cserepes – 1) A *dűlő* in Tállya, mentioned as "noble" in 1798, and as "eminent" in 1867. In 1950, Felső- (Upper) Cserepes was specified as an "outstanding" site for vine cultivation. 2) Legyesbénye has Nagy- (Big) and Kis- (Little) Cserepes *dűlő*-s, both of which were mentioned in 1950 as producing the village's best wine [see the entry for Fulóhegy]. The name Cserepes signifies 'tiler'/'roofer,' and is not known to indicate a family with that surname. It could indicate that numerous ancient tile fragments had turned up while creating the vineyards. This was not unusual, and probably accounts for the same tract name in the Eger wine region.

CSERFÁS – A *dűlő* of Tarcal, mentioned as 1st Class in 1798 and 1867. In a document of 1764 (UC 122:34), concerning vineyards that the Hungarian Chamber transferred to private ownership, the unusual notation was made that Cserfás yields "extraordinary" *aszú* grapes ("*extraordinariae uvae passae producantu*"). This was eight years before the Zemplén County classification of 1772. The name Cserfás refers to the *cserfa* oak tree (*quercetum petrae cerris*), and thus suggests that this *dűlő* was among those many Hegyalja vineyard-tracts created by clearing away forested land on hillsides during the late-13th or early-14th centuries. Nevertheless, it seems usually to have been included anonymously under Tarcal's portion of the old Mézesmáj [see Mézesmáj (c)] until around 1700. The change that gave it individually recognized prominence apparently was ownership by the Klobusiczkys [see that entry, in Part I]. Judging by a document of 1737, a distinction was made between a Nagy- (Big) and a Kis- (Little) Cserfás at one time (UC 145:98). [Note that Cserfás (CHAIR-fosh) is distinct from the Tarcal *dűlő* called Szarvas (SAHR-vush).]

Cserjes – A onetime *dűlő* in Abaújszántó, on the southern side of Sátor-hill, not mentioned in 1798 because Szirmay did not include Abaúj County, but mentioned as "distinguished" in 1867.

It went out of cultivation after phylloxera. The name indicates that a thicket had been cleared away to create the tract.

Csető – The Csetős were nobles of Zemplén County. 1) A respected *dűlő* of Tolcsva, it was not mentioned separately in 1867, though located amidst other tracts rated 1st Class. In 1950, it was included amongst the tracts having the best conditions for wine-growing. 2) Bodrogkeresztúr has a Csadó tract, but this was not recorded in earlier listings, and likely is a corruption of the tract name Csető recorded in 1737 (UC 145:98). But the latter was associated with neighboring Bodrogkisfalud at that time.

Csíkhegy – Csík- (Ribband) hill in Tállya was mentioned as "noble" in 1798 and "eminent" in 1867; and was cited in 1950 for its "outstanding" location for wine-growing.

Csirke – The name means 'chicken,' but in the 14th century the Csirke family had such widespread vineyard holdings in Hegyalja that a *dűlő* with this name most likely refers to them [see the entry for Csirke, in Part I]. The Csirke *dűlő* in Szegi and Bodrogkisfalud was mentioned in passing in 1798 (under the listing for Szegi commune), but was mentioned as "celebrated" in 1867 (under the listing for Szegi and Long communes). In 1950, the Aranyos section of Csirke in Bodrogkisfalud was mentioned as one of village's the two best sites.

Csirkés – A *dűlő* of Tállya, mentioned in 1950 for its "outstanding" location, but not mentioned in 1798 or 1867. The name probably refers to the mushroom known as *csirke*, which suggests forest removal to create a vineyard.

Csojka – A *dűlő* in Mezőzombor, mentioned as 1st Class in 1798 and 1867, and mentioned among the village's "most outstanding" in 1950. The name apparently refers to the Csojka fortress (*castri*) in Bihar County, to the southeast. Csojka existed as early as 1236 and might have acquired this *dűlő* roughly around 1300, when fortresses in the Upper Tisza were also receiving properties in Hegyalja. [See the entry for Csáky, in Part I.]

Csókamáj – A onetime *dűlő* in Bodrogkeresztúr, mentioned as 1st Class in 1798, 1867, and 1950, but no longer in use. Csóka was the name of a bird in Zemplén, while the –*máj* suffix refers to a warm southern slope.

Csók-földe – A *dűlő* in Bodrogolaszi, mentioned in passing in 1798 and 1867. The name, as spelled, signifies 'kiss-land,' but most likely refers to the 15th-century Csok (Czok) family of Sátoraljaújhely, who did possess vineyards.

Csonka – A *dűlő* of Tállya, not indicated under that name in 1798, 1867, or 1950, and therefore not mentioned by any rank. However, it abuts the excellent Hasznos, Bártfai, and Bányász tracts. Csonka ('Stumpy') is a common surname, but since it also signifies something 'broken off from,' the tract perhaps overlapped with the onetime Kis-Hasznos [see the entry for Hasznos].

Csontos – A *dűlő* in Olaszliszka, not mentioned in 1798 or 1867, but indicated among the village's best in 1950. The name signifies 'strong-boned,' but likely is a surname, probably referring to the noble Csontos family of Zemplén, Abaúj, and Sáros counties.

Csuka – The name Csuka, although that of a freshwater fish, most likely refers to the prominent family of that name in the 15th century. 1) A *dűlő* in Tarcal, on the southern side of Tokaj-hill, mentioned as 1st Class in 1798, 1867, and 1950. 2) A document of 1681 mentions the Nagy- (Big) and Kis- (Little) Csuka *dűlő*-s of Olaszliszka (UC 10:88 (a)).

DANCZKA – (or Dancka in modern spelling) A *dűlő* of Mád, not mentioned by name in 1798 or 1867, though its onetime ownership by the Baltic port city of Danzig (Gdańsk) suggests that it was a valued property when Hegyalja was enjoying its peak fame. The town of Eperjes (Prešov) had a vineyard in it in 1672 (UC 154:2). Its regional renown was retained into the communist period. It is one of only a few tract names that has retained its earlier spelling, with the *cz*. [See the entry for Gdańsk, in Part II.]

Darnó – 1) A *dűlő* in Sárospatak, mentioned in passing in 1798 and 1867, and noted in 1950 as "middling" quality, or 2nd Class. 2) A *dűlő* in Bodrogolaszi, on Magoshegy, noted as a lesser tract in 1950 because of its easterly exposure. The name Darnó indicates early ownership by the Prémontré Order, which founded a monastery of that name between Sárospatak and Tolcsva in the early-14th century.

Deák. See the entry for Barát (1).
Délrefekvő-Sulyom. See the entry for Sulyom.

Dereszla – A vineyard hill in Bodrogkeresztúr, not treated as a separate growing site in 1798 or 1867, though noted in the latter instance for its covering of loess. In fact, it is the northernmost loess area along the Bodrog. Its individual renown seems to date to ownership and improvements by Count Wolkenstein after phylloxera. The derivation of the name is unclear, but its origin goes far back in Hegyalja history, as a document of 1255 recorded a '*Dereznek*-pataka' (MOL), or Deresznek-creek, probably a hamlet, in the same vicinity.

Dessewffy – A *dűlő* in Tokaj, on the eastern side of Tokaj-hill, not mentioned separately in 1798 or 1867. It was, though, a well-respected tract, the property of a major aristocratic family of Sáros County. Most likely, it was created (or simply re-named) at the beginning of the 17th century, when John Dessewffy commanded the fortress of Tokaj. But it could have been as early as the mid-16th century, when the family was given the Tarkő fortress (in Sáros), and perhaps a vineyard in Hegyalja that belonged to it.

Diókút – A well-regarded *dűlő* in Erdőbénye, not given individual mention in 1798 or 1867, although the name is found as early as the beginning of the 17th century (UC 108:55). It means 'walnut-source,' which suggests tree removal to create vineyards. Pap (1985) mentioned it as Diós, which could have been in the sense of 'walnut forest.' However, there had been a noble family of that name in Abaúj County, of which the village was a part in bygone times. The family possibly had an earlier connection to the castle of Diósgyőr, 52 km/32 miles west of Tokaj, by today's regional center of Miskolc. The castle's earlier name was just Győr, but it became Diós-Győr in the late-14th century. The *dűlő* in Bénye was not necessarily that old.

Diós. See the previous entry.

DISZNÓKŐ – A *dűlő* of Mezőzombor, on the southern side of Perlite-hillock (*Perlitdomb*), mentioned as 1st Class in 1798 and 1867, and included among the village's "most outstanding" in 1950, with the additional qualifier of "splendidly situated." In 1963 (Dömötör/Katona), it was mentioned among the eight "most well-known" *dűlő*-s of Hegyalja. The name signifies 'hog-stone,' in reference to a large stone that was thought to resemble a wild boar.

Divini-Sulyom. See the entry for Sulyom.

Dobra – A *dűlő* in Sárazsadány, noted in 1950 as producing outstanding wine in its south-facing area. The name refers to Dobra, in Upper Zemplén (now in East Slovakia). The tract may date to ownership by the Rozgonyis of the Varannó Domain in the 14th century (DL 5191, of 1363). But it could be even older, inasmuch as the village of Dobra had existed since the 10th century. [See the entries for Rozgonyi, in Part I; and for Monyorós-Csicsva and Vranov nad Topľou in Part II.]

Donáth – A *dűlő* in Tokaj, not mentioned in 1798, 1867, or 1950, but one of the well-situated sites on the southeastern side of Tokaj-hill. At one time, it was part of the Zsoltáros tract [see that entry], and had two sections, Nagy- (Big) and Kis- (Little) Donáth. Part of it was also known as Tófeli [see the entry for Tófelé]. Pap (1985) attributes the name to St. Donatius, who was venerated in Tokaj as the patron saint of vintners. There was also a noble Donáth family in Abaúj County.

DORGÓ – 1) A vineyard hill and *dűlő* of Tállya, mentioned as "noble" in 1798 (with the spelling 'Dongó'), and as "eminent" in 1867. In 1950, it was referred to as "once famous."
2) A *dűlő* on Gárdony hill in Ond, not mentioned in 1798 or 1867, but remarked in 1950 for producing "the best Ond wine." 3) The Dorgó(-völgy/'vale') of Mád, mentioned by Nagy in 1962, was not listed in 1798, 1867, or 1950. In all three of these instances, the name could be an allusion to the Gálszécs Domain of central Zemplén County. The village of Dargó (now Drahov, in East Slovakia) was part of the Gálszécs Domain, and was owned by several prominent Hegyalja families during 1500-1700. Moreover, the village's name was spelled Dorgó as late as the 17th century. However, a family bearing the village name was involved with wine-growing in Sátoraljaújhely in the 15th century, and might account for one of the Dorgó tract names.

Dörzsik – A *dűlő* in Sátoraljaújhely, not mentioned in 1798 or 1867, although apparently of sufficient quality to be owned by the Trautsohns in 1713 (Balassa, 1991) [see the entry for Trautsohn, in Part I]. The name likely refers to the Sáros County family recorded historically as Derzsi/Derzsik/Derzsák. A Derzsffy was captain of the Tokaj fortress in the mid-16th century. All of the Derzs- names likely originated with the historical person Ders, associated with Zemplén County in the 14th century (DL 52204).

Dukát – A *dűlő* in Tállya, mentioned in 1950 as having a "good name," though it was not a name given individual mention in 1798 or 1867. But the name is of interest in any case. While the name translates to 'ducat,' it might have been a convenient later name. Before the Tatar invasion of 1241-1242, there were dukedoms, referred to as *dukátus* territories. Tállya, with its fortress, might well have been the center of a dukedom, and this tract could be the last reminder of it.

Egri. See the entry for Görbe (3).

ELŐHEGY – Meaning 'fore-hill,' this name has been borne by no fewer than six vineyard spaces in Hegyalja. 1) The most famous hill to bear the name is the one in Sárazsadány, which was known historically as Zsadány-Előhegy, to distinguish it from the others. It might also be the oldest hill of that name, since the onetime community of Zsadány likely had a connection to the early wine-growing family recorded as Sada in 1307 and Zada in 1413. In any case, Szabó/Török in 1867 commented that it "unites all those desirable features of site which one can imagine," while Kossuth, in 1903, wrote that it is "commonly acknowledged" as one of the "pearls of Hegyalja." Also, Hidvéghy noted it for "outstanding" wine in 1950. The tract in Sárazsadány is referred to simply as Zsadányi nowadays. 2) The southern end of Zsadány-Előhegy falls within Tolcsva, and has the famous Kincsem tract [see that entry]. This explains the apparent contradiction that it was mentioned as 2nd Class in 1798 and 1867 (the hill overall), whereas the 1950 report stated that it produces "outstanding" wine (the Kincsem tract). 3) The Előhegy of Olaszliszka was mentioned as 1st Class in 1798, as "eminent" in 1867; and in 1950 was noted as one of the best in the village because of its southern exposure. The Narancsi *dűlő* is situated on it [see that entry]. A sale of a vineyard on this Előhegy in 1474 may be the first sale recorded in Hegyalja between private persons. 4) The Tarcal hill of this name was ranked 3rd Class in 1798 and 1867 (in the latter case under the name Zombori-Előhegy), probably because of its position on the northern side of Tokaj-hill. 5) The name was also used for a vineyard hill in Szerencs as long ago as 1573 (UC 158:29). Fényes praised it highly in 1851. 6) It was also found in Abaújszántó in 1783 (UC 192:6).

Esztáva – This name, peculiar for Hungarian, is found only in Sátoraljaújhely, and is applied to the Felső- (Upper) and Alsó- (Lower) Esztáva *dűlő*-s. Esztáva-hill, under the spellings Zthawa, Ztava and Sztava, was one of the oldest names amongst vineyard hills in northern Hegyalja, going back to at least the 15th century. In 1502, the town of Bártfa purchased the Vajas *dűlő* on 'Zthawa-hegy' hill [see the entry for Bardejov, in Part II]. But the Esztáva spelling was established by at least the end of the 18th century (UC 160:33 (b)), when it belonged to the Szentmiklósi family. The *–va* ending is archaic and suggests a very early history, perhaps even originating with one of the allied groups that came into Hungary with the Magyars; it could even be a topographical relic of the Kabars [see that entry, in Part I]. No mention of the name was made in 1798 or 1867. [Note that Esztáva is not to be confused with the Szávahegy hill on the western side of Sátoraljaújhely. Regarding Száva, see the entry for Turány: On a Saintly Trail, in Part II.]

Falkos – A *dűlő* of Erdőhorváti, not mentioned in 1798, 1867, or 1950. The name likely derives from the village of Falkus (also spelled Falkos and Falkas; and now Falkušovce) in the former Zemplén County. The tract probably dates back to ownership of that village by the Buttkai family in the early-15th century, but possibly even to the mid-14th century, when the village was known as Buttkai-Falkus.

Farkas – The name 'Wolf' likely refers to the Farkas family of Zemplén and Sáros counties. 1) A *dűlő* in Erdőbénye, mentioned in 1950. 2) A *dűlő* in Tarcal, on the northern side of Tokaj-hill, mentioned as 3rd Class in 1798 and 1867. 3) A *dűlő* in Malá Tŕňa, in East Slovakia.

Fegyemes – Possibly one of the oldest tract names in Hegyalja, this has considerable historical interest. Referring to a vineyard hill in Tállya, it was recorded as 'Fedyemes' in 1485 (Gecsényi). Earlier, in 1261, it had been recorded as 'Fidemes.' The latter was also recorded as a toponym in 1055, in the very first document containing Magyar words, the establishment letter of the Tihány Abbey, by Lake Balaton in western Hungary. Indeed an archaic name, it signified 'the cultivated riverside land of the chief priest's wife' (F.J. Badiny, "Az Ékiratok Helyes Hangtana" [The Correct Phonetics of Cuneiform Documents], research paper, Orientalist World Conference, Paris, 1973). The same toponym was also recorded in 1574 as Födémes, in the *urbárium* of the Pozsony Domain (northwestern Hungary, now Bratislava in Slovakia). But the meaning of the old term had long been forgotten, and in Tállya the pronunciation had shifted from *–d* to *–dy*, which is modern Hungarian *–gy*. Thus, the name may sometimes have been skewed as Fegyveres, meaning 'armed,' in reference to weaponry, since it was not unusual for the old domains to have a *fegyveres*-house (*-ház*), or 'armory.' Pap, in 1985, mentioned an old, historical *dűlő* in Tokaj named Fegyveres, but in view of the town's position beside the Bodrog and Tisza rivers, the origin of the name has to be thrown into question.

Fegyveres. See the previous entry.

Fehér- – (or Fejér) The name means 'white.' 1) Fejérhegy – A vineyard hillock in Abaújszántó, whose Nagy- (Big) and Hosszú- (Long) Fejérhegy *dűlő*-s were mentioned in 1950. A document of 1783 shows that there had also been a Kis- (Little) Fejérhegy *dűlő* (UC 192:6). The name was not mentioned in 1798 because Szirmay did not include Abaúj County. The name signifies 'white-hill.' 2) The Fehérkút *dűlő* of Erdőbénye, mentioned in 1950, and in a document of 1739 (UC 83:91). The name signifies 'white-font.'

Fejér-. See the previous entry.

Feketehegy – The name 'black-hill' occurs twice as a toponym, but in three communities. 1) A vineyard hillock in Tarcal, on the western side of Tokaj-hill, was mentioned as 2nd Class in 1798 and 1867. Record of it as an individual *dűlő* can be found as far back as 1573 (UC 158:29). However, in 1737, it was noted as Nagy- (Big) and Kis- (Little) Feketehegy (UC 145:98). 2) Apparently, part of the hill was also in Tokaj, according to the document from 1573. 3) The hillock of this name in Sátoraljaújhely was only mentioned in passing in 1798 and 1867. However, its name was recorded as early as 1481. A Felső- (Upper) Feketehegy *dűlő* was recorded in 1746 (Balassa), but only Alsó- (Lower) Feketehegy has remained. [Also, see the entry for Čerhov, in Part II.]

Felbér – A *dűlő* in Mezőzombor, mentioned as 2nd Class in 1798 and 1867; not mentioned in 1950. The name possibly is a version of the surname Felber found in old documents.

Felhegy – 'Up-Hill' is an extensive vineyard hill in Erdőbénye, much of which was left fallow after phylloxera. It was mentioned in 1950 for its "outstanding" *dűlő*-s, except along its lower portion. A unique episode in the history of Hegyalja hills occurred in 1818, when a violent dispute over Felhegy erupted between the inhabitants of Erdőbénye and those of Baskó, the next village north and farther into the Zemplén hills. Deaths occurred and stiff punishments, both penal and corporal, were meted out.

Felső-Bea. See the entry for Bea.
Felső-Cserepes. See the entry for Cserepes.
Felső-Gát. See the entry for Gát.
Felső-Hetény. See the entry for Hetény.
Felső-Mecsege. See the entry for Mecsege.
Felső-Mocsár. See the entry for Mocsár.
Felső-Mogyorós. See the entry for Mogyorós.
Felső-Thurzó. See the entry for Thurzó.

Fóris – A *dűlő* in Tokaj, it was remarked as "most noble" in 1777 (UC 149:2), just five years after the Zemplén classification. But it was not mentioned by Szirmay in 1798, which probably reflected the fact that it had been absorbed by the Hétszőlő tract [see that entry]. The name is a diminutive form of Florian, and likely refers to a family that acquired Fóris as a surname.

Forrás – A *dűlő* in Tarcal, on the southern side of Tokaj-hill, mentioned as 1st Class in 1798, 1867, and 1950. The name means 'source/spring.' In 1747 (UC 145:123), there were four tracts with this name: Nagy- (Big), two Kis- (Little), and "Hortense Forrás Allya" (Lower Forrás Garden). The recording of two Kis-Forrás tracts was not an error, since one had 19 vineyards in it and the other only eight. The likely explanation is that one of them belonged entirely to Tarcal, while the other was shared with neighboring Tokaj.

FÖVENYES – A *dűlő* in Abaújszántó, on the southern side of Sátorhegy. Not mentioned in 1798 (Szirmay did not include Abaúj County); mentioned as "distinguished" in 1867; mentioned in 1950 among the *dűlő*-s producing the village's "best quality wines." The name refers to quicksand, but this is explained by an earlier Fövenyes creek and hamlet, recorded as 'Feovenyespataka' in a document of 1255 (MOL).

Fulóhegy – A vineyard hill in Legyesbénye, on which most of the village's vineyards were formerly located, notably including the Nagy- (Big) and Kis- (Little) Cserepes *dűlő*-s, which were noted in 1950 as producing the village's best wine. None of these names was mentioned in 1798 or 1867. The name was given as Futóhegy in 1950, which signifies 'runner-hill' and is an understandable garbling of the original name. But the fact remains that the Fuló family was of regional importance from the 14th century until the early-18th century, including a vice-commissioner of neighboring Szabolcs County in the mid-15th century. The hill may have become their property after King Matthias Corvinus, in 1461, made Paul Fuló one of the owners of the Boldogkő fortress, just 21 km (13 miles) north of Legyesbénye. The confusion about the name (Futó- vice Fuló-) might have arisen during the repopulation of the village that began in the early-18th century, following its destruction by the Ottomans several decades earlier.

Fürdős – A *dűlő* in Tallya, not mentioned in 1798 or 1867, but noted in 1950 for its "outstanding" location. The name refers to a 'bathing-place.'

Furmint (also as Formint) – Named for the *furmint* grape variety, this onetime, long-ago vineyard in Erdőbénye was first mentioned in 1623. Presumably, it was included in the Rákóczi classification of the 1640s, but apparently disappeared, at least under that name, by the 18th century. Most likely, it was simply absorbed by an adjoining and better known tract that pre-dated it. A most interesting aspect of its name is that it is also the first record of the *furmint* variety being in Hegyalja, although, as pointed out by Balassa (1991), it might previously have been there under a different name. Moreover, the vineyard was created by none other than László Máté Szepsi [see the entry for Szepsi, in Part I], the presumed font of modern *aszú* wine. Szepsi had taken up residence in Erdőbénye as the Calvinist minister in 1614. It has even been theorized that Szepsi made the first preponderantly botrytis wine while in Erdőbénye. Lastly, this vineyard name demonstrates conclusively that tracts occasionally were named for (usually uncommon) grape varieties [see the entries for Aranka, Kecsi, Lányka, Szegfű, and Talyanka].

Galagonyás – The Rákóczis had a vineyard in this Abaújszántó *dűlő* as late as 1686, and its name appears in a document of 1783 (UC 192:6). But it was not mentioned by Szirmay in 1798, since he did not include Abaúj County. The name refers to 'hawthorn,' probably to indicate the removal of shrubs to create the vineyard-tract.

Galambos – This name refers to pigeons (*galamb*), although in this form it also occurs as a family name. 1) The *dűlő* of this name in Sátoraljaújhely was not mentioned in 1798 or 1867, yet was mentioned as 1st Class in 1950. 2) The Galambos *dűlő* in Mezőzombor was mentioned as 2nd Class in 1798 and 1867. [Also, see the entry for Golopi-hegy.]

Gangalus: Scholar's or Merchant's?

The long extinct 'Gangalus' vineyard-tract name of Tarcal has a couple of things going for it in being mentioned. First, and most unusually, we know exactly when the name came into use: 1747. That is when it was recorded as "*neo assumptum*" (UC 145:123). Second, the name does not seem to have any Magyar, Slavic, or Germanic origin. On the contrary, it appears to be of Greek origin. The ancient Greek *kangelos* (κάγκελος) indicated a barrier, while in Modern Greek *kangelo* (κάγκελο) indicates a railing, but also…a trellis. That's hardly an unlikely name for a vineyard. But the form Gangalus seems both Latinized and Hungarianized; the *–us* ending (instead of the equivalent Magyar *–usz*) suggests Latin influence, while the initial *G* and the use of *a* in place of *e* are the Magyar features. The Hungarian nobility was versed in Latin, the 'official' (administrative) language, and some were familiar with Greek, as well. This leads one to think that Gangalus was a property of a Hungarian nobleman. Or else, it might have been that of a Greek merchant who had become a Hungarian subject (it was the right time-frame). Maybe the Hungarian who recorded the name spelled it as he heard it, using the *–us* ending to show that he had a touch of classicism.

Garai – A *dűlő* in Tokaj, not mentioned in 1798 or 1867, but probably implicitly included in the mention of Mézesmáj [see that entry]. Both a Nagy- (Big) and Kis- (Little) Garai have existed at times, with the latter being the most esteemed because of its position on the south-facing side of Tokaj hill. The Garai family became nationally prominent during the late-14th century, and probably acquired a Hegyalja tract while serving as palatines of Hungary in the 15th century.

Gárdon(y) – A hill and *dűlő* in Ond at least as far back as 1723 (UC 88:125), but not mentioned in 1798 or 1867. It was included among the village's lesser tracts in 1950. Mád was recorded as having a portion of it in 1723 (UC 83:126), perhaps because the population of Ond was still recovering from Ottoman Turkish attacks several decades earlier.

Gát – Felső- (Upper) and Alsó- (Lower) Gát are *dűlő*-s in Sárospatak, neither of which was mentioned in 1798 or 1867. In 1950, it was noted that the the the upper third was of lesser quality, or 3rd Class, while the lower two-thirds were of "middling" quality, or 2nd Class. The names signify, respectively, Upper- and Lower-Bank (embankment).

Gelencsér – A *dűlő* in Abaújszántó, on the southern side of Sátorhegy, it was not mentioned in 1798 because Szirmay did not include Abaúj County. It was noted as "distinguished" in 1867. A separate *dűlő* called Kis- (Little) Gelencsér was recorded in 1784-1785 (UC 143:17). The name signifies 'potter,' but most likely in reference to a family of that name.

Gilányi – A *dűlő* in Tolcsva, not mentioned in 1798 or 1867, but mentioned commendably in 1950. The name refers to the family Ghyllányi (old spelling), originally from Liptó County (now in north-central Slovakia). The family's acquisitions in Hegyalja probably dated to the second-half of the 17th century, when George Ghyllányi was counsel to the Hungarian Chamber and would have been involved with confiscations of vineyard properties following the anti-Habsburg rebellions of that era. He was rewarded with the rank of baron, and apparently with a vineyard property as well.

Göböly – A *dűlő* in Szegi, mentioned in passing in 1798, but noted as "celebrated" in 1867 (under the listing for Szegi and Long). Although the name signifies 'fatted ox' in Hungarian, it may have originated as a Magyar corruption of the German village name of Gübel/Gibel in the Szepesség region (UC 157:73, circa 1670), in the era when communities there had a keen interest in acquiring Hegyalja vineyard property [see the entry for Szepesség, in Part II]. The name is spelled Göböl in some old documents. Also, a noble family with the name Gobol(y) was resident in Abaúj County.

Golopi-hegy – A vineyard hill mostly in Golop, but partly in Tállya, it was not mentioned in 1798 (Szirmay did not include Abaúj County), but it was alluded to in the paragraph about Golop in 1867. It was mentioned in 1950 with the notation that its southern slope, which is in Tállya, is the only favorably situated area. [See the entry for Somos.] Although the name ostensibly refers to

Golop, it might ultimately derive from the Bulgaro-Slav word for pigeon (*gâlâb*/гълъб), *i.e.*, Pigeon-hill [see the entry for Golop, in Part II].

Gömbölyű-Mogyorós. See the entry for Mogyorós.

Gombos – 1) The Gombos *dűlő* in Sárospatak was not mentioned in 1798 or 1867, but was noted in 1950 as "middling" quality, or 2nd Class. A document of 1785 mentioned both a Felső- (Upper) and Alsó- (Lower) Gombos (Balassa, 1991). In the mid-16th century, there was a Gombos-*kert* (Gombos-garden) that was used for mushroom (*gomb*) cultivation. But, by the early-17th century, some vines had been planted, and a 'Gombos-garden cellar' was mentioned. 2) Gomboska (diminutive) *dűlő* in Tállya was not mentioned in 1798 or 1867, but was noted for its "outstanding" location in 1950. 3) Gombos-hegy (hill) is a *dűlő* in Hercegkút. In the latter two instances, the name suggests areas once frequented by mushroom hunters, and thus, vineyards created from forested land. However, in one of these cases, the name might refer to the Gombos family of Sáros County, who were also connected elsewhere in the Upper Tisza. A document of 1761 tells that Emerich Gombos was storing wine at Vinné [see that entry, in Part II].

GÖRBE – Several *dűlő*-s bore the name 'crooked' or 'lumpy,' and all had good reputations. 1) The *dűlő* in Tállya was mentioned as "noble" in 1798 and "eminent" in 1867, and was remarked in 1950 as still having a "good name." 2) Görbe in Tarcal, on the southern side of Tokaj-hill, was mentioned as 1st Class in 1798, 1867, and 1950. More recently, it was joined to the Baksó tract and acquired the combined name Görbe-Baksó. [See the entry for Baksó.] 3) The neighboring one in Tokaj was mentioned in 1764 as being exposed to frigid winds (UC 122:34). Historically, it was also known as Egri, most likely in reference to the noble family of that name in Abaúj and Sáros counties. The Hegyalja part of the family died out early in the 18th century, and in 1749 the tract was sold to a doctor in Tokaj, Sigmund Várady, after which it became more commonly known as Görbe. 4) The Rákóczis had a vineyard in the Görbe tract of Abaújszántó as late as 1686, but the *dűlő* was not mentioned in 1798 because Szirmay did not include Abaúj.

GYAPÁROS – (also spelled Gyopáros) A *dűlő* in Tolcsva, mentioned as 1st Class in 1798 and 1867, and among the village's best in 1950. Kossuth (1903) referred to it as "one of the jewels of the famous Szirmay vineyards [*Szirmay-féle szőlők*]." In 1520, a vineyard in it was purchased by the municipality of Eperjes, which already owned two other Tolcsva vineyards. The name by its typical spelling would seem to refer to 'wool-seller' (possibly an archaic surname); but it was sometimes recorded as Gyopáros, in reference to cottonweed. The name was recorded in 1672 as Gipáros (UC 154:2), which suggests that *Gya-*, not *Gyo-*, was the earlier voicing.

Gyertyános – 1) This *dűlő* in Szegilong was not mentioned in 1798 or 1867, but its southeastern exposure was noted as "most favorable" in 1950. 2) In 1950, the plural form, Gyertyánosok, was used for a *dűlő* in Abaújszántó, apparently because at one time there were two or more of them. Certainly there had been an Ó- (Old) Gyertyános in 1784-1785 (UC 143:17). But neither was mentioned in 1798 because Szirmay did not include Abaúj County. The name Gyertyános refers to the hornbeam tree (*carpino fagetum*), which suggests that tracts with that name were among the many created by clearing forested land on hills during the 14th and 15th centuries.

Gyöpös – A *dűlő* in Tokaj, on the southern side of Tokaj-hill, mentioned as 1st Class in 1798, 1867, and 1950. The name (also spelled Gyepűs in earlier times) definitely marks this as a very old tract. While the name commonly means 'grassy' in modern Hungarian, the term *gyepü* in early Hungarian history signified an open, usually 'grassy' (as opposed to forested) divide, between territories or pieces of land. Thus did the term come to indicate grassy, linear stretches separating vineyard-tracts, though usually set off further by brush or other vegetation along the edge of a tract. It might be supposed that Gyöpös originally was enclosed entirely in that fashion.

Halastó – A *dűlő* in Tállya, mentioned as "noble" in 1798 and "eminent" in 1867. The name signifies 'fish-lake' and apparently dates to the time, in the late Middle Ages, when freshwater fishing was a significant economic activity on the feudal domains of Zemplén County.

Hangács – A *dűlő* in Mezőzombor, mentioned as 1st Class in 1798 and 1867, and among the village's "most outstanding" in 1950. At one time, there were both a Nagy- (Big) and a Kis- (Little) Hangács. Kis-Hangács was mentioned as 3rd Class in 1798 and 1867. The name refers to the Hangács family of Sáros County, which likely dates the *dűlő* name to the 15th century.

Haragos – 1) A *dűlő* in Erdőhorváti, mentioned in 1950 as one of the village's best. The word *haragos* means 'angry,' but it was most likely a later-day corruption of *hólyagos*, or 'blistered,' in allusion to appearance. In fact, several hills in the Upper Tisza region, notably in East Slovakia, still bear the name Hajagos (= Hólyagos), as if it had been a commonly used name for hills of a certain appearance in the late Middle Ages. 2) Kossuth, in 1903, specified the Hajagos (*sic*) of Sátoraljaújhely as one of the altitudinous wine-growing hills that had been left fallow and had reverted to forest two centuries previously.

Harcsa – A *dűlő* in Mezőzombor, mentioned as 3rd Class in 1798 and 1867. The name refers to a fresh-water fish, akin to a catfish. A document near the end of the 17th century mentioned a Harcsafark (Harcsa-tail) tract in Mezőzombor (UC 69:81), but it is unclear whether Harcsa would have been just a shortened form of that name, or that Harcsafark had been a separate section of it.

HASZNOS – 1) The plural form of this name, Hasznosok, came into use on Hasznoshegy hill in Tállya because at one time there were Nagy- (Big) and Kis- (Little) Hasznos *dűlő*-s. The tract mentioned as "noble" in 1798 and as "eminent" in 1867, while in 1950 it was said to still have a "good name." Record of a vineyard purchase in the Hasznos of Tállya is found in a document from 1469. 2) A *dűlő* in Legyesbénye, situated on Monoki-hegy hill, it was not mentioned in 1798 or 1867, but was noted for its good exposition in 1950. These tracts take their name from the once prominent Hasznos family of Mezőzombor. [See the entry for Péter-deák.]

HATALOS – A *dűlő* of Szegi, mentioned in passing in 1798, but as "celebrated" in 1867 (under the listing for Szegi and Long). Its name suggests a connection to the Gathal (= Hatal) family, who were landowners about 34 km (21 miles) northeast of Hegyalja, at present-day Hatalov (now in East Slovakia) by the late-13th century. A small fortress of that name apparently was erected there during the 14th century, probably by the same family, as an expression of their growing local influence. Their importance peaked in the 15th century, which is probably when they acquired vineyard property in Hegyalja. Despite the renown of the Hatalos tract, it was recorded as "*desolatissima*" in 1683 (UC 116:28), probably in connection with anti-Habsburg rebellions.

Határi – A *dűlő* in Olaszliszka, not mentioned in 1798 or 1867, but indicated among the village's best in 1950. Ownership in it by the Szepes municipality of Lőcse in 1594 is testimony to early recognition of its quality. The name 'at-the-border' refers to the tract's location at the edge of the village's lands.

Hátutolsó-Bánya. See the entry for Bánya.

Hegyes – A *dűlő* in Tállya, mentioned as "noble" in 1798 and as "eminent" in 1867; mentioned in passing in 1950. A citizen of Kassa bought a vineyard in Hegyes in 1508, which suggests good repute since the time of the first later-harvested wines of Hegyalja. The name signifies 'pointed.'

Hegyfark – The name 'hill-tail' was used with some frequency for reference to vineyard-tracts at the end of a hill. 1) A *dűlő* in Ond, situated on Kassai-hegy, mentioned in 1950 as one of the village's "most valuable," though it was not mentioned in 1798 or 1867. 2) A onetime *dűlő* in Bodrogkeresztúr, recorded as far back as 1573 (UC 158:29). Nothing was said of it in 1798 or 1867. 3) A *dűlő* in Viničky, in East Slovakia.

Hegymegy – A *dűlő* in Mezőzombor, mentioned as 3rd Class in 1798 and 1867; not referred to in 1950. Bearing the name of the Hegymegy family of Sáros, it is yet another indication of the onetime fashionability in that county for owning vineyard property in Hegyalja [see the entry for Sáros County, in Part II]. As to a noble family having a 3rd Class property, they might have acquired it before later-harvested white wine became typical of Hegyalja.

HENYE – A *dűlő* on a hill of the same name in Bodrogkeresztúr, mentioned as 1st Class in 1798 and 1867 [see the entry for Grassalkovich, in Part I]. It likely dates to around 1600. A document of 1655 shows that George Semsey and his wife, Christina Wesselényi, both of the aristocracy, owned a vineyard in it (UC 155:34). The Serbian Brankoviches also had a property in the early-18th century (UC 79:39). Around 1740, there existed Nagy- (Big) and Kis- (Little) Henye tracts, as well as a Henye-alja (bottom); the latter became known as Lencsés [see that entry]. At one time, part of Henye-alja fell within Tarcal (UC 145:123, of 1747). The name Henye suggests that the tract was owned earlier by the Pethős, a prominent Hegyalja wine-growing family that had owned the village of Pető-Henye in southwestern Hungary before coming to Zemplén in the 16th century. [See the entry for Pethő, below; and in Part I.]

Hercegköves – A *dűlő* in Rátka, not mentioned in 1798 or 1867, but noted in 1950 for producing some of the village's "best wine" on its southeasterly exposed area. The name signifies 'the prince's stony vineyard,' in reference to Prince Trautsohn, the 18th-century owner of the village [see the entry for Trautsohn, in Part I].

Hetény – A *dűlő* in Tállya, mentioned as "noble" in 1798, "eminent" in 1867, and among the village's best in 1950. The part known as Kő- ('stone') Hetény was noted in 1950 as "once famous" and for having an "outstanding" location. The name Hetény has an old history as a place-name, but in this case probably refers to a 15th century member of the family of that name.

HÉTSZŐLŐ – A *dűlő* in Tokaj, located along Tokaj-hill, mentioned as 1st Class in 1798, 1867, and 1950, and included among Hegyalja's eight "most well-known" *dűlő*-s in 1963 (Dömötör/Katona). This prominent *dűlő* was once situated along Mézesmáj, in the latter's older, wider topographical indication [see the entry for Mézesmáj (c)]. Its name means 'seven vineyards,' which is thought to date to about 1500, when it had seven owners. A document from the late-16th century refers to "seven vineyards on the Mezesmal-named vineyard hill belonging to the town of Thokay" (UC 87:61). A document from the late-1500s indicates that all seven had been in the possession of the recently deceased John Bornemissza [see the entry for Bornemissza], and mentions them by name: Nagyszőlő, Németszőlő, Horváthszőlő, Palánt, Kusaly, Tapasztó, Török; with the notation that all seven produce "exceedingly good wine" (UC 87:61). However, the historical composition of Hétszőlő is not exactly clear. It seems that only the Bornemissza parts of the named *dűlő*-s originally formed it, and that some sections were lost, while other adjoining vineyards were attached, as time went by. Notably, Szirmay, in 1798, listed Nagyszőlő,

Németszőlő, and Tapasztó tracts in addition to Hétszőlő. In any case, Hétszőlő became the property of the Hungarian kings, in other words, the Habsburgs.

Hideg- – 'Cold' (*hideg*) is not a propitious qualifier for a vineyard-tract name in Hegyalja, but it was in use nonetheless. 1) The southwest-facing side of Hidegvölgy ('Cold-vale') in Bodrogolaszi was mentioned very favorably in 1950. 2) Hidegoldal ('Cold-side') *dűlő* in Erdőbénye was mentioned in 1950. 3) Hidegoldal in Abaújszántó was not mentioned in 1798 because Szirmay did not include Abaúj County, and in 1950 it was noted as entirely uncultivated. 4) A Hidegoldal was also recorded in Tokaj in 1736 (Balassa).

Hintós – A *dűlő* in Mád, mentioned as 2nd Class in 1798 and 1867, although certain sections apparently caused it to be mentioned among the village's "unfavorably situated" tracts in 1950. The name refers to a four-wheel coach. However, because of its location in one of the earliest significant locales of Hegyalja, one might speculate that the name was a later-day corruption of Huntó, an early-13th century lord at the northern end of the region.

Holdvölgy – 1) A *dűlő* of Mád, mentioned as 2nd Class in 1798 and 1867; not noted in 1950. 2) A *dűlő* of Rátka, not mentioned in 1798 or 1867, but noted in 1950 as being among the village's preferred, southerly exposed tracts. There is a distinct possibility that the two villages cultivated different parts of an area bearing only the one name. The name signifies 'moon-vale' or 'moon-hollow.' But in the case of Rátka, the name Holtvölgy (*sic*) was also used (Borovszki, 1903), apparently in the sense of 'Deadend-valley.'

Hosszú- – The word 'long' occurs with some frequency throughout Hegyalja, usually to indicate a laterally extensive growing site. 1) The *dűlő* of this name in Erdőbénye was mentioned among the village's best in 1950. 2) Hosszúmáj, or 'long-warm-side,' is a *dűlő* shared by Szegi and Szegilong. It was mentioned in passing in 1798 (under the listing for Szegi commune), but called "celebrated" in 1867 (under the listing for Szegi and Long communes). In 1950, it was indicated that the upper section in Szegi is excellent, while the southeastern exposure in Szegilong is "most favorable." 3) Hosszúhegy, or Long-hill, is a vineyard hill in Sárospatak, mentioned in passing in 1798 and 1867, and mentioned in 1950 with the notation that its east-facing section is unfavorably situated. In 1785, both a Belső- (Inner) Hosszúhegy and a Hosszúhegy-fark (-tail) were mentioned (Balassa, 1991). 4) Neighboring Hercegkút also has a Hosszúhegy *dűlő*. 5) Hosszúláz is a former *dűlő* of Sátoraljaújhely not mentioned in 1798, 1867, or 1950. The second portion of the name, *–láz*, is thought to have been borrowed from Slavs to indicate uncultivated land, often forested, either above or below vineyard land (Balassa, 1991). [See the entry for Fehér- regarding Hosszú-Fejérhegy *dűlő*.]

Istenhegy – A vineyard hill in Rátka, mentioned in passing in 1798, 1867, and 1950. Part of it is favorably exposed to the south. The name means 'God-hill,' perhaps in reference to a very old ceremonial site [see the entry for Rátka, in Part II]. In a document from the end of the 17th century, it was recorded as belonging to Tállya (UC 69:81), which seems to have been a temporary situation caused by Rátka's ruination at the hands of the Ottoman Turks at that time. [See the entry for Padihegy.]

Izdenci – (or Izdenczy) A *dűlő* in Tokaj, on the northern side of Tokaj hill, not mentioned in 1798, 1867, or 1950, but generally recognized as a vineyard area having its own historical identity. The name alludes to Martin Izdenczy, who was in charge of the Tokaj fortress under Thököly during the latter's insurrection against the Habsburgs in 1683-1685.

Józan – A *dűlő* of Tokaj, not mentioned in 1798, 1867, or 1950, though existing as long ago as 1573 (UC 158:29). The name means 'sober,' though it likely refers to a family of that name.

Juh- – Considering that cows and hares were represented in old tract names, it is not surprising that sheep (*juh*) were as well. 1) The *dűlő* that has survived is Juharos in Mád, which was mentioned as 2nd Class in 1798 (Juháros) and 1867. The name is an archaic surname, 'sheep-seller,' dating back to as early as 1300, whether or not the vineyard-tract is quite that old. 2) In 1747, a Juhos (signifying a onetime sheep pasture) was recorded at Tarcal (UC 145:123), when it was listed as "Juhos or Lantos." This is a rare record of a tract name going through a transition. 3) Balassa (1991) also noted a Juhos-oldal (side) in Tállya in 1689.

Kakas – 1) A *dűlő* in Bodrogkeresztúr, mentioned as 1st Class in 1798, 1867, and 1950. Both a Nagy- (Big) and Kis- (Little) Kakas were recorded in the Tokaj Domain *urbárium* of 1688; hence the plural form (Kakasok) is also used. 2) A hill and *dűlő* in Mád, mentioned favorably in 1950, but not mentioned in 1798 or 1867. The name 'rooster' (*kakas*) likely refers to a historical figure of the late-13th century, Kakas, who was descended from the 12th century Ratold clan that resided immediately north of Hegyalja. Kakas was an early supporter of the Angevin kings. [See the entries for Angevin and Ratold, in Part I.]

Kalap – A *dűlő* in Erdőhorváti, noted as "very favorably situated" in 1867. The name signifies 'cap' or 'hat,' probably in allusion to the hill's shape.

Kanducs – A *dűlő* in Tokaj, on the southern side of Tokaj-hill, mentioned as 1st Class in 1798, 1867, and 1950. The name was mentioned in a document from the end of the 17th century (UC 69:81), and again in 1736 (Balassa). A document of 1765 noted the Felső- (Upper) Kanducs tract as 1st Class (UC 117:50); that name no doubt separated it from the Kanducs-alja (bottom) mentioned in 1736. The name probably was a version of a surname, perhaps connected to the Kanta/Kandó family [see the following entry]. Sometimes it was garbled, notably as Kendős, which refers to a kerchief and was frequently used in recent times, but also as Gandács earlier. It is to be noted that a 'Kenthes' [*sic*] family in northern Hegyalja donated a vineyard in Sátoraljaújhely to the Pauline Order in 1505 (DL 35797) [see the entry for Pauline Order, in Part I].

Kanta – A vineyard-tract in Bodrogolaszi, not mentioned in 1798, but mentioned as "distinguished" in 1867 (with the misspelling 'Kautha'), and included among the village's best in 1950. The name refers to a family with that surname. The property was confiscated from John Kanta by the Habsburg authorities in 1683 because of his support for the anti-Habsburg rebellion of Emerich Thököly (UC 54:46). The family name was also spelled Kandó, and thus, possibly had a connection to the tract once known as Kandúcs [see the preceding entry].

Kapi – A *dűlő* in Mezőzombor. Situated near the southern end of the Eperjes-Tokaj Hill-Chain, Kapi duplicates the name of a hill at the northern end, just to the northeast of Eperjes (Prešov). Both carry the name of the Kapy family, descended from the ancient Magyar Pukur clan. By the 14th century, the Kapys were (according to Potemkin, 1863), "one of Hungary's most propertied families." Kapi-hill by Eperjes got its name in the early-15th century, when Count Andrew Kapy acquired the fortress upon it. The *dűlő* in Mezőzombor certainly post-dates that, whether because the fortress acquired it, or because of a prominent later Kapy, such as Gabriel Kapy, who was an accounts inspector in Royal Hungary in the mid-17th century. [See the entries for Prešov and Sáros County, in Part II.]

Kásás – A *dűlő* in Olaszliszka, mentioned in 1950, but not in 1798 or 1867. The name would seem to refer to 'porridge' (East European kasha), except that an Affra (female) Kása owned a vineyard in Abaújszántó as early as the mid-15th century.

Kassa – Kassa (now Košice, in East Slovakia) was the first of the Upper Tisza towns to take note of developments in Hegyalja. Located directly north of Abaújszántó, Kassa was aware early of the change in wine-style and improvement in quality that took place around 1500. 1) The Kassa-város (town) *dűlő* in Abaújszántó must have been highly appreciated by the town council when the bishop of Kassa bequeathed it to the municipality in 1508. The name was retained ever after, though it eventually became known as Kassi. 2) Kassa-hegy is a vineyard hill in Ond, mentioned in a document of 1723 (UC 88:125), but not mentioned in 1798 or 1867. In 1950, it was noted as having the village's best vineyard sites on its southern and western slopes. Kassa's early interest, as well as the hill's suitability for wine-growing, give more than sufficient reason to think that Kassa-hegy was the 'Ond's Vineyard Hill' (*Ondzeuloshege*) recorded in 1349 (DL 4087). The hill was also mentioned in a document of 1761 (UC 149:56). 3) Tarcal has a Kassai-hegy hill to its rear, though it was not ranked individually in 1798 or 1867.

Káté – (also spelled Káta) This name is a relic of the Katha clan, one of the oldest in Hegyalja and the surrounding territory. Consequently, we likely are looking at very old vineyard-tracts. 1) The surviving *dűlő* of this name formely belonged to Sátoraljaújhely, but became part of Slovenské Nové Mesto when that section of the town was attached to (Czecho-) Slovakia in 1918, because of its position on the eastern side of the Ronyva creek (the new border). In the past, there were both a Nagy- (Big) and Kis- (Little) Káté. 2) A document of 1747 lists a "Kathy" tract in Tarcal (UC 145:123); but it seems to have disappeared as a separate entity subsequently. 3) The same is true for a Kátai in Mezőzombor in 1683 (UC 58:13). It is of note, though, that the Katha clan seems to have possessed properties at both ends of Hegyalja.

Kecsi – A *dűlő* in Abaújszántó, not mentioned in 1798 because Abaúj County was left out. The Rákóczis had a vineyard here as late as 1686. The name conceivably was shorthand for a vineyard planted with the *kecskecsecsű* variety, mentioned as far back as 1570 [see Grape Varieties, in Part IV]. The variety's onetime significance would explain why it was planted in a major locale such as Abaújszántó. [See the entries for Aranka, Furmint, Lányka, Szegfű, and Talyanka.]

KELETKA. See the entry for Király (2).

Kendős. [See the entry for Kanta.]
Kereknémahegy. [See the entry for Némahegy.]

Kerektölgyes – A *dűlő* in Rátka, its name was documented as early as 1738 (UC 83:86), though it was not mentioned in 1798 or 1867. In 1950, it was mentioned among the village's preferred, southerly exposed tracts. The name signifies 'round oak grove,' another instance suggesting creation by clearing forested land.

Kertész – 1) A *dűlő* in Szerencs, not mentioned in 1798 or 1867 because Szerencs was considered outside Hegyalja, but mentioned among the village's best in 1950. 2) A tract with this name was mentioned in Tokaj in 1676 [see the entry for Mézesmáj (c)]. The name means 'gardener,' but likely indicated a surname, probably the Sáros County family of that name, which held noble rank since around 1600. [Note: Vineyards recorded in the past with names indicating a garden (Kert(i), Hortenses/Hortensis) usually indicated low elevation and lesser quality.]

Keskeny-ág – A *dűlő* in Tokaj, on the northern side of Tokaj-hill, mentioned as 3rd Class in 1798 and 1867. The name signifies 'narrow branch' (as in a 'branch' of a hill).

KINCSEM – A *dűlő* in Tolcsva, situated between that settlement and Bodrogolaszi, on the western end of Zsadány-Előhegy hill. It was not mentioned by name in 1798 or 1867, though probably implicit in the mention of Zsadány-hegye (*sic*). It was mentioned among Tolcsva's best in 1950. Further, Kossuth in 1903 said it was "among the foremost vineyards" of Hegyalja, and related that Kincsem had been so strikingly replanted following phylloxera that a foreign banker offered "a fabulous sum" for it. Fittingly, its name means 'my treasure.'

KIRÁLY(-) – The name 'king' was used to refer to vineyard land that belonged to the king. Such names may be presumed to date mostly from the late-11th to the late-13th century, when royal ownership was at its peak. **1)** Király-hegy (hill) and *dűlő* in Mád were mentioned as 1st Class in 1798 and 1867. In 1950, the hill was included among the village's best, with the additional comment: "The wines of Királyhegy are especially famous. This is acknowledged as the 'king' of Mád's vineyard hills." Király was also mentioned among the eight "most well-known" *dűlő*-s of Hegyalja in 1963 (Dömötör/Katona). The name was also recorded as Nagy- (Big) Király, in earlier times (1683, UC 116:28). **2)** Historically the most esteemed *dűlő* of Malá Tŕňa, in East Slovakia, Királyka (Kraľka in Slovak) has also been the smallest of the village's best tracts. The name could date to royal ownership in the 13th century. However, the name was often corrupted as Keletka, for instance in a document of 1704 (UC 154:45). The latter document mentioned that the tract could produce 40 barrels of wine in a good year, but had produced only four in 1703 because of hail. **3)** In Tarcal, the *dűlő* Királymáj, or 'warm side of King-hill,' was mentioned as 1st Class in 1798, 1867, and 1950. **4)** Királyhegy in Sárospatak was mentioned in passing in 1798 and 1867, but in 1950 was noted as having the town's best *dűlő*-s on its southern and south-southeastern sides. It is certainly a very old vineyard site, as it was the object of a civil dispute in 1338. A document of 1785 mentioned both a Nagy- (Big) and Kis- (Little) Király (Balassa). **5)** In Tarcal, there was a Királygát ('King-embankment') *dűlő* that was not mentioned in any of the listings, although it still exists. This name had nothing to do with a Hungarian king, or even an embankment. A document from 1573 shows that the original name of the *dűlő* was Király-Gál (Kyraly Gaal), in reference to a person named Gál Király. **6)** Nagy- (Big) and Kis- (Little) Király *dűlő*-s in Mezőzombor dated to at least 1573 (UC 158:29), but were not mentioned in 1798 or 1867.

Kis-Bányihegy. See the entry for Bánya.
Kis-Cepre. See the entry for Cepre.
Kis-Cserepes. See the entry for Cserepes.
Kis-Fejérhegy. See the entry for Fehér-.
Kis-Hangács. See the entry for Hangács.
Kis-Káté. See the entry for Káté.
Kis-Király. See the entry for Király.
Kis-Kocsárd. See the entry for Kocsárd.
Kis-Kopasz. See the entry for Kopasz.
Kis-Köveshegy. See the entry for Köves.

Kis-Kút – A *dűlő* in Mád, not mentioned in 1798, 1867, or 1950. The name means 'small well.'

Kis-Lete. See the entry for Lete.
Kis-Meszes. See the entry for Meszes.
Kis-Mézesmáj. See the entry for Mézesmáj (b).
Kis-Mocsár. See the entry for Mocsár.
Kis-Mondolás. See the entry for Mandulás.

Kis-Ősze – A *dűlő* in Tokaj, on the southeastern side of Tokaj-hill, mentioned as 2nd Class in 1798 and 1867. The name signifies 'little grey-hair.'

Kis-Rigócska. See the entry for Rigócska.
Kis-Szárhegy. See the entry for Szárhegy.
Kis-Temető. See the entry for Temető.

Kis-Váradi – 1) A *dűlő* in Tarcal, on the northern side of Tokaj-hill, mentioned as 3rd class in 1798, but not mentioned in 1867 or 1950. The name, meaning 'little Váradi' probably refers to Dr. Sigmund Várady, who had bought a vineyard in the Görbe tract of Tokaj in 1764 [see the entry for Görbe (3)]. 2) A document of 1697 indicates that part of the tract also belonged to Tokaj, and had earlier been known as Kalodás (UC 116:61).

Kis-Vérmány. See the entry for Vérmány.
Kis-Vilmány. See the entry for Vilmánok.
Kőbánya. See the entry for Bánya (1).

KÓCSAG – A *dűlő* in Tokaj, on the southeastern side of Tokaj-hill, mentioned as 1st Class in 1798 and 1867. In 1747, half of the tract belonged to Tarcal (UC 145:123), even though Tarcal did not abut the tract. A onetime Rákóczi property, this *dűlő* was confiscated for the Habsburg empress (and queen of Hungary) by the Hungarian Chamber after the defeat of the Rákóczis in 1711. Spelled Kócsag or Kótsag, the name signifies 'heron.' But older spellings include Kots-ág, Kottság, Kocsógh (UC 145:123), and even Kocsák (UC 81:10 (c)), the latter from 1565; the spelling "Kolchag" (= Kolcsag) is found in the Tokaj Domain *urbárium* of 1581. Balassa (1991) also noted the spelling Kolcsagh from 1736. These spellings suggest that the original name was 'Kots/Kocs-branch' (–*ág*) and referred to early possession by the Kolcs clan of Zemplén, possibly dating to the late-13th century, in the wake of the Tatar invasion. Until into the 18th century, the *dűlő* was also commonly known as Óvár (Old-fort), as if it had at one time belonged to the earliest fortification at the locale; that name is still known. A document of 1707 shows that a Kis- (Little) Kócsag had an identity of its own at that time (UC 116:76), and one of 1747 lists a Kócsag-alja (bottom) (UC 145:123). [Also, see the entry for Mézesmáj (c).]

Kocsárd – The hill of Királyhegy in Sárospatak included the *dűlő*-s Nagy- (Big) and Kis- (Little) Kocsárd, both of which belonged to Károlyfalva after its founding in the 18th century. However, in 1950, Hidvéghy treated Károlyfalva as part of Sárospatak, and mentioned the two Kocsárds as two of the town's best, in other words, 1st Class. Károlyfalva was later attached administratively to Sátoraljaújhely. Consequently, the Kocsárd tracts technically are within the latter's limits now. The name likely is a very old surname, derived from a place-name of the Árpád era.

Kő-Hetény. See the entry for Hetény.
Koldus. See the entry for Nyírjesek.

Kónya – This onetime *dűlő* in Tokaj must have been quite old, since its name refers to the noble Kónya family of Sáros County, and perhaps specifically to the mid-14th century Count Kónya, who was the Lord-Lieutenant of Sáros for several years. In 1716, an Andrew Fazékas had a vineyard in it (UC 152:61); and Balassa (1991) mentions a Kónya-alja (bottom) in 1737. Yet, no mention was made of these in 1798 or 1867, whether because they no longer existed or were implicitly considered part of Kis-Mézesmáj [see the entry for Mézesmáj (c)].

Kőporos – A Hegyaljan colloquialism, the name 'stone-powdery' is a natural for reference to soil at some sites in the region. 1) A *dűlő* of Mezőzombor, mentioned as 3rd Class in 1798 and

1867. 2) A *dűlő* in Hercegkút, mentioned in 1950 as producing the village's lesser wine because of easterly exposure. [Also, see the entry for Bodroghalász, in Part II.]

Kővágó – The name 'stonecutter' became attached to several *dűlő*-s in Hegyalja, perhaps in an early time when large wine-cellars were being built, or maybe even earlier, when stone fortresses were being erected. 1) A *dűlő* in Bodrogkeresztúr, mentioned as 1st Class in 1798, 1867, and 1950. 2) A *dűlő* in Mád, mentioned as 1st Class in 1798 and 1867, and among the village's best in 1950. The name was also recorded as Nagy- (Big) Kővágó in 1723 (UC 26:7 (b)).
3) Kővágók in Tállya was mentioned as "noble" in 1798 and as "eminent" in 1867, and was noted in 1950 as "once famous." In this last case, the plural form (–*k*) suggests that at one time there were at least two separate tracts, whether 'Big' and 'Little,' or 'Upper' and 'Lower.'

Köves – 'Stony' is an apt description for many a Hegyalja vineyard, and thus it has been used in naming sites. 1) Köveshegyek ('Stony Hills') is a name used for a hillock and *dűlő* in Tállya. Earlier, under the name Tályi-Kőhegy, it was mentioned as "noble" in 1798 and as "eminent" in 1867. The use of the plural form (–*ek*) suggests that at one time there was more than one *dűlő* with the name. 2) Köveshegy is a vineyard hill in Sátoraljaújhely, mentioned in passing in 1798 and 1867. However, in 1950, the Nagy- (Big) and Kis- (Little) Köveshegy *dűlő*-s were mentioned as 1st Class. A document of 1505 mentions several owners, and that the "Kenthes" [*sic*] family had donated a vineyard property there to the Pauline Order (DL 35797) [see the entry for Kanducs]. 3) Nagy- (Big) Köves *dűlő* of Mezőzombor was mentioned as 2nd Class in 1798 and 1867. A Kis- (Little) Köves was mentioned in 1723 (UC 83:28 (a)). 4) Another Köveshegy was at Mád (UC 26:7a). 5) The name Köves was being used at Bodrogkeresztúr in 1573 (UC 158:29). [Also, see the entry for Hetény.]

Kövesd – This *dűlő* of Tarcal is mentioned apart from the preceding entry because the origin of the name has nothing to do with stoniness, as is clear from the –*d* ending. The latter shows that it was an early place-name, no doubt the onetime fortress of Nagy Kövesd, in the Bodrogköz, by the northeastern end of Hegyalja. Indeed, the tract was mentioned by its full name in at least one document, of 1747 (UC 145:123). [See the entries for Bodrogköz and Veľký Kamenec, in Part II.]

Középhegy – 1) 'Middle-hill' is a vineyard hill in Mád, not mentioned in 1798 or 1867, but mentioned among the village's best in 1950. 2) A like-named hill was recorded in Tarcal in 1747 (UC 145:123).

Közép-Szárhegy. See the entry for Szárhegy.

KRAKÓ – A vineyard hillock and *dűlő* in Abaújszántó, not mentioned in 1798 (Szirmay did not include Abaúj County); mentioned as "distinguished" in 1867; in 1950, its southwestern slope was mentioned as one of the town's two "most valuable" vineyard areas, and the Krakó-*dűlő* was included among those producing the village's "best quality wines." Krakó's southern side was once a preeminent slope in Abaújszántó, but much of it remained uncultivated after phylloxera in the late-19th century. The name refers to Cracow, the great early market in Poland for Tokaji wine, but earlier it was known as Kis-Sátor, a name that was sometimes still being used as late as 1783 (UC 192:6). [See the entry for Sátorhegy; and for Cracow, in Part I.]

Kún-hegy – A vineyard hillock in Tokaj, on the southern side of Tokaj-hill, mentioned as 1st Class in 1798 and 1867. The name means 'Cuman-hill,' as if in reference to the eastern Cuman people who came into Hungary in the 13th century, but more likely refers to John Kún, a

Transylvanian nobleman who settled in Sáros County in the 15th century. The family became better known in regional history under the name Bydeskúti.

KÚTPATKA – 1) A vineyard hill in Tolcsva, mentioned as 1st Class in 1798 and 1867 (Kútpataka), and included among the eight "most well-known" vineyard-tracts of Hegyalja in 1963 (Dömötör/Katona). The first Hegyalja vineyard purchased by the municipality of Eperjes, in 1505, was located here [see the entry for Térhegy]. The name signifies 'font-creek,' but actually refers to a 14th century hamlet of the same name that abutted Tolcsva. At the beginning of the 18th century, it was also known commonly as Somhegy, or 'Cornel-hill' (UC 154:44). **2)** A *dűlő* in Sárospatak, included in a listing of 1785 (Balassa, 1991), but not mentioned in 1798 or 1867. In 1950, it was noted as "middling" quality, or 2nd Class.

Lajos – 'Louis' is a *dűlő* in Mezőzombor, mentioned as 1st Class in 1798 and 1867; it was not mentioned in 1950. It was also known as Nagy (Great) Lajos, and the Louis referred to was undoubtedly King Louis I 'the Great' (Nagy Lajos), who reigned in the mid-14th century [see the entry for Louis I, in Part I]. This also comports with the tract's quality classification and the fact that Mezőzombor was a very popular locale for wine-growing early on, even before the era of later-harvested white wines.

Lajstrom – A *dűlő* of Tarcal, on the southern side of Tokaj-hill, mentioned as 1st Class in 1798 and 1867. The name signifies 'register/list,' but is a later-day corruption of the name Lestár, recorded as a tract name in a document of 1573 (UC 128:29), and again in the Tokaj Domain *urbárium* of 1688. The Lestárs were a prominent 16th century family. The name had changed to Lajstrom well before the Zemplén County classification of 1772, as a Lajstrom-alja (bottom) was recorded in 1747 (UC 145:123).

Lányka – The defunct "Little Girl" tract of Monok might simply be tossed in with the supplemental list of tract names that follows were it not for the likelihood that it referred to a grape variety [see the entries for Aranka, Furmint, Kecsi, Szegfű, and Talyanka]. The name appears in a document of 1686 (UC 116:50), which was an era when the *fehérszőlő* [see that entry, in Part IV] was one of the chief varieties for botrytis wines. Balassa (1991) pointed out that it was sometimes erroneously called *leányszőlő* (of which *lányka* became the popular diminutive form). The likelihood, therefore, is that the tract was planted with the *fehérszőlő* during the 17th century, for the purpose of enabling a larger output of botrytis wines, but was mistakenly named Lányka. It is unlikely that it was the actual *leányka* variety, since it could be of no help to botrytis wine output. [Regarding the misidentification of varietals, see the entry for Schams, in Part I.]

Lapis – A *dűlő* of Szegi, mentioned in 1798, and as "celebrated" in 1867 (under the listing for Szegi and Long communes). The name likely refers to the Lapispataki family of Sáros County, and the tract possibly had a specific connection to Nicholas Lapispataki, who became a Vice-Lord-Lieutenant of Zemplén County in the late-15th century.

Lapos-Mogyorós. See the entry for Mogyorós.

Lencsés – Apparently, there were two *dűlő*-s with this name in Tokaj, though the name was not mentioned in 1798 or 1867. One was mentioned as "most noble" in a document of 1777 (UC 149:2), and must certainly have been the one on the southern side of Tokaj-hill [see the entry for Mézesmáj (c)]. The other abutted the northwestern side of Tokaj-hill and corresponded to the lower portion of the Henye tract [see that entry]. This second Lencsés certainly was the younger of the two, since the name was only coming into use in the early-18th century; a document of 1747 recorded it as "Henye-allya [bottom] or Lencsés" (UC 145:123). Although seeming to make reference to lentils (*lencse*), the name likely derives from the Lencsés family of Sáros County.

Lengyel – A *dűlő* in Mád, not mentioned in 1798, 1867, or 1950. The name means 'Pole' and could refer to a onetime Polish owner or to a family of that name.

Lete – Monok has both Nagy- (Big) and Kis- (Little) Lete *dűlő*-s, which were mentioned among the village's three best in 1950. Neither was mentioned in 1798, since Szirmay did not include Monok in Hegyalja; in 1867, Szabó/Török included Monok but mentioned no specific growing sites. The origin of the name is uncertain, but the ancient Tekule clan of Sáros County was still using the pagan name 'Lede' as a personal name as late as 1312. Thus, a Lete *dűlő* might have been an early sign of Sáros interest in Hegyalja, perhaps dating to the mid-14th century.

LŐCSE – An historic vineyard-tract of Erdőbénye, it was part of the Sáros-*dűlő*, but developed an identity of its own [see the entry for Sáros]. It was mentioned among the village's best areas in 1950. The name refers to the onetime county seat (now Levoča, in East Slovakia) of Szepes County, no doubt because it had been owned by that municipality [see the entry for Szepesség, in Part II].

Magashegy – 1) 'High-hill' in Bodrogolaszi was mentioned in 1798; mentioned as "distinguished" in 1867; and mentioned among the village's best sites in 1950, particularly its south-facing areas. But in 1950 it was spelled Magos-hegy, which signifies 'seed-hill.' 2) A like named hill in Sátoraljaújhely was mentioned in 1867. In an unusual documentary notation, it was stated that 94 wine-cellars were situated at Magashegy in 1778 (UC 176:18 (c)).

Magita – The hill and *dűlő* of this name in Olaszliszka were indicated among the village's best wine-growing areas in 1950, though not mentioned in 1798 or 1867. The name is found in documents as long ago as 1248 and 1255 (MOL), but it is difficult to relate to Hungarian history. There is a distinct oddness to it, especially the *–ta* ending, which is very suggestive of a Bulgaro-Slav origin. If one considers the Magourata site in northwestern Bulgaria, it seems possible that the initial part of the name could be of Thracian origin. [See the entries for Makra and Rány.]

Magoshegy. See the entry for Magashegy.

Makkos – A *dűlő* in Mezőzombor, mentioned as 3rd Class in 1798 and 1867. The name refers to acorns (once a typical grazing feed for hogs), thus suggesting that the first vineyards were created out of forest land.

MAKOVICA – (historically spelled Makovicza) A *dűlő* in Mád, mentioned as 1st Class in 1798 and 1867. It was also specified as 1st Class in a document of 1777 (UC 149:6), shortly after the Zemplén County classification of 1772. The name indicates a connection to the fortress of Makovica erected in northeastern Sáros County, near the border with Poland, around the time of the Tatar invasion of 1241-1242. The fortress was the foundation for establishing the Makovica Domain, which abutted northwestern Zemplén County. The *dűlő* in Mád likely was acquired for the fortress by the Zudar family by at least the early-14th century. The Zudars died out in the latter part of the 15th century, and were followed by several other noble families, including the Rozgonyis, as owners of the domain and its Hegyalja *dűlő*. The Rákóczis were the lords of Makovica throughout the 17th century. [See the entries for Rozgonyi and Zudar, in Part I.]

158

Makra – A *dűlő* of Makkoshotyka, not mentioned in 1798 or 1867, since no specifics were given about the village. The name reflects a much earlier name for Makkoshotyka: Makramál [see the entry for Makkoshotyka, in Part II]. The Makra- prefix in Makramál referred to Makra peak. Makkoshotyka is a forested area, and the name of Makra peak might have originated in the Bulgaro-Slav *mokra-gora*, or 'wet-mountain-forest.' Other peaks in the area, such as Bogdán and Száva, also evince a Bulgaro-Slav origin [see the entry for Turány: On a Saintly Trail, in Part II].

Mandalin – A *dűlő* of Bodrogolaszi, mentioned in passing in 1798, and as "distinguished" in 1867. The name likely referred to an early German family from one of the Upper Tisza or Szepesség towns [see those entries, in Part II], since the –*in* ending was very typical of surnames in those towns as late as the 16th century.

MANDULÁS – **1)** Tolcsva has the prized *dűlő* of this name. Kossuth in 1903 mentioned it as one of "the classic names" of Hegyalja, and in 1963 (Dömötör/Katona) it was included among the eight "most well-known" *dűlő-s*. It was also mentioned among the village's best in 1950. It is surprising, then, that it was not mentioned by name in 1798 or 1867. **2)** The Mandulás *dűlő* in Tarcal, on the western side of Tokaj-hill, was recorded in the past as Nagy- (Big) and Kis- (Little) Mondolás [*sic*], with both mentioned as 2nd Class in 1798 and 1867, although in 1950 it was said to produce wine about as good as any of Tarcal's best *dűlő-s*. A Mandulás-alja (bottom) was recorded in 1747 (UC 145:123), and presumably was of lesser quality because of low elevation. **3)** Sárospatak also has a *dűlő* with this name, which was not mentioned in 1798 or 1867, but in 1950 was qualified as "middling," or 2nd Class. **4)** Mád also had a tract with this name, as late as 1798, when the Pulszky family of Sáros County had a property in it (Balassa, 1991). The name Mandulás refers to 'almond grove' and suggests that these *dűlő*-s were established in the 14th century, when the planting of almond trees was fashionable in Hegyalja.

Margita – **1)** A *dűlő* in Abaújszántó, not mentioned in 1798 because Szirmay did not include Abaúj County, nor in 1867. Both a Felso- (Upper) and Also- (Lower) Margita *dűlő* were mentioned in a document of 1784-1785 (UC 143:17). However, the earliest name was Szent-Margit (St. Margaret), as shown by the fact that the trading town of Bártfa sold it under that name in 1510. **2)** A Szent-Margita (*sic*) was recorded at Olaszliszka at the end of the 17th century (UC 69:81). **3)** Margitasor ('Margaret-row') was a *dűlő* in Erdőbénye.

Máriás – This *dűlő* is located in Tokaj, on the northern side of Tokaj-hill, and was rated 3rd Class by Szirmay in 1798. Its name is a contender for the most curious name confusion in Hegyalja history, although it might have been deliberate. It has also been known as Máriássy, in reference to a noble family of Sáros County. Because of that connection, it might well have been the original name. But it also became known as Mariás (Marjás in older documents), which is how Szirmay referred to it in 1798. That term was applied to the habit of providing seasonal vineyard workers with a daily meal and weak wine. The practice was widespread by the early 1700s, but might have started by the late-16th century, when owners from outside Hegyalja grew in number and needed to entice workers from amongst their nearby villages (by the mid-1700s, the *marjás* increasingly included fruit-brandy, although doing so was proscribed by Zemplén County). It would seem that someone saw humor in the coincidence of *marjás* and Márjássy (a onetime spelling of the family name), and abbreviated the tract name accordingly – therein lies the deliberateness. [See the entry for Veres (2).]

Mecsege – A onetime *dűlő* in Abaújszántó, the name is of interest because of its peculiarity. It has a superficial resemblance to the name of the Mecsek mountains, west of Hegyalja, but that still does not explain the name. Because of its location, Mecsege possibly has a corrupted derivation from Micsk, a clan important in Abaúj and Sáros counties in the 13th and 14th centuries [compare the Becsk and Becsek names in the latter entry]. Both a Felső- (Upper) and Alsó- (Lower) Mecsege were documented as late as 1784-1785 (UC 192:6), or after the classification of 1772, yet the name was not mentioned in 1867 (Szirmay did not mention it in 1798 because he did not include Abaúj County). It was noted as completely fallow in 1950. [Also regarding Micsk, see the entry for Mestervölgy.]

Medgyes – (or Meggyesek) 1) A *dűlő* in Tállya, mentioned as "noble" in 1798 and as "eminent" in 1867; not mentioned in 1950. In 1737, it was noted that there were both a Nagy- (Big) and a Kis- (Little) Medgyes (UC 145:98), hence the later plural form Meggyes*ek*. Apparently, the parcel had belonged to the Medgyes fortress of Sáros County, which suggests an old origin. The fort had been a seat of the Knights of St. John and is thought to have been constructed in conjunction with the organizational spread of the Roman Catholic Church in the Upper Tisza, or as early as the 13th century. Thus, the knights of Medgyes would have been aware of wine-growing developments in Hegyalja since early times. 2) Rátka also had a Medgyes at one time, as early as 1698 (UC 168:20) and as late as the beginning of the 20th century (Borovszki, 1903). Presumably, it was an extension of the tract of that name in Tállya.

Medve – The well-regarded 'Bear' hill and *dűlő* of Bodrogkeresztúr were not mentioned by that name in 1798 or 1867, although Balassa (1991) found mention of a Medve-völgy ('vale') tract there in 1789. Because both a hill and a valley named Medve existed, a literal reference to bears is the possibility of first resort. It would take the name back to the days of royal hunting grounds and creating vineyards by removing forests. But we might go out on a limb for either of two fallback suppositions: 1) the Medve family of the 14th century that had a connection to the monastery of Lelesz [see that entry, in Part II]; or 2) the Medve fortress of southwestern Hungary (now Croatia), which at one time was owned by the nationally prominent Zrinyi family.

Megyer – This is the name of a hill situated on the northern side of Sárospatak, towards Károlyfalva. The *dűlő* of the same name was mentioned in passing in 1798 and 1867, but mentioned among the town's best in 1950, particularly its south-facing area. The latter, consequently, is amongst the 1st Class tracts of Sárospatak. Its name apparently refers to the Megyer estate of neighboring Szabolcs County, and probably indicates ownership in the 17th century by the Thököly family [see that entry, in Part I]. Certainly, it became an esteemed tract during that century, probably before the Rákóczi classification. Balassa (1991) shows that a presumably separate tract known as Megyer-Tető (-Peak) existed in 1785, and an Alsó- (Lower) Megyer in 1799. The name Megyer is of historic interest because of a tradition recording that it designated one of seven tribes entering Hungary at the time of the Conquest. This seems to be borne out by the several locales called Megyer in early Hungarian history.

Meleg- – 'Warm' is a very favorable prefix. Two significant *dűlő*-s in Hegyalja bear the redundant name Melegmáj (*máj* or *mály* was an ancient Magyar term for 'warm-slope'). This redundancy suggests that the name was given much later than other tract names with that ending, since the old significance of *máj* must have been forgotten and it had come to mean merely 'slope.' 1) The more famous Melegmáj is located between Tarcal and Tokaj. It is also known as Meleg-oldal, or 'warm side,' meaning the southeastern side of Tokaj-hill. It was mentioned as 2nd Class in 1798 and 1867, but as 1st Class in 1950. Two vineyards in this *dűlő* were rented for the Russian Imperial Court in 1746. In 1736, a Melegoldal-Teteje (Peak) was also recorded (Balassa). 2) Another *dűlő* called Melegmáj is in Erdőhorváti. It was mentioned as "very favourably situated" in 1867, and in 1950 was said to be among the village's best. Owners in 1784 included the Pauline Order and Viscount Antal Szirmay (author of the landmark 1798 account of Hegyalja wine-growing). 3) Sátoraljaújhely has had its own Nagy- (Big) and Kis- (Little) Melegoldal, as well as a Melegföld ('warm-land'). Nagy-Melegoldal was mentioned in passing in 1798 and 1867, but as 1st Class in 1950. 5) Another *dűlő* with the name Melegoldal is in Malá Tŕňa, in East Slovakia.

Messzelátó – The name means 'Spy-glass,' as in Spy-Glass Hill, and is found in three locales. 1) The *dűlő* of this name in Bodrogkeresztúr was mentioned as 1st Class in 1798, 1867, and 1950. 2) The one in Erdőbénye was mentioned among the village's best in 1950. 3) The one in Mezőzombor was mentioned as 2nd Class in 1798, 1867, and 1950.

Mestervölgy – A tract located in Tarcal, its name signifies 'Master('s)-vale,' and might date to the Micsk clan [see the entry for Sečovce, in Part II]. The clan became significant in Sáros, Abaúj, and Zemplén counties after the Tatar invasion of the mid-13th century, but especially in the early-14th century, owing to a figure known generally in regional history as Micsk *Bán*, or viceroy (as in the opera *Bánk Bán*, of Ferenc Erkel). However, this Micsk was also called Mester, as if he was highly skilled in a craft (some of the nobility did in fact possess such skills, though in the luxury, decorative category like, say, silversmithing). However, it is uncertain whether vineyards were created from this land at such an early date. Unusually, a document of 1747 listed "Mestervolgy cum [with] Bajuss" and "Kis Temető and Mestervolgy," as though two parts of Mestervölgy were treated as one property along with, respectively, Bajusz and Kis-Temető, at least for tax purposes, which was the context of the document (UC 145:123). In any case, only Bajusz and Temető [see those entries] were mentioned in 1798 and 1867.

MESZES – A hill and *dűlő* in Olaszliszka. The plural form Meszesek has also been used at times because there have been both Nagy- (Big) and Kis- (Little) Meszes tracts. Meszes was mentioned as 1st Class in 1798, and as "principal" in 1867. Additionally, it was mentioned as 1st Class in a document of 1675 (UC 116:15): "*Meszes optima vinea 1 classis.*" Apparently based on old documents written in Latin, the Vay family in the late-19th century stylized the name Nagy-Meszes as 'Meszes-major,' by which it is still known today. The name Meszes refers to earlier times, when a hamlet named Meszes was situated in this locale, and thus the *dűlő* acquired that name [see the last paragraph of the entry for Olaszliszka, in Part II]. Balassa (1991) indicated that some of Meszes belonged to Erdőbénye. In 1950, it was also noted that the lower strip is among the village's lesser areas.

Mészpest. See the entry for Poklos.

MÉZESMÁJ – (a) One of the most vaunted Hegyalja vineyard-tracts, Mézesmáj is situated in Tarcal, on a south-facing slope just west of the town. Both Szirmay in 1798 and Szabó/Török in 1867 mentioned it as 1st Class, and placed its name (probably significantly) right next to that of Szarvas. It seems to have been the only specific Hegyalja growing area mentioned in early Western commentary about Tokaji. In 1816, Jullien wrote (incorrectly): "The wine of the *cru* of the mountain Mezes-Malé does not enter commerce; it is destined in its totality for the caves of the emperor and those of some magnates who possess some vineyards there." In 1839, John Paget noted that "the very finest [Tokaji is grown] only on a small hill, the Mezes-Male, in the parish of Tartzal." The name itself is an archaic Magyar designation signifying 'honeyed warm-slope' (the name is generally found as Mézesmálé and Mézes-Mály in old documents). Indeed, the name "Mezesmal" is found in a Hungarian document of 1280, though in Záhtelek (now part of Nógrádmarcal), about 150 km/93 miles west of Hegyalja. The name was also mentioned as that of a vineyard hill in Buda in 1505 (DL 38658).

(b) A Kis- (Little) Mézesmáj tract in Tokaj was mentioned as 1st Class in 1798 and 1867. One of the earliest indications of a Kis-Mézesmáj acquiring an identity of its own (separate from the notion described below) is from a document of 1707 (UC 116:76).

(c) The Tarcal *dűlő* known as Mézesmáj developed out of a much more extensive stretch of land known by the same name, which ran from Tarcal to Tokaj. It developed its own identity largely because it was the westernmost piece, and separated from the rest by the town of Tarcal. The celebrity of the larger territory probably goes back further than any other wine-growing section of Hegyalja. It certainly was well-regarded by 1411, when a vineyard in Tokaj's part of Mézesmáj was donated to the Pauline Order (this was decades before Tokaji started becoming a later-harvested wine). The Tokaj Domain *urbárium* of 1581 specified six vineyard-tracts on Mézesmáj, and they extended as far east as Szerelmi and Kócsag by the town of Tokaj. Documentation from the late-17th century shows that the name still covered an area broader than it would later on: two documents of 1676 specified the Deák, Donáth, Kanducs, Kapus, Kertész, and Tófelé tracts as being "in Mezesmal" (UC 90:38; UC 111:11); in 1681, "Kanducz in Mizesmal," "Veres szolo in Mizesmal," "Mandolas in Mizesmal" (UC 117:8 (a)); in 1683, "Tófelé in Mezesmal" (UC 116:29); in 1686, "on Mezesmal below the Szarvas vineyard" (UC 116:35). Similarly, a document of 1701 was no doubt alluding to the larger sense of Mézesmáj in noting that "the country's best wine is grown on the outstanding *promontórium*" shared by Tarcal and Tokaj (UC 58:22). [See the entry for Cserfás.]

An older, composite sense of Mézesmáj never entirely disappeared, although its content did change beginning in the 18th century. This seems to have been fomented above all by the singular fame of Szarvas, which is located at the far southern end of Tarcal's portion, abutting Tokaj's portion. Going by Boros (1996), people at Tokaj must have begun distinguishing their portion of Mézesmáj as Nagy- (Big) Mézesmáj and Kis- (Little) Mézesmáj, each consisting of several well-regarded, individual tracts. Specifically, Nagy-Mézesmáj consisted of the south-facing tracts (west to east) Baksa, Talytó, Nyesti, Nagyszőlő, Hétszőlő, Ménesoldal, Szarka, and Kis-Garai; while Kis-Mézesmáj consisted of the southeast-facing tracts (south to north) Szerelmi, Lencsés, Donáth (Tófeli), Kócsag (Óvár), and Palota. Thus, this latter area was far larger than the tract known to Szirmay as Kis-Mézesmáj in 1798.

Mocsár – Although not mentioned in 1798, 1867, or 1950, this *dűlő* of Sátoraljaújhely was mentioned in old documents. Kis- (Little) Mocsár certainly has its own identity today; formerly, there was also a Nagy- (Big) Mocsár. The name means 'bog,' and does not sound propitious for vine cultivation. However, documents from the early-15th century show that Mocharmal (*sic*) was in use as a place-name due north of Hegyalja, at the later village of Mocsármány (now Močarmany, in East Slovakia). The *–mál* suffix would have indicated a warm, south-facing incline, though presumably with boggy land at its foot. This might have been the case with the Sátoraljaújhely vineyard-tract, as well. But, it is also possible that the tract's name reflects a onetime connection to either Mocsármány (Sáros County) or the Zemplén village of Mocsár (now Močar), since these villages at times were owned by significant families in early Hegyalja history, such as the Lapispatakis, Paczoths, Eödönffys, Buttkais, and Rozgonyis.

Mogyorós – *Dűlő* names referring to walnut (*mogyoró*) groves must have been common in Hegyalja during the late Middle Ages, whether they indicated that a few walnut trees grew at the edge of the vineyards or that a number of trees had been torn out to make way for a vineyard. 1) A *dűlő* by this name was noted in Szerencs in 1573 (UC 158:29). 2) Erdőbénye had both a Felső- (Upper) and a Lapos- (Flat) Mogyorós in 1739 (UC 83:91). The latter and the more curiously named Gömbölyű- ('Chubby') Mogyorós were mentioned in 1950 as being among the village's lesser tracts. 3) A document of 1737 also shows a Nagy- (Big) and Kis- (Little)

Mogyorós in Tokaj at that time (Balassa, 1991). 4) A Nagy-, Kis- and Külső (Outer) Mogyorós were recorded at Tarcal in 1747 (UC 145:123). It is possible that there was shared ownership with neighboring Tokaj in that era. 5) Olaszliszka also had a Mogyorós in 1739, but its name originally might not have had anything to do with walnuts. The Monyorós-Csicsva fortress of north Zemplén had a vineyard in Olaszliszka, and the unusual name Monyorós probably came to be referred to by the more familiar-sounding Mogyorós [see the entry for Monyorós-Csicsva, in Part II.] None of the aforementioned names was listed in 1798 or 1867.

Monoki-hegy. [See the entry for Monok, in Part II.]

Mulató-hegy – 'Reveller-hill' is a hill and *dűlő* in Erdőbénye, mentioned in passing in 1798, as 'principal' in 1867, and yet indicated among the village's lesser sites in 1950. The apparent explanation for the latter contradiction is that the prime tract was the one known specifically as Nagy- (Big) Mulató (UC 83:91 – 1739).

Murány – A *dűlő* in Szegi, not mentioned in 1798 or 1867, but indicated in 1950 as excellent in its upper section. The name refers to Murány in Gömör County (now in East Slovakia), which was the center of an old fortress domain created in the late-13th century, after the Tatar invasion of Hungary. In the late-17th century, the domain belonged to the aristocratic Wesselényi family (UC 25:6). Thus, the *dűlő* name may actually be an allusion to them.

Murát – A onetime *dűlő* in Tokaj, not mentioned in 1798, 1867, or 1950. The name is said to refer to a Sultan Murat. If so, this might have been from the period before the 16th century occupation of southern Hungary by the Ottomans, since a Sultan Murat had taken a secular interest in Hungary in the mid-15th century, including the purchase of a residence in Pest, in 1459, for his daughter, who had married a non-Muslim (DL 61919). It seems likely that religion would not have dissuaded this same Murat from purchasing a vineyard property in Hegyalja. But, there was also a Murat Pasha in not too distant Eger in the first-half of the 17th century, and the Rákóczis might have given him a vineyard as a gesture of goodwill. In any case, the house of Savoy acquired the *dűlő* following the Treaty of Karlowitz, in 1699, when the Ottomans departed east-central Europe. [See the entry for Ottoman Turks, in Part I.]

Nagy-Bánya. See the entry for Bánya.
Nagy-Bányihegy. See the entry for Bánya.
Nagy-Boglyoska. See the entry for Boglyos.
Nagy-Cepre. See the entry for Cepre.
Nagy-Fejérhegy. See the entry for Fehér-.

Nagy-hegy – Located in Bekecs, 'Big-hill' has all of the commune's vineyards. The hill was mentioned in passing in 1950, but not at all in 1798 or 1867. [See the entry for Napos.]

Nagy-Káté. See the entry for Káté.

Nagykő – 'Great-stone' *dűlő* in Tolcsva was mentioned as 2nd Class in 1798 and 1867, although Vályi had called it "famous" in 1796. It was still regarded for good quality by Hidvéghy in 1950.

Nagy-Kocsárd. See the entry for Kocsárd.
Nagy-Köves. See the entry for Köves.
Nagy-Kövesd. See the entry for Kövesd.
Nagy-Köveshegy. See the entry for Köves.
Nagy-Lete. See the entry for Lete.

Nagy-Melegoldal. See the entry for Meleg-.
Nagy-Meszes. See the entry for Meszes.
Nagy-Mocsár. See the entry for Mocsár.
Nagy-Mondolás. See the entry for Mandulás.
Nagy-Mulató. See the entry for Mulatóhegy.

Nagy-Palánkos – A *dűlő* in Erdőbénye, not mentioned in 1798, but mentioned among the village's best in 1950. The name refers to the onetime Palánkos family of Hegyalja.

Nagy-Remete. See the entry for Remete.
Nagy-Rigócska. See the entry for Rigócska.
Nagy-Szárhegy. See the entry for Szárhegy.

Nagyszőlő – A *dűlő* in Tokaj, on the southern side of Tokaj-hill, mentioned as 1st Class in 1798, 1867, and 1950. The name signifies 'big-vineyard,' and presumably a sizeable chunk of it went into creation of the Hétszőlő (Seven-vineyard) tract. Part of it later became a property of the Counts Degenfeld. [See the entries for Hétszőlő and Mézesmáj (c).]

Nagy-Temető. See the entry for Temető.

Nagy-Váti – A *dűlő* in Tarcal, on the western side of Tokaj-hill, mentioned as 2nd Class in 1798 and 1867.

Nagy-Véghegy. See the entry for Véghegyek.
Nagy-Vérmány. See the entry for Vérmány.

NAPOS – As suggested by its name, 'sunny,' this *dűlő* in Bekecs faces south on Nagy-hegy hill. It was not mentioned by name in 1798 or 1867. However, it was noted in 1950 as "the only valuable part" of Nagy-hegy (and thus, the only esteemed vineyard-tract of Bekecs). But some considered it among the top dozen or so vineyard-tracts of Hegyalja. Thus, it was historically the southwesternmost tract to enjoy wide fame in the region. Nevertheless, it suffered from neglect after phylloxera, and was used mostly for dessert grape production.

Narancsi – 1) A *dűlő* in Olaszliszka, on the western end of Előhegy, with a southern exposure. The name Narancs [*sic*], or 'orange,' can be found for this tract as early as 1755 (UC 149:28). Contemporary folkore attributes it to an orange appearance when the grapes are at peak ripeness. But the name Narancsi seems to have been a corruption – and the folkore thus aprocryphal – in view of the fact that its name was recorded as Arancsi in 1681 (UC: 10:88 (a)), doubtlessly because it had earlier been a property of the historical Arancsi family, who were in northern Hegyalja by at least the late-16th century. 2) A similar *dűlő* name, Narancs ("Narancz"), was recorded at Tarcal in 1701 and 1747 (UC 116:69 and 145:123); and a Narancs-alja (bottom) in 1765 (UC 117:49). These, too, had probably been Arancsi properties at an earlier time.

Négyszögű – A *dűlő* in Erdőbénye, mentioned among the village's best in 1950. The name signifies 'quadrangular.'

Néma-hegy – 1) 'Mute-hill is a *dűlő* in Sátoraljaújhely, mentioned in passing in 1798 and 1867. 2) Kereknémahegy, or 'Round-mute-hill,' is a tract in Mezőzombor, mentioned as 2nd Class in 1798 and 1867; not mentioned in 1950.

Németszőlő – 1) A *dűlő* in Tokaj, on the southern side of Tokaj-hill, it was mentioned as 1st Class in 1798 and 1867. Historically, part of it went into the making of the Hétszőlő (Seven-vineyard) tract [see the entry for Hétszőlő]. 2) A vineyard in Sátoraljaújhely, on Feketehegy hill, purchased by the municipality of Bártfa in 1502. The name signifies 'German (Német) vineyard,' likely in reference to families with the name Német(h), though possibly in the second case because Bártfa was mostly German-speaking.

Nyavalya – The name of this *dűlő* in Tarcal signifies 'trouble' or 'bother,' which perhaps explains its mention as 3rd Class in 1798 and 1867. Not surprisingly, it is situated on the northern side of Tokaj-hill. A document of 1751 shows that there was both a Nagy- (Big) and a Kis- (Little) Nyavalya at that time (UC 83:138).

Nyergesek – The name refers to 'saddler' (*nyerges*), though probably to the Hegyalja family of that name, who had been active in wine-growing since at least the early-16th century. 1) The vineyard hill of Nyergeshegy in Tállya was mentioned as "noble" in 1798 and "eminent" in 1867. Since the present name is in the plural (*–ek*), there must earlier have been two contiguous *dűlő*-s on the hill, possibly Upper and Lower Nyerges. Vineyards in these *dűlő*-s were purchased by the town of Bártfa in 1487; and from a Cracow (Poland) owner by a Kassa (Hungary) resident in 1506. 2) Balassa (1991) indicates that there was also a Nyerges tract in Erdőbénye in 1700, but Szirmay would not have mentioned it in 1798 because the village belonged to Abaúj County at that time.

Nyírjesek – A *dűlő* in Tállya, not mentioned in 1798 or 1867, but mentioned among the village's best in 1950. The name *nyírjes* refers to a birch tree grove, probably placing creation in the 14th or 15th century, when trees were being removed for vineyards. The plural form, *–ek*, owes to the existence of seven tracts with the core name in 1707 (UC 157:5). Of those, Koldus-Nyírjes is of historical interest because of the fore-name Koldus, meaning 'Beggar.' In any other instance, that might be plausible, but in this one it is a slightly corrupted allusion to nearby Koldu creek, whose name is rather archaic.

Nyúl- – The name 'hare' (*nyúl*) suggests an area visited for hunting, and in turn, the removal of forest or brush to plant vines. 1) Nyulászó, or 'Hare-hunter,' *dűlő* in Mád was mentioned as 1st Class in 1798 and 1867, and among the village's best in 1950. 2) A tract named Nyulas (intimating 'rabbit-place') is situated in Tarcal, on the northern side of Tokaj-hill. 3) Nyúlugró, or 'Hare-jump,' is a tract in Viničky (East Slovakia).

Ökörlánc – A *dűlő* in Tállya, mentioned in 1950, but not in 1798 or 1867. The name means 'ox-chain,' possibly indicating some other agricultural use before becoming a vineyard site.

Omlás – A *dűlő* in Erdőbénye, not mentioned in 1867, though it probably was implicit in the mention of Mulatóhegy hill [see that entry]. It definitely had achieved an identity of its own by 1585, when the important Szepes town of Lőcse purchased a vineyard in it; and it was still known by that name a century later (UC 69:81). The name suggests friable soil.

Ördög – 'Devil' may seem a suitable name for a vineyard, but in this case it likely referred to the Ördög (Eördögh) family of Nagy Bári (now Bara, in East Slovakia), just beyond the northeastern edge of Hegyalja. 1) A *dűlő* with this name was noted in Tarcal in the 18th century (UC 122:52), but was not mentioned in 1798 or 1867. 2) Ördögkősor (Ördög-stone-row) was a *dűlő* in Erdőbénye, but Szirmay did not include Abaúj County in his account of 1798.

OREMUS – A vineyard hill in Sátoraljaújhely. Mentioned in 1798; mentioned in 1867; mentioned as 1st Class in 1950. At one time there were both Nagy- (Big) and Kis- (Little) Oremus tracts, and a document from the beginning of the 17th century noted the excellence of Kis-Oremus: "*vinea praestantissima*" (UC 108:55). As a vineyard site, Oremus probably dates to at least the 13th century, in connection with the Roman Catholic Pauline Order [see that entry, in Part I]. The Pauliners had established a cloister in Sátoraljaújhely by 1221, and they returned shortly after the Tatar destruction of 1241-1242, at which time they helped see to the resettlement of the town, including the expansion of vineyard land. The Latin name Oremus ('let us pray') suggests that the Pauliners developed this vineyard hill in that period. Kis-Oremus was probably the vineyard created out of forest land just below the Pauliner property in the mid-15th century (DL 15742). The Pauliners continued to possess Oremus into the early 1500s, after which it was confiscated and its vineyards became properties of the landed nobility. It holds a special place in Hegyalja history because, according to legend, the first *aszú* wine from botrytized grapes was produced from its vintage, probably around 1620. At that time, Susanna Lórántffy, the wife of Prince George Rákóczi I, had a large vineyard on Oremus under the direction of László Máté Szepsi [see the entries for Lórántffy and Szepsi, in Part I]. However, in a document of 1686, Oremus was mentioned as a "*főbor* producing" hill (UC 154:11), which leaves open the possibility that even well into the 17th century *aszú*-wines had yet to replace *főbor* everywhere in Hegyalja [see the Part IV Essay].

Őszhegy. See the entry for Uszhegy.

Ösztvérek – A *dűlő* in Erdőbénye, it was mentioned in 1798 despite Szirmay's general exclusion of Abaúj County. It was mentioned as "principal" in 1867, but in 1950 at least part of it was not considered among the village's very best. The plural form (*–ek*) indicates that at one time there were 'Upper' and 'Lower' or 'Big' and 'Little' Ösztvér *dűlő*-s; but the singular form Ösztvér was used in 1867. The name refers to 'mule' (*ösztvér*).

Óvár. See the entry for Kócsag.

Paczoth – A onetime *dűlő* in Tolcsva, mentioned as 1st Class in 1798 and 1867. The name refers to the Paczoth family of Sáros County. Through involvement with the Szepes Chamber [see that entry, in Part I], the Paczoths acquired an interest in neighboring Zemplén County, and Hegyalja, in the 16th century. The vineyard-tract in Tolcsva apparently acquired its name during the time of John Paczoth, who was the royal judge at Tokaj in the mid-16th century, and is known to have acquired a holding in Tolcsva in 1564. The family also had property in the northern Hegyalja commune of Kistoronya (now Malá Tŕňa) in the mid-16th century. The Paczoths died out at the end of the 17th century, but the *dűlő* retained their name.

Padihegy – 'Bench-hill' in Rátka was mentioned in 1950 for producing some of the village's "best wine." It was not mentioned in 1798 or 1867, but in 1867 it was almost certainly the hill referred to as Rátkai-hegy, since the village's only other vineyards were said to be on neighboring Istenhegy [see that entry]. As with the latter, Padihegy was mentioned at the end of the 17th century as belonging to Tállya (UC 69:81), probably because Rátka had yet to recover from the recent Ottoman destruction. The name Padihegy was an abbreviated version of the original name, Vargapadihegy, or 'Cobbler's Bench Hill' (Borovszki, 1903).

Pajzos – The name of a hill and *dűlő* in Bodrogolaszi. Not mentioned in 1798 or 1867, the tract might have lagged in achieving self-standing recognition. A colloquial designation 'Pajzos' could have developed from a collection of adjacent vineyards as late as the 19th century. The name itself is quite old in Hungarian history, having been recorded as a surname as early as 1454. But it might have come to Hegyalja only after the departure of the nobility of the Szerémség region [see that entry, in Part II], when the Ottomans began their occupation of southern Hungary in 1526. The name mirrors that of a locale at the western end of Szerém (now near Croatia's border with Serbia). The family's arrival time in Hegyalja is uncertain. But they were in Sáros County [see that entry, in Part II] by the mid-17th century; and by 1745, they had land just north of Hegyalja, in Kolbása (now in East Slovakia). Presumably, they could already have had property in Hegyalja before those dates. However, in 1899, Anna Pajzos of Sáros married a member of the noble Dókus family, who had been prominent Hegyalja owners since at least the 17th century, and the Pajzos tract might have been created in part from Dókus vineyard land. (The spelling of the family name varied in the past as Payzsoss, Paizsoss, Pajzsos, and Pajsos.)

Paksi – This *dűlő* on the southern side of Tokaj-hill is shared by Tokaj and Tarcal. It was mentioned as 1st Class in 1798, 1867, and 1950. The name refers to the Paksi family of Zemplén County.

Palandor – A *dűlő* in Olaszliszka, not mentioned explicitly in 1798 or 1867, although a document of 1739 demonstrates that it had its own identity by that time (UC 83:91). In 1950, Hidvéghy noted it as a lesser quality (3rd Class) tract. The name 'Paul-Andrew' (Pál-Andor) is suggestive of an early connection to a church or monastery. In any case, it was at one time part of an ecclesiastic estate administered by the Szepes Chamber [see Part I].

Palásti – A *dűlő* in Erdőbénye, mentioned among the village's best in 1950. The name is that of an aristocratic family of northern Hungary in the late Middle Ages.

Pál-deák – This onetime *dűlő* in Tarcal refers to a classically educated person, a scholar (*deák*), named Paul (Pál), possibly Pál Melith, a nobleman who acquired vineyard land in Tarcal in the early-17th century. The *dűlő* was not mentioned in 1798, 1867, or 1950.

Pálosok – A *dűlő* in Sátoraljaújhely, not mentioned in 1798, 1867, or 1950. The name refers to onetime ownership by the Pauline Order [see that entry, in Part I]. The plural ending (–*ok*) suggests that this was a *dűlő* created from at least two neighboring tracts whose name included 'Pálos.'

Palota – 1) The 'Manse' *dűlő* in Tállya was mentioned as "noble" in 1798 and as "eminent" in 1867; and in 1950 was said to still have a "good name" for its wines. 2) A *dűlő* of the same name has been at Tokaj since as early as 1573 (UC 158:20) [see the entry for Mézesmáj (c)].

Papalj. [See the entry for Makkoshotyka, in Part II.]

Paperdő – A *dűlő* in Erdőbénye, indicated in 1950 as not being among the village's very best. The name signifies 'priest's forest,' and thus suggests that a forest had been cleared to create the first vineyard at the site.

Parlag – A *dűlő* in Erdőbénye, mentioned among the village's best in 1950. The name means 'fallow,' but most likely reflects onetime ownership by the Parlag farmily (also spelled Parlak in old documents), who were actually the 'Horváths of Parlag,' in reference to the Zemplén village of Parlag (now Prieloha, in East Slovakia), further north. The family's interest in Hegyalja could date as far back as 1461, when King Matthias Corvinus made Francis Parlaghi (*sic*) one of the owners of the nearby Boldogkő fortress in Abaúj County (DL 24835).

Patkó – 'Horseshoe' *dűlő* in Tolcsva was not mentioned in 1798 or 1867, nor in 1950, though the simplicity of its name, probably alluding to the tract's original shape, suggests a long existence.

PATÓCS – A hill and *dűlő* in Tállya, mentioned as "noble" in 1798 and "eminent" in 1867, and cited as "once famous" in 1950. The name originated as a pagan personal name and then became a surname; and it is likely that the *dűlő* was owned by a family of that name at an early date.

Pécsy – (or Pécsi) A *dűlő* in Tokaj, on the northern side of Tokaj-hill, mentioned as 3rd Class in 1798 and 1867. The name refers to the noble Péchy (or Pécsy) family of Sáros County, who became landlords in Zemplén County in the 16th century. This tract, along with other family vineyards in Szegi and Mezőzombor, were confiscated by the Imperial Habsburg authorities in 1686 because of the Pécsys' support for the anti-Habsburg rebellion of Emerich Thököly in 1683-1685 (UC 36:78, UC 90:54).

Pendics – (or Pendits) A *dűlő* in Abaújszántó, on the southern side of Sátorhegy, not mentioned in 1798 because Szirmay did not include Abaúj County; mentioned as "distinguished" in 1867; and mentioned in 1950 among the *dűlő*-s producing the town's "best quality wines." Earlier, there were two *dűlő*-s, respectively Nagy- (Big) and Kis- (Little) Pendics (UC 154:50, UC 26:7 (a)). The name most likely was a surname, derived from the Hungarian form, Pentele, of the Christian personal name Panteleimon.

Percze – (also spelled Pertze) A vineyard hillock and *dűlő* in Mád, mentioned as 1st Class in 1798 and 1867, yet noted in 1950 as having some "unfavorably situated" land. The name presumably was a surname, probably that of the noble Pertzel family of Sáros County.

PERES – A vineyard hill and *dűlő* of Erdőbénye, mentioned in 1798; mentioned as "principal" in 1867; and noted in 1950 as a quality area except for the lower portion. Further, Kossuth in 1903 called Peres one of "the classic names" of Hegyalja. In earlier times, Peres was also called Tolcsva or Tolcsvahegy hill, apparently because it originally fell within the borders of neighboring Tolcsva. The name Peres alludes to the Csicsva fortress, built by the Rozgonyis in 1310, further north in Zemplén County [see the entry for Monyorós-Csicsva, in Part II]. It was the name of the village adjoining the fortress. Thus, Peres is in every way a "classic" name.

Perőc – A *dűlő* in Tarcal, on the western side of Tokaj-hill, mentioned as 2nd Class in 1798 and 1867 (Perócz), yet noted in 1950 as producing wine about as good as the town's best *dűlő*-s. The name seems to connect the tract to the Jászó fortress of Abaúj County, which included a village called Perecze, whose inhabitants probably worked the tract. [See the entry for Jasov, in Part II.]

Pestere – A onetime *dűlő* in Tarcal, not mentioned in 1798, 1867, or 1950. Its name suggests a possible Bulgaro-Slav origin (*peshtera* = cavern); it would be a typical magyarization to have changed the final *a* to an *e*. [See the entry for Bulgarian Empire, in Part II.]

Péter-deák – 1) A *dűlő* in Tarcal, not mentioned in 1798, 1867, or 1950. The name dates to around 1600 and refers to Peter Hasznos of nearby Mezőzombor, who was the chief judge at Tarcal. He was otherwise known as 'Peter *deák*,' the latter term being an honorific for a well-educated person. [See the entry for Hasznos.] 2) Balassa (1991) noted that there was a Péter-deák tract in Tállya in 1563, obviously with no connection to Peter Hasznos.

Pethő – (or Pető) A *dűlő* in Tolcsva, not mentioned in 1798 or 1867, but it lies between the 1st Class *dűlő*-s of Ciróka, to its east, and Mandulás and Kútpatka, to its west. It bears the name of the Pethő family, who came to Zemplén from western Hungary in the 16th century. They acquired the Sztropkó Domain, through which a considerable amount of Hegyalja wine was shipped to Poland. Because of their vineyard ownership (and this one does not seem to have been their only property), they took a keen interest in the Polish trade. [See the entries Bel- and Henye.]

Petrács – This *dűlő* in Tolcsva was not mentioned in 1798 or 1867, probably because it lacked an identity distinct from an adjacent tract. The name most likely represents a slight alteration of the surname Petrás, in reference to a noble family of both Zemplén and Sáros counties.

Pogánykút – A *dűlő* in Hercegkút, noted in 1950 as producing "the [village's] better wine." The name signifies 'pagan-font,' but likely refers to the noble Pogány family of Sáros County, perhaps as early as the 16th century, when they were also resident in the Gálszécs Domain of Zemplén County [see the entry for Sečovce, in Part II]. A point of historical interest is that a document of 1785 shows three *dűlő*-s by this name in neighboring Sárospatak at that time: Belső- (Inner), Középső- (Middle) and Alsó- (Lower) Pogánykút (Balassa, 1991). This probably reflected Hercegkút's close relationship to Sárospatak [see the entry for Hercegkút, in Part II].

Poklos – A *dűlő* of Szegi, mentioned in 1798 as Poklos and Mézpest (originally Mészpest); mentioned in 1867 as Poklos-Mézpest (under the listing for Szegi and Long communes); and mentioned simply as Poklos in 1950, when it was also cited for its excellent upper section. The compound form of the name in 1867 shows that two adjacent *dűlő*-s had fused during the early-19th century. Poklos apparently was a surname, also found as Puklus. The name Mészpest refers to the Zemplén village of that name (now part of Oborín, in East Slovakia), probably going back to its ownership by the Soós family, who acquired Szegi around 1500 [see the entry for Soós, in Part I]. Historically, Poklos-Mészpest did not always fall within Szegi. Balassa (1991) documented that Mészpest fell within the limits of Bodrogkeresztúr in 1702, as did Poklos in 1765. The same name turns up in a document of 1573 (UC 158:29). Further, a document of 1683 places Poklos in Bodrogkeresztúr and Bodrogkisfalud, although the explanation in this case seems to be that a separate tract called Kis- (Little) Poklos belonged to Kisfalud (UC 116:28). The Tokaj Domain *urbárium* of 1688 mentions both a Nagy- (Big) and Kis- (Little) Poklos.

Ponczi – A *dűlő* in Tarcal, on the northern side of Tokaj-hill, mentioned as 3rd Class in 1798 and 1867. The name might derive from the Pinczi family of Zemplén and Sáros counties; in Sáros, the family name evolved from Pinczi to Pinczik to Ponczák.

Por-törő: Dusting off a Name

This long defunct tract name of Tarcal is found in a document of 1747 (UC 145:123), and is included here on the theory that it might be one of the oddest cases of name garbling in Hegyalja history. Literally meaning 'dust-buster,' it must have been an archaic occupation, 'pulverizer' or 'grinder,' since it occurs, without the hypen, as a surname (Portheöreö) in the 1601 *urbárium* of the Tőketerebes Domain. But was that the origin of the tract name? A tantalizing possibility is that it was a more familiar sounding inversion of the syllables of Toporó in northern Zemplén [see Stropkov, in Part II]: Toporó→Portoró→Portörő. The Toporó fort belonged to the Perényi family, and likely received a vineyard-tract in Hegyalja, much as did the neighboring Makovica Domain of the Zudars, whose tract still bears its name [see the entries for Perényi and Zudar, in Part I]. This would place the origin of the tract in the early-15th century.

Pósa – A *dűlő* in Viničky, East Slovakia, considered among the village's best, although not mentioned in 1798 or 1867 because the village was not treated as part of Hegyalja. The name refers to the Pósa clan, dating back to the Árpád dynasty, before the 13th century.

Püspöki – A *dűlő* in Tarcal, on the northern side of Tokaj-hill, mentioned as 3rd Class in 1798 and 1867. The name suggests onetime ownership by a bishopric (*püspök* = bishop).

Raffai – A *dűlő* in Erdőbénye, mentioned among the village's best in 1950. The name probably refers to Nicholas Ruffi, who was associated with the Nagy Mihály Domain in the early-15th century [see the entry for Michalovce, in Part II]. This would seem to be an Italian connection amongst Hegyalja vineyard-tract names, assuming that the Ruffis were amongst the 14th-century Italian nobility or ecclesiastical officials brought to the Upper Tisza region.

Rákóczi – The onetime vineyard of this name was located in Sárospatak, and had been a Rákóczi property. Nevertheless, it was noted in 1686 as "not large, not even good" (UC 154:11).

Rakottyás – A *dűlő* in Olaszliszka, not mentioned in 1798 or 1867, but indicated among the village's best in 1950. The name refers to the Rakottyás family that hailed from a hamlet of that name that existed around the 15th century, a few miles north of Hegyalja, by Kolbása.

Rány – A hill and *dűlő* shared by the neighboring communities of Olaszliszka and Vámosújfalu, mentioned as 1st Class for both in 1798. In 1867, the part in Olaszliszka was named as one of the village's "principal" *dűlő*-s, and again in 1950 was indicated as one of its best. A document of 1791 shows that Vámosújfalu had both a Nagy- (Big) and Kis- (Little) Rány at that time (UC 207:10). The name is a mystery, although the location of Rány-tető ('peak') along the eastern edge of the hill group by Tolcsva suggests an origin with the Bulgaro-Slavs, from *ran-*, or 'early,' as if to indicate 'First-light Hill' or 'Crack-of-dawn Hill.' This comports with the settlement of Bulgaro-Slavs from Macedonia in the vicinity of nearby Sárazsadány [see the latter entry, in Part II].

Rátkai-hegy. See the entry for Padihegy.

Remete – 1) A vineyard hill and *dűlő* in Tállya, mentioned as "noble" in 1798, "eminent" in 1867, and in 1950 was still recorded as having a "good name." This *dűlő* was probably the Nagy- (Big) Remete *dűlő* recorded in 1573 (UC 158:29). 2) Balassa (1991) found mention of Remete in Tarcal as early as 1637. There was a Felső- (Upper) Remete in 1747 (UC 145:123), and Alsó- (Lower) Remete was a *dűlő* mentioned by Kossuth in 1903; apparently, the former went out of cultivation after phylloxera. Although there is a village named Remete in Abaúj County, which existed as early as 1344, the name of the *dűlő* could indicate the Pauline Order as an early owner, since the word means 'hermit,' as in St. Paul the Hermit.

Rézló – The onetime 'bronze-horse' *dűlő* in Tolcsva was mentioned in 1950, though not in 1798 or 1867. It was possibly quite old because the name conceivably is a corruption of the pagan personal name Razlo, which was in use until around the 14th century. The tract might have had a specific connection to the village of 'Razlo' or 'Raslofolde' (later Raszlavice/Raslavice) in Sáros County, at the far northern end of the Eperjes-Tokaj Hill Chain. That locale at one time was a fortified site, and forts in the Upper Tisza region often had a vineyard in Hegyalja.

Rigócska – This name, meaning 'little thrush,' designates a hill in Erdőhorváti that had both a Nagy- (Big) and Kis- (Little) Rigócska *dűlő*. They were mentioned in a document of 1784 (UC 143:16), but not in the listings of 1798 or 1867.

Rosenberg – The reason for including this long-defunct *dűlő* of Tállya is to emphasize how far the fame of Hegyalja spread in Hungary after the later-harvested wines began to be produced. The name refers to present-day Ružomberok (in west-central northern Slovakia), when it was still a predominantly German-speaking town and known as Rosenberg (the Hungarian name was Rózsahegy). In view of the considerable distance from Hegyalja (around 193 km/120 miles), the town council obviously did not want to be left without its own source of Tokaji. Presumably, it already existed at the time of the Rákóczis mid-17th century classification; a document of 1737 mentioned the 'Roszenbergh' *dűlő* (UC 145:98). The name is documented as late as 1764 (UC 122:34), but Szirmay did not mention it in 1798. It might have disappeared subsequent to the Zemplén County classification of 1772. Considering that it was located in Tállya and owned by a wealthy municipality, it most likely was a very good wine-growing site.

Rudnok – A *dűlő* of Sárazsadány, on Előhegy hill, noted in 1950 as one of the village's most important vineyard areas. The name refers to the village of Rudnok (now Rudník, in East Slovakia), which indicates early ownership by the Jászó (Jasov) fortress, in Abaúj County, *i.e*, villagers from Rudnok cultivated it. In 1733, the tract was recorded as 'Rudnákos.' [See the entry for Jasov, in Part II.]

Sajgó – A hill and *dűlő* in Bodrogkeresztúr, mentioned as 1st Class in 1798, 1867, and 1950. However, a document of 1675 indicates that part of it fell within the boundaries of Bodrogkisfalud (UC 116:15) and was 2nd Class. The name most likely is a slight corruption of the surname Salgó, a prominent Sáros County family in the late Middle Ages.

Sarkad – A *dűlő* in Mád, its –d ending suggests an origin during the early period of the Hungarian kingdom, or before 1300. It was mentioned as 3rd Class in 1798 and 1867, and in 1950 as "unfavorably situated." The name indicates a 'corner' (*sarok*) position on a hill.

Sáros – The county of this name was of considerable importance in the rise of Hegyalja, as regards both consumption and exports [see the entry for Sáros, in Part II]. Thus, a vineyard-tract with this name does not come as a surprise. But it does not mean that the county, as such, was an owner. Instead, it indicates onetime ownership by the fortress of Nagy Sáros (now Veľký Šariš, in East Slovakia), at the northern end of the Eperjes-Tokaj Hill-Chain. 1) Certainly the chief vineyard-tract of this name was the one in Erdőbénye. A significant part of it became the famous Lőcse tract [see that entry]. 2) But Erdőbénye did not exist until the 15th century, and the Nagy Sáros fortress likely had land in Hegyalja since at least the late-13th century, following the Tatar invasion. The onetime Sárosi vineyard of Tarcal might be the explanation (UC 154:54, of 1738).

Sashegy – 'Eagle' (*sas*) hill in Tállya traditionally had two highly regarded *dűlő*-s, respectively Sastető (Sas-peak) and Sasalja (Sas-bottom). They were mentioned as "noble" in 1798 and "eminent" in 1867, with Sastető mentioned among the village's best in 1950.

Sátorhegy – 'Tent-hill' would be a most significant name in Hegyalja history simply because the two hills of that name have demarked the extent of the region for at least six centuries. But additionally, the wines are of note. 1) The Sátor *dűlő* in Sátoraljaújhely is, of course, situated on Sátorhegy, which was mentioned as 1st Class in 1950, although not mentioned in 1798 or 1867. 2) Despite its historical importance, the identically named hill in Abaújszántó, at the southwestern end of the region, was not mentioned by Szirmay in 1798 because it was in Abaúj County. But it was mentioned as "distinguished" in 1867, and in 1950 its southwestern slope was included as one of the commune's two "most valuable" vineyard-tracts and among those producing its "best quality wines." A document of 1784-1785 recorded an Első- (First), Kis- (Little) and Hosszú- (Long) Sátor (UC 143:17). 3) Sátorfark is the name for the 'tail-end' (*fark*) of Sátorhegy in Abaújszántó. It was bartered to the municipality of Bártfa in 1511. 4) Additionally, a Sátorhegy in Tállya was purchased by the town of Bártfa in 1486.

Serédi – (or Serédi-Vay) A *dűlő* in Tolcsva, indicated in 1950 amongst Tolcsva's well-regarded tracts, although it was not given individual recognition in 1798 or 1867. Whatever the reason for that omission, the tract had an individual identity since the 16th century. It bears the name of Gaspar Serédi, a loyal military leader of Emperor Ferdinand when the Habsburgs were warring to gain control of what remained of Royal Hungary. The Tokaj Domain was bestowed on Serédi in 1541, and he came into possession of a vineyard-tract in Tolcsva in that same period. He can perhaps be considered the first Hungarian recipient of Habsburg largesse in return for fealty. Later on, the Vay family acquired Tolcsva and the *dűlő*, and their name also became associated with it, in the form Serédi-Vay.

Seres – *Sör* (or *ser*) is Hungarian for beer. The settling of Germans throughout the Upper Tisza and adjoining Szepesség region led to widespread production of beer. A result was that the Latin term for brewer, *braxator*, became a surname, and later took Hungarian forms. 1) A *dűlő* in Sátoraljaújhely, on Feketehegy hill, bore the name Seres, which is a variant of Sörös, the name of a noble family of Sáros County. A vineyard there was purchased by the town of Bártfa in 1502. Neither the hill nor the tract was mentioned in 1798 or 1867. 2) A more formal and probably older form, Serfőző, belonged to a *dűlő* in Tarcal, which also was not mentioned in 1798 or 1867.

Siller – Except for this onetime vineyard of Tarcal, the ancient Hegyalja tradition of producing red and reddish wines is not apparent from tract names. But *siller* is the old Hungarian term for rosé wine, particularly the kind made by mixing white and red grapes. The Siller vineyard probably got its name because it was planted with white and red varieties exactly for the purpose of making such wine. It was mentioned in a document of 1765 (UC 117:49), which was just two decades after a purchase of Hegyalja red (or reddish?) wine for the Russian Imperial Court [see the entry for Paraskevich, in Part I]. The Siller vineyard's location in Tarcal, otherwise a prime area for botrytis white wines, suggests that the making of more or less red wines must still have been habitual virtually throughout Hegyalja in the 18th century. [See the entry for Olaszliska, in Part II.]

Sípos – A *dűlő* in Tállya, not mentioned in 1798 or 1867, but noted in 1950 for its "outstanding" location. The name means 'piper,' but likely refers to the Sípos family.

Sóhajó – A *dűlő* in Tarcal, on the western side of Tokaj-hill, mentioned as 2nd Class in 1798 and 1867. A document of 1768 referred to both a Nagy- (Big) and Kis- (Little) Sóhajó. There are two choices for explaining the name. Meaning 'groaner,' it could be supposed that there had been a severely aching cultivator way back when. Alternatively, it might have started out as *só-hajó*, or 'salt-boat,' perhaps because a retired boat had been placed there. River traffic on the Bodrog would have included salt from the mine at Sóvár (now Solivar), to the north, in Sáros County, at the northern end of the Eperjes-Tokaj Hill-Chain. In turn, that would suggest a connection to the important 'Sóvári Soós' family of the late Middle Ages. [See the entries for Soós, in Part I; and for Solivar and Sáros County, in Part II.]

172

Somlyód – Although not mentioned in 1798 or 1867, this vineyard-tract of Végardó has had an exceptionally well-documented and fascinating history. Further, it apparently was well-respected in early times. The name itself reflects a very old Magyar word for hillside (Somló, or Somlyó, hill north of Lake Balaton, in western Hungary, has been a famous wine-growing locale for centuries). Further, the –d ending takes this name back to the earliest period of Hungarian history, that of the Árpád kings. Although within the boundaries of Végardó, Somlyód belonged to the domain of the Sárospatak fortress, and thus, for a long time, it was treated simply as part of Sárospatak, as indicated by documents of 1631 (UC 40:39) and 1686 (UC 154:19), especially since Végardó was but a minor neighbor. It had been a significant tract in that era. It was where Francis Dobó had the "Somolyód" vineyard that was included in his will at the end of the 16th century. Susanna Lórántffy also had a vineyard in it. Two of her letters from 1634 show that the vintage there started on October 9 that year, and that "Azzu Szeoleo" (*aszú*-grape) wine was made. From her property alone, 259 barrels were filled that year. The entire tract had yielded 425 barrels in 1632. But Somlyód's fortunes declined in the second-half of the century. A document of 1686 noted that the tract was large but with rather few vine-stocks (UC 154:11). When the Trautsohns became the owners in the early-18th century, the tract was producing no more than 15 barrels even in a good year, and was disregarded for several decades. But Dujardin, Trautsohn's estate manager, ordered its reconstruction in 1747, which brought its output back to significance, with 120 barrels produced in 1750. In 1776, the Szepes Chamber bestowed it on the new settlements of Hercegkút (Trautsohnfalva) and Károlyfalva, but the German colonists left it uncultivated. A document of 1790 mentioned "pasturage on the deserted Somlyód vineyard-hill" (UC 191:12 (a)). It is hardly any wonder that the tract was not mentioned by Szirmay in 1798. [See the entries for Dujardin and Trautsohn, in Part I.]

Somos – Apparently, the cornel (*som*) tree, or sour-cherry, enjoyed popularity in Hegyalja at an early date, or at any rate before the almond [see the entry for Mandulás]. 1) A *dűlő* of this name in Bodrogolaszi, on Magashegy (Magoshegy) hill, was mentioned in passing in 1798, but as "distinguished" in 1867. Remarked as one of the village's best in 1950, the parts with southeastern and southwestern exposure were singled out. 2) A *dűlő* in Szegi, mentioned in passing in 1798, and as "celebrated" in 1867 (under the listing for Szegi and Long). 3) A Nagy-Somos *dűlő* was recorded in Bodrogkisfalud in 1683 (UC 116:28). 4) Somos *dűlő* in Golop was not mentioned in 1798 because Szirmay did not include Abaúj County, but in 1950 the upper section called Somos-oldal (side) was noted as yielding the village's "best wine." Because of Golop's position near the Hernád river valley, just west of Hegyalja, the name might refer to the Sáros County village of Somos (now Drienov, in East Slovakia) because of seasonal labor brought from there. 5) A *dűlő* called Somszeg (Som-angle) existed in Tállya in the early-18th century (Balassa, 1991).

Sulyom – 'Water-caltrop' is inexplicable as a vineyard name, but it exists at Abaújszántó. It might have been a slight corruption of *sólyom* (hawk); and in fact, it was recorded as "Solyom" at the end of the 17th century (UC 69:81). Further, the Sólyomkő ('Hawk's Rock') fort was located directly north in the Hernád valley since the 15th century, and probably would have acquired vineyard land in Hegyalja (this was also long enough ago to account for a misinformed change in name). The Sulyomok (plural form) tracts are located on Sulyomhegy hill. Documents of 1783, 1784, and 1785 show that four tracts incorporated the name Sulyom at that time: Hosszú- (Long) Sulyom; Délre-fekvő (South-facing) Sulyom; Sulyom-Tető (Peak), and Sulyom-Alja (Bottom) (UC 192:6 and UC 143:17). None were mentioned by Szirmay in 1798 because he did not include Abaúj County. Nor did Szabó/Török mention them in 1867, perhaps because, generally, the name was not associated with the town's best tracts. However, Hidvéghy in 1950 indicated that Sulyomtető ('Hawk's Peak'?) was amongst the best. Additionally, he mentioned a Divini-

Sulyom *dűlő*, a name that referred to the old Divini (or Divényi) family of Sáros County. [See the entry for Zsolyomka.]

Szappanos – Although not mentioned in 1798 or 1867, a vineyard in this *dűlő* in Tokaj was rented for the Russian Imperial Court beginning in 1747. The name signifies 'soapmaker,' though likely in reference to a family of that name. The spelling Szapanyos is found in a document of 1765 (UC 117:50).

Szárhegy – This name, meaning 'spur-hill,' has been used at several sites in Hegyalja. 1) The hill and *dűlő* in Sárazsadány were mentioned as "excellent" in 1867 (Sárhegy), and as "outstanding" in 1950. 2) Those in Erdőbénye were mentioned amongst the village's best in 1950. 3) A vineyard hill in Sátoraljaújhely, was mentioned only in passing in 1798 and 1867, but in 1950 the *dűlő*-s Nagy- (Big) and Kis- (Little) Szárhegy were mentioned as 1st Class. Only a Közép- (Middle-) Szárhegy has remained. 4) Közép- (Middle) Szárhegy in Mád is now usually called just Közép-hegy [see that entry].

SZARVAS – A *dűlő* in Tarcal, on the southern side of Tokaj hill, Szarvas has enjoyed singular fame since the late-17th century. However, it is not known when the tract acquired an identity of its own, that is, separate from the Tarcal portion of Mézesmáj [see that entry (c)]. The earliest 'best' conjecture to work with is that King Matthias Corvinus created it in the last part of the 15th century and gave it the name Szarvas because he had come into possession of the Szarvas estate in Békés County, to the southwest, in 1472 (DL 45503). However, a document of 1505 shows that in this same era there was a vineyard-owning family named Szarvas in northern Hegyalja (DL 35797); and in 1672, Andrew Szarvas was associated with the monastery of Lelesz [see the entry for Leles, in Part II].

Certainly the Szarvas tract's connection with the Rákóczis during the 17th century must have added to any luster that already attached to its name because of great suitability for botrytization. But when the Habsburg General Spork demanded 15 barrels of wine in 1674, he said that it should be from Mézesmáj; he did not specify Szarvas. A short time later, though, a document of 1701 indicated that Szarvas had become renowned in the meantime (UC 58:22) [see the entry for Timon, in Part I]. A document of 1764 shows that its fame had spread well beyond Hungary by that time: "*vinea nobilissima et per totum Submontanu* [Hegyalja], *imo Europan celeberriuma*" (UC 122:35). Needless to say, the Szarvas *dűlő* was mentioned as 1st Class in 1798 and 1867. Further, it headed the list of Tarcal's 1st Class vineyard-tracts in 1798, and was singled out as "celebrated" in 1867. In 1950, Hidvéghy called it "the most famous" Hegyalja *dűlő*. In 1963 (Dömötör/Katona), it was mentioned among the eight "most well-known" *dűlő*-s.

If not singularly and objectively 'the best' of all Hegyalja vineyard-tracts, Szarvas in any case became the most storied of them, chiefly because it had been the most important property of the Rákóczis, and consequently was confiscated after 1711 on behalf of the Hungarian king, the Habsburg emperor, Joseph I. Szarvas was expanded in 1749 and 1751, during Maria Theresa's reign, through acquisition of adjacent vineyards in the tracts Arnyék, Nagy- and Kis-Mura, Messzelátó, Veres, and Decsi. Curiously, it was only after this time that the *furmint* variety became dominant in Szarvas, since Matolay (1744) had reported finding "only very little" of it there. During the 1800s, and most of all after the inception of the Dual Monarchy (Austria-Hungary) in 1867, Szarvas became identified with the expression 'Imperial Tokay,' owing in no small part to the property's formidable official title, "K.u.k. Hofweinbergverwaltung zu Tarczal." After the dissolution of the Austro-Hungarian Empire in 1918, and continuing until the Second World War, Szarvas was cultivated under the direction of The Royal Family Vineyard Administration. In 1950, the property was transferred to the newly formed state enterprise,

Tarcal Farm, and was directly under the supervision of the Viti-Vinicultural Research Institute in Tarcal, for which reason it became the prime source for the *aszú-eszencia* wines of the communist era. The name Szarvas translates as 'Stag.' [Note that the Szarvas (SAHR-vush) name is distinct from that of the Tarcal *dűlő* called Cserfás (CHAIR-fosh).]

Szegfű – The 'carnation' *dűlő* in Sárospatak was mentioned in 1798 and 1867, with the spelling Szögfő, but without a qualitative indicator. A document of 1785 shows that there had also been a Belső- (Inner) Szegfű (Balassa, 1991). Balassa speculated that the name might have resulted from the tract having been planted with the *szekfű* grape variety of earlier times. Though it was a minor variety in Hegyalja generally, the name suggests that it was a semi-aromatic sort, and had a distinctive aroma appreciated by some growers. [See the entries for Aranka, Furmint, Kecsi, Lányka, and Talyanka.]

Szemere – A *dűlő* in Szerencs, with southern exposure, not mentioned in 1798 or 1867, because Szerencs was generally considered outside Hegyalja then, but mentioned among the village's best in 1950. The name alludes to the very old Huba clan, which adopted the surname Szemere in the first-half of the 16th century. The *dűlő* probably dates to the latter period.

Szemince – The vineyard hill of Bodroghalász, noted in 1950 as the site of all of the village's vineyards. Szemince is a contraction of Szent Vince (St. Vincent). The name apparently was bestowed by the Dominican Order when they built their monastery on the site around 1255, in the wake of the Tatar invasion. Presumably, the earliest vineyards on Szemince were created at that time.

Szemszúró-hegy – A vineyard hill in Sátoraljaújhely, not mentioned in 1798, but mentioned in 1867, and called 1st Class in 1950. The name signifies 'eye-piercing-hill.'

Szent-Ignác – The St. Ignatius *dűlő* in Sárazsadány was mentioned in passing in 1798, but as "excellent" in 1867.

Szent-Kereszt – The 'Holy Cross' *dűlő* in Tarcal's northern portion of Tokaj-hill was not ranked or mentioned in 1798 or 1867, although the name definitely was in use in 1737 (UC 153:112). At that time, the Szepes Chamber bestowed it upon the Piarist Order, although it is unlikely that the Piarists named the tract since there had been a cloister on the hill earlier. But it is difficult to specify the origin of the name since 'Holy Cross' was widespread as a church, monastery, and place-name in the 13th and 14th centuries. The *dűlő* may have been established by the Eödönffy family of Vinna, with Szent-Kereszt as the original name [see the entry for Vinné, in Part II; also see the entry for Vinnai, below]. However, the Perényi family had a village named Szent-Kereszt as far back as 1321. Adding to the confusion, 'Holy Cross' was the name of the Lelesz Convent, which had Hegyalja vineyard properties. For a time before the Piarist acquisition, the *dűlő* belonged to the Pettkó family, and had become known by their name as well; but that name disappeared subsequently.

Szent-Margit. See the entry for Margita.

Szent-Tamás – A *dűlő* in Mád, mentioned as 1st Class in 1798 and 1867, and mentioned among the village's best in 1950. The name 'St. Thomas' apparently connects it to the Pauline Order.

SZENTVÉR – The 'Holy-Blood' *dűlő* in Tolcsva was mentioned in 1963 among the eight "most well-known" *dűlő*-s of Hegyalja (Dömötör/Katona). Oddly, it was not mentioned by that name in

1798 or 1867. In the absence of other Tolcsva tract names referring to religious devotion, it is likely that Szentvér was the vineyard bestowed on the Pauline Order by the nobleman Michael Buttkai in 1506. However, a document from the end of the 16th century indicates that the Homonna Domain also had a vineyard here ("Zent Ver") at that time (UC 31:15).

Szent-Vincze – A *dűlő* in Sárospatak, not mentioned in 1798, but mentioned in 1867. A document of 1785 shows that there had been both a Felső- (Upper) and Alsó- (Lower) Szent Vincze (Balassa, 1991). The name Saint Vincent refers to a patron saint of wine-growers. Apparently, it at one time belonged to the Dominican Order of Sárospatak.

SZERELMI – A *dűlő* in Tokaj on the southern side of Tokaj-hill, mentioned as 1st Class in 1798 and 1867. It was also mentioned as "most noble" in a document of 1777 (UC 149:2). The present form of the name signifies 'lovely,' but it is a corruption of the name Szerémy, as shown by the spelling 'Szeremi' in the Tokaj Domain *urbárium* of 1688, and also in a notation of 1620 (Balassa, 1991). The name likely dates to George Szerémy, the court priest of John Szápolyai in the 16th century. It is attractive to think that the name refers to the once famous Szerém wine area of southern Hungary (now the Sremska district of northern Serbia), as an intention to emulate the namesake region, and possibly that this was created with settlers and vine cuttings brought from Szerém. But there is no information by which to demonstrate it. Earlier spellings included Zereny (UC 158:29), and more oddly, Szerenne, in the 1581 *urbárium* of the Tokaj Domain.

Szilvölgy – 'Elm-vale' is a *dűlő* in Tarcal, on the southern side of Tokaj-hill, mentioned as 1st Class in 1798 and 1867. The name suggests the clearing of forest land to create the tract. But the name was also recorded once, in 1747, as Szélvölgyi, or 'Wind-vale' (UC 145:123), which is another example of how easily names could become altered.

Szőlőhegy – 1) 'Vineyard-hill' is a natural choice of name in a small commune, and in the case of Vámosújfalu it is the site of all of the village's vineyard tracts. But in 1950 it was noted that most of them were of lesser quality because of northeastern exposition. 2) The southern slope of the slightly differently named Szőlőshegy tract in Monok was mentioned in 1950 as one of the village's three best sites.

Szunyogh – A *dűlő* in Erdőhorváti, not mentioned in 1798, but mentioned as "very favourably situated" in 1867. The name refers to the Szunyogh family.

Talyanka – A *dűlő* in Ond was recorded by this name in 1761 (UC 149:56), and likely was existing at the time of the 1772 classification, but was not mentioned in 1798 or 1867. The name would seem to refer to Italians or Walloons [see the entry for Tállya, in Part II], except that it was recorded as 'Takanka' in 1723 (UC 88:125). But if Balassa (1991) is right in thinking that the vineyard-tract Szegfű might have borne the name of an unusual grape variety, it could also be that we are looking here at a corruption of the varietal name *tamianka*, as a reference to muscat-type grapes [see the mention of *Tömjén* in the entry for Grape Varieties, in Part IV]. [Also, see the entries for Aranka, Furmint, Kecsi, Lányka, and Szekfű.]

Tályi-Kőhegy. See the entry for Köves (1).

Tapasztó – A vineyard in Tokaj, on the southern side of Tokaj-hill, mentioned as 1st Class in 1798 and 1867, and as "most noble" in a document of 1777 (UC 149:2). Historically, part of it went into the creation of Hétszőlő [see that entry]. The name signifies 'plasterer.'

Tar Balázs – A onetime *dűlő* in Tarcal, not mentioned in 1798 or 1867, but recorded as far back as 1573 (UC 158:29). The name refers to a member of the Tar (Thar) family of Zemplén County, Blasius Tar.

Tárczi – A *dűlő* in Tarcal, on the southern side of Tokaj-hill, mentioned as 1st Class in 1798 and 1867. The name refers to the Tárczi (or Tárczay) family of Sáros County, possibly going back to the early-15th century, but definitely to the beginning of the 16th, when the family possessed the Tarkő fort in Sáros. A "Tarczy Allya" (bottom) was also listed in 1747 (UC 145:123).

Tehéntánc – 1) The 'cow-dance' *dűlő* of Tokaj was not given individual recognition in 1798 or 1867, but it was mentioned in documents of 1676 (UC 90:38) and 1785 (Balassa, 1991). In 1676, it was recorded as belonging to Bodrogkeresztúr, whereas by 1785 it belonged to Tokaj. Regarding the name, while disappointingly little has come down in the way of folkloric explanations of tract names, Pap (1985) related one about Tehéntánc. In bygone times, there was a custom of setting out an open wooden tub of wine and letting harvesters help themselves to it during the course of the day. One afternoon a cow on the grounds got to the tub while no one was looking, drank copiously, and began prancing around madly, to the great amusement of the harvesters. 2) Surprisingly, Hidvéghy, in 1950, included this name in his discussion of distant Sárospatak. But perhaps it should not be surprising if cows in other parts of Hegyalja also were inclined to be bibulous and rowdy. He noted it for 'middling' quality, or 2nd Class (but cows obviously would not have agreed).

Temető – The Nagy' (Big) and Kis- (Little) 'Cemetery' *dűlő*-s in Tarcal are on the northern side of Tokaj-hill, and were mentioned as 3rd Class in 1798 and 1867. [See the entry for Mestervölgy.]

Terézia – (or Terézhegy) A *dűlő* in Tarcal, mentioned as 1st Class in 1798 (*Clivus Theresiae*) and 1867, and in 1950 as producing wine about as good as the village's best *dűlő*-s. The original name was St. Teresa, in honor of Empress Maria Theresa, for whom it was created in 1751 by acquiring property on the eastern side of the Mézesmáj tract [see the entry for Grassalkovich, in Part I]. A chapel was erected on its peak. Thereafter, the hillock itself became known simply as Terézhegy hill. The esteemed *dűlő* is on the hillock's southern side.

Térhegy – (also known as Bartalos-Térhegy, or just Bartalos) A hill in Tolcsva, mentioned in 1950, but not in 1798 or 1867. Kossuth (1903) said it could be included among the best tracts of Hegyalja. He knew it as Bartalos-Térhegy, in which the forename referred to a family that owned it in early times; indeed, a serf named Barnabás Bartalyus sold a vineyard in the Kútpatka tract to the municipality of Eperjes in 1505. Curiously for an excellent tract, the old term *tér* indicated land suitable for plowing and field crops; but the hill might have acquired its name at an early date merely from the arable land at its foot, whereas the higher areas proved suitable for vineyards at a later time.

Thurzó – Of considerable historical significance in Hegyalja, this name refers to the Thurzó family of the Szepesség region and Cracow, who became interested in Tokaji wine nearly as soon as it began acquiring renown. [See the entry for Thurzó, in Part I; and for Szepesség, in Part II.] 1) The family owned a *dűlő* in Tarcal, on the southern side of Tokaj-hill. Although Kossuth in 1903 mentioned the *dűlő* simply as Thurzó, a distinction between Felső- (Upper) and Alsó- (Lower)

Thurzó had been made for a long time previously, since at least 1683 (UC 116:28), and as late as 1747 (UC 145:123). Felső-Thurzó was noted as 1st Class in 1798 and 1867. 2) Neighboring Tokaj had a Kis-Thurzó tract in 1736 (Balassa).

Tófelé – This name was applied to vineyard-tracts in several Hegyalja communities during the late Middle Ages. The name means 'towards-the-lake,' in reference to fishing ponds that belonged to the various domains. These tracts were probably small, and thus were attached later to larger neighboring ones. A mention of one that had retained its identity rather late was located in Tokaj, and was named in documents of 1683 (UC 116:28) and 1737 (Balassa) [see the entry for Mézesmáj (c)]. It later disappeared. A document of 1695 suggests that it increasingly became known as Bornemissza (UC 116:60) [but, see the entry for Donáth]. [In her work of 1914, the researcher Spotkovszky noted that a document of 1679 mentioned a "Toseli" vineyard that abutted the famous Gyapáros tract of Tolcsva, and assumed that this reflected onetime ownership by an Italian by that name. But the vineyard name likely was Tófeli (= Tófelé), since the letter *f* in early Hungarian orthography can easily be mistaken for *sz* (the Hungarian *s*).]

Tokaj-hegy – A long vineyard hill bearing Tokaj's name, although originally it was known as Tarcal-hegy. It stretches from Tokaj to Tarcal, and has excellent wine-growing tracts, for the most part within the borders of Tarcal. However, all the significant *dűlő*-s of the town of Tokaj are arrayed along it, with the best ones having a southern exposure, followed by those with a southeastern exposure, and lastly those with a northerly exposure. [See the entry for Mézesmáj (c).]

Tökösmáj – A *dűlő* in Tállya, mentioned as "noble" in 1798 and "eminent" in 1867. Its history includes a vineyard purchase in it by the town of Bártfa in 1487. The name signifies 'warm-hillside-with-a-pumpkin-patch.' But Balassa (1991) found it mentioned as Tőkésmál in 1563, which would signify 'planted with vine-stocks' (*tőkés*).

Tolcsvahegy. See the entry for Peres.

Töltvény – A *dűlő* in Tokaj, not mentioned in 1798, 1867, or 1950, but mentioned as "most noble" in a document of 1777 (UC 149:2). The name derives from *tölt-*, or 'fill,' and was used to designate a piling up of stone and earth into a large mound upon which vineyard-guards would erect a hut for their use, and from which they could easily survey the area under their purview.

Tompakő – A *dűlő* in Sátoraljaújhely, mentioned in 1798 (Tompa) and 1867, and mentioned as 1st Class in 1950. The name means 'blunt-stone.' It can only be speculated that the name originated with the very old Tumpa clan of the Árpád era.

Újhegy – Meaning 'New-hill,' this name probably refers to a vineyard area developed relatively late in Hegyalja history, though possibly still in the 15th century, most likely by clearing forested land. 1) The one in Bodrogkeresztúr was mentioned as 1st Class in 1798, 1867, and 1950. 2) The one in Rátka was not mentioned in 1798 or 1867, but was noted in 1950 for being among the preferred, southerly exposed tracts, and for producing some of the village's "best wine."

Úrágya – A *dűlő* in Mád, not mentioned in 1798 or 1867, but mentioned among the village's best in 1950. The name means 'the lord's bed,' and is thought to refer to early royal ownership, not to a religious affiliation. A document of 1723 contains one of the strangest instances in Hegyalja history of garbling the name of a vineyard-tract: Ó-Ragya, meaning Old-Pockmark (UC 83:127).

Urbán – A *dűlő* in Mád, not mentioned in 1798 or 1867, but noted in 1950 amongst the town's *dűlő*-s having "the best repute" for its wine, even though at least in part "unfavorably situated." The name refers to Orbán, a patron saint of wine-growers in parts of Hegyalja, as shown by the listing of the tract name in that form in a document of 1761 (UC 149:56).

Uszhegy – (or Őszhegy) A vineyard hill and *dűlő* in Mád, mentioned as 2nd Class in 1798 and 1867. The name refers to the Usz clan of Sáros County, which suggests a very early origin, possibly even prior to the Tatar invasion of 1241-1242, and thus, some of the earliest interest shown in Hegyalja by notables from Sáros. [See the entry for Usz, in Part I.] Subsequent to 1867 (Szabó/Török), probably after phylloxera, the name Őszhegy (Gray-hill) came into general use, no doubt because nobody any longer remembered the Usz clan. (Inexplicably, Hidvéghy, in 1950, mentioned an Őszhegy for neighboring Tállya, but none for Mád. Tállya's lands do not even border Mád's Uszhegy/Őszhegy, and no such tract was mentioned amongst Tállya's in 1798 or 1867.)

Vajas. See the entry for Esztáva.

VÁRHEGY – The name means 'fortress-hill,' and considering the importance of constructing fortresses in the half-century after the Tatar invasion of 1241-1242, it is not surprising that a number of hills in Hegyalja and elsewhere received this name. In the case of Hegyalja, it might not always have been because a fortress had been situated on the hill, but simply because the hillside belonged to a fortress. Five such hills can be specified in Hegyalja: **1)** The foremost of them was that in Tállya, which was mentioned as "noble" in 1798; as "eminent" in 1867; and as "once famous" in 1950. But it might have been mostly fallow by 1867 and completely wiped out by phylloxera after 1885, because Kossuth said of it in 1903 that it had once "produced the glory of Francis Rákóczi II's table and the pearl of his princely gifts" but had long since passed into memory. In the meantime, though, it has been recovering. 2) A hill of the same name in Bodrogkisfalud was mentioned in 1798 and 1867 (under the listing for Kisfalud). Its fame rested largely on the Barakonyi-oldal *dűlő* (Barakonyi-side tract), which was mentioned as one of the village's two tracts that produce the "most outstanding" wine. It once belonged to the prominent Hantos family of Zemplén, but the name Barakonyi refers to an earlier family and suggests an origin in the 14th century. 3) A vineyard hill in Erdőbénye, mentioned only in passing in 1798, but called "principal" in 1867. 4) A vineyard hill in Tolcsva, mentioned as 2nd Class in 1798 and 1867, and among the village's best in 1950. At the beginning of the 18th century, it was also known commonly as Előhegy (UC 154:44). 5) A onetime vineyard-tract was on the hill of the same name in Sátoraljaújhely. The hill had indeed been the site of a fort in the mid-14th century. As a vineyard hill it was mentioned in passing in 1798 and 1867. Presumably, it included the Váralja ('fortress-bottom') *dűlő* mentioned in a document of 1567 (UC 40:35). The Váralja tract was bestowed on the Pauline Order in 1665, though it perhaps had belonged to them earlier, as well, before the Protestant Reformation in Hungary.

Varjas – A *dűlő* in Szegi, mentioned in 1798, and as "celebrated" in 1867 (under the listing for Szegi and Long communes). The name derives from 'raven' (*varjú*), but probably refers to the Varjas family, going back to the 15th century.

Vashegy – A vineyard hill in Bodrogkisfalud, mentioned in 1867, though not in 1798. The name means 'iron-hill,' as an allusion to reddish color, though possibly in reference to the Vas(s) family.

Vay. See the entry for Serédi.

Véghegyek – A *dűlő* in Erdőhorváti, mentioned as "very favourably situated" in 1867, and included among the village's best tracts in 1950. The name is in plural form and signifies 'last/end hills,' in reference to there having been more than one tract named Véghegy. The hill on which the tracts were situated is Véghegy, in singular form.

Veres – The name 'red' (*veres*) occurs among Hegyalja names because of reddish soil.
1) The onetime Veresföld ('redland') *dűlő* in Sátoraljaújhely was mentioned as 1st Class in 1798 and 1867, under the name Veres-Haraszt, although the latter perhaps referred to only a part of the area. It was also mentioned as 1st Class in 1950. 2) A vineyard in the Veres *dűlő* of Tokaj was rented for the Russian Imperial Court beginning in 1746. In 1681, Draheim [see that entry, Part I] listed it among "the most select [*selectissimas*] vineyards" of Tokaj. Later, it blended into the Máriás tract [see that entry]. 3) The Veresek *dűlő* in Mád was mentioned as 3rd Class in 1798 and 1867; and in 1950 was noted as being "unfavorably situated" on its northern side. The plural form (*–ek*) indicates that at one time there were two contiguous vineyards; and indeed, a document of 1688 mentions a Nagy- (Big) Veres (UC 149:22). 4) Both a Veres and a Veres-alja (bottom) were recorded at Tarcal in 1747 (UC 145:123).

Vérmány – This name refers to 'blood' (*vér*) to indicate the red soil color of the Nagy- (Big) and Kis- (Little) Vérmány *dűlő*-s in Sárospatak. The name was mentioned in a document of 1785, but not in 1798 or 1867. In 1950, it was noted that the Vérmány tracts are unfavorably situated, particularly their north-facing areas.

Verőmáj – A *dűlő* of Erdőbénye, mentioned in passing in 1798, mentioned as "principal" in 1867, but noted in 1950 as not having recovered from phylloxera because of its steep slopes. The name implies 'sun-beaten warm slope.' Interesting, too, is that its location was rather westerly, almost out of the Zemplén hills and towards the Hernád river valley. Verőmáj is a veritable reminder that Erdőbénye was once part of Abaúj County.

Vida – A southerly exposed *dűlő* of Szerencs, mentioned among the village's best in 1950. It was not mentioned in 1798 or 1867 because Szerencs was generally considered outside Hegyalja. The name doubtlessly refers to the Vida family, and could date to the 14th century.

Vilmánok – Mentioned among the best vineyard areas of Mád in 1950, the present-day name is in plural form (*–ok*) because in the past there were a Nagy- (Big) and a Kis- (Little) Vilmány, the latter being mentioned as 2nd Class in 1798 and 1867. The name refers to the wine-growing village of Vilmány in the Hernád river valley, in neighboring Abaúj County, probably because laborers were brought from there to cultivate some of the vineyards in past centuries.

Vinnai – (or Vinnay) A *dűlő* in Tarcal, on the northern side of Tokaj-hill, mentioned as 3rd Class in 1798 and 1867. The name dates to the 16th century and refers to the Vinnai (or Vinnay) family from Vinna (now Vinné, in East Slovakia) [see that entry, in Part II]. The Vinnai family likely was identical to the one known earlier as Eödönffy (*i.e.*, the family took the name of their estate as a surname, in place of their ancestor Eödön, of nearby Nagy Mihály) [see the entry for Michalovce, in Part II]. [Also, see the entries for Gombos and Szent-Kereszt, above.]

Vióka – A *dűlő* in Sátoraljaújhely, mentioned as 1st Class in 1950. The origin of the name seems to be that of a curious old surname recorded as Vioga and Vijóka in the past.

Virginás – A *dűlő* in Mezőzombor, mentioned as 1st Class in 1798 and 1867; not mentioned in 1950. The origin of the name is indeterminate, though possibly a reference to the 'Holy Virgin,' which of course suggests an early attachment to a religious order.

Vitéz. See the entry for Szarvas.

Zombori – Several vineyard areas in the southeastern part of Hegyalja incorporate the name Zombor, most likely in reference to the commune of Mezőzombor. 1) Zombori-Király (King) *dűlő*, in Mezőzombor itself, was mentioned as 1st Class in 1798 and 1867, and among the village's "most outstanding" in 1950. 2) The *dűlő* called Zombori (Zombori-Előhegy in the past) is in Tarcal, on the northern side of Tokaj-hill, and was mentioned as 3rd Class in 1798 and 1867. 3) Zomborka was a *dűlő* in Ond as late as 1761 (UC 149:56). In its case, though, the name might have been a surname, since there was such a family in nearby Heves County, to the west.

Zsadányi. See the entry for Előhegy (1).

ZSÁKOS – A vineyard hill in Erdőbénye, praised in 1950 for its "splendid" site, although little of it was under cultivation. The 1950 report also noted that in pre-phylloxera times it "was known as the most renowned of Bénye's vineyard territory" and produced the village's "most outstanding wine." Onetime ownership by the Rákóczis and Greek merchants (Stegner) may be supposed. Nonetheless, Zsákos was a lasting victim of phylloxera, especially in its upper part. Apparently, Zsákos at one time included more than one *dűlő*, since in 1867 Szabó/Török also mentioned it as Zsákosak (*–ak* being the plural form). The origin of the name is uncertain. Superficially, it would seem to derive from 'sack' (*zsák*). But it was recorded in 1733 as 'Sakos,' which suggests that the later name was a corruption. A document of 1436 mentions an estate called 'Sakos' in Transylvania (DL 29781), which indicates early use of the name as a toponym. But it could also derive from a family name, as Martin Saák (*sic*) was the chief judge at Tarcal in 1720 (UC 94:14).

Zsebrik. [See the entry for Monok, in Part II.]

Zsoltár(os) – A *dűlő* in Tokaj that was listed in 1736 (Balassa), though not mentioned in 1798 or 1867. A vineyard in this tract was rented for the Russian Imperial Court in 1746.

Zsolyomka – A *dűlő* in Sátoraljaújhely. Its name may be a variation of the name Sulyom [see that entry].

Zsuzsonka – A vineyard hill and *dűlő* in Erdőbénye, not mentioned in 1798 because Szirmay did not include Abaúj County, but mentioned in 1950 as a quality area except for its lower portion. The name means 'little Suzie' and might have referred to Susanna (Zsuzsanna) Lórántffy, since it is known that László Máté Szepsi was also involved with wine-growing at Erdőbénye. [See the entries for Lórántffy and Szepsi, in Part I]

Zúgó – The name of a vineyard hillock in Tokaj, on the southeastern side of Tokaj-hill. In 1798 and 1867, the *dűlő* on the eastern side of the hill was mentioned as 2nd Class, and the one on its northwestern side as 3rd Class. In 1736, a Zúgó-alja (bottom) was also recorded (Balassa). The Zúgó *dűlő*-s date to at least 1600. The name signifies 'mill-race.'

* * *

Supplemental List of Onetime Tract Names, by commune

Most of these names are from documents of the Hungarian National Archives (MOL), and are cited by document number; Bor. refers to the Borovszky volume of 1903; Bal. refers to the Balassa book of 1991.

Abaújszántó: Alsó-Gyűr, Herke (**end of 17th c.** – UC 69:81); Hám (**1723** – UC 83:28 (a)); Felső- & Nagy-Bogár, Középső- & Nagy-Gyűr, Kőpad, Vigyorgó (**1783** – UC 192:6)

Bodrogkeresztúr: Hegysárky, Kéry, Kis-Vári (**1688** – *urbárium*); Köles-Tarló, Lapisi-Palánt, Lépes, Pipiske (**end of 17th c.** – UC 69:81)

Erdőbénye: Nagy- & Kis-Herceg (**1789** – Bal.)

Erdőhorváti: Középhuta (**1903** – Bor.)

Mád: Hársas (**1675** – UC 116:15); Kertiszőlő (**end of 17th c.** – UC 69:81); Gyurkó Pál, Nagy-, Kis- & K.K.- [*sic*] Hegy, Kiskút, Nőtelen, Pelsőczy [Pelőczy], Suba (**1723** – UC 83:127 & 26:7 (b))

Malá Tŕňa (Kistoronya): Symonhegye (**1466** – DL 16377); Bolygó (**1698** – UC 116:62)

Mezőzombor: Christof, Fridrik, Keczer, Kuntz, Zolten (**1565** – UC 81:10(c)); Bartha, Filpesi-Köves, (**1573** – UC 158:29); Musay (**1581** – *urbárium*); Békealja, Berekalja, Berkenyés (**end of 17th c.** – UC 69:81); Felső Kis Köre, Jobbágy (**1717** – UC 69:18); Kamenka (**1723** – UC 83:28 (a))

Olaszliszka: Bónis-féle (**1679** – Bal.); Balázs-pap, Bata, István-pap, Nagy-Haraszt, Kis- & Nagy-Tölgyes [Tőgyes], Torna (**1681** – UC 10:88 (a)); Farkashát (**1700** – UC 145:36)

Ond: Barát, Boldizsár, Fodor-Csél, Károly, Kucs [Kwtss], Zala, Zendy, Zoltán (**1573** – UC 158:29); Olajfás, Zombrika (**1723** – UC 83:126)

Rátka – Széles (**1738** – UC 83:86)

Sárospatak: Felső & Alsó Hostáti (**1634** – Bal.); Cinege, Szava (**end of 17th c.** – UC 69:81); Kis- & Nagy-Cinege (**1737** – UC 145:98); Bancsi, Cirkáló, Collegiumi, Csonka, Fűrdős, Gangosi, Gergelyhegye, Görög-Zsiga, Gregósi, Felső-Hárselő, Hosszúhágó, Kácsád, Alsó-Kácsád, Károlyi, Korgosi (later Korgó), Krucsai, Nagy-Mihály, Nyiri-sor, Szarvas-Ugró (**1785** – Bal.); Csermőke (**1789** – Bal.)

Sátoraljaújhely: Sárhely (**end of 17th c.** – UC 69:81); Barka (**1734** – Bal.)

Tállya: Szerencsés, Tolvaj (**1670-1673** – UC 157:73); Pipiske (**end of 17th c.** – UC 69:81); Kandu-Nyírjes (**18th c.** – UC 122:52); Békás (**1768** – UC 156:47); Görvényes, Szeles (**1737** – UC 145:98)

Tarcal: Czekevölgy [see the entry for Cseke] (**1565** – UC 81:10(c)); Csákvölgye, Szabó-Péter (**1573** – UC 158:29); Árnyék, Burja, Csajka, Kis-Ványai, (**1737** – UC 145:98); Booth [Bóth], Fenyő, Város Vége (**1747** – UC 145:123); Kundri (**1751** – UC 83:138); Ivankó-Dorogy, Magyaros [probably Mogyorós], Toppan (**18th c.** – UC 122:52); Désán, Fűz-tőke, Jeremiás, Pulykás (**1765** – UC 117:49)

Tokaj: Kulcsár, Lisztes, Nyilas, Polyékes [Polekas, Poleka, Polyankas] (**1573** – UC 158:29); Pincefelől (**1581** – *urbárium*); Borbely, Henderke, Hornáti, Vidlány (**1672** – UC 154:2); Alj-szőlő, Clastrom-felett, Csepegő, Palántalja, Városfeli (**1674** – UC 116:11); Kapus, Kert(i), Vitány (**1676** – UC 111:11); Kapitány (**1684** – UC 90:54); Izsák, Kis-Oltár, Lisztes (**1688** – *urbárium*); Tormás (**1690** – UC 1:35); Elsőjárás (**end of 17th c.** – UC 69:81); Barka, Csepegő, Dobó, Gatya, Hitvány, Kalodásalja, Ménes-oldal, Nyestalja, Posta, Sánczy, Verebes (**1736** – Balassa); Házfelőli, Nagy-Verebes (**1737** – UC 145:98); Kövesdi, Forrai, Szarka, Usura (**1753** – UC 94:36); Bartus, Bodor (**1765** – UC 117:50); Poczdajka (**mid-18th c.** – UC 122:52)

Tolcsva: Csekő (**18th c.** – UC 122:52) [see the entry for Cseke]

PART III

ESSAY

The Development and Classification of Hegyalja Vineyard-Tracts

Many Hegyalja vineyard-tracts had taken shape at least two centuries before the advent of later-harvested wines towards the end of the 15th century. During the 13th and 14th centuries, Hungarian kings gladly granted fortification rights in the Upper Tisza region, and this resulted in population buildup and the creation of new vineyards in Hegyalja. Documents show that by the early 1300s, individual vineyards were being sold by reference to the names of the tracts in which they were situated. From then through the 15th century, documents burgeon with vineyard-tract names. It is in this period, too, that persons and municipalities further north began acquiring land in Hegyalja, sometimes occasioning new tract names for certain sections of older ones.

After the mid-16th century, the situation for wine-growing at times was less secure, and resulted in ups and downs both in the total producing area and the number of tracts still in use. Periodic Ottoman Turkish forays into the Upper Tisza were especially negative for communes in the southernmost part of today's Hegyalja, especially the Szerencs hills [see that entry, in Part II). In the second-half of the 17th century, the anti-Habsburg rebellions disrupted production, and resulted in confiscations from rebellious nobles by the Szepes Chamber (the agent of the Habsburgs). In 1676, for instance, 245 vineyards in 19 Hegyalja locales were confiscated (UC 58:9). Some recovery in the 18th century was followed by retraction in the early-19th century because the partitions of Poland towards the end of the 18th resulted in a sharp decrease in prices.

Kossuth, in 1903, noted that one could see vineyard land that had been left fallow and had overgrown with woods for 200 years, or since around 1700. He is easily borne out by comparing Szirmay's vineyard-tract classification of 1798 to documents from the preceding century-and-a-quarter and noticing the disappearance of tract names. Kossuth further stated that vines had gone out of cultivation on a "significant" amount of land even before phylloxera, in reference to the preceding decades of the 1800s; he especially noted the negative situation at Bodrogkeresztúr, Bodrogkisfalud, Bodrogzsadány (now Sárazsadány), and parts of Erdőbénye and Tolcsva. He attributed this primarily to the decline in sales to Poland. Although Kossuth commented that it was "the more difficultly, and thus more costly, worked vineyards" that suffered most, nothing is known as to whether tracts were affected relative to the sort of wine produced from them. It may be suspected, for instance, that it was in the second-half of the 1800s that areas typically planted with red varieties practically vanished from most of Hegyalja.

After the Second World War, at the outset of the communist period, a detailed survey of the Hegyalja vineyard-tracts was made, with a view towards reconstructing them, if only in part. Achievement, though, was feasible only relative to the availability of farm labor and potential profitability (especially hard-currency earnings from exports to the West). Plus, government agricultural authorities wanted a quick recovery in terms of output. The result was a shortsighted decision to put off, or ignore, the recommended reconstruction of old tracts, and instead to create new tracts on crop land at the bottom of the vineyard slopes. Not many of the recommended old sites were actually brought back into production, with the exception of some lower slopes where botrytization tended to be abundant. Nevertheless, an attempt was made to bring a few of the better tracts on the middle part of the steeper slopes back into use if they were susceptible to the creation of terraces that allowed for mechanized cultivation. At the same time, there was a positive effort to take some tracts out of use if they were located in low-lying pockets or basins subject to frosts or to becoming waterlogged. [See the Appendix Essay.]

*

The origin of tract names varies as to time period, but not enough documentary information is available by which to separate those periods with any precision. It does appear, though, that certain types of names were characteristic of periods whose dates can be approximated.

A handful of names, which perhaps represents the oldest stratum, derive from ancient Magyar clan names, from the pre-13th century Árpád Dynasty. But these are disappointingly few, such as Baksó (Baksa) in Tarcal, Káté (Katha) in Slovenské Nové Mesto (East Slovakia), Berkec in Szerencs, probably Uszhegy in Mád, Lete in Monok, and possibly Szemere (of the Huba clan) in Szerencs. But there is no indication of the conquerors of Hungary, unless it is the onetime Ondzeuloshege (*sic*) in Ond, in reference to the chieftain Ónd, but even that is indeterminate. [Also, see the entry for Fegyemes.] However, tract names that include the word 'king' (*király*) likely date to the Árpád kings, possibly to as early as the 11th and 12th centuries. In that period, royal fortresses characterized Zemplén, and vineyards would have belonged to them, hence use of the name 'king.' But this period ended around 1300, after which families acquiring domains would not have used the name 'king' or 'royal' in naming newly created vineyard-tracts.

Probably amongst the oldest *dűlő* names are those with the suffix *-máj* (also written as *–mály* or *–mál* in the older documents). As an archaic Magyar term denoting the sunniest, warmest slope of a hill, this class of names likely pre-dates the Tatar invasion of 1241-1242. Foremost among them is the famous Mézesmáj between Tokaj and Tarcal, but there are others: Barnamáj (Erdőbénye), Csókamáj (Bodrogkeresztúr), Hosszúmáj (Szegilong), Királymáj (Tarcal), Melegmáj (Erdőhorváti), Tökösmáj (Tállya), Verőmáj (Erdőbénye). Not surprisingly, in view of the meaning of *–máj*, most of these were considered amongst the best in their communes.

The *–máj* names are just a particular instance within the category of names relating to physical features. The main difference is that the broader category often relates to hill names rather than to individual tracts, although in the case of a few hillocks the name may have been coextensive with a tract, at least initially. This is a populous category, since it can refer to the shape of a hill or some particular feature of a tract, such as soil color. Thus, the names are wide in range, for instance: Agyag in reference to 'clay' land (Tarcal); the renowned Disznókő, in reference to a stone thought to resemble a boar (Mezőzombor); Feketehegy, or 'black-hill' (Tarcal); Hidegoldal, or 'cold-side' (Erdőbénye); Hosszúhegy, or 'long-hill' (Hercegkút); Köveshegy, or 'stony-hill' (Sátoraljaújhely); Kőporos, or 'stone-powdery' (Mezőzombor); and of course, the two hills known as Sátorhegy, or 'tent[-shaped]-hill,' respectively in Sátoraljaújhely and Abaújszántó, which have given popular definition to the north-south extent of Hegyalja for several centuries. However, unlike the *–máj* names, these names may vary widely as to the period when they came into use. Some hills probably bore their names before they became the site of vineyards, as is possible in the cases of Magita, Makra, and Rány.

Another old category of names is those with a religious origin. The exemplar, and certainly the one with the greatest name recognition, is Oremus in Sátoraljaújhely. But it is a fairly numerous category: Bahomalja (Tállya), Barát (Tarcal, Tokaj), Istenhegy (Rátka), Pálosok (Sátoraljaújhely), Püspöki (Tarcal), Szemince (Bodroghalász), Szent-Ignác (Sárazsadány), Szent-Kereszt (Tarcal), Szent-Margit (Abaújszántó), Szent-Tamás (Mád), Szentvér (Tolcsva), Szent-Vince (Sárospatak), Urbán (Mád). Most of these reflect either initial planting or early ownership by Roman Catholic religious orders. Most also likely date to the post-Tatar invasion period of the late-13th century, although a few could date to earlier Árpád kings, some of whom were quite active in establishing monasteries and religious orders in order to bolster Christianity against lapses into semi-pagan rites. King Kálmán around 1100 was notable in that regard, and a handful of piously named tracts might be that old.

A more recent stratum of vineyard-tracts is recognized by names that likely originated towards the end of the 13th century and the early decades of the 14th century. They were created in connection with the spread of fortresses and feudal domains meant to forestall more devastation by Asiatic invaders. Some of their names actually indicate the particular domains upon which they were bestowed: Ciróka (in Tolcsva) of the Homonna Domain; Darnó (Sárospatak) of the Tőketerebes Domain; Dobra (Tolcsva) of the Gálszécs Domain; Kövesd (Tarcal) of the Nagy Kövesd fort; Peres (Erdőbénye) of the Csicsva fort [all of those in Zemplén County]; Makovica (Mád) of the Makovica Domain; Bodonyi (Tarcal) of the Bodon fort; Sáros (Erdőbénye) of the Nagy Sáros fort [all of those being in Sáros County]; Berkec (Szerencs) of the Kővár Domain; Perőc (Tarcal) and Rudnok (Sárazsadány) of the Jászó fort; Sólyom/Sulyom of the Sólyomkő fort [all of those in Abaúj County]; Murány (Szegi) of the Murány Domain [Gömör County]. As well, there were vineyard hills named Várhegy, or 'fortress-hill,' because fortresses were actually located on or by the site (Bodrogkisfalud, Erdőbénye, Sátoraljaújhely, Tállya, Tolcsva).

All of the above categories can be thought of as 'ancient period' in origin, because they date to when Hegyalja supplied largely itself and a limited regional market in the Upper Tisza. This began to change with population growth. The category of names bridging the old and the new periods is that which refers to the clearing of previously wooded land to make way for new vineyard-tracts. Perhaps the most obvious of these, as well as the most celebrated historically, is Cserfás (in Tarcal), in reference to the removal of oak trees. But there are references to other trees, such as beech (Bikkoldal, in Tolcsva), birch (Nyírjesek, in Tállya), elm (Szilvölgy, in Tarcal), and hornbeam (Gyertyános, in Szegilong), as well as shrubbery (Cserjes and Galagonyás, in Abaújszántó). The names of fruit trees also occur. Tracts received the names Birsalmás (Mád), Mandulás (Sárospatak, Tarcal, Tolcsva,), Mogyorós (Olaszliszka, Szerencs), Somos (Bodrogolaszi, Szegi, Golop), respectively in reference to quince, dwarf-almond, walnut, and cornel trees. Orchards might have been removed because wine-growing was seen as the economic future. Names referring to hunting and game also suggest the clearing of forests. Finally, the communes of Erdőbénye, Erdőhorváti, and Végardó actually refer to their setting amidst onetime forest land (erdő/ardó), as is also true of Makkoshotyka (makk = acorn).

The indisputably 'modern period' of vineyard-tract names begins after 1500, and reflects the greater commercial importance of Hegyalja wine in the Upper Tisza region. One aspect of this development was that tracts began to acquire the names of particular families. The Csirke family was a harbinger of this trend already in the 14th century, but the tendency intensified as vineyard ownership in Hegyalja became a status symbol. The tracts Bornemissza (in Tokaj), Gilányi (Tolcsva), Hangács (Mezőzombor), Pethő (Tolcsva), and Thurzó (Tarcal) are prime examples. This was accompanied by names relating to ownership by towns further north, both in Hungary and in Poland, that had a stake in Tokaji wine, notably Bártfai (in Tállya), Danczka (Tokaj), Kassai (Ond), Krakó (Abaújszántó), Lőcse (Erdőbénye), and Rosenberg (Tállya).

It would appear, too, that the several vineyard-tracts bearing the name of a grape variety are also modern, not least of all in that the name did not grow out of habit and tradition, but was bestowed by the person who first planted the varietal. But there does not seem to have been more than a handful: Aranka (Szerencs), Furmint (Erdőbénye), Kecsi (Abaújszántó), Lányka (Monok), Szegfű (Sárospatak), Talyanka (Ond). [Also, see the entry for Siller.]

The first known classification of the Hegyalja vineyard-tracts dates to the mid-17th century and was initiated by the Rákóczis. It is likely that it was accomplished in connection with the regulations for Hegyalja that the Rákóczis promulgated in 1641. However, record of it has not survived. It probably did not cover all of the communes included within Hegyalja by the laws of 1893 and 1908, and instead would have been confined to those areas that fell within the domains possessed by the Rákóczis. But as this would have included the Regéc, Tokaj, Sárospatak, and Sátoraljaújhely domains, the great preponderance of Hegyalja would have been included. The vineyard-tracts were ranked as 1st, 2nd, and 3rd Class, and although the classification did not survive, several documents from the late-17th century mention the ranking for a few of the tracts; and these could only reflect the Rákóczi classification.

A second official effort at classification was made in 1772. However, this was conducted by Zemplén County, and so left out the areas of Hegyalja that belonged to Abaúj County (at that time: Abaújszántó, Erdőbénye, Erdőhorváti, Golop), as well as Zemplén villages that not everyone thought of as part of Hegyalja. In all likelihood, it did not dispute much about the Rákóczi classification, though it would have added and deleted tract names due to changes that had occurred. It is known that the 'composition' of tracts sometimes increased or decreased; that is, a smaller tract might be attached to a larger neighboring one and lose its name, or a large tract might eventually be recognized as two or three separate tracts, each carrying its own name. And, as noted by Kossuth (1903), not a few tracts simply went out of cultivation after 1700.

The 1772 classification no doubt was the basis for the tract rankings given in 1798 by Antal Szirmay in his book on Zemplén County wine-growing. That book in turn became the reference point for later commentators on tract quality. The Szabó/Török account in the *Tokaj-Hegyaljai Album* of 1867 is virtually a restatement of Szirmay. Szirmay's influence is obvious even in the 1950 viticultural report of Hidvéghy. All of this likely was in a straight line of descent from the Rákóczi classification.

Szirmay's account, though, was not 'complete.' For one thing, of course, Abaúj County was left out. Further, while Szirmay gave a fairly full report on *dűlő*-s for the major Hegyalja settlements of Zemplén County, he concentrated on 1st and 2nd Class tracts and neglected 3rd Class. Szabó/Török in 1867 added some tract names, mostly because they included several communes that Szirmay left out, but at the same time, they did not mention several others mentioned by Szirmay even though they still existed. Both works were inconsistent in specifying 1st, 2nd, and 3rd Class tracts; both gave short shrift to the smaller Hegyalja communes; and even in the case of the larger communities, it is apparent that the authors occasionally hurried to summarize, and resorted to a terse *et cetera*. The Hidvéghy report of 1950 respects Szirmay and Szabó/Török on 1st and 2nd Class tracts, but gives more specificity about 3rd Class. However, since Hidvéghy's report was a technical one that did not have classification as an object, he did not refer to each and every tract mentioned by Szirmay and Szabó/Török.

We must also keep in mind several other historical points about the old classifications of *dűlő*-s. First, in early times, when opinions began forming, the varietal complement was significantly different from what it would be after 1800 [see the varietal names and the entry for Grape Varieties, in Part IV]. Second, some of the vineyard-tracts gained fame because they grew particularly good grapes of one or another variety; and so, their fruit or wine was sought for blending with grapes from vineyards where other varieties yielded good results. Third, some tracts became famous as exceptional producers of *főbor* (the predecessor of *szamorodni*) in the early period of later-harvested wines, but were less reliable when the commercial emphasis switched to the sweeter and more botrytis-dependent *aszú* wines. But such questions were not addressed by Szirmay or Szabó/Török, and it can only be supposed that they might have had some influence on the Rákóczi classification.

*

Just as it is not known why the Rákóczis decided to classify the vineyard-tracts, and why three classes were specified, so too, nothing is known about the criteria used. Presumably, the basis was largely empirical, since a century-and-a-half had passed during which it had been noticed which tracts were best for leaving the berries to shrivel on the vine. An indication of this is the mention in 1764, eight years before the Zemplén County classification, that the Cserfás tract produces "extraordinary" *aszú* grapes (UC 122:34). In accounting for such a qualitative outcome, it was practically instinctual to consider vineyard exposition; and the early use of the suffix *–máj* in vineyard names is a sure indication that a southerly exposition had long been paramount. To be sure, vineyards with easterly, westerly, and even northerly expositions were created, but these were not held to be among the best, and many fell by the wayside as the centuries went by.

The extent to which soil or land features might have played a role in the early classifications is unclear. A document of 1674, addressing the vineyards of the town of Tokaj, referred to three types of land: stony (*köves*), 'humpy-bumpy' (*görbe*), and cloddy (*göröngyös*) (UC 116:11). But these were aspects related to working the land, rather than soil types per se. In a similar vein, Keler, in 1726, mentioned stony, gravelly, and clayey land, which he associated respectively with the high, middle, and lower growing areas. But, by 'clayey' he seems to have meant not so much soil type (since he noted that it could be black, yellow, or gray), as land whose color stood out because of a dearth of any grade of stony overlay. And Bél, around 1730, was reminiscent of the 1674 document in stating that "smooth" (*sima*), or 'uniform,' land was preferable, which obviously was the antithesis of the 'humpy-bumpy' land.

Yet, long before 1700, one soil type had become regarded as preferable, all else being equal. This was the type called *nyirok* by the local people [one searches in vain for the term in old documents]. *Nyirok* is a clayey loam soil derived from volcanic rock, especially riolite, trachyte, and andesite. Of course, a variety of more detailed descriptions are found in the Hungarian literature on Hegyalja, but two provide particularly helpful images. First, Spotkovszky (1914) called it a "[stone-]fragment-free, plastic clay" and noted it as "water-retentive to a great degree," to the point that it can be "gluey" (she supposed this latter aspect accounted for the name *nyirok*, signifying 'moist-stuff'). Second, Balassa (1991) referred to it as "compact, hard, but fat soil, which is slightly tarry [*i.e.*, sticky in consistency], [such that] the two-pronged hoe that has dug into it can only be cleansed of it with difficulty." (Looking back at the 1674 document, it would seem that "cloddy" land was rather the opposite of *nyirok*, and therefore not very desirable.) It might just be added that the relative compactness of *nyirok* was also a factor, since insufficient or excessive compactness was unfavorable for moisture retention.

Parenthetically, the general preference for *nyirok* may not have resulted from empiricism alone. The merits of clayey soil for wine-growing had been passed down from the ancient Greeks, and could already have been a Balkan influence in Hegyalja when the Magyars arrived. That is, most of the existing vineyards might have been situated on such land. For instance, this might have been the case with the *nyirok*-clay hill of Rány [see that entry]. By the time of the Rákóczi classification, the educated class of Hegyalja owners would have been familiar with clayey soil in theoretical terms directly from the works of Greek and Roman authors.

But the prospective vineyard purchaser had choices other than *nyirok*. Loess was also a notable soil type. It was colloquially dubbed *sárgaföld*, or 'yellow-land,' presumably to distinguish it from the dark shades associated with *nyirok*. Loess had respected sites of its own, usually at a lower altitude than the *nyirok* lands, and invariably with southern exposure. It distinguishes the southern line of Hegyalja, but most of all, from Tarcal to Tokaj, where the most famous exemplar historically was Mézesmáj (in its broadest sense) [see Mézesmáj (c)]. Further, there are many transitional areas between *nyirok* and loess, with the two mixing to greatly varying degrees. Sometimes, mostly in southern Hegyalja, the loess and loess-*nyirok* soils are splotched with lime, whether of limestone or marly loess origin (Hidvéghy). Historic tracts notable for lime-content are Hasznos (in Legyesbénye), Hegyfark (Ond), Istenhegy (Rátka), Napos (Bekecs), Sasalja (Tállya), Úrágya (Mád), and Zsebrik (Monok).

Yet another soil type was called 'stone-dust' (*kőpor*), because of stone that had been ground to a dust. Presumably, it was the sight of this type that caused Townson (1797) to mention a soil "remarkably fine and light, just like Tripoli, it is quite a powder…it has nothing of the nature of sand." 'Remarkable' though it might be as such, it was not esteemed, on account of lesser heat retention. The (Hungarian) Pallas Encyclopedia (1893-1896) called it "the poorest" of Hegyalja soils. Additionally, there are rarer, localized soil types, such as the 'burnt-land' (*égevény föld*), of direct volcanic origin, found most notably in the Gyapáros, Rézló (Tolcsva) and Zsákos (Erdőbénye) tracts, and (according to Szabó/Török in 1867) the 'obsidian soil' area of the first.

Some tract names actually refer to soil and ground features. Tarcal and Abaújszántó have tracts named Agyag ('Clay'). Sometimes soil color is indicated, especially brown and red in the case of *nyirok*. In Erdőbénye, *Barna-* ('Brown') *máj* refers to the brown color of profoundly *nyirok* soil. Other names allude to iron content in *nyirok* by referring to red (*veres*), such as Veresek ('Reds') in Mád, Veresföld ('Red-land') in Sátoraljaújhely, and Vérmányok ('Blood-reds') in Sárospatak. Even 'stone-dust' has representatives: Kőporos in Hercegkút and Mezőzombor. Stoniness was another feature from which tract names originated, such as Köveshegyek ('Stony-hills') in Tállya, Nagy-Köves ('Big-Stony') in Mezőzombor, Hercegköves ('Prince's Stony') in Rátka.

Additionally, a variety of identifiable mineral material, not only riolite, trachyte, and andesite, but also quartz, feldspar, and others, is scattered throughout Hegyalja in different proportions. In some tracts, one will predominate; in other tracts, two might be found but not others; while in still others all can be found, though in different parts of the tract. Oftentimes it was to mineral content that nuances were attributed by which to distinguish, supposedly, the wine of one part of a tract from another. This could also account for personal taste preferences. But mineral composition as such is not known to have had an impact on classifications, nor even on the old vineyard names.

*

In the Introduction to Part III, it was remarked that elevation holds the middle ground, so to speak, between exposition and soil in terms of 'room for maneuver,' that is, choosing one's property so as to minimize negative conditions for wine quality. While this might not usually call for a separate discussion of 'height above sea level,' the size of Tokaj-Hegyalja and the history of 'average' elevation just during the century between the phylloxera episode and the constraints of the communist era is alone reason enough to look at the issue more closely. Specifically, is 'the higher the better' a useful rule of thumb? Or, what are its limitations?

In 1773, Sylvester Douglass, on the word of his Hungarian informants, noted: "the general rule is, that the exposure most inclining to the south, the steepest declivities, and *the highest part* of those declivities, produce the best wine" (emphasis added). Nevertheless, in the two centuries after him, the well-observed trend was for the Hegyalja vineyards to descend to lower altitudes. Kossuth (1903) stated that this had already occurred at some locales even decades before Douglass. It was brought on by trade restrictions in the 18th century, and was exacerbated by price declines that of course had their most negative impact on the vineyards most costly to work, which were those highest up and usually with the greatest degree of slope.

But the losses did not end in the 18th century. According to a firsthand account of 1817, the previous four vintages had been so poor that the highest vineyards were being given over to forest and brush (Borovszki, p. 443). Capping it all was phylloxera, emigration, and the world wine glut of the Interwar Period, which left the upper slopes 'high and dry.' Thus did Hidvéghy note, in 1950, that the vineyards generally had "slid down" the slopes. Irrespectively of political regime, which in fact included several types from 1900 to 1990, what did this actually mean for the quality of Tokaji in the 20th century?

Some excellent altitudinous vineyard areas were lost, especially after phylloxera. We have only to consider that many tracts with the forename Upper (Felső) never recovered. However, this tendency did not affect all locales and tracts equally. Further, not all high tracts were superior, since some were created during Tokaji's heyday to take advantage of its name, and had failings as regards exposition or soil. Indeed, Dombi (1758) commented that the highest areas yield thin, sharp wine. In his day, this might in part have been because of varietal factors, including not only the white sorts being grown, but also red ones. In any case, it is clear that many high tracts were ill-suited. Kossuth, too, in 1903, intimated that many high tracts had been left fallow long ago not just because of inconvenient position, but also because they were "less well-exposed."

If one wants to get down to the nitty-gritty of elevation and its relation to wine quality, it has to be noted that the predominance of the esteemed *nyirok* soil, with good stone covering, was on the middle slopes. Spotkovszky (1914) reported that "the most expensive" vineyards were on "the middle third" of the hills. Even during the the crisis of the mid-1810s, it was the vineyards of the middle slopes that the Hegyalja growers struggled to preserve: "the [vineyards] on the waist of the hills we hold on to and are at pains for, in good hope, until time teaches us otherwise."

As to the elevation of the 'middle-zone,' somewhat varying figures are found. Brezovcsik (1974) stated the widest range, from 120 meters/394 feet to 200 meters/656 feet above sea level, which he said had also been true "long ago" (*Tokajhegyalja Borgazdasága*). Presumably, he meant pre-phylloxera times. Szabó-Jilek (1962), though, stated that, historically, the mid-level was 150 meters/411 feet to 190 meters/623 feet. The discrepancy perhaps is explainable by the locales used as a gauge, as well as by historical varietal factors, such as the switchover to *furmint* and *hárslevelű*, since different varieties have been preferable at varying heights. Brezovcsik noted that the range of 120 meters to 175 meters/574 feet "always" yields the best quality "in mediocre or poorer years," and that "the most intensive budding" takes place in the 120-150 meter range.

In any case, the general preference for the middle-zone was greater reliability in botrytis vintages. Any strong preference for the range of 150 to 200 meters at particular sites or locales mostly had to do with greater stoniness and consequent heat retention. Below the 120-meter level, stoniness declined greatly, while at the same time, cold air sank there. It was obviously an empirical awareness of that disadvantage that caused so many tracts to have their lowest portion identified separately and tagged with the suffix –*alja* (bottom), especially during the 17th century, when botrytis wine came to the fore. Brezovcsik questioned whether "such locations [below 120 meters] should be used at all for the planting of vineyards."

Above the range of 190-200 meters, one is in what can be called the 'upper part' of the middle slopes. Referring back to Spotkovszky and her 'division' of the slopes into thirds, it can be said that the range from 250 meters/820 feet or 687 to 300 meters/984 feet, constituted the 'upper third,' even if it did not constitute a literal third of Hegyalja elevation. Nagy (1962) stated that vineyards at 250 meters/820 feet to 280 meteres/ 919 feet, were generally the highest area cultivated, with 300 meters being rare. This is in line with Kossuth's (1903) notation that the vineyards on Hajagos hill, at Sátoraljaújhely, had been abandoned long ago. Újhely always had Hegyalja's highest vineyards, and historically, the very highest, perhaps even over 300 meters, would have been on Hajagos, which reaches 660 meters/2,165 feet.

In general, any superiority displayed by some of the higher tracts had to do with stone covering. All things being equal, larger and more widespread stones were preferable; and, on average, this was found most frequently in the more altitudinous areas. Nevertheless, the higher and stonier land varied considerably as to the size of the stones, not to mention sub-soil, erosion, and exposition. Also, because of Hegyalja's northerly position as a wine region, it is just as important to have higher hills to the rear to protect against cold air from the north either early or late in the growing season. Certainly, many of the higher vineyards of past times would not have had that protection (that is certainly one implication of Dombi's statement about thin wine being rather characteristic of the altitudinous area). Further, the advantage that some high sites might have had in earlier times was seriously diminished once the *furmint* became dominant, since it is a late-ripener and does not bear cold well. The *furmint* is decidedly more at home in the middle-zone.

Kossuth (1910) saw no general falloff in the quality of Hegyalja botrytis wine because of the loss of some high vineyards following phylloxera. Moreover, the loss of what excellent land there was at the higher elevations was countered after phylloxera by considerable improvements in other aspects of viticulture; besides which, improvements in varietal composition vis-à-vis botrytization occurred during the two centuries when the more altitudinous vineyards were being abandoned. No one has dared to say it, but it is quite possible that the best wines produced during 1900-2000 were as good as the best produced during 1700-1800.

This does not refute, though, that 'average quality' might have declined by some fraction during the past 200 years because of a decrease in average altitude, nor the contention that contemporary Hegyalja will remain short of its full potential until certain of the upper slopes are 're-taken.' One can certainly wish for renewed interest in the best of the high slopes (*e.g.*, Zsákos in Erdőbénye), no matter the techniques used to re-create them. And those techniques will vary because of Hungary's new free-market economy and ongoing research on viticulture.

*

According to Dömötör/Katona (1963), the most vaunted *dűlő*-s that survived were Király at Mád; Disznókő at Mezőzombor; Szarvas at Tarcal; Hétszőlő at Tokaj; Ciróka, Kútpatka, Mandulás, and Szentvér at Tolcsva (stated in that order). But, in comparing that 'short-list' to the Hidvéghy report of 1950 and older notations, it is obvious that an offhand 'historical memory' hardly does justice to a region as extensive as Hegyalja. A more complete listing of 'the best of the best,' based on historical reputation, would be as follows (alphabetically by commune and tract):

Abaújszántó: Fövenyes, Krakó
Bekecs: Napos
Bodrogkeresztúr: Henye
Bodrogszegi: Aranyos, Hatalos
Erdőbénye: Lőcse, Peres (or Tolcsva-hegy), Zsákos

Mád: Danczka, Király, Makovica
Malá Tŕňa (Kistoronya): Királyka (or Keletka)
Mezőzombor: Disznókő
Olaszliszka: Meszes
Sárazsadány: (Zsadány-) Előhegy
Sárospatak: Szentvér
Sátoraljaújhely: Oremus
Tállya: Dorgó, Görbe, Hasznos, Patócs, Várhegy
Tarcal: Cserfás, Mézesmáj, Szarvas
Tokaj: Hétszőlő, Kócsag, Szerelmi
Tolcsva: Ciróka, Gyapáros, Kincsem, Kútpatka, Mandulás

It could be said, simply, that a greater percentage of people in the Upper Tisza region were aware of the qualitative import of these names than those of other tracts in Hegyalja. This would have included not only the bourgeoisie, but even peasants from the many villages where day-laborers were procured, especially since the esteem of the tract may have been reflected in higher wages.

Tracts of various soil gradations can be regarded equally in terms of the quality of their wine, in relation to the 1st, 2nd, and 3rd Class breakdown of the historical classifications. But the particulars are thought to impart the characteristics associated with the best wines of certain communes. For example, the loess soil on the southern slopes at Tokaj are known to give the sweetest wines of Hegyalja. Or again, the stonier soils on southerly exposed *nyirok*, for instance at Tarcal, give the most generous, or 'heady,' wine. At this point, though, even a scientific researcher would be moving beyond objective classification, into the realm of consumer preference (even if an 'informed preference'). Consideration of Szabó/Török (1867), Kossuth (1903), and Hidvéghy (1950) yields a good impression of the complexities involved.

It is also worth considering Bél (c. 1730), who wrote, "every good property [of the land]...rests on the moderate qualities of the respective soil." He did not want his readers to be in doubt about his meaning of "moderate": "[the land] should be neither overly dense, nor loose, but rather, it should come closer to being crumbly; it should not be lean, nor greasy, but should strongly approach being fat [rich]; it should not be flat, nor steep, but rather, situated higher, and smooth."

Finally, the viewpoint of Hungarian experts as regards Hegyalja *dűlő* classification has differed relative to Western notions about classifications. Dömötör/Katona (1963) had this comment:

> The enumeration of *dűlő*-s and the distinguishing amongst growing-sites were
> not value-rankings in terms of wine quality [as opposed to site advantages].
> Just as it cannot be decided whether the most pleasant floral smell is that of
> the violet, the lilac or some other flower, so too, everyone will place the wine
> of this or that parcel at the head of the list according to their taste.

While it might be objected that the authors threw in gratuitous comments here and there to appease a politically oriented editor who could not countenance an implication of 'innate superiority' (or 'nobility'), it is worth remembering the analoguous comment made by Bél over two centuries before Communist Hungary: "everyone esteems the wines of [Hegyalja] according to [the location of] their property or the evaluation of their taste."

*   *   *

PART IV

WAYS and MEANS:

grape varieties, wine types, techniques, characteristics

"The chemical composition, the nature, the processes taking place during the preparation, handling and maturation of Tokaji wines are so divergent from those of other wines that it is not possible either to compare them or to draw generalized inferences [that apply to Tokaji]."

Ákos Ásvány, enologist, 1983

INTRODUCTION

Judging from the sparse inhabitation of Hegyalja when the Magyars arrived at the end of the 9th century, vineyards and wine-making could only have been minor in extent. Further, there is compelling reason to think that most of the wine was of a more or less red hue. Nearly 600 years would pass before Tokaji wine as we know it today began to take shape.

Hegyalja's wine-making history during the past millennium is best understood within the context of what came before. In terms of viticulture, a virtual gulf separated the Upper Tisza region from the rest of the former Kingdom of Hungary. While Hungarian, Slovak, and other Central European historians habitually credit the Romans with either introducing or decisively influencing cultivation of the vine and wine-making in the Carpathian basin, this does not hold true for the Upper Tisza and Hegyalja. The Romans did not push much further to the northeast than the Danube, and certainly did not occupy the Upper Tisza. Instead, this area was under Avar domination after the 7th century, and by at least the 9th century the Avars were but satraps of the medieval Bulgarian Empire. It is likely that the small fortresses existing in and around Hegyalja at that time were erected mostly with Roman encroachment from the southwest in mind.

Not surprisingly, the oldest stratum of grape varieties in Hegyalja vividly reflects this past. There is no sign whatsoever of an early presence of Western grape varieties, only Balkan varieties. But the Bulgaro-Slavs not only brought grape varieties. They also introduced the Balkan method of vinifying them by a long fermentation on skins and stems, sometimes even in the case of white grapes. The later Hegyalja habit of 'soaking' the skins of overripe grapes in white grape must or wine likely was cued by this old Balkan practice. Red wine of Balkan type continued to be a Hegyalja wine-type, even if only minimally an export article, as late as the mid-19th century.

*

The turning point in favor of white wine came in the latter part of the 15th century, when records demonstrate that the vintage was put off until late-September. This resulted in the production of more or less sweet wines from grapes that had become overripe on the vine; and the white varieties happened to be more suitable than the red ones for later harvesting. It is shortly thereafter, in 1524, that Sperfogel made the comment that Tokaji is better than it ever was before.

Nevertheless, Hegyalja's star only began to rise when southern Hungary was occupied by the Ottomans, starting in 1526, and the premier southern wine region of Szerém (now the Srem region of Serbia) was no longer accessible to buyers from Poland. The most prized Szerém wine was mature white wine, and consequently, Hegyalja had no interest in deviating from that type in replacing Szerém on the Polish market. The propensity for well-aged wine grew with the ascendancy of sweetish Tokaji, and was reinforced further after the inception of botrytis *aszú*.

While later-harvested grapes may have been referred to as *aszú* berries even in the early years, for the most part these were ordinary shriveled grapes, not botrytized grapes. Botrytization did not begin attracting particular notice until after 1560, when a third hoeing was introduced and the vintage was pushed well into October. But the decisive change happened roughly around 1600, when a delay, probably owing to warfare with the Ottomans, pushed the vintage into October-November. That vintage was conducted after the grapes had been widely attacked by the fungus we know as botrytis, or 'noble rot.' This fungus imparted a different quality of sweetness to the *aszú* wines, and again favored the white grape varieties then typical of Hegyalja.

*

The history of Hegyalja grape varieties is the topic least visited by Hungarians and non-Hungarians alike, perhaps because only three varieties were authorized from 1908 until 1990: *furmint*, *hárslevelű*, and *sárga muskotály*. But many varieties were grown in Hegyalja before that time, and several reveal aspects of the earlier history of Tokaji wine.

Four central facts stand out in the varietal history of Hegyalja as it pertains to the region's development as a producer of specialty white wines. First, the Hegyalja region initially was, and has ever remained, within the eastern European sphere of grape varieties, which have Pontic (Black Sea) or Balkan origins. These differ from the grape varieties grown in Western Europe, oftentimes in their 'semi-aromatic' nature in the case of white varieties.

Second, during the past thousand years, white grape varieties only gradually became predominant over red in Hegyalja [see the entry for Paraskevich, in Part I]. It is likely that Hegyalja wine in early times was more often red or reddish in color than white. This red wine culture grew out of the Balkan tradition. This is shown not only by the grape varieties, but also by the manner in which white grapes were vinified for later-harvested wines, namely, by long contact with skins and stems, which was the Balkan method for red wine (and sometimes for white).

Third, during the past 500 years of later-harvested Tokaji white wines, the dominant white grape varieties have changed. During the past 200 years, *furmint*, *hárslevelű*, and *sárga muskotály* came to the fore. For the 300 years before that, the dominant varieties for sweet white wine were *fehérszőlő*, *kövérszőlő*, and *gohér*, with *furmint* gaining ground only in the second-half of the 1700s, and *hárslevelű* in the 19th century. 1750 to 1850 was a period of deliberation and change.

Fourth, the constant in the varietal complement for sweet wine during the past 500 years has been its adhesion to the varietal notions behind the Greek Malvasia wines of the Middle Ages. The Malvasia tradition consisted mostly in using a mix of varieties, but always featuring 'semi-aromatic' ones, while minimizing the 'aromatic' muscats. Also, Malvasia was made from grapes usually over-ripened on the vine, not raisined after harvesting. The importance of this 'Malvasia model' to educated producers (aristocrats, religious orders) of later-harvested white wines in Hegyalja is readily understood from the Europe-wide commercial significance of Malvasia wine from the 13th to the 18th century, especially its popularity on the important Polish market.

*

Wine-making in Hegyalja is unusual for the northern zone of European wine-growing. As with varietals, a Balkan origin is apparent. Three facts stand out about practices at the time of the Magyar Conquest. First, the grapes were trampled outdoors, in the archaic Balkan peasant habit [see the entry for Cepre, in Part III]. Even later, wine-presses were not used. Second, the must was brought indoors after the outdoor work, into small, rude structures. Examples have not survived, because of their fragility, but it is known that such structures served as domiciles and work-sheds in the 9th century [see the entry for Bodrogköz, in Part II]. Third, goatskins were the containers for wine, and a small, partially submerged space dug out of earth or stone was adequate to preserving small-scale wine output. These features were straight out of the south-central Balkan tradition of the Middle Ages. [See the entry for Balkan Influences.]

Amongst smallholders, the primitive structures evolved into a larger and sturdier cellar, dug into mounds or hillsides. This was encouraged first by the replacement of goatskins by wooden barrels, which may have been the single greatest change brought about by the early settlers from western and southern Europe. Later, the growing commercial importance of wine caused a further upgrading of the cellar, with greater size and solidity. However, even the improved cellar retained its role as a space for wine maturation and storage, not for wine-making. But the cellars were now being dug deeply into tuff and rock, and this had an indirect influence because of stable low temperatures of 8-12° C (46-54° F).

As long as wine-presses were not used, the typical cellar remained adequate even as Hegyalja moved into its modern era and later-harvested wines. The varying ripening times of the dozen or so major varieties meant staggered harvesting and wine-making, so that the cellar still did not need to be the site of must-making, etc. Later, their limited size might even have encouraged the separate processing of partially botrytized, whole-clusters for wines of *főbor* type, from the processing of the fully botrytized, selected-berry wines called *aszú*. However, larger cellars were being built by the nobility and religious orders by the 12th century, and this began to take place purposefully around the 15th century, again reflecting the commercial need for storage space.

The growth in commercial importance of *aszú* favored the characteristic intermediate product of the Hegyalja vintage, *aszú*-dough, a smooth paste of botrytized berries. The *aszú*-dough was prepared outdoors, and was added to must/wine for fermentation into sweet wine. The sweetness could be varied by adjusting the proportions according to a formula suggested by the typical Hegyalja containers. The dimensions of the cellar entrances required a small barrel, which led to the 136- to 140-liter *gönci*. The 28-30 liter *puttony* became the typical grape collection container, and the number of *puttony*-s of *aszú*-dough added to a volume of must or wine equal to *gönci* capacity determined the *puttonyos* level of an *aszú* wine, usually 2-, 3-, 4- or 5-*puttonyos*.

The *puttonyos* system aside, all evidence indicates that the production of the botrytis wines was never uniform. There were aspects in which producers could exercise judgment: whether to use must, new wine, or old wine as the liquid in which to 'soak' the *aszú*-dough; the length of time for the soaking; if and when to add *eszencia*; and aging time. Further, post-phylloxera legislation, driven by enological knowledge, did not establish requirements for these aspects. Any choices made by a commercial producer were acceptable as long as the resultant wine, after legislation of 1924 and 1936, met the constituent requirements for each kind of botrytis wine.

*

Significant health benefits have long been attributed to Tokaji. But Hungarian enologists paid rather scant attention to this subject, which fascinated a limited number of consumers. The enologists concentrated instead on aspects that would be of greatest help to producers in turning out high-quality wines that would retain that quality after sale. But in recent decades, especially since the 1970s, as researchers delved ever deeper into Tokaji's chemical nature, knowledge also started coming to light with regard to the specific effects that it can have on health. Of course, this has benefited from general, international research on the healthful properties of wine.

Research to date has demonstrated that Tokaji is virtually in a class of its own among white wines. It has health benefits usually associated only with red wines, and further, has some of its very own. But much remains to be learned about how the content of the healthful constituents is affected by each of the traditional production techniques. What this research will eventually mean for the making of Tokaji botrytis wines is not yet clear. Hungarian enologists have already suggested that some of the healthful properties of Tokaji might be useful as indicators of authenticity and even vintage quality. But whether or not there will be any commercial use for such data likely will depend, ultimately, on whether consumers show an interest.

*   *   *

PART IV

THE A-Z LISTING

Note: 1) The term 'specialty wine' has been used throughout this text to refer to the Hegyalja wines dependent on botrytized grapes. It is a convenient English substitute for the Hungarian term borkülönlegesség, *which translates more at 'wine-delicacy,' but is somewhat awkward to the English ear.* [See the entry for Wine-delicacy, below.] *2) The sources of certain enological statements are referenced in parentheses; full information is found in the Bibliography.*

*

Acetaldehyde. Protracted aging in barrel, with exposure to oxygen, results in a relatively high content of acetaldehyde in the Tokaji botrytis wines, despite a sparing use of sulfur (sulfur promotes greater acetaldehyde content) [see the entry for Sulfuring]. Traditionally matured Tokaji can reach more than 250 mg/l of acetaldehyde (compared to 20-50 mg/l in a new wine that has been sulfured to only a minor extent). This unusual feature of Tokaji provoked some wonderment amongst Western enologists during the communist period, and thus some skepticism as to how Tokaji was being produced. But acetaldehyde had been noticed in Tokaji before the communist era. In 1936, Czech technicians (Fiala/Sedláček) noted that it was present in all the samples of "old Tokaji wine" analyzed. They concluded that it was a "decidedly characteristic mark." (Incidentally, their report also constitutes a proof that long maturation in barrel was typical of Hegyalja even before the communist era.) [See the entries for Furfural and HMF.]

Aging-period. [See the entry for Barrel Aging.]

Alcoholization. [See the entry for Fortification.]

Aldehydes. Aldehydes are typical primarily of fortified, oxidative wines, such as Port and Sherry. However, they are also among the distinguishing components of Tokaji botrytis wines that are aged by the traditional method [see the entry for *Darabbantartás*]. It can thus be said that Tokaji is the sole example of a wine that has the aldehydic character of an oxidative wine, yet is not such a wine as measured by redox-potential. The presence of aldehydes in Tokaji during the communist era helped to fuel Western speculation about the use of concentrated must. But aldehyde content was recognized in Tokaji before the communist era. [See the entries for Acetaldehyde, Furfural, HMF, and Redox-potential.]

Amber color. [See the entry for Color.]

Amino Acids. [See De-amination, HMF, Maillard Reaction, Nitrogenous Compounds, and Umami.]

Antioxidants. These substances have gained attention because they reduce the oxidation of low-density lipoprotein cholesterol ('bad cholesterol') and thereby protect against arteriosclerosis. They are typically associated with red wine because they usually derive from phenols. But research has revealed that Tokaji *aszú* wines possess antioxidative capacity at a level comparable to – and in some cases above – red wines. Further, other research has shown that, while certain phenols may be exclusive to red wine, Tokaji has some antioxidant advantages of its own [see the entries for SOD and Vitamin E]. (Gvozdjáková, 1996)

Hungarian research of 2000 demonstrated that Tokaji *aszú* wines possess antioxidative capacity at rare high levels for white wine (Nikfardjam, 2000). Antioxidant capacity (as measured by the so called TEAC test) in *aszú* wines from the 1998 and 1999 vintages reached as high as 5.9, 6.1, and 7.4 mmol/l, although TEAC values above 5 mmol/l had never previously been reported for white wines. The results were in line with Tokaji's relatively high content of phenols. However,

198

not all of the antioxidants in Tokaji are related to phenols as such [see the aforementioned entries, as well as Resveratrol].

Aszú. The most well-known of Tokaji specialty wines, *aszú* entails separating botrytized grapes from the rest of the harvest; mashing them into a compact paste called *aszú*-dough; soaking the dough in must or wine for 12 to 48 hours; squeezing the mass to obtain the liquid to be fermented; providing a secondary fermentation in barrel; and finally, aging in barrel for several years [see the entry for Barrel Aging]. Historically, the two measures involved in making *aszú* wines were the collection butt called *puttony* and the *gönci* barrel. The *puttony* has a capacity of 28-30 liters (7.5-7.9 gallons) and the *gönci* barrel has a capacity of 136-140 liters (36-37 gallons). By increasing the number of *puttony*-s of botrytized grapes added to the equivalent of a *gönci* barrel of ordinary must or wine, a sweeter *aszú* wine is obtained. In laws of 1924 and 1936, *aszú* wines were given specific compositional parameters in place of actual *puttony*-s, as a quality safeguard. [See the entry for *Puttonyos* System.]

Aszú only achieved its status gradually, and was not the wine that first earned fame for Hegyalja; instead, that was *főbor*, the harbinger of *szamorodni*. In fact, *aszú* did not originally have a specific connection to botrytized grapes. Its earliest use in the name of a wine type was *aszú-szőlő bor* (shriveled-grape wine), which would simply have been a wine from grapes harvested very late, but not late enough to have undergone much, if any, botrytization, since the term referred to any wine made in part from shriveled grapes. In earlier Hungarian usage, the word connoted 'dried out' and was used in reference to various vegetal growths (even trees) in the process of desiccation. More generally, the term referred to a deprivation of water, as shown by the term *aszúpatak*, or 'dry creek' (DL 17090, DL 36040). [See the entry for Herodotus, in Part I.]

Aszú wines, *i.e.*, wines from shriveled berries, were around for perhaps a century before special note was taken of botrytis. Credit for the idea of using botrytized berries as the *basis* for a wine is traditionally given to László Máté Szepsi, a Protestant cleric who otherwise was employed as chief wine-grower by Susanna Lórántffy, wife of George Rákóczi I, probably sometime around 1620. But his innovation may have been of a more particular kind, something involving technique [see the entry for Szepsi: Mystique and Mystery, in Part I]. The fact that a regulation of 1655 *required* that *aszú* (botrytized) berries or bunches be collected separately from the rest of the harvest indicates that botrytis wines were being made in some quantity even earlier in the 17th century. Had Szepsi been the first to notice and make use of botrytized berries, *aszú* wines would not have become widespread in Hegyalja until long after 1655. There is no evidence to support the idea that Szepsi suddenly started a 'craze' for botrytis, not even amongst aristocratic owners. It may even be supposed that the changeover from *főbor* to *aszú* lagged despite the 1655 'requirement.' That is one explanation for the fact that as late as 1686 the Oremus vineyard-tract, so famous in *aszú* history, was mentioned as a "*főbor* producing" hill (UC 154:11).

Generally, the commercial propagation of botrytis *aszú* vinification most likely was spurred more by merchants than by growers, since merchants were far more attuned to markets, especially the Polish market. The characteristic system of 2-3-4-5- and 6-*puttonyos* levels of *aszú* wine came about gradually, but might already have been known by Szepsi's time, and indeed, might have developed while Tokaji sweet wine was still being made from ordinary shriveled, non-botrytis berries. Thus, while the earliest trade records referencing *aszú* wines do not mention *puttonyos* levels, a Polish mercantile document mentions a 4-*puttonyos* wine of 1646. It would be extraordinary if the 'discovery' of botrytis by Szepsi around 1620 had evolved into the fully developed *puttonyos* system within just a quarter-century's time.

A 'botrytis wine,' yes, but something else is to be said about where Tokaji *aszú* 'fits' amongst wines. Namely, it is the last, ultimate, most distant outgrowth of Aegean traditions for sweet wines, a hybrid of Malvasia and *diakhyton* (διάχυτον). As with the original Malvasia wines, *aszú* has relied on semi-aromatic (non-muscat) varieties of eastern origin, with most of the grapes left to over-ripen or wrinkle *on the vine* (except for certain supplemental varieties that benefited from being 'sunned' after harvesting). But they were then vinified by the technique for the *diakhyton* of ancient Greece. First, before fermentation, the sun-dried grapes were immersed in the juice of over-ripe grapes. This conforms to Columella's description of Mago's recipe for sweet wine. Though a Carthaginian, Mago was relating an Aegean/Minoan technique [see the entry for Columella, in Part I]. The technique persisted in the Aegean, where its sole survivor today is the *visanto* of Santorini. The Italianate name *visanto*, an acquisition from the Middle Ages, must not throw us off the scent; the technique has no link to Italy. For *visanto*, the sun-dried grapes are plunged into the juice of ultra-ripe grapes repeatedly for 24 hours, which parallels the *áztatás* ('soaking') of Hegyalja [see Soaking]. Indeed, the immersion is called, in Greek, '*potisma*,' or 'soaking.' Moreover, Pethe (1808-1813) wrote that the 'soaking' of *aszú*-dough in must is "usually just for 24 hours." How these defining overlaps came about will remain shrouded in history. What was the role of ethnic migrations, of geographical contacts and imitation, of book knowledge (such as Columella)? But the fact remains that *aszú*'s conceptual 'home-ground' is the Aegean Sea. Botrytis is just a happenstance of latitude and setting. [B. Krimbas, "Le Vin et les cépages malvoisie," *Bulletin de l'OIV*, March 1947; G. Venetsanos, "*Visanto*: Traditional Technique and Enological Facts," *Trofima kai Pota* (Food and Beverages), June 1999.]

Aszú-dough. Called in Hungarian *aszú-tészta* (literally, *aszú*-dough or *aszú*-paste), this is the characteristic intermediate product of the Hegyalja vintage, and the basis for all *aszú* wines. Obtained after the self-expressed juice for *eszencia* has been taken off, *aszú*-dough is made by mashing the botrytized (*aszú*) berries into a homogenous mass of skins, stems, seeds, and pulp for immersion in must or wine [see the entry for Soaking]. Halász (1962) described the traditional "test" for the proper result: "take a handful and press the dough between the fingers until nothing but pips remain in the palms...the skins [are] so soft that they will 'disappear'...and become part of the *aszú*-dough." But, he added, this will not happen without the grapes having been affected by 'noble rot.' Originally, the dough was made by trampling by foot, but during the 1950s feet were replaced in large-scale wineries by a machine specially designed for the task, particularly so as to avoid cracking the seeds. *Aszú-tészta* is also referred to as *aszú-pép*, or *aszú*-mash, and, in colloquial parlance, occasionally as *aszú-lekvár*, or *aszú*-jam. Yet another colloquial term for it is 'kasha' (*kása*) [see #6 in the entry for Balkan Influences].

Aszú-Eszencia. This name has been associated with the top commercially available Tokaji wines since at least around 1800. The earliest known mention of the term is from the early-19th century, when a wine from the famous 'comet vintage' of 1811 was marketed as *aszú-eszencia*. The name and the type of wine probably originated in the second-half of the 18th century, since Gabriel Gyöngyösi did not mention such a wine in 1736, when he warned against over-production of *aszú* and *eszencia*. Also significant is that Antal Szirmay did not mention the term *aszú-eszencia* or describe a wine like it in his book of 1798.

The name would seem to connote a cross between *aszú* and *eszencia*. Indeed, the aspect which wines called *aszú-eszencia* have always had in common is a rare level of sweetness, namely, sweetness beyond what could be expected of even a 6-*puttonyos aszú* wine. Furthermore, in the early-20th century, some *aszú* wines were 'upgraded' to this notion of *aszú-eszencia* simply by adding a generous dosage of genuine *eszencia*, especially in the case of *aszú* wines that had lost sweetness during protracted aging. But according to John Dercsényi, in 1825, that was not the origin of *aszú-eszencia*. Instead, he mentioned 8-, 10- and 12-*puttonyos aszú* wines, *i.e.*, the use of additional quantities of *aszú*-dough, and always in increments of two *puttony*-s above 6-*puttonyos aszú*. Unfortunately, Dercsényi did not describe how these wines were actually fabricated. It is clear that the sheer volume of liquid and *aszú*-mash would have been too great for the capacity of most vats used for fermenting *aszú* wines of only 3-, 4-, 5- or 6-*puttonyos* level. On the other hand, he made no mention of admixing genuine *eszencia*, while his specification of the gradations (8-, 10-, 12-) does indicate a greater use of measurable quantities of *aszú*-dough, not merely notional levels of sweetness. (Obviously, this *aszú-eszencia* could only have been produced by the largest aristocratic growers, possessed of considerable facilities.)

Because of their great sweetness, 8-, 10- and 12-*puttonyos* wines were a true transition between *aszú* and *eszencia*. Sometimes they were colloquially referred to as *eszencia*, as is clear from Dercsényi's notation that the 12-*puttonyos aszú* was known as "the queen of *eszencia*-s," in other words, the next in line to the 'king,' *eszencia* itself. But the relative frequency of *aszú-eszencia* in 19th century production and trade is unclear, since it is practically impossible to discern when mentions of *eszencia* might actually have been casual, shorthand references to *aszú-eszencia*. Nevertheless, the extreme rarity of genuine *eszencia* in the 19th century suggests that a good bit of *aszú-eszencia* was drunk under the mistaken impression that it was *eszencia*, whether or not this was a deception on the part of the merchants involved. And the further removed from Hungary one was, the greater the likelihood of the misunderstanding. (Despite the late appearance of the terms *eszencia* and *aszú-eszencia*, there is a possibility that Rákóczi's gifts of '*eszencia*' to European royalty around 1700 actually conformed to Dercsényi's super-*aszú*.)

The sort of *aszú-eszencia* specified by Dercsényi seems to have fallen victim to phylloxera. During the first-half of the 20th century, this category of *aszú* wine was dormant, at least in its original conception as a wine made with a surpassing quantity of *aszú*-dough. There was the occasional addition of *eszencia* to a 5- or 6-*puttonyos aszú* wine, which might be thought of as an 'exaggerated' sort of *aszú-eszencia*. But the term was not touched upon by the Hungarian legislation of 1924 and 1936, when specifications were set out for the other Hegyalja botrytis wine types. Even enological books of the period did not discuss it, presumably reflecting its general neglect in wine-making.

Aszú-eszencia was revived commercially during the communist period. This might have reflected some thought that had been going on among Hungarian enologists during the previous decades. But another factor may have been the ambition of the enologists to produce something of exceptional quality even under the constraints of the era. Also, the Viti-Vinicultural Research Institute at Tarcal had under its direct supervision the Szarvas vineyard, the most famous Hegyalja vineyard-tract. *Aszú-eszencia* would be just the product to highlight Szarvas and the skill of the Institute's enologists. Accordingly, in the 1960s, *aszú-eszencia* was defined officially by the National Wine-Expert Committee: "*Aszú* wine from eminently suitable land and vintage, of such outstanding quality that its qualitative value can no longer be expressed by indicating the number of *puttony*-s." In effect, Dercsényi's understanding had been resurrected, in that *aszú-eszencia* could not be made merely by adding *eszencia* to an *aszú*: it was to be strictly an *aszú* wine in its fabrication, and dependent on seasonal conditions. In the post-communist era, the definition was altered to reflect strictly technical criteria: *aszú-eszencia* could be applied to any wine that surpasses 6-*puttonyos aszú* in sugar and non-sugar extract requirements, so that it qualifies notionally as at least a 7-*puttonyos aszú* wine. [See the entry for *Puttonyos* System.]

Aszú-máslás. [See the entry for *Máslás*.]

Áztatás. [See the entry for Soaking.]

Bakator. Though it was never a significant variety in Hegyalja, at least not during the past 500 years, the *bakator* has long held a certain fascination for Hungarian ampelographers and wine historians. This is because of its name alone, which was long thought to indicate that the variety had been brought from Italy at some time in the distant past. Supposedly, *bakator* was a corruption of an Italian name, *baccador* or *bocca d'oro*, in reference to the color gold (*oro*). But this explanation was undermined first by the absence of such a name in Italy, and later by the discovery that Bakator existed as a surname in Hungary centuries ago. (Pap, in 1985, referred to a view that attributes the name to the Kabars [see that entry, in Part I].) Even more devastating to the folklore, *bakator* is not at all of a yellowish hue, but a rosy pink. Because of the variety's apparent antiquity in Hegyalja, it might be useful to search amongst Greek and Balkan varieties, perhaps beginning with ones such as *roditis* and *bakouri*. But whatever might be discovered by pursuing that line, it is clear that to the extent *bakator* ever flourished in Hegyalja, it was in the pre-1500 era when more or less red wine was still a prominent product there.

Balafánt. (a) This white variety is singular in the history of Hegyalja grape varieties because at one time it had some significance, but enjoyed that popularity for a relatively brief period, roughly from 1800 to 1900. Interest in it must have peaked around 1875, when it was mentioned along with *fehérszőlő* and *gohér* as one of the "valued" varieties of Hegyalja. But, according to Kossuth (1903), this status was based primarily on yield: "The *balafánt* is perhaps the most abundantly producing variety among the old Hegyalja grape-types, for which feature, as well as because it does not detract from the character [typicity] of Hegyalja wine when it is scattered around in a plantation, it is especially liked by the smaller wine-growers."

(b) It is also notable about the *balafánt* that it may have arrived in Hegyalja from a westerly direction. Speculation about that is fueled primarily by the name, which Hungarian researchers have variously thought might reflect a French name, *belefaint*, or a German one, *blaufahnler*, whether or not the *balafánt* had an ampelographic tie to either of those (in favor of *blaufahnler* is that it has both light and dark variants, and in 1855 *balafánt* was mentioned as having both a white and a black variant). Complicating matters further, the genuine *belefaint* has also been supposed to have had a connection to the *picolit*, which does not seem likely for the *balafánt*. These supposed ties to West Europe are based on the fact that Hungarian growers began taking an interest in French and other Western grape varieties towards the end of the 18th century. But this did not happen in Hegyalja. Thus, Kossuth seems to have been mistaken in calling *balafánt* one of "the old Hegyalja grape-types," unless he simply meant that it was a pre-phylloxera variety.

Balkan Influences. Tokaji wine is the northernmost occurrence of Balkan wine tradition, no matter that Hungary is not a Balkan country. Research in Greek and Bulgarian source materials [as cited below, but not in the Bibliography] demonstrate some specific overlaps between antique viti-vinicultural practices in the southern Balkans and those of Hegyalja. The Hegyaljan habits and their possibly significant Balkan 'antecedents' are as follow:

1) Hegyalja: The trampling of the grapes originally took place outdoors amidst the vineyards.

Balkans: In north-central Greece (Macedonia), it was common in the Middle Ages, demonstrably as far back as the 11th century, for the grapes to be trampled in the vineyards and the must transferred from there to indoor facilities. (I. Papangelos, "Vineyard and Wine in Medieval Chalkidiki," in *Istoria tou Ellinikou Krasiou* [History of Greek Wine], Athens, 1990. Papangelos noted that this practice had also been common in other parts of Greece.)

2) Hegyalja: The earliest form of *főbor* [see that entry], a later-harvested wine, included grapes in various stages of ripeness, certainly over-ripe ones, but also ripe and under-ripe ones, all vinified together. This was because of the considerable varietal diversity in the vineyards. Several years of maturation were needed for the wine to achieve peak quality.

Balkans: The *omfakitis* (ομφακίτης) of the ancient Greeks "was produced from mixing over-ripe and under-ripe (green) grapes," and was drunk "after the passage of some years and was considered among the best dessert wines." (V. Logothetis, *Symvoli tis Ambelou kai tou Oinou eis ton Politismon tis Ellados kai tis Anatolikis Mesoyeiou* [Contribution of the Vine and Wine to the Civilizations of Greece and the Eastern Mediterranean], Thessaloniki, 1975.) Logothetis also noted the sweeter *diakhyton*, from over-ripe and raisined grapes [see the entry *Aszú*: Aegean Echo].

3) Hegyalja: Grapes used for later-harvested, sweet wines were left to shrivel on the vine, not raisined outdoors or indoors after harvesting.

Balkans: The original and usual method for the Greek Malvasia wines, which dated to antiquity conceptually, was to over-ripen the grapes on the vine, rather than to 'sun' them after harvesting. (B. Krimbas, "Le Vin et les cépages malvoisie," *Bulletin de l'OIV*, March 1947; V. Logothetis, *Ai Malvaziai* [The Malvasias], Thessaloniki, 1965).

4) Hegyalja: The storage of wine in goat-skins was usual in the early history of Hegyalja, in the era of the Árpád Dynasty.

Balkans: This method of storing wine is recorded throughout ethnographical and historical works touching on wine practices in Bulgaria and Greece. It dates to antiquity, and even in recent centuries was common amongst traders using pack-animals, as well as by peasant smallholders. (See chapter 6, in I. Zaikov, I. Dionisiev, G. Petrov, *Kniga za Vinoto* [A Book About Wine], Sofia, 1982; the chapter offers a discussion of the skill required to prepare skins for wine storage.)

5) Hegyalja: The *aszú*-dough for *aszú* wines in earlier times was prepared by stamping the mass of botrytis-affected grape skins, stems, seeds, and pulp in sacks of coarse cloth. This may have been carried over from the production of white wine in earlier times, when red and white grapes were harvested together.

Balkans: At Siatista, in south-central Macedonia, Greece, a renowned *white* sweet wine (still produced in minor quantities) is made from a must obtained mostly from shriveled *red* grapes, with the mass of solids passed through pouches of clean goat's wool. (G. Georgakopoulos, "*Stabilisation des Vins Doux: Grèce*," Paris, 1959.) It was also traditional in Albania to tread grapes in fiber sacks to obtain a white wine despite inclusion of some red grapes: "Often blue grapes would also be put into the sack [along with white], but after pressing, the juice would be separated immediately from the skins and thus the must could not absorb the color." (B. Andrásfalvy, "Forms of Albanian Viticulture," *Acta Ethnographica*, Vol. XI, No. 3-4, 1962.)

6) Hegyalja: The thoroughly mashed, 'homogenized' skins, stems, seeds, and pulp are colloquially referred to as 'kasha' (*kása*), to indicate the thick, porridge-like consistency.

Balkans: In southwestern Bulgaria, notably in the Bulgarian part of 'Ottoman Macedonia,' the term 'kasha' (каша) is used in precisely the same way. (L. Peneva-Sâbeva, "Traditional Wine-growing and Wine-making in Petrich and Melnik," *Bulletin of the Ethnographic Institute and Museums*, Sofia, 1971.) 'Kasha' is a very old Slavic word, dating back to before Slavs first migrated south into the Balkans, hence its presence from north to south in east-central Europe; but as a vinicultural term, it was not used by wine-producing northern Slavs, such as the western Slovaks ('Great Moravians'), even though they knew kasha as a food.

7) Hegyalja: The *aszú* wines are produced by 12-to-48 hours of contact with the solids of botrytized grapes, but with seeds removed as soon as they float to the surface.

Balkans: The standard traditional procedure for red wine, and even some white wine, was a long fermentation on skins and stems, with expeditious removal of seeds from the liquid. (This fact is found widespread in the ethnographic literature on wine-making in the south-central Balkans.)

8) Hegyalja: *Aszú* wine was made by fermenting the mashed botrytis grapes in the must or wine of ordinary grapes, and then giving the wine several years of aging in the unique Hegyalja cellars.

Balkans: The fermenting of shriveled grapes in must or wine dates to antiquity. In the Bulgarian section of Ottoman Macedonia, at Melnik (populated by Greeks for over a millennium), the most famous wine was a semi-sweet red made from grapes shriveled on the vines of the best vineyards, and fermented in must or new wine from ordinary ripe grapes. This was followed by up to 20 years of aging in the special Melnik cellars. (Stefan Stanchev, *Melnik*, Sofia: 1965.)

9) Hegyalja: Douglass, in 1773, reported that the by-product *máslás* wines were being obtained by pouring "the common juice" over the *aszú* marc, which then was to be "wrung with the hands." The same method was reported by Bél around 1730 and in a Hungarian periodical of 1838. Moreover, in 1839, Paget noted *aszú* being made in that way: "the grapes are at once placed in a vat and gently pressed with the hand" (either after *eszencia* collection or if none was taken). But whether *máslás* or *aszú*, the use of hand-squeezing at this late date in Tokaji history is remarkable.

Balkans: The technique dated to Greek antiquity: "[Dionysus] untaught, without winepress and without treading, squeezed the grapes firmly between hand and wrist, interlacing his fingers until he pressed out the inebriating issue…" (Nonnos, *Dionysiaca*). In 1809, Lord Byron's traveling companion noted the same at Zitsa, in northwestern Greece (Epirus): the best white wine was "not trodden out, as [the monastery prior] told us, by the feet, but pressed from the grape by hand." (John Cam Hobhouse, *A Journey Through Albania and Other Provinces of Turkey in Europe*, London, 1813.)

10) Hegyalja: Small cellars dug into tuff, with temperatures typically at 8-12° C (46-54° F), may date to at least 900 in northeastern Hegyalja (particularly the area now in Slovakia). These cellars provided excellent, clean conditions for wine maturation. Later, the larger of them had lateral wings or passageways.

Balkans: At Melnik, small cellars were being dug into sandstone since the early Middle Ages, possibly as early as the 7th century. This practice expanded later on: "The tunnels are in endless labyrinths. In some places, there are subterranean springs with icy water, which serve to preserve [wine] production hygiene at a high level." (I. Zaikov, *et.al.*, *op.cit.*) Cellar temperatures are in the range of 10-12° C (50-54° F).

11) Hegyalja: The most idiosyncratic product of the region has been *eszencia*, a very low-alcohol wine, achieved after multiple years of aging. It is produced by collecting the droplets that are squeezed spontaneously from piled-up botrytis grapes, and collected in barrels to ferment. [See the entries for Nectar and *Protropon*.]

Balkans: The ancient Greek *protropon* (πρότροπον) wine was made in like manner: "produced from the effluent must of unpressed grapes, of ripe or over-ripe grapes. The must flows drop by drop and is gathered in long-necked containers, in which they are left to ferment." (Logothetis, *op.cit.*, 1975). Such wine was still typical of the island of Zakynthos [see that entry, in Part II], as late as the last decades of the 19th century: the island's *lianorogi* ('small-berry-wine') was "made from choice white grapes [small and very sweet], not subjected to the pressure of the feet, or of the press; the must is obtained merely by the pressure of the grapes on each other heaped together." (John Davy, *Notes and Observations on the Ionian Islands and Malta*, London, 1881.)

12) Hegyalja: *Eszencia* was added to *aszú* and other botrytis wines as necessary to enrich them in sugar, extract, and overall character.

Balkans: In ancient Greece, the oldest wines were used "as a seasoning for improving other wines" (Pliny, *Natural History*). That is, such wines were reserved as an enhancement of younger wines which, because of seasonal conditions, were deficient. At that point, the old wines were so sugar-rich as to be thick and dense.

As to how elements of Balkan wine culture, including grape varieties, survived in Hegyalja despite settlers from western Europe, it is apparent that the migration was too staggered over time and too scattered amongst villages to have a significant impact on what already existed.

[The foregoing overlaps turned up fortuitously during decades of research on east European viti-viniculture. Extensive research on the subject could yield insightful rewards about wine history.]

Balkan Touch: In the Sack

Hungary has never been counted amongst the Balkan countries. But if there is a giveaway about Hegyalja being the farthest northern outpost of Balkan wine-making culture, surely it is the oldtime use of fiber sacks in the trampling of *aszú*-dough. While it did not start out with sacks made from plant fibers, still, there is every reason to think that the idea arose because of the Bulgaro-Slavs who were brought to the vicinity of Hegyalja in the 9th century. People from the ancient ovine lands of the Balkans generally employed goatskins for storing wine; and the Magyars and Kabars no doubt recognized such 'vessels' when they arrived in Hegyalja. However, other uses had also been found for goatskins during wine-making in the Balkans. Whenever the initial trampling of grapes took place in the vineyard, the resultant grape 'kasha' [see #6 in the previous entry] could be transported in the skins to indoor spaces. It just happened that well-prepared skins reduced the risk of aerobic bacterial damage during the transport (K. Mitrakos, S. Papras, "Historical Aspects of Viticulture and Viniculture in Ambelakia, Thessaly," in *Istoria tou Ellinikou Krasiou* [History of Greek Wine], Athens, 1990.) Additionally, the use of animal or plant fibers as 'filtering' material during must-making proved effective in preventing red grapes from 'coloring' a largely white 'kasha' [see #5, above]. This feature probably was valued in the early days of Hegyalja's later-harvested white wines, when some red grapes were no doubt collected along with the white.

Barrel Aging. After centuries of it being taken for granted that Tokaji should receive long aging in barrel, the topic became the subject of intense debate in the post-communist era. Proponents of giving *aszú* and *szamorodni* wines minimal time in barrel went so far as to charge that the longer maturation times during the communist era were an aberrant departure from traditional practice. During that era, maturation ranged from two or two-and-a-half years for *szamorodni*, to eight years for a 5- or 6-*puttonyos aszú*. But this was certainly the rule before communism. In 1937, the enologist Pettenkoffer stated: "The Hegyalja sweet wines ferment slowly and their secondary fermentation lasts for years, in between longer or shorter cessations." In 1903, Kossuth stated that eight to ten years was the typical maturation time for *aszú* wines, while Spotkovszky, just a decade later, reported three years for *szamorodni* and "at least 5-6" years for *aszú*. Further, in 1985, Pap mentioned an old rule of thumb: an *aszú* needs at least as many years in the barrel as the number of *puttony*-s of *aszú*-dough used to make it (for example, a 5-*puttonyos aszú* needs five years in barrel). Current Hungarian law requires a minimum of two years of barrel maturation for *aszú* wines, and at least one year of further maturation in bottle. There is pressure to remove limitations altogether, which is not quite a new idea, since there were thoughts along those lines even during the communist era [see the next to last section of the Appendix Essay].

Habits with regard to barrel maturation evolved after Tokaji became a later-harvested wine, that is, after around 1500. Early on, small Hegyalja growers sold off their wines quickly, since initial maturation was taking place in full barrels (not partially filled ones as in the *darabbantartás* technique). Any further aging of the wines in full barrels was just as well accomplished in the cellars of merchants further north in the towns and domains of the Upper Tisza region, or even in Poland. But the question had to be reconsidered after the wines of the Szerémség region were no longer available to the Poles after the Ottoman occupation of southern Hungary in the 16th century. It happened that the most popular Szerém wine in Poland was a well-aged white wine. Thus, during the 17th century, a great deal of cellar expansion was taking place in Hegyalja, as was highlighted by the construction of the vast Rákóczi cellars in Sárospatak and Erdőbénye. Clearly, cellars of such size were oriented towards more or less lengthy aging of wines.

The influence of botrytis, in particular, on wine-aging times is not documented. If the prevalent story of Szepsi's botrytis *aszú* is approximately accurate, he probably produced it around 1620, and it would have been a decade old when he presented it to Susanna Lórántffy in 1631. A variant of the story tells that it was actually produced in 1608, in Erdőbénye, in which case the wine would have had 23 years of age on it [see the entry for *Furmint*]. Be that as it may, the types of wine broadened during the next century-and-a-half, and cellar-masters certainly began to consider each type individually in terms of aging and effects on quality. As well, as the markets for the wines became more differentiated, major growers and traders were compelled to take into account the varying preferences about wine age amongst the consumers to whom they catered. Furthermore, aging had become a reference point for distinguishing Tokaji from those of nearby places that resembled it only for the first year or two [see the Part II Essay]. It can thus be stated that lengthier barrel aging was the norm by at least the 18th century, when fraudulent Tokaji became a serious problem; that is, a significant aspect in making bogus Tokaji consisted precisely in lending it the impression of a long-aged Hegyalja botrytis wine.

A considerable problem for long-aged botrytis wines at Tokaji was caused by an otherwise beneficial feature of the Hegyalja cellars, namely, their coolness. This induces a quicker evaporation of alcohol than water through the pores of the barrels, which is the opposite situation of relatively warm cellars (as in Mediterranean countries under typical oldtime conditions). However, nothing is known about techniques that might have been used by Hegyalja cellar-masters in earlier times to minimize this tendency. What, for instance, was the effect of rubbing the interior of barrels with bacon fat, as was done several centuries ago? (Komoróczi, 1944)

It is impossible to say, too, what practices the Macedonian Greek traders might have introduced in this regard. Those from places like Siatista and Melnik certainly were used to dealing with the problem for centuries before Tokaji became a sweet wine [see the entry for Balkan Influences], and had come up with effective methods. In short, there existed in the south-central Balkans, at the time of the advent of Tokaji botrytis wines, a variety of procedures for minimizing the loss of alcohol in cool cellars during long years of aging in barrel. What is not known is if and how the Greek traders in Hegyalja might have imparted their knowledgeability.

Barrels. [See the preceding entry, *Darabbantartás*, and Gönci; also, see Zemplén Hills, in Part II.]

Biogenic Amines. Also known as polyamines, the biogenically active amines occur in relatively significant amounts in Tokaji wines (Hajós, 2000; Sass-Kiss, 2000). Indeed, Hungarian enologists have suggested that polyamine content might eventually prove serviceable as an indicator of authenticity, vintage quality, and vinification and maturation technique.

Tokaji's unusual amine content is in line with its extraordinary content of nitrogenous compounds. While these compounds are also notable in non-botrytis Tokaji wines, botrytis elevates their presence. Thus, *aszú* wines from 1993, 1997, and 1998 had polyamine content several times higher than non-botrytis varietal wines from either of the two major Hegyalja grape varieties (*furmint* and *hárslevelű*). Also, polyamine content was found generally to increase with the *puttonyos* level of *aszú* wine from a given vintage. Further, research has indicated a correlation between the total content of polyamines and the aging of *aszú* wines. The content increased not only with the quality of the botrytis vintage, but also with time in barrel according to the traditional *darabbantartás* technique. But the parameters have yet to be explored fully, especially as regards the precise polyamine contributions made by *darabbantartás* aging.

The specific biogenic amines involved are tyramine, putrescine, cadaverine, histamine, phenylethylamine, and spermidine. They play a role in a number of body processes, notably cell metabolism and synthesis of protein, RNA, and DNA. Spermidine is also useful in digesting food so as to maximize the use of nutritive elements, and consequently, it can be an especially valuable part of the daily diet for elderly persons. However, although Tokaji's content of polyamines is below the level at which they would generally have negative physiological effects, some persons might experience headaches or allergic reactions, perhaps depending on the amount of wine consumed. As with Tokaji's phenol content, the ratio of the individual biogenic amines varies from vintage to vintage [see the entry for Phenols].

Bolgár. [See the entry for *Szlankamenka.*]

Bor. Being of Turkic origin, the Hungarian word for 'wine' is one of several terms showing that the Magyars had some familiarity with wine-growing before arriving in Hungary. It is singled out here because in Hegyalja it has also been used to connote 'must.' Researchers need to be aware of this when considering whether wine or must was meant in some early accounts.

Borkülönlegesség. [See the entry for Wine-Delicacy.]

Botrytis. The indispensable requirement for the production of the Tokaji specialty wines is the occurrence of *botrytis cinerea*, otherwise known as 'noble rot.' It is a particular form of the desiccation (*aszúsodás*) of grapes while still on the vine. Its 'nobility' as a form of rotting lies chiefly in that, given the right seasonal conditions and consequent appropriate progression of over-ripening, *botrytis cinerea* brings about pervasive shriveling, but without causing damaging mold formation. Also, a feature that distinguishes botrytized grapes from grapes dried on straw mats is that acids as well as sugars are consumed, which makes for gentler, though still vivid, acidity in botrytis wines (Pettenkoffer).

The seasonal conditions conducive to the onset of botrytis are a growing season that has brought the berries to a perfectly ripened state, followed by humid late-summer mornings that promote the onset of botrytis, and finally, a long, dry autumn that allows botrytis to spread healthfully. Consequently, botrytis wines cannot be produced every year. In Hegyalja, about three years out of ten are botrytis vintages. The relative abundance of noble rot in those years will largely determine how much *aszú* is made relative to *szamorodni*, keeping in mind, too, that the yield of *eszencia* is also affected by seasonal conditions. But even in botrytis years, wines will differ in quality from vintage to vintage. The best years occur when grape bunches ripen fully and then have good conditions for super-maturation before botrytis sets in. Of course, this also favorably affects the quality of the must or new wine in which the botrytized berries (in the form of *aszú*-dough) are fermented.

As far as is known, botrytis was first noticed in Hegyalja. It would not have happened earlier than the last decades of the 1500s, since it was not until then that a third hoeing pushed the vintage back far enough for botrytis to have set in to any extent. Even so, it is unlikely that such berries were separated from grapes that were desiccating without botrytis. That is, the practical effect on wine-making was not immediately recognized. Although the story of Ladislaus Máté Szepsi's 'discovery' of botrytis may be apocryphal, it may be fact that, in line with the Szepsi legend, it took an exceptionally delayed vintage, with an abundance of botrytis, for the effect of 'noble rot' to become palpable in the resultant wine, and thus valued in its own right. Only after that point, too, was attention paid to which grape varieties were the best hosts for botrytis.

As an aside, note needs to be made of the ancient Greek wine called *saprias* (σαπρίας), which could be translated as 'the rotter.' Because the name refers to 'rotten' or 'decayed' (*sapros*), some writers on ancient wine and food have thought that *saprias* was or might have been a botrytis wine. But Classical literature provides no substantiation that any grape desiccation other than the ordinary sort was known in antiquity. Instead, *saprias* referred to a technique of multi-year aging that brought the wine to the verge of 'decay,' but in the nicest way, hence the usual translation of *saprias* as 'the mellow wine.'

Botrytis: Stellar Conditions

By all accounts, the ideal botrytis vintage was the 'comet year' of 1811. In 1823, a Hungarian scientist noted, "Even now, a similar vintage is the daily wish of Tokaji owners." Little is known about conditions during that growing season. Temperature data for Budapest show that air temperature during the July-October period was 2-4° C above average. Hegyalja experienced an Indian summer with fine weather into fall. The renowned Hungarian patriot, Louis Kossuth, a native of Monok, was nine-years-old at the time, and in 1883 recollected that persons separating out the *aszú* berries had to wash their hands four times a day because their fingers repeatedly became stuck together from the great quantity of sugar: "I saw it myself, experiencd it on my own fingers." Seasonal conditions also favored a banner year for the non-botrytis harvest, thus giving exceptional must or new wine in which to soak and ferment the *aszú* material. Such a vintage must have resulted in a great proportion of *aszú* being produced (relative to *szamorodni*), and much *aszú-eszencia*, since 1811 is the earliest known instance of a wine being marketed under that name. 'Comet *aszú*' quickly gained fame, and quickly sold. When Habsburg Emperor Ferdinand V sought some for his coronation, in 1830, he could find only three barrels in all of Hegyalja. But bottles were stored by growers and merchants, and considerable sums were paid for them well into the 20th century. "Today, too, through more than 150 years, the Tokaji 'Comet *aszú*' has held its primacy in fame, in quality" (Szabó-Jilek, 1977).

Breadiness. One of the organoleptic features traditionally expected in properly matured Tokaji wine is an aromatic overlay like the crust of freshly baked dry rye-bread (of pumpernickel type). As with baked bread itself, this occurrence is a manifestation of 'browning.' The term in Hungarian is *bródigság*, which is compounded from the German for 'bready' (*brodig*) and Magyar for –ness (*ság*); but it is also known in Hungarian as *kenyér-íz* ('bread-taste'). It is exemplified, and most readily noticeable, in the best traditionally aged dry *szamorodni* wines. [See the entries for De-amination and Maillard Reaction.]

Bródigság. [See the previous entry.]

Browning. The 'browning' of sugars is one of the most widespread chemical processes to which comestibles are submitted to enhance flavor and palatability. Textbook examples include toffee and caramel, while less obvious examples include honey, the crust of baked bread, the crust of seared meat, etc. As in those examples, browning is usually the result of subjecting sugars to heat or oxygen. However, a rare form of browning requires neither, and this is the Maillard reaction, which is typically undergone by the Tokaji specialty wines during their traditional maturation process. [See the entry for Maillard Reaction.]

Cellar fungi. [See the entry for *Claudosporium cellare*.]

Cellars. (a) Perennially the feature most captivating to visitors, the cellars where Tokaji wine is matured have a very old history that is closely intertwined with the development of the region's wine types, from the time of more or less red dry wine stored in goatskins, to the era of more or less sweet white wines dependent on botrytized grapes and stored in partially empty barrels. It was certainly in this last era, though, that the cellars gained decisive influence, as is apparent in a Hegyalja proverb mentioned by Vincze (1958): "the cellar makes and mends the wine."

In surveying cellar-types throughout Hungary, Vincze raised the possibility that the differences in characteristic regional types might ultimately be of an "ethnic nature." He did not probe that subject for any of the regional types, but the question is bound to arise when considering his separate classification of the traditional smallholder's cellar in Hegyalja and the surrounding area: "hole-cellar without cellar-house" (*pinceház nélküli lyukpince*). In other words, only a door separated the cellar from the outside. Vincze stated that this type was originally dug out of limestone, tuff, or loess, "in imitation of housing styles in some areas." Indeed, the earliest wine cellars in Hegyalja were of a small and rudimentary type that grew 'organically' out of habits for constructing shelters for people and crops, as is known to have been the case in the adjacent Bodrogköz [see that entry, and the second paragraph for Bara, in Part II]. This takes the 'ethnic origin' of the habit back to the Avar-Slav element present in the area at the time of the Magyar Conquest.

Later, this type of cellar was elaborated with an entranceway, called a 'neck' (which can be likened, figuratively, to that of an igloo, but higher, wider, and longer – it was not necessary to crawl). It was meant to strengthen the opening after goatskins had been replaced by barrels, since barrels could ruin an opening that was not buttressed. An 'ethnic' influence might be presumed in this case, too, inasmuch as the switch to barrels amongst smallholders was probably led by Walloon, Italian, and German settlers. In any case, while an entranceway was needed, it did not have to be large. This is shown by the fact that the early Hegyalja cask, the *antal*, was only half the size of the later *gönci* barrel. (As desirable as it would be to have extant examples of the earliest types of cellars, their susceptibility to caving in made such preservation impossible.)

(b) Basically, there have been only two kinds of cellars: 'simple' and 'complex.' The two developed in tandem from the time of the Árpád kings, and the 'complex' sort never displaced the 'simple.' Both have in common their steady temperature, in the range of 8-12° C (46-54° F), which owes to their having been built into tuff and rock. [See #10 in the entry for Balkan Influences.] [For detailed information about cellar architectural types, see Alkonyi (2001, English), Balassa (1991, Hungarian, with English summary), and Vince (1958, Hungarian).]

The construction of substantial cellars specifically for wine must have begun by at least the time of King Stephan I ('St. Stephan of Hungary'), at the beginning of the 11th century. At that time, the fortress at Zemplén covered 11 hectares (27 acres), and excavations showed that cellars were quite extensive beneath it. Being a royal property, and set amidst important vineyard land, some of which would later be part of Hegyalja, there can be little doubt that King Stephan was storing wine in the fort. A century later, his descendant King Kálmán had large cellaring facilities built at Tarcal, in southern Hegyalja. (Both the Zemplén and Tarcal cellars were close to vineyard-tracts whose names indicate early royal ownership. [See the entry for Király (1), (2), and (3), in

Part III.]) This likely was followed by cellars at Sátoraljaújhely, which Kálmán had given to the Ratold clan from Italy. Thereafter, cellars of varied size multiplied with the profusion of settlers and wine-growing following the Tatar invasion of the mid-13th century.

However, it is only after the inception of later-harvested wines, but most especially the rise in importance of botrytis wines after 1600, that the large cellar also became 'complex.' The motivation was commercial, and the gradual adoption of the *gönci* barrel (still small, but twice the size of the earlier *antal*) made it imperative for magnates and municipalities with extensive vineyard land to expand their cellaring facilities several-fold. This was typified above all by the Rákóczis at Sárospatak and Erdőbénye. The 'complex' nature of these cellars lay in their lengthy and interconnecting passageways, and sometimes, being built on two levels underground. The most 'complexity' possible for the common sort of cellar (the "hole-cellar without cellar-house") was to have one or two short wings or branches off the main cellar. However, not unlike the complex cellar, the simple cellars of the smallholders sometimes were 'layered,' such that their single passageway might lie above or below one-to-three others.

(c) The 'curiosities' of the construction and types of Hegyalja cellars were rather superficial to their role in the history of Tokaji wine. What ultimately made them special was their contribution to the nature of the wine, the so called 'Tokaji Character' [see that entry]. The cellars gained special importance in connection with the maturation technique known as *darabbantartás* [see that entry]. Historically, one of the most characteristic features of the Tokaji specialty wines has been their long secondary fermentation and aging. The cellars are notable not only for their steady temperature, but also for the propensity for beneficial molds to build up on the cellar walls and enhance a hygienic environment for wines produced by an oxidative technique. [See the entry for *Claudosporium Cellare*.] Although the origin of the habit of directly exposing the Tokaji specialty wines to the cellar air is not known, it likely dates to the early days of Tokaji *aszú*'s fame, when the Polish market showed a preference for such wine [see the entry for Rumpolt, in Part I].

Because of their special importance, the cellars have been the object of observation over the centuries, including enological research in recent decades. As emphasized by Pap (1985), various sections of the complex cellars can be expected to nurture wines to slightly different sensory results during the course of *darabbantartás* maturation. Lengyel (1950) referred to an experiment showing differences between the relatively more and less humid areas of the cellars: in the more humid areas, both acids and alcohols showed changes in the course of aging, and the resultant wines gave a more intense sense of an older wine; in the less humid areas, changes occurred only in the quantity of alcohol, which was attributed to a faster secondary fermentation. Also, the cool conditions of the cellars cause a relatively faster loss of alcohol than water. Requinyi (1948) stated that *darabbantartás* maturation results in losing 1 to 2 percent alcohol annually, "not counting losses showing up due to racking and other handling." This was a consideration behind the regulation of 1936, which allowed for adding wine spirits, up to a specified maximum, so as to replace the lost alcohol and enhance the wine's stability [see the entry for Fortification].

'Classic' (Tokaji). The term *klasszikus*, or 'classic,' has been invoked with some frequency by Hungarian enologists in reference to Tokaji wine since the time of the phylloxera episode. It seems originally to have connoted re-creating all the viti-vinicultural conditions by which Tokaji could recover its former quality, that is, its 'classic' features. However, during the communist period, there was discussion about offering very young *aszú* and *szamorodni* wines [see the Appendix Essay], and in that context *klasszikus* came more specifically to connote the sort of barrel aging Tokaji had usually received during the previous three centuries. The term has continued to be used in that sense in the post-communist period because of the ongoing debate over what is a proper maturation for Tokaji. [A convenient solution to the debate conceivably could entail a legal definition of 'Classic Tokaji' for use on labels. This would give recognition to producers who persevere with the time-honored methods despite delayed financial reward, while at the same time not encumbering use of the Tokaji name by other producers. It would also give enophiles a courtesy choice. As it happens, chemical research is now yielding enological information upon which objective criteria for 'Classic Tokaji' can be based. For instance, see the entries for Biogenic Amines and Phenols.]

***Claudosporium cellare* (etc.).** A marvelous feature of the Hegyalja cellars is their extensive capacity, owing to environmental factors such as temperature and moisture, to support fungi on the cellar walls (and even as a 'turban' on the necks of upright bottles). The predominant one is *claudosporium cellare* (also known as *rhacodium cellare*), which is credited especially with creating a hygienic atmosphere in which wines are able to develop even when left in partially bunged, partially empty barrels for a period of time, per the *darabbantartás* technique. Hungarian research has shown that this particular mold does not have a direct effect on the aroma of Tokaji, but more than 50 other fungi are also present, and their aggregate influence on the nature of the long-aged botrytis wines has not been studied.

Color. The initials COS, standing for the Latin words *color odor sapor* (savor), were a typical marking used by Polish traders on barrels of Tokaji that met their commercial standards. In the post-communist era, color, in particular, became the focus of the debate between producers who wanted to produce a medium yellow wine (with minimal barrel-aging) and Hungarian authorities [see National Wine-Qualifying Commission, in Part I] who insisted on amber-gold or old-gold wine (entailing longer barrel aging). The former group couched the debate largely in terms of what color was 'traditional,' which was to say the color of Tokaji before the communist period and its amber-colored wines. But, from the strictly historical standpoint, there can be no debate.

The written record makes it clear that the Tokaji botrytis wines were amberish going back to at least the 17th century. Going *backwards* through time, it is found that pre-Second World War Hungarian wine literature consistently refers to Tokaji as "brownish yellow." It was also said to be "of brownish-yellow, amber color" in 1936 with reference to the Czechoslovak corner of Hegyalja (Fiala/Sedláček). The 1875 *Larousse Grand Dictionnaire Universel* described Tokaji as "amber." Alexandre Odart, in 1845, advised that attempts to replicate Tokaji in the Midi would entail producing a wine with "*une jolie couleur ambrée*." John Paget saw it slightly differently in 1839, but even so, as "topaz." In 1824, Alexander Henderson noted Tokaji as "brownish yellow." In 1730, Voltaire, in Canto I of his poem *La Pucelle d'Orléans* called Tokaji "*jaunissante*," a description used as wheat comes to its fully ripe golden-brown color; hence, Hungarian translations of Voltaire as 'dark-yellow' and 'amber' (as in "amber waves of grain" in the song 'America the Beautiful'). Perhaps the oldest indication comes from correlating the comments made respectively by Michael Olofsson Eneman in 1711-1712 and John Cavel in 1677 with reference to the Ariousian wine of Chios. Eneman likened it to Tokaji ("Ptokaiska"), while Cavel had described the Chian as "amber." Other evidence of Tokaji's traditional color is the fact that all of its would-be imitators in the New World endeavored to market wines in amber shades. [See the entry for Slovakian Tokaji.] None of this is contradicted by the occasional poetical reference to Tokaji as "golden" (as in the case of Isadora Duncan in her autobiography). The range of amber color does encompass 'old gold,' and such glints are always notable in Tokaji by candle-light.

Finally, let it be noted that the aforementioned Ariousian wine had been famed since antiquity, and dark 'white' wines retained their allure into the late Middle Ages, when Tokaji made its debut. We need only consider the Italian Vin Santo and Greek Malvasia wines to understand that Tokaji did not have to be any less amber or more yellow than those to gain widespread approval.

Among the old descriptions of Tokaji's color, the one penned in 1773 by Sylvester Douglass (*An Account of the Tokay and Other Wines of Hungary*) is conspicuous for having muddied the waters: "The colour should neither be reddish (which it often is) nor very pale, but a light silver." In view of his other notes about Tokaji, it seems likely that Douglass was not stating his own observations and opinions, but rather was faithfully recording what he heard from Hungarian interlocutors in Hegyalja. But just what did *they* have in mind? By "reddish," they most likely were referring to wine actually of a reddish color, not merely to long-matured Tokaji *aszú* wine that had developed garnet glints from aging in Zemplén oak. Nearly half a century after Douglass, more or less reddish wine was still very much a Hegyalja product, so much so that in 1816 André Jullien cautioned West Europeans that red Tokaji is not the Tokaji they were to seek. As for Douglass's specification of "light silver" as the desirable color, the only way to make sense of it is to consider that his upper-class, worldly Hungarian hosts were thinking of the typical silver ore of Hungary and Central Europe, argentite, which is a silver sulfide splotched with brownish yellow. [To view a sample of argentite, go to: http://www.mindat.org/min-326.html.]

Concentrated must. Of considerable concern to some Westerners during the communist period was that the Tokaji botrytis wines reportedly were being made at least in part with the use of concentrated must, instead of relying entirely on botrytis for sweetness. The sweetness of a wine can be increased by heating the grape must so as to evaporate water and thereby increase the sugar content of the must. Doing so will create the aldehyde HMF (hydroxymethylfurfural) in the resultant wine, and in 1965, Maynard Amerine, the doyen of California enologists, concluded that the presence of HMF in Tokaji was proof that concentrated must was being used. But the presence of HMF in Tokaji had been noticed by the Dutch scientists Kniphorst and Kruisheer in research they conducted during 1935-1937, at which time they concluded that it appeared to be a natural though unusual occurrence, a feature intrinsic to Tokaji. Later Hungarian research showed that some HMF occurs naturally in Tokaji because of its unusually high content of nitrogenous compounds and the Maillard reaction [see that entry]. In the meantime, the communist era had entered a new phase, in which the newly formed Tokaj-Hegyalja State Farm Wine-Facility could exert greater enological supervision. In 1987 [personal correspondence], András Bacsó, then director of enology for the Wine-Facility, responded to the continuing allegation as follows: "In the interest of protecting the quality of the *különleges* [delicacy] quality wines, it was always prohibited historically and is also prohibited now, and is also professionally impermissible 'nonszensz' [*sic.*, nonsense] that concentrated-must be used. Thus, if you, or anyone else in the world, should buy a bottle of Tokaji Szamorodni or Aszú, <u>you can be sure that there is not even a drop of concentrate in it</u>" [underlining in original]. [See the entry for Sulfuring; and the discussion of concentrated must in the Appendix Essay.]

Csemegebor. [See the entry for Dessert Wine.]

Darabbantartás. This Hungarian term means 'holding in piece' and refers to maturation in barrels that are not entirely filled and are left only partially bunged. In recent centuries, the practice was used throughout the maturation of the Tokaji specialty wines: "...it is necessary that during the process of [Tokaji's] development, the casks should never be filled up to the bung-hole, or too tightly bunged" (Szabó/Török, 1867). But Hungarian enologists in the 20th century determined that this was much longer than necessary for the development of true 'Tokaji character' [see that entry]. By the 1970s, the use of *darabbantartás* was reduced to one-to-three months, though it could be repeated several times during the course of maturation (Kádár, 1973).

The beginning of this practice is difficult to date. It has to be presumed that it was not being done prior to the 16th century, since it was not a practice taken to Cotnari, in Moldavia (Romania), when settlers from Hegyalja were brought there to impart wine-growing skills. In Hegyalja, the shift in favor of this technique must have started by at least the second-half of the 17th century. This is convincingly demonstrated by Eneman's likening of Tokaji to the amber-colored wine of Chios in 1711-1712 [see the entry for Color]. Townson's emphatic statement in 1797 (based on his 1793 visit to Tokaj) that *eszencia* should be kept in *full* barrels intimates that this was not the case with *aszú* by that time. The use of *darabbantartás* most likely occurred in tandem with the adoption of the *gönci* in place of the *antal* (or *átalag*) as the typical aging vessel, in the second-half of the 17th century. This changeover represented a doubling in barrel capacity; to have kept an *antal* only partially filled would have been a huge waste of limited cellar space. (It can be wondered, therefore, whether the large cellars built by the Rákóczis in the 17th century were linked in part to the spread of the *darabbantartás* technique.)

There is some evidence that *darabbantartás* might have begun in the late Middle Ages, though not necessarily in Hegyalja initially. Winemakers of the day were anxious to preserve the quality of wine in barrels that had already been tapped, and in northern lands they might have intuited that the air in the barrels could be used, paradoxically, to retard oxidation, almost like an 'innoculation' (but the 'paradox' may be no more so than the case of 'tempering' in cookery). A cookbook published in Frankfurt in 1581 by the Hungarian-German Marx Rumpolt included a section for cellar-masters and considered the problem of wine spoilage in partially empty barrels. The book appeared in Hungarian translation in 1681, while Hegyalja cellar practices were still being worked out. [See the entry for Barrel Aging, above; and the entry for Rumpolt, in Part I.]

De-amination. This term refers to the breakdown of amino acids, which is a significant process in Tokaji botrytis wines because of their elevated levels of nitrogenous compounds [see the latter entry]. The process has been found to foster 'Tokaji character,' particularly the typical aspect of aroma reminiscent of the crust of dark rye breads. De-amination also contributes to the broadly felt mellowness and satisfying, long aftertaste of umami. However, de-amination takes longer than the two-year minimum maturation in barrel currently required by law for *aszú* wines. Research was conducted on Tokaji's content of amino acids at the Magarach enological institute in the Crimea in the early 1960s, and a definite correlation was found between the breakdown of these amino acids and the manifestations of "Tokaji bouquet." Specifically, de-amination of easily oxidized amino acids ushered in optimal Tokaji character, whereas de-amination of the other, remaining amino acids detracted from that character (Almashi, Nilov, 1964).

Dessert Wine. Mention of 'dessert wine' needs to be made because in Hungarian wine legislation this category (*csemegebor*) has always excluded Tokaji, which instead was treated as a 'wine-delicacy' (*borkülönlegesség*). The legal significance is that certain procedures permitted for 'dessert wine,' notably the use of concentrated must, have never been sanctioned for Tokaji. [See the entry for Wine-delicacy.]

Diakhyton. [See the entry for *Aszú*: Aegean Echo.]

Eszencia. (a) This is the legendary nectar of Tokaj-Hegyalja, produced from the dense 'syrup' expressed solely by the weight of the botrytized berries piled upon each other. The liquid can be collected either from the bottom of the grape collection tubs, or by piling the grapes on a specially designed table top with holes through which the liquid slowly drips. In 1937, Pettenkoffer stated that 1/2-to-2 liters of *eszencia* are obtainable from a *puttony* (28-30 liters) of botrytized berries; in 1973, Kádár stated 1-to-1-1/2 liters. The better the botrytis vintage, the less the *eszencia* produced from a quantity of grapes, since less liquid will drip from a richer, denser mass of *aszú* berries. Ever since legislation of 1936, *eszencia* must contain at least 250 grams of natural sugar and 50 grams of non-sugar extract per liter. Because of the extremely high content of sugar, *eszencia* rarely reaches 7-8 percent alcohol by volume (and that only after multiple years of fermentation), and more typically is in the range of 4-6 percent. Current Hungarian law stipulates no higher than 5 percent. The primary purpose of *eszencia* has always been to enrich *aszú* wines, if deemed necessary. This is usually done by adding it prior to fermentation. The enologist Soós (1956) called *eszencia* "the most natural material for correcting *aszú* wine, since it is no less than an *aszú*-syrup."

(b) The name *eszencia* was given by German-speakers (though probably natives of Hungary), and indeed, most early mentions of it are in the German form, *essentz* or *essenz*. Magyars may have been calling it *nektár* colloquially, since some continued to do so, but in general they adopted the German name, though with a Latinate twist on the end. The Magyars also gave it a more formal name, *legfőbb bor*, signifying 'head-most' wine, perhaps in the sense of the first vinifiable liquid obtained from botrytized berries. But that name disappeared in the 19th century. The name *nektár* suggests Greek influence in the naming [see the two entries for Nectar].

It appears that *eszencia* was a late introduction in the botrytis wine tradition of Hegyalja. It is likely that it did not antedate the Zemplén County requirement of 1655 that all botrytized grapes be collected separately, simply because the separate production of *eszencia*, by its nature, requires a large quantity of botrytized grapes. The earliest written mention of it (*essentia*) is from 1707, when Alexander Nedeczky wrote to Francis Rákóczi II of Peter the Great's fondness for it. However, by 1736, Gabriel Gyöngyösi was complaining about over-production of *eszencia* (as well as *aszú*). All of this suggests that *eszencia* may not have been made until late in the 1600s, and definitely that it only became significant around that time. It might be conjectured that *eszencia* was not much needed before the preeminence of botrytis *aszú* wines, and that its importance grew in tandem with the use of the *puttonyos* classification system. Yet, as late as 1798, a Zemplén County decree referred to "the *so called* Essentia" (emphasis added), as though *eszencia* had only secured its place in Hegyalja terminology in rather recent generations.

The timing of *eszencia's* ascent raises the intriguing possibility that it was promoted, if not introduced, by the Greek merchants who began settling in the region in the late 1600s (the 'Greek tax' levied by Zemplén County beginning in 1689 indicates that Greek traders must already have been resident in Hegyalja in significant numbers for at least a couple of decades). The procedure for making *eszencia* is identical to that for the ancient Greek wine called *protropon* (πρότροπον), and the technique was still known to Greeks of the modern era. In that regard, it is notable that the technique was never adopted at places in Hungary that produced later-harvested wines but *did not* have a resident Greek merchant community. Further, it was the habit of the Greeks to use such richly dense and viscous wine to improve other wines, which is exactly what came to be done with *eszencia* in Hegyalja. Of course, this ideally suited a merchant's need to supply an *aszú* wine of, say, 5-*puttonyos* instead of 3-*puttonyos* sweetness.

Also notable in the history of *eszencia* is a mention in 1792, by I. Mátyus, that the chief grape variety used for it was the 'Augster,' or *gohér*. This is the only mention of a varietal preference for *eszencia*, and it specifies *gohér* even as *furmint* was gaining importance in Hegyalja. Considering the Greeks once again, and the possibility that the *gohér* is a variant of the Greek *goustoulidi*, it is impossible to overlook that small berries of the latter variety were used on the island of Zakynthos to produce the dessert wine *lianorogi* by the *protropon* technique, as described by the English visitor John Davy in 1881. Could the introduction of both the variety and the technique be traceable to Greece? [See *Gohér* (b), and #11 in Balkan Influences.]

(c) Most Europeans in the 19th century believed implicitly that to purchase *eszencia* one need only have sufficient funds, and perhaps the right contacts. They were not aware of the ameliorative use to which genuine *eszencia* typically was put in Hegyalja cellars, nor even that in the cellars it was kept in much larger bottles than those for *szamorodni* and *aszú*. Nor were Europeans aware that another product, *aszú-eszencia*, was casually referred to simply as *eszencia* [see the entry for *Aszú-eszencia*]. Genuine *eszencia* was hardly ever sold as a commercial wine, and instead entered commerce mostly through the pharmaceutical trade, which explains extant apothecary bottles bearing its name. A related misconception was the identification of *eszencia* with the term 'Imperial Tokay' [see that entry].

Misunderstandings about *eszencia* also influenced erroneous beliefs about its fate under communism. Those beliefs likely led to the preoccupation behind Alec Waugh's 1959 statement that "Tokay exists no more." In 1977, the American enologists Amerine and Singleton wrote more explicitly: "Little, if any, Essenz has been produced since World War II" (*Wine: An Introduction*). Their statement confuses commercialization with production. While the old pharmaceutical sales may have disappeared, *eszencia* was still being produced for its usual role, namely, to improve other botrytis wines. There was no break in the tradition of producing it. Further, it still made an occasional, honorary appearance before selected persons at international wine contests in Hungary, and of course found its way to the 'proletarian elite' of the Eastern Bloc, just as it did earlier to the tables of the Austro-Hungarian aristocracy.

Not only was true *eszencia* rarely available, it was not relished by everyone who tasted it. Certainly there were misgivings about it in its early years, before it had been able to clear. In any case, the most intriguing specific comment made about it was that of Dr. Robert Druitt, who found "a decided remembrance of green tea" typical of "its admirable aroma" ("Report on Cheap Wines," 1864).

Eszencia: Literary Aside

The allure of *eszencia* was felt by Hungarians, too. In "The Gentry," a short story of 1897, author Kálmán Mikszáth recounts his visit to the onetime Tokaji trade center of Eperjes (Prešov) to take part in a wedding, and mentions *eszencia* in taking humorous aim at provincial Sáros County pretensions. As a gustatory high point on the wedding day, one of the guests presents all of the attendees with a three-deciliter bottle of the "liquid gold that is called Tokaji *eszencia*" from the year of their birth. In the moment, Mikszáth is in awe of "the dazzling luxury" of the gesture, but events of the next day show that not everything had been as it appeared. A reader must then question the genuineness of the *eszencia*, especially since it would not have been available from every vintage, and thus had to have been labeled with fictitious vintage dates. Further, because of the modest financial means of everyone involved, the provider of the bottles likely had them filled with, at best, a 2- or 3-*puttonyos aszú* available in Eperjes, or at worst, a bogus Tokaji laced with spirits, which was rife in the post-phylloxera years when the story was written, because of the scarcity of genuine Tokaji of any kind. But, far from being fooled, the guests implicitly understood the 'play.' As natives of Sáros ("the county…of hallucinations") they knew that their role – and their social obligation – was to enjoy the contents of the bottles as if it were the *eszencia* of their imagination.

Falsification. The problem of bogus Tokaji plagued Hegyalja from the early-18th century to the early-20th century. To some extent, it was represented by wines produced outside Hungary but sold under the name 'Tokay.' But, for the most part, those wines were just making opportunistic and euphemistic use of Tokaji's name, and were less often a ruse by which to lure unsuspecting consumers. Further, that became ever more the case as time passed: nobody purchasing California or Australian 'Tokay' thought they were getting a wine from Hungary, just something similar to it. The really insidious problem occurred in Hegyalja itself, especially following the Rákóczi wars early in the 18th century and after the phylloxera episode at the end of the 19th century, when demand for Tokaji outpaced production capacity owing to decline in vineyard land and loss of population (labor).

However, falsification in Hegyalja was not accomplished in the same way during the period between, roundly, 1700 and 1900. The most variegated and 'elaborate' era undoubtedly was during the 18th century, when the Macedonian Greek merchants dominated the trade [see the entry for Rosa, in Part I]. There is little if any specific indication that they went out of their way to bring quantities of non-Hegyalja wine into the region, although, in an era when the confines of the region were still being debated, these merchants probably gladly included grapes, must, or wine from just west and northeast of modern Hegyalja, since there was a resemblance in the wines right after fermentation. But the Greeks no doubt availed themselves of the panoply of methods that they were familiar with in their homeland, and which oftentimes harked back to antiquity. This included such procedures as boiling a small portion of must and adding it to new wine that had not finished fermenting; or, taking off a small amount near the end of fermentation, boiling it, cooling it, and then pouring it back into the still-fermenting wine; or, using baked gypsum to make the wine feel denser; or, adding certain herbs. The merchants did not necessarily regard these treatments as pernicious, and even regarded the effect as beneficial in the case of certain grape varieties. There is even the possibility that they introduced the use of *eszencia*, another of their age-old 'tricks,' in connection with 'falsification' [see the entry for Protropon].

Later, in the early-19th century, the use of imported raisins became the most common form of abuse, as is made clear by Széchenyi's ironic comment in 1830 about the surfeit of Syrian raisins stockpiled in Hegyalja [see the entry for Széchenyi, in Part I]. This may have been the favored ploy of the Armenian traders, who seem to have enjoyed their halcyon years in between the respective periods of Greek and Jewish dominance of the Tokaji trade. It would certainly explain Komoróczi's remark about the 'grand scale' of falsification by the Armenian traders [see the entry for Armenians, in Part I]. (The Greeks do not seem to have relied on raisins, although they may have dried some locally harvested grapes indoors, which was a common practice in their Macedonian homeland. It is unlikely, too, that they would have imported raisins from anywhere other than some of the Aegean islands, such as Ikaria.)

The falsification epidemic following phylloxera was different, and distinctly 'modern,' in being, so to speak, 'chemistry-based.' It consisted of bringing in large quantities of wine of diverse origin, 'correcting' it with sugar, caramel coloring, and spirits, and then labeling it 'Tokaji.' The national legislation of 1893 and 1908 makes it quite clear that these were the concerns of the day.

A final note about falsification concerns its 'social' dimensions. Merchants were not alone in trying to make the most of Tokaji's occasional scarcity. Komoróczi (1944) pointed out that smallholders frequently were complicit in going along with the wishes of the merchants in terms of the grapes or must or wine they delivered. This was particularly true during the 18th century. But Kossuth (1903) indicated that smallholders in the late-19th century were of a quite different mind, perhaps exactly because of earlier experience of the backlash from falsified Tokaji on the European market. Certainly after phylloxera, falsification was the bane of smallholders, with no 'up-side' whatsoever. Their readiness to participate in cooperatives that saw to strict adherence to the national laws aimed at protecting the integrity of Tokaji wine is testimony to that. As for the aristocracy, their intense opposition to the Greek merchants suggests that they did not take part in any sort of falsification during earlier times, although they likely were aware of dubious practices on the far side of the Polish border, such as the occasional addition of brandy.

Fehérszőlő. (also as *fejérszőlő*) [Note: Also see the entries for *Kövérszőlő* and *Tumidula*.]
(a) Once the kingpin grape variety for sweet white wine in Hegyalja, the 'white (*fehér*) grape' began losing ground first to *gohér* in the late-17th century, and then to *furmint* in the late-18th century. But it was still mentioned as one of the region's four main varieties (along with *furmint*, *hárslevelű*, and *gohér*) in the *Tokaj-Hegyaljai Album* of 1867. However, its star had actually

been in steep decline for some time by then, since at least around 1800. The main cause was the growing preference for *furmint*; and although *fehérszőlő* hung on for a while because of its great sweetness and pleasant aroma, the more *furmint* came to the fore, the more the relatively earlier-ripening *fehérszőlő* became less than a completely satisfactory partner for botrytis wines. Curiously, Szirmay in 1803 stated that the *fehérszőlő* did not produce *aszú* berries, although this was contradicted by other commentators, perhaps because of name confusion with the *kövérszőlő*. Thus, the later-ripening and more botrytis prone *hárslevelű* gradually replaced the *fehérszőlő*. Following phylloxera, it became a variety of the past in Hegyalja.

(b) When considering the antiquity of white grape varieties in Hegyalja, it is impossible not to think of the *fehérszőlő*. The variety's pedigree is not well understood. Obviously, the task of tracing its background is complicated because the name 'white-grape' lends itself to much confusion with other Hegyalja grapes that have borne the word 'white' as a qualifier. Further, several early commentators virtually equated the *fehérszőlő* with the *leány-szőlő* (now *leányka*), though erroneously [see the entry for Lányka, in Part III]. This might explain Szirmay's statement that the variety did not produce *aszú* berries.

Some Hungarian ampelographers have thought that the variety in its modern form originated in Transylvania. In 1570, though, Szikszai Fabricius equated it with the *uva argitis spinaria* of ancient Greece, which was stated again in a Latin-Hungarian dictionary of 1767. Although the *argitis* was not described by Pliny or Columella, the scholar Isidore of Seville, in Book XVII of his early-7th century work, *Etymologiae*, mentioned the *argitis* as a Greek white variety that rots under the influence of moisture. The name *argitis* signifies 'silver-grape' in Greek, which refers to a grape that is ultra 'white.' Keler (1726) in fact described the *fehérszőlő* as "whitish green" (*weisslich grün*); and Szabó in 1826 noted that it remains "pale-colored" (*halovány színű*) even at ripeness. While no grape in modern Greece is referred to by a name indicating 'silver,' many are called 'whitey' (*asproudi*). But no matter the question of a specific connection to Greece, we again have a variety of Pontic/Balkan type, and one of great significance to the development of Hegyalja as a producer of later-harvested wines, including *főbor* [see that entry]. It could also have been the main variety used early on for wines in which *aszú*-dough was fermented.

Ferenczi Heat-Treatment. (*Ferenczi-féle melegkezelés*) Devised by the enologist Alexander Ferenczi to stabilize the Tokaji specialty wines, the heat-treatment began with pasteurization at 83° C (181° F) for one or two minutes for the purpose of destroying microbes that might occasion unfavorable micro-biological reactions during the remainder of the process. Subsequently, the wine was held in isothermic containers for one to four weeks at 35° to 45° C (95-113° F), depending on the nature of the wine. Notably, the Ferenczi heat-treatment was administered after the wines had already matured fully in barrel (in terms of 'Tokaji character' as yielded by traditional aging). At that point, the wine had nothing further to gain from the microorganisms that were to be eliminated by the procedure. Thus, the wines were still able to benefit from *chemical* evolutions that take place in bottle. The latter was not known to Western commentators on Tokaji, with the result that much Tokaji was drunk without further bottle-aging.

Főbor. Literally meaning 'head-wine,' this was the earliest name for wine akin to *szamorodni*. *Főbor* was the wine that first brought attention to Hegyalja around 1500; it was in all likelihood the reason that Sperfogel, in 1524, made specific note of the improvement in the region's wine. However, at that time it signified a later-harvested wine that did not necessarily include botrytized grapes; most of the shriveled grapes would simply have been ones that had raisined partially on the vine before harvesting. Later, though, towards 1600, some large producers probably hoped and looked for some botrytization because introduction of a third hoeing resulted in an even later vintage. Once the concept of *főbor* started to include botrytized grapes, the stage was set for the concept of botrytis *aszú* wine to develop. In fact, Balassa (1991) considered that *főbor* "almost completely disappeared" after *aszú* reached the peak of its commercial importance for Hegyalja in the early 1700s. Nearly a century would pass before its 're-emergence' as *szamorodni*. In the interim, *ordinárium* was evolving towards what *főbor* had become and took over for it commercially [see the entry for *Ordinárium*].

Although *főbor* was the forerunner of *szamorodni*, it was not precisely the same as the latter. *Főbor* always remained a wine that did not necessarily have to be made with botrytized grapes, which meant that it could be made from more vintages by just letting the grapes shrivel. Thus, too, whereas *szamorodni* developed in tandem with greater attention to the appropriateness of specific grape varieties, and always in favor of later-ripening ones, *főbor* was connected historically to the earlier period of considerably greater varietal diversity in the Hegyalja vineyards. This meant that grapes in various stages of ripeness were used in producing it, everything from under-ripe to over-ripe grapes. In that way, *főbor* brings to mind the *omfakitis* wine of the ancient Greeks, although in the case of the former, the emphasis was on over-ripe grapes. In common with *omfakitis*, though, *főbor* made with few or no botrytized grapes likely benefited from the inclusion of under-ripe grapes because of greater acidity to enhance 'freshness' of savor. [But, see the entry for *Aszú*: Aegean Echo.] Finally, the history of the *darabbantartás* method [see that entry] suggests that *főbor*, unlike *szamorodni*, was not aged by that technique during most of its history.

Fordítás. Though a by-product of botrytis *aszú* wine, *fordítás* came about much later, certainly long after *máslás* [see the latter entry]. The name has not been found earlier than 1826. It comes from the verb 'to turn' (*fordít-*), in allusion to the procedure of pouring ('turning') must or wine over the trampled 'remains' of the process for a previously made botrytis wine. Notations from the mid-19th to the mid-20th century indicate that the primary method was to pour must over the remaining *aszú*-dough (which at that point was *aszú* marc), letting it 'soak' for 4-8 hours, treading on it again, and finally, pressing. Since much sugar still remained in the *aszú*-dough, the wine obtained was considered as 'second-*aszú*' (*másod-aszú*). But another method was to use the marc of *szamorodni* wine in particularly good (sugar-rich) botrytis vintages.

Although Pettenkoffer, in 1937, indicated that must was generally used, Kádár, in 1973, stated that must *or* wine could be used. Pap, in 1985, specified the use of old wine (probably from the previous vintage) in making *fordítás*, but this might have reflected the general practice during the communist period. Balassa (1991) noted that for a time during the 19th century, there was some confusion between *fordítás* and *máslás* in common parlance because both could be made by pouring ('turning') wine over 'remains' (whether marc or lees). He supposed that the term *fordítás* acquired a more specific meaning, namely the use of marc, precisely in order to differentiate the two after the Polish market's interest in *máslás*, as a 'lees wine,' had declined.

Fordítás was defined as a marc wine in 1936. As a commercial wine, it enjoyed considerable popularity, rather like a preeminent semi-sweet wine, and had a good market in Central Europe. Pettenkoffer noted, though, that "the quality of *fordítás* and *máslás* depends on the quality of the *aszú*- [vintage], as well as the quality and quantity of the wine poured over [the remains]." The term *fordítás* disappeared commercially during the communist era, although such wines were used in making *édes* (sweet) *szamorodni*, and sometimes even *aszú* wines, since it was a sugar-rich wine.

Fortification. It needs to be emphasized immediately in discussing the addition of spirits to Tokaji that it never had the purpose of fortification in Sherry and Port, in which alcohol is added to halt the initial fermentation at the desired level of sugar content. In Hegyalja, the addition of grape spirits was made towards the end of barrel maturation, in order to replace alcohol lost over the years and thereby serve as a protection against re-fermentation [see the entry for Cellars]. Historically, it is very likely that some traders, particularly those who had warehouses in southern Poland, added common brandy. However, any addition of alcohol was strongly opposed by the conservative growers of Hegyalja [see the entry for Punchification]. Nevertheless, the national wine law of 1893 gave open-ended permission to add wine spirits for the purpose of stabilizing the wines, thereby helping to market them. But abuse by traders caused this permission to be rescinded in the subsequent law, of 1908.

A regulation of 1936 required that Tokaji be marketed in bottle with a state control band, which changed the equation because state inspection became mandatory before the wine could be marketed. This meant that the addition of spirits, if resorted to, could be controlled. Thus, the regulation allowed highly refined, faultless Tokaji wine spirits of 92-percent alcohol by volume to be added to *szamorodni* and *aszú* wines so as to raise the wines' alcohol by not more than 4 percent in volume, and in no case to surpass a total of 18.5-percent alcohol by volume. From the Hungarian perspective, it was certainly better to have the addition of spirits take place in Hegyalja than performed by foreign merchants. By, in effect, discontinuing the wholesaling and retailing of any wine in barrel as 'Tokaji,' and requiring strict enological supervision, the regulation ended 'tampering' with Tokaji outside Hegyalja, which had been a foremost concern since phylloxera. However, enological concern grew about the upper limit on the use of spirits, and that such use should not be organoleptically apparent to consumers. Consequently, the law of 1959 reduced the maximum to 16.5 percent alcohol by volume, and a subsequent regulation did not permit addition greater than 3 percent in volume. [See the entry for Regulation.] In practice, though, *aszú* wines were rarely marketed with more than 15-percent alcohol by volume. The regulations of 1936 and 1959 regarding spirits remained in effect until 1980, at which time all use of spirits was prohibited because more effective means of preventing re-fermentation had been developed.

An aspect of Tokaji wine-making history that has not been explored is the relationship between *máslás/fordítás* wines [see those entries] and the replacement of lost alcohol in *aszú* wines. Because of their higher alcohol content, the best quality *máslás* or *fordítás* wines could have been added after maturation so as to give a boost to alcohol and sugar in a long-aged *aszú* wine.

Furfural. This is an aldehyde typical of brandy, seldom of wine. But its presence in Tokaji is unusually high due to the Maillard reaction. Since furfural browns in color in contact with oxygen, it contributes to amberish color in traditionally matured Tokaji. [See the entries for Acetaldehyde, HMF, and Maillard Reaction.]

Furmint. (a) The principal grape of modern-day Tokaj-Hegyalja is *not* the grape that made Tokaji's reputation. The wine's fame was established during the 16th and 17th centuries, whereas *furmint* did not begin receiving special attention in the vineyards until the 18th century, and did not achieve dominance until after 1800. *Furmint* supplanted the *fehérszőlő* and *gohér*, mostly on the strength of its later ripening and greater susceptibility to noble rot. This happened in conjunction with *aszú* wine becoming more important to growers than *főbor*, since more botrytized grapes were needed for *aszú* wines. [See the entry for *Főbor*.]

Furmint likely had its first boost in Hegyalja after a third hoeing was introduced towards the end of the 16th century and a very late vintage was possible. Yet, it remained a minor variety. Szikszai Fabricius, who resided in Sárospatak, did not mention it in his 1561-1576 listing of numerous Hegyalja varieties (unless he knew it by a different name). Documents indicate that *furmint* was being given consideration at Erdőbénye in the early 1600s, at which time there was a vineyard plot with that name [see the entry for Furmint, in Part III]. But, in 1623, it was remarked as being detrimental to other varieties, and was not mentioned at all in a varietal inventory of 1635. An entire century passed before the *furmint* was mentioned again. In 1726, Keler noted that the variety was a good producer of *aszú* ("*trucken-beer*") grapes in Hegyalja. It was at this time that *furmint* began to gain notice in the region, albeit slowly. Around mid-century, the major landlords were more frequently planting it, although this was a weak 'trend' (it would be a few more years before it became a major variety in the Habsburg vineyard-tract of Szarvas, in Tarcal). However, in 1796, Dercsényi listed *furmint* second to *gohér*. Its advantage was not only susceptibility to noble rot, but also, more basically, the variety's tough skin, which allowed it to withstand wet or icy frosts that could ruin other varieties left on the vine into late fall. As Légrády noted when commenting on this advantage in 1844, growers "did not have to hurry the vintage for fear of frost destruction." Further, his comment that the *furmint* was "in fashion" in Hegyalja at that time is good reason to date the variety's major upswing to the early-19th century.

Furmint's dominance was clinched by the phylloxera episode that reached Hegyalja in 1885. An important part of reconstructing the vineyards was to exclude the numerous varieties less suitable for producing botrytis wines, which resulted in increasing *furmint's* presence throughout Hegyalja. Further, this entailed looking more closely at the numerous clones of the variety. Expert opinion mostly favored the variants *hólyagos* ('blistered,' in reference to skin texture) and *madárkás* ('birdling-like,' in reference to small bunches). These two variants had been significant as far back as Szirmay in 1798, and were deemed especially suitable for the upper middle slopes, where the resistance of *furmint*'s skin to frosts was desirable.

The *furmint* is a fairly populous family of types and clones. There is even a red type, which was also found in Hegyalja at one time. But most variants belong to the white, or *fehér furmint*, sub-variety. These include *hólyagos* and *madárkás*, as well as *nemes* ('noble'), *király* ('king'), and others. The preferred clones are of a large-berry type because they produce more *aszú* berries and better botrytis wine. Consequently, small-berry types, such as *madárkás*, receded in cultivation.

The classification, or ranking, of Hegyalja vineyards could not have had any connection to their suitability for the cultivation of the *furmint* in particular. Those determinations were already made before the variety was significant. On the other hand, the gradualness of the variety's expansion, beginning in the 18th century, might have influenced thinking about which locales belong in Hegyalja and which do not; namely, locales where *furmint* was unimportant might have been viewed as not being producers of genuine Hegyalja wine. However, there is little information by which to track the variety's spread through the communes. The only known instance of the *furmint* having an effect on 'delineation' is when Czechoslovakia, beginning in the 1930s, tried to expand its piece of the Hegyalja region beyond the Hungarian legislation of 1908 by planting the large-berry *hólyagos* on soil that was similar, but did not really conform, to Hegyalja type, so as to achieve passable quality 'Tokaji' wine from less appropriate soil. Finally, it needs to be emphasized that the choice of *furmint* cannot be separated from the question of aging the botrytis wines. Because it gives a hard wine that botrytis alone could not sufficiently soften, a long period of barrel aging became ever more preferred. This would explain why, in the earliest period of botrytis wines, small growers were usually satisfied to release them to traders after a year; that is, varieties of 'softer' character than *furmint* were yielding the wines.

(b) Much has been written about the origin of *furmint*, and the attribution usually is to Italian or Walloon settlers who brought it along with other vine cuttings from their homelands. The name *furmint* itself is thus attributed to names of medieval West European grape varieties (for instance, Italian *formia*). The basic problem with imputing a West European origin to the grape itself, as distinct from the name, is that the *furmint* belongs to the Pontic (Black Sea)/Balkan family of grape varieties, and thus does not have an origin in Western Europe, but instead, in a direction east or south of Hungary. Clearly, then, the *furmint* was not brought from Italy or elsewhere in Western Europe. But, on the other hand, this does not mean that it was brought to Hegyalja by Bulgaro-Slavs prior to the 10th century.

Furmint might have made its way first to the Szerém region of southern Hungary (now Sremska in the Vojvodina region of Serbia), and later to Tokaj-Hegyalja when its growers were seeking to emulate the once highly esteemed Szerém wines and brought vine cuttings from there. This might have occurred during the 15th century or earlier, but certainly after Walloons had settled in the Szerém region in the 13th century. The Serbian name Fruška Gora in Sremska signifies 'Frankish Hill,' and it was most likely those early 'Franks' (Walloons) who first bestowed a grape name that became the *furmint* of Magyar-speakers. The terms *fromenau* and *formentau* were used as grape names in Western Europe to indicate a 'wheaten' color (as with the medieval English beverage 'frumenty'). However, this does not mean that the Walloons brought this grape variety to Hungary, just that they transferred a color conception and name to the Hungarians.

Gohér. (a) Truly, here is a forgotten grape with a noteworthy history. Its insignificance during the past century-and-a-half belies its once central position in Hegyalja. As an early-ripening sort, it was very susceptible to over-ripening by late September. It was also semi-aromatic. Thus, *gohér* was a foundation for making later-harvested wines in the region's early days as a producer of sweet white wines; and being susceptible to botrytis, its role only increased as botrytis-affected *főbor* and *aszú* wines grew in importance. Even in 1857, when *gohér's* importance in Hegyalja was waning, the best *szamorodni* was said to be made solely from it and *furmint*. Further, a notation from 1782 specified *gohér* as a preferred variety for making *eszencia* (Hegyalja was not specified, but the *eszencia* technique was not used elsewhere in Hungary).

Gohér's significance in the 17th and 18th centuries is shown by the fact that by the mid-18th century it had been taken from Hungary to Astrakhan (around the mouth of the Volga where it enters the Caspian Sea). In 1771-1776, P.S. Pallas, a German explorer of southern Russia, made detailed notes about vine culture in Astrakhan and mentioned two varieties known by the name *hungarian*: "Hungarian grapes, both white and black. Both round, thin-skinned, and remarkably sweet. They ripened in August, at which time they burst and began to drip their juice. The white kind grew everywhere, but the black was very scarce. Because of their propensity to burst, they were used exclusively to make wine; but the wine pressed from them was quite superior in quality." Pallas did not know the name *gohér*, but he was describing that variety; and a black variant was known in Hegyalja. This was at the time of *gohér's* heyday, which coincided with the period when the czars kept a purchasing agency in the region. The czars had valued Astrakhan grapes since at least the early 1600s, and because of their connections in Hegyalja they apparently saw to the transplantation to Astrakhan of one of the most valued Hegyalja varieties.

In 1794, the Hungarian poet Michael Csokonai Vitéz mentioned only *gohér* and *furmint* in his poem, *A Vizital*. Despite the poem's name, 'Water-drink,' it had a bacchic theme and very much suggests that Csokonai Vitéz had the Hegyalja region and Tokaji wine in mind. In 1796, John Dercsényi noted that *gohér* was the most widespread variety in Hegyalja. It continued as a significant variety for several decades more, but as Csokonai Vitéz's poem shows, *furmint* was now advancing. Early in the 19th century, the *gohér* was increasingly replaced by the later-ripening, but similarly semi-aromatic *hárslevelű*, in order to accommodate the late-ripening *furmint*. Even so, *gohér* was mentioned as a significant variety in Hegyalja as late as 1867 (in the *Tokaj-Hegyaljai Album*). It took the phylloxera episode to spell its end.

221

(b) The *gohér's* origin would make for intriguing ampelographic research. Its name is a corruption of the German name *augster*, which signifies ripening in August. Besides the name, the *gohér's* sweetness and superior quality suggest that it might have been a variant or scion of the Greek *goustoulidi* (also named for August, *avgoustos*), which as late as the early 1800s was still being used on the Ionian island of Zakynthos for a sweet wine called *lianorogi* (or *lianoroïdi*) that involved the *eszencia* technique (identical to that for ancient Greek *protropon* wine), though with less shriveled, relatively juicier berries [see #11 in the entry for Balkan Influences]. [Photos of *gohér* and *goustoulidi* (provided respectively from Hungary and Greece) show them to have virtually identical bunch shape, berry shape and compactness, and color.]

But no matter the kinship with *goustoulidi* in particular, there is a good chance that *gohér*, as a semi-aromatic variety, had its origin among the various early-ripening Greek grapes that were associated with the sweet Malvasia wines. The connection between *gohér* and Malvasia wine is seen in the alternative Hungarian name '*malozsa gohér*,' meaning '*malvasia gohér*,' recorded in 1804. Further, in praising it most highly in 1803, Szirmay attributed the *gohér's* origin to the Peloponnesus and likened it to Malvasia grapes: "*Malvaticisque simillimas*" (like virtually all Europeans of his era, Szirmay mistakenly assumed that a single grape variety known as *malvasia* accounted for all Greek wine traded under that name [see Lambert-Gócs, *The Wines of Greece*]). Another indication of the variety's origin from the area of the Ionian Sea is that it was also recorded by the synonym *ragusaner*, indicating a provenance from Ragusa, today's Dubrovnik.

Conceivably, the *gohér* might have been brought from there to Hegyalja, most likely around 1500, by aristocratic growers who were intent on 'modeling' Tokaji after Malvasia, the sweet wine most famous in Central Europe at that time. On the other hand, the *goustoulidi* could have been brought by the Greek vine-dressers that were brought to Hegyalja by King Béla IV following the Tatar invasion of 1241-1242, since they might have come from the northwestern Peloponnesus, or even nearby Zakynthos. In either case, it is noteworthy that Greek Malvasia was typically made, not from grapes that had been harvested and then spread in the sun [see the entry for Straw Wine], but rather from ones that had reached super-maturation on the vine, which has ever been the Hegyalja method. [See Louis I, in Part I; and Dalmatia and Zakynthos, in Part II.]

Gold Content. Around the time that later-harvested wines began to be made in Hegyalja, toward the end of the 15th century, stories spread of vines containing gold, literally. Paracelsus came to investigate in 1524 and did not find golden vines, but posited that the basis for the purported occurrences must be mineral content in the vines. Gold-colored, hardened areas on vines were still reported from time to time as late as the 18th and 19th centuries, and investigation pointed to solidified resinous material as the cause. It was also said that golden droplets sometimes fell from the vines; according to Balassa (1991), this was particularly associated with the *fehérszőlő* variety. The credibility of the old legends in popular lore was due to the erroneous belief that since the soil of Hegyalja is volcanic and heterogeneous, it might sporadically contain gold that had spewed from the depths of Earth eons ago and perchance might seep into vines in a thoroughly pulverized form that could dissolve but subsequently harden occasionally. Certainly the most fabulous of the gold stories was that a completely gold grape was found in the Aranyos ('Golden') vineyard-tract in Tokaj during the time of the Rákóczi rebellions, and that Francis Rákóczi II sent it to Czar Peter the Great as a gift. This was related by J. Matolay in 1730.

Gönci Barrel. Traditionally one of the key measures used in Hegyalja wine-making, the *gönci* barrel has a capacity of 136-140 liters (36-37 gallons). The *puttonyos* level of *aszú* wines was determined by the number of *puttony*-s of botrytized grapes fermented in an amount of must or wine equivalent to the volume of the *gönci* [see the entry for *Puttonyos* System]. The small size of the *gönci* was tailored for the small entranceways of the typical cellars of Hegyalja and the

Hernád river valley. Its name refers to the village of Gönc, just to the northwest, on the far side of the Zemplén hills [see the entry for Gönc, in Part I]. The earliest mention of the barrel is from 1576, which suggests its fabrication by the Germans who were settled there. Later, it was also produced at several other places, notably in the Szepesség region after iron hoops started replacing wooden ones, in the early-19th century. The *gönci* gradually replaced the earlier *antal*, which had only half its capacity, and became typical in trade as well as wine aging and storage.

The landmark date in the history of the *gönci* is 1716, when the Szepes Chamber officially notified all of the counties in its purview, which included the entire Upper Tisza region, that their wine producers were to use barrels of *gönci* capacity for trade with Poland because of preference for it there. This mostly affected Zemplén County, and in 1737 a county regulation required use of the *gönci* for Hegyalja wine, though partly as a means of trying to stem falsification (the barrels were also to be marked in a distinctive manner). An inventory taken in Szepes County in 1755 referred to *aszú* wines stored in "old" (*antiqui*) *antal*-s, as if to imply 'old-style' casks. Certainly after this period, the *darabbantartás* technique of aging Tokaji must have become habitual amongst all commercial growers [see the entry for *Darabbantartás*].

Grape Varieties. Hegyalja has seen a profusion of grape varieties during its history. Görög had as many as 50 of them in his varietal collection in the early-19th century; Szabó in that same period numbered them at 63 in the community of Mád alone. But only a small number have been of importance since the advent of later-harvested white wines around 1500.

White Varieties: As far as the later-harvested white wines are concerned, various notations since the 16th century give a picture of how the varietal complement for those wines changed over time. The turning point was when a third hoeing was initiated in the second-half of the 16th century. This resulted in later harvesting, which happened to favor the inherent potential of the best white varieties in the vineyards. By the mid-17th century, botrytis-based wines had come to the fore and induced further varietal evaluation, based on proneness to botrytization.

It happens that accounts specifying the major varieties in Hegyalja do not occur until the cusp of the botrytis era, or the late-16th century. The following chronological listing (with author's name in parentheses) of some key notations mentions the botrytis-prone white varieties, in the order given by the respective author, and other quality white varieties suitable for use in making botrytis wines. (Note that mentions of the *fehérszőlő* in some instances might reflect the apparently old tendency to see it as a variant of the *kövérszőlő*.)

c. 1570 (Blasius Szikszai Fabricius): *fehérszőlő*, *gohér*, *muskotály*; plus, two other varieties suitable for sweet wine, namely, *malozsa* (*i.e.*, 'malvasia') and *kecskecsecsű*; the first two would retain prominence for over three centuries more; no mention was made of *furmint* or *hárslevelű*, though that does not mean they were not present in the vineyards

1744 (János Matolay): *furmint*, *fehérszőlő*, mentioned as the exclusive sorts for *aszú* (at least for the botrytis portion); also mentioned *hárslevelű* and *gohér* [see the entry for Szarvas, in Part III]

1758 (Sámuel Dombi): [in Latin] *augusta* (*gohér*), *albula* (*fehérszőlő*), *tumidula* (*kövérszőlő*, though possibly *furmint* was meant); plus *gemma* (*gyöngyszőlő*) for additional sweetness

1798 (Antal Szirmay): *furmint*, *gohér*; plus the sweet *kecskecsecsű*

1821 (János Nagyváthy): *gohér*, *furmint*, *fehérszőlő*, *muskotály*, *hárslevelű*

1848 (Zemplén County determination): the "better quality" sorts were specified as *furmint, gohér, muskotály*; the name *leányszőlő* in this era may have been a synonym for *fehérszőlő*; plus, the sweet but not botrytis-prone *gyöngyszőlő*; notably, *hárslevelű* was not included even at this late date

1867 (Szabó/Török): *furmint, fehérszőlő, hárslevelű, gohér, muskotály*; plus *kecskecsecsű*

1875 (Károly Keleti): *furmint, fehérszőlő, muskotály, hárslevelű*; plus *malozsa* for extra sweetness

1893 (Hungarian legislation): *furmint, hárslevelű, fehérszőlő, gohér, muskotály*; plus *kecskecsecsű* at Sátoraljaújhely

1903: (János Kossuth): *furmint, hárslevelű, muskotály, fehérszőlő, gohér*; but the latter two were mentioned as being of little significance

1908 (Hungarian legislation): *furmint, hárslevelű, muskotály*; henceforward, these were the only authorized varieties for the Tokaji specialty wines, until the addition of *zéta* in 1990

It is readily apparent from this listing that the 'evolution' in varietal complement in Hegyalja did not proceed along a straight path. This fact becomes even clearer from the history of the individual varieties and comments made about their significance at various times by other observers of Hegyalja [see the entries for *Balafánt, Fehérszőlő, Furmint, Gohér, Gyöngyszőlő, Hárslevelű, Kövérszőlő, Malozsa*, and *Muskotály*]. Although a shift in favor of certain varieties, notably *furmint*, might have been expected at the beginning of the 18th century, following the massive vineyard destruction during the last Rákóczi rebellion, there is no information by which to confirm it, especially not with regard to *furmint*.

The main explanation is that in a region the size of Hegyalja, changeovers in varieties did not occur at an equal pace throughout the region. A remarkable example is when David Szabó, in 1838, wrote about the varieties at Mád and mentioned *furmint, hárslevelű*, and *balafánt* as the only ones used in *aszú* wine production there, while *gohér, fehérszőlő*, and *muskotály* were present but of no significance. That stands in considerable contrast to what Nagyváthy said ten years earlier and Zemplén County ten years later about Hegyalja overall.

Change was quicker to take place on the large properties of major owners than in the vineyards of smallholders, but even that was not universally true if we consider that the already renowned Szarvas tract had yet to shift to *furmint* in the mid-18th century. Further, it is not apparent when commentators might have been influenced by particular informants, or even their own views about the suitability of particular varieties (in other words, 'wishful thinking' about the varietal direction of the region). For instance, it is difficult, in view of the notations made by others, to give credence to Matolay in 1744, when he said that only two varieties were used for *aszú*.

Several white varieties other than the chief ones used for botrytis wines also merit a note in connection with Hegyalja's varietal history, as follows:

1) the *kecskecsecsű*, which was once of significance in Hegyalja (see the listings of 1570, 1798, 1867, and 1893, above), equates to the Greek *aigomastos*, or 'goat-teat' [see the entry for Kecsi, in Part III];

2) the *tömjén-szőlő* ('incense-grape') likely was the *tamianka* (same meaning) of Bulgaria;

3) the *demjén* likely was the *dimiat/damiat* of southern Bulgaria (Thrace); the name originated with the *zoumiatiko* (in reference to 'juiciness') of northern Greece (Macedonia); the broadness of *demjén*'s bunches and the "chubby" roundness of its berries (Balassa) are also characteristic of *dimiat/zoumiatiko*

(O. Davides, *Elliniki Ampelologia*, Athens, 1982) [unaware of *dimiat*, Balassa thought the variety might be Italian, though he found no name resembling it amongst Italian varieties];

4) the *juhfark* ('sheep-tail') is a direct translation of Greek *provatonouros*;

5) the *tök-szőlő* ('gourd-grape') equates to the *kolokythas* of Greece.

Red Varieties: It is all too easy to overlook the onetime significance of red varieties in Hegyalja. Balassa (1991) expressed surprise at the preeminence of dark-colored varieties in early times. [See the entry for Olaszliszka, in Part II; and for Siller, in Part III.] It is not known exactly which ones were important during the 9th-15th centuries. However, Balassa lists several that must have been known widely in Hegyalja during that era: the *fekete*, or 'black,' which reminds of the many Greek cultivars with the name *mavroudi* ('blackie'), especially since Dercsényi (1796) noted its "many" variants. Likewise, the *rózsás* ('rosy') recalls the populous Greek *roditis* ('rosy') group, all the more so because Görög (1829) commented on its "strikingly beautiful color." The red *bolgár* likely was the *pamid* of southern Bulgaria and northern Greece [see the entry for *Szlankamenka*]. The dark *porcsin* seems to correspond to the *zarchin* of northwestern Bulgaria [see the entry for *Porcsin*]. Both a black and a white *ökörszemű* ('ox-eyed') existed in Hegyalja, and the name mirrors that of the red Greek *voïdomatis*, sporadically a supplemental variety for Aegean sweet wines. Also, Balassa considered Greece as an origin of the *romonya*, but concluded that it was probably from Italy, unaware that the name Roman*í*a was applied to southern Greece in the Roman era, or that the island of Zakynthos [see that entry, in Part II] was exporting a claret under the name Roman*í*a in the 16th century [Lambert-Gócs, *The Wines of Greece*].

Zemplén County legislation of 1848 still allowed six red varieties (black-muscat [see the following entry], black-*porcsin*, red-*bogár*, red-*furmint*, red-*kecskecsecsű*, *rózsás*); Szabó/Török mentioned that the *porcsin* was still of some significance in 1867; and the national legislation of 1893 permitted two red varieties at Sátoraljaújhely (*porcsin*, *rózsás*).

[For other varieties in Hegyalja history, see: Balassa (1991), pp. 115-153; and Pap (1985), pp. 25-34.]

Any review of the varietal history of Hegyalja is bound to lead to the conclusion that much light could be shed on the origins of Hegyalja wine-growing if extensive ampelographic research were to be done across national boundaries in southeastern Europe. But even without that, it seems clear that the preponderant influence in Hegyalja came by way of the Balkan lands. As with general historians of Hungary and Slovakia, Balassa discounted the extent of Balkan influence in the Upper Tisza.

Conversely, there is no sign of an early Western influence on the varietal complement of Hegyalja. Even Western settlers (Walloons, Italians, Germans) in the late Middle Ages seem not to have brought any varieties that gained esteem in Hegyalja at large, much less displaced the varieties of Balkan and Black Sea origin. Further, Balassa noted that Hegyalja stayed on its own varietal path even into the 19th century: "the great wave of grape varieties, which flowed from the West in the first-quarter of the 19th century, did not reach Tokaj-Hegyalja." The region was so far out of the Hungarian mainstream, that not one person in Zemplén County subscribed to the 1813 Hungarian translation of Chaptal's work, which included descriptions of French varieties.

In conclusion, Hegyalja's varietal history vividly underscores the fact that the Upper Tisza region had an identity of its own throughout the history of the former Kingdom of Hungary. Further, it demonstrates that Hegyalja was but an offshoot of the south-central Balkan varietal inventory.

Balassa (1991) was mystified by a passage in the law of 1655 that referred to "black and *aszú* berries" as the "most valuable." He considered that 'black' might have referred to the color of the *aszú* berries, but was not satisfied with that in view of the fact that a variety called 'black-grape' (*feketeszőlő*) was recorded in Tarcal and Tokaj in 1620. Red *aszú* wine could be made from certain varieties, as was done with *kadarka* at Ménes (now Miniş, Romania). But there is no evidence by which to suppose such a wine in Hegyalja. However, there is another aspect, though it would not clear up the situation in 1655. Balassa notes that when the National Assembly of 1807 considered the question of Hegyalja grape varieties, the *fekete muskotály* ('black muscat') "was listed amongst the best and recommended" varieties. How and when did this variety reach Hegyalja? In the area around Siatista, in Greek Macedonia, the *moskhomavro* ('musky-black') had been the basis for a most remarkable white (!) sweet wine, traditionally given up to 20 years in cask. Siatista was in the area of central Macedonia from which so many Greek traders came to Hegyalja beginning in the late-17th century, or perhaps even earlier [see the entry for Rosa, in Part I]. In that era, no law would have excluded the *moskhomavro* from being brought and planted in Hegyalja.

Gyöngyszőlő. (also as *gyöngyfejér*) Now insignificant, the *gyöngyszőlő* merits mention because in 1758 Samuel Dombi listed it, by its Latin name, *gemma*, as one of the four major varieties of Hegyalja (the others being *gohér, fehérszőlő*, and *kövérszőlő*). Oddly, this was the only time that the variety was mentioned as being so prominent. The explanation might be that Dombi was taking into account the region overall, rather than just 1st and 2nd Class vineyards or those of the nobility. In any case, the *gyöngyszőlő* had been closely associated with Hegyalja, and it was an abundant producer. It was also very sweet. But it was an early-ripening sort and did not develop botrytized berries, which probably caused it to lose favor as *furmint* gained importance. Still, it was considered a quality variety and was not excluded from Hegyalja until the wine law of 1893.

Hárslevelű. (a) The 'linden-leaf' variety has played the major supporting role to *furmint* since around the mid-19th century, and was duly specified as one of the three authorized varieties for the Hegyalja specialty botrytis wines in the national legislation of 1908. Ever after, the variety accounted for roughly one-third of plantings. Once the *furmint* became the absolutely preferred variety for botrytis wines, *hárslevelű* offered several advantages. Not only was it a good producer of *aszú* berries, it also ripened in the same time-frame as *furmint*, which was not true of its predecessors. It was also complementary to *furmint* in the vineyards, since *hárslevelű* proved very well-suited to the lower middle slopes; that is, lower down than *furmint* plantings.

Surprisingly, opinion in favor of *hárslevelű* seems to have built up very gradually, maybe even erratically. It came to Hegyalja relatively late, and almost certainly well after the introduction of botrytis *aszú* wine. Keler mentioned it in his book of 1726, and noted its suitability for yielding *aszú* berries ("*Trucken-Beer*"). Favorable mentions of *hárslevelű* were also made by Dercsényi and Szirmay around 1800. Nevertheless, the Zemplén County General Assembly subsequently ordered the removal of *hárslevelű* from the Hegyalja vineyards in 1804, and ignored it as late as 1848. This might have been prompted by concern that this relatively new variety would push aside others that until that time had been deemed the best Hegyalja grapes. In fact, *hárslevelű* eventually did replace *fehérszőlő* and *gohér* entirely. [See the Part IV Essay.]

Besides susceptibility to botrytis, an advantage of the *hárslevelű*, at least in the long run, was its scent. The variety belongs to the Pontic/Balkan group, and is semi-aromatic. Although not muscats in kind or intensity of aroma, the semi-aromatic sorts do have relatively vivid and distinctive aromatic material. *Hárslevelű* in particular was usually likened to elder-flower and elder-honey, although Dercsényi's (1796) description as "full of spice" (*fűszerszámos*) justly gives more leeway. But describe it as one might, *hárslevelű* wine won over many admirers in Poland, and not even resistance from the Zemplén County General Assembly could overcome the preference in that market, especially since most vintages yielded only normally ripened berries from which table wines were produced.

(b) The varietal name *hárslevelű* has some mystery to it. A notation of 1861 pointed out that, in contradiction to the name, the variety's leaf does not resemble that of the linden. Actually, even at that late date the variety was also known by names that alluded to other features, such as 'fish-grape' (*halszőlő*) because of bunch shape, and 'elder-flower-fragrant' (*bodzavirágszagú*) because of smell. In 1855, David Szabó noted that some people called it *hasadt-levelű* ('torn-leaf') because of a German corruption of the Hungarian *hárs*. Szabó may have been on to something. Perhaps *hasadt* had been part of the name in earlier times, maybe even *hasadt-szőlő* ('burst-grape') in reference to rotting. In medieval Hungary, the linden was a very popular tree, and some people in that era might have heard *hasadt* (HUSH-ot) as *hárs* (HAARSH).

Yet another name known for *hárslevelű* was *erdélyi*, indicating provenance from Transylvania (Erdély in Hungarian). This dovetails with the variety's Pontic/Balkan connection, and also with the fact that the town of Tokaj was situated along a major route from Transylvania to the Upper Tisza region. This would mean that *hárslevelű* was introduced from the east, and not from the Szerém wine region to the southwest (now in Serbia). In turn, that would explain why the variety bears the name *lipovina* (*lipova* = linden) among the Croats and Serbs: the reference to the linden was simply borrowed from the Hungarian name when this variety reached them.

HMF. Tokaji wines are unusual for their content of the aldehyde hydroxymethylfurfural (HMF). A spotlight was cast on this feature in the West during the communist era. HMF is usually a sign that concentrated must has been used, and since Western chemical analyses detected HMF in Tokaji, it was assumed that the Hungarians must be using concentrated must. But Hungarian enological researchers found an unusually high content of HMF occurring naturally in Tokaji because of its high content of nitrogenous compounds and sugars, which interact to yield HMF through the Maillard reaction. Further, HMF increases with the age of the wine; and the *aszú* wines traditionally received 4-8 years in barrel. Indeed, HMF had also been noticed in Tokaji before the communist era. The Dutch scientists Kniphorst and Kruisheer recorded HMF in Tokaji during research conducted from 1935 to 1937, and admitted the possibility that HMF might be intrinsic to Tokaji, rather than a result of using concentrated must or caramel coloring, both of which were prohibited by Hungarian law. However, the Ferenczi heat-treatment used during the communist era increased HMF. HMF is a minor contributor to the amberish color of traditionally matured Tokaji. [See the entries for Acetaldehyde, Furfural, and Maillard Reaction.]

Hydroxymethylfurfural. [See the previous entry.]

Imperial Tokay. The term 'Imperial Tokay' was used to refer to *aszú* wine produced on Habsburg vineyard property for use at the Imperial Court, but also, outside Hungary, as an erroneous reference to *eszencia* generally. The two tended to become identified over time in the mind of the Western connoisseur. The notion 'Imperial Tokay' came along relatively late in the history of Habsburg rule. Even though they had ruled Royal Hungary since 1541, and had vineyard properties in Hegyalja, their properties were so scattered that there could be no territorial (or '*cru*-based') notion of a 'Habsburg vineyard estate.' Only after consolidation of the Habsburg vineyards around the Szarvas tract in Tarcal, in the mid-18th century, did the Imperial vineyards have a territorial unity [see the entry for Grassalkovich, in Part I]. But even that did not mean that all Tokaji drunk at the Imperial Court was 'Imperial Tokay.' In 1839, John Paget pointedly noted that "the Emperor himself is often obliged to purchase his Tokay from others." Capping the tendency to exalt the Szarvas estate, the property acquired the title K.u.k.

Hofweinbergverwaltung zu Tarczal after the creation of the Austro-Hungarian Empire in 1867. The term 'Imperial Tokay' spread quickly thereafter.

Kabar. Authorized in 2006, this is the latest grape variety to expand the list of those that may be used in making the Hegyalja specialty wines. Since it is a cross of *hárslevelű* and *bouvier* (*chardonnay* x *silvaner*), it can be thought of as *hárslevelű*'s counterpart of *furmint*'s offspring, *zéta* [see that entry]. Besides being botrytis-prone, it is valued for its high sugar content, which owes to relatively early ripening. The name is a nod to the Kabars of early Hegyalja history [see the entry for Kabars, in Part I]. During its development, it was more prosaically called Tarcal 10.

Kosher Wine. Jewish commercial interest in Hegyalja beginning in the 18th century most likely originated from earlier acquaintance with the region as a source of wine for their communities in the Upper Tisza region and Galicia [see the entry for Jews, in Part I; and for Dukla, in Part II]. The wines were made in accordance with Jewish religious requirements, and only by Jews. However, the grapes were purchased from non-Jewish growers of the smallholder class, and processed in the rented facilities of non-Jews. But, in 1791, Zemplén County prohibited Jews from purchasing botrytized fruit for making kosher wine, lest it occur at the qualitative expensive of non-kosher *aszú* wines. Thus, the kosher wines were usually made from ordinary grapes or else, in years not propitious for botrytis, from late-harvested but non-botrytized berries. The latter, in effect, harked back to wine-making habits around 1500, when the first (semi-)sweet wines were simply late-harvest wines, possibly from shriveled grapes, but without botrytis. However, the County began backing away from the prohibition in 1819, particularly in the case of Hungarian subjects. Kosher wine production became a significant market for the grapes of Hegyalja smallholders beginning in the 19th century, as large numbers of Galician Jews starting settling in the Upper Tisza region, especially in Zemplén County (10,000 Jews in Zemplén north of Hegyalja by the mid-19th century). The kosher wines were simply carted northward by minor merchants.

Kővérszőlő. [Also see the entries for *Fehérszőlő* and *Tumidula*.] (a) This grape appears to have been one of the main white varieties in Hegyalja during the late Middle Ages. Its importance can be gauged from the fact that it was the chief variety brought by Hegyaljan vine-dressers who were settled in the Cotnari region of Moldavia in the 15th century, with the intention of making white wine similar to that of Hegyalja. Because of late ripening, it was in all likelihood the variety that first led to later-harvested white wines in Hegyalja, towards 1500, when later harvesting began. Owing to its susceptibility to noble rot, it must also have been the main source of *főbor* when it was becoming more dependent on botrytized grapes, and certainly critical to the establishment of botrytis wine as Hegyalja's signature product. This was mirrored at Cotnari. The *kövérszőlő* apparently had some importance until the middle of the 18th century, but confusion between it and the *fehérszőlő* seems to have caused it to recede thereafter. There is no indication of a later presence in Hegyalja, or at least not in any quantity or under that name. But, in a historical irony, the *kövérszőlő* became an object of interest to Hungarian viti-vinicultural researchers during the communist period because of its sugar content and strong propensity for botrytization. This interest continued into the post-communist era among some growers, and in 1998 resulted in the variety being authorized for use in making Hegyalja botrytis wines. However, the new *zéta* variety approximates the chief advantages of the *kővérszőlő*, and consequently, it is questionable whether the latter will stage a significant comeback.

(b) The name *kövérszőlő* means 'stout/fat grape' (in Cotnari it became *grasă*, or 'fat'). Its history in Hegyalja is obscured because use of that name seems to have disappeared there during the 16th century, excepting, possibly, the use of the Latin equivalent *tumidula* once in 1758 [see that entry, below]. It seems that, somehow, the name *fehérszőlő* came to be used for the *kővérszőlő* as well as for the actual *fehérszőlő*, presumably because of a similarity seen by growers. But the historical commentary relating to Hegyalja does not support an identity of the two. Notably, skin color and propensity for botrytization differ. The greenish-yellow color of the *kövérszőlő* differs from that of the white-green of the *fehérszőlő*; and Szirmay (1798) wrote that the latter does *not* host botrytis, which is hardly the case for the *kövérszőlő*. This confusion in varietal terminology might account for Görög, in 1829, and Légrády, in 1844, mentioning the flesh of *fehérszőlő aszú* berries as "greasy" (*zsíros*), which is the connotation of the Romanian name *grasă*. [See the entry for Schams, in Part I.]

Legislation. [See the entries for *Puttonyos* System and Regulation; and for Zemplén County, in Part II.]

Lőre. Although an ancient Latin term (*lora*), Balassa (1991) considered that the Hegyaljans picked it up from Germans, not from Italian settlers or from ancient Latin literature. It was originally used to designate a small wine for field hands, made by fermenting a mixture of water and the marc of ordinary wine. But variations developed, notably *fő-lőre* (head-*lőre*), in which *aszú* marc was substituted; and *máslás-lőre*, in which the remains from *máslás* production were used [see the entry for *Máslás*]. [Also, see the mention of *olaszbor*, in the entry for Italians, in Part I.]

Maillard Reaction. This term refers to a specific and peculiar type of 'browning,' namely, a chemical process in which amino acids act on sugars, so that the sugars are 'browned' in color, aroma and flavor without either oxidation or heating, which are the usual causes of browning in comestibles. Since Tokaji contains an unusually high content of nitrogenous compounds, the Maillard reaction proceeds extensively when the wine is matured for several years, as in the traditional method. Accordingly, the reaction has an influence on the character of such Tokaji wine ("Maillard reaction products are known to develop specific aromas or odors." Johnson/ Peterson, 1974, p. 25.) Hungarian enological research of 2000 indicated that the Maillard reaction also contributes to high content of phenols and antioxidants in *aszú* wines. (Nikfardjam, 2002)

During the communist era, lack of knowledge about Tokaji's nitrogenous compounds and the Maillard reaction among Western wine commentators led to the erroneous attribution of all browning manifestations in Tokaji to concentrated must and/or pasteurization. Although some contemporary enophiles might view browning as detracting from *terroir*, the peculiar susceptibility of Tokaji to undergo the Maillard reaction, *precisely because of* its innate chemical nature, clearly is a uniquely innate 'secondary' manifestation of the Hegyalja *terroir*. It is, though, necessarily a 'delayed' manifestation, not one that comes about soon after vinification. [See the entry for Tokaji Character.]

Malozsa. a) At one time, a white grape variety known as *malozsa* (or *malosa*) was grown in Hegyalja to a minor extent. This might have dated to the 15th century or earlier, and it continued into the early-19th century. It was a very sweet grape, supposedly linked to the renowned Malvasia wines of Greece. It is possible that the corruption of the name from *malvasia* to *malozsa* occurred because of the Greek white variety *malagouzia*, which was also called *malouzia* and *malaouzia*. (The Greek name places the accent on the last syllable. This suggests imitation of *monemvasia*, the original Greek name for Malvasia wine, and the name of one of the semi-aromatic grape varieties associated with it.) However, the *malozsa* was usually grown in Hegyalja as a table grape, and any attraction it had for wine-growers was thoroughly undermined by the *hárslevelű* during the 19th century. [Also, see the entry for *Gohér*; and for Dalmatia, in Part II.]

b) The Malvasia name was also borrowed for a specific kind of wine. Malvasia's influence may have come through the earlier Szerémség tradition, when that tradition 'relocated' to Hegyalja after the Ottoman occupation of Lower Hungary. But it could have been even earlier because of

Malvasia's fame, and exports of it to Poland through Hegyalja by Greek traders. The Malvasia tradition would explain the Hegyalja practice of letting grapes reach an over-ripe state on the vine, including some shriveling, rather than being spread in the sun after harvesting. [See the entry for *Aszú*: Aegean Echo; and the Part IV Essay.] In Greece, the original practice had been to let the grapes become super-mature on the vine, mainly by letting Malvasia-appropriate early-ripening varieties hang until a late harvesting date. (However, since white Malvasias were always made from two or more varieties, certain of the minor varieties included were semi-dried after harvesting to augment their sugar content and aroma.) In fact, it was mostly this practice that differentiated the Malvasias from the sweeter Greek wines called *liasto* ('sunned'), not to mention the ultra-sweet *visanto* (anciently *diakhyton*) of Santorini. Hegyalja's *malozsa* wines, too, were from super-mature grapes of varieties that ripened earlier than the *furmint* of later Tokaji history.

Máslás. The oldest by-product botrytis wine of Hegyalja, 'duplicate' wine is a lesser-quality botrytis wine – but a superior table wine – made from a mixture of non-botrytis wine and the lees of either *aszú* or *szamorodni* wine. The former is poured over the latter, allowed to soak a sufficient number of hours to extract remaining sugar and aromatic material, and then pressed and fermented. The 'duplication' lies in having obtained a wine bearing a certain resemblance to *aszú* and *szamorodni*, and the more so the better the quality of the poured wine and the wine that provided the lees. Historically, *máslás* reflected an effort not just to use the botrytis vintage to maximum advantage, but also to satisfy the very substantial market that existed for wine of that name in Poland. Although given legal definition in 1936, *máslás*, like *fordítás*, disappeared as a commercial wine name during the communist period, though it continued to enter commerce by being used in making *édes* (sweet) *szamorodni*. [See the entry for *Fordítás*.]

Contrary to the impression of long-standing clarity about the meaning of *máslás*, the term's history is in fact unusually checkered. As late as as 1570, it was used rather like the name *lőre* [see that entry], as a general designation for weak, watery wine. But the term took a step up in quality connotation thereafter, for application to wine that resulted from pouring good ordinary wine over the lees of *főbor* (the predecessor of *szamorodni*). Even so, *máslás* was still a 'lees wine.' By the early-18th century, though, it had also become a 'marc wine,' made by pouring must or common wine over the marc of *aszú*. This continued to be a common understanding of *máslás* well into the 19th century, even though it was being replaced by the term *fordítás* to refer to the marc wine from either *aszú* or *szamorodni*.

Poland was not only the greatest market for any wine called *máslás* after the inception of later-harvested wines in Hegyalja. It also compounded the nomenclatural confusion. By at least the 18th century, wine merchants in Poland were pouring ordinary wine (whether or not from Hegyalja) over the lees left in barrels of Tokaji *aszú* wines, and then marketing it as *máslás*, but with indication of the *puttonyos*-level of the particular *aszú* wine. This led to the term *aszú-máslás*. The tendency to equate *máslás* with the lower *puttonyos*-levels (1-, 2-, 3-) of *aszú* wine became common even in Hegyalja because of the strong Polish commercial influence. But this usage fell off during the 19th century, when Poles increasingly preferred *szamorodni*, and the term *fordítás* came into use for 'marc wine.' *Máslás* then recovered its earlier meaning as a 'lees wine' distinct from *fordítás*, and was so defined in the legislation of 1936.

Máslás: In Other Words

There is no satisfying translation for *máslás*. The Poles did not even bother trying; they simply gave it a Polish 'accent' (*maślacz*). Alkonyi's (2000) translator gave it as 'copy wine,' but it has been translated herein as 'duplicate wine,' so as to emphasize 'double,' since *más* in Hungarian means 'other' and *másod-* indicates 'second.' But these terms leave a lot to be desired. For that matter, so does *máslás* itself. All imply 'replica wine' or 'facsimile wine,' and that is a far cry from what results from pouring must or wine over the remains of a previously made wine, no matter how hard it is squeezed. This problem gets into the question of whether there could be *any* adequate 'enological' term for it. Maybe we need to borrow from other fields: literary – 'shadow' *szamorodni*; theatrical – 'stand-in' *szamorodni*; psychology – 'alter-ego' *szamorodni*. Or, how about something just plain plebeian, such as 'mime-wine'?

Másod-aszú. [See the entry for *Fordítás.*]
Maturation-time. [See the entry for Barrel Aging.]

Muskotály. (*Sárga Muskotály*) (a) One of the three authorized varieties for the Tokaji specialty wines in the legislation of 1908, the yellow (*sárga*) 'muscat lunel' is valued above all for its aromatic contribution. However, this contribution is necessarily of considerable subtlety, as the variety occupies barely three percent of the planted area in Hegyalja, as has been the case for centuries. Nothing substantial is known about the decision in its favor, except that it was regarded as a slight flavor enhancer. Gas chromatography has shown that the muscat smell overlaps coriander seed; hence, it can be understood why *muskotály* was treated almost like adding a spice to the botrytis wines. Presumably, its qualities were first appreciated by the nobility, who were probably impressed as well by the variety's ancient pedigree. It is clear from the small amount of *muskotály* planted in past centuries that the Hegyaljans never had in mind to become a competitor in the market for Muscat wines. However, during the late-19th century, it became fashionable amongst wealthy growers with multiple vineyards to make *muskotályos aszú* (muscat-*aszú*) wines in years of extensive botrytization. Such wines enjoyed a miniscule but lucrative market ever after, and thus were made even during the communist era.

(b) There is no mystery about the *muskotály*. It has indeed been around since antiquity, when the Greeks knew it by the name *psithian* (ψίθιος) and the Romans by the name *apiana*, both in reference to the marked aroma (the name *apiana* alluded to the observation that bees liked it). Pliny (*Natural History*) described it as having "a peculiar flavour which is not that of wine" (though that may depend on one's thoughts about coriander seed). This is also why the older names eventually were replaced by ones referring to 'musk.' The muscat was always associated mostly with Greece. For instance, early French ampelographers recorded as *muscat de Corfou* the variety that their more nationalistic successors dubbed *muscat de Frontignan*. But, while the variety's path westward through the Mediterranean is obvious and very old, its journey northward into Central Europe is unclear. It could have arrived by way of Dalmatia in the Middle Ages, or else had come earlier from the Aegean area. In any case, it was in Hungary under the name muscat by the end of the 14th century, and in Hegyalja by the 16th century.

Muskotály may have had a varietal forerunner in Hegyalja. A notation from 1730 mentions the "*tömjénszőlő* (thurea)" variety, or 'incense-grape.' This equates to the Bulgaro-Slav name *tamianka* used for grapes of muscat type. [See the entry for Grape Varieties, above; and for Talyanka, in Part III]. It suggests that the *muskotály* had been in the region under a different name, a name coming from the Balkan lands to the south. This could have dated as far back as the Bulgaro-Slavs who were brought to Hegyalja from the vicinity of Thessaloniki in the 9th century.

Nectar. Although it was an alternative name for *eszencia* among Hungarians in the past, the term 'nectar' (*nektár*) is not well-documented. Balassa (1991) thought it must have come into use in the late-18th century, and had primarily a literary usage, more so than as a colloquialism. He pointed out, for instance, that it was the term used by Francis Kölcsey in 1823 when including mention of Tokaji in writing what became the Hungarian national anthem [see the entry for Kölcsey, in Part I]. But a case can be made that Hegyaljans might have been using the term colloquially over a century earlier, even though the term *eszencia* had been adopted, and adapted ('latinized'), from the Hungarian-German term *essentz*, for commercial purposes. In 1842, *eszencia* was remarked as the "wine differentiated by the long-standing name of nectar." In 1798, a Zemplén decree referred to "the *so called* Essentia" (emphasis added), which suggests that another name for it had been in common use. That other name would only have been 'nectar.'

Nectar: Macedonian Bequest?

Balassa intimated that the educated nobility of Hegyalja must have lifted 'nectar' out of an ancient Latin or Greek literary work. But this is not necessarily so. It is quite possible that it was taken right out of the mouths of the Macedonian Greek merchants who had come to the region in the 17th century. Of course, the survival of ancient terms among the Greeks of the modern era was spotty. For instance, the term *protropon* [see that entry] disappeared even though the technique for making it did not. But 'nectar' had survived. Indeed, in his book of 1717 – note that date relative to the history of *eszencia* – the French traveler Joseph Tournefort found that the term was still being used as the proper name (*i.e.*, Νέκταρ/Nectar) for a particular wine on the island of Chios, which had been famous for its wines, including a sweet one, since antiquity (*Relation d'un voyage du Levant*). To this, it need only be added that the sweet wine of Chios was one of the wines that Macedonian Greek merchants, such as those in Hegyalja, had earlier been exporting to Poland. [See the entry for Chios, in Part II.]

Nitrogenous Compounds. A characteristic of Tokaji wine is its high content of nitrogenous compounds (Kádár, 1973). Hungarian wines generally surpass other European wines in this respect, but Tokaji exhibits levels well above the Hungarian average. This makes the specialty wines very susceptible to production of HMF through the Maillard reaction. [See the entries for De-amination, HMF, and Maillard Reaction.]

Noble Rot. [See the entry for Botrytis.]

Ó-Aszú. 'Old' (*ó*) *aszú* was a vinous curiosity that began to be marketed in bottle under that name in the late-19th century. Of course, the Tokaji speciality wines were 'old' in the sense of having been aged to maturity for 4-10 years in barrel, and 'old' vintages of bottled wine could be found in merchants' cellars. But *ó-aszú* was distinguished by having been purposely kept in barrel so long that its sugar had fermented out to virtual dryness. It enjoyed a cachet among a small number of Hegyalja clientele, mostly in Poland, but died out in the early-20th century, partly because it was increasingly viewed by Hungarian professionals as an aberration.

Olaszbor. [See the entry for Italians, in Part I.]
Omfakitis. [See #2 in the entry for Balkan Influences; and the entry for *Főbor*.]

Ordinárium. After later-harvested wines became the standard-bearer of Hegyalja, wines produced from grapes that were not harvested in a shriveled state were referred to by the Latin term *ordinárium*. Thus, Pap (1985) found that the term did not come into use until around 1600. In any case, these 'regular' wines, or wines made 'in the ordinary way,' were produced in every vintage and were the commercial mainstay of Hegyalja until into the 18th century [see the entry for Gyöngyösi, in Part I]. Surpluses of them were a reason for fermenting *aszú*-dough in wine, instead of in must, in making *aszú* wines, and for expanding output of better *máslás* wines.

Balassa (1991) found the term *ordinárium* on its way out of usage by the early-19th century, although Schams used it as late as 1832. By that time, though, it was usually expected that an *ordinárium* had been made in part with shriveled grapes, and even botrytized ones in the case of botrytis vintages. Poland took ever more interest in such wine the more that shriveled grapes became integral to it. This evolution in the term set the stage for *szamorodni*, a wine that was necessarily based on botrytis. In short, *ordinárium* was a major factor in holding the Polish market during a generally difficult period for Hegyalja wine due to Habsburg and other European trade policies, as well as market-dampening political developments in Poland.

Szamorodni, though, effectively consigned this old-fashioned term to the dust-bin. A good reference date is 1867, the year of the *Tokaj-Hegyaljai Album*, which discussed *szamorodni*, but not *ordinárium*. By the end of the century, if the latter term was used at all, it was in its earliest sense, as just a table wine. Consequently, in the 20th century it was completely replaced by *pecsenye bor*, or 'roast wine,' to refer to high-quality dry table wine suitable for the desired Sunday meal of roast meat (*pecsenye*). [See the entry for Wine-delicacy.]

Oxidative aging. [See the entries for Barrel Aging, *Darabbantartás*, Redox-potential, and Yeast Film.]
Pasteurization. [See the entry for Ferenczi heat-treatment.]
Pecsenye Bor. [See the entry for *Ordinárium*.]

Phenols. One of the distinctive features of Tokaji botrytis wines is their high content of phenols. Phenol content in wine has gained interest because it raises the quantity of antioxidants [see that entry], but it is almost exclusively associated with red wine, not merely because of red skin color but also because of long skin contact with the must during maceration. For white wine, the skins are usually removed, but in vinifying the botrytized white grapes for Tokaji *aszú* they are mashed as whole grapes and then soaked in must or wine for 12-48 hours, which yields a relatively high content of phenolic substances. Analysis in 2000 of several 1998 and 1999 *aszú* wines of 5- and 6-*puttonyos* level showed a phenol content in the range of 537 to 1,725 mg/l (averaging 886 mg/l), although values above 800 mg/l had never previously been reported for white wines and were considered strictly the province of red wines. (Nikfardjam, 2000)

Results from both 2000 and 1976 demonstrated that the specifics of phenol content may vary with vintage, soaking time, and maturation, as reflected in differential gains and losses among individual phenolic acids. The 2000 results showed generally predominant amounts of coutaric and caftaric acid in 5-*puttonyos aszú* wines from the 1990s, with differences in quantity being attributed mainly to vintage and vinification factors. However, it may be worth noting as one of Tokaji's identity marks that a greater amount of coutaric than caftaric acid was found in all samples, compared to the reverse relationship recorded in chemical analyses that have been reported for some other wines, both white and red.

In 1976, gas chromatography analysis of 1963 5-*puttonyos* and 6-*puttonyos aszú* wines did not find coutaric and caftaric acids, while two other phenol compounds were detected that were not reported in the counterpart wines from the 1990s: the anti-carcinogen ellagic acid, and scopoletin, which has proved effective in helping to reduce blood pressure. The 1963 wine also showed more of the antioxidant gallic acid than did those from the 1990s. The 1976 research attributed the presence of these phenols to *aszú* wine's ability to extract lignins and hydrolysable tannins from oak as it ages in the small *gönci* barrel. Hence, too, the older 1963 5-*puttonyos aszú* that had been fully matured in barrel before bottling contained significantly more scopoletin, gallic acid, and o-coumaric acid (another antioxidant) than the 1973 6-*puttonyos aszú*, which had not completed its barrel maturation at the time of the 1976 research/analysis. (Kerényi, 1976)

Another aspect of the phenols is that, while the individual constituents are not detectable as such on the palate, their overall content in Tokaji does have a palpable manifestation in flavor, namely, a hint of astringency (as in, say, dark chocolate), which may vaguely recall the tannic feel of a red wine. In the best vintages, this is underscored by acidity while simultaneously countered by sweetness and, with appropriate aging, umami [see the latter entry].

Phylloxera. The greatest calamity in Hegyalja history since the Tatar invasion of 1241-1242, the invasion of this dreaded vine pest began in 1885. Between that year and 1890, the vineyard area under cultivation dropped precipitously. Precise figures vary, perhaps depending on which villages were included, but in any case, less than one-fifth, and perhaps as little as one-sixth, of the pre-phylloxera area survived, or less than 1,000 hectares (2,470 acres); Keleti's data showed about 5,700 hectares (14,080 acres) for 1873. In his account of 1903, Kossuth stated that "we can say that the reconstruction of Tokajhegyalja is 3/4 complete," an estimate that perhaps was a bit high. In any case, there was a notable qualitative improvement in many of the reconstructed vineyards, due to the adoption of contemporary viticultural principles. Further, only a very small part of the renewed tracts consisted of direct-producing American varieties, as opposed to the old varieties grafted onto American root-stocks. [See the entries for Kosinszky and J. Szabó, in Part I.]

A lasting setback caused by phylloxera was the abandonment of some excellent south-facing sites at higher elevations. This was caused in part by prudence, because it had been noticed that the lower slopes in general had fared much better against phylloxera, and especially the loess areas that were more typical of the lower and middle slopes along the important southern line of Hegyalja, from Mezőzombor through Tarcal and Tokaj. Additionally, the reconstruction of the higher areas was hampered by large-scale overseas emigration, not only of Hegyalja smallholders, but also of laborers (primarily Slovaks and Rusyns) from further north who had relied on the seasonal income they earned in the region. But despite the setbacks and changes, the Hegyalja growers, as noted by Kossuth, found that wine quality in the post-phylloxera era had not suffered a general deterioration. [See the entry for J. Kossuth, in Part I.]

Porcsin. (also as *purcsin*) (a) This dark grape variety had a long history in Hegyalja, from at least the 15th century until the late-19th century. Because of the frequency of its mention in listings of Hegyalja's varietal inventory, it was almost certainly a basis for the region's old tradition of producing red and black wines. Even though it is not of particularly high quality on its own, it can make a positive contribution in combination with other varieties. Balassa (1991) mentions a curious story (undocumented), according to which Szepsi made his first *aszú* in 1608 using *porcsin* grown in the Oremus vineyard-tract in Sátoraljaújhely. While Balassa notes that this hardly seems possible given that the *porcsin* is not prone even to shriveling, it is nevertheless a somewhat late-ripening variety whose free-run, white-colored must or wine could have been used as the liquid in which to soak the botrytized fruit of white varieties [see the entry for Furmint, in Part III]. The story might simply have become garbled over time.

(b) Hungarian ampelographers of course have not put much effort into researching the now obscure *porcsin* (pronounced POR-chin), while the older literature on Hegyalja sometimes assumes that the variety may have come from Italy because it seems to bear the Italian word for a mushroom. But the story is more complex, and seems to reflect the ancient past of Hegyalja. The old descriptions and notations about the *porcsin* (as related by Balassa) are remarkably reminiscent of the old *zarchin* (зарчин) variety indigenous to northwestern Bulgaria, *e.g.*, blackish color, tight grape-clusters, round berries, very tough skin, very sweet, resistance to rotting [see A. Timov, L. Timova, *Zarchin*, Sofia: Bulgarian Academy of Sciences, 1966]. The *zarchin* (pronounced ZAR-chin) is also known colloquially as *darchin*, which is even closer to 'por-chin' in sound. In light of such information, it can be wondered whether Italians who settled in Hegyalja altered a Balkan name to approximate a word they knew. That is, they might not have brought the variety from Italy, but at most lent an Italian name to a pre-existing variety (Balassa found no Italian grape with a name approximating *porcsin*).

Protropon. In connection with the *eszencia* of Hegyalja, it is clear that the ancient Greek wine known as protropon (πρότροπον) was a reference point, although it is unknown for whom, since the date and place of the first *eszencia* remains a mystery. The central feature of *protropon* was that the self-expressed juice of over-ripened grapes was allowed to ferment on its own, sometimes to a wine of low alcoholic degree. This technique might have come to the attention of a few educated Hegyalja owners by around 1600. For instance, Szepsi, who read Latin, might have learned of it by reading ancient authors. However, there is no actual indication of *eszencia* before around 1700. Since the *protropon* technique was still known to some wine-traders in Greece at that time, it also has to be taken into consideration that it might have been demonstrated by Greek merchants resident in Tokaj. The Greeks certainly knew that wine of this type was useful for improving other wines. [See the two entries for Nectar; and #11 in the entry for Balkan Influences.]

Punchification. This Anglicization is used here in place of the old colloquial Hungarian term *pancsolás*, which actually derived from the word 'punch.' It was a derogatory description for altering the nature of Tokaji wine by mixing it with anything else, whether wines from elsewhere or products from sources other than the vine, or most of all, by boosting alcohol content with the addition of brandy. The term increasingly came into use during the 19th century because of dishonest commercial practices, especially the utter falsification of Tokaji wine by relying on wines from outside Hegyalja to achieve desired quantities. Punchification was a major factor behind the strict Hungarian regulations of Tokaji enacted in 1893 and 1908, and memory of it was a factor in delaying until 1936 the adoption of a regulation that allowed a scientific method of stabilizing Tokaji by minimal use of grape-spirits [see the entry for Fortification].

Puttony. [See the following entry.]

Puttonyos **System.** The term *puttonyos* became the foundation for grading the levels of sweetness in *aszú* wines. It grew out of the habit of collecting the botrytized grapes in the wooden container known as a *puttony* ('butt'), which had a capacity of 28-30 liters (7.5-7.9 gallons). The *puttonyos*-level of the wine was determined by how many butts of botrytized grapes (in the form of *aszú*-dough) were 'soaked' in 136-140 liters (36-37 gallons) of must or wine [see the entry for Soaking]. Usually, this would be 3, 4, or 5 *puttony*-s. Two factors determined *puttonyos* level. First, there was the relative abundance or scarceness of botrytized grapes in a given vintage, or generally, the quality of the vintage. Second, there was consideration of taste preferences and price acceptability among customers in specific markets. These two factors also influenced the use of *eszencia* as a corrective for sweetness and flavor.

The time period during which the *puttonyos* system developed is not known. The fact that a 4-*puttonyos* wine was in Poland in 1646 proves that it was in use during the first-half of the 17th century, and indeed was already a typical way of marketing Tokaji *aszú* by that time. This in turn suggests that the system might have pre-dated the botrytis wines and was developed during the preceding period when *aszú* wines from shriveled (but non-botrytized) grapes began to be produced. Since both the *puttony* and the *gönci* barrel were being used in Hegyalja by the second-half of the 16th century, it might be that the *puttonyos* system came into use around that time. But it did not immediately become the sole way of indicating quality. A document of 1735 inventoried the estate of the late administrator of the Ungvár Domain [see the entry for Uzhhorod, in Part II] and recorded his stocks of *aszú* wines simply by three quality classes: first - *primae classis seu praestantissimae*; second - *classis secundae seu mediocris*; and third - *classis tertiae seu infirmae* (UC 105:6).

Nor was the *puttonyos* system ever an absolute indicator of quality. It was long observed that a 4-*puttonyos aszú* from a superior botrytis vintage could surpass a 5-*puttonyos aszú* from a lesser one, etc. This continued to hold true, but the parameters for disparity amongst wines of the same *puttonyos* level from different vintages were reduced by a law of 1924 that replaced measurement by actual *puttony*-s with legally specified minimum levels of sugar and total extract content per liter. Lest sugar comprise too much of total extract content, the parameters were further narrowed by a law of 1936, in which minimum sugar levels remained the same, but total extract content was replaced by minimum non-sugar extract content per liter, as follows:

1- or 2-*puttonyos aszú*: at least 30 grams of natural sugar and 25 grams of non-sugar extract
3-*puttonyos aszú*: at least 60 grams of natural sugar and 30 grams of non-sugar extract
4-*puttonyos aszú*: at least 90 grams of natural sugar and 35 grams of non-sugar extract
5-*puttonyos aszú*: at least 120 grams of natural sugar and 40 grams of non-sugar extract
6-*puttonyos aszú*: at least 150 grams of natural sugar and 45 grams of non-sugar extract

The requirements specified in 1936 were repeated in a communist-era law of 1959, except that 1-*puttonyos aszú* was eliminated. For that matter, in actual practice, 2-*puttonyos aszú* also ceased to be produced in large-scale commercial trade, since it had in effect been replaced by sweet *szamorodni* wine. However, 2-*puttonyos aszú* hung on amongst smallholder vintners, and also in general commercial production in the Slovakian corner of Hegyalja.

Redox-potential. One of the most remarkable features of Tokaji pertains to the enological measure known as redox-potential. The name 'redox' refers to the antithetical processes of 'reduction' (*red-*), which is wine maturation in the relative absence of oxygen, and 'oxidation' (*-ox*), which is wine maturation with exposure to oxygen. Redox-potential is stated in terms of 'rH-value' and usually ranges from 14 to 24. A high rH-value typically indicates that the wine has been matured by an oxidative technique, which means that further exposure to oxygen will not enhance the wine. Conversely, a low rH-value indicates a 'reductive wine,' or one that has potential for further beneficial contact with oxygen.

Traditionally matured Tokaji is exceptional in being aged by an oxidative technique, yet emerging with a low rH-value, like that of a reductive wine: in studies, "the rH-value of the *aszú* wines throughout their storage and maturation was low, around 14-15 rH, which although a surprising occurrence, demonstrates that Tokaji *aszú* wine is truly a completely unique wine-specialty, since this property sharply differentiates it from the partially similar Xeres, Port, Sherry, Madeira type wines, which are characterized precisely by their high redox-potential, rH-value" (Ferenczi, 1966). This quality of the *aszú* wines, in comparison with Port, etc., is thought to begin with the formation of reductive material during the process of botrytization; to be increased by the phenols acquired in the 'soaking' process; and finally, to be enhanced during maturation because of the yeast film and the cool cellar conditions. [See the entries for *Darabbantartás*, Phenols, and Yeast Film.]

Regulation. Tokaji wine has been the subject of regulations since the Rákóczi era in the mid-17th century. Of special note with regard to wine-making was a Zemplén County ordinance of 1655 that required the separate harvesting of botrytized berries. However, it was only in the post-phylloxera period that national legislation was promulgated to safeguard the authenticity, character, and quality of Tokaji. At that time, the reputation of Tokaji was being threatened by bogus products. The first national law on wine was promulgated in 1893, and is notable for treating the Tokaji wines apart from the production of other sweet wines in not allowing the use of partially raisined grapes or spirits. Under the 1893 law, seven white grape varieties were permitted in Hegyalja, plus several other varieties, including two red ones, at Sátoraljaújhely. But a law of 1896, which was aimed at improving quality in the course of the reconstruction following phylloxera, reduced the permissible Hegyalja varieties for wine to three white ones: *furmint*, *hárslevelű*, and *sárga muskotály*. However, none of these measures could stop the production and sale of bogus Tokaji. In 1904, the Ministry of Commerce forbade the blending of

Tokaji wine with any other wine, and this restriction was included in the revised wine law of 1908, except that blending could take place outside Hegyalja as long as the resultant wine was marketed without any indication of an origin in Hegyalja. In connection with Hegyalja origin, the 1908 law is known especially for demarcating the region by including only the *hillside* vineyard areas of 31 communes. [Also, see the entry for Zemplén County, in Part II.]

The law of 1893 had proscribed the use of sugar in producing Tokaji, and in 1908 this prohibition was extended to concentrated must as well. However, the preservation of the natural sugar content in Tokaji had remained a concern because of the threat of re-fermentation; and consequently, to ensure that content, a regulation of 1936 allowed the addition of wine spirits of no less than 92-percent alcohol in volume, but only in an amount up to 4-percent of total volume, with the wine's total volume of alcohol not to exceed 18.5-percent [see the entry for Fortification]. The regulation also established specific sugar and non-sugar extract content for each of the botrytis wines [see the entry for *Puttonyos* System]. Further, it required that all Tokaji wines must enter commerce with a state control band, and that to do so the wines must be submitted for testing to the appropriate authorities in Hegyalja for chemical analysis [see the entry for National Wine-Qualifying Institute, in Part I]. The major law on wine during the communist era was that of 1959, which again treated Tokaji apart, and mostly was a reiteration of the foregoing laws. It still allowed the use of spirits, except that the total volume of alcohol in the wine could not exceed 16.5 percent; subsequently, the total addition was also reduced from 4 to 3 percent of total volume. But the addition of alcohol was barred in 1980 because other methods had been developed for preventing re-fermentation and the resultant loss of natural sugar.

Resveratrol. Among antioxidants not particularly associated with phenols, Tokaji botrytis wines contain resveratrol derivatives (trans- and cis-resveratrol, and trans- and cis-piceid), a flavonoid group tentatively linked, on the basis of *in vitro* research, to the prevention of cancer and dementia. The amounts of resveratrol derivatives found in Tokaji during cooperative Hungarian/German enological research exceeded those in the German botrytis wines analyzed, and also the amounts that have been recorded in studies of non-botrytis white wines produced by reductive (non-oxidative) techniques, and even some red wines, *e.g.*, Beaujolais and some French and Californian cabernets and merlots (Nikfardjam, 2002). Tokaji's content of resveratrol derivatives appears to be linked to the long 'soaking' of *aszú*-dough [see the entry for Soaking].

Slovakian Tokaji (Tokajské). The production of Tokaji wine in Slovakia had been an issue for Hungarian wine authorities for decades, and became a front-burner one after the end of communism in 1989. It is perhaps a unique circumstance that a well-defined, 'integral' wine region should be divided by a state border (and perhaps also testimony that wine-appellation regions carry no weight whatsoever among statesmen working on territorial partitions). But this has been the case with Hegyalja since 1918, when the Austro-Hungarian Empire was dismantled and its territory redistributed to new states. Three northeastern locales of Hegyalja were separated from Hungary and allocated to what would become the Slovakian portion of the appellation region [see the entry for Slovakia, in Part II]. This did not immediately entail any divergence from the production of Tokaji per the Hungarian law of 1908. Further, there was a tendency for the few Slovakian producers (all of whom were Hungarian-speakers) to keep up with developments in Hegyalja. Additionally, the area was again in Hungary during 1938-1944.

But divergences occurred later, as intensive research went forward in Hungary, whereas in Slovakia it tended to stagnate, especially as regards the enological aspects of Tokaji production. Notable in the communist period was the inclusion of grape varieties other than *furmint*, *hárslevelű* (*lipovina* in Slovak), and *sárga muskotály* (*muškát žltý*). Along with those, *leányka* (*dievčie hrozno*), Italian riesling (*rizling vlašský*), and *gewürztraminer* (*tramín*) made up about 10 percent of the grapes used for the botrytis wines, although these three did not produce botrytized grapes, and thus were only usable for must or wine in which to ferment botrytized grapes. Another feature of Slovakian Tokajské has been the continued production of 2-*puttonyos aszú*, which disappeared from the Hungarian commercial roster of *aszú* wines. As a final note, Slovakia in the communist era used the same aging techniques as in Hungary and pre-communist Slovakia. Thus, Blaha (1952) noted Tokaji as being "of dark-yellow, amberish color."

The Slovakian terms for the botrytis wines are: *výber* = *aszú*; *putňové* = *puttonyos*; and *samorodné* = *szamorodni*; *suché* = dry; *sladké* = sweet; *druhák* (colloquial) = *máslás*.

Soaking. (*Áztatás*) (a) One of the most singular aspects of Hegyalja wine-making is the practice of 'soaking' the *aszú*-dough (skins, stems, seeds, and pulp of botrytized berries mashed together) in the liquid of non-botrytized fruit, whether must or wine. As a characteristic regional habit, it is definitely older than the *darabbantartas* method of aging. However, how much older is uncertain. For instance, it is not known whether it was already being done when the region first started producing later-harvested white wines around 1500. However, it does appear to be an indigenous technique, definitely unknown in other Hungarian regions. Most notably, there is no information to suggest that such a technique was being used to make the Szerém wines that Tokaji replaced on the Polish market in the 16th century. Yet, soaking would appear to be a variation on antique wine-making habits from Thrace and Macedonia that were brought to Hegyalja in the Middle Ages by the Bulgaro-Slavs who dominated the Upper Tisza region of the later Kingdom of Hungary [see #7 in the entry for Balkan Influences; and the entries for Bulgarian Empire, and Macedonia, in Part II]. The antiquity of the notion is shown by one of Columella's prescriptions for making sweet wine in his *De Re Rustica* [see the entry for Columella, in Part I].

The purpose of soaking is to draw out all the rich properties in the mass of botrytized berries, particularly the sugar and non-sugar extract material (although the literal meaning of *áztatás* is 'soaking,' in this figurative sense it is perhaps more at 'steeping'). During the process, the vat is closed, but the solids are stirred from time to time, and the seeds are removed as they float to the surface. Hungarian sources show that soaking time has never been uniform, and certainly not from one botrytis vintage to another, but practically always with more time for *aszú* than for *szamorodni*, as follows:

Year (Source)	Aszú	Szamorodni
1808-1813 (Pethe)	"usually 24 hours"	[not yet a habitual wine type]
1810 (Szirmay)	"48 hours is always enough"	[not yet a habitual wine type]
1867 (Szabó/Török)	12-48 hours	"several hours"
1903 (Kossuth)	"usually" 6-8 hours	"about 6 hours (sometimes more)"
1914 (Spotkovszky)	10-14 hours	6-8 hours
1937 (Pettenkoffer)	"at least" 12 hours	6-12 hours
1948 (Requinyi)	8-24 hours	6-10 hours
1956 (Soós)	12-36 hours	6-12 hours
1959 (Rakcsányi)	12-36 hours	6-12 hours
1963 (Nagy)	12-48 hours	"several hours"
1973 (Kádár)	12-24 hours, but up to 36	implies 12 as usual
1973 (Farkaš)	24-36 hours	12-24 hours
1974 (Brezovcsik)	6-12 hours, but up to 24	as little as 6 hours
1977 (Mercz)	12-36 hours	4-8 hours
1985 (Pap)	12-48 hours	6-8 hours

Historically, it seems that even longer immersion periods might have been used for *aszú*. Balassa quoted a notation of 1791 that allowed for as long as three days (72 hours).

Vintage circumstances required flexibility as to the length of soaking time. Thus – as noted by Szabó/Török in 1867, Pettenkoffer in 1937, and both Rakcsányi and Nagy in 1963 – relatively longer soaking time may be needed if the weather is very cold, since fermentation is slower to commence (Rakcsányi specified 24-36 hours in cold weather, and only 12-16 in warm). Similarly, soaking time would be less in the better quality botrytis vintages, since more of the desired properties were gained more quickly. Also, if wine was used instead of must as the soaking liquid for *aszú*, enrichment of the liquid again could be achieved more quickly. However, as a general principle, soaking was not continued long after fermentation began, lest any textural or tactile harshness be occasioned, such as undue astringence from too much non-sugar extract.

(b) There is a question as to whether must or wine was the original liquid in which the *aszú*-dough was soaked. A major reason for supposing it was must is that Columella (Book XII. Xxix. 1-3), described an *aszú*-like technique, which he learned about from the Carthaginian agricultural writer Mago, in which the use of must was specified [see the entry for Columella, in Part I; and for *Aszú*: Aegean Echo, above]. The oldest Hungarian descriptions, from the early 1700s, use the word *bor* (wine), but in the old parlance of Hegyalja it also indicated must. Moreover, Keler (in German) in 1726 and Szirmay (in Latin) in 1798 referred to must. Douglass, in 1773, obviously meant must in saying that "the expressed juice" of non-botrytized grapes was used. Neverthelesss, it was probably at a very early time in the history of *aszú* wine, perhaps even before it became 'by definition' a botrytis wine, that wine was also used, since several of the grape varieties important in Hegyalja's earlier history ripened ahead of others. Usually this would have meant newly fermented wine (that is, from the same vintage but from the earlier-ripening grape varieties). In 1818, Bright mentioned the use of "good wine" in the soaking process. In 1839, Paget mentioned "good must, or new wine obtained in the ordinary manner."

By at least around 1700, 'old' wine (usually from the previous vintage) was also used occasionally. Doing so could improve quality in some years, and also, older wine hastened an *aszú* wine's acquisition of mature Tokaji character, which was particularly desired on some markets. This practice also spared the use of *eszencia* toward that end. Further, the production of *aszú* wines in a lesser botrytis year could be maximized by using old wine; this reflected the onetime tendency to get as much *aszú* wine as possible out of a vintage. Related to all of these circumstances, as regards both new and old wine, was the general consideration of trade needs and stock management. However, the use of old wine also became associated with the production of falsified wine, since lending 'mature' character to new wines, including those made from shriveled but non-botrytized grapes, was one ploy in the crafty merchant's quiver.

Coming to the more recent and 'enological era' of Tokaji wine, the *Tokaj-Hegyaljai Album* of 1867 mentioned must as the soaking agent. This was repeated by Kossuth in 1903, and by Spotkovszky in 1914. During the Interwar Period, in 1937, Pettenkoffer gave the choice of "good quality must or new wine." In 1948, Requinyi specified must. In 1956, Soós stated, "they sometimes used to use new or old wine instead of must. However, must is more appropriate." In the middle of the communist era, in 1973, Kádár noted that "must, new wine or old wine" could be used depending on "enological and operational" factors, but that the usual practice was new wine because by the time of the botrytis harvest, ordinary must had already been used up for the production of non-botrytis wines. As regards old wine, Rakcsányi in 1959 stated that it was used only "occasionally"; Kádár in 1973 put it as "exceptional cases"; and Farkaš in 1973 noted "only to enrich the extractive or aromatic material." However, in 1977, Mercz indicated that wine (apparently either new or old) was a better choice than must "in the case of weaker quality *aszú* berries." Obviously, too, mixtures of new and old wine were possible for large growers or merchants. But regulations never laid down any requirement as to soaking 'agents.'

SOD. Noteworthy among the antioxidants in Tokaji *aszú* that are not particularly associated with phenols is the enzyme superoxide-dismustase (SOD). Research in 1995 demonstrated that a Slovakian 1983 5-*puttonyos aszú* contained a considerable amount of SOD, and surpassed all but one of the five red wines analyzed (Gvozdjáková, 1996). In addition to the usual benefits of antixoxidants, SOD is known to foster good skin tone [see the entry for Eugènie, in Part I].

Straw Wine. One of the historical anomalies of Hegyalja is that 'straw wine' (*szalmabor*) has never been of any significance. The term refers to wine made from ripe grapes that are gathered and exposed to the sun, whether or not on straw mats in particular [see the entry for Botrytis]. The anomalous aspect is that Hegyalja received settlers from various lands where such wines were typical. Instead, the habit that caught on for making later-harvested wine was to let the berries over-ripen on the vine, which was done in parts of Greece since antiquity, and was the earliest tradition behind Malvasia wines [see #3 of the entry for Balkan Influences; and *Malozsa*]. However, Balassa (1991) stated that the drying of grapes after harvesting had been a technique that a few minor growers knew about and used on rare occasion. It may also have been encouraged by Greek traders (and used by them in vineyards they owned) to simulate Tokaji botrytis wine in years of poor botrytization. This may even have been one of the reasons that Zemplén County took issue with the practices of the Greek merchants, even if it was only 'borderline' falsification.

Sulfuring. Among the notable features of oldtime Hegyalja wine-making was the minimal use of sulfur in fermenting the botrytis wines. Indeed, none was used until well into the 20th century, and it only became standard practice during the communist era. Even then, the purpose of sulfuring was limited to adding just enough so as to guard against harmful microorganisms, promote the development of aromatic material, and ensure the reductive nature of the wine [see the entry for Redox-potential]. Experiments had shown that an addition of as little as 100 mg/kg of sulfur-dioxide to the crushed grapes was sufficient to accomplish these purposes (*Tokajhegyalja Borgazdasága*, 1974). This moderate use ensured minimal impact on the other aspects of the traditional aging process for the botrytis wines. Also to be noted in connection with sulfuring, is that because the production of concentrated must entails a relatively large addition of sulfur, Western allegations that concentrated must was permitted in making Tokaji botrytis wines during the communist era are enologically implausible [see the entry for Concentrated Must].

Szamorodni. This is the wine produced from entire grape bunches that have been partially affected by botrytis. Indeed, the name *szamorodni* comes from Polish and signifies 'self-grown' (*i.e.*, 'as comes off the vine'). All of the grapes are harvested at one time, with no individual collection of botrytized grapes. In line with the collection procedure, initial fermentation proceeds as for most wines, except for an initial 'soaking' of around 6 to 12 hours with the skins and stems. Depending on the extent of botrytization in the grape bunches, the resultant wine may be dry (*száraz*) or sweet (*édes*). The sweet kind can equate in sugar content to a theoretical 2-*puttonyos aszú*, for which reason the latter ceased to be produced and bottled commercially in Hungary during the course of the 20th century. Owing to sufficient sugar, alcohol, and non-sugar extract content, wines that earlier would have been marketed as *fordítás* or *máslás* were sometimes marketed as *édes* (sweet) *szamorodni* during the communist era, or else were used in making it. Beginning with the law of 1936, and continuing with that of 1959, *szamorodni* had to contain at least 13 percent alcohol by volume and 22 grams per liter of non-sugar extract.

Szamorodni's advantage in the eyes of traders was its reliability as a commercial product, since it could be made, whether dry or sweet, in more vintages and in greater quantity than could *aszú* wine. Additionally, in comparison to *aszú*, it did not need as much time in barrel, and was more stable owing to higher alcohol content. From the point of view of small growers, the emphasis on *szamorodni* production tended to focus their attention on vineyards situated in the lower middle part of the slopes, where botrytis was more reliable than further up. Also, they did not have to feel compelled to eliminate varieties less pronte to botrytization. Of course, this delayed change in varietal composition in the region at large. Notably, *szamorodni* probably sustained the botrytis-prone but early-ripening *gohér* [see that entry] well into the 19th century.

Szamorodni was the (delayed) successor to *főbor*, the chief historical difference being that *szamorodni* has always been used to refer to a botrytis wine, whereas *főbor* went back to the time of the first later-harvested wines, when shriveled but non-botrytized grapes were used. According to Balassa (1991), the name *szamorodni* replaced that of *főbor* around 1800. This would account for Sylvester Douglass making no mention of *szamorodni* in his book of 1773. Meanwhile, though, the name *ordinárium* was being applied to wine from fresh and shriveled grapes. When botrytis became regarded as essential to such wine, a new name was needed, and a Polish name obviously would have a greater impact in the Polish market that was most keen to have that wine, and that name was *samorodno*. For a time in the early-19th century, the Magyars did have a corresponding term, *termés-bor*, signifying 'wine-as-it-is-harvested.' But, since in that era many inhabitants of Hegyalja, including the nobility, were acquainted with one or another Slovak-Rusyn dialect of the Upper Tisza region, a variation on the Polish term, *szamorodni*, easily took hold amongst the Hungarians, too, once its commercial importance was realized.

Szerednyei Barrel. Although the Gönci barrel predominated in the history of *aszú* wine, and was a key measure used in making it, the somewhat larger Szerednyei barrel, of 200-liter (53-gallon) capacity, was also used occasionally to store Tokaji during the aging process. It, too, could fit through the small entranceways of the traditional cellars. The name refers to Szerednye (now Serednye in Ukraine), a wine region about 66 km (41 miles) northeast of Hegyalja.

Szlankamenka. (a) The name of this grape is yet another reason to take into consideration the Bulgaro-Slavs at the time of the Conquest by the Magyars. Although the scribe Anonymous referred to the Bulgarian Zalán in telling of the Conquest, his account has been doubted. Yet the *szlankamenka*, 'a mere grape variety,' suggests that in the lower Tisza region there was indeed a locale known as 'Zoloncaman' (=Zalán-kamen), ruled by a historical Zalán.

(b) The Balkan 'pedigree' of the variety is displayed by the fact that it is the same as the Bulgarian *pamid*, actually Greek *pamidi* (a name derived from ancient Greek *pan+methi*, signifying 'all-inebriating'). Balassa (1991) was puzzled by a long-ago Hegyalja variety known as *bolgár* and *bogár*, and wondered in particular whether there could have been any association with Bulgaria. One of his sources, Keler (1726), definitely believed that to be the case. Since it occurred in "white, red and blue" variants, there is a strong possibility that the *bolgár* was in fact the *pamid*, which has the same color variants (an indication of a very long varietal history). The variety could have been brought to Hegyalja as early as the 9th century, when Bulgaro-Slavs were brought from north of Thessaloniki, from the Strymon/Struma river basin, where the *pamid* is still a typical variety [see the entry for Macedonia, in Part II].

Tokaji Character. (a) Hungarian enologists have used the expression 'Tokaji character' (*Tokaji jelleg*) since the second-half of the 19th century to allude to the expected sensory characteristics of Tokaji botrytis wines, including color, aroma, and flavor. What they were alluding to, of course, were the features that most set Tokaji apart. However, Dömötör/Katona (1963) had this to say of it: "This character cannot be specified adequately with words, but anyone who has tasted it never forgets it…[words] will be only a pale replica of the reality [of the experience]." This view, though, hardly originated with enologists, but instead followed from a long history of empirical observation by Hungarians and non-Hungarians alike. We have only to consider Sylvester Douglass in 1773: "nobody who has ever drank [Tokaji] genuine, can confound it with any other species of wine." Despite the difficulty of nailing Tokaji character down with words, some perceptive remarks have been made over the centuries, and even Dömötör/Katona did not back away from tagging the Tokaji botrytis wines with descriptive terms.

Visual: More or less dark yellow has been typical as far back as the late-17th century. This has frequently been termed 'amber.' Just how dark the yellowness should be can vary according to type of wine, such as darker in *aszú* and lighter in *szamorodni*, and to the wine's age, lighter in youth and darker at barrel-maturity. Some (non-enologist) Hungarian authors, such as Wekerle (1888), have occasionally mentioned 'golden yellow' (*arany-sárga*), but whether they had in mind something much different than Voltaire's "*jaunissante*" (in the sense of wheat reaching its full golden color) is questionable in view of other comments about color [see the entry for Color]. Dömötör/Katona stated that the color can range "from the light golden-yellow of new *aszú* through the brownish toned old-gold color of ripe *aszú*-s, to the reddish-brown color of archival [*muzeális*] *aszú*-s," with "every shade" in between. Szirmay warned that if the *aszú* berries were soaked for more than 48 hours, "the beautiful gold color is lost, and [the wine] picks up a reddish color from the film of the *aszú* grapes." Paget (1839) emphasized a "bright" appearance. Further, texture should be visibly apparent when the wine is poured or swirled: "It should, when poured out, form globules in the glass, and have an oily appearance" (Douglass, 1773). In 1825, Dercsényi, too, noted 'oiliness' as a feature.

Aromatics: 'Browning' has long been deemed an expected and correct feature of Tokaji. The oldest and most persistent association (at least for the Hungarians) has been an aspect of the crust on freshly baked rye-bread of pumpernickel type, which they summed up by the German term *bródig*, or 'bready.' The wine-writer Henderson apparently agreed with this and mentioned it in writing of Tokaji in 1824. Soviet researchers in the 1960s demonstrated that this in fact results from the de-amination of certain amino acids in Tokaji [see the entry for De-amination]. However, it is certainly simplistic to think that browning aromas end with bread crusts. Dömötör/Katona mentioned chocolate and carob as occasional marks of mature Tokaji, and those fit comfortably under the rubric 'browning aromas.' Dry tea leaves present other manifestations of browning, and Robert Druitt did bring "green tea" into Tokaji's profile in 1864. Although he specified *eszencia*, it can be argued that the best *aszú*-s carry a whiff of tea, whether green or other, at various times during their maturity. "Honey and vine-blossom" were mentioned by Dömötör/Katona as characteristic of new *aszú*, but even honey includes a browning component to its smell. Finally, Tokaji's content of hydroxymethylfurfural needs to be noted because of the brown-candy (toffee, caramel) aromas mentioned by Western writers.

Flavor: Without diminishing the contribution of appearance and aromatics in giving Tokaji its distinctiveness, most often the inimitable aspects of flavor are what will enable enophiles to set it apart in their memory most surely from other wines. Dercsényi used the unusual term *terjékes*, which translates best as 'extractive.' This is the feature that explains some of the enological reasoning, and concerns, behind the 1936 law that specified a non-sugar extract content for the *aszú*, *eszencia*, and *szamorodni* wines. It might also account for Wekerle's (1888) use of the descriptions "chalky" and "denseness" [see the quotation at the end of the Part IV Essay]. All of these terms apply to the wine while it is in the mouth. The capstone, though, is the 'tang' after the wine has been swallowed. It is most likely what Redding had in mind by "an earthy twang," and unquestionably what explains Jullien's (1816) remark that Tokaji cleanses the palate of all foods that have preceded it. The Hungarians have never used a word quite like tang or twang, but Douglass tells us that they did have a term for it: "When swallowed, [Tokaji *aszú*] should have an earthy astringent taste in the mouth, which they [his Hungarian informants] call the *Taste of the root*" (sic), (*gyökér-íz* in Hungarian). The same was implicit in Dömötör/Katona's mention of "earth-taste" (*föld-íz*), as one of the "chief characteristics" associated with properly aged Tokaji. This tang, in combination with 'extractive-ness,' explains why the enologist Pettenkoffer (1937) wrote that Sauternes wines are "softer and smoother" than Tokaji. Additionally, Szabó-Jilek (1962) included as integral to "traditional" Tokaji character "a certain taste of age," but not of an exaggerated sort that brings out "acrid medicinal tastes" or causes Tokaji to forfeit much of what sets it apart from other wines.

(b) It might be presumed that 'Tokaji character' is at odds with, or detracts from, *terroir*. However, the notion actually adds a whole other dimension to the usual meaning of *terroir*, and is dependent on the traditional vinification and aging methods, which are the means by which the most individual aspects of Tokaji's inherent chemical consistency are brought forth (note the quotation from Ásvány at the head of Part IV). In centuries past, those peculiarities could only be inferred from anecdotal information about remarkable physiological effects. But, in recent years, the precise nature of these features has begun to be understood scientifically, and appear traceable largely to the traditional maturation of Tokaji wines. Since several years of maturation are involved, this gives an entirely different cast to the question of *terroir* in the case of Tokaji, one that involves significant, latent chemical manifestations of *terroir* that take time and specific prerequisites to reveal themselves. [See the entries for Biogenic Amines, HMF, Phenols, and Umami.]

The concept 'Tokaji character' has always downplayed the flavors usually associated with particular varietal wines in their youth. Writing in 1903, Kossuth stated that "the wine of any foreign grape sort [experimented with in the wake of phylloxera] in Hegyalja takes on Hegyalja character to a greater or lesser extent." For emphasis, he mentioned the case of a varietal *othello* wine grown in Hegyalja: "even the characteristic foxy taste was unable to suppress the wine's Hegyalja character." This aspect explains why other varieties yielded characteristically Hegyaljan wines even before *furmint* came to the fore 200 years ago. The subject of 'Tokaji character' still has relevance. Efforts to discard the techniques which engender its appearance carry the threat of yielding Hegyalja wines that too closely resemble wines that can be produced in nearby locales, to the west, north, and northeast, which were long ago excluded from Hegyalja. Here, it need only be added that those wines resembled Tokaji only in their youth.

Tokaji Character: A Personal Slant

Much as I have tried to keep my *self* out of this book, it is impossible to drink Tokaji for over 40 years – both during and after the communist period – and not address 'Tokaji character.' Not that I stray far from what was said above in (a), but I cannot pretend not to have some thoughts of my own. Descriptions of color can vary according to cultural and personal understanding of colors, and I have never found what I would consider a 'profoundly' amber color to be indispensable to Tokaji; Odart's somewhat poetic description of a "*jolie*" amberish shade best comports with my expectations. While I would not go so far as to say that Tokaji's remarkable flavor features cannot be found clothed in lighter hues, pineapples provide me with my line-in-the-sand where color is concerned: the orangish-yellow on a ripe pineapple is my limit on lightness; the pineapple-yellow of the ripe flesh is over the edge for me. This does not reflect my color preferences, but rather my sense that the distinctiveness of Tokaji's color is degraded, and my experience that the pineapple-yellow wines prove deficient in that combination of fatness and tang that does so much to set Tokaji apart. As regards fatness, this has always been the feature that enables Tokaji's 'extractive-ness' (noticeable in a slight astringency and 'chalkiness') to be so eminently palatable and memorable. Indeed, some poorer *aszú*-s are marked exactly by a chalky textural sensation that stands alone, as it were, in mid-palate. Another shortcoming is when the superficial glide of alcohol 'substitutes' real fatness, which is most noticeable when lingering vinosity overshadows any semblance of a tang. And about that tang – it seems to manifest itself mostly in two species when it is right: apricot *lekvár* (a very thick Hungarian jam) or medium-dark orange (and not bitterish) marmalade, with the latter more usual (it seems to me) in older *aszú*-s. Otherwise, the tang is such that the sensors of the entire rear top and side surfaces of the tongue are perceptibly stimulated at an equal level of intensity long after the wine has been swallowed (Jullien comes to mind again). Aromas and flavors are very variable in their specifics, even in the case of 'browning.' Toffee may turn up for the English, but so can maple-candy/syrup for Americans. More allusive are tea and honey. One would need to have a large fund of experience in either category to identify the guises in which they turn up in Tokaji, *a là* Druitt. It happens that even before I read Druitt, teas and tisanes frequently crossed my mind when sniffing at a glass. Tisanes bring us to the verge of floral aromas, and such do appear even in mature wines, which is not surprising if we think again of honey and the many flowers that can influence its smell (let us be clear that Tokaji is not only about 'browning' aromas). One of the most charming aromatic nuances can be dried tobacco (though I hesitate to specify Virginia flue-cured or Maryland air-cured). This gets into browning, fruitiness, and the sweet spices all at once. But I am not inclined to consider tobacco as integral to Tokaji character. Lastly, its survivability aside, there certainly is Tokaji that is past its prime and has begun to forfeit its distinctiveness, if not its Tokaji character in all respects. Red flags go up for me when I see brownish cinnamon or prune-juice shades; detect coffee or California dark raisins on the nose; or find astringency upstaging residual fatness.

Tumidula. Hungarian writers in past centuries sometimes gave Hungarian grape names in Latin form, and one case where it is unclear which variety was indicated is *tumidula*. In the early-18th century, the geographer Matthias Bél, in writing of the western Hungarian region of Sopron, is presumed to have meant *furmint* by it since the variety was known from Croatia north to Sopron. Also, in 1758, Samuel Dombi mentioned *tumidula* among the four main Hegyalja varieties, and some historians have assumed that he, too, must have meant *furmint*. Yet, this was before *furmint's* rise to prominence in Hegyalja. Further, *tumidula* signifies 'bulge-ling' or 'little sweller' (*dagadtka* in Hungarian), which is hardly a credible Latin translation of *furmint*. The name *furmint* was thought to be of Latin origin, and therefore would have been translated in a recognizable form, along the lines of, say, *frumentum*. For another, none of the known synonyms for *furmint* (including its non-Hungarian names) suggest the equivalent of *tumidula*.

As indicated in the entries for the varieties *furmint*, *fehérszőlő*, and *kövérszőlő*, the historical relationship between these varieties and/or their names is unclear. Judging from the contradictory comments about the latter two, it seems certain that the one was often confused for the other. But the Latin name *tumidula* suggests that there was also confusion between *kövérszőlő* and *furmint*. Since *tumidula* also connotes 'stout' or 'plump,' the name suggests something rather like the *kövérszőlő*, or 'fat/stout-grape.' The latter seems to have been a significant Hegyalja variety in the 15th century [see the entry for Cotnari, in Part II], but steadily receded thereafter, probably yielding to the related *fehérszőlő*, and both of those to *furmint* eventually. This is to say, too, that Bél and Dombi were not necessarily indicating the same grape variety by the name *tumidula*. Here, it is worthwhile to emphasize that Schams, in 1834, wrote to Zemplén County specifically about the problem of the misapplication of varietal names. [See the entry for Schams, in Part I.]

Umami. Sometimes translated as 'tastiness,' this Japanese term refers to the fifth sense of taste. Unlike the other tastes, umami is felt widely in the mouth, rather than in a specific area, and sparks a tactilely provocative mellowness throughout the mouth, which enhances palatability and encourages savoring. Chemically, umami has been linked to glutamates, which are the salts of glutamic acid. Exemplars of umami among solid foods are dried mushrooms and Parmigiano-Reggiano cheese. As regards wine, merely keeping a wine in barrel or bottle will not result in umami; in other words, 'mellowness' in the sense of 'no rough edges' does not equate to umami. Instead, a true vinous manifestation of umami depends on the wine's amino acid content. Tokaji botrytis wines, owing to their unusual content of amino acids, and particularly their relatively high content of glutamic acid, have a rare potential for umami. However, bringing this potential to fruition requires several years in barrel during which the requisite de-amination can take place (Almashi/ Nilov, 1964). Umami can thus be considered prominent among Tokaji's 'delayed' manifestations of *terroir* [see the entry for Tokaji Character].

Vitamin E. Among the antioxidants in Tokaji *aszú* that are not particularly associated with phenols, the presence of vitamin E (α-tocopherol) is notable. Research in 1995 showed a Slovakian 1983 5-*puttonyos aszú* to have 822.6 mg/l of vitamin E, which was significantly greater than younger non-botrytis Tokaji wines and all but one of the other white wines analyzed. Further, the 1983 *aszú* possessed two-fifths more vitamin E than the average for the five 1994 red wines analyzed, including one-fifth more than the highest of those. (Gvozdjáková, 1996)

Wine-delicacy. (*Borkülönlegesség*) This term, and the notion behind it, has been central to Hungarian enological conceptions, and thus to legal requirements as well, regarding the Tokaji specialty wines. 'Delicacy' in this case refers less to the esteemed organoleptic features of the botrytis-based wines, than to rare or unique, and painstaking, procedures involved in making them. Dömötör/Katona (1963) commented: "The preparation of the Tokaji wine-delicacies, even if not diabolical, is still a quite complicated task." The notion, perhaps influenced by the German term *delicatesse*, grew out of the distinction the Hungarians have long made between so called *szűrt* and *csinált* wines. These latter terms do not translate well, and the closest figurative meanings in English are, respectively, 'drawn-off' and 'done-up.' This can be thought of as 'natural' versus 'unnatural,' but without the value judgments we usually assign to those terms. A *szürt* wine can be thought of as 'plain' wine, one made without any delays or fuss, simply from the juice 'drawn-off' from the grapes just gathered. But a *csinált* wine results from elaboration entailing extra procedures, time, and effort, hence a wine that has been 'done-up.' In this sense of employing techniques otherwise superfluous to making wine, a wine-delicacy reflects 'sophistication' or 'embellishment,' or even, if one prefers, 'artificiality' in a judgmentally neutral sense. Certainly a wine that can be made only in certain years is a prime candidate for treatment as a wine-delicacy, and that aspect of course explains, too, why Hungarian enologists and legislation have always treated the Tokaji specialty wines in the *borkülönlegesség* category, separate from *csemegebor*, or 'dessert wine' [see the latter entry].

Yeast-film. Called *hártya*, this film is a covering of dead yeasts that forms on the surface of the Tokaji specialty wines as they age in barrel by the *darabbantartás* technique. Along with cellar temperature, the film prevents extensive oxidation of the wine [see the entry for Redox-potential]. This film is not to be confused with the *flor* of Sherry, as the *hártya* has no visible volume.

Zéta. A cross of *furmint* and *bouvier* (*chardonnay* x *silvaner*), this variety was originally called *oremus* and was introduced into Hegyalja in 1951. It joined the regional pantheon of approved varieties in 1990, and was renamed *zéta* in 1999 so as to avoid confusion with the vineyard-tract known as Oremus [see that entry, in Part III]. The variety is very susceptible to botrytis, and is also very high in sugar because it is relatively early-ripening. Although similar to the *kővérszőlő* in those respects, *zéta* is not considered its all-around equal in quality. [See the entry for *Kabar*.]

*   *   *

PART IV

ESSAY

The Historical Development of Hegyalja Wine Types

Tokaj-Hegyalja is alone amongst the botrytis-wine producing regions in the range of wine types it offers. But this array did not emerge all at once. About 350 years elapsed, roughly from 1475 to 1825, for the wine types to settle into place. It can even be argued that the process was not really complete until the national legislation of 1924 and 1936, when the types were defined according to enological criteria.

Főbor, malozsa, aszú-szőlő bor, aszú, aszú-eszencia, eszencia, legfőbb-bor, szamorodni, ordinárium, máslás, fordítás. It is a formidable cavalcade of names, and cavalcade is the right word for it in view of the fact that we are dealing with a historical procession of wine types. However, the procession was not quite 'orderly.' Most of the names went through transitions in meaning, such that it is not always clear in reading old accounts or documents whether a given name refers to an earlier or later meaning of the term. For instance, when Habsburg General Spork demanded 15 barrels of *főbor* in 1674, did he actually expect to receive what we know as *aszú?* Similarly, when the Oremus vineyard-tract was mentioned as a producer of *főbor* in a document of 1686 (UC 154:11), was *aszú* to be understood? The late-17th century was, after all, well into the era when *aszú* had supplanted *főbor* as the premier wine type of Hegyalja. But, even so, definite answers cannot usually be given to such questions.

*

Just how did Hegyalja acquire the habit of producing later-harvested white wines in the first place? The first step was taken in the late-15th century, when records show that the vintage was taking place later than previously. Instead of mid-September, the grapes were being collected in late-September or early-October. The reason for the change is not known. It might have been occasioned by historical events, especially warfare. It was the period when King Matthias was defending the Upper Tisza against Polish armies. This protracted effort called for manpower and thus could interfere with what had been considered the timely collection of grapes in Hegyalja.

Other factors could have been involved, though. It might already have been noticed that some of the major white grape varieties had more remarkable qualities when harvested later. This would have happened if climatic cooling had been taking place in Hegyalja. In the same era, wine-growing was receding in the more northerly areas of the Upper Tisza, such as the northern half of the Eperjes-Tokaj Hill-Chain, largely for that reason. Further, some of the religious orders of Hegyalja might have begun harvesting some grapes later, under Adriatic (Dalmatian) influence.

However, the region as a whole certainly did not become committed to later-harvested white wine at anything like an equal pace. It would seem that the southern line of locales from Tokaj to Abaújszántó was the earliest area where later harvesting took hold. Pap (1985) shows that some of the earliest information testifying to the change comes from Tállya. Also, Tállya and Abaújszántó figure prominently in the wine purchase records of Bártfa for the decade 1500-1510. At the very least, it was along the southern line that the first delay in harvesting made a palpable difference in the wine, which is why the towns of the Upper Tisza purchased most of their vineyards in the south around that time. Thus, too, the long-lasting contention that the 'real' Hegyalja was centered along the southern line can be dated to roughly 1500.

As to the nature of the wines resulting from later harvesting, no wine names definitely go back far enough to tell us anything specific. However, if the *fehérszőlő, gohér*, and *kövérszőlő* (the latter being the variety taken from Hegyalja to Cotnari in this era) were the major white grapes, Sperfogel's comment, in 1524, about the improved quality of Tokaji is reason to suppose a mellower, semi-sweet wine of more pronounced aromatic flavor. Some raisining may have occurred, but even so, the wines probably conformed largely to what we would call 'late-harvest' wine today. The importance of the change can be seen from the eagerness of the towns of the Upper Tisza to acquire their own vineyard-tracts in Hegyalja around 1500, which was before the Ottomans occupied Lower Hungary and cut off access to the popular Szerém wines.

*

After later harvesting had become routine, two wine names turn up: *főbor* and *malozsa*. It may be presumed that those names originally indicated two different kinds of wine. But there was some overlap, and this increased the more that the role of shriveled grapes increased in Hegyalja. The 'convergence' would ultimately lead to modern-day *aszú* wine.

Főbor had a dual connotation. Literally meaning 'head/chief' (*fő*) wine,' it signified the main wine made, but also implied the 'principal' (*fő*) harvest. Early on, this would have included grapes in various stages of ripeness, because of the different ripening times of the grape varieties grown. There was nothing new about such a habit; it was the same as for the *omfakitis* of the ancient Greeks [see #2 in Balkan Influences; and the entry for *Főbor*]. Thus, use of the name might have antedated considerably any recorded mention of it. As time went on, though, more shriveled grapes were being included, possibly as a result of greater observation of the different grape varieties. Eventually, *főbor* was largely expected to include shriveled grapes, as made clear by Keler in 1726 (he used the German equivalent, *hauptwein*).

The second name, *malozsa*, is notable as the only truly exogenous name in the history of Hegyalja wine types. Balassa (1991) was inclined to see an Italian loan-word in it, perhaps to make Italian influence seem more palpable than was indicated by anything else he had found. But the overwhelming evidence points to an origin in Greece. *Malozsa* recalls the Malvasia wines, and for good reason. That wine, coming mostly from Crete and the Cycladic islands in that era, had enjoyed a great market in Central Europe in the late Middle Ages, and Macedonian Greek merchants frequently shipped it through Hungary, even through Hegyalja on the way to destinations in southeastern Poland. The Hungarians also had familiarity with the name from their ties to the Dalmatian coast, where wines meant to replicate Malvasia were made.

The name *malozsa* could have been in use in Hegyalja earlier than *főbor*. Dalmatia was quite important to Hungary during the reign of Matthias Corvinus in the second-half of the 15th century, and even under Louis I in the late-14th century. *Malozsa* might originally have had a varietal connection to the *gohér*, since the latter was also known as the *malozsa gohér*, and Szirmay (1798) mentioned its relationship to the '*malvasia*' variety. This could date the wine name *malozsa* to as early as the influx of Greek vine-dressers from the Peloponnesus in the second-half of the 13th century. The *malagouzia/malaouzia/malouzia* variety likely was already established in the northwestern Peloponnesus by that time, because of Malvasia's fame.

The names *főbor* and *malozsa* died out early in the 18th century, but not before leaving behind a joint legacy. From *főbor*, Hegyalja kept the habit of fermenting shriveled grapes amidst the juice of ripe grapes. From *malozsa*, which was understood to indicate grapes with concentrated sugar, no matter the variety, a preference for over-ripe grapes dominated, while under-ripe grapes were eliminated. From both, the tradition of allowing grapes to lose moisture on the vine continued.

This was an alternative method of ancient Greece, not the ubiquitous Roman practice of always shriveling the grapes, indoors or outdoors, after harvesting. These features promoted another name, *aszú-szőlő bor*, or 'shriveled-grape wine.' The term had existed earlier, but it had to wait in the wings until the 'fusion' of *főbor* and *malozsa* gave it a solid identity and commercial role. *Aszú-szőlő bor* would become the immediate progenitor of modern *aszú*.

*

Nearly a century might have passed before habits changed much in fabricating the later-harvested wines. General von Schwendi's formidable confiscation of 4,000 barrels in the 1560s hardly seems probable for anything other than a rather typical late-harvest wine, if only because of the constraint of having an easily seizable quantity of such magnitude. Moreover, when he took vine cuttings from Hegyalja to Alsace, he did not bring along any ideas other than late-harvesting.

General von Schwendi happened to appear on the Hegyalja scene just as it was about to take a second major step in the development of its wine types. This was the introduction of a third hoeing, which Szirmay tells us began to be practiced after 1560. The reason for the change again is not known. However, it may be more than coincidental that it occurred after the Ottoman Turks had begun the occupation of southern Hungary in 1526 and the previously famous Szerémség region lost its place on the market, especially the Polish market. In endeavoring to replace those wines in Poland, Hegyalja looked to the Szerémség for 'hints.' A third hoeing and an even longer delay in harvesting may have been the lesson learned for pleasing the Poles.

The third hoeing extended the growing season even longer, with vintage-time beginning in late October. As with the first delay in harvesting some seven decades earlier, the third hoeing must have been adopted at a varied pace in the region. But it is clear that this time the more northerly areas would have had the most benefit from the delay, since shriveling had time to proceed more extensively (it was in this era that places farther north in the Eperjes-Tokaj hills were abandoning wine-growing because of climatic cooling). Likewise, tracts throughout Hegyalja, even in the south, that had less than ideal expositions could now accumulate enough warmth to undergo significant shriveling of grapes on the vine.

However, the proportion and relative importance of shriveled, *botrytized* grapes after the third hoeing was introduced is a matter of conjecture. It probably varied a good deal from vintage to vintage, and just how late the collection was made. Even in 1634, Susanna Lórántffy mentioned that the *aszú* vintage on Somlyód hill, near Sárospatak, had begun on October 9. Judging from that date, it can be wondered whether the shriveled (*aszú*) berries had in fact been attacked by botrytis to any significant extent, or were just shriveled as for *főbor* and *malozsa*.

At any rate, in the case of the second delay in harvesting, we know the major grape varieties involved, from Szikszai Fabricius, circa 1570: *fehérszőlő, gohér, muskotály, malozsa, kecskecsecsű*. All were of Balkan or east Mediterranean origin; all were early-ripening compared to the eventual major Hegyalja varieties; all were very sweet; and all were susceptible to shriveling nicely on the vine. Therefore, it may be presumed that the *főbor* wines produced after the second change in vintage date were substantially the product of shriveled grapes, more so than merely over-ripe ones. It was very likely the type of wine that gained the praise of the pope at the Council of Trent in 1562 (no matter if it seems a slight contradiction of Szirmay's dating of the third hoeing). Certainly it was the kind of wine that the Polish market wanted.

By the late-16th century, Poland had replaced the Upper Tisza region of Hungary in the concerns of growers and traders of Hegyalja wine. There is a distinct possibility that the Polish market varied in its preferences with regard to sweetness, and also, affordability. This circumstance might have impacted Hegyalja wine types in two ways. First, it would have perpetuated the production of the earliest kind of *főbor*, since it could be produced from virtually any vintage. Second, it might well have led to the *puttonyos* system even before botrytized grapes became the basis for *aszú-szőlő* wine. The record of a 4-*puttonyos* wine in Poland in 1646, not even a generation after the legendary 'discovery' of botrytis *aszú*, is an indication that the system came into use while shriveled but non-botrytized grapes accounted for Tokaji's growing renown.

*

Since the term *aszú* originally intimated nothing more than desiccated grapes, its use in connection with Hegyalja wine types always has to be in doubt when encountering it in accounts earlier than the late-17th century. Notably, the term *aszú-szőlő bor* had no necessary connection to botrytized grapes. Balassa (1991) presented information showing that as late as 1793, 1799, and 1807 it was sometimes equated with *malozsa, i.e.,* wine from over-ripe and ordinary shrunken grapes.

Nevertheless, wine types based on botrytis can usually be presumed when the term is used after 1655. That was the year that Zemplén County required the separate harvesting of *aszú* berries. In view of the Rákóczis' delineation of Hegyalja and classification of its vineyards in the preceding decade (as well as the contribution of László Szepsi to the advent of modern *aszú* wine several decades earlier), there can be no doubt that botrytis wine had now come to the fore. By 1736, Gabriel Gyöngyösi wrote in opposition to the over-production of *aszú* wine at the expense of usual wines, and that would hardly have been the case if ordinary shriveled grapes were still generally associated with the name *aszú*.

Little can be specified about change in varietal content during the transition from *főbor* of the non-botrytis type to *aszú* of botrytis type. Clearly, though, the *fehérszőlő* and *gohér* must have maintained primary importance throughout, with other varieties having some significance only locally. We need only consider that *gohér* cuttings were taken from Hegyalja to Astrakhan for the czar's vineyards early in the 18th century. At the same time, there was still little sign of *furmint*. Further, it is likely that some red grapes were still being included (red wine was being produced at Olaszliszka in the early-17th century). Indeed, one reason for continuing the use of sacks in producing later-harvested white wines may have been to ensure that red color would not be imparted to the wine [see #5 in the entry for Balkan Influences].

But how did the fabrication of *főbor* change before it led to *aszú-szőlő* wine? The 1655 regulation made *aszú* absolutely dependent on botrytis, which *főbor* had not been, and thus, a wine that required certain seasonal conditions in order to be produced. But if, as seems likely, the *puttonyos* system had come into use in the second-half of the 16th century (because of the introduction of both the *puttony* and the *gönci* barrel), then *főbor* had to have become a wine produced by 'soaking' shriveled, but mostly non-botrytized berries in the must of non-shriveled ones. In this scenario, modern-day botrytis *aszú* was but the end result of what *főbor* had become in the late-16th century. It is why a differentiation by name was needed for a new wine type.

'Soaking' is one of the unique aspects of Tokaji production, and there is no reason to wonder at it. The basic idea for it certainly antedated *főbor*, as it was an integral part of Hegyalja's Balkan wine heritage. Historically, the long contact of pulp with skins and stems, including forceful 'jamming' of the solids, was associated mostly with red wines. But it had also been employed for wines of rosy hue (produced from red and white grapes), and occasionally even for white wines. It was valued by smallholders for yielding a more extractive wine, and one with more alcohol for better conservation. This thinking had a degree of transferability to white wines from shriveled grapes [see the entry *Aszú*: Aegean Echo]. Nevertheless, it was probably only when the aristocracy of Hegyalja became familiar with Columella, roughly around 1600, that empirical tradition began to be shaped by rigorous observation of 'soaking' and its effects on the specialty wines. This is one of the chief possibilities for the contribution made by Szepsi early in the 17th century.

[The Hungarian ethnologist Bertalan Andrásfalvy wrote that the Balkan red wine culture did not reach Hungary until the Ottoman occupation in the 16th and 17th centuries, mostly in connection with Serbian immigration and the *kadarka* grape variety, and mostly in southern and central Hungary ("Red Wine in Hungary: The Balkan Connection of our Viniculture," *Ethnographical Reporter*, Vol. 39, 1957). But, as demonstrated repeatedly in this book, Hegyalja had a different history than other Hungarian wine regions, with far deeper Balkan roots, and connections to Bulgaria and Greek Macedonia, not Serbia.]

Though it might not have made a difference, at least initially, in defining *aszú* as a wine type, it seems that the aging of wines underwent a change that largely coincided in time-frame with the receding of *főbor* and the ascent of modern *aszú*. This is seen above all in the Rákóczis' construction of large cellaring facilities at several locales in Hegyalja. Those cellars in part reflected the increasing replacement of the *antal* by the *gönci* barrel. The latter was twice as capacious as the former, which suggests that the technique of keeping an empty space in the barrels (*darabbantartás*) was becoming usual. Moreover, the fact that the Swede Eneman likened Tokaji to the amber-colored wine of Chios in 1711 demonstrates that this method of aging had become associated with Tokaji in foreign markets well before the end of the 17th century. Its dominance was clinched by the Szepes Chamber's requirement of 1711 that only the *gönci* barrel was to be used in exporting wine from Hegyalja and the rest of the Upper Tisza.

*

When Polish President Ignacy Mościcki married in 1933, bottles of 250-year-old Tokaji were opened. A newspaper report of the day commented that if the wine was good, it could only have been *eszencia*. The problem with that supposition has to do with timing. 250 years would take the wine back to 1683, whereas there is no mention of the name *eszencia* until 1707, and even in that case the only reason for supposing that it was genuine *eszencia* is that it was a gift from Prince Francis Rákóczi II to Czar Peter the Great of Russia.

We are confronted here with the possibility that the name of a Hegyalja wine type originated apart from the origin of the wine type itself. That is, the name might have been bestowed by persons who had nothing to do with the creation of *eszencia*. Specifically, the name arose first amongst Hungarian-Germans, whereas the technique was of ancient Greek origin.

The timing of *eszencia*'s appearance inevitably leads to contemplating the population of Greek wine traders in the town of Tokaj in the late-17th century. Their sizeable number is clear from Zemplén County's imposition of a 'Greek tax' as early as 1689. The ancient Greeks had known wine of *eszencia* type by the name *protropon*. This name had been lost to the later-day Greeks, but not so the technique itself. It was valued for producing a syrupy wine with which to improve or enrich other wines. The name by which the Greek traders would have called such wine was 'nectar' [see that entry], and they probably transmitted the name to the Hegyaljans: a Zemplén County record from 1842 referred to *eszencia* ("*legfobb bor*") as the "wine differentiated by the *long-standing* name of nectar" (emphasis added). This makes it highly doubtful that the term nectar only began to be used at the end of the 18th century, and only as a poetic device at that.

The key date for *eszencia* is 1655, when it was required that *aszú* grapes be harvested separately. That is when botrytis *aszú* became the most characteristic wine of Hegyalja. Before that time, the availability of botrytized fruit would have been insufficient for *eszencia* to be made, since a large quantity was needed to produce even a small quantity of *eszencia*. This timing dovetails with the rise to prominence of the Greek traders. Furthermore, there is no information by which to think that Szepsi would have invented *eszencia*, not even on an experimental scale. Unlike the 'soaking' process for *aszú*, he would have picked up no ideas from Columella about *protropon*.

It is unlikely that *eszencia* was the first outcome of the 1655 regulation. Rather, the first new idea was probably to produce *aszú* wines using more than five *puttony*-s of botrytized grapes, simply because aristocratic owners would have had much greater availability of such grapes. Wines like that would explain a palatable 250-year-old wine being drunk at the Mościcki wedding in 1933, without it having been an *eszencia*. They were the sort of wines that later became known as *aszú-eszencia*, as specified by Dercsényi in 1825. Their fabrication makes it virtually impossible to know just which wines called *eszencia* in the 18th and 19th centuries were truly that wine type.

Nevertheless, when Keler mentioned *eszencia* in 1726 and Gyöngyösi in 1736, they have to be understood as meaning genuine *eszencia*. In the era of *aszú*'s great fame – not to mention the first era of falsification – *eszencia* was highly desirable for its 'corrective' role. Its availability as a wine in its own right, though, is uncertain. After the collapse of the anti-Habsburg aristocracy in the early-18th century, there was no motive for using *eszencia* to curry favor for the Hungarian cause abroad (nothing suggests gifts of *eszencia* during the Hungarian revolution of 1848-1849).

As to its commercial sale, it does not seem as though *eszencia*, as opposed to *aszú-eszencia*, was ever much available (if it had been, Thomas Jefferson certainly would have had the merchant Bollman procure some for him). All indications are that special connections and non-commercial channels were needed to obtain any at all. During the 19th century, practically the only people paying for *eszencia* did so at pharmacies, for tiny quantities. But its name endured famously because of its legendary qualities, as well as its mistaken identification with 'Imperial Tokay.'

*

Aszú was not the only outgrowth of *főbor*. Although the latter name lost its allure, the original technique had not been lost. It was perpetuated above all by the smallholders of Hegyalja. This happened because of less selectivity about the grape varieties to be used. The ripening time of the varieties was not crucial. Whether or not botrytized fruit was involved could be left to chance; and consequently, quantity over quality was quite acceptable. Moreover, there was definitely a market for such wine.

It should be emphasized that the smallholders were not unaware that more money could be made by basing their wines on botrytis. But they lacked the financial resources to expand their cellars and equipage, and preferred selling their botrytized fruit to the Greek wine traders. Besides which, the feudal system that prevailed through the 17th century meant that the owners of the land per se – the aristocracy – enjoyed the right of 'first pick' of the smallholders' grape output. The result was that the best wine a smallholder could make was from a random mixture of fresh and shriveled (botrytized or not) berries. In effect, this harked back to the earliest sort of *főbor*.

In 1773, Sylvester Douglass indicated wine of this type as one of the four products of Hegyalja (the others were *eszencia, aszú,* and *máslás,* in that order). He did not give it a name. The name *főbor* had practically disappeared by that time, or at least was no longer used by his aristocratic informants. But he emphasized that this type was "made by taking all the grapes together at first," and that it was "chiefly prepared by the peasants." The phrase "all the grapes together" indicates a wine in which grapes of various varietal origin and ripening times were crushed simultaneously, as had been the case with the earliest *főbor*.

Their lowly status notwithstanding, the "peasants" (smallholders) just happened to keep alive a tradition that would become of inestimable importance to the economic survival of the botrytis wines in the late-18th and early-19th centuries, when Hegyalja was plagued by trade barriers and falsified wines. The smallholders' gradual accommodation to varietal changes caused botrytis to become a feature of their wines, too (at least in botrytis years), and this set the stage for a thoroughly updated version of *főbor*, so much so that it deserved a new name.

The 'peasant' origin of this wine was reflected in the first name attached to it: *ordinárium*. While Douglass did not use that name, it must have been the wine he had mind as the "fourth kind" of Hegyalja wine, since he referred to it as "the common *Vin du pais*," even though shriveled grapes were included along with ripe and under-ripe ones. But whether or not Douglass had heard the name, *ordinárium* was how this wine was commonly being called in Hegyalja towards the end of the 18th century. The French scientist Chaptal's mention of it as a Tokaji wine type in 1805 shows that the name had even become known outside Hungary. Indeed, while Douglass assumed that this sort of wine was "entirely consumed in [Hungary]," it had in fact been increasingly gaining a foreign market, particularly in Poland. The lower price of *ordinárium* made it attractive, and it swiftly gained favor amongst Poles. In its new form (*i.e.*, overlapping the evolved sort of *főbor*), it shared in the character of *aszú* more than it ever had before. This was no doubt attributable in part to use of *darabbantartás* aging, which yielded both the dark yellow or amberish color and browning aromas otherwise associated with typical *aszú*.

However, Polish traders, familiar with the harvesting of *ordinárium*, apparently found the new form an even easier sell on their home market by anointing it with a name that would have more cachet than 'the ordinary one,' and would convey to Poles a better idea of what the wine actually was. Thus did the name '*samorodno vino*' become this wine type's commercial name in Poland. Moreover, its attractiveness to the Poles inevitably resulted in the Hegyaljans replacing the name *ordinárium* by *szamorodni*. Dercsényi indicated that this was occurring by the end of the 18th century [see the entry for *Ordinárium*].

Although the *szamorodni* name took hold because of marketing factors, it was appropriate that *ordinárium* be rechristened. It had come far from its origins in *főbor* and really was a new wine type: it was now invariably a botrytis wine, virtually as dependent on seasonal conditions as *aszú*. In turn, the role of 'soaking' became critical, and required as much attention and care as in the case of *aszú*. Plus, there was the aforementioned difference in barrel aging.

Szamorodni production had some effects on Hegyalja besides ensuring the Polish market during the difficult period following the partitions of Poland. For one thing, it brought more small producers into the realm of commercial wine. A few had dabbled in production of 1-, 2-, and 3-*puttonyos aszú* wines, since there had been a ready market amongst the Greek traders, and also in the small towns of the Upper Tisza if the smallholder was able to cart the wines himself. But virtually any grower with a cellar could turn out *szamorodni*, which did not require much more in the way of facilities and equipment than had the old *ordinárium*. It may even be conjectured that this new stimulus to greater and more widespread commercial involvement was a factor in causing the smallholders increasingly to resent aristocratic privilege in Hegyalja wine-growing and trade, and to demand free trade. That trend and the rise of *szamorodni* grew in tandem.

Szamorodni seems also to have had a varietal impact in Hegyalja. As an outgrowth of *főbor*, *ordinárium* originally had the same varietal 'profile': just about anything planted in the vineyards would do. But as a botrytis wine, selection had to be more rigorous for *szamorodni*. While this must have been helpful to *furmint*, that variety by 1800 was securing its place because of *aszú* alone and did not really need a boost from a new botrytis wine type. Instead, the indisputable beneficiary of *szamorodni* was the *hárslevelű*. Planting of that variety had been prohibited by Zemplén County in 1804, and was still frowned upon as late as 1848. But the variety's capacity for botrytization on the lower middle slopes endeared it to smallholders as they became more dependent on *szamorodni*. By the mid-19th century, the preference of the Poles both for *szamorodni* and for table wine from *hárslevelű* compelled Zemplén County to accept the variety.

*

In summary, the pattern of development from late-harvest to botrytis wines can be diagrammed as follows:

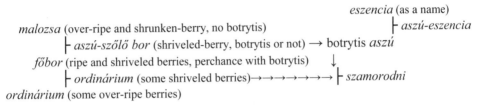

*

As proud a place as the foregoing names hold in Hegyalja history, none compares in age or durability with *máslás*. It can safely be presumed that it was in use long before Tokaji became a later-harvested white wine, and even before it was a white wine at all. The name means 'duplicate,' in reference to a wine made by using the remaining solids of a previously made wine. Originally, that wine would have been of any color, made from ordinary ripened grapes. But the name *máslás* would eventually be brought into the ranks of the botrytis white wines.

The durability of the *máslás* name owed to its flexibility. Indeed, far more than the other wine names used in Hegyalja, its meaning was ever in flux. Choose a century, and be prepared to encounter a different content to the term *máslás*. Komoróczi (1944) considered that in the early-17th century it might even have been used in lieu of *aszú* in Poland sometimes. It could be said that *máslás* was the 'residual' name amongst the others. That is, it was always of use, but always shifting in meaning in order to accommodate new names. Its content did not achieve stability until national legislation in the post-phylloxera period.

The chameleon quality of *máslás* goes back to its humble origins. It had been a 'wash-over' wine, a wine created to stretch the harvest by pouring water over the marc of the first fermented wine, squeezing again, in fiber (skins in distant times and sacks later on), and then fermenting the result into a low-alcohol wine. It was the *defterias* of the ancient Greeks, the *secundarium* of the Romans. Consequently, for about three centuries, from the decades following the Tatar invasion in the late-13th century, until the predominance of botrytis *aszú* wine, around the mid-17th century, the name *máslás* was used rather interchangeably with *lőre*, the term for weak wine made simply by mixing water and the marc of ordinary wine, and letting the mixture ferment.

The idea of pouring an unfermented liquid over the remains of a fermented one to get more out the vintage of the vintage never lost favor. Even the aristocracy found it convenient as a way, first, of giving sustenance and refreshment to their laborers and providing a quaffable beverage for their rural taverns, and later, of supplying an improved inexpensive table wine to customers in the Upper Tisza region of Hungary. This required a change, though, since the original *máslás* was utterly unacceptable for most urban consumers. But *főbor* made it possible to upgrade *máslás* by pouring water over sweeter and richer remains. This procedure led to a substitution of wine for the water later on, thus giving rise to an improved *máslás* wine that started gaining a market in Poland in the 16th century.

By the time botrytis *aszú* wine came along in the 17th century, the marc of *aszú* also began to be used. This can be considered the acme of *máslás*, and it became very much sought after under that name in Poland. Indeed, the curious hybrid term *aszú-máslás* came into use, which explains why *aszú* might sometimes have been called simply *máslás* in Poland in that era, as pointed out by Komoróczi (*i.e.*, much as *aszú-eszencia* was shortened to *eszencia* colloquially). The notion reached a contorted peak when merchants in Poland began pouring wine over the *aszú* lees left in their barrels and marketing the result as *máslás*, with indication of a *puttonyos* number, according to the *puttonyos* level of the *aszú* wine lees used.

Paradoxically, the corruption of the term was the best thing that ever happened to *máslás*. It compelled the Hegyaljans to think about what the term should mean. The problem was resolved by the introduction of yet another term: *fordítás*. Created towards the mid-19th century, the name *fordítás* represented an effort to narrow the meaning of *máslás* to that of a wine produced from the lees of *aszú* or *szamorodni*, while excluding the use of marc (which was to define *fordítás*). It might be thought of as a 'demotion' of *máslás*, but the clarification did secure it a specific and permanent place in the roster of Hegyalja botrytis wines.

*

The wine types had a background role in the delineation of Hegyalja. As the names of the wines became more 'fixed' in meaning, it grew easier, at least theoretically, to determine which locales did justice to those names. However, the size of the region and the differential recovery amongst locales following the Rákóczi wars in the early-18th century delayed a thorough, fair estimation.

From the time of the first later-harvested white wines in the late-15th century, until the introduction of a third hoeing in the second-half of the 16th, the use of 'Hegyalja' as a geographical term in connection with wine was fraught with confusion. Even the term *főbor* did not clarify matters, not even after it was understood to include botrytized grapes. *Főbor* could also be produced west of the Zemplén hills, in the Hernád valley, and to the northeast, in the Bodrogköz. Exporters to Poland were less inclined to make a distinction about place than about kind of wine.

The decisive change in this situation came in the 18th century, when any notional connection between *aszú* wine and *főbor* was severed. *Aszú* had become entirely associated with botrytis wine, such that it could only be produced in certain years. That had not been the case with *főbor*, nor even the so called *aszú-szőlő* wine, both of which also encompassed shriveled but *non*-botrytized berries in non-botrytis years. But even the narrower understanding of the term *aszú* did not resolve the delineation problem entirely, for again, the Hernád valley and some of the Bodrogköz locales could grow botrytized grapes of the same varietal kinds.

The telling factor turned out to be the aging of the botrytis wines, and specifically, barrel aging by the *darabbantartás* technique. Even with as little as two years of age, the Hernád and Bodrogköz wines lost their resemblance to Hegyalja wines. Hence, the production of bogus Tokaji wine in the 18th century was largely focused on trying to simulate the character of well-aged *aszú*. The surest method was to add some *eszencia* to a cheaper, manipulated wine. This was convenient, too, for as we have seen, Gyöngyösi in the early-18th century spoke out against producing too much *eszencia*, and Zemplén County was anxious to keep it out of the hands of the Greek traders.

Máslás had the unfortunate distinction of lending itself as the basis for the most convincing of the fraudulent *aszú*-s. This was particularly pernicious on the Polish market where, as noted above, Polish traders thoroughly bastardized the *máslás* concept by pouring any wine over the lees of *aszú* and selling it as '(2-, 3-, 4-, 5-)-*puttonyos-máslás*.' This continued until *szamorodni* began sweeping the Polish market in the early-19th century. In the meantime, the popularity of *máslás* hindered a careful delineation of Hegyalja if only because it was not in Zemplén County's immediate interest to issue hasty proscriptions against use of the Hegyalja name by communities whose main 'fault' might be little more than small size and lack of name recognition.

To the extent that wine types might have influenced a 'dilution' of territorial notions of Hegyalja, *szamorodni* appears to be the most likely suspect. When the Rákóczis delineated the region in the mid-17th century, botrytis *aszú* would have served as the standard for inclusion (keeping in mind that some people were still using the term *főbor* rather than *aszú*). This is demonstrable because the only basis on which the Rákóczis were able to have the vineyard-tracts classified was the propensity for extensive and exceptional botrytization [see the entry for Cserfás, in Part III]. *Szamorodni*, though, cast a somewhat different light on the subject. Some areas that could reliably produce good *szamorodni* might generally have been rather minor producers of *aszú* in quantity, and mediocre (2nd Class) in quality. This pertained especially to the areas at the southwestern and northeastern ends of Hegyalja. It was above all the commercial imperative caused by *szamorodni*'s hold on the Polish market that held the delineation question in limbo.

Fortunately, the potential for detrimental effects of a geographical 'dilution' of the Hegyalja name could be parried. It was accomplished by national legislation between 1893 and 1936. Two key measures were the elimination of locales that did not measure up in typicity, and the stipulation that only hillside vineyards were to be used for the botrytis wines, with no use of must or wine from the adjacent lowlands. But also, the wine types ultimately were given legal definition, with specific requirements for sugar and non-sugar extract content. After being subject to vagaries for over three centuries, the nomenclature for the botrytis wine types had been carved in stone.

* * *

APPENDIX ESSAY:

Tokaji Wine Production during Hungary's Communist Era

Current developments in Hegyalja are viewed against the background of the communist era. Typically, this leads to utterly negative generalizations to the effect that the region's tradition of 'fine wine' came to an end. But what it actually meant for Hegyalja, in concrete terms, is little known to Western commentators on Tokaji. Making matters worse, those of their Hungarian informants who were active in Hegyalja under communism supply anecdotal material which is lopsidedly selective in decrying former conditions, either because of how the questions are asked or translated, or because of their present employers or own financial interests. Furthermore, such information is available on a firsthand basis mostly from the latter half of the era, since the generation most active during the first half has largely died out. Another drawback of the anecdotal information is that, whereas Hegyalja is a large region, the providers of the anecdotes can only report on experiences and details at their local 'station.' It is to be hoped that Hungarian agricultural historians will undertake research in a broad variety of documents and records from the era and present their findings. In the meantime, the following is offered as overview and context.

*

If we are to be objective in assessing the communist era in Hegyalja, two aspects must be kept in mind in reviewing it. First, it needs to be recognized that the era was *not* a unitary period of 40 years during which the conditions for the wine industry were static and in all respects negative for Tokaji wine, no matter the economic distortion that characterized the period as a whole. Second, it is necessary to distinguish viti-vinicultural developments that occurred specifically because of the communist regime, from those that might have occurred irrespectively of regime.

For the sake of convenience and prudence, the communist period in Hegyalja may be divided into two roughly equal parts, from 1949 until 1971, and from 1971 until 1989. Although other, sub-periods presumably could be delineated, notably, the years up until the 1956 Hungarian Revolution, not enough documentary information is available to specify them accurately, whether in terms of time-frame or characteristics. That is, the sets of chief features by which to recognize sub-periods are not fully identifiable at this time, and it will be a difficult task in that it involves economic, organizational, and technical aspects of Hegyalja wine production, not to mention records of the professional (enological) assessment of particular wines from various vintages.

The significance of 1971 as the key division is not arbitrary. It was the year in which the Tokaj-Hegyalja State Farm Wine-Facility (*Tokaj-Hegyaljai Állami Gazdaság Borkombinát*) was established. This represented the one clear break in the circumstances of Hegyalja wine production to be found during the communist era. Far from being a matter of happenstance, it occurred in tandem with the New Economic Mechanism (NEM) that was initiated at the end of the 1960s [see the entry for Kádár, in Part I]. The aim of the NEM was to reduce central-planning by allowing individual enterprises to be decision-makers, with elements of supply-and-demand at work. In short, the NEM was the single major divide in the economic history of Socialist Hungary, and the creation of the Tokaj-Hegyalja Wine-Facility was its manifestation in Hegyalja.

*

For Western connoisseurs, the chief discomfort about Tokaji wine after 1949 was the elimination of the vineyard properties of the former nobility, and its presumed flipside, a headlong descent into the anathema of collectivized production. The properties of the Habsburgs, and those of princes, counts, and barons were indeed seized by the state, as were those of prominent Horthyite (pro-Nazi) owners. The best properties were retained for state or cooperative farms, as entities,

256

while the rest were redistributed to peasants who had no vineyards. But the amount of land involved was not major relative to the total vineyard area under cultivation (Boros, 1996).

The first two decades of communist rule in Hegyalja was a period of fits and starts, not least of all with regard to dealing with the smallholders who cultivated most of the vineyard land, whether as their own or within the framework of 'joint-cultivation' associations. This had to do with the ideological issue of assimilating them into socialized wine-growing. Instead of collective farms with their state-owned land, cooperative farms and specialized wine-growing units or work-teams composed of local smallholders were seen as the most expedient method of achieving this end, and they had been formed in most Hegyalja communes by 1960 (those in the smaller villages usually joined with cooperatives in nearby larger communities).

However, the overall effect of the change in regime, especially until the 1956 revolution, was decidedly negative. The fundamental setback was that investment in industry became the top priority, and agriculture took a far backseat. This system also entailed obligatory deliveries of grapes or must at minimal prices. For the smallholder, there was no incentive (historically, though, this was hardly a first in Hegyalja, and indeed was, practically and ironically, a return to the 'first-dibs' rights that the aristocracy enjoyed on smallholders' output before the 19th century). Parcels situated on higher or steeper land were abandoned, or rather, were left abandoned, since this problem had been lingering since phylloxera and the 1930s' Depression. As for the peasant beneficiaries of the redistribution of vineyard land, they usually did not have requisite knowledge or experience, and consequently, they frequently allowed the land to go fallow. By 1961, there was less vineyard land being cultivated in Hegyalja than at the end of the Second World War, and the average quality of the remaining land was lower.

At the same time, though, it was realized that Hegyalja could make an important contribution to the national economy, both in hard-currency earnings and in trading with the Soviet Bloc. After the 1956 revolution, the new government under Kádár gave more leeway to smallholders. Cooperatives became more of an end in their own right rather than a stepping-stone to collectivization, and the position of the membership bore at least some small resemblance to the cooperatives of the Interwar Period. The growers now found themselves selling their product, whether grapes, must, or wine, to cooperatives that were reorganized according to a mixed-bag of 'socialist economic principles' and season-to-season pragmatism. But, even so, uncertainty about the future crippled initiative, especially in reconstructing vineyards on good but steep slopes.

For all of that, the communist ideal of total collectivization was never even approached, and actually receded as a goal as time went by, particularly during the second-half of the era. In 1961, 11 percent of 4,900 hectares of vineyard land were worked only by individuals; in 1973, individuals worked 40 percent of the 6,500 hectares of vineyards. Eventual collectivization remained a theoretical goal (even if cynically so for politicians), at least until the NEM period, but this would have to await not merely the passing of the older generation of growers (as a matter of political expediency after the 1956 revolution), but also certain changes in viticulture.

*

Someday it might be argued that the entire 40-year period of communism was but the next to last stage in reconstructing Hegyalja subsequent to the phylloxera episode of 1885-1890 (the last stage beginning with the reemergence of capitalism in 1990). Although progress had been made in the first-half of the 20th century, particularly in terms of total acreage under cultivation, the replanting was very uneven by locale and site. Notably, many high-quality vineyard-tracts were left out during the Interwar Period, often because owners (some of them in East Slovakia) lacked sufficient funds and commercial motivation due to the worldwide Depression and wine glut.

Further, Hegyalja overall (excluding the nobility) had never recovered in terms of reconstructing the vineyards according to modern precepts, such as planting in rows, soil/wind erosion prevention, and the selection of the best cultivars. The First World War, the dismemberment of Austria-Hungary, the economic troubles of the Interwar Period, and of course the Second World War, all hampered efforts at qualitative reconstruction. During the early years of communism, reconstruction efforts were resumed by the same technical specialists as previously, with the aim of restoring and updating vineyard cultivation. In 1950, for instance, a detailed cadastral survey of Hegyalja was completed. However, because of the government's favoritism towards industry in that period, funds were not allocated to carrying out much of the work recommended by the survey, and deficient organizational clarity hampered even the planning of such activity.

As far as land was concerned, the priority in Hegyalja at the advent of communism remained what it had been previously: to find a way to update the vineyards while being faced with a shortage of agricultural labor (first because of emigration, and then because of labor siphoned off to industry), and being situated in one of Hungary's poorest regions. By the mid-1950s, it was clear that this would entail mechanization, which in turn would require a thorough overhaul in the planting of vineyards. During the 1960s, one aspect of this was to experiment with various vine-training and vine-spacing possibilities. But, owing to the size of Hegyalja, its varied growing conditions, and the fact that only three in every ten years was a botrytis year, it was going to take decades to obtain reliable results by which to make sound decisions about reconstruction.

Meanwhile, Hegyalja was deemed a potentially valuable resource for earning hard-currency by selling the region's specialty wines in Western countries, while also sending a large quantity of table wine for barter trade with socialist trading partners in East Europe. Consequently, the solution arrived at by centralized authority in the wine industry during the 1960s was a makeshift 'reconstruction,' whereby vineyard area was to be expanded and viticultural practices updated, not usually by bringing abandoned tracts on the slopes back into production, but just the opposite, by planting new vineyards on the 'skirt' (*szoknya*) lands, or 'level-country' (*sík-vidék*), at the bottom of the hills. These lands had always been considered inferior for vines, and instead were used mainly for field crops. Moreover, earlier legislation on Hegyalja had specified that only the slopes, whether upper or lower, could be used for the production of the specialty wines. Duly, experts spoke out against the skirts, even in the state-run print media. But a command-economy could carry out its plans in the face of the professional criticism and local opposition.

Central authority was attracted to the skirts because they easily accommodated the foreseen progression of mechanization, and ultimately, collectivization (that is, ownership by the state and cultivation by state employees). As for the old legal provision for 'slopes-only' cultivation, the regime could finesse the issue by claiming that the product of the skirt-vineyards would be treated apart from that of the hillside vineyards, and be used only for table wines destined for the Soviet and other East Bloc markets. Indeed, the major communist-era law addressing Hegyalja, that of 1959, specifically stated that the specialty wines could be produced only from 1st and 2nd Class vineyard-tracts on the hillsides, as classed in the cadastral survey of 1950. (This desire to optimize the availability of botrytized grapes by expanding sources of common wine was mirrored in the Slovakian area of Hegyalja. However, the solution there was to expand the territory of the Slovakian portion by including several villages that had not been recognized as part of Hegyalja earlier, and in so doing to include lesser quality land, and grape varieties not authorized in Hungarian Hegyalja. This was an object of the 1959 Slovakian legislation.)

It did not take long for even the proponents to realize the folly in having created the skirt-vineyards. The growing season was short because of late budding and early ripening, and the sugar-content of the grapes was low. Even worse, the theory that more botrytized grapes from the hill vineyards would be harvested by leaving table wine production to the skirts proved illusory. In the socialized sector, the need to harvest the skirt-vineyards earlier than the hillside vineyards typically led to harvesting the latter at too early a date, just for the sake of convenience and cost-savings in the use of labor and machinery. By the early 1980s, some of the cooperatives were eliminating skirt lands from vine cultivation, and returning them to other agricultural uses.

*

Throughout these decades, profitability, and especially the ability to earn hard-currency, was at the core of decision-making for the state economic apparatus, the cooperatives, and the Tokaj-Hegyalja State Farm Wine-Facility alike. Modest positive steps were taken as early as the 1960s. This mostly had to do with strategies for making the most progress possible in vineyard reconstruction with limited resources. Efforts were focused on micro-regions that were not only best suited to large-scale viticulture, but also of good quality. The major drawback of this approach was that the steepest slopes had to be brushed aside. However, the actual quality 'loss' only pertained to certain south-facing tracts with ideal soil type and stone covering (an eminent example would be the Zsákos tract [see that entry, in Part III]). Moreover, the experience of the post-phylloxera period had demonstrated that, because of the complexities of its fabrication, Tokaji's quality was dependent on more than just high altitude and great degree of slope.

Thus, the creation of terraces suitable for mechanization became a priority. Terraces were not a new idea in Hegyalja, and in fact had antecedents in the 19th century, and even the 18th. But since this was a relatively expensive proposition, it was reserved for the lower- and upper-middle slopes where it could be accomplished most effectively, with higher yields of sugar-rich grapes. Some famous sites, such as Szarvas, enjoyed precedence. Yet another measure to concentrate resources was to ignore areas deemed less worthwhile for reconstruction, notably the Szerencs hills area in southwesternmost Hegyalja, but also in areas situated more deeply in the Zemplén hills, farther from the Bodrog river and having a less warm growing season. Likewise, areas that suffered from erosion or were subject to micro-climate hazards were disregarded as not being worth the investment of money or labor.

In the most practical terms, all of this came down to trying to find a balance between grape yields and wine quality. A lot of experimentation took place, especially with varietal clones in connection with the various vine-training systems (such as Lenz-Moser). This is a notable instance in which it may safely be said that wine-growers in Hegyalja would have been looking at the same issues and choices irrespectively of regime, if only because of the veritable explosion of new cultivation ideas in Western Europe and the New World (the difference, of course, is that independent commercial producers would have been far more diverse in their perception of 'correct solutions'), not least of all depending on the location of their properties. Communist officials did favor higher yields, but they were held in check by the threat that the regime would not see the results it wanted in hard-currency earnings from investment if the quality of the botrytis wines nose-dived because of yield increases.

As regards yields and quality, some post-communist Hungarian accounts assert the utter negativity of developments. But the later-day reviews of the era make no distinction between average yields and those on the upland (1st and 2nd Class) areas and those on the lowland ('skirt') parts, let alone 'technicalities' such as terrace, training, and drainage systems. Furthermore, are we speaking of botrytis or non-botrytis years? What of different soil types?

What of the different clones? What of all of the factors joined together? The most authoritative statement from the period itself was made in 1974 by the technical expert László Brezovcsik: "The contemporary cultivation methods do not exclude the possibility of quality production, but in connection with this the appropriate level of budding must be ensured. In Hegyalja, with the *furmint*, *hárslevelű* and *muscat lunel* [*muskotály*] varieties, it is not permitted to produce more than 100 quintals [10 metric tons] [of grapes] per hectare. We can consider 80 quintals [8 metric tons] per hectare normal on areas in good condition" (*Tokajhegyalja Borgazdasága*). Later, in 1983, it was shown, on the basis of 1970-1982 results, that 8 metric tons per hectare was also the yield at which the Tokaj-Hegyalja State Farm Wine-Facility, under the more market-like conditions of the New Economic Mechanism, made a profit (Boros, 1996).

*

Somewhat paradoxically, finances became more of a threat to quality as economic conditions were loosening under the NEM, precisely because enterprises, including the Wine-Facility, had to make decisions that favored their own profitability. For instance, as a matter of cost savings, barrels were not always replaced when they should have been. But, as yet, no studies have appeared that address, in a point by point manner, how the Facility or the cooperatives performed their balancing acts. All indications are, though, that a significantly greater dropoff in 'average quality' took place in table wines than in the specialty botrytis wines.

From the point of view of profitability, threats posed by the quality-versus-quantity dilemma could be offset by savings in making common wines for the East Bloc. Even prior to the Wine-Facility, this was, after all, the stimulus for planting the skirt vineyards. When mention is made of low-quality wines being produced in Hegyalja, these are the wines to which the statements apply. Conversely, when the literature of the period speaks of Tokaji being exported to 50 or 60 capitalist countries, this was the market for the preponderance of botrytis wines. The Soviet Union was not a significant, nor even a desired, market for *aszú*.

After the inception of the Wine-Facility, which had to respond to market factors in order to stay afloat under the New Economic Mechanism, a new marketing strategy had to be found. Thus, 'flexibility' became a byword. The Facility, with the assistance of the state wine export agency, had to make a critical assessment of where their various wines could be marketed, in terms of countries, demographics (income levels), and tastes. This "market-segmentation" (*piac-szegmentálás*), as it was called, became the guiding principle for the Wine-Facility.

There was nothing systemically 'socialistic' about this approach. Large Western cooperatives in this same period were demonstrating that a cooperative could turn out a wide range of products, and could aim them at specific markets (the preeminently apt example, vis-à-vis Hegyalja and the Wine-Facility, was the obligatory cooperative on the Greek island of Samos [Lambert-Gócs, *The Wines of Greece,* 1990]). For the Wine-Facility, the size of Hegyalja and the existence of several large and contemporary wine-making units were practically ideal for the "market-segmentation" approach. Further, one of the peculiarities of the communist era in Hegyalja was that progress in the vineyards (wine-growing per se) and in the cellars (wine production and maturation) was out of sync. Namely, adaptation in wine fabrication with regard to product differentiation could be achieved almost immediately, whereas viticultural adaptation was a long-term proposition.

*

Hungarian viti-vinicultural specialists during the communist period had little or no knowledge that Tokaji wine was an object of scrutiny by Western observers, much less any idea of the extent to which this scrutiny was misinformed. The scientists mostly dealt with international colleagues through the International Office of Vines and Wines (OIVV), which was a means of staying in direct touch with the West that the Hungarian specialists greatly valued. On the other hand, their familiarity with popular Western wine-writing was meager or non-existent. Unbeknownst to Hungarian enologists, Tokaji was the subject of numerous adverse statements from the pens of Western wine-writers, and some enologists too, none of whom, however, offered any proof of their allegations and speculations. This can be dated at least as far back as Alec Waugh's 1959 pronouncement that, "Tokaji exists no more," and continued as an omnibus accusation against the communist regime throughout the next three decades. Even today, many Western writers refer to the communist period as nothing less than a break in Tokaji tradition.

The embarrassing fact, for the West, is that a variety of proofs of the general continuity of tradition were readily at hand for even a superficial researcher. Amber color in the communist era wines offers easily documented proof. Virtually all descriptions from *before* the 20th century refer to Tokaji as amber or yellow-brown [see the entry for Color, in Part IV]. Further, the production of the botrytis wines as described in enological texts during the communist period coincided with those from pre-war times. One need only compare the *Borászat* (Enology) volume edited by Kádár in 1973 to Pettenkoffer's *Borgazdaság* (Viniculture) of 1937, or for that matter, either of those to the text of Kossuth in 1903, of Szabó/Török in 1867, and of Szirmay in 1798. It is to be noted, too, that there is no discrepancy to be found between those accounts and the description of Slovakian Tokaji production by Farkaš in 1973 (the same year as the Kádár volume), or in the pre-communist work of Fiala/Sedláček in 1936. Communist Czechoslovakia would have been under no obligation to go along with the purported Hungarian transgressions against traditional Tokaji production techniques just because of 'socialist solidarity.'

*

Under any regime, post-war Hungary would have been anxious to resuscitate Tokaji's reputation and maximize its export potential. Despite the error of planting flat-land vineyards, it was characteristic of the period that viti-vinicultural research that had been ongoing before the Second World War was resumed and carried forward. Communism had very little effect on the directions taken by such research. However, Western commentators during that period repeatedly charged the communist regime with two major 'transgressions,' namely, the use of pasteurization and the use of concentrated must. (Ironically, they had no idea about vineyard-land issues other than their preconceptions about collectivization, which were wrong.)

The chief technical concern in wine-making in Hegyalja since the mid-19th century was the stabilization of the Tokaji speciality wines. In past centuries, the sweet wines had too frequently arrived abroad and re-fermented, to the detriment of Tokaji's good name. To forestall this, a minor degree of fortification had been specified since 1936, though only at the point when the wines were bottle-ready. However, many growers did not like this solution, and enologists looked primarily to some form of heat treatment as a better one. The Hungarian chemist Preysz had experimented with heating Tokaji wines as early as 1861. But the technical requirements for large-scale use of his findings were beyond either the comprehension or the means of most growers. The large producers who had an export market steadfastly clung to painstaking adherence to tradition in not sending wines forth without a 'proper' maturation.

In the early period of communist rule, the enologist Ferenczi worked out a special 'heat-treatment' to stabilize the wines. By his method, it was possible to allow the wines to age fully in barrel by the old technique, so that all beneficial biological processes had taken place, and then to subject the wines to a protracted, low-level heat-treatment that stabilized them biologically while also allowing them to continue to go through chemical evolutions in bottle, to the benefit of the wines [see the entry for Ferenczi Heat-Treatment, in Part IV]. Addressing this issue in 1988, the enologist Ákos Ásvány, of the National Wine-Qualifying Institute, had this comment: "domestic and foreign experts alike can testify that the quality of the *aszú* and *szamorodni* wines does not decrease in bottle, but improves significantly year by year, as the large number of components in them continually form new chemical substances" (see Correspondence, in the Bibliography).

But, in the West, the use and particulars of the Ferenczi treatment were unknown, and the image of standard pasteurization became a major charge against 'Communist Tokaji.' Tokaji was thought of as a 'mummy,' dead-on-arrival, incapable of maturing further. The heat-treatment was also said to have very negative effects on taste. The strongest statement was made in 1976 by Terry Robards: "In comparison tastings with Sauternes from good vintages and German Rhines and Mosels of at least Beerenauslese degree of sweetness...even an Aszú of five *puttonyos* will rarely match the others. Tokaji is not quite as soft and velvety, perhaps because the Hungarian Government now pasteurizes it to stabilize it for shipping" (*The New York Times Book of Wines*). But the textural feature to which Robards referred was nothing new. The Hungarian enologist Pettenkoffer had noted the same in 1937, in pre-communist Hungary: "The [Sauternes] wines are softer and smoother than the Tokaji or Rhine sweet wines, but not as fat."

*

Equally troubling to Western observers was their belief that the sweetness of Tokaji wine was now dependent at least in part on concentrated must. Connoisseurs and enologists in the West routinely alleged or suggested that concentrated must was being used, and they seemed almost to reinforce each other's concerns. In the case of the connoisseurs, this had to do mainly with the more or less 'toasty' or 'toffee-ish' aromas associated with the browning of sugars. For the enologists, it had to do with Tokaji's content of hydroxymethylfurfural (HMF), which is usually taken as incontrovertible proof that concentrated must has been used.

Perhaps the most damaging misinformation about Tokaji in the communist era appeared in 1969, when A. Massel wrote that Hungarian law actually *permitted* the use of concentrated must in Tokaji (*Applied Wine Chemistry and Technology*). But Massel had mistakenly assumed that Hungarian law allowing the use of concentrated must in 'dessert-wines' (*csemegeborok*) also applied to Tokaji. In fact, Hungarian law did not treat the Tokaji botrytis wines as 'dessert wines,' but instead as 'wine-delicacies' (*borkülönlegességek*), under which the use of concentrated must was *im*permissible. (The use of concentrated must in making Tokaji table wines was permitted within certain parameters, and this became routine in the case of ones made from the skirt vineyards because of their usually low sugar-content.)

The smells of browning and the content of HMF derived in the first place from the chemical nature of Tokaji, specifically its unusually high content of nitrogenous compounds. As a result of the Maillard reaction, those compounds react with sugar to produce HMF and cause browning without heat being applied to the sugars (which is responsible for HMF in concentrated must). This had nothing to do with the communist regime. Tokaji's content of HMF had been noticed in 1935-1937 (Kniphorst/Kruisheer), prior to the communist era, and it was concluded that these likely were natural occurrences in mature Tokaji. Furthermore, the level of HMF increases with time in barrel; and the Tokaji specialty wines did receive several years of aging. However, later on, the Ferenczi heat-treatment also increased the level of HMF (one might wonder whether Ferenczi's method would therefore have been banned under other political regimes).

Finally, the use of concentrated must in the specialty wines would have had a couple of implications that are not borne out by the record. First, it would suggest that wines falsely called *aszú* could have been turned out from *any* vintage, not just those which produced botrytized fruit. Yet, there were the expected gaps in *aszú* vintage dates; bottled *aszú* wines were turned out only from years when major botrytization occurred. Second, the use of concentrated must would imply that *eszencia* was not available to boost sweetness. Yet, there is no evidence of a cessation in *eszencia* output. Also, since *aszú* wines during the communist era sold slowly, there would have been no impetus to over-produce and stockpile them by resorting to concentrated must.

*

There can be little question that during the first-half of the communist period, even after the 1956 revolution, there was tension between Communist Party officials in Hegyalja on the one hand, and viti-vinicultural specialists, as well as many smallholders, on the other, as to future directions in the region. Nevertheless, the Party did not squelch debate, since all parties were concerned to put Hegyalja on its best footing for success on the world market and the earning of hard currency. After the Tokaj-Hegyalja State Farm Wine-Facility was created in 1971, its vested interest was in producing reliably fine specialty wines. Further, with the exception of the borderline legality in planting the skirt vineyards, the government did not abrogate the long-standing laws and regulations pertaining to Tokaji, fail to enforce them, or promulgate laws that undermined those. Moreover, it was during the communist period, in 1980, that the addition of spirits was banned.

Many of the same specialists who were active in the pre-war period continued their work after the communists came to power. In the sphere of grape-growing, studies as to the most suitable vineyard-tracts and the best clonal selection had the enthusiastic stamp of approval from Party functionaries, even if their focus was not centered on achieving 'top quality' relative to previous eras. It is especially notable that this work went on in the early communist period, despite being at odds with the agricultural 'principles' of the Soviet pseudo-agronomist, Trofim Lysenko, who was an opponent, on ideological grounds, of notions of 'superior' pieces of land or plant varieties.

Likewise, in wine-making, enologists in Hegyalja were exploring an array of topics as broad as the many distinctive aspects of Tokaji production. Heading the list was, of course, stabilization of the wines, which culminated in the Ferenczi heat-treatment. But virtually every detail of producing *aszú* and *szamorodni* wines was being studied, including the factors that account for 'Tokaji character,' the proper role for the *darabbantartás* technique, the contribution of the molds on the cellar walls, the differential effects of drier and more humid parts of the cellars, etc.

Most surprising of all is that research was conducted to *reduce* barrel aging. This is totally at odds with the belief of Westerners who since 1990 have averred that aging had been unduly *lengthened* during the communist era. But, as early as 1950, enologists were experimenting "for the purpose of fast maturation of the *aszú* and *szamorodni* wines" (*Vinicultural Research Institute Yearbook*). In 1963, Dömötör/Katona stated: "We acknowledge the primacy of the traditionally matured *aszú*, but emphasize that, alongside it, it is also necessary to ensure an appropriate role for Tokaji *aszú* that has been readied at an early age, and thus, capable of being commercialized even after one year of age." That was still in the first-half of the communist era, and while Dömötör/Katona might have been at the far edge of realism about aging the botrytis wines, their statement was a harbinger of the aforementioned "market segmentation" outlook: insofar as the regime was stepping into the cellars of Hegyalja, it was not averse to sending forth whatever kind of *aszú* was wanted in capitalist markets, provided that all legal requirements for *aszú* were met.

Beyond the technical realm, the processing and commercialization of Tokaji took an unexpected turn during the second-half of the communist period. The shortcomings of having a monopolistic buyer of must from smallholders had become all too clear. The state purchasing agency dictated prices that were only marginally remunerative. Yet, the state could hardly afford to see smallholders go under, since they worked much of the vineyard land in Hegyalja. One result under the NEM was to allow cooperatives to produce and bottle wines that competed with those of the Tokaj-Hegyalja State Farm Wine-Facility. The cooperatives at Mád and Tolcsva, two of the major Hegyalja vineyard areas, took advantage of this and marketed their own bottled wines.

As the New Economic Mechanism continued to unfold, it was suggested in the mid-1980s that smaller groups of producers be allowed to join together to produce and bottle wine. However, this would have faced practical difficulties because many smallholders had cast off their barrels and vats during the early years of communism. They would have needed extraordinary financing, including hard currency with which to make purchases of equipment from Western countries.

*

Even observers who make no presumptions about the effect of regime might wonder if Tokaji during the communist era was equal to that of earlier times. Direct qualitative comparisons were impossible since the Hegyalja cellars were ransacked during the war. But it is hard to imagine wines much better than the *aszú-eszencia*-s of the Tarcal Viti-Vinicultural Research Institute, or even the 5-*puttonyos aszú* wines from the best vintages when given good cellaring. A 1956 5-*puttonyos aszú* carefully stored in Hegyalja was still an exceptional wine in 1999; *et cetera*.

For that matter, though, just when during the history of Tokaji botrytis wines was quality 'best'? How are the changes in grape varieties or the ups and downs in cultivated area to be addressed? Plus, the vicissitudes of Hegyalja history encumber the specification of a particular era as the acme of quality. This pretty much leaves us, today, with our own idealized notions.

Balassa (1991) attributed a decrease in *aszú* quality (which "does not reach that of the 18th century") to the skirt vineyards, though he gave no information as to how or in what time period the fruit of the skirts entered into *aszú* production. A different assessment was made several years earlier, in 1984, still in the communist period, by no less an authority than Ásvány. He stated that the post-war *aszú*-s did not reach the intensity of bouquet of the best pre-war wines, and attributed this to the totality of changes that had taken place, not to any particular one.

Since many changes resulted from factors that would have come into play no matter the form of government, the role of communism, as such, in decreasing 'average quality' in *aszú* seems mostly tangential. Still, the regime stood in the way of specialists who might otherwise have made wines as good as any in the past, and of greater stability. But even so, the wines of the communist period lived up to the encomium bestowed by Alexander Wekerle in 1888:

> "Golden-yellowish color, strength without any harshness, and flavor of its own kind: a pleasant, discrete, chalky taste, sweetness wrapped in full-bodiedness, in *aszú* almost in denseness. These are the marks of Tokaji wine, whose matchless features are besides that apparent in the way its strength, taste, smell, and flavor, beginning with the first touch on the lips and the tip of the tongue, proceed through the entire mouth cavity, throat, and stomach, pleasurably stirring every organ of taste."

*   *   *

BIBLIOGRAPHY

[Regarding Hungarian archival documents, see the closing note.]

PRIMARY SOURCES

History

Gyula Antalffy, "Szeptemberben érett, Októberben édes ['Ripe in September, Sweet in October' (an adage)], in *Élet és Irodalom* (Life and Literature), September 20, 1985.

Iván Balassa, *Tokaj-Hegyalja Szőleje és Bora* [The Tokaj-Hegyalja Vineyard and Wine] (Tokaj, 1991).

I. Bartha "Borkereskedés Problémai Hegyalján a XIX. Század Első Felében" [Hegyalja Wine Trade Difficulties in the first-half of the 19th c.], *Agrártörténelmi Szemle*, Vol. XVI, No. 1-2 (1974), pp. 264-276.

Sándor Bodnár, "A Tokaj-Hegyaljai Borok Minőség és Eredetvédelme" [The Quality and Origin Control of the Tokaj-Hegyalja Wines], *Borgazdaság* [Viniculture], Vol. XXXIV, No. 4 (1986), pp. 148-152.

László Boros, *Tokaj-Hegyalja Szőlő- és Borgazdaságának Földrajzi Alapjai és Jellemzői* [Geographical Foundations and Characteristics of Tokaj-Hegyalja's Vineyard and Wine Economy] (Budapest, 1996).

Samu Borovszki, ed., *Zemplén Vármegye* [Zemplén County] (Budapest: Apollo Literary Soc., 1903).

J. Dömötör, J. Katona, *Magyar Borok-Borvidékek* [Hung. Wines/Wine Regions] (Bp: Mező. Kiadó, 1963).

G. Fábián, ed., *Tokajhegyalja Borgazdasága* [Tokaj-Hegyalja Viniculture] (Bp: M. Mező. Múzeum, 1974).

Piroska Feyér, *Szőlő- és Bor-Gazdaságunk Történetének Alapja* [The Foundation of our Viti- and Vinicultural History] (Budapest: Akadémiai Kiadó, 1970).

György Komoróczi, *Borkivitelünk Észak Felé* [Our Wine Exports to the North], (Kassa: Kazincy, 1944).

János Kossuth, "Bortermelés és Gyümölcstermelés" [Wine- and Fruit-growing"], in Borovszki (above).

Lajos Nagy, ed. *Tokaji Útikalauz* [Tokaji Journey Guide] (Miskolcs: Panorama, 1963).

Miklós Pap, *A Tokaji* [Tokaji-an] (Budapest: Gondolat, 1985).

Irén Spotkovszky, *A Tokaj-Hegyalja Szőlőgazdaságának Geografiája* [The Geography of the Viticulture of Tokaj-Hegyalja] (Budapest: Patria, 1914).

J. Szabó-Jilek, ed., *Munkás Évek* [Industrious Years] (Budapest: Viticultural Research Institute, 1962).

J. Szabó-Jilek, *Nagy Hírű Boraink: A Tokaji Borok Életútja* [Our Wines of Great Fame: The Path of Tokaji Wine] (Budapest: Mezőgazdasági Kiadó, 1977).

J. Szabó and I. Török, *Tokaj-Hegyaljai Album* (Pest: Vinicultural Society of Tokay-Hegyalja, 1867).

Antal Szirmay. *Notitia historica, politica, oeconomica montium et locorum viniferorum comitatus Zempleniensis* [Historical, political, economic notes on the wine-bearing hills and places of Zemplén County] (Kassa: Ellinger, 1798).

István Vincze, "Magyar Borpincék" [Hungarian Wine Cellars], *Néprajzi Értesítő* [Ethnographical Reporter], Vol. 40 (1958), pp. 83-103.

Viti-Viniculture (Technical)

K. Almási, V. Nilov, "Aminokisloty Tokajskikh vin" [Amino acids of Tokaji wine], in *Vinodelie I Vinogradarstvo* [Enology and Viticulture], No. 4 (1964), pp. 10-15.

Ákos Ásvány, "Tokaji borok hydroxi-metil-furfurol tartalmáról" [Concerning the hydroxymethylfurfural content of Tokaji Wines] in *Borgazdaság* [Viniculture], Vol. 31, No. 4 (1983), pp. 151-152.

Pál Csepregi, János Zilai, *Szőlőfajtáink* [Our Grape Varieties] (Bp: Mezőgazdasági Kiadó, 1976).

Sándor Ferenczi, *A Szőlő, a Must és a Bor Kémiája* [The Chemistry of Grapes, Must and Wine] (Budapest: Mezőgazdasági Kiadó, 1966).

A. Gvozdjáková, "Srdce-Vino-Antioxidanty: Tokajské vino v novom svetle" [Heart-Wine-Antioxidants: Tokaji wine in a new light], in *Kvasný Průmysl* [Fermentation Industry], Vol. 42, No. 9 (1996), 278-279.

G. Hajós, *et. al.* "Changes in biogenic amine content of Tokaj grapes, wines and *aszú*-wines," in *Journal of Food Science*, Vol. 65, No. 7 (2000).

S. Hidvéghy, "Szőlőtalajvizsgálatok Tokajhegyalján" [Vineyard Soil Studies in Hegyalja], in *Szőlészeti Kutató Intézet Évkönyve* [Vit. Research Inst. Yrbk.] (Bp: Mezőgazdasági Kiadó, 1950), pp. 175-190.

John E. Hodge, "Origin of Flavors in Foods: Non-enzymatic Browning Reactions," in H.W. Schulz, ed., *The Chemistry and Physiology of Flavors* (Westport, CT: AVI Publishing, 1967).

Ms. Z. Jeszenszky, P. Szalka, "A Magyar Borok Oximetil-furfurol Tartalma" [The Oxymethylfurfural Content of Hungarian Wines], *Borgazdaság*, Vol. 23, No. 1 (1975), pp. 22-26.

Gyula Kádár, ed., *Borászat* [Enology] (Budapest: Mezőgazdasági Kiadó, 1973).

Z. Kerényi, "Tokaji borkülönlegességek aroma-anyagainak gázkromatográfiás vizsgálata' [Gas-chromatographic examination of the aromatic material of Tokaji wine-specialties], *Borgazdaság*, Vol. 25, No. 1 (1977), pp. 26-29.

Béla Lengyel, "Tokaj-hegyaljai borok érlelésével kapcsolatos megfigyelések" [Observations in connection with the maturation of Tokaj-Hegyalja wines], in *Szőlészeti Kutató Intézet Évkönyve* [Vinicultural Research Institute Yearbook], Vol. X (Budapest: Mezőgazdasági Kiadó, 1950).

M.S.P. Nikfardjam, G. László, H.Dietrich, "Polyphenols and Antioxidative Capacity in Hungarian Tokaj Wines" (Research Paper, Hungary, 2002).

--, "Resveratrol-Derivatives and Antioxidative Capacity in Wines made from *botrytized* Grapes" (Research Paper, Hungary, 2002).

P. Nyerges, "Adatok a Tarcal Borpince Mikroflórájához" [Contributions on the microflora of the Tarcal wine-cellar], in *Borgazdaság* [Viniculture], Vol. 8, No. 3 (1960), pp. 73-76.

Sándor Pettenkoffer, *Borgazdaság* [Viniculture], (Budapest: Patria, 1937).

L. Rakcsányi, "National Report: Hongrie," in *IXe Congrès International de la Vigne et du Vin*, Vol. III, Oct. 1959, pp. 101-110.

A. Sass-Kiss, E. Szerdahelyi, G. Hajós, "Study of Biologically Active Amines in Grapes and Wines," *Chromatographia Supplement*, Vol. 51, 2000.

SECONDARY SOURCES

History

László Alkonyi, *Tokaj: The Wine of Freedom* (Budapest: Spread Bt., 2000).

I. Balassa, "A Szőlőművelés és Borkezelés Változása a XVI-XVII. Században Tokaj-Hegyalján" [Change in Viti-Viniculture in Tokaj-Hegyalja in the 16th-17th c.] *Agrártörténelmi Szemle*, Vol. XV, no. 1-2 (1973), pp. 1-10.

Márta Belényesy, "Szőlő- és Gyümölcs-termesztésünk a XIV Században" [Our Grape and Fruit Cultivation in the 14th c.], *Néprajzi Értesítő* [Ethnographical Reporter], Vol. XXXVII (1955), pp. 11-28.

S. Bodnár, "A T-H Állami Gazdasági Borkombinát Borgazdasági Tevékenysége" [Wine-Growing Activity of the Tokaj-Hegyalja State Farm Wine-Facility], *Borgazdaság*, Vol. XXX, No. 3 (1982), pp. 88-92.

P.J. Crampton, *A Concise History of Bulgaria* (Cambridge University, 1997).

M. Détshy, "A Sárospataki Vár Kertjei és Szőlői" [Sárospatak Fort Gardens and Vineyards], *A. Szemle.* 1973, #1-2.

E. Fügedi, "Bártfai XVI. Szd. Eleji Bor- és Lókivitel Néhány Kerdése" [Several Questions about Bártfa's Wine and Horse Exports at the beginning of the 16th c.], *Agrártörténelmi Szemle*, Vol. XIV, no. 1-2 (1972), pp. 41-80.

L. Gecsényi, "Városi és Polgári Szőlőbirtokok…a Hegyalján a XV-XVI. Század Fordulóján" [Municipal and Citizen Vineyard Holdings…in Hegyalja at the turn of the 15th-16th c.], *Agrártörténelmi Szemle*, No. 3-4 (1972), pp. 340-351.

Zoltán Halász, *Hungarian Wine Through the Ages* (Budapest: Corvina Press, 1962).

R. Hanák, A. Kišon, *Rajonizácia Viniča v ČSSR* [Vineyard Regionalization in the ČSSR] (Bratislava: 1962).

Charles Keleti, *Viticulture de la Hongrie 1860-1873* (Budapest: Athenaeum, 1875).

Andrea Kiss, "Some Weather Events in the 14th c." (http://www..sci.u-szeged.hu/eghajlattan/akta99/KissA.html).

I. Kiss, "Szőlő Monokultúra a Hegyalján, XVI-XVII. Század" [Vineyard Monoculture in Hegyalja, 16th-18th c.], *Agrártörténelmi Szemle*, Vol. XV, No. 3-4 (1973), pp. 383-388.

Csaba Lévai, "Thomas Jefferson and his Hungarian wines: study of an attitude" (research paper, 1993).

Ferenc Maksay, *Urbáriumok XVI-XVII. Század* [*Urbária*, 16th-17th c.] (Akadémiai Kiadó, 1959).

István Molnár, "Bortermelés" [Wine-growing], in *Az Osztrák-Magyar Monárchia* (Bp: 1880), Vol. 3.

László Molnár, "Tokaji Borok a Cárok Asztalán" [Tokaji Wines on the Table of the Czars], www.tankonyvtar.hu, 1998.

A. Paládi-Kovács, "Paraszti Bortermelés Néhány Abaúji Faluban" [Peasant Wine Production in Several Abaúj Villages] (Debrecen: Kossuth Lajos Tudományegyetem, 1967).

Sándor Szakáll, "Bevezetés és Földrazji Áttekintés" [Introduction and Geographical Overview (of the Szerencs Hills)], in *Topographia Mineralogica Hungariae,* in Vol. III (1998), pp. 7-10.

Sándor Takáts, *Rajzok a Török Világból* [Sketches from the Turkish Occupation (of Hungary)], Vol. III (Budapest: Magyar Tudományi Akadémia, 1917).

J. Žadanský, *Tokajské Vino a Jeho Tajomstvá: Tokajské Vinohradníctvo a Vinárstvo v Slovenskej Časti Zemplína* [Tokaji Wine and its Secrets: Viti-Viniculture in Zemplén's Slovakian Part (Nitra: Slovak Ag. Univ., 2002).

------------, "Z dejín tokajského vinohradníctva a vinárstva" [From the history of Tokaji viticulture and viniculture] *Historica Carpatica*, Vol. 29-30, 1999, pp. 25-35.

Viti-Viniculture (Technical)

M.A. Amerine, V.A. Singleton, *Wine* (Berkeley: U. of California Press, 1965).

Susan Bardócz, "Polyamines in Food and their Consequences for Food Quality and Human Health," *Trends in Food Science* & Technology, Vol. 6, 1995, pp. 341-346.

Jozef Blaha, *Československa Ampelografia* (Prague: Oráč Roľnícke Vydavateľstvo, 1952).

Ján Farkaš, *Technológia a biochémia vína* [Technology and Biochemistry of Wine] (Prague: Alfa, 1973).

A. Fiala, J. Sedláček, *Vinárství v čs. Oblast Tokajské...* [Wine-making in the Cz.-Sl. Tokaj Region...] (Brno, 1936).

A. Johnson, M. Peterson, *Encyclopedia of Food Technology* (Westport, CT: AVI Publishing Co., 1974).

L. Kniphorst, C.Kruisheer, "Identification of 2,3-Bylene, Glycol, Acetylmethylcarniol and Diacetyl in Wine..." in *Zeitschrift zür Lebensmittel Untersuchung und Forschung* [Food Analysis/Research Review], Dec. 1937, pp. 477-485.

Z. Jeszenszky, "Karamell kimutatása borokban gél- és gás-kromatográfiás módszerekkel" [Detection of caramel in wine by gel- and gas-chromatography], *Borgazdaság*, Vol. 33, No. 3 (1985), pp. 105-110.

A. Massel, *Applied Wine Chemistry and Technology* (London: Heidelberg Publishers, 1969).

A. Mercz, *A Must és a Bor Egyszerű Kezelése* [Simple Treatment of Must and Wine] (Bp: Mező. Kiadó, 1977).

Géza Requinyi, *Borászat* [Enology] (Budapest: Magyar Természet-tudományi Társulat, 1948).

Albin Scholtz, István Soós, *Borgazdaságtan* [Vinicultural Science] (Budapest: Mezőgazdasági Kiadó, 1956).

Correspondence
Ásvány, Ákos: Enologist, National Wine-Qualifying Institute. July 6, 1984; Jan. 21, 1988.
Bacsó, András: Enologist, Tokaj-Hegyalja State Farm Wine-Facility. June 8, 1987.
Bodnár, Sándor: Enologist, May 15, 2009; March 27, 2010.
Kállay, Miklós: Enologist, St. Stephan Food Science Faculty, Bp. Dec. 16, 2002.
Kerényi, Zoltán: Enologist, Viti-Vinicultural Research Institute, Kecskemét. Sept. 30, 2000.
Kiss-Sass, Agnes: Enologist, Central Food Science Research Institute, Bp. Dec. 5, 2002.
Kozma, Pál: Director, Research Institute for Viticulture and Viniculture, Pécs. Oct. 1, 2003.
Lanarides, Panayiotis: Director, Ampelographic Institute, Lykovrysi, Greece. Sept. 6, 2003.
Szalka, Péter: Enologist, National Wine-Qualifying Institute. March 25, 1993.
Urbán, András: Enologist, Inst. for Vini-Viticulture, U. of Horticulture, Bp. Oct. 6, 1981; Aug. 5, 1982.

Regional History

J.Beňko, J. Durkaj, *Stropkov a Okolie* [Sztropkó and Environs] (Košice: East Slovakian Press, 1978).
Dezső Csánki. *Magyarország Történelmi Földrajza a Hunyadiak Korában* [Hungary's Historical Geography in the time of the Hunyadis] (Budapest: Magyar Tudományos Akadémia, 1890).
Ödön Potemkin, *Sáros Vármegye Leírása* [Description of Sáros County] (Pest: 1863).
Sándor Tóth, *Sáros Vármegye Monografiája* [Monograph of Sáros County] (Budapest: 1910).
F. Uličný, *Dejiny Osídlenia Šariša* [History of the Settlement of Sáros] (Košice: E. Slovakian Press, 1990).
B. Varsik, *Osidlenie Košicke Kotliny* [Settlement of the Košice Basin] (Slovak Academy of Science, 1973).
Ilona Walter, "The Settlement History of the Bodrogköz," *Agrártörténelmi Szemle*, Vol. XVI (1974).

Antique Western Accounts

Richard Bright, *Travels from Vienna through Lower Hungary* (Edinburgh: A. Constable & Co., 1818).
Sylvester Douglass, *An Account of the Tokay and Other Wines of Hungary* (Royal Soc. of London, 1773).
Alex. Henderson, *The History of Ancient and Modern Wines* (London: Baldwin, Craddock & Jay, 1824).
André Jullien, *Topographie des tous les Vignobles Connus* (Paris: Huzard, 1816).
Larousse Grand Dictionnaire Universel du XIXe Siècle (Paris: Pierre Larousse, 1875), vol. 15.
Alexandre Odart, *Ampelographie* (Paris: Chez Bixio, 1845).
John Paget, *Hungary and Transylvania* (London: John Murray, 1839).
Cyrus Redding, *A History and Description of Modern Wines* (London: Whittaker, 1836).
Robert Townson, *Travels in Hungary* [in 1793] (London: G.G. & J. Robinson, 1797).

Note: Hungarian Archival Documents

An array of old documents can be accessed online at the Hungarian Archives (Magyar Országos Levéltár) website: www.arcanum.hu/mol. Simply write the name of the village, vineyard-tract, family, etc., in the box marked 'Keresés' (Search) and press 'Mehet' (Go Ahead). If the words 'Nincs Találat' (No Hit) appear, it means that nothing by that spelling was found. In the older documents, of course, variations in spelling can occur. Many of those instances have been noted in the entries in this volume.

Most of the useful historical material, especially regarding vineyard-tracts, is found in the category of *Urbaria et Conscriptiones*. These are the documents numbered with the UC prefix. A category useful for earlier history in general is that of diplomatic papers, *Diplomatikai Levéltár*. These are the documents numbered with the DL prefix. In several cases in this volume, only the letters MOL are shown, because although hits turned up, they were not in the UC or DL categories, and carried no other numbers.

To be emphasized is that the researcher does not see the *actual* document online. Further, the UC documents usually are summaries (oftentimes translated from Latin), with the degree of detail being variable. The DL documents are always given in their entirety, in the original language, usually Latin.